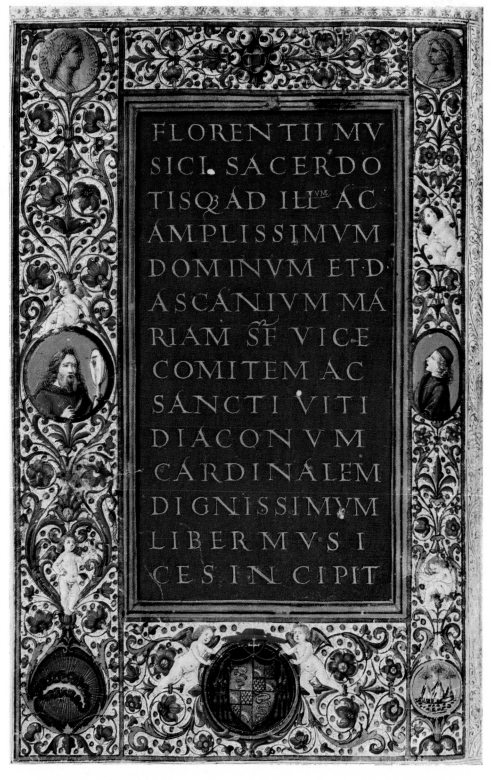

Title page of Florentius, *Liber musices*, dedicated to Cardinal Ascanio Sforza, with his coat of arms and devices, illuminated in the workshop of Attavante degli Attavanti. Milan, Biblioteca Trivulziana, MS. 2146 (p.48).

Josquin des Prez

Proceedings of the International Josquin Festival-
Conference held at The Juilliard School at Lincoln
Center in New York City, 21–25 June 1971

Sponsored by the American Musicological Society
in cooperation with
the International Musicological Society
and the Renaissance Society of America

Edited by
EDWARD E. LOWINSKY

in collaboration with
Bonnie J. Blackburn

London
OXFORD UNIVERSITY PRESS
NEW YORK / TORONTO
1976

Oxford University Press, Ely House, London W. 1

GLASGOW NEW YORK TORONTO MELBOURNE WELLINGTON
CAPE TOWN IBADAN NAIROBI DAR ES SALAAM LUSAKA ADDIS ABABA
DELHI BOMBAY CALCUTTA MADRAS KARACHI DACCA
KUALA LUMPUR SINGAPORE HONG KONG TOKYO

ISBN 0 19 315229 0

© Oxford University Press 1976

*Printed in Great Britain
by W & J Mackay Limited, Chatham*

Preface

There are times in the life of scholarship when it takes a concerted team effort to create the momentum needed to determine new directions of study and research in a given field for the next generation or two. That time had arrived for the study of Josquin after the work of two great scholars had been completed, Albert Smijers' edition of the *Werken* and Helmuth Osthoff's two-volume monograph, *Josquin Desprez*. It is the fate of pioneering efforts that they form the basis of future work as well as its unavoidable targets. The second edition of Josquin's music, already being considered and debated by an international team of musicologists, will differ from its predecessor in content and in form. The biography of Josquin, the investigation of his compositions, the exploration of the sources of his music, both in the material and spiritual sense of the word, the analysis of his personal style, the inquiry into its evolution—these and related problems require new departures that will at times confirm, at times diverge from the conclusions offered in the first great monograph. This is in the nature of things. But history recognizes the special merit of the pioneers, and rightly so. The papers assembled here, notwithstanding the critique they may occasionally express of the authors of the first edition and the first monograph, are also the most eloquent tribute to their achievement.

The present volume constitutes the report of the Conference and, in a departure from conventional practice, substantially more. The generous offer of Oxford University Press, nine months *before* the Conference, to publish its Proceedings, and the considerable expense for the publisher in producing and the reader in acquiring such a work, imposed a special obligation to issue it in the most perfect form attainable. Many authors revised and developed their original papers, partly in response to the opportunity to elaborate on their topics without the time limit imposed by a scholarly meeting, partly in answer to queries and suggestions, partly as a result of research undertaken at various European archives after the Conference was over. The goal of excellence superseded all other considerations. Three papers have been incorporated that could not be delivered at the Conference itself: one on Czech sources of Josquin's music by Jitka Snížková that, hopefully, may lead to further investigations of East European sources; one by Jeremy Noble on benefices received by Josquin during his service at the Papal Chapel that may well serve as a model for the study and interpretation of benefice documents, a much neglected but essential source for a full picture of artistic life of the period; and a third one, in which Virginia Woods Callahan, a classical scholar, solved the riddle of 'Ut Phoebi radiis', a humanistic poem set to music by Josquin that had so far defied all efforts to interpret its text and the seeming nonsense syllables contained in the second verse.

The special aspects of this volume of Proceedings, the wealth of music examples, tables, and illustrations may in part explain the long time it has taken to bring it out. Not infrequently the difficulty of the problems involved led to extended correspondence and consultation with the authors. At other times proposals to shorten a paper had to be made. No mechanical rules were applied. Pertinence and conciseness were the only standards. One speaker elected to publish his paper outside of the Proceedings. Professor Leeman L. Perkins's article, 'Mode and Structure in the Masses of Josquin', appeared in the *Journal of the American Musicological Society*, XXVI (1973), 189–239. The willingness of our foreign speakers to use English as Conference language placed the responsibility on the Editor to render their papers in the most idiomatic form. Finally, the proofs were read once by the authors, twice by the editors, who checked them a third time. The patience and the cooperation of the authors are beyond praise.

The interconnection between the papers devoted to one single composer and the wealth of new facts and new ideas brought together here suggested a special effort to make them more easily accessible to scholars and students. This is the purpose of the editorial footnotes referring the reader to related papers. Dr. Bonnie J. Blackburn is responsible for forging the key to the thirty-three papers, the three workshops, and the symposium in the form of an Index *nominum et rerum*.

To our profound regret, three of the speakers whose papers appear in these pages do not live to see their work in print. Walter H. Rubsamen, who returned to the subject of his youth in his comparison of Josquin and Pierre de la Rue, which continued to occupy him throughout his life, died on 19 June 1973. May his hope to publish the works of La Rue be fulfilled by a worthy successor! Geneviève Thibault passed away in Strasbourg on 31 August 1975, where she was arranging a travelling exhibition of French and English musical instruments of the eighteenth century. Her radiant personality, her scholarship and organizing talents, and her generous support of musical scholars and scholarship will be missed in international musicology. Finally, Friedrich Blume died on 22 November 1975. He survived by over four years the warnings of his doctors in 1971, which he resolutely dismissed, not to expose himself to the rigours of transatlantic travel. His presence at the Conference symbolized the span of generations; remembering in his opening address the young people in his 'Collegium

Musicum Vocale' at the University of Berlin, with whom he performed Josquin and whose enthusiasm led him to found *Das Chorwerk*, he was pleased and impressed by nothing as much as the great number of students who had flocked to New York from all corners of the United States to celebrate the commemoration of Josquin des Prez.

It had been the general consensus at the Conference that the most fruitful innovation—one that in the meantime has become the model for a whole number of musicological conferences—was the interweaving of music and scholarship, not only in the four brilliant concerts given by four of the world's finest ensembles for early music, but above all in the three workshops, where musicians and musicologists met face to face to debate the numerous problems of performance and interpretation. The lively debates have been transmitted in these Proceedings, but the cost of adding the records of the music with the diverse interpretations offered by the four ensembles proved in the end too high. Yet without the music, the workshops made little sense; without the workshops the Proceedings would lose a most characteristic feature. At that point the Martha Baird Rockefeller Fund for Music, which under the stewardship of Donald L. Engle had already made a very substantial contribution to the Conference itself, came to the rescue. I wish to express my warmest gratitude to the Fund, its Board of Trustees, and its new Director, Miss Maude E. Brogan, for their generous response to my appeal which permits us now to present the discussions on performance problems complete with three recordings, one for each of the workshops.

It was not possible to record all the music played at the workshops. In consultation with the Directors of the workshops, I selected what appeared to be the most instructive examples of a particular view and style of performance and interpretation. As a whole, the three records present, I believe, a faithful mirror of the various artistic persuasions of the four ensembles and their conductors as well as of the problems involved in performing Josquin as seen by the musicologists involved. These recordings do not offer smooth concert performances. They have the spontaneity and occasional roughness of a rehearsal and are at times enlivened by unintentional background noises. But they offer the student for the first time Josquin's works in different settings and diverse interpretations according to principles and insights developed in the debates. I must not omit thanking that remarkable acoustical engineer of The Juilliard School of Music, Mr. Henry Friend, for the splendid tapes made of the workshops, indeed of the whole Conference, without which neither the discussions nor the performances could have been preserved.

In the workshop discussions the participants referred to many writers of the past. Editorial footnotes have been added to aid the reader by locating the precise references. I trust I will be forgiven for appending a few footnotes with personal observations of an analytical or bibliographical character, both in the workshops and symposium. In the latter, these footnotes appear in brackets to separate them clearly from footnotes added by the speakers themselves. In a few music examples, with the kind permission of the authors, I have added editorial accidentals in parenthesis in accord with the rules and principles developed in my *musica ficta* paper in the symposium.

As Director of the Conference, I expressed my thanks to the committees and the many persons who have aided me in the preparation of the Conference, officially and unofficially, in my welcoming address. It remains for me to recall the essential contribution made by Len Alexander, General Manager, whose work in New York, at the scene of action, was responsible for the smooth functioning of the complex operation of the five-day event, in which he enjoyed the able support of the managerial staff of The Juilliard School of Music. I wish also to thank my Chicago staff that typed hundreds of letters, made phone calls, handled the registrations, was equal to any challenge and emergency—and there were many of them—and worked beyond reasonable hours to take care of the infinity of organizational details. That staff consisted of one person, Dr. Bonnie J. Blackburn. Her name is also inscribed on the title page of this book. Neither the Conference nor the Proceedings would have been possible without her.

The history of this volume would be incomplete were I to omit mentioning the man who believed in this enterprise when it was only a plan, who managed the production of this volume through its most difficult phases, meeting the unenviable task of steering a fair middle course between the wishes of a demanding editor and the exigencies of a budget constantly shrinking under the assault of inflation with fortitude, equanimity, and, as the reader will acknowledge, a high degree of success. I wish to pay tribute to the Music Books Editor of Oxford University Press, Anthony Mulgan.

In conclusion, we are forever indebted to the institutions and the individuals whose generosity made it possible to carry through the original plans for the Festival-Conference and for the present volume of Proceedings in all details. Their names are gratefully recorded in the List of Donors.

E.E.L.

List of Donors*

American Council of Learned Societies
American Musicological Society
Antiquae Musicae Italicae Studiosi
Deutsche Forschungsgemeinschaft
Deutscher Musikrat
Ingram Merrill Foundation
Koninklijke Vlaamse Academie voor Wetenschappen, Letteren en Schone Kunsten van
    België
Martha Baird Rockefeller Fund for Music, Inc.
Mary Duke Biddle Foundation
Maya Corporation
Ministry of Cultural Affairs, Recreation, and Social Welfare, Holland
Ministry of Culture, Belgium
Ministry of Foreign Affairs, Italy
National Endowment for the Arts
National Endowment for the Humanities
New York State Council on the Arts
Scherman Foundation, Inc.
University of Chicago
University of Kentucky Research Foundation
Margaret Day Blake
Richard F. French
Ellen T. Harris
Stewart R. Mott
Samuel F. Pogue
David Rockefeller, Jr.
Hope R. Spencer
Clementine M. Tangeman

* The programme of the Conference carried a complete list of all donors, great and small, including the names of those who helped in the fund-raising efforts. The present list is confined to the sources of major donations.

Contents

Illustrations

List of Recorded Examples

WORKSHOP ON THE MOTETS

1. 'Monstra te esse Matrem', *a cappella* (Schola Cantorum Stuttgart) (p. 651)
2. 'Monstra te esse Matrem', voices and instruments (Capella Antiqua München) (p. 651)
3. 'Absalon fili mi' (low pitch, as notated in London, British Museum, MS. Royal 8 G VII), *a cappella* (Schola Cantorum Stuttgart) (p. 654)
4. 'Absalon fili mi' (high pitch, as printed by Kriesstein, Augsburg, 1540), *a cappella* (Capella Antiqua München) (p. 654)
5. 'Stabat Mater' (*prima pars*), *a cappella* (Schola Cantorum Stuttgart) (p. 658)
6. 'Stabat Mater' (*prima pars*), *a cappella*, with instrumental *cantus firmus* (Cappella Antiqua München) (p. 658)

WORKSHOP ON THE SECULAR MUSIC

1. 'Adieu mes amours', voices and instruments (New York Pro Musica) (p. 664)
2. 'Adieu mes amours', instruments (Capella Antiqua München) (p. 669)
3. 'Plus nulz regretz', *a cappella* (Capella Antiqua München) (p. 674)
4. 'Plus nulz regretz', instruments (New York Pro Musica) (p. 674)
5. 'Je ne me puis tenir d'aimer', voices and instruments (New York Pro Musica) (p. 683)
6. 'Je ne me puis tenir d'aimer', *a cappella* (Capella Antiqua München) (p. 690)
7. 'Fortuna dun gran tempo' (version without *musica ficta*), instruments (Prague Madrigal Singers) (p. 692)

WORKSHOP ON THE MASSES

1. *Agnus* II of the 'Missa L'homme armé super voces musicales', superius alone, in Petrucci's version (Prague Madrigal Singers) (p. 706)
2. Same, with all three voices, in Petrucci's version (Prague Madrigal Singers) (p. 706)
3. Same, version of Berlin MS. 1175, superius alone (Prague Madrigal Singers) (p. 707)
4. Same, version of Berlin MS. 1175, all three voices (Prague Madrigal Singers) (p. 707)
5. *Agnus* II and III of the 'Missa L'homme armé super voces musicales', experiment in tempo relations (Prague Madrigal Singers) (p. 709)
6. *Kyrie* of the 'Missa L'homme armé super voces musicales', experiment in tempo relations (New York Pro Musica) (p. 709)
7. Ockeghem, 'Malheur me bat' (Prague Madrigal Singers) (p. 712)
8. *Et in Spiritum* of the 'Missa Malheur me bat', using B♭ and G♯ in final cadence (Prague Madrigal Singers) (p. 712)

The Opening
Session

Josquin des Prez: 'Vive le roy' (Fanfare for Louis XII)
(New York Pro Musica Wind Ensemble)

CLAUDE PALISCA (President, the American Musicological Society):
Honoured guests, ladies and gentlemen: It is a rare privilege for me to
open this commemoration of the 450th anniversary of the death of Josquin
des Prez on 27 August 1521 in Condé-sur-l'Escaut. This morning's program
began with a 'hail to the king'; it closes with two lamentations. I should think
that the opening fanfare better captures the spirit of this occasion than the
closing music. We have more reason for a *jubilation* than a *deploration*. For,
though we are commemorating Josquin's death, we are also rejoicing in
his resurrection. So, as they used to shout when a king died: *Josquin est
mort; Vive Josquin!*

It is normal, of course, in such observances as this to seek rounder
numbers than we have reached. Having missed Josquin's 500th birthday
through ignorance, we would have had to wait until the year 2021 to
commemorate his death with round numbers.

But today the convergence of many factors makes the time ripe and also
right for this event. We owe it to the foresight of Professor Edward Lowinsky to have recognized three years ago that if we were to look to the calendar
for a pretext, this was the last chance in the lifetime of most of us for a
retrospective exposition of Josquin's work.

New York—rather than Condé-sur-l'Escaut, that village in France, once
part of the county of Hainaut, where Josquin died—New York may seem
on the face of it to have no strong claim for the honour of hosting this
homage to the great composer. But as every schoolboy knows, before it
was seized by the English in 1664 for the Duke of York Manhattan was
New Amsterdam, an island bought from the Indians for some $24 worth of
trinkets by the Dutch West India Company, an agency of the Hapsburg
rulers of the Austrian Netherlands, descendants of the very Hapsburgs
who were sovereign over the county of Hainaut when Josquin died. New
Yorkers share this common heritage with Josquin; but Josquin was also
the most international of the great composers—claimed not only by the
Netherlands, but by France, Belgium, and Italy. In his own day he was

embraced variously as 'gallus', 'hennuyer', 'belgus', 'picardus', 'veroman-dus', and 'd'Ascanio'. For this reason too this most international of cities claims the honour of saluting him.

I do not expect to convince you that we chose this building on Amsterdam Avenue for these reasons. The most compelling attraction in New York as a site of this festival is this great citadel of the performing arts, Lincoln Center, and particularly this building, which perhaps more than any lends the Center architectural distinction and holds the key to its future—The Juilliard School.

Long a distinguished conservatory of music, now a school of music, drama, and dance, The Juilliard School in recent years has been very much involved with musicology and the repertory of early music. In 1963 it accepted the challenge of bringing to elementary school music some of the fruits of musical scholarship through extending the repertory of music sung and played by children to as far back as the Middle Ages. Several of us here participated in that effort—Gustave Reese, Paul Henry Lang, and I, and one whose memory pervades this festival, Noah Greenberg, who particularly was entranced by the prospect of school children singing Renaissance music accompanied on drums and bells and castanets. The Juilliard repertory project was undertaken on the initiative of President Peter Mennin and Dean Gid Waldrup of The Juilliard School, with the support of the United States Office of Education. Recently editions of music from the Middle Ages to the present not previously available for school use have been published for Juilliard by the Canyon Press of Cincinnati in an attractive and practical format. Musical research, then, is no stranger to this institution, which this week is host to the Josquin Festival-Conference. Here to welcome you officially to this great institution is Professor Peter Mennin, composer and President of The Juilliard School.

MENNIN: My role this morning is blessedly short. It is with pleasure and anticipation that I welcome you to the International Josquin Festival-Conference. I say 'anticipation' because it is rare to have such a distinguished group of scholars, musicians, and delegations from different parts of the world. Actually, it is not my role to comment on the composer some of you have come so far to hear and to honour. I wish to welcome you to the School and to the City of New York, and I hope that you give us the opportunity to make your visit as pleasant as possible. I shall not comment on the music because the musicians and the spokesmen who follow will do so with eloquence and reverence and also with pleasure. Thank you very much for honouring us with your presence.

PALISCA: I am glad Dr. Mennin included New York City in his welcome, as I have not wanted to trouble the beleaguered officials of New

York City to greet you; but I am sure they have been eager to welcome you.

I shall, however, ask a representative of the United States government to address you, in recognition particularly of the fact that this is an international conference—almost 100 musicians and scholars from abroad are actively participating, and numerous visitors from many countries from Iceland to Israel have registered.

Josquin des Prez is the oldest composer ever honoured by a festival or conference in the New World. This is fitting, because his contemporaries, looking back to the immortal poets of ancient Greek civilization, conceived of the art of composition as the fashioning of complete and perfect works that could withstand the ravages of time and leave something lasting behind after the artist dies. Josquin must have felt this duty to create music that would pass every test of artistic significance in his place and time—and also transcend them. We do not know what notice he took of that great event around his 50th year that was to expand the world he knew: the landing of Columbus in the West Indies. Those great patrons of music, Isabella of Castile and Ferdinand of Aragon, had the vision and sense of adventure to sponsor that momentous voyage. Within two years of Josquin's death, in 1523, the Flemish musician Pedro de Gante (1480–1572) established the first music school in Mexico. Well may we mark this week not only 450 years since Josquin's death but 450 years of European music and possibly of Josquin's music in the Western Hemisphere.

The expedition that eventually brought Western music to the New World was financed by what today we call a matching grant, negotiated by Christopher Columbus with almost as much difficulty as that negotiated by Professor Lowinsky in Washington. The Spanish crown supplied around 1,400,000 maravedís, while Columbus invested about 250,000 of his own (totalling approximately $14,000, not counting salaries). Even so, it probably cost the Queen less than did her chapel of twenty adult singers and twenty-five boys and numerous instrumentalists each year.

I shall not draw comparisons between the cost of our great space explorations of recent years and the federal government's investment in music, which actually has been considerable. Rather I point with satisfaction to the fact that the National Endowment for the Humanities is the principal supporter of this festival with a one-to-one matching grant for half of our budget, while from the National Endowment for the Arts we received a smaller outright grant, to which was recently added a very generous subsidy from the New York State Council on the Arts.

From his earliest reconnoitring trips to Washington, Edward Lowinsky found there two eager allies, Dr. Walter Anderson, Director of the music program of the Arts Endowment, and Dr. William R. Emerson, Director of research grants for the Humanities Endowment. We are most gratified that both are attending this morning's session, and Dr. Emerson has agreed to address a few remarks to you on behalf of the Foundation on the Arts and the Humanities. Dr. Emerson shares with us an interest in history, the field in which he earned his doctorate at Oxford and in which he later taught at Yale and Harvard. Before joining the Endowment he was Assistant to the President of Hollins College. He is now Director of the Division of Research and Publication of the National Endowment for the Humanities.

[*Dr. Emerson brought greetings from the National Endowment for the Humanities.*]

The Josquin Festival and the American Musicological Society as its principal sponsor have been blessed with the cooperation of two other organizations, the International Musicological Society and the Renaissance Society of America. We are indebted to these two organizations for enlisting the participation of their members.

Professor Ludwig Finscher of the University of Frankfurt has been our liaison not only with foreign speakers on this program but also with the three performing groups from abroad. Many of you know him, I am sure, from his numerous articles on the classical period, his edition of Gluck's *Orphée et Euridice*, his edition of the works of one of the most gifted contemporaries of Josquin, Loyset Compère, and from his thoughtful contributions concerning performance practice, particularly of Josquin's music. On that subject you will hear from him this afternoon. Now he brings us a greeting from the International Musicological Society.

FINSCHER: On behalf of the International Musicological Society, I have the honour to present this Society's greetings to the International Josquin Festival-Conference. It is, I believe, the first time that an international scholarly congress is dedicated to a composer earlier than Bach or Monteverdi, and—although the most immediate reason for this congress has been the commemoration of the 450th anniversary of Josquin's death— this fact alone suffices to illustrate the tremendous importance which Josquin's work has gained in the world of musicology and in the world of music. That at least some of Josquin's music today is no longer a buried treasure, enshrined in the vaults of libraries and hidden in the pages of a just-finished complete edition, but a living force in our musical life, and that at least a vague feeling, if not a conscious recognition, of the unique genius of this composer has spread unto a large musical public, has been, above all, due to the efforts of musicologists since musicology has begun to play an active part in contemporary musical life. But in doing this, musicology has taken the responsibility to justify its efforts not only before itself but before the general public too; not only to investigate Josquin, the man and the musician, as an historical phenomenon and as one of the first and one of the greatest incarnations of creative musical genius, but to help and guide performers and public alike in the understanding of Josquin's music as a living part of music history. The International Josquin Festival-Conference has taken an important step in this direction: by coordinating and presenting the research and efforts of Josquin scholars from all over the world and thereby embracing the present state of Josquin research and stimulating further and even greater activity, and by trying to bridge the traditional gap between musicology and the application of its results by performing artists in the organization of workshops, in which musicians and musicologists are to combine their efforts for the sake of Josquin's living presence in the musical life of today. The International Josquin Festival-Conference is the first musicological congress to define its role in the world of music in this way. The International Musicological Society most emphatically welcomes this effort and presents its very best wishes for the progress of the Josquin Festival-Conference and for a stimulating and successful cooperation of all its participants—*in signo Josquini.*

PALISCA: The other society that has favoured us with its support is the Renaissance Society of America. Musicologists can take satisfaction in the flourishing condition of the Renaissance Society, and its excellent quarterly and annual volume of studies, which have always welcomed articles and reviews in the field of music.

It is uncannily appropriate that the new President of the Renaissance Society is Professor Gustave Reese, for his chapter of some 100 pages, 'Josquin des Prez and his Contemporaries', in *Music in the Renaissance,* published seventeen years ago, has served most of us in the English-speaking world and also in other countries as a guide and introduction to the music of Josquin and to its context in the history of music. To Professor Reese goes a large share of credit for the Josquin renaissance that succeeded the Palestrina renaissance.

REESE: It gives me great pleasure to be one of those who are extending a welcome to you today. I would under any circumstances regard it as a privilege to be in a position to do this, but I derive a special kind of satisfaction from the fact that I am addressing you on behalf of an organization that is not primarily musical but, rather, cross-cultural. The Renaissance Society of America concerns itself with all aspects of Renaissance culture and has followed the excellent example of its older sister-organization, the Mediaeval Academy of America, in paying due respect, in its own activities, to music and musicology. It is heartening to note that the director of the International Josquin Festival-Conference has, for his part, provided that alongside the papers we are going to hear about the music itself—papers of a kind that will quite naturally predominate—we shall be presented also with studies on 'Art and Architecture in Lombardy at the time of Josquin des Prez' written by Dr. Maria Luisa Gatti Perer and on 'The Literary Texts of Josquin's Chansons' by Dr. Brian Jeffery. What we may perhaps call the ecumenical aspect of scholarship is to be agreeably in evidence.

And while we glance beyond the borders of music, we might remind ourselves that 1971 marks not only the 450th anniversary of the death of Josquin, but also the 500th anniversary of the birth of Albrecht Dürer—of Dürer who, like Josquin, shared the by no means uncommon medieval and Renaissance fascination for the goddess Fortuna and showed this in works subtle both in their art and in their symbolism. Some years ago, the director of our Festival called attention to Josquin's concern for the goddess and, in the process, he showed that certain procedures in the *Agnus Dei* of the 'Missa Fortuna desperata' may well have a symbolical significance connected with conceptions of Fortuna current at the time. The Mass is among the works we are going to hear, as is also the secular piece, 'Fortune d'estrange plummaige/Pauper sum ego'. It would not surprise me if that remarkable piece, 'Fortuna dun gran tempo', were to come up for comment in our discussions. In view of the attention the goddess is bound to receive, it would perhaps not seem excessive for me, in the course of welcoming you, to express the hope that she will be gentle and unmoody in her treatment of all of you and in her attitude toward every aspect of our Josquin Festival.

PALISCA: Our next speaker, Professor William S. Newman, was President of the American Musicological Society during most of the two years of gestation of this festival. He could hardly have embraced the idea of a week-long conference on Josquin with more enthusiasm had Josquin left ninety sonatas instead of that number of motets. From the very first suggestion that the American Musicological Society be the official sponsor of this event, Bill Newman unhesitatingly set out to move foundations, the Internal Revenue Service, and the machinery of our own Society to conspire with Edward Lowinsky to produce this splendid gathering and program. In recognition of his close association with the planning over many months of this event, I shall ask Professor Newman, as Past President of the American Musicological Society, to bring you the greetings of the Executive Board of that Society. As Bill's successor and for the present the guardian of his presidential files, I have had the opportunity to admire the meticulous attention, fine judgement, and warm humanity that marked each action and letter recorded and preserved there—and they number in the thousands.

I shall relinquish to Professor Newman also the pleasure of introducing Professor Edward Lowinsky, the creator of this festival, the one who conceived it, urged it upon our many patrons, long studied and carefully planned it, and who seemed to have thought of everything to make it the brilliant success we wish it to be. Through one of the many instances of secret diplomacy in this project, Bill Newman reserved that introduction for himself. I am happy to present that very essential member of the team that prepared this festival—Professor William S. Newman of the University of North Carolina.

NEWMAN: Honoured guests, distinguished colleagues, ladies and gentlemen: Among those on stage to bring greetings, I have the double privilege of welcoming you on behalf of the American Musicological Society and of introducing the distinguished procreator of this Festival-Conference.

My own actual share in this notable project is simply that of the erstwhile midwife during most of its prolonged labour and complicated birth. Edward Lowinsky originally proposed his idea of an international homage to Josquin some two and a half years ago, when the Society's Executive Board met in New Haven in late 1968. Within but a few weeks, he had already developed and shaped the idea to the point where travel, special meetings, correspondence, long-distance calls, and applications for funds were requiring nearly all of his time and considerable AMS collaboration.

Naturally, the first problem to be resolved, if there was to be a Festival-Conference at all, was that of funds—funds, funds, and more funds—indeed, astronomical funds that, in the face of higher costs, trickier logistics, and wider offerings, would dwarf, for example, the once 'astronomical funds' required to finance the International Musicological Congress in New York ten years ago. How Ed attacked this problem, as with all the other problems that arose, must be an object lesson for us all. I, for one, have never known greater enterprise, resourcefulness, or determination. Unless you are experts at fundsmanship—Ed always insisted he was a rank novice— you would never believe the number and variety of foundations, government agencies, and individuals, both here and abroad, that he discovered to be at least receptive to approach, most often by the unending legwork of personal interviews.

But funds represent only one of the main problems that had to be surmounted. Not for a single moment did Ed lose track of the goal that constitutes the *raison d'être* of this Festival-Conference—that is, the fuller recognition and understanding of Josquin, after four and a half centuries, as (to borrow that sixteenth-century analogy Ed most likes to cite) the Michelangelo of Renaissance music. Indeed, throughout those thirty months of intensive preparation Ed has managed to keep his own important research going on Josquin and related topics, as most of you know from his continuing stream of new publications, and from the fascinating offprints some of you have been lucky enough to receive from him. Special emphasis should be placed, too, on that idea of Festival-Conference, for it was that combination—of festival with conference, of music closely integrated with scholarship—that was to lend special distinction to the project.

Before the middle of 1969, Ed was able to shift his headquarters from Chicago and New York City to Milan in Italy in order to meet in person, in their own national centres, with many of the foremost European musicians and scholars who would be participating two years later—this week. Meanwhile, a committee of his United States colleagues was starting along parallel lines to work with the specialists in this country. By now the financial footing was at least looking promising enough to justify such planning, notwithstanding many a down with the ups yet to come, such as the devastating Italian postal strikes that made correspondence a nightmare of delays while Ed was centred in Milan, or the terrifying mire of new federal and state tax laws that threatened to sink the whole project, along with many other joys of the humanities, throughout much of 1970.

But my present object is hardly to take you through the involute history of this project, even if that history could at least be summarized within a short introduction. From this point on, in the story, any summary would need to branch out to include the participation and leadership of a growing number of notables—of Ludwig Finscher, Gustave Reese, Claude Palisca, Donald Grout, and all those others who have contributed so richly to the prospects for this week. No, the hope is simply to convey some of the flavour of the experience and some of the fortitude of the man responsible for it.

In short, representing the American Musicological Society, may I extend a hearty welcome to all who are here, and may I present to you the Director of the International Josquin Festival-Conference, Edward Lowinsky.

LOWINSKY: Ladies and gentlemen: It is you who have made the International Josquin Festival-Conference a reality: you, who have come from Canada, Austria, Belgium, Holland, Germany, and Iceland, and from all corners of this country; you, the speakers and workshop directors who have come from France, Germany, Italy, Holland, Belgium, England, Israel, and from a dozen American universities; you, the artists who have come from Prague, from Munich, from Stuttgart, and our very own New York Pro Musica—founded by the unforgettable Noah Greenberg— you, the members of the committees, the presidents and officers of the three societies sponsoring and co-sponsoring the event, above all the two presidents of the American Musicological Society, William Newman and Claude Palisca; you, the directors and officers of the foundations whose support furnished the indispensable economic groundwork for this enterprise; you, the donors, encouraged by the very first grant of the American Council of Learned Societies, and especially the National Endowment for the Humanities, whose generous matching grant set in motion the great train of gifts from private foundations and individuals, down to the $5 gift of an enthusiastic high school student from the State of Washington;

you, the members of the New York Public Library and the Toscanini Memorial Archives; and last but not least, you, our hosts, the President, the Board of Trustees, and the members of The Juilliard School whose magnificent Theater, hardly a year old, is our home for the five days of the Conference. Nor can I omit mention of that gracious lady, Alice Tully, whose name adorns the hall in which our concerts are held and who, with an extraordinarily generous gift, put us over the hump when we were struggling to match the grant of the National Endowment for the Humanities.

I also owe thanks to the many experienced people who assured me that it was utterly utopian to expect to raise the huge budget needed for the ambitious plans of the Festival-Conference in this day of economic slump and national malaise: for they strengthened my determination. And I owe thanks to a few rare friends who told me from the beginning that, yes, I could do it, and they would help. I must name at least a few individuals whose contribution cannot be judged from the appearance of their names as committee members or as donors: Barry S. Brook of the City University of New York and his gracious wife Claire, who not only cleared my path to a number of foundations but also gave a whole series of dinners in their home to interest people in the Josquin Festival; Richard French of the Union Theological Seminary, who was helpful in many ways and who insisted that the Conference would draw not 300 people, as I thought, but 900—and his words, uttered two years ago, proved quite prophetic; Ludwig Finscher, head of a strong German delegation of scholars and artists, who put an enormous amount of time and energy into the multifarious negotiations with individuals, ensembles, foundations, ministries; who advised me on every phase of the plans, helped me recruit, persuade, cajole, finance—and was indispensable from beginning to end.

Finally, and above all, this Festival is due to the enthusiasm of the young people, the students of music and musicology in this country, who make up nearly fifty per cent of this great audience. I had wished for nothing so much as for their participation. But their registrations exceeded my most sanguine expectations. A hard-working committee on student participation helped.

It was in anticipation of lively student participation that I asked the foreign speakers to deliver their papers in English. Our students have a reading knowledge of foreign languages, but the ability to read in a foreign language is not tantamount to understanding a native speaker. I wish to thank our foreign speakers warmly for their kindness in consenting to read their papers in English. The extraordinary number of students here should be regarded as a response to their generosity in taking the young into consideration.

It is, after all, for the young that we build; it is the young in whose hands

lies the cultural heritage of the world; it is the young whose hearts and
minds we need, if we are to succeed in turning mankind from the insanity
of war to the arts and the works of peace. It is the young, who, in an age of
disillusion and disenchantment, must be given examples of how it is still
up to us, each one of us, to arouse the great constructive, cultural forces
here and abroad, to celebrate the great hours of humanity. To the greatest
hours of humanity belong the creative lives of mankind's artists, poets, and
musicians. And of the greatest musicians of any age, Josquin des Prez is a
figure so towering that his name cannot be left out of any enumeration of
great composers, however small the number of them might happen to be.

The response to the idea of a Josquin commemoration was enormous
from the beginning, and it was not confined to the young. When, in the
summer of 1969, I invited the then 82-year-old Higinio Anglés to be one
of our speakers, he wrote me on 12 August 1969—and I shall read the main
part of his letter as he wrote it, in German:

Über Ihren wunderschönen Plan für die 'International Josquin Festival-Conference' 1971 freue ich mich ausserordentlich; leider mein Alter und meine Gesund-
heit werden mir nicht erlauben, 1971 in New York persönlich zu erscheinen.
Trotzdem wenn Sie es wünschen und jemand bereit ist mein Referat dort
vorzulesen, bin ich bereit etwas über 'Josquin in der Musik Spaniens' zu schreiben.

Four months later Anglés died. This Conference honours his memory.

Knud Jeppesen of Denmark, too, had hopes to contribute to our Conference. But the recent publication of his magistral three-volume work on
the Italian frottola so consumed his energies that he had to decline regretfully.

The first Josquin scholar to whom I wrote was, needless to say, Helmuth
Osthoff of the Johann Wolfgang von Goethe-Universität, Frankfurt am
Main, the author of a two-volume work on Josquin, the first monograph
on the composer and the only one to date. I asked him to share the direction
of the Conference with me. To his and to my own infinite regret Professor
Osthoff's state of health prevented him from accepting this invitation. A
few weeks ago I sent him an advance copy of the program. I had the
pleasure of receiving a letter from him, the main part of which I am going
to share with you:

Die Qualität und Reichhaltigkeit des Programms ist erstaunlich, nicht zuletzt
die verschiedenen musikalischen Ensembles und die Verwendung vieler nach-
gebauter Instrumente der Zeit! Es ist schon sehr schade, dass ich nicht mit dabei
sein kann. Ich kann nur mein aufrichtiges Bedauern wiederholen, dass ich *lediglich*
aus gesundheitlichen Gründen nicht anwesend sein kann. Aber ich werde in der
Zeit vom 21. bis 25. Juni mit meinen Gedanken oft nach New York herüber-
schweifen, und ich wünsche Ihnen und allen Teilnehmern einen vollen Erfolg.
Eine besondere Freude ist es mir, dass das musikwissenschaftliche Institut der
Universität Frankfurt durch eine stattliche Gruppe von Teilnehmern vertreten
sein wird.

Ich bitte Sie, den Konferenzteilnehmern meine besten Grüsse und Wünsche zu übermitteln, und seien Sie selbst aufrichtig gegrüsst von

Ihrem
(signed) Helmuth Osthoff

I have asked Ludwig Finscher, Helmuth Osthoff's successor at the Goethe University of Frankfurt am Main, to compose the text of a cablegram to Professor Osthoff in the hope that this Conference will want to salute the great Josquin scholar on this occasion. I call on Professor Finscher.

FINSCHER: The International Josquin Festival-Conference salutes Helmuth Osthoff to whose lifelong study of Josquin and his music, and to whose meticulous scholarly care and deep artistic insight we owe the most vivid and masterly drawn portrait of the artist and his achievement. To the great Josquin scholar, whose attendance should have distinguished our meeting, would his health have permitted him to travel, the participants of this congress express their deep gratitude for his work and send their heartfelt wishes. (The salute to Osthoff was accepted by acclamation.)

LOWINSKY: When it comes to the older generation, not all is regret. One of the greatest musical scholars of our time, a man of universal interests, and in addition a student and editor of Josquin, Friedrich Blume, has come all the way from Germany to New York notwithstanding his doctor's warnings that the trip might be a hazard to his health. He will be properly introduced by the President. But I could hardly forego welcoming him and Mrs. Blume and thanking both of them for honouring us with their presence at this festive occasion.

Among the many generous and imaginative responses that we have received from friends and colleagues, I should single out the photographic exhibit that the President of the Société Française de Musicologie, Madame Thibault-Chambure, undertook, aided by Daniel Heartz and Frédéric Thieck, to give us a visual image of time, place, and environment of Josquin; the precious facsimile edition of Petrucci's second book of Josquin's Masses specially printed for the speakers of this Conference by the Antiquae Musicae Italicae Studiosi at the initiative of their President, Professor Giuseppe Vecchi of Bologna; the decision of the Executive Board of the American Musicological Society to present to our foreign guests Helen Hewitt's beautiful edition of Petrucci's *Canti B* with its substantial number of Josquin chansons.

Although I neglected to have, in true Renaissance fashion, a horoscope cast, it appears that a particularly felicitous constellation is favouring our enterprise. Could even the most inspired astrologer have predicted that the Music Division of the Library and Museum of the Performing Arts, in the exhibit arranged by their fine group of librarians led by Thor Wood,

Frank Campbell, and Susan Sommer, would be able to produce a new, unknown copy of the first print of polyphonic music containing a number of works by Josquin, Petrucci's famous *Odhecaton*, printed in Venice in 1501 and reprinted in 1503 and 1504, of which so far only six copies have been known to survive? Our thanks go to all of them and in particular to Mrs. Sommer, Curator of Rare Books, who is responsible for an unusually thoughtful and imaginative exhibit. Would anyone have been able to foretell that by the time our Conference takes place the Pierpont Morgan Library would have received, ordered, and catalogued the Carey Collection of musical autographs, some of whose unbelievable riches, together with previous treasures, will be shown to our speakers and conductors as a special exhibit at a time when the Library is usually closed? For such generosity we cannot be sufficiently grateful to the Director, Dr. Charles Ryskamp, and to Herbert Cahoon, Curator of Manuscripts, and his staff, who are preparing the exhibit.

We are indebted not only to individuals and institutions: The Belgian, Dutch, German, and Italian governments—the last unfortunately too late to be included on the program—have aided the Conference with generous grants.

But surely the most felicitous constellation under which the Conference operates concerns the work of Dutch musicologists who have—just in time for our celebrations—completed, in precisely fifty years of hard and dedicated labour, the edition of works by Josquin des Prez.

It was a historic moment when the Board of the Dutch Musicological Society in 1919, right after the end of the First World War, decided to bring out an edition of Josquin's works and entrusted it to the young Albert Smijers, who, only two years earlier, had acquired his Doctor of Philosophy degree from the University of Vienna, where he had studied under the guidance of Guido Adler.

It is hard today to do full justice to the heroic dimensions of Smijers' work. Should anyone have used such a word in his presence, Smijers, always calm, gentle, imperturbable, would have smiled. But under the calm surface was an iron will and an unshakable steadiness of purpose. Smijers travelled all over Europe in search of the sources of Josquin's works, written and printed. Only a few catalogues were then available. His travels became veritable expeditions. He discovered many now famous manuscripts and was the first to describe them.

Smijers was a man of few words. His letters, always hand-written, ordinarily consisted of only a few lines. His edition of Josquin is concise and economic, but, if we consider that it was essentially the work of one man, of a surprising excellence. Smijers never hesitated to change his views or his editorial techniques. He began the edition with unreduced note values and old clefs; he changed to reduced note values and modern clefs. When, in 1926, he published as first Mass the 'Missa L'homme armé super voces musicales', he based it on MS. Cappella Sistina 154, written between 1550 and 1555, the only one among the many sources that transmits the *Credo* in its entirety: all other sources lack the final part of the *Credo*. Thirty-one years later, in 1957, the year of his death, when he published a new edition of the same Mass, Smijers used instead the Petrucci print of 1502, placing the final section of the *Credo* in Cappella Sistina 154 in an appendix, and characterizing it as almost certainly spurious—testimony of a strong sense of self-criticism, the mark of a true scholar.

It is to the credit of the Dutch Musicological Society that it carried Smijers' work to completion under the leadership of his one-time student and later assistant, Professor Myroslaw Antonowycz, later aided by Dr. Willem Elders, who had begun his studies under Smijers and completed them under René Lenaerts. It is to these men that we owe a complete edition of the works of Josquin des Prez.

Smijers, through his own revisions of earlier editions, indicated the need for a new edition. The Dutch Musicological Society has already announced plans for a second edition. The present Congress could not have been held at a more auspicious moment. For it is my conviction—and our Dutch friends and colleagues, I believe, will agree with me—that it is impossible today to produce a new edition of Josquin's works that is truly up-to-date without international cooperation. Now that the first edition has been completed, nothing would be more beneficial than a lengthy pause, an interval that should be filled with well-planned international working conferences in which all aspects of a new edition would be subjected to dispassionate, thorough, many-sided scrutiny and from which, without haste, might emerge the guidelines for a new edition.

The present Conference, with a number of specialized papers and a three-hour symposium on editorial problems, will, I trust, furnish the initial impetus to such a discussion.

But the concerns of this Congress are spanned more widely. This is a Festival as well as a Conference. The *leitmotif* of the whole event is the most thorough integration of art and scholarship. The concert programs are designed to give a vivid idea of the character, genius, versatility, and evolution of a great musical artist; they are conceived with a view toward letting us hear as many unrecorded works as possible without being pedantic—for you will find old favourites in these programs as well—they are intended to create a full artistic image against whose background the scholar's search for the essence of the man and his art makes an entirely different sense.

It is time that scholars and musicians met face to face. For we witness a growing dichotomy between the musical ensembles performing, recording, and creating the *public* image of the composer, and the scholars writing, researching, and creating the *scholarly* image of the composer. The two images cannot and should not be the same; but they ought to be related. Musicians and scholars should keep in touch. They have a lot to learn from each other. We scholars must learn that whenever a group of gifted musicians led by an imaginative conductor presents a composer's work in a new interpretation, we discover something about that composer that cannot be learned in any other way. The musicians must learn that unless they keep conversant with current scholarship they may not even know whether what they perform as Josquin is in fact by Josquin. A number of works that now are part of the Josquin edition will not appear in a truly critical second edition. One of the most famous Masses by Josquin, the 'Missa Da pacem', has been proven to be a work by Noel Bauldewyn in a masterly monograph by Edgar Sparks that is just in process of publication by the American Musicological Society. Current scholarship will furnish the performers also with better and more authentic readings of Josquin's scores; it will provide them with new insights into the manifold performing possibilities in Josquin's own time, and it will disclose the use of a more colourful harmonic palette by applying *musica ficta* more in tune with contemporaneous practice.

The workshops have been set up precisely for such an encounter between performers and scholars. We scholars talk too much about performance practice and too little about interpretation. The performer has, after all, a problem that is peculiarly his own: how to interpret old music for a present-day audience. The ideal performer struggles in equal measure for vitality of interpretation as for ever increasing insight into the intentions of the composer and the performance traditions of the period. If he disregards the latter, it should not be from ignorance, but as a responsible artistic choice. Such choices are important. It is not the task of musicology to deprive us of them.

The more profound a composer is, the more does his music lend itself to a variety of interpretations. We have chosen the four ensembles that will give us the four concerts of Josquin's music not only for their excellence, but for their differences of national and individual temperament and for the wide spectrum of interpretative possibilities of Josquin's music which they will reveal to us. I wish to thank them for having come to New York for this occasion, for it is unquestionably they who will leave us with the most vivid memories. They deserve our thanks also for the way in which they have consented to help in illustrating the lectures, building the workshops, and celebrating Josquin's memory this very morning by the performance of two lamentations on his death by two younger contemporaries and two lamentations by Josquin himself.

And now it is time for music to speak.

Nicolas Gombert: 'Musae Jovis ter maximi' *(Schola Cantorum, Stuttgart)*
Hieronymus Vinders: 'O mors inevitabilis' *(Capella Antiqua, München)*

PALISCA: No commemoration is complete without a proper *encomium*. We are deeply grateful that Professor Friedrich Blume, braving the wrath of his doctors, undertook the long trip from Schlüchtern, Germany to deliver that oration. No one more completely epitomizes the ideals of this conference-cum-festival than he. In 1929 he inaugurated a series of editions under the title *Das Chorwerk* dedicated to the proposition that music of earlier times must be sung and played as well as read silently and analyzed. It is significant that he chose for the first volume of that series, which now numbers more than one hundred, his edition of a work of Josquin des Prez, the 'Missa Pange lingua', a work that he justified for this honour by describing it as one of the half-dozen most important Masses in six centuries of polyphony. He followed up that volume with his own editions of two more Masses, including the 'Missa de Beata Virgine', which you will hear on Thursday evening, a volume of Josquin's secular songs, and three volumes of his motets. Most of us here who grew up before the age of the Xerox machine sang and played our first Josquin from these handy, scholarly, and supremely practical editions. The masterfully concise paragraphs of introduction to these volumes would make a fine anthology of quotations by themselves, or in the language of the stylebook of *MGG*, a complete *Würdigung*.

It is a unique privilege and great pleasure for me to introduce the first President of the International Musicological Society, distinguished editor of *Die Musik in Geschichte und Gegenwart*, and corresponding member of the American Musicological Society, Professor Friedrich Blume.

Here Professor Blume read the paper which follows.

PALISCA: Our universal and everlasting thanks, Professor Blume, for these inspiring and judicious words and for putting into broad perspective the tasks that lie ahead.

After this commemorative eloquence, we proceed to the eloquence we are here to commemorate.

Josquin des Prez: 'Planxit autem David' *(Prague Madrigal Singers)*
Josquin des Prez: 'Nymphes des bois' *(Déploration d'Ockeghem) (New York Pro Musica)*

Josquin des Prez:
The Man and the Music

FRIEDRICH BLUME

When, early in May of the year 1927, we studied, and finally performed, the 'Missa Pange lingua' of Josquin, no one foresaw that this event would set rolling a snowball destined to grow into an avalanche. 'We' in this case means my students, both of musicology and related areas, at the old Berlin University (now called Humboldt University). I had organized a 'Collegium Musicum Vocale' with these young men and women, and all were full of enthusiasm and the excitement of discovery.

The performable music from the fifteenth and sixteenth centuries then accessible to us and responsive to our needs was rather limited. The *embarras de richesses* we are enjoying today in the field of newly edited 'old' music (whatever 'old' may mean in this context) had not yet begun to make itself felt. At the beginning we were not too particular in our choice; we took whatever we could get hold of. Our major stumbling block was always the lack of scholarly editions that could also be used for musical performance. Available editions, as a rule, were meant for church use and consisted mostly of 'favourite pieces'. Worse yet, to render the music true to its original intent seemed far less important than to display the editor's fancy. So it came about that we directed our efforts first of all to copying suitable music from the 'Denkmäler', 'Kritische Gesamtausgaben', and the like. Soon we discovered many singable compositions of the fifteenth and sixteenth centuries and resuscitated many a fine work of a famous old master (Ockeghem, for instance) whose name figured in textbooks, but whose compositions were virtually unknown.

Josquin supplied us with a test case. Once, early in the history of the Collegium Musicum, a very young man, score in hand, addressed me: 'Herr Doktor, können wir nicht das hier einmal singen?' What did he bring along, carrying it like a holy relic? Browsing in the Musikabteilung of the old Prussian State Library in Berlin, he had stumbled upon the fifth volume of Ambros's *Geschichte der Musik* of 1889 and had fallen in love with Josquin's 'Missa Pange lingua'. He had copied and mimeographed it for the members of the Collegium Musicum; we sang the Mass, and we were all fascinated by it.

I am not telling this story just to amuse you but to offer a tiny contribution toward the genesis of modern historical musicology. The discovery of Josquin's Mass was a spontaneous experience for the young man, for all of us; for a moment it illuminated the approach to the history of music by practical performance. It is a test case for the close connection between youthful enthusiasm for 'old' music and the urgent need for modern editions. Later, in 1927, we performed the 'Missa Pange lingua' (this was possibly the first performance in four centuries), and in July 1929 the same work was presented to the general public as No. 1 of a new series, *Das Chorwerk*. I founded *Das Chorwerk* on a homage to Josquin, as it were. (The series is still being published and has grown in the meantime to 111 issues.) Thus the snowball was set rolling. From that time on, innumerable choruses have devoted their efforts to Josquin and many practical editions of old music have included works by him.

On the basis of this 'discovery', Josquin grew rapidly to the stature of one of the greatest musicians in history—the same Josquin about whom we had known so little!

What did the name of Josquin mean to the student of the history of music at that time? All our knowledge came either from Kiesewetter's *Die Verdienste der Niederländer um die Tonkunst* (1829), or from Ambros who, in the third volume of his *Geschichte der Musik* (1868), drew for the first time a comprehensive picture of the 'Era of the Netherlanders', as he entitled his chapter. It is, with all its errors and omissions, one of those 'classical' essays in music history that one should re-read now and again. By the way, in those days 'Netherlands music and musicians' was a generally accepted term for any music and musicians between the Ciconia-Dufay period and the end of the sixteenth century insofar as they originated in the Low Countries, which then comprised Belgium, the southern parts of Holland, and some parts of Northern France. The recent controversies concerning Josquin's place of birth and native language have, as far as I can see, produced no definitive results. Modern scholarship seems inclined to recognize Josquin as having been born in Picardy or Vermandois, at all events in French-speaking territory, and not in the Flemish-speaking Hainaut, as older scholars would have it.[1]

After Josquin's 'rediscovery', research on the man and his music developed at an incredibly fast pace. The edition of his works, it is true, had been started in the year 1921 by Albert Smijers. It has been continued with many and long intermissions into the 1960s, and has now been completed with the issue of a Supplement (1969). A thorough check of the total number of compositions handed down to posterity under the name of Josquin proved that in his own lifetime as well as later in the sixteenth century a considerable number of works of dubious authenticity, even spurious works,

[1] [On this point, see below, pp. 92-3 and 208—Ed.]

have beclouded the tradition. If I am not mistaken, there is a recognized stock of twenty Masses by Josquin complete and authentic. However, I understand that this number should perhaps be reduced by one, insofar as the 'Missa Da pacem' has recently been suspected to be a composition by his contemporary, Noel Bauldeweyn.[2] Apart from these twenty—or nineteen—complete Masses, there are six single Mass movements. But about eight or nine complete Masses and three single movements, certainly not composed by Josquin, have crept into the traditional corpus of works, mostly owing to the carelessness of the music printers of the period, who sometimes interspersed the names of well-known composers rather frivolously among the pieces of music they printed. In some cases the true composers have been identified by industrious scholars, but as a rule the authorship of such movements or cycles remains in doubt.

The situation is similar with regard to the motets ascribed to Josquin. Tradition enumerates no fewer than ninety-five motets of the most different types, the lion's share set for four or five voices, some rare pieces for two to three, and a goodly number for six voices. With a few exceptions, all these motets are composed in two separate sections, some even in more, as for example 'Qui velatus facie fuisti' with six, 'Vultum tuum deprecabuntur' with seven, or the famous lament of David 'Planxit autem David' with four extended sections. These 'secundae' or 'tertiae partes', as they are called, can be used independently, because as a rule they are self-contained. Also, certain works such as the 'O admirabile commercium', with its four subsequent *partes* 'Quando natus es', 'Rubum, quem viderat', 'Germinavit radix Jesse', and 'Ecce Maria genuit' (*Werken*, Motetten, Bundel ii, nos. 5–9), do occur in certain sources as single pieces, one printed after the other, each with its own number. In other cases, certain favourite *partes* appear singly, quite separate from their context, such as the popular 'Mente tota', *quinta pars* of 'Vultum tuum deprecabuntur', on which Antoine Févin wrote a Mass. This brings the number of single motet sections up to more than two hundred, all of them regarded as authentic. But, as with the Masses, a considerable number of motet sections of dubious authenticity, as well as identifiable works by other composers, have been smuggled into the traditional heritage. I guess their number to be some fifty or sixty, and unfortunately several of them have been printed in the *Werken*, as, for example, 'O bone et dulcis' (no. 18) or 'Nunc dimittis servum tuum' (no. 93), both for four voices. For the motets the same holds true as for the Masses: now and then it has been possible to ascertain the true composer of the piece in question, but the authorship of most of the dubious or non-authenticated compositions remains in the dark. Some of the most famous composers of Josquin's time as well as of the following generation have been

---

[2] [See Edgar H. Sparks, *The Music of Noel Bauldeweyn* (American Musicological Society, Studies and Documents, No. 6; New York, 1972), esp. Ch. III.—Ed.]

suggested as authors for these controversial pieces, among them Willaert, Mouton, Senfl, Stoltzer, Brumel, Richafort, Verdelot, and so forth, but in most cases these are mere conjectures. Ten years ago Professor Antonowycz, in an article on the Josquin *Werken* in the Dutch journal, displayed a classic example: the motet 'Sancti Dei omnes', originally believed by both Smijers and Antonowycz to be a work by Josquin and on this basis incorporated into the *Werken*, but edited by Paul Kast from a version ascribed to Mouton in *Das Chorwerk* (no. 76) as early as in 1959, proved to be, by virtue of Antonowycz's own analysis, a composition of Mouton.[3]

An example such as this indicates how complicated the relation of tradition and style can be—and often is. If an eminent specialist on Josquin like Professor Antonowycz can be deceived by a motet handed down under different names in different sources, how can a poor non-specialist presume to judge questions like these?

Suffice it to say that for the secular works the same problems and questions hold true. The total of fifty-eight secular compositions at present regarded as authentic is paralleled by some twenty to twenty-five dubious or non-authenticated pieces ascribed to various composers of the era but mostly remaining anonymous.

As matters stand, one conclusion offers itself: further progress in Josquin research and in the study of the music of the whole age will largely depend on detailed inquiry into the catalogue of the authentic works of the master. This will probably be the most burning problem, for how should the scholar pursue serious studies of Josquin's music, and how should the amateur find an approach to this outstanding musician, unless they know that the composition in their hands is really by Josquin? I leave aside the still more complex question whether not only the piece itself but also its version is original or not. The late fifteenth and early sixteenth centuries, as all of us know, were periods when quotations from, and arrangements of the works of other composers, or even a composer's own works, belonged to the basic techniques of a composer's workshop. Many cases are known of authentic compositions being varied in some way or other, for example by the addition of newly invented voice-parts. I should like to remind you of the well-known case of the 'Ave Maria, gratia plena, Dominus tecum, Virgo serena' (no. 1 in the *Werken*) that, apart from its original version for four voices, exists in arrangements for six and eight voices.[4] 'Miserere mei,

---

[3] M. Antonowycz, 'Die Josquin-Ausgabe', *Tijdschrift van de Vereniging voor Nederlandse Muziekgeschiedenis*, xix (1960–1), pp. 6–31; esp. pp. 11–12.

[4] See Osthoff, *Josquin Desprez* (2 vols.; Tutzing, 1962–5), ii, pp. 86 and 111. Smijers published Senfl's six-part arrangement in the *Werken* (Motetten, Bundel i, Appendix); the eight-part arrangement in Verona, Società Accademia Filarmonica, MS. 218, draws only on Josquin's superius. The six-part version of Munich, Bayerische Staatsbibliothek, MS. mus. 41, adds two voices to Josquin's original version; it is published in the *Werken*, Motetten, Bundel i, as no. 1a.

Deus', composed for Duke Ercole I of Ferrara in 1503 or 1504, has been provided with a *sexta vox* by one Antoine Bidon, a fellow countryman of Josquin, who also sang in the Duke's chapel.[5] It will, therefore, remain a constant challenge to Josquin research to set up an inventory of indubitably authentic works and to eliminate all dubious and spurious works handed down erroneously under his name. I know how demanding and how pretentious it would be to establish a 'Thematisch-systematisches Verzeichnis', a Köchel, as it were, for Josquin. Still, it seems to me that without such an inventory, research on Josquin will remain seriously hampered by unreliable ascriptions.

This is a bibliographical problem derived from the present state of Josquin research, as I see it. On its solution depends the answer to the next and no less urgent problem, the definition of Josquin's individual style viewed in the perspective of the general style of his day, and the development of his style within his large oeuvre. Most studies on Josquin published within the last decades are concerned to some degree with the question of style. Most of them proceed by describing characteristic details of the authentic works, but they also draw on details from dubious works or on works by other composers. Among the host of scholars who have worked, or are working in this field, I want to single out one distinguished man, Professor Helmuth Osthoff, well known as the author of the comprehensive two-volume monograph on Josquin. In his paper read at the Utrecht Congress in 1952,[6] a contribution that was the result of decades of meticulous investigation into this complex and delicate question, he tried to establish a scheme of three stages in Josquin's style and its development. This was a tentative effort, of course; but it is important enough to be quoted in outline at least. According to Osthoff, Josquin's style, in its first decades—that is, during the approximately twenty-five years from 1459 to 1486, when Josquin joined the Papal Chapel in Rome—is characterized by a rather imprecise relationship between the words and the music; the part-writing tends to be abstract, often complex, full of so-called 'instrumentalisms'; the cadences dispense with thirds and fifths; final notes often appear in an isolated position, with archaic suspensions. In the middle stage, coinciding with the Roman years, from 1486 to (at most) 1501, the relation between words and music grows closer; musical symbols appear for single words or affections; the 'instrumentalisms' gradually disappear; systematic imitation often replaces free contrapuntal invention; and the cadences use thirds and fifths. The late style is marked by a close affinity between the words and the music; melodic invention often depends on the meaning of the words.

   [5] [See Lewis Lockwood's article in these Proceedings, pp. 103–37.—Ed.]

   [6] Helmuth Osthoff, 'Zur Echtheitsfrage und Chronologie bei Josquins Werken', *Internationale Gesellschaft für Musikwissenschaft, Kongressbericht Utrecht 1952* (Amsterdam, 1953), pp. 303–9.

The techniques of canon and *cantus firmus* are relegated to the background; the complex rhythmic textures and the 'instrumentalisms' disappear more and more; they are replaced by frequent syllabic declamation of the words.

All of this is good and useful to know. However, important questions remain. First of all, there is a question of methodology: does it make sense to study the different stages of one composer's style, to the exclusion of the individual style of contemporaneous composers? Are the stylistic traits of a certain period confined to the individual composer, or are they valid for the generation as a whole, or compatible with local developments? These are old questions—the relationship between personal style, generic style, and so forth—and they are full of imponderables. In the specific case of Josquin, they are the more significant since we know so little about the composer's life and works.

Here another problem intervenes—the question of chronology as connected with the analysis of style. The industrious and meticulous research of the last twenty years notwithstanding, further inquiry into the chronology of Josquin's life and works is urgently needed. Unfortunately, our knowledge of biographical dates is as limited as that of the dates of single works. Normal procedure would require us to fix, first of all, the biographical data, scant though they be, and then with their aid investigate whether any of the master's works could be connected with them. Only when we succeed in establishing a skeleton of biographical and compositional data can we hope to arrive at an understanding of the development of Josquin's style. The tradition that has been established concerning Josquin's works does not offer much help; it may even lead us astray, as the example of the Masses shows.

Josquin des Prez is, as we all know, the first musician in history whose compositions have been published in a coherent series of individual prints, prints, that is, containing no works save his own. Ottaviano Petrucci published three books of Josquin's Masses in 1502, 1505, and 1514. In contrast to custom, these volumes contain exactly what their title says: *Missae Josquin, liber primus, secundus*, and *tertius*, and not one work by another composer. A supplementary volume of 1505, *Fragmenta missarum*, intersperses compositions by Josquin with Mass movements of other composers. Here we have the example of a fixed date for the long series of Josquin's Masses; unfortunately, it is no more than a *terminus ad quem* and does not offer us any information on the dates when these Masses really were composed.

From this situation resulted what, in my opinion, is an error concerning the dates of the Masses in general. In his three volumes Petrucci published seventeen of the twenty complete Masses of Josquin that have traditionally been considered genuine. One of the three that escaped Petrucci's attention, 'Allez regrets', seems to have eluded everyone else; as far as I can see, it was printed for the first time in the *Werken*. The two remaining Masses—'Da pacem' (if still considered authentic) and 'Pange lingua'—were published for the first time by the Nuremberg printer Johann Ott, in 1539, in his *Missae tredecim*. Taking their point of departure from Ott's solitary print, some scholars (beginning as early as the 1860s with Ambros) have been led to the assumption that the Masses 'Da pacem' and 'Pange lingua' represent the latest group of such compositions. Osthoff proposed to include also the 'Missa de Beata Virgine', praised by Glareanus as the 'perfectissimum corpus', the most familiar of Josquin's Masses during the sixteenth century. However, the style of 'Da pacem' and 'Pange lingua' by no means agrees with that of 'de Beata Virgine'. Ott's isolated print does *not* prove that the two Masses really are late works, but another *terminus ad quem* can be deduced from the fact that the 'de Beata Virgine' Mass was printed by Petrucci in 1514 in his *liber tertius*, and some movements of this same Mass make their appearance in a manuscript written for Pope Julius II, that is between 1503 and 1513 (MS. Cappella Sistina 23).

It was my intention to show you with this one example how closely connected the problem of chronology is with the problem of style, and how the lack of reliable dates for Josquin's life and works can easily lead to wrong inferences. For, if the theory of the so-called 'group of late Masses' should prove to be unfounded, the chronology of the Masses linked with this last stage also collapses.

Chronology and style of the motets are beset by corresponding doubts and questions. Professor Lowinsky, in his brilliant article on Josquin and Ascanio Sforza,[7] has discussed a similar example, with the following result: 'Now if we must assume that the young Josquin could write [the Passion motet] *O Domine Jesu Christe* in the style said to belong to his late phase, if we must further accept the fact that he wrote *Huc me sydereo*, a work that has all the aspects of his middle period, in his last years, then the whole foundation of the stylistic evolution of Josquin begins to crumble.'

Josquin was, it seems, the first great composer in history to place the motet well to the fore, whereas the older composers, Ockeghem, for example, regarded the Mass as the weightiest form of religious music. The traditional number of motets listed under Josquin's name amounts to approximately ninety-five. They offer the greatest variety of texts and styles, but only a handful can be dated with any certainty. The 'Déploration d'Ockeghem', now that the date of his death has been discovered, can be dated as having been written after 6 February 1497.[8] The 'Salve Regina'

---

[7] 'Josquin des Prez and Ascanio Sforza', *Congresso Internazionale sul Duomo di Milano: Atti*, ed. M. L. Gatti Perer (Milan, 1969), ii, pp. 17–22.

[8] [See 'Johannes Ockeghem overleed op 6 februari 1497', Addendum to *Johannes Ockeghem en zijn tijd*, Catalogue of Exhibition at Dendermonde, 14 November–6 December 1970 (Dendermonde, 1970), pp. 279–80.—Ed.]

for five voices can be given to the year 1502, provided it was *this* 'Salve Regina' that Sigismondo Cantelmo, Count of Sora, sent to the Duke of Ferrara with a letter of 24 February 1502.[9] The 'Miserere' for five voices composed for Ercole I of Ferrara—if it was *this* 'Miserere'—can be connected with Josquin's service at the court of Ferrara in about 1501 to 1505.[10] The motet 'Memor esto' for four voices is reported to have been written for King Louis XII as a reminder to keep his promise of securing a prebend for the musician;[11] if this information is correct, the motet could have been composed between about 1501 and 1507. Finally, if the five-voice 'De profundis' with the triple canon is indeed the funeral music for Louis XII, it must have been written in 1515.[12] Professor Lowinsky, in his article on Josquin and Ascanio Sforza, has managed most ingeniously to connect three of Josquin's works convincingly with particular events and to suggest that they were composed at the behest of Ascanio Sforza: 'Fama malum' by Virgil for the wedding of the Duke of Milan in 1489, the 'Missa Hercules Dux Ferrariae' for a visit of Ercole I to Rome in 1487, and the motet 'Absalon fili mi' as an offering of condolence to Pope Alexander VI, when his son Juan Borgia had been murdered in 1497.[13] But this is all we know of occasions and dates when these seven particular motets (and one Mass) out of almost a hundred may have been composed. For all the rest, dates may be guessed on the basis of more or less plausible assumptions, on anecdotes, or on dubious stylistic observations.

The fact is that Josquin did not create a standard style either in his motets or in his Masses. The texture may be more or less contrapuntal or homophonic, the use of canon frequent or rare, *cantus firmus* may or may not be present, the relationship between words and music may be loose or strict. Most surprising is that foretaste of Baroque tone-painting in Josquin's music that might well be the chief ground why his contemporaries compared him to Michelangelo. In Psalm 92, 'Dominus regnavit', there is a representation of the waves of the sea in unmistakably graphic motives and an impressive syllabic declamation, whereas a related work, the setting of Psalm 37, 'Domine, ne in furore tuo', appears to steer clear of specific expression of the psalm's powerful and dramatic words. Modern interpreters of Josquin's motets should not forget that since the Baroque era the power of affective musical language increased to such an extent that our ears may have grown deaf to what struck the Renaissance listener as the faithful expression of the words in musical configurations.

Lest I allow myself to be sidetracked by enticing views on the problem of Josquin's relationship to the Renaissance and humanism, permit me to conclude my remarks anent Josquin's motets by stating that the problems

---

[9] Osthoff, i, p. 51.   [10] Ibid., p. 57.   [11] Ibid., p. 41.

[12] Ibid., pp. 48–9; see also Herbert Kellman's article in these Proceedings, pp. 189–90.

[13] Lowinsky, 'Josquin des Prez and Ascanio Sforza', pp. 19–21.

of chronology and style are no less stubborn here than they are regarding the Masses or the secular works. These last can be simple or full of artifice, they can follow the courtly style or adapt themselves to popular tunes and rhymes, they can embrace French or Italian taste. They, too, steer clear of a standard style or formula. Finally, there are motet-like compositions after Virgil, such as 'Fama malum', 'Dulces exuviae', or contemporaneous poems in Latin with a humanistic mixture of secular and religious, such as 'Illibata Dei Virgo nutrix' (which contains Josquin's name in the guise of an acrostic), or 'Ut Phoebi radiis' (on the syllables of the hexachord).[14] Whereas some of Josquin's chansons can be related to certain persons, such as the Duchess Margaret of Austria, residing in Malines as regent for the Low Countries, or to certain events such as the Anglo-Empire alliance of 1507, most secular compositions lack hints at external dates; they are the more difficult to arrange in chronological order since diversities of style betray their relationship with different traditions, for example, the frottola and lauda, whose dates of origin are as dubious as are the dates of Josquin's imitations,[15] or his attempts to develop a new motet style from these Italian models.

Our knowledge of Josquin's works—the meticulous research of the last decades notwithstanding—is weak on all points; whether on the catalogue of his authentic compositions or on the large body of dubious and spurious works, on their chronology or on their problems of style, and equally weak on all three sections of his oeuvre: the Masses, the motets, and the secular compositions. This is one reason why our picture of Josquin's personality —insofar as we have one—is unsatisfactory: we are only beginning to understand his role in the history of music, and despite all attempts at scrutinizing his personality and ascertaining his ties to the persons surrounding him, and regardless of the enormous increase in our knowledge of details, Josquin the man remains obscure. The 'last word' has certainly not been spoken on the historical phenomenon called Josquin des Prez. Biographical details have been handed down from generation to generation, they have been checked by reference to historical sources, and they have been sifted and criticized. Bibliographical details of the sources on which our knowledge of the works rests are being investigated to the farthest corners, libraries and archives explored from basement to attic. But it is not the biographical and bibliographical details on which the historical picture of a great artist rests; or, at least, they are not absolutely essential. The essence of a great artist lies in his creative accomplishments, and the assessment of the oeuvre depends on the knowledge of its evolution, i.e. on the knowledge of its chronology, and its stylistic growth.

[14] [The riddle of this text with its nonsense syllables has been solved by Virginia W. Callahan; see her paper in these Proceedings, pp. 560–3.—Ed.]

[15] [On the likely date of origin of the four-part homophonic lauda and frottola, see Edgar Sparks's article in these Proceedings, p. 345, n. 3.—Ed.]

Professor Lowinsky, in his study on Josquin and Ascanio Sforza, has summed up with admirable understanding and empathy the general evolution of Josquin's style and personality: Josquin's 'chief significance in the history of music lies in his slow evolution from a great contrapuntist to the first composer to put all of his musical gifts into the service of expression of human affections'. I like this view and am ready to follow so enticing a picture. But I find it hard to disregard the fact that this enlightened appreciation rests on the shaky ground of sparse reliable biographical dates. Of course, nobody knows this better than Professor Lowinsky himself, who continues, 'Unfortunately, Josquin's biography contains many voids; there are numerous years in his life for which we have no certain information. Nor do we have an assured chronology of his works.'[16]

It is this problem on which further progress depends, and I am convinced that a conference like the present one will be able to lend fresh impetus to Josquin research. As far as I can see, we owe this idea to Professor Lowinsky who, in the strictest sense of the word, is the *spiritus rector* of this assembly; he can be assured of the gratitude of all concerned, of all Josquin enthusiasts. If I may speak in the name of the foreign guests, thanks are also due to the American Musicological Society and to the Rennaissance Society of America who are sponsoring this conference and whose hospitality has enabled so many foreigners, especially Europeans, to attend the event.

There is one idea that struck me when perusing the outlines of the 'Festival-Conference'. It is the idea of not confining the plan to a mere sequence of learned papers and to the specialists' discussion of the problems of editing, but combining the most recent results of Josquin research with musical performance and workshops. The preliminary announcement reads: 'The workshops will be directed by scholar-musicians.... The four ensembles and a few musicologists will co-operate in exploring various ways of performing.... In the centre of the workshops stands experimental demonstration....' This reminds me of our first and very modest beginnings in resuscitating Josquin not by research but by simply singing his music and, then, by editing it. We did not know much of historical performance practice, nor did we have the means to carry out experiments. We did what the spirit of music suggested to us and, thus, we found a practical approach leading us to a deepened enthusiasm for Josquin. And it is that same enthusiasm for Josquin that has brought us together in this 'Festival-Conference'.

[16] Lowinsky, 'Josquin des Prez and Ascanio Sforza', p. 17.

I Biographical Background and Historical View

Ascanio Sforza's Life: A Key to Josquin's Biography and an Aid to the Chronology of his Works[*]

EDWARD E. LOWINSKY

Introduction

The greatest paradox in Josquin's biography is the sharp contrast between his universal fame and the sparsity of biographical data. The greatest mystery is the time of his youth and his development to maturity.

Ever since Claudio Sartori's discovery, published in 1956, that Josquin did not come to Milan in 1474 to take a post as singer in the newly founded chapel of Duke Galeazzo Maria Sforza of Milan, as had been generally assumed, but that he had been a singer in the Duomo of Milan since 1459,[1] it was clear that the solution to the mystery of Josquin's youth lay in the archives of Milan. And a mystery it is; for the greatest composer of his age appears in the records of the Duomo with the modest monthly salary of two florins, the average payment of the singers, and fifteen years later in the account books of the court with a monthly salary of five ducats, compared to the seven, eight, ten, and twelve ducats earned by other members of the chapel.[2] What adds to the mystery are the frequent and lengthy absences from service,[3] and the hiatus of seven and a half years in Josquin's life from April 1479 to September 1486, when he entered the Papal Chapel in Rome.

Scholars have wondered with justification what the reasons were for the inferior financial position of the young genius. Sartori is of the opinion that 'Josquin was not particularly appreciated in Milan',[4] indeed that he was not even called to Milan, but went there on his own initiative to offer his

[*] I am deeply indebted to Dr. Bonnie J. Blackburn, who shared with me in the laborious task of exploring the rich mine of materials at the Archivio di Stato in Milan and of copying the documents. Her unceasing enthusiasm was a constant source of pleasure and inspiration.

[1] Claudio Sartori, 'Josquin des Prés cantore del Duomo di Milano', *Annales musicologiques*, iv (1956), pp. 55–83.

[2] Ibid., p. 64, n. 1.   [3] Ibid., pp. 65–6.   [4] Ibid., p. 82.

services. Another hypothesis offered was that Josquin, before his entrance into the court chapel of Milan, even though over thirty years of age, had given only scarce proofs of his talent. '[T]here seems no way to escape the conclusion', writes Nino Pirrotta, 'that, for all his potential gifts, Josquin had a late start as a composer.'[5] Pirrotta believes that the fault lay with his environment, and he goes on to say: 'Whatever may have diverted the brilliant and enterprising young man from the path which would later commit his name to history, his example dramatically raises the question of the degree to which the atmosphere of the Italian courts and towns during the second half of the 15th century was actually favorable to the artistic development of a young composer of polyphonic music.' In a recent article, Clement Miller surmised that the absence of Josquin's name in Gafurius' writings before the *Practica musicae* of 1496 'gives further support to the thesis that Josquin's reputation as a composer did not begin before about 1490.'[6]

How can such views be reconciled with the appearance of Josquin's name right after that of Ockeghem in the famous 'singer's prayer', 'Omnium bonorum plena', by Loyset Compère, in which Dufay is referred to as a living master, and which therefore must be dated before 1474? Ludwig Finscher, biographer of Compère and editor of his complete works, holds this to be a work of Compère's youth and thinks it might have been composed as early as 1470.[7]

One avenue of research had never been tried. From a poem of Serafino dall'Aquila, 'Ad Jusquino suo compagno musico d'Ascanio', and two compositions in Petrucci's books of frottole, in which Josquin is called 'Josquin d'Ascanio', we know that the great Cardinal Ascanio Sforza, brother of Ludovico il Moro, Duke of Milan, had been Josquin's patron—no one knows where, when, nor how long. If we could trace Ascanio Sforza's life and movements, might we not find out when Josquin served him and

---

[5] Nino Pirrotta, 'Music and Cultural Tendencies in 15th-Century Italy', *Journal of the American Musicological Society*, xix (1966), pp. 127–61; p. 128.

[6] Clement A. Miller, 'Early Gaffuriana: New Answers to Old Questions', *Musical Quarterly*, lvi (1970), pp. 367–88; p. 376. Perhaps one might refer here to a little noted passage in Gafurius' *Angelicum ac divinum opus musice*, published in Milan in 1508 and presenting for the most part a summary of Gafurius' *Practica musicae*, which was published in 1496 but in parts written in the early 1480s (ibid., p. 374; see also idem, 'Gaffurius's *Practica musicae*: Origin and Contents', *Musica disciplina*, xxii (1968), pp. 105–28). It contains a reference to conversations Gafurius had 'gia molti anni passati' with 'Iusquin despriet et Gaspar dignissimi compositori' (Book V, ch. 6). Obviously, this is a reference to conversations between Gafurius on the one hand and Josquin and Weerbeke on the other. Since the only years in which the three lived together in one place were the years in Milan from 1473 to 1475, Gafurius' personal acquaintance goes back at least to the early period of Josquin's service at the court of Milan.

[7] Ludwig Finscher, *Loyset Compère (c. 1450–1518), Life and Works* (American Institute of Musicology, 1964), p. 140.

whether the many gaps in his biography might be related to this service?[8] But no book, not even one single good article, exists on the cardinal. At the time of my first visit to Milan in 1968, I discovered that the Archivio di Stato in Milan possesses thousands and thousands of documents containing the diplomatic correspondence between Ascanio, as cardinal in Rome, and the government in Milan, for Ascanio's position was religious in name, but in fact political; he functioned chiefly as the head of Milan's diplomatic mission in Rome. It seemed an almost quixotic undertaking to study this huge mass of documents dealing with politics and diplomacy in the hope of finding a clue to the cardinal's interest in music. But to make progress in Josquin's biography it was necessary to form a picture of Ascanio's personality and life and above all to record minutely his movements in an effort to coordinate them with the known facts as well as with the voids in Josquin's biography. At the same time the archives needed to be searched for new documents on Josquin.

Two new documents on Josquin from 1473 and 1474

Emilio Motta had already thoroughly combed the Milanese archives for his study on music and musicians at the Sforza court.[9] An updated and expanded version of musical life at the court was written by Guglielmo Barblan in the *Storia di Milano*.[10] These writers did very valuable work; but they missed a huge number of documents, including two letters dealing with Josquin.

The first document is a chancellery minute, dated 20 September 1473 and issued from Pavia, one of the seats of the dukes of Milan (see Pl. 1). The letter is directed to the Cardinal of Novara, who is requested to prevail on his secretary to relinquish formally his claim on a certain benefice in Gozzano that he had obtained. The reason stated is: 'we have had it given to our singer, Josquin':

[8] In an earlier paper delivered at the International Congress on the Duomo of Milan in 1968, I attempted to connect certain special works of Josquin with certain events in Ascanio's life as described in Ludwig Pastor's *History of the Popes* and in the diaries of Johann Burchard, the German-born Master of Ceremonies of Alexander VI. (For the compositions in question see Edward E. Lowinsky, 'Josquin des Prez and Ascanio Sforza', *Congresso Internazionale sul Duomo di Milano, Atti*, ed. Maria Luisa Gatti Perer, 2 vols. (Milan, 1969), ii, pp. 17–22, and this paper, pp. 67–8). After the close of the Congress, I took the opportunity to initiate the exploration of the documents from the Sforza era in the Archivio di Stato. I returned for a stay of eight months in 1969. I wish to thank Prof. A. R. Natale, Director of the Archivio, and members of his staff, Dr. Adele Bellù and Mr. Enrico Gavazzeni, for their kind assistance. I also wish to thank my friends, Miss Maria Pia Ceruti and Mr. Mario Fara, for counsel and for help in making extracts, and sometimes complete copies of documents.

[9] Emilio Motta, 'Musici alla Corte degli Sforza', *Archivio Storico Lombardo*, 2nd ser., iv (1887), pp. 29–64, 278–340, 514–61.

[10] 'Vita musicale alla corte sforzesca', *Storia di Milano*, ix (1961), pp. 787–852.

Pavia, 20 September 1473. To the Cardinal of Novara. Most Reverend Father in Christ, etc. We request your Reverend Lordship to have your secretary, who upon his supplication was granted the benefice of Gozzano, which we had given to Josquin, our singer, prepare those free deeds of renunciation that are needed for the free resignation, and thereupon collation from the Holy Father, because to have given him only the signed supplication does not render it secure, though he claims to have been well counselled on this. But it is necessary that your secretary have made here a letter of proxy for renouncing [a benefice]. Thus, may it please Your Lordship to have it done, for that will please us very much.[11]

Josquin's name appears in the list of singers at the Duomo for the last time in December 1472; it reappears in a list of the court chapel dated 15 July 1474. It is found also in an undated list which can with great probability be ascribed to the year 1473.[12] Sartori makes much of the fact that Josquin remained in the service of the Cathedral until the end of 1472, whereas other singers had passed into the ducal service before. 'Perhaps', writes Sartori, 'his delay is due to lack of interest on the part of the duke. He was certainly the youngest of the French singers, the least well known. Perhaps he was already considered an Italian, in view of his long residence in Milan.'[13] The letter of September 1473 puts an end to all of these speculations. Galeazzo Maria Sforza, Duke of Milan, had conferred a benefice upon Josquin at a time prior to September 1473.[14] To do so, he did not

[11] Papie. xx. Septembris 1473.

Cardinali Novariensi.

Reverendissime in Christo pater et domine pater nobis optime. Pregamo vostra Reverendissima Signoria che vogli fare che quello vostro secretario qual impetro lo benefitio da Gozano, El quale nuy havemo facto dare ad Joschino nostro cantore, faci quelli instrumenti liberi de renuntiatione che bisognano per havere la libera resignatione, et deinde collatione dal sancto patre, peroche lo haverli dato solamente la supplicatione signata non lo rende securo, come dice esserne ben consigliato. ma bisogna chel secretario vostro li faci qua carta de procura ad renuntiandum etc. piacia aduncha ad vostra Signoria farla fare, che ne sara gratissimo. (Archivio di Stato, Milan, Fondo Sforzesco, Carteggio Generale, Novara, cart. 825). Abbreviations have been resolved, *u* and *v* normalized, and punctuation added.

A later hand added on the upper left margin the following précis: '1473. 20 settembre. Al Cardinale di Novara: Perche faccia munire il cantore ducale de ricapiti necessarij onde avere dal Santo Padre la collazione del beneficio di Gozzano'. A modern hand added on the upper right margin: '1473 sett. 20'. The marginal notes prove that the document was not unknown to archivists. They also suggest that the name of Josquin was not familiar to the Milanese archivists.

[12] See the facsimile in *Storia di Milano*, ix, p. 827. Reasons for dating it as of 1473 are given there, p. 826. The four surviving lists of singers have been published several times. They are conveniently available in Sartori's article (pp. 64–6).

[13] Sartori, 'Josquin des Prés', p. 81.

[14] The letter shows that the duke's active interest may predate the letter of September by several months, for he had already succeeded in making the cardinal's secretary file certain documents in favour of Josquin, but they were not found to be executed in the form required to achieve legal effect.

hesitate to ask the Cardinal of Novara to yield preference to a singer of the duke's over his own secretary, who apparently had had earlier promise of, and claim on, the benefice in question.

This document changes with one stroke the whole biographical picture. Far from being an underrated and poorly paid singer, Josquin, still a young man, must have been held in high esteem; otherwise the duke of Milan would not, as early as 1473, in addition to calling him together with other foreign musicians from the Duomo to his personal service, have bestowed a benefice upon him. Of course, much depends on the nature of the benefice, on which the letter is silent. Fortunately, the Milanese archives yielded a second document, previously unknown, concerning the same benefice. It is a letter from Johannes Albus de Bressanis, passport official, to the duke, sent in care of the duke's secretary, the powerful Cicco Simonetta, by special delivery, or, in the parlance of the time, 'cito, cito' (see Pl. 2). The document is dated 25 February 1474 and reads in translation as follows:

To the most Illustrious and most Excellent Lord, the Duke of Milan, etc. To my most singular Lord. In care of the Magnificent Lord Cicco. By special delivery.

Most Illustrious and Most Excellent Prince, my most Dread Lord. A short time ago I received a letter from Your Lordship instructing me to obtain information from the vicar of the bishop [of Novara] what the income was from the canonry at Gozzano held by Josquin, the singer of Your Lordship. To this I respond and say that I have been informed by that vicar and also by others who have furnished me more precise data, and I find that the income amounts to one hundred florins per year, if he makes his residence there; if not, he can appoint a caretaker for four or five ducats a year. To the best of my knowledge there is no other singer who has a benefice in these parts, neither in Novara nor in the whole diocese of Novara. 25 February 1474.

> Faithful servant Johannes albus
> de Bressanis, passport official,
> with greetings.[15]

[15] (Address on back): Illustrissimo Principi & Excellentissimo domino domino duci Mediolani etc. domino Meo singularissimo. Ad Magnificum dominum Cichum. Cito. Cito.

Illustrissime Princeps. & Excellentissime domine domine Mi Metuendissime. In questo di o havuta una da la illustrissima vostra signoria nela qual cuntiene che me debia Informare dal vicario del vescovo quanto a Intrata Lo canonicato che Tiene Joschino cantadore de la prelibata ad Goçano. respondendo a quella dico che o havuta da esso vicario Informatione & da altri ancora che me ano piu certamente Informato. Trovo che a Intrata Fiorini cento per anno façendo ressidença & non façendola se afficta ducati quatro o vero cinque per caduno anno, & non Intendo ne trovo che altro cantadore habia in queste parte alcuno benefficio ne in novara nec nel diocesis novarese. 25 Februarii 1474.

> Servitor fidelis Johannes albus de
> bressanis bulletarum officialis
> cum recomendacione

(Archivio di Stato, Milan, Fondo Sforzesco, Potenze Sovrane 1634, n. 17).

A benefice amounting to 100 florins, 95 or 96 of which would go to Josquin if he appointed a caretaker for the canonry, is a splendid income. It must be measured against the sixty ducats that Josquin made as his yearly salary at the court.[16] Adding these figures up (100 florins = 100 ducats),[17] Josquin had a yearly income of *c.* 160 ducats, equivalent to the salary of the best paid man in the ducal chapel. Surely, Josquin must have given proof of extraordinary talent to receive so generous a benefice at the very start of his career as singer at the court of Milan.

[16] Nevertheless, the salary of five ducats monthly must have been considered an adequate living wage for one person. A measure of comparison is offered by the supplication of an Italian trombonist, who writes to the duke that his salary of four ducats monthly is not sufficient to take care of his wife and children: 'Illustrissimo et clementissimo Signore constreto de grande bixogno ricorre con ogni fede, et speranza di vostra signoria lo vostro schiavo et fidelissimo servitore perino trombono: Exponendoli como lanimo suo sie servirla vivere et morire ne li soy servitij: Sed se vede inhabile servirla nel modo [che lui] desidera: E questo e per havere pocha provixione la quale e solum de ducati 4. il mese. li quali non li pono satisfare ad imparare vivere luy ne sua dona e fioli . . . (Archivio di Stato, Milan, Potenze Sovrane 124).

[17] Originally, I had reckoned 100 *fiorini* equal to 82 ducats. On restudying the problem, I found that only the *fiorino de Reno*, the Rhenish florin, had the diminished value—diminished in relation to the ducat—but without the qualifying attribute 'Reno' one must assume either the *florenus largus* (= 81 soldi) or the *florenus da camera* (= 80 soldi). The ducat came to 80 soldi.

The brothers Gnecchi, in their fundamental work (1884), still today regarded as authoritative, assert (p. LIV) that the names *zecchino, fiorino, ducato d'oro*—from the time of Francesco Sforza (1450–66) to the middle of the sixteenth century—all meant one and the same monetary unit. Edoardo Martinori, in his encyclopedic work (1915) under the entry *ducato milanese*, identifies it with the *fiorino d'oro*.

The proclamations of the mint of Milan gathered by Emilio Motta constitute the most authentic sources of information regarding the various currencies of coins, gold and silver, during the diverse periods of Milanese history. The Milanese monetary system changed radically with the reign of Galeazzo Maria Sforza (1466–76) to whom the brothers Gnecchi attribute the honour of having created 'un compiuto e ben regolato sistema di monetazione' (p. XLV). A 'decreto sul valore delle monete d'oro e d'argento' of 28 May 1474 (doc. 276) distinguishes between *fiorini larghi* (= 81 soldi), *fiorini da camera* (= 80 soldi), and *fiorini de Reno* (= 63 soldi), and Motta observes that the *fiorino da camera*, the most usual currency, had increased in value from 64 to 80 soldi. This is corroborated by a *grida* issued on 31 October 1465 (doc. 229) that speaks of *floreni seu ducati de camera*, again identifying florins and ducats and equalling them with 64 soldi. In the light of all this, one aspect of the letter gains new significance: it mentions both florins and ducats—florins for the value of the benefice, ducats for the caretaker's fee. The writer, it would seem, was accustomed to using the terms interchangeably. Literature: Francesco ed Ercole Gnecchi, *Le Monete di Milano* (Milan, 1884); Emilio Motta, *Documenti Visconteo-Sforzeschi per la storia della zecca di Milano* (Milan, 1893–96; reprinted from the *Rivista Italiana di Numismatica*, 1893–96); Edoardo Martinori, *La Moneta. Vocabolario Generale* (Rome, 1915).

Benefices held by Josquin's colleagues between 1473 and 1476

In a well known letter to the bishop of Novara of 29 January 1473, written when he was deliberating on the establishment of a chapel of foreign musicians that would rival the best in Italy, Galeazzo had expressed his intent to provide rich benefices for his musicians. He asked the bishop to intervene with the Pope for the purpose of obtaining benefices amounting up to 300 gold ducats in each of the six main cities of the Duchy of Milan—altogether a sum of 1800 gold ducats.[18] If Galeazzo had in mind to form a chapel of thirty singers (there are thirty-four on the first list, probably dating from 1473), and if he thought of bestowing a benefice upon each singer, the average benefice would have insured an income of sixty ducats annually. Some of his singers, however, were married; they would have to be provided for by other means: the donation of a house, income from certain ducal territories, even—in the case of the chapelmaster, Antonio Guinati—a concession to work various mines.[19] We do not know whether Galeazzo's ambassador succeeded in persuading the Pope to concede all these benefices. But of the fifty singers named in at least one of the four extant chapel lists, documents survive from the years 1473 until 1487 to show that twenty-seven, that is slightly more than half of them, had some type of benefice, the most common being a canonicate. The yearly income from these benefices might range from as high as 200 ducats to as low as eight. Some singers held multiple benefices of small amounts.

To ascertain with greater precision the relative rank of Josquin in the ducal chapel, judged by the value of his benefice, a systematic study of the archival records was necessary. Of the fifty singers found in the lists of

[18] Pavia. 29 January 1473. To the Bishop of Novara.
Monsignor. Since we have for a long time taken delight in music and song, more so than in any other entertainment, we have taken measures to engage singers to establish a chapel; and so far we have brought here a goodly number of singers from beyond the Alps and from diverse countries; and we have laid the foundation for a famous and worthy chapel, to whose members, beyond the good and decent stipend that we gave them, we wish to accord some benefices in our realm, that is, in Milan, Pavia, Piacenza, Parma, Cremona, Novara, in the amount of at least 300 gold ducats for each city. To this purpose we want you to seek audience with His Holiness and petition him in our name that he may deign to concede to the bishops and vicars of each of these cities the right, at the opportune time, to confer upon these singers [benefices, curate or non-curate, and in any calendar month, also in those reserved for the Holy See] up to the sum mentioned for each city. And you will attest to His Holiness that it is our intent to add an endowment from our own means to make this a worthy and much honoured chapel. And pursue this matter with dispatch so that we may obtain this privilege. (Archivio di Stato, Milan, Potenze Sovrane 124; facsimile in *Storia di Milano*, ix, p. 824; transcribed in Emilio Motta, 'Musici alla Corte degli Sforza', p. 310, from another copy which includes the words in brackets.) A curate benefice is one having the care of a parish, that is, with obligation of residence at the place that grants the benefice.
[19] See Motta, 'Musici alla Corte degli Sforza', pp. 517–18.

cantori de camera and *cantori de cappella* from 1473 to 1475, no more than thirteen can be shown to have held benefices in the time span from 1473 to 1476, the year of Galeazzo's assassination,[20] and only four singers in addition to Josquin can be found to have received benefices as early as 1473. And few singers enjoyed as high an income as Josquin, fewer still a higher one.

A good standard is Gaspar van Weerbeke, who probably arrived in Milan in 1471 and was entrusted by the duke with the task of staffing his chapel. Twice he went to Burgundy and Flanders to engage singers.[21] Newly discovered documents show that the duke asks on 17 August 1473 for a pension of forty ducats on the *prepositura*—office of a parish priest—of S. Lorenzo in Lodi in his behalf. A benefice of ten ducats was added in March 1474, a pension of eight ducats in December 1475.[22] In 1474 the duke wishes him to receive benefices resigned by Henrico Knoep, of whom we shall hear presently. The picture is too fluid to be precise on the amounts involved. Yet, Josquin with his benefice amounting to 100 ducats awarded him in 1473 appears to rank even above Weerbeke.[23]

Another famous contemporary of Josquin and colleague at the ducal chapel in Milan was Loyset Compère. A previously unknown document

---

[20] Their names are, in chronological order:
   1) Cardino de Bosco, Normando, March 1473
   2) Guglielmo (= Guielmus Gigardus?), March 1473
   3) Enrico Guinati, called Sagristano, March 1473
   4) Gaspar Weerbeke, August 1473
   5) Zorzo Brant (= Giorgio Branda), February 1474
   6) Gileto Cossu, clerk of Cambrai, February 1474; Zanin Anon (= Jo. Anon or Hanon, clerk of Cambrai) shares one of Cossu's benefices obtained April 1476.
   7) d. Raynero (= Raynero de Precigneyo), February 1474
   8) Nicolo Ochet, alias Prugli, April 1474
   9) Henrico Knoep, August 1474
   10) Jo. Cordier, clerk of Tournai, October 1474.
   11) Ginet (= Gineto Morelli), September 1476.
Two singers ask for benefices, but no documents have been found concerning the disposition of their requests:
      Zanin Lomon (= Ottinet, clerk of Cambrai), November 1474
      Aluyseto (= Loyset Compère, clerk of Arras), September 1476.
[21] See Gerhard Croll, 'Gaspar van Weerbeke', *Musica disciplina*, vi (1952), pp. 67–81; p. 68; idem, 'Gaspar van Weerbeke', *MGG*, iv (1955), cols. 1407–12.
[22] From a document of 14 January 1475 we learn that Gaspar was born out of wedlock, for dispensation had to be sought for him *super defectu natalium*; Archivio di Stato, Milan, Autografi III 93/3.
[23] The position of trust and appreciation that Weerbeke enjoyed at court is evident from the events following upon his departure for the Papal Chapel in Rome. In a letter of 20 April 1482 published by Motta (p. 326) the duke instructs his ambassadors in Rome to persuade Gaspar to return to his service. To this end he tells them to promise him benefices in the Duchy of Milan 'fin ad tal summa, che sera conveniente'.

of 25 September 1476[24] shows that the duke wishes to award a benefice in the church of S. Georgio de Catasijs in Pavia to 'Aluiseti clerici atrabatensis cantoris prelibate dominationis vestre'. Although the duke's lieutenant runs into trouble when he finds that the benefice is held by the rector and that 'we do not have the power to install a new rector', the very fact that the duke wished to award a benefice to Compère three years later than Josquin demonstrates both the esteem that the younger Compère enjoyed and the higher rank held by Josquin. Josquin's late arrival in the ducal chapel, rather than being caused by the supposed low esteem in which he was held, may on the contrary have been owing to a special request of the rapidly depleted chapel of the Cathedral for the continuing services of the gifted and versatile young musician.

There were singers who received higher benefices than Josquin, but they were few. Entirely unknown as composers, they may well have been virtuoso performers. Outstanding among these is Galeazzo's manifest favourite, Henrico Knoep, clerk of Liège, who seems to have collected benefices with equal ease and avidity, leaving the whole chapel behind him in the number and value of his pensions, benefices, canonicates, houses, and gardens. A description of his numerous holdings would exceed the framework of this study.[25] Suffice it to say that from a notice on his successor published by Motta[26] we learn that he was a tenor—obviously Italian love for the particular timbre of the tenor voice began early. At one time, the chapter of a church, at which Knoep held a canonicate, attempted to force him to take up residence in the parish, to do his duty as a canon, whereupon the duke informed the chapter that 'we shall under no circumstances permit him to leave, because he is exceedingly dear to us both for his upright character and his outstanding talents, in music as well as in a number of other fields: nor do we believe that another could easily be found of the same excellence and loyalty toward us and our state.'[27] One wonders whether the words 'in a number of other fields' and 'toward... our state' might not suggest that Knoep also functioned occasionally in a diplomatic capacity—music and diplomacy being mixed not infrequently in Renaissance courts where artists were wont to find an open door and an open ear.

[24] Archivio di Stato, Milan, Potenze Sovrane 124. The date of this document confirms Ludwig Finscher's supposition that Compère must have stayed in Milan until the end of 1476. He writes in his work on *Loyset Compère*, p. 17: 'In the choir-roster of 30.3.1475 Compère turns up again, and finally in a letter dated 4.12.1475. After that there is no trace of him in Milan, and he obviously departed consequent on the reduction in size of the court chapel choir after the murder of duke Galeazzo Maria in December 1476'. See also below, pp. 40–2.

[25] It is my intention to report fully about the Milanese musicians on the basis of published and newly found documents in a monograph on Josquin des Prez.

[26] Motta, 'Musici', p. 332, n. 2.   [27] Ibid., p. 332.

One gains the impression from reading the old documents that many of these benefices were obtained by the persistent enterprise of the would-be holder. Much of our knowledge comes from supplications addressed to the duke, in which the singer asks for a certain benefice. Josquin's case is different. That the documents dealing with his benefice have not been discovered so far is probably due to the unusual character of the case. It was not handled through the ordinary official channels and is therefore not to be found in the correspondence dealing with such matters. Josquin's benefice was treated as a matter of state, in which the duke personally intervened, and in which the Secretary of State, at the duke's instructions, obtained official information on the precise income of the benefice in question.

The idea that has taken hold in recent Josquin scholarship that the young artist went unrecognized, that he was called from the Duomo to the court only at the very end, that he was poorly paid, because his musicianship was not appreciated, that indeed he may have been a late bloomer, who began composing at a relatively late age—all of these notions may now safely be relegated to the realm of fable on the strength of the two letters presented. It is quite possible that new letters may be found in Milan or Novara concerning Josquin's benefice. But what we have suffices to create an altogether new picture of Josquin as a young artist.

An unknown list of singers departing in 1477

It has been generally assumed that the great musical chapel founded by Galeazzo Maria in 1473 was disbanded after his assassination on 26 December 1476. A list of singers attached to a letter of safe conduct issued by Bona and Gian Galeazzo, unknown so far, sheds new light on the situation. The letter is dated 6 February 1477 and instructs the duke's officials to let the bearer travel with two companions and his baggage free of any taxes.[28] It is issued to Antonius Gmaeck—obviously a Flemish name. No singer by this name is found in the four lists of the ducal chapel, nor does the letter itself indicate that he is a musician. However, after the notation at the end of the letter, 'in simili forma infrascriptis', that is, 'in similar form for those named below', the following twelve names are listed: Antonio de Cambrai, Antonio de brabante, Pierort, Victor de Bruges, Johannes de Frania, Cornelio de Lillo, Gineto, Loyseto de Compera (*sic*), Michaeli, Johanne happaert, Daniele de Schak, Colin de lanoy. Seven of these are musicians who are known from one or more of the singer lists. Three composers, all Frenchmen, appear for the first time: Colin de Lannoy, Johannes de Frania (in other documents his name is spelled Franeau, Franier, and Fresneau),[29]

---

28 Archivio de Stato, Milan, Archivio Ducale, Registri Ducali 28, fol. 60ᵛ.

29 Fresneau was cited as a student of Ockeghem by Guillaume Cretin in his famous 'Déploration'. The only documents referring to him known so far stem from France and

and Johannes Happaert (known as Jannes Japart from another document).[30] Finally, there are two names that may be identical with names on the singer list. Antonio de Brabant may be the Antonio de Bruges of the 1474 list. For Michele we have no fewer than three candidates: Michael de Feyt in the first three lists, Michael da Torsi in the same three lists, and Michael da Carpi in the last list.

This letter must be read together with a document dated Milan, 7 January 1477, showing that twelve days after the duke's death a decision had been reached not to dismiss all singers but rather to select the best of them, among whom should be Cordier.[31] On the sixth of February, that is one month later, somewhat less than half the duke's singers received their letters of safe conduct to leave Milan. At least five of them may have gone directly to Ferrara, with whom Milan had cordial diplomatic and personal relations and which was famous for its fine musical establishment.[32]

We may consider these documents proof for the beginning of the dissolution of the ducal chapel. They are of importance for Josquin's biography inasmuch as they contribute to the invalidation of the erroneous image modern scholarship has formed of the lack of success and esteem suffered

show him on the list of the 'chapelains ordinaires' of the royal chapel. Nanie Bridgman, in her article in *MGG*, iv (1955), cols. 926–7, states that he appears in the accounts for the last time in September 1475. This ties in well with the fact that his name does not appear in the Milan singer lists, the last of which is dated 4 December 1475. We may assume that he came in the beginning of 1476. His name is found in various Milanese documents of the year 1476 in connection with benefices promised to him. In one of them, dated 14 November 1476, he is described as a 'priest from Cambrai, our singer, and a modest and virtuous person' (Archivio di Stato, Milan, Potenze Sovrane 124).

[30] A note from 4 July, without year, but with great certainty belonging to the year 1476, refers to benefices of Philippus de Raymundis 'promissa d. Janni Japart' (Archivio di Stato, Milan, Miscellanea Storica Sforzesco 25). Nanie Bridgman begins her article on Johannes Japart in *MGG*, vi (1957), cols. 1753–4, with the statement, 'Über sein Leben ist nichts bekannt'. In the meantime, Lewis Lockwood, in an article on 'Music at Ferrara in the Period of Ercole I d'Este' in *Studi musicali*, i (1972), p. 119, has established that Johannes Japart was in Ferrara from 1477 to at least 1479, thus corroborating Fétis' belief that Japart served at the court of Ferrara ('paraît avoir été attaché en qualité de chantre à la cour de Ferrare', he says in his article on Japart in *Biographie universelle des musiciens*, 2d ed., iv (Paris, 1862), p. 429). Fétis seems to be the only historian of music who saw that four-part chanson by Josquin beginning with the words 'Revenu d'oultremonts, Japart, Je n'ai du sort que mince part', whose existence was doubted by Osthoff ('wenn sie existiert haben sollte'; *Josquin Desprez*, ii, p. 154). That this seemingly lost chanson really existed is much more likely now that Japart's presence at the court of Galeazzo Maria has been established. It tells us something about Japart that Josquin addressed a chanson to him, the only living musician so distinguished.

[31] Archivio di Stato, Milan, Registri Missive 130, fol. 11ᵛ.

[32] They were: Antonio de Cambrai, Cornelio, Michele de Feys, Daniele, and Johannes Japart. See Lewis Lockwood, 'Music at Ferrara in the Period of Ercole I d'Este', *Studi Musicali*, i (1972), pp. 118–19.

by the young Josquin at the court of Milan. If indeed Josquin had been so little appreciated, Bona and Gian Galeazzo would certainly have let him go, as they did a fine chanson writer such as Johannes Japart and an important composer like Loyset Compère.[33]

Life and personality of Ascanio Sforza

There is a second myth that affects Josquin's biography. It is the common belief[34] that Cardinal Ascanio Sforza was a niggardly patron. Usually, the time of Josquin's service in the cardinal's household is assumed to fall into the years 1490–3. But such a late date raises the question why Josquin, at the age of fifty, when he served in the most prestigious musical establishment of Christendom, the Papal Chapel, and when his fame was uncontested, should have entered into the service of an uncongenial and stingy master.

The belief that Ascanio was a miser has no foundation other than a loose interpretation of a few lines from Serafino's sonnet addressed to Josquin and a similarly loose interpretation of an anecdote concerning Josquin's 'Missa La sol fa re mi', supposedly referring to Ascanio's brushing aside the composer's plea for remuneration with a brusque 'Lascia fare mi'.[35] Not a single contemporary document refers to Ascanio in connection with this Mass, nor is there any evidence that Ascanio was a penny-pincher. He was acquisitive—as were all Sforzas and indeed most princes, both inside and outside of Italy—but that is another matter. Acquisitiveness and generosity go well together in the lives of great Renaissance patrons. And Ascanio was a prime example, for he was ever hungry for new sources of income, and he was one of Rome's greatest spendthrifts. All histories of secular or papal politics of the period confirm that; they also report that no class of the populace mourned his passing more deeply than the beggars of Rome.[36]

Ascanio was born in 1455 as the fifth of the six sons of Francesco Sforza (1401–66), powerful *condottiere* and subsequently Duke of Milan, the first from the house of Sforza.[37] Ascanio was destined for an ecclesiastical

[33] Ludwig Finscher's surmise that Compère left Milan in the wake of the duke's assassination (see above, n. 24) is borne out by this document.

[34] See, e.g., André Pirro, *Histoire de la musique de la fin du XIVe siècle à la fin du XVIe* (Paris, 1940), p. 173; Gustave Reese, *Music in the Renaissance*, 2nd rev. ed. (New York, 1959), p. 229; Helmuth Osthoff, *Josquin Desprez*, i, p. 34.

[35] See James Haar, these Proceedings, pp. 564–6.

[36] See Nicola Ratti, *Della famiglia Sforza*, 2 vols. (Rome, 1794–5), i, p. 90, n. 25, and the description of his funeral in *Johannis Burckardi Liber Notarum*, 2 vols., ed. Enrico Celani (*Rerum Italicarum Scriptores*, new ed., xxxii/1; Città di Castello, 1906), ii, 484–5.

[37] A full-length monograph on Ascanio Sforza, though long overdue, does not exist. One has to assemble the data concerning his career from various sources such as Ludwig Pastor's *Storia dei Papi*, iii (Rome, 1942) (this translation, based on Pastor's seventh German edition, was 'entirely redone' by Angelo Mercati, prefect of the Vatican Archives), the

career and given a careful classical education;[38] he was a mere youngster when he was made protonotary apostolic. This was his official ecclesiastical title when he was exiled from Milan together with three brothers in 1477 for conspiring, after the assassination of his oldest brother, Duke Galeazzo Maria, to unseat the widow, Bona of Savoy, who ruled as regent for her young son, Gian Galeazzo.[39] That was still his title when Ludovico, in 1479, supported by two other brothers, captured the government from the hands of Bona and tried and executed Cicco Simonetta, the faithful old secretary of Francesco Sforza, of Galeazzo Maria, and of Bona of Savoy.[40] It seems that Ascanio, not having been made a part of this conspiracy, undertook some rash moves of his own and in consequence was exiled again, first to Ferrara, then to Naples. This period of exile, lasting from 7 March 1480 to September 1482, was the most unhappy period of his life. Even though the Duke of Ferrara treated him like a brother, he was an exile. In Naples, where he was not treated with similar affection, he was truly miserable.[41]

Finally, toward the end of the year 1482, his abject pleas for readmission to the good graces of the court of Milan and especially those of his brother Ludovico il Moro, who now ruled as regent for his nephew, were granted, and in a curious, lengthy formal document, written in Latin and dated 29 December 1483, he had to swear an oath of allegiance to the Duke of Milan.[42] From that moment on the union between Ludovico and Ascanio was unbreakable.

The huge diplomatic correspondence between Ascanio and Milan contained in the Fondo Sforzesco at the Archivio di Stato in Milan reveals that Ascanio, made cardinal in 1484, was from beginning to end a willing and obedient instrument of the foreign policy of the State of Milan,

---

sixteen-volume work *Storia di Milano* undertaken by the Fondazione Treccani degli Alfieri per la storia di Milano (Milan, 1952–66), and the concise book by Caterina Santoro, *Gli Sforza* (Varese, 1968). A popular, but dependable, summary of Ascanio's political activities is available in Maria Bellonci's *The Life and Times of Lucrezia Borgia*, trans. Bernard and Barbara Wall (New York, 1953).

[38] 'He pursued his language and his literary studies under the celebrated rhetorician, Bartholomeo Petronio of Cremona,' writes a Cremonese literary chronicler, Franciscus Arisius, in *Cremona Literata seu in Cremonenses Doctrinis, & Literariis Dignitatibus Eminentiores Chronologicae Adnotationes* (Parma, 1702), i, p. 334.

[39] See *Storia di Milano*, vii (1956), p. 316.

[40] Ibid., pp. 334–9.

[41] See the beginning of his letter to Bona of Savoy of 15 May 1482, in which he refers to his 'common and continuous affronts, troubles, worries, and painful afflictions' ('Alle commune continue Iniurie, affanni, molestie: e rencrescevoli despiaceri mei...'; Archivio di Stato, Milan, Potenze Sovrane (Sforzesco) 1465).

[42] 'Instrumentum assignationis: et feudalis Investiturae factarum Illustrissimo et Reverendissimo domino Ascanio Mariae sfortiae vicecomiti...'; Archivio di Stato, Milan, Potenze Sovrane (Sforzesco), 1465.

identifying himself completely with the house of Sforza. Needless to say, he owed his election to the cardinalate to the diplomatic efforts of Ludovico il Moro.

No sooner had Ascanio become cardinal than Ludovico started laying the groundwork for making Ascanio pope. Twice Ascanio came close to achieving this ambition. After the death of Innocent VIII in 1492 he and Cardinal Giuliano della Rovere, later Julius II, were among the chief contenders for the highest office of the Church. Between these two ambitious, capable, hot-tempered men arose an enmity of nearly mythical proportions. Seeing that he could not gain the papal seat for himself, Ascanio threw the election to Roderigo Borgia, a man whom Giuliano despised. When Borgia was made Pope Alexander VI, Giuliano went into exile, first to his fortress at Ostia, then to the court of France. And it was France that toppled the house of Sforza in 1499–1500, carrying Ludovico and Ascanio into captivity. Ludovico died a prisoner of the French in 1509, but Ascanio was freed in 1503 through the intervention of Cardinal d'Amboise because the latter hoped to further his own aspirations for the papal election through Ascanio's influence.

Ascanio, upon his return, was received by the Roman populace with tumultuous jubilation.[43] A number of cardinals favoured his election. Ascanio had promised Amboise his vote, and Amboise gained thirteen votes in the first scrutiny, but Cardinal Carafa obtained fourteen, and Giuliano della Rovere fifteen. In the following votes Amboise lost, and Giuliano gained. Finally, he lacked only two votes to gain the necessary two-thirds of the votes present. But, in the words of Ludwig von Pastor, 'in the last hour the ambitious dreams of della Rovere were destroyed by his ancient enemy, Ascanio Sforza'.[44]

The parties agreed on a compromise candidate, Cardinal Piccolomini, who reigned as Pius III for less than one month. And again, the cardinals met, but this time della Rovere was in the lead from the beginning on; he placed all of his cards, political, diplomatic, financial, unscrupulously on the table. When it became clear that he would gain the two-thirds majority, Cardinal d'Amboise threatened a schism. But at this moment della Rovere's lifelong foe, Ascanio Sforza, in a decision that showed greatness of spirit, turned to throw his support to his old adversary, so as to achieve unanimity of the election and to preserve the unity of the Church—and Amboise followed suit.

When Ascanio died two years later, Julius II commissioned Andrea del Sansovino to build Ascanio a funeral monument, universally considered one of the noblest sculptures of Renaissance Rome, still to be seen in the church of S. Maria del Popolo.[45]

[43] See *Storia di Milano*, viii, p. 93.   [44] Pastor, *Storia dei Papi*, iii, p. 648.
[45] For an illustration of Ascanio's funeral monument, see Osthoff, *Josquin Desprez*, i, pl. 9.

Ascanio and music

Ascanio was without doubt the wealthiest cardinal at the time of Alexander VI. His yearly revenues from rich prebends came to 30,000 gold ducats[46]—a fabulous fortune that the cardinal used to keep a magnificent palace, a huge household, a stable of the finest horses, and kennels of well trained dogs for his favourite sport, the hunt. He spent his money not only on sumptuous entertainments but also in support of art and letters.

Did Ascanio care for music? A recent writer on Ascanio specifically denied this.[47] But persistent digging has unearthed enough information to relegate also the notion of Ascanio, the insensitive, ignorant, unmusical patron of a great genius, to the realm of fable. All children of Francesco Sforza had a thorough literary, humanistic, and musical education. A charming letter to the Duchess Bianca Maria on her youngest son, Ottaviano, hardly three years old, reports that 'the little *angeletto* is always happy, singing and playing, and always asking for Barbante, his maestro, with his *violeta*'.[48] Ascanio's older sister Ippolita was a fine singer and dancer. When she, in 1465, went to Naples to marry Duke Alfonso of Calabria, son of the King of Naples, her dancing teacher, the famous Johanne Ambroso da Pesaro, who accompanied his noble pupil, wrote back to the duchess that Ippolita 'had made two new dances that she had thought out herself to the music of two French chansons and that his Majesty, the King, had no greater pleasure than to watch her dance and hear her sing.'[49]

As a young nobleman of fifteen years, Ascanio had a steward who could sing French and Italian songs.[50] Seven years later, in 1477, when Ascanio and his brothers went into exile after their plot to overthrow Bona of Savoy, Regent of Milan, had been foiled—on the way to their separate places of confinement, Ascanio being sent to Perugia—they were received by the Duke of Ferrara 'con grandissimo onore'. A Ferrarese chronicler describes how they dined with the duke while Giovanni and Francesco, two blind musicians, singing to the lira, were competing in singing their praises and in

[46] In June of 1500 Alexander VI issued a bull imposing a tithe upon all lands of the Church, the College of Cardinals, and the officials of Rome in order to raise an expedition against the Turks. Ascanio is taxed 3,000 ducats, one thousand more than the next cardinal, Giuliano della Rovere, the future Julius II; see Burchard, *Liber Notarum*, ii, pp. 226–7. At his death, Ascanio was Vice-Chancellor of the Church, Bishop of Pavia, Bishop of Novara, Bishop of Cremona, Commendatory of the monastery of Chiaravalle in Milan, and Abbot of the monastery of S. Ambrogio in Milan.

[47] Albert Seay, in his study, 'The "Liber Musices" of Florentius de Faxolis', *Musik und Geschichte. Leo Schrade zum sechzigsten Geburtstag* (Cologne, 1963), pp. 71–95, says (p. 95) that Ascanio's 'relations with Josquin make it evident that he had no comprehension whatsoever of the abilities of that genius then in his retinue'—a statement not backed up by any evidence.

[48] *Storia di Milano*, ix, p. 804; facsimile on p. 806.   [49] Ibid., p. 814.

[50] Letter from Ascanio to his brother, Duke Galeazzo Maria Sforza, of 20 October 1470; Archivio di Stato, Milan, Potenze Sovrane (Sforzesco), 1465.

performing beautiful songs—'the two blind men were brilliant artists', he added.[51] When he was again exiled to Ferrara in 1480, this time alone, Ascanio sent his steward back to Milan to bring him, together with a number of personal articles, his 'clavicordio'.[52] This precious note informs us of his possession of a 'clavicordio' and his wish to have it with him in exile. It is not too bold an assumption that he had learned to play the keyboard instrument just as Ottaviano had learned singing with Maestro Barbante to the *violetta* and Ippolita had studied voice and dance.

Pietro Giannetti, physician and poet, who in his youth had joined Ascanio, first in his exile to Perugia, later in Naples, wrote a Latin poem in praise of the cardinal; he described his magnificent palace in Rome, his immense gardens, his stables full of fast horses, his kennels replete with speedy hunting dogs. Turning to Ascanio's huge staff of servants and his court, Giannetti singles out two musicians, a German lute player, identified in the margin as Enricus, and Bachieca, an Italian singer to the lute.[53] In 1493, on the occasion of the birth of Ludovico's son Massimiliano, Ascanio sent an ensemble of Spanish viol players to the court of Milan whose playing, according to a letter of 6 March 1493, was most skilful and sweet.[54] In 1497, when Ascanio lay gravely ill for many months and there was serious doubt whether he would recover, the King of Naples sent him 'one of his personal physicians by the name Maestro Antomazo, in whom His Majesty placed the greatest confidence, and with him came a gentleman of His Majesty with a head chef and with many candied almonds and wines, and with a clavicymbalum in which an organ was inserted that made a very sweet sound.'[55] This extraordinary musical gift increases the likelihood that Ascanio was himself a keyboard player.

[51] Bernardino Zambotti, *Diario Ferrarese dall'anno 1476 sino al 1504*, ed. Giuseppe Pardi (*Rerum Italicarum Scriptores*, new ed., xxiv/7 (Bologna, 1934), p. 34).

[52] The information comes from a letter of safe-conduct issued by the Duke on 13 July 1480 to Joannemaria Barbarino, Ascanio's head steward, who is transporting 'cesti duy, cappa una, et clavicordio uno' (Archivio di Stato, Milan, Registri Ducali 38, fol. 66).

[53] 'Est tibi germanis cytharoedus missus ab oris
    Qui fidibus curas pellere mente potest;
  Est et apollinea perdoctus in arte Bachiecha...'
See Giuseppe De Luca, 'Il "*libellus carminum*" di un poeta Sforzesco', *Archivio Storico Lombardo*, liv (1927), pp. 96–113; pp. 101–2.

[54] See Attilio Portioli, 'La Nascita di Massimiliano Sforza', *Archivio Storico Lombardo*, ix (1882), pp. 325–34; p. 333.

[55] 'La maesta regia ha mandato alla sua Signoria Reverendissima uno suo medico nominato maestro Antomazo, nel quale pare chepsa maesta habia grandissima fede, et cum epso e venuto uno zentilhomo de la predicta maesta cum uno coco principale et cum molte sorte de confecti et vini et cum uno Clavacimbalo nel quale e inserto uno organo che e molto suave instrumento...'; letter of Stefano Taberna, Milanese ambassador to the Pope, to Ludovico il Moro of 7 March 1497; Archivio di Stato, Milan, Potenze Sovrane (Sforzesco) 1465.

Ascanio must have played a significant role in commissioning music, which we have already discussed with regard to Josquin[56] and which may be further surmised in other works mentioned below. However, the only documented commission known to me at present concerns a motet in honour of the election of Alexander VI. Johannes Burchard reports that on 9 December 1492, the second Sunday of Advent, Mass was celebrated in the Sistine Chapel, as usual. The singers of the Papal Chapel, at the suggestion of the 'Cardinal Vice-Chancellor', wished to perform after the Offertory a piece in praise of the Pontiff. The Pope, however, preferred that the work be sung in his private chambers. Burchard quotes the text of the eulogy under the following heading: 'Epigramma Joannis Tinctoris, legum doctoris atque musici, in laudem et gloriam SS. D. N. Alexandri Pape VI'.[57] The poem begins with the words 'Gaude Roma vetus'.

It may be assumed that Tinctoris set the music to the poem; since Burchard pays hardly any attention to music,[58] it is quite possible that he confused the poet with the composer, although it is not to be ruled out that Tinctoris wrote both text and music. This notice has already entered Tinctoris scholarship,[59] but it has not been connected with Ascanio's name, since Burchard speaks of him only as 'cardinalis vicecancellarius'. We must recall that Tinctoris was in Naples during the time of Ascanio's sojourn there in 1481–2. Surely, they met—and the same may be assumed of Josquin and the other musicians in Ascanio's retinue. Now, in 1492, Tinctoris was evidently in Rome, and Ascanio wished perhaps to draw him there. At any rate, the commission might have had such an effect with a more music-loving pope. The work is seemingly lost.

The most important information on Ascanio's relationship to music comes from a letter written by a secretary of Antonio Stanga, the Milanese ambassador, to Ludovico il Moro. The secretary reports that Stanga had fallen ill and that Ascanio sent him 'la sua musica a cantare e sonare' 'per tenerlo meglio recreato', that is, Ascanio sent him 'his singers and players to keep him better entertained'.[60] And it is from this casual remark contained in a routine report sent to Ludovico on 8 April 1499 that we know that Ascanio had what to all intents and purposes must have been a private musical chapel.

That Ascanio's love for music went even further may be concluded from the musical treatise commissioned by him and written by a musician named Florentius and directed 'ad Illustrissimum ac Amplissimum Dominum, et

[56] 'Josquin des Prez and Ascanio Sforza'.

[57] Johannes Burchard, *Liber Notarum*, i, p. 376.

[58] On this point see Osthoff, *Josquin Desprez*, i, pp. 23–4.

[59] Heinrich Hüschen's article on Tinctoris in *MGG*, xiii, cols. 418–24; esp. 419 and 423–4. See also Osthoff, *Josquin Desprez*, i, p. 24.

[60] Letter of 8 April 1499; Archivio di Stato, Milan, Potenze Sovrane (Sforzesco), 1465.

D. Ascanium Mariam Sfortiam, Vicecomitem ac Sancti Viti Diaconum, Cardinalem Dignissimum'. Albert Seay, in his essay on this treatise, dated it after 1492—and more specifically, for additional reasons, between 1495 and 1496—because that was the year Ascanio attained the office of Vice-Chancellor at the court of the newly elected Pope Alexander VI.[61] But the title *Vicecomes* in the dedication means viscount; it is a hereditary title borne by all sons of Francesco Sforza from their birth on. The Latin term for Vice-Chancellor is *vicecancellarius*, and it is the absence of that title that gives us a *terminus ad quem*. The treatise cannot have been completed before 1484 because Ascanio is addressed as cardinal, and not after 1492, because then he would have had to be called *vicecancellarius*. Now Florentius, in his dedication, refers to the time when he was with Ascanio in Naples and in Rome (*cum Neapoli Romaeque tecum una essemus*). This means that either Florentius or Ascanio had left Rome. Ascanio was in fact absent from Rome for almost a year, to be precise, from 10 November 1487 to 7 October 1488. It is also possible that Florentius had left Rome either before 1487 or after 1488.

Florentius' treatise, MS. 2146 of the Biblioteca Trivulziana in Milan, is one of the most beautiful illuminated treatises on music in existence. It is written by an exceptionally fine humanistic hand, as may be seen in the two opening pages of the treatise (Frontispiece and Pl. 3) that show Ascanio's coat of arms and emblems. The execution of so splendid a manuscript was expensive; Florentius would certainly not have undertaken it had he not been sure both of Ascanio's great love of music and his generosity. In his dedication, the writer assures his patron that even though he is no longer with him, he is animated by the same good will toward him that had inspired him before.[62] He excuses himself if he did not write his book 'with that talent, art, and high concept of the subject matter that the acumen of your mind and the admirable discipline of your nature ordinarily use in the reading and emending of books'. He confesses lack of self-confidence 'for it was not easy in writing on so vast a topic and in addressing so great a prince to determine whether anything new could be added to the literary monuments [of the past]. Therefore, before I put forth anything original, I wanted to investigate with greatest diligence the writings of earlier authors, so that I, true to your command, would leave nothing untried that has any bearing on this art.'

It appears not only that Ascanio Sforza had asked Florentius for a treatise

---

[61] Albert Seay, 'The "Liber Musices"', p. 74. This error, together with the erroneous date of writing, has been taken over by Klaus-Jürgen Sachs in his recent article on 'Florentius de Faxolis' in the Supplement to *MGG*, xvi, cols.310–11.

[62] 'Most fervently do I wish you to believe that my disposition toward your Reverend Lordship is no different from what it had been when I was with you in Naples and in Rome' (for the Latin text of the dedication, see Seay, ibid., pp. 76–7).

on music, but that he had specifically requested an encyclopedic treatment of the subject. The character of the treatise, and its arrangement, may well reflect Ascanio's ideas.[63] In particular, the great initial chapter 'On the praise, power, utility, necessity and the effect of music' mirrors with admirable clarity the new concept of music emerging in the Renaissance[64]—the very concept that we need to understand if we are to comprehend the immense changes in Josquin's evolution as a composer. Of course, the 'effects of music', traditionally mentioned in the theory of music, become a *topos* in the 1480s. I have shown elsewhere that Tinctoris wrote a treatise on the twenty effects of music (neatly divided, however, between the religious and the secular), Gafurius concentrated on it in his *Theoricum musicae* of 1478 and 1480, and even Ramos lost all his native scepticism when dwelling on the miraculous effects of music as recounted by the ancient writers.[65] The ancient legends were called upon to account for the new excitement, the new psychological dimension that the music listener of the time experienced, and no composer exceeded Josquin in the range and the strength of emotions that he was capable of eliciting from the combination of Flemish counterpoint and Italian harmony.

Nevertheless, it is astonishing, in a treatise dedicated to a cardinal, that music is praised with hardly a word on its role in the liturgy of the Church. But was Ascanio in the first place a man of the Church? His contemporaries agree in regarding him more as a diplomat than a religious personality; indeed, he had not really studied for the priesthood before becoming cardinal, and it took a special dispensation from the Pope for him to receive the title 'Diaconus' to legitimize his election to the cardinalate.[66] The traditional position of music in the quadrivium, too, receives short shrift in Florentius' treatise. This must provoke amazement in a work written in the 1480s. It suggests that the educated man of the time was dissatisfied with the old answers, that he raised with a new urgency the old question: 'What is music and on what rests its peculiar power over Man?'

[63] Seay's interpretation of the origin of the treatise in a desire on the part of the cardinal 'to supply him with a backlog of small talk about music and some smattering of fact about the procedures therein' (p. 94) does equal injustice to the seriousness and thoroughness of the book and the frame of mind of a Renaissance prince. One cannot grasp so great a period by cutting down its patrons of art to the size of the host in a twentieth-century book on etiquette.

[64] Seay views this chapter with apparent incomprehension: 'Florentius has given much space to all the legends about music, the stories from mythology and the mystic figures of the past, a space far out of proportion to any of the rest of the sections' (ibid., p. 93). I have dealt with this problem in my study on 'Music of the Renaissance as Viewed by Renaissance Musicians', *The Renaissance Image of Man and the World*, ed. Bernard O'Kelly (Columbus, Ohio, 1966), pp. 129–77; see especially pp. 150–2.

[65] 'Music of the Renaissance', p. 151.

[66] Reported in a letter of 5 April 1484 from the Milanese orators in Rome to the duke; Archivio di Stato, Milan, Archivio Ducale, Carteggio, Roma 95.

It is significant that the patron of Josquin des Prez should have been interested in this question. And it is only in the light of Ascanio's great love of music and his independent musical establishment that Josquin's service at Ascanio's court makes any sense.

Where was Josquin from 1479 to 1486?

We have no information on the composer's whereabouts between spring 1479 and fall 1486, at which period he appears for the first time in the account books of the Papal Chapel. This seven-and-a-half-year period in the life of the mature composer, that is, the period between his approximately thirty-ninth and forty-sixth year, is the most crucial time span in Josquin's life of which we have no information whatever. If we consider that Ascanio went into exile for the second time in 1480, that he became cardinal and went to Rome in 1484, where he acted in a diplomatic capacity in the conflict between the League (Milan, Florence, and Naples) and the Pope, and that he signed the peace treaty with the Pope for Milan on 11 August 1486,[67] then the very interesting possibility emerges that Josquin was in Ascanio's retinue during his exile, that he returned with him to Milan in 1482 and accompanied him to Rome in 1484, and that his fame as composer and singer brought it about that he was allowed to divide his time between the cardinal's private musical chapel and the Papal Chapel, which he entered in September 1486, hardly one month after the war between Milan, Florence, and Naples on the one hand and the Church on the other had been concluded. The very fact that Josquin enters the Papal Chapel immediately after the war between the League and the Pope was over suggests that he was with Ascanio in Rome from 1484 on. In view of his identification with the house of Sforza, his entry into the Papal Chapel depended on the conclusion of the war of the League with the Holy See. Had he been a free agent, there is no reason why the beginning of his services should have coincided so precisely with the settlement of Milan's political relations with Rome.

What facts can we adduce to support a thesis that would be of great utility in constructing a biography of Josquin des Prez free of the huge gaps it has contained so far?

We must first establish the circumstances under which Ascanio went into his second exile. Was he indeed in a position to maintain a great retinue? It does not conform to modern notions that a person exiled from his own country should be provided by his own government with the financial and diplomatic means for a luxurious maintenance and a brilliant and numerous cortège. But Bernardino Zambotti, author of a 'Ferrarese Diary from 1476 to 1504', presents precisely this picture in his report of 7 March 1480:

[67] *Storia di Milano*, vii, p. 375.

The Most Reverend Monsignor Ascanio came today to Ferrara. Our Most Excellent Duke went to meet him on horse with his whole court up to the river Po and he was accompanied to the Palazzo Belfiore near the Certosa, where he was lodged for some days. And our Duke has already reserved the House of Pendalgi for him [where all men of learning and high standing were housed] and he [the Duke of Ferrara] is receiving one hundred ducats for rent since Ascanio is here confined on orders of the Duchess of Milan.[68]

The chronicler goes on to enumerate such a mass of provisions for men and horses sent by the duke to Ascanio in the value of another hundred ducats that the conclusion is obvious: Ascanio came with a huge retinue.

We know that Florentius, the author of the music treatise dedicated to Ascanio, was with him in Naples. The same is true for Pietro Giannetti, the poet-physician, whose Latin poem praises two singers to the lute that Ascanio, at a later time, had with him. If a poet-physician like Giannetti and a modest and obscure musician-priest like Florentius were then in Ascanio's train, the likelihood of Josquin's being with him looms larger.

Serafino and Ascanio

We must now inquire into the life of Serafino dall'Aquila, the poet to whom we owe the sonnet 'Ad Jusquino suo compagno musico d'Ascanio': to Josquin, his companion, Ascanio's musician. For it is this poem on which all modern accounts of Ascanio, the stingy, unsympathetic patron of a great genius, rest. Moreover, three years in Josquin's biography (1490–3) are tied to Serafino, because the latter is said to have been in Ascanio's service at that time. The key question is, was Serafino really in Ascanio's service from 1490 to 1493? All Josquin scholars give these years after Mario Menghini, who draws his conclusions from the earliest biography of Serafino, written by his friend, the poet Vincenzo Calmeta, and published in 1504.[69] But Calmeta offers no dates other than those of Serafino's birth in 1466 and death in 1500. If we are to succeed in finding the precise period of Josquin's service with Ascanio in Rome, we must attempt to construct a more detailed chronicle of Serafino's life based on Calmeta's description of the poet's wanderings and of his various patrons as well as the historical events mentioned in connection with them.[70]

[68] Zambotti, *Diario Ferrarese*, p. 73. Ugo Caleffini, in his Ferrarese chronicle, claims that Ascanio came to Ferrara accompanied by 200 men; see Lewis Lockwood, these Proceedings, p. 108.

[69] Mario Menghini, ed., *Le Rime di Serafino de' Ciminelli dall'Aquila* (Bologna, 1894). Calmeta's biography is printed on pp. 1–15.

[70] Such a chronology has been attempted by Barbara Bauer-Formiconi in her recent book, *Die Strambotti des Serafino dall'Aquila* (Munich, 1967), pp. 11–17, who was able to fill in many of the dates for events mentioned by Calmeta. However, she errs in placing Ascanio's trip to Milan in the year 1489.

Let us begin with the last years. When Louis XII entered Milan, Serafino went to Rome and stayed with Cesare Borgia. Louis XII entered Milan in 1499, one year before Serafino's death. How long had Serafino stayed in Milan? Calmeta says that he came to Milan from Mantua in the company of Francesco Gonzaga, Marquis of Mantua, for Ludovico's investiture as Duke of Milan. This event falls into the year 1495.[71] When and from where did Serafino come to Mantua? According to Calmeta, the Duke of Calabria, future King Ferdinand of Naples, had to go to the Romagna to oppose Charles VIII, whose army had invaded Italy and threatened Naples. He took Serafino with him and at the request of Elisabetta Gonzaga left him at the court of Urbino. This event falls into the year 1494. From Urbino, after a happy stay of 'many months', Serafino went to Mantua, a move coinciding with the return of Ferdinand's army to Naples in the month of November, 1494. Serafino had stayed at the court of Naples for three years. That brings us back to the year 1491. Thus we have already exploded the notion that Serafino's stay with Ascanio fell into the years 1490 to 1493.

At this point, we are aided by a happy find in the Milanese archives. A letter of 4 November 1490, from Frater Christophorus of Novara to an official in the ducal Chancellery, contains the following lines on Serafino Aquilano:

If the poet Serafino has written anything new, I shall use every diligence to have the music copied with the words, and I shall gratify you gladly, but I do not know where he stays, because he has left the service of the Most Reverend Monsignor Ascanio.[72]

This letter reveals that in 1490 Serafino had already left Ascanio's service and that his—and therefore Josquin's—stay with Ascanio predates 1490.[73]

---

[71] Calmeta's biography is rather sketchy and in part inaccurate for the period 1497 to 1500. Calmeta himself had been secretary to Ludovico's wife, Beatrice d'Este. When she died in January of 1497, he left Milan and went to Rome, but, he says, Serafino stayed on with Hybleto dal Fiesco until Louis XII entered Milan and Fiesco died; thereupon he went to Rome, taking refuge first with Cardinal Giovanni Borgia, later with Cesare Borgia (Menghini, *Le Rime*, p. 12). Bauer-Formiconi documents Serafino's presence in Mantua in February and August 1497 in the service of Francesco Gonzaga; he also made trips to Venice (1497, before July), Urbino (August–September 1498 and December 1499), and Genoa (after September 1498). Only at the very end of 1499 did he go to Rome, where he died on 10 August 1500 (*Die Strambotti*, pp. 16–17).

[72] 'Si Seraphino poeta havera ancora facto cosa nova usaro omne diligentia per haverla notata et le parole, et ve gratificaro volentera, ma non intendo ove sia la stantia sua poy che e partito dal Reverendissimo Monsignore Ascanio...' (Archivio di Stato, Milan, Archivio Ducale, Carteggio, Roma 102). Throughout the vast diplomatic correspondence between Rome and Milan, Ascanio continues to be informally called 'Reverendissimo Monsignore' or 'Reverendissimo et Illustrissimo Monsignore' from his early years through his service as cardinal.

[73] Calmeta says that he left Ascanio's service after carnival (Menghini, *Le Rime*, p. 5).

It also proves that Serafino wrote his own music to his verses, and that they were in demand in the ducal circles of Milan.[74]

'Now he began', to quote Calmeta, 'to give himself to the company of people who were not of his social standing, he spent an active night life, slept wherever he happened to be; any other house rather than that of Ascanio was his refuge and wherever he was (be it whosoever) he recited not only his compositions but gave copies thereof, so that throughout Rome no other poems were recited than his'.[75] Serafino spent about one year of this nomadic life in the Eternal City, after which he reconciled himself with Ascanio and re-entered the cardinal's service.[76]

Calmeta says that Serafino entered Ascanio's household for the first time shortly after arriving in Rome, an event that Barbara Bauer-Formiconi places in April 1484.[77] Now Ascanio, created cardinal in March of 1484, came to Rome only in August of that year, in order to participate in the conclave that elected Innocent VIII. Thus we may date the beginning of

[74] This illuminates a point raised by Nino Pirrotta, who translates the title of Serafino's poem 'Ad Jusquino, suo compagno musico d'Ascanio' with '[To] Josquin, his fellow musician under Ascanio' and goes on to say: 'If we are shocked by the equation implied in this title between the art of Josquin and Aquilano's own musicianship, a 15th-century man who had little familiarity with polyphony may not have been prepared to include Josquin's works at all in his notion of music' ('Music and Cultural Tendencies', pp. 138–9). I would point out that

1) it is more likely that the title should be translated 'To Josquin, his companion, Ascanio's musician';

2) Calmeta, the early sixteenth-century biographer of Serafino, reports that the poet enjoyed a musical education under the Flemish musician Gulielmus Guarnerius, mentioned by Gafurius in both the *Tractatus praticabilium proportionum* of *c.* 1482 and the *Practica musicae* of 1496 (see Clement A. Miller, 'Early Gaffuriana', pp. 375 and 378–9);

3) the above letter concerning Serafino's music to his own words implies the possibility of one of those simple, attractive three- or four-part settings that the Italian musicians of that period cultivated. At the very least Serafino must have been the composer of the melodies to his poems, but a polyphonic setting, in view of his study with Gulielmus Guarnerius, is not to be excluded;

4) the spheres of popular music and the great polyphony of the time were constantly bridged (a) by the polyphonists' use of popular tunes, (b) by the presence of popular polyphony assumed by Pirrotta himself and called by him quite appropriately 'the "unwritten" tradition of music' (ibid., p. 138, n. 42).

[75] Menghini, *Le Rime*, p. 3.

[76] During this year, according to Calmeta, Serafino became involved with Hieronymo Estouteville, son of the late Cardinal of Rouen, who was thrown into jail by Innocent VIII; Serafino also fell under suspicion. From a letter of the Milanese ambassador to Rome we learn that this event falls into April 1490 and that Ascanio took it upon himself to effect Estouteville's liberation (Archivio di Stato, Milan, Archivio Ducale, Carteggio, Roma 101; 8 April 1490). 'After some time' (probably not more than a year and a half) Serafino received permission to go back to his family home in Aquila, whence he went to the court of the Duke of Calabria.

[77] *Die Strambotti*, p. 12.

Serafino's service in the fall of 1484.[78] Three years from this date brings us precisely to Calmeta's next statement: 'It happened in those times that Cardinal Ascanio went to Lombardy, Serafino staying in Milan'. This means obviously that Serafino accompanied Ascanio when he went to Milan in November 1487 to take over the reins of government during Ludovico's lengthy and serious illness. He also returned to Rome with the cardinal in October 1488.[79] Serafino's service in Ascanio's household may now be stated with assurance as extending from fall 1484 to carnival of 1490 and a brief period in 1491.[80] This would serve as corroboration for Josquin's being in Ascanio's service in Rome from 1484 on, which increases the likelihood of his having been in Ascanio's retinue before his arrival in Rome.

Serafino and Ascanio did not get along well—Serafino's biographer, his friend and fellow poet Calmeta, is our witness. The mordant rhymes of

---

[78] The reason why musicologists as well as historians of literature have agreed to assign the year 1490 as the date of Serafino's entry into Ascanio's service lies in a statement of Calmeta's which was neither carefully written by him, nor carefully read by them. At one point in his account he announces: 'He was 24 years old, and was of strong build', etc. Calmeta's readers added 24 to his birthdate, 1466, and arrived at 1490. They failed to do two things: (1) to determine what grammatical and logical connection there was between Serafino's entry in Ascanio's household and the age of twenty-four; (2) to construct a chronological order of Serafino's life based on the historical data furnished by Calmeta. The second we have done; it leads in natural sequence—supported by one new document found in the Milanese archives—to 1484. Concerning the former, two observations are in order: the announcement of Serafino's age occurs *after* Calmeta's report of Serafino's unhappy three years in Ascanio's service and the growing animosity between Serafino and the cardinal, increased by the poet's indiscreet habit of satirizing his patron in 'sonetti faceti e mordaci'. Specifically, the statement of Serafino's age follows upon this sentence: 'As he continued thus to be swept along in these diverse happenings for approximately three years, he took in the end to a certain style of living that resulted in his ensnaring ever more the attention of the common people. He was 24 years old, of robust build, and very dexterous and good in sports, running and jumping'. Certain it is that the statement of age cannot be connected with Serafino's entry into Ascanio's household. The least we must do is place it three years later, that is after three years in Ascanio's service, which would bring the date of entry to 1487, not 1490. But we must take Calmeta's style of writing into account. He is not presenting the reasoned, documented, dated biography of a professional historian but the rambling account of a friend and fellow poet, who shuns precise dates throughout, and obviously writes from memory, occasionally getting the precise nature and sequence of events scrambled.

To arrive at a reasonable chronology of Serafino's life, we had best discard the sentence on his age on the ground that it is not fitted into a coherent sequence of biographical events, and at any rate could at most be applied to the end of his first three years in Ascanio's retinue.

[79] Burchard notes that Ascanio left Rome on 10 November 1487 and returned on 7 October 1488 (*Liber Notarum*, i, p. 239).

[80] Calmeta, in speaking of Serafino's 'three years' in Ascanio's service, refers only to the Roman years *before* the trip to Milan, that is, the years 1484–7.

Serafino are responsible for Ascanio's poor reputation. Historians of music have uncritically accepted Serafino's poetic judgement. But we must consider that the two men were of vastly different temperaments. When the horns sounded, the dogs barked, and the cardinal rode out to hunt, the poet was hiding under his bed, trembling, imploring God to liberate him forever from his cruel destiny.[81] One can well imagine the cardinal's sardonic laughter. Indeed, in the same poem, in which Serafino describes his panic at the sounds of the hunt, he vows that he will 'flee from him who has no pity for him'—a vow that he kept, as Calmeta affirms.[82] Serafino was as certainly the butt of Ascanio's jokes as the latter was the target of his satirical rhymes. A study of these rhymes suggests the possibility of a deep-seated misunderstanding and growing conflict between the poet and the cardinal.

The surface of Serafino's verse is often humorous, sometimes comical, perhaps deceptively so—for behind the humorist hides the malcontent. The cardinal may have viewed him as an entertainer—he was a brilliant *improvvisatore*; he may have granted him the proverbial freedom that kings accorded their fools. And the fools were allowed to say things to their kings that might have cost a courtier's head. This may explain the extraordinary liberty that Serafino could take in some of his rhymes against Ascanio, but also his profound dissatisfaction at finding himself in so ambiguous a position. Surely it must have vexed him that he was not recognized and celebrated at Ascanio's court as poet. But the function of court poets has been at all times, and certainly was at that period, the glorification of the prince, be he secular or ecclesiastic. For this Serafino did not have the stomach. It was the symbol of his extraordinary and unprecedented freedom that he could poke fun at his master. Ascanio, on the other hand—a fiercely proud man notwithstanding the sense of humour that he certainly had—could not brook Serafino's taking liberties with him, unless his position was clearly defined as that of the proverbial fool, albeit a rhyming fool. To assure that nobody could misunderstand Serafino's liberties with him, Ascanio surely exercised the master's prerogative of ridiculing his audacious servant as the occasion arose. To each humiliation Serafino had only one recourse, another satire. Mutual resentment was bound to increase—particularly when Ascanio found out that Serafino was distributing the satires against him throughout Rome—and it is easy to see who would keep the upper hand in this unequal match of wit versus power. Essentially, the built-in conflict between Ascanio and Serafino was beyond repair; Calmeta's account is testimony to that.

The relationship between Ascanio and Serafino deserves deeper study than it has received so far. The present attempt at a new interpretation

[81] See his poem 'Quando sento sonar tu tu, tu tu' (Menghini, *Le Rime*, p. 117).
[82] 'Fuggendo chi di me pietà non ha'; ibid.

should, however, suffice to put an end to the uncritical manner in which Serafino's poems have been used in Josquin's biography as the only source for an assessment of the personality of Ascanio, whose generosity, connoisseurship in the arts and music, and judgement of genius have been contested on such a brittle foundation.

Serafino and Josquin

None of the preceding explains the controversial sonnet of Serafino to Josquin, often quoted but rarely translated.[83] We offer it in a literal English rendering:

> To Josquin, his companion, Ascanio's musician
>
> Josquin, don't say the heavens are cruel and merciless
>   That gave you genius so sublime.
>   And if someone is well dressed, do not mind,
>   For this is the privilege of buffoons and fools.
>
> Take your example from these, I pray:
>   Silver and gold that bear their value in themselves
>   Appear unclothed; but wood is overlaid[84]
>   When stage or temple are bedecked.
>
> The favour to those others lent fades fast;
>   A thousand times a day, however pleasant,
>   Their status turns from white to black.[85]
>
> But who has talent may wander through the world in his own way;
>   Like the swimmer wrapped in a vest of cork:
>   Put him under water, yet he fears not drowning.[86]

[83] Charles Burney gave a free, rhymed translation in *A General History of Music* (1789; ed. Frank Mercer, New York, 1957), i, p. 752.

[84] Serafino refers to the Renaissance habit of painting the wood in halls and churches.

[85] The original says 'de nero in bianco'. Traditionally, when votes were taken, black meant approval, white defeat. In English, the sense comes out better in reverse, although we have at least a partial parallel in the expression 'to draw a blank'.

[86] Iusquin, non dir che'l ciel sia crudo et empio
>   Che te adornò de sí sublime ingegno,
>   Et se alcun veste ben, lassa lo sdegno
>   Che di ciò gaude alcun buffone o scempio.
> Da quel ch'io te dirrò prendi l'exempio:
>   L'argento e l'or che da se stesso è degno
>   Se monstra nudo e sol si veste el legno
>   Quando se adorna alcun teatro o tempio.
> El favor di costor vien presto manco
>   E mille volte el dí, sia pur giocondo,
>   Se muta el stato lor de nero in bianco.

An unforced interpretation of the poem yields nothing more than the poet's wish to comfort a friend, whose genius is universally admired, when he finds him in a depressed mood, seeing around him the easy success of courtiers strutting about in fine dress. Great artists, at all times, have been known to suffer from fits of depression and melancholy.[86a] Serafino is the only contemporary witness to paint Josquin in this light. This trait, ignored by the commentators, is what makes his sonnet especially valuable for us, since we have so few contemporary accounts of the composer. But there is nothing, even in this poem of Ascanio's deprecator, that would provide evidence of the Cardinal's stinginess or lack of appreciation for Josquin.

Now that we know that Serafino set his own verses to music, his praise of Josquin's 'sublime genius' takes on added meaning. We may well search his poems for further information on his interest in music and on his possible musical bonds with Josquin. Both questions are answered in one single poem, an inconspicuous sonnet on the Virgin Mary. Here is the poem in the manner presented by Menghini:

> La vita ormai resolvi e mi fa degno,
>> Sol, regina del ciel, mia fida scorta;
>> L'alma è già inferma, or falla alquanto accorta,
>> Redutto sol d'ogne smarrito legno.
>
> Solvi, superna dea, mio fosco ingegno,
>> Fa ch'io te segua e fa la via qui torta,
>> Sol ben cognosca, e sol trovi io la porta
>> Utile a ognun che ha qui smarrito el segno.
>
> Fa la superna corte io veda alfine;
>> Mi combatte qui amor, fortuna e morte;
>> Lasso fa tu sol con tue man divine.
>
> Retoglimi a costor, fa ch'alfin porte
>> Utile fior de sí pungenti spine,
>> Relaxando penser d'ogne altra sorte.
>
>> Sol in te spero forte
>> Misericordia, o sol, rendomi solo,
>> Regina, a te, fa tu sol m'alzi a volo.[87]

Ma chi ha virtú, gire a suo modo el mondo,
  Come om che nota et ha la zucca al fianco,
  Mettil sotto acqua, pur non teme el fondo.
(Menghini, *Le Rime*, p. 112).

[86a] See Lowinsky, 'Musical Genius', *Dictionary of the History of Ideas*, 5 vols. (New York, 1973), ii, pp. 312–26, esp. p. 320, for the reference to Marsilio Ficino, who—on the basis of Aristotle's Problem XXX, 1—introduced 'the idea of the melancholy man of genius' to Renaissance Europe.

[87] *Le Rime*, p. 140.

The sonnet contains an extraordinary number of solmization syllables. If one reads them horizontally:

lines

1   La re sol mi fa
2   Sol re mi
3   La fa la
4   Re ut sol etc.

they make no musical sense. Read vertically, however, they result in the following melody:

Ex. 1

We recognize in the first four notes the beginning of the *Salve Regina* melody (L.U., p. 276); the second four notes intone the same motive, one tone lower; the last six notes are almost identical with the ending of the *Salve Regina*:

Ex. 2

Vir - go Ma - ri -   - a

Remains only the three-note figure F, E, A in the middle unaccounted for. Even this motive occurs as a three-note ligature no less than three times in the Marian antiphon: two times as E, D, G, once as D, C, F. True, they appear as *mi re sol* rather than *fa mi la*, which is a sequential elaboration of the three-note figure of the chant.

James Haar, having established the relationship between Josquin's 'Missa La sol fa re mi' and the *barzelletta* 'Lassa far a mi' attributed to Serafino, points in a footnote to the present poem and notes the 'word-play on solmization syllables...; every line in fact begins with one'.[88] If neither he nor Claudio Gallico, who also refers to this sonnet,[89] noticed the play with the motives of the *Salve Regina*, the reason certainly lies in the way in which the poem appears in the modern edition. Menghini lists as one of the sources a collection of Serafino's poems printed by Besicken in Rome in the year 1503, of which only a few incomplete copies remain. The most complete copy extant, lacking only the title page, is in the Biblioteca Riccardiana in Florence. In this early edition the poem carries the inscription (mentioned by Menghini in a footnote): 'Sonecto XCIX artificioso sopra la musica dove piu uolte e inserito. Vt: Re: Mi: Fa: Sol: La. Alla nostra donna' (see Pl. 4). The *Salve Regina* motives embedded in the sonnet present the 'musical artifice' involved.

[88] See below, p. 564, n. 3.
[89] Claudio Gallico, *Un libro di poesie per musica dell'epoca d'Isabella d'Este* (Mantua, 1961), pp. 42–3.

Besicken's typography, however, uncovers another musical secret. He is the only printer to align the first syllables of each quatrain and tercet and the first syllable of the second line of the irregular third tercet in such a manner that the following reading results:

La

Sol

Fa

Re

Mi

In the 1526 print of Serafino's *Rime* the capital letters L S F R appear at the left under each other and separated from the rest of the word, save for the last letter, R—an arrangement that hides what Besicken's typography reveals. The typography and subtitle pointing to a musical artifice render it likely that Besicken had Serafino's autograph before him. Thus Professor Haar's thesis of a connection between Josquin's Mass and Serafino's poems appears further strengthened.

Haar refers to a letter of the commendatory of the monastery of S. Bassiano, discovered by Claudio Gallico in the Archivio Gonzaga in Mantua, in which he asks Giacomo D'Adria, Secretary of the Marquis, to send him 'that artful sonnet of our Serafino—I mean the one that contains the whole musical system' (that is, the six solmization syllables). This letter is dated 3 June 1495.[90] We have seen that Serafino came from Naples to Mantua in 1494 and 'after a happy stay of many months' accompanied Francesco Gonzaga to Milan for the occasion of Ludovico Sforza's formal investiture as duke, an event that fell on 26 March 1495.[91] Manifestly, Serafino's 'artful sonnet' enjoyed a vogue at the music-loving court of the Gonzaga. If, as is likely, the poem originated at the time of Josquin's and Serafino's service at the court of Ascanio, we may well surmise the pleasure that all three took in this ingenious combination of poetry, music, and the praise of the Virgin, under whose special patronage the six Sforza brothers were placed, each one of them having been baptized with the middle name Maria. There is a certain connection between this poem with its acrostic and Josquin's famous motet in honour of the Virgin, 'Illibata Dei Virgo', bearing the composer's name as an acrostic and hinting at the name of the Virgin through the ostinato motive *la mi la*.[92] Indeed, Josquin's tribute to Mary, named in musical syllables, may have held a special meaning for Ascanio Maria Sforza, who must have been fond of the witty play with solmization syllables practised by two of the artists at his court, the poet-musician and the composer. Two observations may be in order:

1) The 'Missa Hercules Dux Ferrariae' in which Duke Ercole's name is expressed in solmization syllables (and thus flows from the vowels of his

[90] See below, p. 565, n. 3, and Gallico, pp. 42–3. [91] *Storia di Milano*, vii, p. 406.
[92] See Myroslaw Antonowycz, these Proceedings, pp. 545–59.

name into the music) may have been composed, as we have attempted to show, in the year 1487, when the duke paid a state visit to Rome and Ascanio was designated by the Pope as one of his two hosts for this function.[93] Serafino's sonnet to the Virgin with its wealth of solmization syllables (flowing from language into music) is mentioned in a letter of 1495 and may have been written during his and Josquin's service at Ascanio's court. This is the period that sees the beginnings of humanism in music, that is, the period in which music and language become ever more closely tied to each other.[94] Ascanio, a great music lover, is also a humanist, a poet of sorts, a man of letters who writes Latin as well as Italian and was brought up with French, as was his brother Galeazzo Maria. He was certainly intrigued by the phenomenon of solmization. In Josquin's works music (the *soggetto cavato dalle vocali*) reveals names (those of the Virgin and of the duke); in Serafino's poem, language reveals music. Solmization, the musical alphabet for choirboys as well as musicians in general, thus became the bridge between music and language. Josquin and Serafino showed that the bridge could be crossed in both directions.

2) The conjunction of Serafino's praise of the Virgin with its play on solmization and the Mass of Josquin seems reflected in a work of the Florentine musician Francesco Layolle, whose motets have just been brought out in an edition by Frank D'Accone. In a five-part setting of the 'Stabat Mater' the second tenor sings an ostinato motive, in proportional reduction, through all three *partes* of the work. The motive consists of the *la sol fa re mi* of Josquin's Mass.[95] The only precedent for the connection of Josquin's motive with the praise of the Virgin appears to be Serafino's sonnet, which may well have been known to Layolle.

Where was Josquin from February to September 1487 and from October 1487 to June 1489?

The strange absences of Josquin from the Papal Chapel have often been wondered at. Although he had begun his service in September 1486 and had served no more than five months, he is absent from February 1487 through May 1489, with the exception of one month, September 1487— that is, altogether a period of twenty-seven months.[96] Having found the

---

[93] Lowinsky, 'Josquin des Prez and Ascanio Sforza', p. 19.

[94] See Report on the Roundtable on 'Verse Meter and Melodic Rhythm in the Age of Humanism', *Report of the Eighth Congress of the International Musicological Society, New York, 1961* (Kassel, 1962), ii, pp. 67–71.

[95] *Music of the Florentine Renaissance*, iii–vi (American Institute of Musicology, 1969–73), v, pp. 136–48. D'Accone, although not connecting the work with Josquin's Mass, notes that in one source the second tenor bears the inscription 'super la sol fa re mi' (ibid., p. XXII).

[96] For a list of dates revised by one month, see Jeremy Noble, these Proceedings, pp. 76–7.

clue to the gap of seven and a half years in Josquin's biography in Ascanio's life, we turn to the same source for illumination.

Ascanio left Rome on 10 November 1487 and is reported back in Rome only on 8 October 1488—a lengthy absence for a cardinal from the centre of his activities. Only an event of overriding importance could have caused such a long leave. Ascanio had received disquieting news from home. Ludovico il Moro had fallen gravely ill. From the often euphemistic accounts, it appears that he may have suffered a stroke. The first document on the illness is a letter from Duke Gian Galeazzo to the then ambassador of Milan at the Papal Court, the Bishop of Como, of 13 August 1487,[97] in which he speaks of the 'laceratione grave' that Ludovico had suffered (perhaps during a fall accompanying the stroke). The slowness of recovery was disturbing. When his brother was still incapacitated two months later, Ascanio went to Milan to look after Ludovico himself and to pick up the reins of government that had fallen from the hands of the head of state—head if not in name, certainly in substance.[98]

Who accompanied Ascanio on his trip to Milan? If he had a numerous retinue in 1479, when he was exiled from Milan, if he was then accompanied by poets and musicians, if he sent his steward to get his *clavicordio*, surely now, in his new status as cardinal, reconciled with his brother and with the government, he was riding home with a retinue far more magnificent and lacking in nothing that physical luxury, ceremonial splendour, and artistic enrichment could afford.

Calmeta reports that Serafino went with him. If Ascanio had Serafino with him, with whom he had at best an ambivalent relationship, he certainly took Josquin and his whole musical establishment to Milan. He may have left them there after he departed, to keep his brother 'better entertained' on his road to full recovery, just as he did later with the Milanese ambassador. This is the more likely since Josquin's services were certainly demanded at the nuptials of Gian Galeazzo with Isabella of Aragon in February 1489, as we shall see presently. This would sufficiently explain the long absence of Josquin from the Papal Chapel; it would also open an exciting vista on the composer's return to Milan at a time when Leonardo da Vinci worked at the court and when the visual arts made the great advances so vividly described in the paper of Professor Maria Luisa Gatti Perer.[99]

[97] Archivio di Stato, Milan, Archivio Ducale, Carteggio, Roma 100.

[98] A letter dated 21 November 1487 announces Ascanio's arrival in Milan on that day and speaks of the 'continued improvement' of Ludovico. It is directed to the 'Commissario Potestatique Papie' and 'in simili forma' to fifteen other cities and municipalities in Lombardy (Archivio di Stato, Milan, Potenze Sovrane (Sforzesco), 1469). It was obviously calculated to reassure the citizenry.

[99] See below, pp. 138–47.

But it would not account for Josquin's absence from the Papal Chapel during the months of February through August 1487. In view of Ascanio's involvement in the peace negotiations of the League with the Pope concluded on 11 August 1486 and Josquin's entry into the Papal Chapel one month later, the following hypothesis may not seem too far-fetched. We have assumed, in principle, that Josquin divided his time in Rome between service in the Papal Chapel and in Ascanio's household. By February 1487, half a year after the war of the League had been concluded, Ascanio must have had time sufficient to get settled in his palazzo in Rome and to create his own musical establishment. Before then, he had his hands full with the negotiations. Now he might have called Josquin to his exclusive service, allowing him only one other month in the Papal Chapel, the month of September, when Ascanio was perhaps absent from Rome to avoid the summer heat.[100]

We wish there were records—and perhaps there are and they will be discovered one day—of Ascanio's social life in Rome. All indications are that he must have had a court of his own of incomparable brilliance. Being a notable music lover and residing now at one of the great music centres of Renaissance Italy, we may imagine all sorts of festivities, concerts, plays (with music) having taken place at his palace with the noble representatives of the Church, the diplomatic corps, and the artistic community in attendance. Josquin may have directed the musical activities; many of his motets, chansons, and instrumental compositions may have been composed for these occasions. It must have been this role that earned him the name 'Ascanio's Josquin'.

From May 1494 to 1500 the accounts of the Papel Chapel are missing. If, as I believe, Josquin wrote the extraordinary motet 'Absalon fili mi' for Alexander VI upon the death of his son, Juan Borgia,[101] then he was still in Rome in 1497. When the accounts resume in 1501, Josquin's name never appears again. In 1500, Ludovico and Ascanio were made prisoners of the King of France. While we are not informed on the precise whereabouts of Josquin in those years, we know that he was in France.[102] In 1503 Ascanio returned to Rome, and Josquin is found back in Italy, in the employ of the Duke of Ferrara, an old and close friend of Ascanio's.[103] In 1504, Josquin left Italy, never to return again. In 1505 Ascanio died.

The parallels between the movements of Ascanio and the voids in the biography of Josquin are too precise, too long, and too frequent to be

---

[100] Absences from Rome, usually beginning in July and ending in September or October, can be documented for the years 1489, 1490, 1491, 1492, 1494.

[101] Lowinsky, 'Josquin des Prez and Ascanio Sforza', pp. 20–21.

[102] See Helmuth Osthoff, *Josquin Desprez*, i, pp. 45–6.

[103] See Lewis Lockwood, these Proceedings, p. 114.

dismissed as pure coincidence.[104] They postulate a long and affectionate relationship between a great patron of music and the greatest composer of the age—a relationship that may already have begun in Ascanio's youth. Further archival investigation and stylistic analysis of Josquin's works are still needed.

Ascanio's life and the chronology of Josquin's works

The question now arises what all this contributes to the understanding of the master's music. A whole series of great works of Josquin's find, I believe, entirely new illumination from the changed biographical picture.

One of the few unanimously accepted facts in the difficult chronology of Josquin's works is that the 'Missa L'ami Baudichon' is the earliest Mass that Josquin wrote, the only one that shows closeness to Dufay's style, as Osthoff has demonstrated convincingly.[105] No one has proposed a date for this Mass. I submit that it was the first Mass composed by Josquin for Galeazzo Maria Sforza as he entered his chapel in 1473, and on these grounds:

1) Dufay was still alive, and his influence at its peak.

2) The Mass is based on a little ditty with a motive consisting of three stepwise descending lines in major—the whole Mass is written in the Ionian mode on C. The tune is similar to our 'Three Blind Mice'. It appears in the *Kyrie* in the following form:

Ex. 3   Kyrie I

3) It is unlikely that Josquin would have thought of writing a Mass on the tune of a little French street-ballad while he was composing for services at the Cathedral of Milan.

[104] Not always do the voids in Josquin's biography coincide with the movements of Ascanio. Sometimes the opposite is the case. For example, in the year 1489, when Ascanio is away from Rome travelling from 15 June to 25 December (Burchard mentions Ascanio's presence on these two dates, but not in between), Josquin is recorded as present in the Papal Chapel from June through December 1489.

[105] *Josquin Desprez*, i, pp. 112–15.

4) Galeazzo Maria, on the other hand, was exceedingly fond of French songs. We have a letter from Scaramuccia Balbo to Duke Francesco Sforza of 28 March 1452 in which he reports about the progress that Galeazzo, then eight years old, was making in his education. He writes that aside from Latin, he 'attends very well to his singing lessons; he has learned eight French chansons, and learns new ones daily.'[106] The name of his teacher was Guiniforte Barrizza. Galeazzo's love of French popular song continued undiminished. On 16 November 1472 he sent a letter to Antonio Appiano in Vercelli asking him to procure for him from the Duchess of Savoy 'Robineto notato su l'ayre de Rosabella'.[107] This is the French song 'Hé Robinet, tu m'as la mort donnée', written in form of a two-part quodlibet under the famous melody 'O rosa bella, o dolce anima mia'. The French text is quite mischievous; the Italian is an ardent love song. The Duke had heard this song sung by the 'Abbate, Maestro de la Capella de questa Madama', whose musicians Galeazzo frequently borrowed before founding his own chapel. The 'Abbate' is Antonio Guinati, whom the Duke shortly thereafter persuaded to head his own chapel.[108] He was so eager to get the music—and with all the French words—that he instructed Antonio as follows: 'as soon as you have it in your hands, send it to me immediately through the present messenger, and see to it that he puts in those same words that the Abbate sings. Arrange it so that we have this chanson tomorrow'. The quodlibet occurs in only one source; the French voice appears as the opening number of the chansonnier El Escorial MS. IV.a.24; it fits with the superius of the 'O rosa bella' setting by Dunstable or Bedingham, found later on in the manuscript.[109]

In those same years Galeazzo instructed his Venetian ambassador to send him a copy of the songs of Giustiniani, the famous popular love songs in the Venetian dialect, and find him a boy, between twelve and fifteen years old, to sing them to the lute.[110] We can well imagine that Galeazzo must have been delighted with Josquin's Mass on a French folk-song. This Mass, the only one Josquin wrote in the Ionian mode, has a clarity and simplicity of texture inspired by the simple folk-tune, a rhythmic bounce and melodiousness, and above all a tone of carefree joy that are rare in Josquin's music. It breathes the youthful optimism of a young genius who feels his powers, and it reflects the atmosphere of that *joie de vivre* that characterizes an Italian court of the fifteenth century and in particular the court of Milan at the period of the youthful, strong-willed, art- and music-

---

[106] *Storia di Milano*, ix, p. 818.

[107] Motta, 'Musici alla Corte degli Sforza', p. 303.   [108] Ibid., p. 313.

[109] See Martha K. Hanen, 'The Chansonnier El Escorial, MS. IV.a.24' (Ph.D. dissertation, University of Chicago, 1973), music volume, no. 1. A brief quotation from the quodlibet appears in Tinctoris' *Proportionale musices* of c. 1474; see ibid., text volume, p. 41.

[110] See Motta, 'Musici alla corte degli Sforza', pp. 542–3 and 553–5.

loving Galeazzo Maria. Its composer did deserve a benefice of 100 florins.

Works that can be related to Ascanio would have to be placed six to nine years later. In 1480, when Ludovico took over the reins of government in Milan by force, while preserving the appearance that he was acting as regent for the young Gian Galeazzo, Ascanio was exiled and suffered all the pains of an ambitious, proud, powerless man who had hoped to take part in the new government. We have already proposed the thesis that Josquin accompanied Ascanio into exile. Indeed, after Galeazzo Maria's assassination, after the gradual dissolution of the musical chapel, in view of the moderate interest in music shown by Bona, Gian Galeazzo, and Ludovico il Moro, Ascanio was the only Sforza left with a strong commitment to music. Both places of exile, Ferrara and Naples, were great centres of music about 1480 and Josquin could profit from the new musical experiences offered at these two courts.

I believe that three Masses in particular were written by Josquin to express Ascanio's despair, the Masses 'Fortuna desperata', 'Malheur me bat', and 'Faisant regretz'. Each time Josquin used a three-part chanson, the first by Busnois, the second by Ockeghem (although some sources contest his authorship), and the third by Walter Frye. The first two Masses stand between *cantus firmus* and parody technique and are placed by Osthoff a few years before Josquin's entry into the Papal Chapel—which agrees very well with the dates of Ascanio's exile, 1480–2. The essential points are these:

1) In both Masses the model is a lament on the cruel and capricious turns of fortune in form of a chanson.

2) In both Masses the light and transparent texture of the 'Missa L'ami Baudichon' gives way to the characteristic density and genuine polyphony that Josquin must have learned from Busnois and Ockeghem.

3) Now we begin to hear the darker colours of vocal scoring, the imaginative harmonic progressions that we connect with Josquin's style, the enlargement of the harmonic compass, the strong dissonances, the ostinato-like repetitions of unusual harmonic phrases, the astonishing cross-relations, and the creation of an idiom that is as far beyond the austere modality of Ockeghemian vintage as it is removed from the clear and centred language of tonality.

4) Here emerges the characteristic melancholy vein in Josquin's music that is entirely absent in the 'Missa L'ami Baudichon' but pervades Josquin's music from now on to the end.

The 'Missa Faisant regretz' is based on Walter Frye's chanson 'Tout a par moy', the first three lines of which, in Herbert Kellman's translation,[111] run as follows:

[111] See below, p. 199. The text is cited after the edition of the chanson by Dragan Plamenac, 'A Reconstruction of the French Chansonnier in the Biblioteca Colombina, Seville—I', *Musical Quarterly*, xxxvii (1951), pp. 530–31.

> I remain quite apart so that I shall not be seen,
> I shall not appear again, so mournful am I,
> I keep to myself like a numbed soul . . .

These are sentiments well in tune with the feelings of an exile. Like a man struck by misfortune who will keep mumbling the same words, so does the tenor sing the four notes 'Faisant regretz' of the second section of the chanson throughout the whole Mass[112] in various rhythms, on diverse tone levels, and with differing solmizations, now *fa re mi re*, now *sol mi fa mi*, now *mi ut re ut*. The two lines of the second section read:

> Faisans regrets de ma dolente vie
> Et de fortune qu'ainsy fort me guerroie.
>
> (Mourning my sorrowful life,
> And the [mis]fortune that assails me so fiercely.)

Thematically, the three Masses belong together. Each one is based on a chanson singing of the bitter blows of misfortune. Stylistically and technically, the 'Missa Faisant regretz' fits well with the two other Masses. Indeed, I am inclined to date it the earliest of the three—an assumption that also agrees with the model. Gustave Reese differs from those who consider Frye a member of the Busnois-Ockeghem generation. 'In fact', he asserts, 'he may well have been one of Dufay's older contemporaries.'[113] I believe the style of his works[114] supports this judgement. The ostinato dominates not only the tenor; it contends with repetition, sequence, imitation, and canon for primacy in shaping the form of the Mass. Osthoff criticizes the rigidity of construction; he also notes the loose relationship between text and music and views the Mass more as an experiment, particularly when compared with a great work of art such as the 'Missa La sol fa re mi', likewise based on ostinato technique.[115] Under these circumstances, I do not understand why he groups this work together with the two 'L'homme armé' Masses and the 'Missa La sol fa re mi'. The work has not the rich sonority of the 'Fortuna desperata' or the flowing melody and felicitous expressivity of the 'Malheur me bat' Masses. But it is certainly to be regarded as an introductory study in melancholy expression, a vein so fully

[112] Josquin borrowed the idea of the ostinato from Alexander Agricola, his Milanese colleague, who wrote a chanson based on Walter Frye's model, and incorporated the ostinato motive F D E D into the contratenor of the second section 'Faisant regretz'. That Josquin borrowed from both Frye's and Agricola's chansons is evident from his use of the superius of Frye's rondeau, which does not appear in Agricola's chanson (see Sylvia W. Kenney, *Walter Frye and the Contenance Angloise* (New Haven and London, 1964), p. 109).

[113] *Music in the Renaissance*, p. 93.

[114] See *Walter Frye, Collected Works*, ed. Sylvia W. Kenney (American Institute of Musicology, 1960).

[115] Osthoff, *Josquin Desprez*, i, p. 163.

developed by Josquin throughout his life in all genres of composition. It might be added that Frye's chanson occurs in a number of Italian manuscripts.[116]

The 'Missa Una musque de Buscaya', in which Osthoff finds 'archaic' traits and which he treats together with the Masses 'Fortuna desperata' and 'Malheur me bat', also has a similar stylistic physiognomy. Osthoff emphasizes its polyphonic density, the widespanned lines, the extremely long notes of the *cantus firmus* in the *Credo*. Elsewhere in this volume I have referred to the unusual harmonic colours and *musica ficta* problems contained in this Mass.[117] The text of the underlying chanson[118] contains a refrain in the Basque tongue, and Biscaya is a Spanish province, the bay of Biscaya forming the northern boundary of the Basque provinces. This leads to the assumption that Josquin composed the 'Missa Una musque de Buscaya' during Ascanio's exile in Naples, which, since 1442, was governed by the house of Aragon and whose culture showed a strong admixture of Spanish elements.[119] The peculiar harmonic language of the Mass, too, points to Spanish and Neapolitan influence.[120]

In a paper delivered at the Congresso Internazionale sul Duomo di Milano I proposed dates for other works of Josquin in connection with important events during Ascanio's stay in Rome:

1487 for the 'Missa Hercules Dux Ferrariae'. This is the year in which Duke Ercole I of Ferrara paid a state visit to the Holy See. 'Ascanio was one of two cardinals appointed to receive the duke in the name of the Sacred College in Rome.'[121]

1489 for 'Fama, malum', a motet on verses by Virgil composed for the celebration of Gian Galeazzo's nuptials with Isabella of Aragon. During the brilliant festivities planned by Leonardo da Vinci[122] various representations were staged, one of which showed Mercury 'flying from heaven and introducing Fama'. The chronicler relates that the representation was accom-

---

[116] For the sources, see Kenney, *Walter Frye, Collected Works*, p. VI.

[117] Symposium, pp. 743–5 below.

[118] *Werken*, Wereldlijke Werken, Bundel iv, pp. x–xi. On the Basque origin of 'Una musque de Buscaya', see Stevenson, below, p. 218.

[119] Under the reign of Alfonso the Magnanimous, the literary language at court was Castilian. After his death, Italian emerged, but Castilian poets still worked at court; see Isabel Pope, 'La musique espagnole à la cour de Naples dans la seconde moitié du XVe siècle', *Musique et Poésie au XVIe siècle*, ed. Jean Jacquot (Paris, 1954), pp. 35–61; p. 38.

[120] Martha Hanen, 'The Chansonnier El Escorial, MS. IV.a.24', chapter IV on *Musica ficta* (pp. 153–66), discusses the bold and unusual accidentals added in this manuscript both by the original scribes and later by performers. She makes a convincing case for the provenance of the chansonnier at the court of Naples in the 1460s—a thesis variously suggested and debated before.

[121] 'Josquin des Prez and Ascanio Sforza' p. 19.

[122] Alessandro Visconti, 'Leonardo in Milan and Lombardy', *Leonardo da Vinci* (New York, 1961), p. 113.

panied by the singing of a *carmen Latinum*. Since the nuptials were celebrated in Milan in the month of February, and Josquin did not return to the Papal Chapel until June, our assumption that he stayed on in Milan gains further substantiation.

1497 for 'Absalon fili mi', the text of which combines three lamentations of Old Testament fathers (David, Job, Jacob) mourning the loss of their sons. The occasion was the murder of Juan Borgia, Duke of Gandia and son of Alexander VI, on 15 June 1497.

To these dates I wish to add two more: 1497 for the four-part motet 'Ave Maria... Virgo serena' and the 'Missa de Beata Virgine' for four and five parts, and 1499 for 'Fortuna dun gran tempo'.

In January 1497 Ascanio fell ill; it was the most serious and lengthy disease of his life and Ludovico demanded almost daily reports on his brother's state of health.[123] Indeed, he sent his own physicians to Ascanio's bedside; the King of Naples, too, sent a physician (together with the amenities and the rare musical instrument mentioned before); two Spanish physicians also attended him (all these in addition to Ascanio's own physicians, of course); but the illness dragged on through February and March. Still in April, although slowly recovering, he was confined to bed for the larger part of the month. At the first signs of improvement Ascanio made plans for a pilgrimage to Loreto. On 30 March one of Ascanio's oldest and most faithful servants, Gasparo dal Paradiso, wrote to the duke that Ascanio assured him, upon his inquiry, that he 'felt better than ever (since the beginning of the illness), saying that with God's help he hoped to be free soon to make the pilgrimage to the Blessed Virgin Mary at Loreto, if God and the Glorious Virgin bestowed this grace on him.... '[124]

On 23 September 1497 Ascanio finally left Rome for Loreto; he returned on 21 October. Burchard, in his often mentioned Diary, notes with laconic brevity: 'On Saturday, 23 September, at the crack of dawn, the Reverend Cardinal Ascanio, Vice-Chancellor of the Holy Roman Church, left Rome to go to the Church of the Blessed Virgin Mary in Loreto, as he had vowed (*ex voto*).'[125] And a month later, he wrote: 'On this same day, Saturday,

---

[123] A special file on 'Sforza, Ascanio Maria. 1497. Febbraio a Maggio. Sua grave malattia a Roma' in the Milanese archives (Potenze Sovrane (Sforzesco) 1465) contains almost one hundred letters dealing with Ascanio's illness. Ludovico asks for reports from everyone: physicians, attendants, relatives, friends. He sends a reprimand to Cardinal Lonate of Milan for not writing him about Ascanio's illness, and the elderly cardinal, with trembling hand, writes a lengthy apology to the duke, assuring him he would give his life for the recovery of Ascanio.

[124] '...et adimando io la Signoria sua como la se sentiva la me resposta cum leto animo stare meglio che mai sij stata, (dapoi ha questo male) dicendo sperava cum la gratia de dio in brevi essere libera per inviarsse ad madona sancta maria da loreto che dio e la glorioxa vergene li faci tanto de gratia...'; ibid.

[125] Burchard, *Liber Notarum*, ii, p. 54.

21 October, the Reverend Ascanio, Vice-Chancellor, returned to Rome from Loreto, having fulfilled his vow (*voto soluto*).'[126] I propose that Ascanio took his singers with him and that Josquin composed the great Lady Mass and his most famous motet, the 'Ave Maria' written in the Ionian mode, one of his most radiant works, for this occasion.[126a]

Little need be said about the 'Ave Maria'. Jacquelyn Mattfeld, in her exemplary study on the liturgical motets of Josquin,[127] defines it as a votive antiphon, and traces the sources of the text. The work shows Josquin in full command of his technical resources. Unsurpassed master of vocal scoring, he weaves the voices in canon and imitation, he brings them together in full harmony on points of climax, he lightens the texture by separating high and low voices in paired imitation, he speeds up at various points in the course of the work, by faster motion, triple metre, syncopated imitation, he starts at a deliberate pace in an open texture and ends with slow solemnity in an invocation that for simplicity and clarity of tonal writing, beauty of the full sound of the four voices, and intimacy of feeling has no match in contemporary literature. The whole motet breathes an ease of companionship between word and tone equal to that reached in the lament of Absalom and the 'Déploration d'Ockeghem', for which I propose the same year, 1497.[128] All three works show perfect technical mastery, stylistic maturity, and profundity of expression; in all of them the leading role of the text is incontestably established.

The exceptional character of the 'Missa de Beata Virgine' in Josquin's Mass oeuvre is well known. It is the only work in which each movement is based upon a different chant, the only one adding the ancient Marian tropes to the *Gloria*.[129] The special character of this Mass suggests a special occasion, a particular commission. The Mass has usually been placed in the last phase of Josquin's life. 'Since Glareanus says that Josquin composed the work "ad extremam vergen[s] aetatem", one is perhaps justified in shifting it more toward the upper time limit (1513)', writes Osthoff.[130] But in his wide-ranging analysis he speaks of a number of contrasting features which, I believe, accord better with the date proposed here. He shows the funda-

---

[126] Ibid., p. 57.

[126a] See D'Accone, below, p. 613, for a note on Pope Paul III travelling to Loreto in 1539 accompanied by an 11-man chapel.

[127] 'Some Relationships between Texts and Cantus Firmi in the Liturgical Motets of Josquin des Pres', *Journal of the American Musicological Society*, xiv (1961), pp. 159–83; pp. 170–2.

[128] The recently discovered date of Ockeghem's death, 6 February 1497; see *Johannes Ockeghem en zijn tijd* (Dendermonde, 1970), pp. 279–80, allows us to join this unique lamentation on the death of a composer with 'Absalon fili mi' and the present 'Ave Maria'.

[129] For the six Marian tropes, see Gustave Reese, these Proceedings, p. 592.

[130] *Josquin Desprez*, i, p. 181. The Mass was first published in Petrucci's third book of Masses by Josquin in 1514.

mental contrast between *Kyrie* and *Gloria*, written for four parts in free imitatory paraphrase technique, and the chain of canons beginning with the *Credo*, which initiates the transition from four to five voices; he emphasizes the strange difference between vocal melody in certain parts of the Mass and 'instrumental' melody in others; he contrasts its prevailing constructive design with the generally sharper correspondence between music and text; he underscores the polymodal character of the work, originating in the different modes of the underlying Gregorian melodies. Osthoff believes that the ostinato technique, which was so significant in the early Masses, but occurs only occasionally in the 'Missa Ave maris stella', has vanished completely in our Lady Mass. However, even this 'early' trait can still be encountered throughout the *Christe eleison*, at the end of the *Gloria* (mm. 242–7), in free form in the *Credo* (mm. 132–50, and at the end, mm. 232–48), *Sanctus* (mm. 16–21), *Osanna* (mm. 97–118), and in the second *Agnus Dei* (mm. 63–70 and 80–85, the final phrase).

The 'Missa de Beata Virgine' is a work of immense richness, technically as well as spiritually. Its very vitality, its wealth of sonorities, the unprecedented mixture of minor and major modes, its combination of four and five voices, and its rich invention in precise proportion to its extraordinary length, obstruct a feeling of that last clarity—what the German language calls 'Abgeklärtheit'—of the unity and integration that are ordinarily the mark of a master's last period, and that in fact are present in the 'Missa Pange lingua'.[131]

Having become Duke of Milan in his own right after the death of Gian Galeazzo in 1494—by many rumoured to have been the victim of slow poisoning by his uncle—Ludovico, through his growing arrogance, ended up in complete political isolation. France, the Pope, and Venice contracted to destroy the proud Sforza, whose only support came from a man lacking both in money and troops—the Emperor Maximilian, married to Bianca Maria Sforza, Ludovico's niece. Il Moro's troops proved to be no match to the combined military forces of France and Venice. On the dawn of 2 September 1499 Ludovico fled Milan, having previously entrusted his sons and his money to Ascanio, who had left Rome for Milan on 14 July 1499 and, putting aside his cardinal's hat and donning armour, remained his brother's sole, unshakeable support, a tower of strength in the unfolding tragedy.

Ludovico's fall from power made a profound impression on his contemporaries. A lament[132] composed at the time introduces him as saying:

131 See Osthoff's detailed analysis, ibid., i, pp. 191–9. See also Friedrich Blume's remarks, above, p. 24. Richard Sherr, in the Mass Workshop, has suggested that the manuscript Cappella Sistina 23, which contains the *Gloria* and *Credo* of the 'Missa de Beata Virgine', may date from before 1503; see below, pp. 712–13.

132 'Pianto e lamento de lo illustrissimo signor Ludovico Sforza, che già fu duca de

I am that Duke of Milan
Standing in sorrow and tears.
I who was lord am now subject,
I have become a German.[133]
I said one God only was in heaven
And one Moro on earth,
And I made war and peace
According to my whim.[134]

Great reversals in the fate of the powerful have traditionally been connected with the revolutions of Fortune's wheel. Already in 1496 the Milanese chronicler Cagnola remarked that Fortune had shown herself somewhat 'bald' to Ludovico in that year[135]—referring undoubtedly to the traditional depiction of Fortuna-Occasio as a woman with a forelock and a bald head—he who does not grasp her by the forelock as she comes by has lost her.

I suggest that Josquin's 'Fortuna dun gran tempo', brilliant symbol of Fortune's inconstancy, was composed in 1499, under the immediate impression of the fall of the house of Sforza. The question now is whether the style of Josquin's 'Fortuna' justifies placing it in the year 1499. The advanced character of Josquin's design in an instrumental work for three parts, each with its own key signature, the chains of imitations in the circle of fifths, the bold modulatory plan involving E♭, A♭, D♭, the symbolic power of Fortuna mirrored both in the rondo form and the 'mutations' of *musica ficta*, and above all the flawless mastery and elegance with which the design is carried out[136]—all point to a relatively late date.

One might ask whether it is reasonable to assume that Josquin created a symbol of Fortuna under the impact of Ludovico's tragic fall from power

---

Milano, composto per uno suo fedele Cangilero homo valentissimo'; see Caterina Santoro, *Gli Sforza*, pp. 328–9.

[133] Probably a reference to Ludovico's intention to flee to Germany under the protection of Maximilian. He was captured by the French on his way to Germany.

[134] Son quel duca de Milano
    che con pianto sto in dolore
    son sugieto che era signore,
    hora son fatto Alemanno.
    Io dicevo che un sol Dio
    era in cielo e un Moro in terra,
    e sicondo el mio disio
    io faceva pace e guerra;...

[135] Santoro, *Gli Sforza*, p. 316.

[136] For a detailed analysis, see Edward E. Lowinsky, 'The Goddess Fortuna in Music, with a Special Study of Josquin's *Fortuna dun gran tempo*', *Musical Quarterly*, xxix (1943), pp. 45–77, esp. pp. 45–53.

in a form so light and graceful. But this means to misunderstand the character of Josquin's composition, which lies precisely in the change from the beginning to the end. If it was his purpose to show Fortuna's deceit, could he have done better than create an alluring image of her, as he did in the animated rhythms and elegant lines of the beginning, written in the major mode, while showing the unpredictable tragic finale in the slow ending, the dark hues of minor and the middle register, and the strange harmonic evolution from C major to F minor?

Neither is there any difficulty in explaining how a piece presumably written in the fall of 1499 could have been printed as number 74 of Petrucci's *Odhecaton* published in Venice on 15 May 1501. Venice was a place likely to be interested in this piece for more than one reason: its intrinsic value, the eminence of its maker, its advanced artistic design, its symbolic significance, and very probably also because the connections between Josquin and the house of Sforza were universally known—after all, it is Petrucci who attached the name Josquin d'Ascanio to two frottole of the composer—and because the connection between the Fortuna piece and the fall of the house of Sforza was understood by many.

Such an interpretation is corroborated by another Venetian piece whose significance and origin have been shrouded in obscurity so far. An early sixteenth-century manuscript of Venetian keyboard dances, discovered and edited by Knud Jeppesen, contains a dance with the title 'Son quel Duca di Milano'. Its text and music are reported as 'otherwise unknown'.[137] We recognize in its title the first line of the 'Pianto e lamento de lo illustrissimo signor Ludovico Sforza'. The ornamented dance would seem to be based on a popular tune to the verses of 'Son quel duca di Milano' that might have run as follows:

Ex. 4   Son quel duca de Milano   top line of keyboard version

derived melody!

Son   quel   du - - ca   de   Mi - la - no   che 'con   pian-

-to   sto in   do - lo - re   son   su - gie -

[137] *Balli antichi veneziani per cembalo*, ed. Knud Jeppesen (Copenhagen, 1962), no. 21 and p. XVI.

- to___ che e - ra si - gno - re ho - ra son___

fa - to A - le - man - no.

If one wonders about the transformation of the lament into a gay tune, and later an even livelier dance, one must remember that Ludovico's fall was greeted in Venice with cheers. 'Il Moro has always been and will always be the perpetual enemy of the Venetian Republic', was the saying in Venice.[138]

A companion piece to Josquin's 'Fortuna' is Serafino's 'Sonetto per il Moro quando fu preso' (Sonnet for *il Moro* when he was captured),[139] of which I offer a literal translation:

> He who knows not how Fortune lifts and lowers
> The miserable mortals in one instant,
> If he but looks at me and my misfortunes
> Will see that he is mad who makes himself her servant.
>
> Once I was high, looked down on those below me,
> And fancied to belong to the immortals.

[138] *I Diarii di Girolamo Priuli*, ed. Arturo Segre (*Rerum Italicarum Scriptores*, new series, xxiv/3; Bologna, 1921), p. 31.

[139] Menghini, *Le Rime*, p. 180. This is the title that the sonnet bears in the 1516 edition of Serafino's *Rime*, published by Giunta in Florence, the earliest printed source. Menghini considers it of doubtful authority, because of this late appearance in print. Were we to apply such stringent criteria to Josquin's works, we would be deprived of most of the master's mature and late works.

> Chi non sa come a un punto alzi et abassi
>   Fortuna i tristi e miseri mortali,
>   Se in me si specchia e ne' mie longhi mali
>   Vedrà che matto è chi suo servo fassi.
> Già fui sí alto ch'io sprezava i bassi,
>   Et esser mi credea fra li immortali;
>   Ma poi che questa iniqua aperse l'ali
>   Caddi qual giú da' monti e' gravi sassi.
> Perso ho l'ingegno, i sensi et ogni possa,
>   Né spero piú di rilevarmi in piede,
>   Sí rotti ho i nervi, le medolle e l'ossa.
> Però chi in cima di sua rota siede
>   Exemplo pigli dalla mia percossa;
>   Ché savio è quel che inanzi al mal provede.

But when the wicked one opened her wings,
Down, down I fell from heavy rocks and mountains.

Lost have I mind and senses, all my power.
And I despair to set myself on foot again
So broken are my nerves, my marrow, and my bones.

Therefore who sits on top of Fortune's wheel,
Let him but take a warning from my ruin
For wise is he who can provide for evil times.

This sonnet was followed by another one entitled 'Sonetto per il medesimo' (A sonnet for the same) that ends with this sentiment:

...be there no one who puts his faith
In worldly things, for in one single instant
Fortune forces to weep him who is laughing.[140]

'Fortuna sforza a lacrimar chi ride' runs the last line in the original, and one wonders whether the poet wished to symbolize the collision between Fortuna and Sforza in his choice of words.

This is the time at which Leonardo da Vinci, who had steadily worked in Milan from 1483 on, wrote the following note in his sketchbook: 'The Duke has lost his state and his goods and his liberty, and none of his works has been finished by him'.[141]

Serafino's and Josquin's Fortuna pieces belong together in space, time, and occasion. Implicit in this is the assumption that Josquin stayed in Rome from 1499 to 1500, for which time the account books of the Papal Chapel are missing. Ascanio left Rome on 14 July 1499, when the Pope sided with France. In a letter of 9 June of the same year Ascanio wrote to Ludovico that Alexander VI had said 'that the whole house of Milan had to be over-thrown and ruined'.[142] Did Ascanio, under the hectic circumstances and with the storm clouds gathering over the house of Sforza, ask Josquin to go with him? It is not likely. Ludovico and Ascanio were captured on 10 April 1500, the former on the way back from Germany in an attempt to regain power, the latter near Piacenza by the Venetians, who handed him over to the French. They went into captivity in France. And in 1501 we have documents showing Josquin in France.[143] In April 1503 Josquin joined the chapel of Ercole I d'Este of Ferrara, old friend of Milan, and left in April 1504.[144] In the month of May 1504, as Herbert Kellman's surprising discoveries have shown,[145] Josquin arrived in Condé-sur-l'Escaut. Far

---

[140] Menghini, *Le Rime*, p. 181.
[141] Visconti, 'Leonardo in Milan and Lombardy', p. 124.
[142] '...che tutta la casa de Milano sia disfacta et ruinata'; Santoro, *Gli Sforza*, p. 320.
[143] Osthoff, *Josquin Desprez*, i, p. 51.
[144] See Lewis Lockwood, these Proceedings, p. 114.   [145] See below, p. 207.

removed from the brilliance and beauty, the perpetual strife and intrigue of Italian courts, the master lived the last seventeen years of his life in a quiet Netherlandish town, in the company of simple, steady, hard-working, and devout citizens. It is here that he came to rest, here that he wrote his great psalm motets, new in their simplicity, clarity, and heart-felt piety.

The foregoing is no more than a sketch for an extended study of Josquin's life and music. It is fragmentary both in regard to biographical facts and stylistic analysis. Yet I hope to have been able to convey a glimpse of a new vision of Josquin's life and work. The study of Ascanio Sforza, his life and personality, will enable us, I am confident, to comprehend Josquin's music in a way that reflects the unusual life of an introspective, deep, immensely gifted artist close to a powerful figure of the time who was only one heartbeat away from the papacy, who hungered for power, riches, pleasures, artistic beauty, and for music to almost equal degrees.

Ascanio's life, with its ups and downs, with its phases of triumph and despair, with the brightness of its feasts and the gloom of its crises, culminating in the final tragedy of the Sforzas' downfall and the imprisonment in France—this colourful, dramatic and eventually tragic life is the background against which Josquin evolved as a composer, commanding from the beginning a stupendous technique, but developing in slow stages, each one of which holds its own fascination and its own masterworks, a musical language of ever growing expressivity.

Josquin loosened the musical tongue of his age, and all who listened felt touched and addressed in ways they had not known or felt before. We can understand him better if we study his long connection with an Italian Renaissance prince, a man of intense passions, fierce pride, great culture, and infinite artistic sensibilities. For it is with Ascanio that he learned of human passions and developed the musical language expressing them. And it is in liberating himself from Ascanio—he left Italy before Ascanio's death—that he arrived at his own, deeply felt religious views, and composed works so strongly rooted in the Christian tradition that they were capable of inspiring Catholics and Protestants alike.

New Light
on Josquin's Benefices

JEREMY NOBLE

It was Franz Xaver Haberl, in the epoch-making study of the Papal Chapel which he based on his archival researches in Rome,[1] who first published documentary evidence of Josquin's presence there. He found it in the series of bound volumes of *Mandati* relating to the expenses of the papal household which is preserved in the Archivio di Stato.[2] For music historians the principal interest of these account-books (or *libri bulletarum*, to give them their original title) lies in the fact that the monthly payments to the chapel generally list its members by name, thus enabling us to reconstruct in considerable detail the changing personnel and fortunes of that institution.

This is precisely what Haberl did, but since he was, as he implies, more interested in discovering new facts about known composers than in listing the comings and goings of relative nonentities,[3] he seems not to have examined every single monthly list, but instead to have taken a representative sample every three months or so. The result, unfortunately, is a host of small errors of dating. In the case of Josquin, however, Haberl was quite well enough aware of the importance of his discovery to present it with special care. According to his reading of the evidence, Josquin's name first appears in the lists in September 1486, disappears from February until September 1487 and again from October of the same year until June 1489,

---

[1] Fr. X. Haberl, 'Die römische "schola cantorum" und die päpstlichen Kapellsänger bis zur Mitte des 16. Jahrhunderts,' *Vierteljahrsschrift für Musikwissenschaft*, iii (1887), pp. 189–296. Also published as *Bausteine für Musikgeschichte*, iii (Leipzig, 1888). Page references are to the former publication.

[2] Rome, Archivio di Stato: Camerale I, vols. 824 ff. The volumes covering the period of Josquin's service are 851–5. The entries are not in the hand of the deacon of the chapel, Dominus Raphael de Arena, as is stated by Helmuth Osthoff (*Josquin Desprez*, i [Tutzing, 1962], p. 21), but are copies of 'orders to pay' addressed to the Treasurer by a much more important Raphael—Raffaele Riario, Cardinal of S. Giorgio, a relative of Sixtus IV who was appointed papal *camerarius* or chamberlain in 1483 and retained the post until 1517 (cf. W. von Hofmann, *Forschungen zur Geschichte der kurialen Behörden* [Rome, 1914], ii, p. 87). This is proved by the unusually full entry for September 1489 (Camerale I, Vol. 853, fol. 159): 'Raphael Sancti Georgii Diaconus Cardinalis domini pape camerarius Reverendo patri domino Falconi de Sinibaldis prothonotario apostolico et thesaurario generali....'

[3] Haberl, 'Die römische "schola cantorum"', pp. 217–18.

and is then present until April 1494, when the series of *mandati* is interrupted by a six-year gap; when it resumes, Josquin's name is no longer among the singers.[4]

Haberl's account is substantially correct, but Helmuth Osthoff, in his valuable recent monograph,[5] considered that it needed qualification, insofar as there were months when the entry in the *mandati* made a summary reference to the *officiales et cantores capelle* without specifying them by name, and other months, particularly during the reign of Alexander VI, when no entry for the chapel appears in the *mandati* at all. Awareness of these factors led Osthoff to a perhaps over-cautious presentation of the evidence, making Josquin's service appear even more intermittent than it in fact was; 'each singer', he concluded, 'performed his duty month by month, while Josquin appears as a restlessly fluctuating element in the chapel'.[6]

However, Osthoff seems not to have observed that in those cases when a summary entry is given, without individual names, it always makes specific reference back to a previous entry which does contain them, in some such words as the following: '... qui cantores continentur in precedenti mandato presentis (or dicti) mensis', followed by a folio reference.[7] Summary entries of this kind therefore provide just as strong evidence for the presence or absence of a particular singer as do the more specific entries to which they make reference, and for most of the months in which Osthoff regards Josquin's presence merely as very probable it can in fact be regarded as certainly attested.

But apart from this question of interpretation Osthoff has unfortunately introduced a further small error of dating. It seems to have escaped his attention that the system employed in the *libri bulletarum* entails that each month's provision for the papal chapel is included in the accounts for the *succeeding* month. Thus, to take a concrete instance, a page belonging to the May accounts and headed 'Mensis Maij 1485' contains an entry formulated as follows: '... similiter solvi faciatis infrascriptis officialibus et cantoribus capelle sanctissimi domini nostri pape summam pecuniarum infrascriptam viz. pro eorum provisione mensis Aprilis proxime preteriti.... '[8] For this reason, all of Osthoff's dates need to be shifted one month earlier.

Furthermore, light is shed on the mysterious gaps of a month or two that occasionally occur in the *mandati* during Alexander VI's reign by the discovery that one of them at least can be filled from a source in the Archivio Segreto Vaticano itself. Under the call number Miscellanea, Arm. XV. 161 is preserved a separately bound fascicle entitled in a later hand 'Ordini di pagamenti del Card. di S. Giorgio, Camerlengo di S. C., per la Coronazione

[4] Ibid., p. 244–6.   [5] Osthoff, *Josquin Desprez*, i, pp. 21–2.   [6] Ibid., p. 28.
[7] E.g., Camerale I, Vol. 851, fol. 263—the payment for November 1486—which refers back specifically to the October list of singers entered on fol. 253 of the same volume.
[8] Camerale I, Vol. 851, fol. 75.

di papa Alessandro VI'.[9] This is evidently the section (fols. 12–29) missing from Vol. 855 of the Archivio di Stato series, withdrawn at some early date for special treatment and never reunited with its parent volume. It supplies us with the chapel lists for November and December 1492, hitherto thought to be missing; in November Josquin's name appears as 'Ju. despres', in December as 'Judo. despres'.[10] Possibly other gaps of a single month can be ascribed to a similar cause.

When allowance has been made for the above-mentioned factors, it can be seen that the situation is almost exactly as Haberl formulated it. Josquin's service falls into two main periods—September 1486 to January 1487 inclusive and June 1489 until at least March 1494 insofar as the evidence survives[11]—together with a single unattached month in between these two periods, namely September 1487.

★ ★ ★

The practice of supplementing the salaries of chapel singers by conferring benefices upon them was extremely widespread by the later fifteenth century. It was not confined to the Papal Chapel. Kings and princes throughout Christendom sought to attract the best talents to their service by inducements of this kind, offering such pecuniary *beneficia* as happened to lie within their gift with a disregard for the spiritual *officia* they were supposed to accompany which might be considered cynical if it had not been taken so completely for granted—and not least by the papacy itself. 'Canonries were the staple commodity of the papal market', a distinguished historian has said,[12] but if the Pope stood head and shoulders above any competitors in the lavishness with which he dispensed benefices, this was

---

[9] I should like to thank the Rev. Charles Burns, whose generous assistance is well known to all users of the Vatican Archives, for drawing my attention to this document.

[10] Josquin's name is written in the earlier series of entries, up to and including September 1487, in the form 'Jo. de pratis'—'Jo.' presumably standing either for 'Jodocus' or (less correctly) 'Josquinus', although it normally stands for 'Johannes.' In the entries from June 1489 onwards it appears in a mixture of Latin and French: 'Jodo(cus)', usually abbreviated to 'Ju.' (which is in practice indistinguishable from the 'In.' that stands for 'Innocentius'), followed by 'de prez', 'de prezis', 'desprets' and other similar spellings. This is, so far as I am aware, the only case in the chapel lists where two such completely different linguistic forms are used for the same individual, though there are cases where an alias is either substituted or added, as when 'Jo. Corbie' (May 1456 onwards) becomes 'Jo. Jorlandi' (May 1457), or when 'Ber. Vacqueras' is given the sobriquet (October 1484) 'alias de Bassia'.

[11] It should be pointed out that a volume (the last for Innocent VIII's reign) containing the entries from September 1491 to June 1492 is missing from the Archivio di Stato series between 854 and 855. However, since every singer present in August 1491 is also present in July 1492, perhaps we may assume that Josquin was not absent from the chapel during this period.

[12] F. W. Maitland, *Roman Canon Law in the Church of England* (London, 1898), p. 67.

due not to greater worldliness but to greater—much greater—opportunity.[13]

Clement IV's bull *Licet ecclesiarum* of 1265 had set forth for the first time the theoretical right of the Pope to dispose of all benefices—a right which was claimed to co-exist with the rights of the ordinary collators, lay or religious, in most cases, but to be exclusive in certain special classes of benefice 'reserved' to the papal authority.[14] These included, for example, benefices vacated by incumbents dying at the Holy See (*apud sedem apostolicam*). In time, with the steady growth of centralization in the medieval church, the 'reserved' classes of benefice were enormously extended, particularly during the period of exile in Avignon; their conferment became a principal mode of papal patronage—a patronage from which all curial officials, and among them the *cantores capellani* with whom we are concerned, benefitted. Or at least were intended to benefit, for the practice led to such legal confusion, such tangled webs of conflicting claims and conflicting authorities, that many of the benefices so eagerly sought and bestowed with such generosity never took effect and brought their recipients nothing but trouble and expense.[15]

A very large number of bulls[16] referring to beneficial matters survives in the various series of official registers of the papal correspondence, and of these a small but significant proportion inevitably refers to musicians. These *litterae beneficiales* are essentially legal documents. They are completely formalized in expression and exceedingly involved in style—a direct result of their need to forestall all possible legal objections to their validity. They can, however, provide us with biographical information, if handled with an awareness of their implications. Haberl recognized this, and included a number of footnote references to them,[17] but an examination of his article makes it clear that he used only the relatively small series of registers (253 volumes) known as the Diversa Cameralia.[18] It was in the course of exploring some of the other sources so abundantly preserved in the Archivio Vaticano and the Archivio di Stato in Rome that the following

[13] The most accessible general account in English of the growth of the system is to be found in Geoffrey Barraclough, *Papal Provisions* (Oxford, 1935).

[14] Ibid., p. 9.

[15] Ibid., p. 34. Cf. also Abbé F. Baix, 'De la valeur historique des actes pontificaux de collation des bénéfices', *Hommage à Dom Ursmer Berlière* (Brussels, 1931), pp. 57–66.

[16] Throughout this paper the word 'bull' is used not in the strict technical sense, but to cover papal letters in many different forms.

[17] Haberl, 'Die römische "schola cantorum"', pp. 225–32.

[18] For an account of this series, cf. Ursmer Berlière, *Inventaire analytique des Diversa Cameralia des Archives Vaticanes (1389–1500) au point de vue des anciens diocèses de Cambrai, Liège, Thérouanne et Tournai* (Rome, Namur, Paris, 1906), especially pp. iii–ix. Six volumes of the series refer to the reign of Innocent VIII, four to that of Alexander VI. It seems possible that Haberl's use of the series was circumscribed by the progress of the hand-written card-index of the Diversa Cameralia, the so-called 'schedario Pietro Sella', which is still the main guide to the collection's contents.

documents relating to Josquin came to light (together with a large number relating to other members of the Papal Chapel which I hope to publish once the information contained in them has been compared and analysed).

The first of the three newly-discovered bulls addressed to or relating to Josquin is registered in a volume in the Archivio di Stato entitled 'Liber expectativarum pontificatus nostri anno 50'[19] (i.e., the fifth year of Innocent VIII's papacy, which began on 12 September 1488, the anniversary of his coronation). *Gratiae expectativae* were, as their name implies, benefices conferred prospectively, as soon as they should become available in the future. It was the practice in the later Middle Ages for the Pope to distribute many thousands of such 'expectative graces', especially at the beginning of his papacy, to the poor and otherwise unbeneficed clerks who flocked to Rome in hope of receiving them.[20] The present volume, however, records expectative graces of a more prestigious kind: benefices (canonries for the most part) granted to curial officials and members of the Pope's own household, and so phrased as to give them special legal precedence.

Our document is contained on fols. 297-9 (cf. App. A). It is dated (at the end) 9 September 1489 and is addressed to Josquin himself, whose name appears here, as elsewhere in these official documents, as 'Judocus de Pratis'. As seems to be customary, he is immediately given the style of the benefice which the document is designed to confer on him, i.e., 'canon of the church of St. Omer at St. Omer in the diocese of Thérouanne'. He is further described, in the standard phrases, as a member of the papal household ('continuus commensalis noster') and a singer-chaplain ('cantor capellanus') in the Papal Chapel. A rather unusual provision is inserted ('et presentes. . . valere') back-dating the effect of the bull to 1 November 1486. This seems particularly odd in a document which by its very nature is prospective. Presumably it is intended to confer legal precedence on Josquin's claim over any similar grant made *since* 1 November 1486, but the choice of that particular date does tend to confirm that Josquin's service with the chapel goes back at least that far.

The document continues with the normal formula of absolution, needed to ensure that its validity could not be challenged on grounds of the recipient's spiritual condition, and the brief *motu proprio* clause, before coming to the gist of the matter. It both confers and provides[21] Josquin with the aforementioned canonry at St. Omer. It reserves to him a prebend

---

[19] Rome, Archivio di Stato, Camerale I, Vol. 1099.

[20] G. Mollat, *La Collation des Bénéfices ecclésiastiques sous les Papes d'Avignon (1305-1378)* (Université de Strasbourg: Bibliothèque de Droit Canonique, i; Paris, 1921), pp. 69-78. Also Camille Tihon, 'Les expectatives in forma pauperum particulièrement au XIVe siècle', *Bulletin de l'Institut Historique Belge de Rome*, v (1925), pp. 51-118.

[21] Normally speaking, the Pope provides, while the bishop collates (or confers); cf. Barraclough, p. 121. But in the case of 'reserved' benefices the Pope assumes the functions of the normal collator.

(a canon's stipend) and an official position, excluding the principal one in the church, which would in this case be that of provost.[22] It also (*necnon*) reserves to him a benefice, to the estimated annual value of 40 *livres tournois* with cure of souls or 30 without, whose collation belongs to the Benedictine monastery of St. Ghislain in the diocese of Cambrai. It goes on, again in absolutely standard formulas, to debar the Bishop of Thérouanne, the Chapter of St. Omer, and the Abbot and Convent of St. Ghislain from undertaking any action that might impede the effect of the bull.

Before we summarize the second part of the document, a word or two on the background to these ecclesiastical appointments seems appropriate. By 'the church of St. Omer at St. Omer' is meant the collegiate church originally dedicated to the Virgin Mary and nowadays again known as Notre-Dame.[23] It was founded by St. Omer (Audomarus) about the year 660, and he himself was buried in it; during the Middle Ages his tomb attracted pilgrims and the church took his name, just as the abbey church in the lower part of the town, though originally dedicated to St. Peter, became known as St. Bertin, after St. Omer's disciple of that name. The chapter of St. Omer consisted of thirty canons with a provost at their head. According to the *pouillés* (tax registers) for the diocese of Thérouanne published by Auguste Longnon,[24] this latter office was exceptionally well endowed, being taxed on an estimated revenue of no less than 800 *livres* per annum—a sum which made that benefice an ecclesiastical plum of almost episcopal magnitude and no doubt explains why it was held at this date by a member of the Burgundian ducal family, albeit an illegitimate one. The canons received a prebend of 80 *livres* apiece (still valuable as canonries went). Such a prebend, combined with the 30 *livres* from a benefice *sine cura* in the gift of the abbey of St. Ghislain, would amount to a very considerable annual income.

While St. Omer lay just within the northern border of the County of Artois (with its capital at Arras), St. Ghislain was one of the principal Benedictine houses of the County of Hainaut, far away to the east.[25] It may seem strange to find two churches, geographically so distant from one another, linked in this way, but with more evidence before us, we shall be able to suggest the reasons for it.

The second part of our document records, though still within the context

[22] On the distinctions between *dignitas, personatus, officium*, etc., see Mollat, *La Collation des Bénéfices*, pp. 2–3.

[23] For an excellent summary history of this church and its rival, St. Bertin, see Canon O. Bled, 'Abbatiale et Collégiale', *Mémoires de la Société des Antiquaires de la Morinie*, xxxii (1914–20), pp. 5–112.

[24] Auguste Longnon, ed., *Pouillés de la Province de Reims* (*Recueil des historiens de la France publié par l'Académie des Inscriptions et Belles-Lettres: Pouillés, Tome VI, première partie*; Paris, 1908), p. 642.

[25] Dom Ursmer Berlière, *Monasticon Belge*, i (Maredsous, 1890–7), pp. 244–70.

of the letter addressed to Josquin, the instructions (*litterae executoriae*)[26] sent to the three commissioners charged with putting its provisions into effect and seeing that its recipient was duly inducted into his new state. These commissioners, or commissaries, are the Bishop of Tournai, a canon of Cambrai named 'Nicolaus Rombert', and the Official (i.e., the Bishop's deputy in legal matters) of the diocese of Thérouanne. Of these, only the last can be regarded as an absolutely formalized choice. The first two, in spite of their official connections with the Low Countries—Tournai and Cambrai respectively—turn out on closer investigation to belong to that numerous band of northerners employed in the papal Curia. There had in fact been a schism in the see of Tournai since the previous bishop, Ferry de Clugny, died in Rome in 1483.[27] By virtue of the right of reservation already mentioned above, Sixtus IV appointed as his successor one Jean Monissart, who had previously served as councillor to two Dukes of Burgundy, Philip the Good and Charles the Bold,[28] but was now resident in Rome as master of the papal household (*palatii apostolici magister domus*). This nomination, which took place in October 1483, was hotly contested by Charles VIII of France, who regarded Tournai as an outpost of French influence in the north and had no wish to see its ecclesiastical affairs in the hands of a man who might be expected to favour his Burgundian enemies. Indeed, he went so far as to get his own candidate, the royal councillor Louis Pot, elected by the canons of Tournai and received in the diocese. This schism became a principal point of contention between the papacy and the French court,[29] and it was not ended by Monissart's death in August 1491.[30] However, the later stages of the conflict go beyond our concern, which is merely to establish the identity of Josquin's commissioner. Although Monissart was never able to take personal possession of his see, he is constantly referred to in the diary of Johannes Burchard, the papal master of ceremonies, as 'episcopus Tornacensis', and there can be no doubt that it is he who is meant in our document.

Nicholas Rombert (more usually spelled Rembert or Rambert) occu-pied a less august rank in the curial hierarchy, but his connections with

[26] Barraclough, *Papal Provisions*, pp. 137f; Mollat, *La Collation des Bénéfices*, p. 116.

[27] É. de Moreau, *Histoire de l'Église en Belgique*, iv (Brussels, 1949), p. 58.

[28] Cf. his epitaph, as quoted in Burchard's diary: *Johannis Burckardi Liber Notarum*, ed. Enrico Celani (*Rerum Italicarum Scriptores*, new ed., xxxii/i; Città di Castello, 1906–42), p. 313, note 1. Also in Thuasne's less accurate edition: *Johannis Burchardi Diarium*, ed. L. Thuasne (Paris, 1883–5), i, p. 416, note 1.

[29] The instructions issued by Charles VIII to his ambassadors in 1491 make this very clear. They are reprinted in the *Ordonnances des Rois de France de la troisième race*, ed. Pastoret, xx, pp. 290f, and as document 37 in the Appendix to Vol. i of Thuasne's edition of Burchard (see especially pp. 552–3).

[30] Not 1484, as Moreau (iv, p. 465) states, following *Gallia Christiana*, iii, col. 236A. Burchard's diary (see note 28 above) is quite explicit and circumstantial.

music are closer, or at least better attested. From the notarized copy of his will preserved in the chapter archives of Notre-Dame at St. Omer[31] we learn that he was baptized, and therefore presumably born, at Doudeauville, a village in the Pas-de-Calais some 24 kilometres south-east of Boulogne; but the first known dated reference to him occurs in 1475 and 1476, as a *contratenorista* in the choir of St. Peter's at Rome[32] (i.e. the small choir employed by the canons of the basilica, not to be confused with the Pope's much larger personal chapel, even though the latter sometimes recruited its singers from the former). However, no further references to Rembert as a singer have yet come to light. He appears to have taken up the career of a curial lawyer and administrator, without altogether abandoning his connections with musicians. In 1481 he is referred to as a priest of the diocese of Thérouanne and rector of the church of St. Martin outside Aire in that diocese, but this in no way implies his residence there.[33] Indeed he is soon afterwards specifically referred to as a *familiaris*, or member of the household, of the new Pope, Innocent VIII,[34] and we can trace even in the published documents the gradual accumulation of benefices that marked the successful progress of his curial career. Already by 1 December 1484 he is named as a canon both of Cambrai and of St. Omer.[35] In 1488 we find him acting as proctor for one 'Johannes Trutoris' in the matter of paying annates for a canonry in the church of St. Gertrude at Nivelles.[36] 'Trutoris' can surely be no other than a mistranscription (either by the original scribe or by his modern editor) of 'Tinctoris', particularly since a marginal note informs us that the said Johannes is resident in Naples. By 1493, at the latest, Rembert appears to have been both a notary of the Sacred Rota and an *abbreviator litterarum apostolicarum*.[37] Various documents associate him with benefices at Notre-Dame, Antwerp,[38] and at St. Géry, Cambrai,[39] but the culmination of his beneficial career evidently came with his appointment as Dean of St. Omer in 1494, in succession to Simon Godefroy.[40] He died on

[31] St. Omer, Bibliothèque Municipale: Archives capitulaires, II. G. 484. Rembert begins by commending his soul to God, the Virgin Mary and various saints, including 'Monseigneur sainct Bertont patron de léglise paroissiale de sainct Bertont de Doudeauville en laquelle je fus baptisié'.

[32] Haberl, 'Die römische "schola cantorum"', p. 237n.

[33] Berlière, *Inventaire analytique*, no. 760.

[34] Ibid., nos. 777–8.

[35] Ibid.

[36] E. Brouette; *Les 'Libri Annatarum' pour les pontificats d'Eugène IV à Alexandre VI: Tome IV—Pontificats d'Innocent VIII et Alexandre VI (1484–1503) (Analecta Vaticano-Belgica,* xxiv; Brussels/Rome, 1963), no. 193.

[37] Hofmann, *Forschungen*, ii, p. 183. The information comes from lists given in Burchard's diary under the dates 4 and 5 June 1493; cf. Celani edition, pp. 433, 435.

[38] Berlière, *Inventaire analytique*, no. 794.

[39] Brouette, *Les 'Libri Annatarum'*, no. 267; Berlière, *Inventaire analytique*, no. 801.

[40] *Gallia Christiana*, iii, col. 482C.

11 January 1504 (new style), and the account rendered to the chapter by his executors refers to him as being at that time an apostolic protonotary, dean and canon of St. Omer, and prior *in commendam* of the priory of Rumilly-le-Comte, 26 kilometres south-west of St. Omer and quite close to his native village. He was buried near the tomb of St. Omer, having presented a bronze screen for the choir and left provision in his will for the construction of a chapel on the south side of the nave.[41]

Whether Josquin did in fact succeed in taking possession of his canonry, even with such influential backing as Rembert's, could be determined only by an examination of unpublished primary material.[42] As we shall see, certain factors speak against it, but since these apply equally to the benefices conferred upon him in two further newly discovered documents, it will perhaps be best to detail their contents first, before considering the common factors which might have hindered, if not prevented, all of them from taking effect.

*   *   *

The two remaining documents come not from the Archivio di Stato, but from the much larger and more important collection of papal registers contained in the Archivio Segreto Vaticano itself, and more particularly from the series of so-called Registri Vaticani.[43] The contents of this immense collection of official papal correspondence are considerably more miscellaneous than that of the *liber expectativarum* referred to above, but inevitably a high proportion is concerned with beneficial matters, and among these is a fair sprinkling of bulls pertaining to papal singers. So far only two have been found referring to Josquin, but each adds some details to the total picture of his career.

Both date from the papacy of Alexander VI (1492–1503). The earlier (cf. App. B and Pls. 5–7) is dated 8 November 1493, not from Rome but from Corneto (the modern Tarquinia), which the Pope and his son Cesare had then reached in the course of a tour round their towns and fortresses in

[41] For his will cf. note 31 above. L. Deschamps de Pas, 'L'Église Notre-Dame de Saint-Omer d'après les comptes de fabrique et les registres capitulaires', *Mémoires de la Société des Antiquaires de la Morinie*, xxii (1890–92), and xxiii (1893–96), notably xxii, pp. 186–7; Emmanuel Wallet, *Description de l'ancienne cathédrale de Saint-Omer* (Saint-Omer and Douai, 1839), p. 33.

[42] The remaining archives of Notre Dame are preserved, as mentioned above, in the Bibliothèque Municipale of St. Omer (no published inventory). The chapter acts for the relevant period are contained in II. G. 355 [1479–97] and II. G. 356 [1497–1525] and might well repay detailed examination.

[43] For a general guide to the collection cf. *Sussidi per la consultazione dell'Archivio Vaticano* (*Studi e Testi*, 45; Rome, 1926). Also Leonard E. Boyle, O.P., *A Survey of the Vatican Archives and its holdings* (Pontifical Institute of Mediaeval Studies: Subsidia Mediaevalia, i; Toronto, 1972), pp. 103–13—unfortunately published after the researches in Rome on which this paper is based had been completed.

1. Minute of letter from Galeazzo Maria Sforza to the Cardinal of Novara of 20 September 1473 on a benefice for Josquin. Milan, Archivio di Stato, Archivio Sforzesco 825. (p. 34)

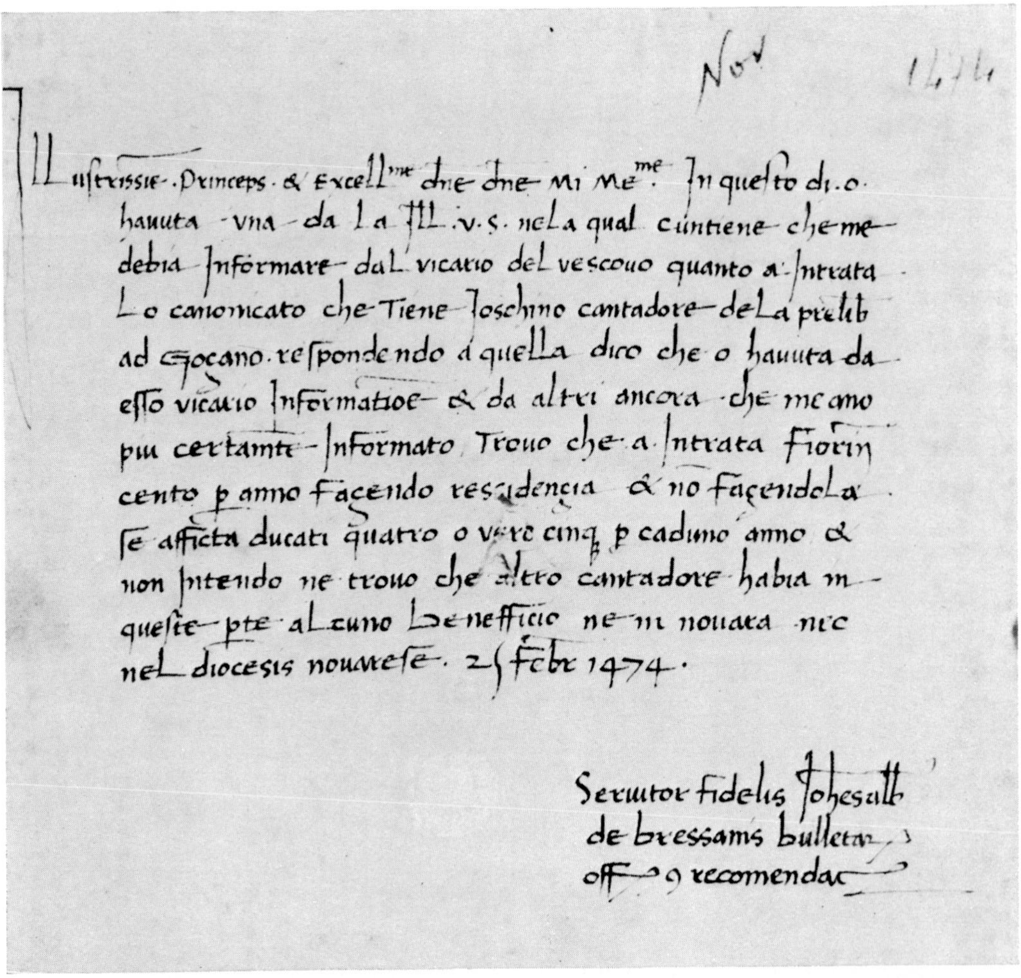

Nov 1474

Illustrissie. Princeps. & Excellme dne dne mi mee. In questo di o
hauuta vna da la Ill. v. s. nela qual cuntiene che me
debia Informare dal vicario del vescouo quanto a Intrata
Lo canonicato che Tiene Joschino cantadore dela piellb
ad Cocano. respondendo a quella dico che o hauuta da
esso vicario Informatioe & da altri ancora che me ano
piu certamte Informato. Trouo che a Intrata Fiorin
cento p anno facendo residencia & no facendola
se afficta ducati quatro o vere cinq p caduno anno &
non Intendo ne trouo che altro cantadore habia in
queste pte alcuno beneficio ne m nouara nec
nel diocesis nouarese. 2 Febr 1474.

Seruitor fidelis Johesalb
de bressams bulletar
off g recomendac

2. Letter from Johannes Albus de Bressanis to Galeazzo Maria Sforza of 25 February
1474 on Josquin's benefice. Milan, Archivio di Stato, Potenze Sovrane 1634.
(p. 35)

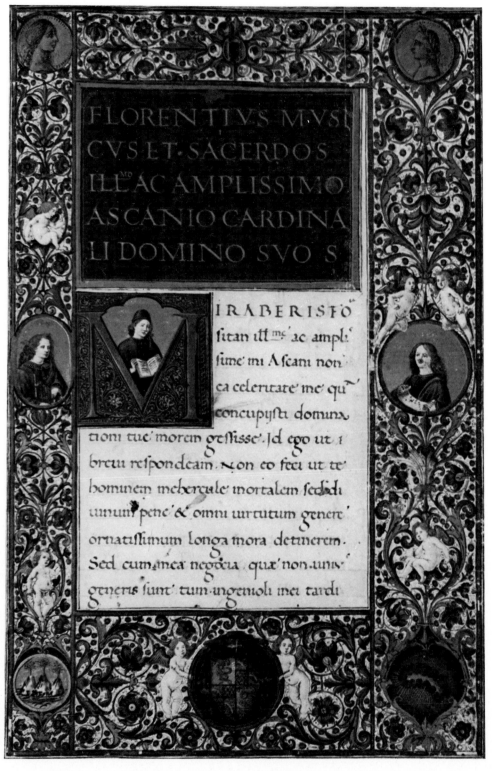

FLORENTIVS MVSI
CVS ET·SACERDOS
ILLᴹᴼ AC AMPLISSIMO
ASCANIO CARDINA
LI DOMINO SVO S

IRABERISTO
sitan ittᵐᵉ· ac ampli
sime mi Ascani non
ea celeritate me qu̅
concupysti domina
tioni tue morem gessisse. Id ego ut i
breui respondeam. Non eo feci ut te
hominem mehercule mortalem sed di
uinum pene & omni uirtutum genere
ornatissimum longa mora detinerem.
Sed cum mea negocia que non unius
generis sunt· tum ingenioli mei tardi

3. Florentius, *Liber musices*, opening page with beginning of dedication to Ascanio
Sforza. Milan, Biblioteca Trivulziana, MS. 2146. (p. 48)

Sonecto·xcix artificiale p la musica
doue piu uolte e inserte·Vt:Re:Mi:
Fa:Sol:La·   Alla·nostra donna·

La uita hor mi resolue: mi fa degno·
  Sol regina del ciel mia fida scorta·
  Lalma e gia iferma: hor falla alqua reccorta
Redocto sol dogni smarrito legno·
Solui superna dea mio sosco ingegno·
  Fa chio te segua: e fa la uia qni corta
  Sol ben conosca: e sol troui io la porta
Vtile a ognun che ha qui smarrito el segno·
Fa la superna corte io ueda al fine·
  Mi combatte qui amor: fortuna e morte
  Lasso fa tu sol con tue man diuine·
Retoglimi a costor: fa chal fin porte
  Vtile fior de si pungenti spine
  Relaxando penser dogni altra sorte·
      Sol in te spero forte·
Misericordia: o sol rendomi solo
  Regina a te: fa tu sol malzi a uolo·
      Finis·

4. Serafino dall'Aquila, 'La vita ormai resolvi'. [*Opere*], Besicken, Rome, 1503.
(p. 58)

5. Bull of Alexander VI dated 8 November 1493 concerning a benefice for Josquin. Vatican City, Archivio Segreto Vaticano, Reg. Vat. 782, fol. 33ᵛ (continued on plates 6–7). (p. 84)

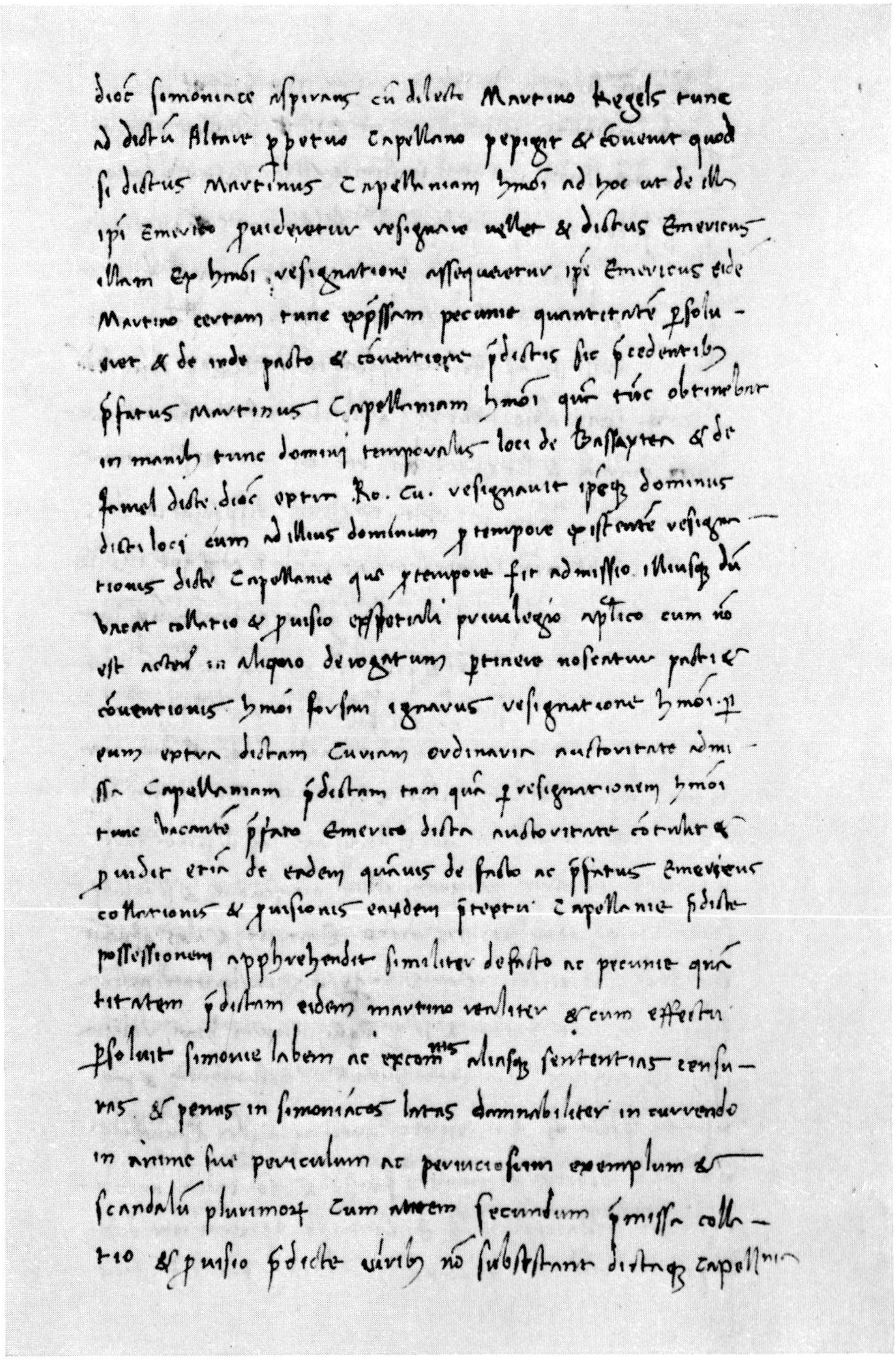

6. Reg. Vat. 782, fol. 34.

ad huc ut pfertur bracare noscentur Nos pfatoz Indoco
q̃ etiam cotinuus comensales nr̃ epistr̃t p̃missoz obsequoz
et meritoz suoz in tuitu spatem gratiam facere volentes
ipm̃q̃ Indocum nqbuis epcom̃nis suspensionis et interdicti
aliasq̃ ecc̃ sentencijs censuris et penis niue ut aliqomin
quinuis occasione ut causa latis sigb quomolibet innodatus epistr̃t ad effectum p̃sentium duntaxat cõsequẽdū
havq̃ sene absoluentes et absolutũ fore censentes necnon omnia et singula b̃n ecc̃ cum .cū. et sine cura
que dictus Indocus etiam epqbuis dispensationibus
apticis obtinet et expectat ac inqb et nǒq̃ que ius sibi
quomolibet comparit querūq̃ gẽoq̃ et qualiucūq̃ sent
eaq̃ fructuum vedd. et pro. nec an. ua. ac hm̃ dispe-
sationum tenores p̃sentib̃ p q̃p hijs habentes disc̃etioni
nr̃e p ap̃ticн sc̃ripta mandam̃ quatin̄ uos et duo uel
unus ur̃m si dictus Indocus eundem Emericum sup
eisdem relatis coram .nobis accusare seq̃ in form̃ iuris
inscribere uoluerit postquam illum accusauerit et se inscripserit ut pfertur vocatis dictō Emerico et alijs qfuerit
euocandi sup eisdem relatis inquratis audovitate nr̃a
diligentius uevitatem et si p inquisitionem hm̃or uelatu
ip̃a veperueritis uevitate subnit — collationem et pro
uisonem p̃distaq̃ et indefecter querimq̃ nulla et inualida
nulliusq̃ voboris ut momẽti fuisse et esse eandem audovitate nr̃a declaretis ipm̃q̃ Emericum n. detenentione diste
Capellanie realiter amonentis put de iure fuerit faciendū.

7. Reg. Vat. 782, fol. 34ᵛ.

8. First letter of 4 August 1502 from Girolamo da Sestola, alias 'il Coglia', to Duke Ercole I d'Este. Document No. 10. (p. 126)

9. Second Letter of 4 August 1502 from Girolamo da Sestola, alias 'il Coglia', to Duke Ercole I d'Este. Document No. 11. (p. 127)

10. Letter of 14 August 1502 from Girolamo da Sestola, alias 'il Coglia', to Duke Ercole I d'Este. Document No. 14 (continued on plate 11). (p. 130)

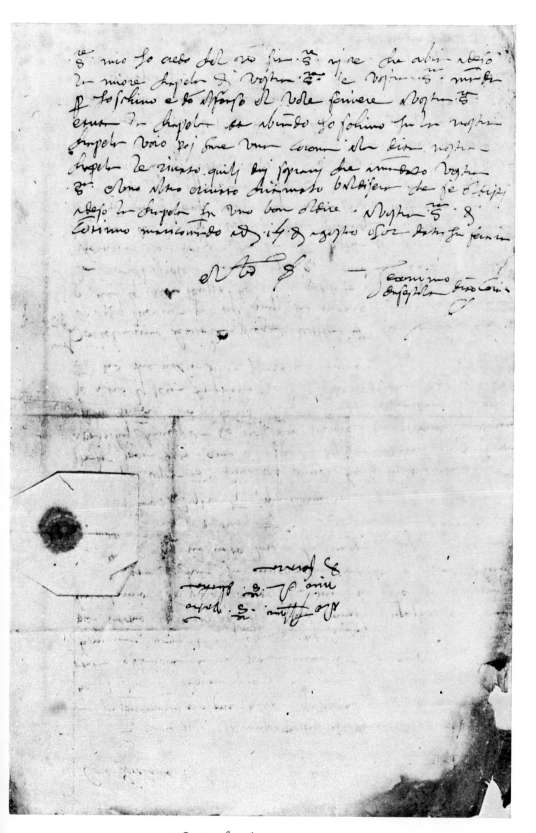

11. Letter of 14 August 1502, page 2.

12. Letter of 27 January 1504 from Ferrarese ambassador to Venice, Bartolomeo de' Cartari, to Duke Ercole I d'Este. Document No. 23. (p. 134)

the country north of Rome.[44] The document this time is not in the form of *litterae gratiosae* addressed to Josquin himself but of *litterae executoriae* addressed to the relevant commissioners: the deans of the collegiate churches of Condé (where Josquin himself was eventually to become Provost), and of Soignies, both in the diocese of Cambrai, and Johannes de Porta, canon of Cambrai.[45] Josquin has brought to the attention of the Pope that one Emericus de Honstat, the present incumbent of a perpetual chaplaincy at the altar of St. Theobald in the parish church of 'Bassaytea' in the diocese of Cambrai, has obtained this position by means of a simoniacal agreement with the previous incumbent, Martinus Kegels. The commissioners are empowered, if Josquin lays the above charge in legal form, to inquire into the matter and, if his case seems to be justified, to remove the said Emericus from his chaplaincy (which according to Josquin is without cure of souls and is worth at most 15 *livres tournois* per annum) and to induct or cause to be inducted Josquin or his chosen proctor.

It seems reasonable to suppose that for Josquin to have got wind of simoniacal irregularities at the parish level he must have had some local connection with the area. 'Bassaytea', however, proved at first rather difficult to identify, not least because the curial scribe, no doubt working from an original in an unfamiliar hand, had unwittingly changed a letter. The consultation of modern gazetteers of France and Belgium failed to produce this name or a plausible cognate, but a more nearly contemporary source revealed the reason for this. In the fourteenth-century *pouillés*, or ecclesiastical taxation lists, for the diocese of Cambrai[46] there appears, in the archdeaconry of Brabant and the deanery of Hal, a parish called 'Bassa Yttra'. From the seventeenth-century antiquarian Jacques Le Roy we learn that the ancient fief of Ittre (in Latin, Yttra), which lies some seven kilometres north-northwest of Nivelles, was from an early date divided into two parts, Haute and Basse (Alta Yttra and Bassa Yttra), the former of which lay in the County of Hainaut, the latter in the Duchy of Brabant.[47] Basse-Ittre, as the more important of the two villages, has nowadays lost its prefix and become Ittre *tout court*, though Haut-Ittre is still known as such, and so spelled.

From the fourteenth-century *pouillé* already referred to, we discover that

[44] Michael Mallett, *The Borgias* (London, 1969), p. 119.

[45] He died on 13 June 1515, according to his executors' accounts, preserved together with his will at Lille (Archives du Nord, 4. G. 1397).

[46] Longnon, *Pouillés*, p. 329. For his text of the *pouillés* of the diocese of Cambrai, Longnon relied (p. lii of his Introduction) on the Belgian sources published by Canon Reusens in *Analectes pour servir à l'histoire ecclésiastique de la Belgique*, xxviii (1900).

[47] *Topographia historica Gallo-Brabantiae* (Amsterdam, 1692), pp. 42–4. Le Roy here quotes verbatim the unpublished notes of Jean Blondeau of Nivelles (see his prefatory epistle to the reader): 'La Terre d'Ittre, est divisée en haute & basse, Haut Ittre est du Comté de Haynau, Bas Ittre est Brabant.'

the parish church of Basse-Ittre was well endowed in the late Middle Ages. The benefice itself was taxed on an annual valuation of 23 *livres tournois*, and there were also four dependent chaplaincies; J. Tarlier and A. Wauters,[48] describing a somewhat later period, though without specifying their sources, list no fewer than six, including one dedicated to 'St. Thibaud' in the gift of the *seigneurs* of Ittre. Ittre lies in an area that has for centuries suffered from the tensions between two ethnic and linguistic groups, sometimes expressed in merely local terms, sometimes in the clash of nations—the battlefield of Waterloo lies only a few kilometres to the north-east. As a result the village has been ravaged not once but many times, and the church of Josquin's day destroyed. However, Le Roy preserves some details that help to explain why it should have been so well endowed. It was, he tells us, the proud possessor of an ancient wooden statue of the Virgin which produced miraculous cures;[49] this attracted pilgrims from far and wide, and no doubt endowments as well.

The Cambrai *pouillé*[50] also has a certain amount to tell us about the two collegiate churches whose deans were charged with executing their particular commission, though it does not of course help us to identify them as individuals. Of the twenty-four canons who made up the chapter at Condé-sur-l'Escaut at this period, thirteen (the so-called canons 'de Hannonia'—of Hainaut) were assessed at 25 *livres tournois* each per annum, while the eleven canons 'de Brabant' were assessed at 20. The three offices of dean, provost, and treasurer were assessed at 20, 16, and 25 *livres* respectively, but no doubt the first two at least of these *dignitates* were each held in addition to a canon's prebend. In theory, and probably in practice too, the patronage of all these benefices was vested at this period in the Duke of Burgundy, insofar as he united the titles of Count of Hainaut and Duke of Brabant.[51]

The same is true of the slightly larger and considerably richer collegiate church of St. Vincent at Soignies, which held thirty prebends assessed at 50 *livres*, of which the dean and provost held two each.[52] The topographical

[48] J. Tarlier and A. Wauters, *La Belgique ancienne et moderne . . . Deuxième livraison: Canton de Nivelles (communes rurales)* (Brussels, 1860), p. 42.

[49] Le Roy, *Topographia*, p. 42: 'Cette Église est célèbre pour l'Image Miraculeuse de Nostre Dame, qu'elle conserve, & pour plusieurs bénéfices qui y sont fondez.'

[50] Longnon, *Pouillés*, pp. 326–7; the canonries and other dignities of Condé have here been mistakenly printed under the general heading of St. Vincent de Soignies. See also M. Hénault, ed., *Département du Nord: Ville de Condé-sur-l'Escaut: Inventaire Sommaire des Archives Communales antérieures à 1790* (Lille, 1897), Introduction, pp. xvi–xvii.

[51] Moreau, *Histoire de l'Église*, p. 73. Osthoff's statement (*Josquin Desprez*, i, p. 72) that eleven prebends were in the gift of 'the sovereign' and ten others in that of 'the Lords of Condé' mistakenly paraphrases Hénault, who is referring to the period after the French conquest (1678).

[52] Longnon, *Pouillés*, pp. 326–7.

writer Jacobus Lessabaeus (Jacques Lessabée or de Leussau) in a description
of Hainaut published at Antwerp in 1534 but probably compiled earlier[53]—
in other words during the decade after Josquin's death—refers to both
churches as being particularly noted for their music. Of Soignies he remarks
(his stilted Latin can only be translated freely): 'I doubt whether there is in
all Hainaut a nobler chapter, or one more famous for its vocal music, for
even that of Cambrai is not far ahead of it in this respect. Nor has this come
about without fortune's favour; not only the pleasant situation of the place,
but also its truly royal endowments induce singing musicians to flock hither
like bees to a hive, where they may find rich provision'.[54] Guicciardini,
writing a little later in the century, confirms both the beauty of the place
and its musical reputation: 'Sogni ha vicino il bellissimo bosco di Sogni ...:
è buona terretta, & ha un' nobile & celebrato Collegio di Canonici,
nominato del nome di S. Vincentio. ... Partorisce particularmente questo
luogo molti bonissimi musici con voci eccellenti, & perfette; & qui
ordinariamente ricompensa, & da provvisione il Re a suoi cantori'.[55] (The
king Guicciardini refers to is of course not the King of France but 'il gran'
Re Cattolico, don Filippo d'Austria', to whom his book is dedicated.)
Guicciardini's entry on Condé[56] oddly contains no mention of its collegiate
church, but Lessabaeus has no hesitation in ranking it as the third most
musical chapter of Hainaut,[57] presumably after Cambrai and Soignies.

The reasons for choosing the Deans of Condé and Soignies, let alone
Johannes de Porta, canon of Cambrai, to deal with the simoniacal chaplain of
Ittre are not very obvious, though it is true that Soignies lies reasonably close
(some 15 kilometres south-west). But coming as they do from the three most
musically famous collegiate chapters in the area, it seems at least possible
that they may have been chosen for their acquaintance with Josquin's stature as a musician, and perhaps their sympathy for him as a claimant.

★ ★ ★

[53] Jacobus Lessabaeus, *Hannoniae urbium et nominatiorum locorum...anacephalaeosis*
(Antwerp, 1534). The original Latin text was republished by Baron de Reiffenberg in
Monuments pour servir à l'histoire des provinces de Namur, de Hainaut et de Luxembourg, i
(Brussels, 1844), pp. lv–lxxxii; a French translation by G. Decamps and A. Wins was
privately printed for the Société des Bibliophiles Belges séant à Mons (Mons, 1885) on
the occasion of the society's fiftieth anniversary.

[54] 'Sonnegiae: ...Atque haud scio an tota Hannonia generosius habeat sodalicium ac
vocalius, nam Camaracenam hac parte laudem haud multis prae se parasangis hactenus
habuit. Fit enim non omnino reflante superum numine, ut sedis locique amoenitatis non
solum gratia, verum etiam munificentiae plane Basilicae cupiditate solicitati, vocales
Musici undique eo confluant, haud secus atque in alvearia apes, ubi proventum faciant
uberrimum'; Lessabaeus, *Hannoniae urbium*, fols. A[6–6ᵛ].

[55] Lodovico Guicciardini, *Descrittione di tutti i Paesi Bassi* (Antwerp, 1588 ed.), p. 388.

[56] Ibid., pp. 380–81.

[57] 'Condatum: ...sodalitio tertia rei musicae laurea nobilitato'; Lessabaeus, *Hannoniae
urbium*, fol. B3.

The last, and latest, of our documents relating to Josquin is dated (from Rome again this time) 9 November 1494 (cf. App. C). This at once adds a further seven or eight months to the period during which Josquin's association with the Papal Chapel can be documented. Indeed, if we may assume that the marginal correction dated 'die xviiii 1495 febr.' was made at Josquin's own request, we can add nearly a year to his previously known stay in Rome.

The bull again consists of *litterae executoriae* addressed to a three-man commission, consisting this time of the Deans of Cambrai and of Nivelles (i.e., of the collegiate church of St. Gertrude in that town),[58] together with the Official of the diocese of Cambrai. It charges them with seeing to the induction of Josquin into the canonry and prebend at St. Géry, Cambrai, recently held by one Nicolaus Menent, who has died *extra Romanam Curiam*. The normal absolution clause ('a quibuscunque. . . absolventes et absolutum fore censentes') is included, and the marginal note opposite this in the Vatican register apparently refers only to the correction of a scribal error by which it had been made to apply to Menent rather than to Josquin: 'ipsumque Nicolaum' has in fact been altered to 'ipsumque Iudocum'. Any substantial alteration of this kind to the official record naturally required the highest authorization, which in this case is provided by the Pope himself and transmitted by his private secretary Lodovicus Podocatharus.[59]

In size and wealth St. Géry was the second of the three collegiate churches in the city of Cambrai, with 48 canons each having an annual revenue taxed at 42 *livres tournois*—as against the chapter of the cathedral (Notre-Dame) which had fifty canons, each with a prebend taxed at 85 *livres* 9 *sous*, and Ste.-Croix with twelve canons, each with a prebend at 19 *livres* 2 *sous*.[60] Was Josquin deliberately attempting to mislead the curial officials in asserting that the annual value of Menent's benefice did not exceed 24 *livres* ('ut dictus Iudocus asserit')? Such liberties with strict truth are apparently not uncommon in supplications for benefices,[61] but there may be other explanations for the discrepancy which could only be determined by work on

[58] The chapter of St. Gertrude's was headed by an abbess ('La Dame de Nivelles') who was a great lady of the realm, but there were both male and female provosts and a male dean; cf. Alfred d'Hoop, *Inventaire général des archives ecclésiastiques du Brabant. Tome I: Églises collégiales* (Brussels, 1905), p. 200.

[59] Podocatharus, a native of Cyprus, had been secretary to Rodrigo Borgia when he was Vice-Chancellor, and continued as his private secretary after his election to the Papacy as Alexander VI. Nominated bishop of Capaccio, a diocese in southern Italy, on 14 November 1483 (cf. Burchard, ed. Celani, i, p. 148, note 2), he was created a cardinal on 28 September 1500 (ibid., ii, pp. 242–3), taking the title of S. Agata in Suburra. He died at the age of 75 in August 1504, and was buried, like most curial cardinals, in S. Maria del Popolo (ibid., ii, pp. 458–9). See also Hofmann, *Forschungen*, ii, pp. 123–4 and 195.

[60] Longnon, *Pouillés*, pp. 280–5.

[61] Examples may be found in the article by Baix cited in note 15 above.

primary, unprinted sources, and in any case the published *pouillés* date from about a hundred years earlier.

Of the three commissioners, the first is easily identifiable. The Dean of Cambrai (i.e., of the cathedral chapter) was throughout this period one Gilles Nettelet, of whom *Gallia Christiana*[62] informs us that he was a doctor of the University of Paris and a theological writer of some distinction. Of his colleagues, namely the Dean of Nivelles and the Official of Cambrai, the latter has not yet been identified by name, but the former may well have been another papal singer and composer, Marbriano de Orto. There is clear documentary evidence that by 1496 at the latest De Orto was recognized, at least in Rome, as the Dean of St. Gertrude's at Nivelles;[63] earlier than that the evidence is complicated and contradictory, and it will be examined in a separate study.

* * *

Further investigation of archives, both in Rome and elsewhere, may well bring to light more evidence concerning benefices conferred on Josquin in partial remuneration for his services with the Papal Chapel; to that extent this paper can only be regarded as an interim report, and its conclusions subject to revision. However, if one looks at the benefices discussed above from the standpoint of political rather than ecclesiastical geography, one common factor emerges clearly: all of them lie within territory that belonged, either *de jure* or *de facto*, to the ducal house of Burgundy or its Hapsburg heirs.

The period between the death of Charles the Bold, the last Valois duke of Burgundy, in 1477 and the Treaty of Senlis in 1493 is, as it happens, a particularly confused one as regards the territorial ownership of the areas in question. In strict feudal theory, no doubt, those parts of the Burgundian dominions which had been held as fiefs of the French crown should have reverted to it upon Charles's death without a male heir, but national and quasi-national interests were in practice already too strong by the end of the fifteenth century for this to take place without a struggle. For one thing, the prosperous and semi-independent towns of the Low Countries were loth to see their privileges undermined by French centralization. But the crucial factor that prevented a swift annexation of at least the French-speaking territories was the decision of Duke Charles's daughter, Mary of Burgundy, to accept the hand, and with it the protection, of the Archduke Maximilian. It was this marriage, solemnized in August 1477, which ensured that even after Mary's early death (March 1482), the conflict continued, transformed now into a struggle between the French crown and the Hapsburgs.

[62] iii, col. 72B.

[63] Two bulls dated 30 July 1496, both contained in Reg. Vat. 872 (fols. 111–2 and 221–2^v), refer to him in this capacity, but suggest that his appointment has met with opposition.

Of Josquin's papally-conferred benefices one—the canonry at St. Omer—lay within the much-disputed county of Artois. Artois, together with its northern neighbour Flanders, had come into Burgundian possession as the inheritance of Margaret of Flanders, the wife of Philip the Bold, upon her father's death in 1384; the fact that they had already descended in the female line gave some colour to the claim that these territories at least should now be permitted to come directly to Mary of Burgundy and not revert to the French crown. Louis XI nevertheless invaded first Picardy and then Artois immediately after Charles's death in 1477, taking Arras, its capital, and Bapaume. St. Omer, however, held out against his troops both then and during further fighting in 1479.[64] By the Treaty of Arras (December 1482) Maximilian's infant daughter, Margaret of Austria, was betrothed to Louis's young son, the Dauphin Charles, and Artois and other territories were ceded to France as Margaret's dowry. It was specifically stipulated, however, that the frontier town of St. Omer should not be handed over until the marriage itself was consummated; in the meantime it was to be held by the Estates of the town, and kept neutral in the event of war.[65] After Louis's death in the following year Maximilian attempted to regain Artois, and during the fighting which followed, St. Omer was in fact taken by the French (27 May 1487) and held until February 1489.[66] But this period of less than two years appears to be the only one during which St. Omer was actually in French possession. In 1491 Charles's betrothal to Margaret was repudiated by France, in favour of a marriage with Anne, heiress to the duchy of Britanny. Further conflict ensued, which was brought to an end on the eve of Charles's expedition to Italy by the Treaty of Senlis (May 1493), by which, *inter alia*, France renounced its claim to direct rule over Artois, though not its sovereignty.[67] Thereafter the county remained under Hapsburg control until it was eventually annexed to France by Louis XIV.

The remaining places that concern us were all in more unequivocally Burgundian territory. The abbey of St. Ghislain was situated, as has already been mentioned, in the county of Hainaut—an Imperial fief to which France made no serious claims at this period, though it was invaded by Louis XI. St. Ghislain itself lies on the river Haine, only some 16 kilometres above its confluence with the Scheldt at Condé-sur-l'Escaut. The abbot at the time of Josquin's expectative benefice (1489) was the aged Jean Fabri, but his

[64] L. Deschamps de Pas, *Histoire de la Ville de Saint-Omer* (Arras, 1880), pp. 80–3.

[65] For the text of this treaty, cf. *Chroniques de Jean Molinet*, ed. G. Doutrepont and O. Jodogne (Brussels, 1935–7), i, pp. 378–406. The clauses relating specifically to Saint-Omer are on pp. 382–5.

[66] Deschamps de Pas, *Histoire*, pp. 85–90.

[67] Molinet (Doutrepont and Jodogne ed., ii, pp. 354–71) preserves the terms of the treaty; cf. especially pp. 355–6.

coadjutor, Dom Quentin Benoît, had already assumed much of his authority, and we find him frequently attending the meetings of the Estates of
Hainaut at the capital, Mons (10 kilometres to the east) and representing
the interests of his order at the archducal court at Malines and elsewhere.
Benoît is moreover reported to have been an intimate of the dowager
duchess, Margaret of York, the widow of Charles the Bold, whose normal
residence was at Binche, also in Hainaut. The abbey must clearly be regarded
as entirely within the Burgundian orbit, both geographically and politically.[68]

The village of Basse-Ittre, we have seen, lay just within the duchy of
Brabant, in fact within a small salient of land almost enclosed within the
county of Hainaut.[69] It was in any case deep within Burgundian territory,
only 22 kilometres south-southwest of Brussels. Condé and Soignies, whose
deans formed part of the commission for this benefice, were both in Hainaut;
both chapters were represented, like the abbey of St. Ghislain, at the
meetings of the Estates at Mons.[70]

Cambrai, where Josquin's third benefice was situated, was of course an
independent episcopal city within the Empire, whose territory, the Cam-
brésis, lay to the south of Hainaut; but unlike such other episcopal towns as
Tournai and Thérouanne it seems never to have been a centre of French
political influence. In general it attempted to remain neutral in the quarrels
between France and Burgundy, but one may note that its bishop from
1480 to 1502, the famous Henri de Berghes, was very much a Burgundian
adherent.[71] This prelate, a humanist and statesman, was first Abbot of
St.-Denis in Hainaut, then, after a period as coadjutor, appointed Bishop of
Cambrai in 1480. At Christmastide 1487 we find him in Rome, celebrating
Mass in the Papal Chapel on 23 December and assisting the Pope at vespers
on Christmas Day itself.[72] Burchard says merely that he was either going to
or returning from Jerusalem on a pilgrimage, but Dom Baudry, following
other sources, suggests that he was there as an unofficial ambassador for
Maximilian.[73] This seems likely, in that Henri de Berghes was to become

[68] The fullest information for the period in question is preserved in the manuscript
annals of Dom Pierre Baudry (1702–52), of which the text has been published, up to 1600,
by Baron de Reiffenberg in *Monuments pour servir à l'histoire des provinces de Namur, de
Hainaut et de Luxembourg*, viii (Brussels, 1848), pp. 199–835. Cf. also *Gallia Christiana*, iii,
cols. 90D–100B.

[69] See the quotation in note 47 above. Map I in Maurice-A. Arnould, *Les Dénombrements
de foyers dans le comté de Hainaut, XIVe–XVIe siècle* (Brussels, 1956), shows the situation
clearly, as do those of Brabant (between pp. 64 and 65) and Hainaut (pp. 368 and 369) in
the edition of Guicciardini cited in note 55 above.

[70] L. Devillers, *Inventaire analytique des Archives des États de Hainaut*, 3 vols. (Mons,
1884–1906), Introduction to Tome i, p. xxxii.

[71] For a general account of his career, cf. *Biographie Nationale de Belgique*, ii, cols. 207–9.

[72] Burchard, ed. Celani, pp. 213f; ed. Thuasne, i, pp. 279 and 282.

[73] Baudry, *Annales*, ed. Reiffenberg, p. 582.

one of the principal councillors of Maximilian's son Philip, celebrating the prince's marriage to Juana of Aragon and accompanying the young couple to Spain. His solidarity with the Burgundian interest is confirmed by the the fact that in 1493 he was appointed Chancellor of the Order of the Golden Fleece.

In spite of the frequency in anti-papal invectives of the time of complaints against the awarding of benefices to 'foreigners', it seems likely that such complaints were exaggerated, and that the 'foreigners' in question were quite often natives of the region concerned who happened to have made their careers at the Roman Curia rather than on home ground. It would in any case have been quite contrary to common sense for clerics to sue for, or for the Pope to award, benefices in places where a strong local interest would automatically be ranged against them.[74] We must therefore consider it proved, I think, that already during the period of his service in Rome Josquin looked upon the Burgundian territories in the Low Countries, and more particularly in the County of Hainaut, as his homeland.

Whether this need imply that he was actually born there is another matter. That the question of nationality had real significance at this date is strikingly demonstrated by a recently discovered document concerning the composer Compère (printed in full, since its details are interesting, in App. D). This is a decree of Charles VIII, dated April 1494, granting French nationality to Compère, who, as a native of Hainaut, did not possess it, and had requested it in order to safeguard the benefices in France which he had acquired in the royal service. If Josquin was indeed born in the Vermandois[75] (at or near St. Quentin), it seems odd that all the benefices he receives from Rome should be in the Burgundian-Hapsburg domains; Vermandois, together with Picardy, had been French since 1477. St. Quentin, moreover, lay within the little diocese of Noyon, and in the two documents printed here as App. B and C Josquin is described as a 'clerk of the diocese of Cambrai'—which strongly implies that he was born as well as ordained in that diocese. If, on the other hand, he was like Compère a native of Hainaut, as Ronsard and others described him,[76] it would be perfectly natural not only that he should have chosen to end his days there, at Condé, but also

---

[74] Barraclough, *Papal Provisions*, p. 45.

[75] As the Swiss humanist Aegidius Tschudi asserted in his song-collection (St. Gall, Stiftsbibliothek, Mus. MS. 463/464), doubtless relying on information from his friend Glarean. Cf. Osthoff, *Josquin Desprez*, i, p. 4; Hans-Christian Müller, art. 'Tschudi' in *MGG*, xiii, cols. 928–9.

[76] In the now lost Superius of the *Livre de Meslanges* (Le Roy & Ballard, Paris, 1560), for which cf. Eitner, *Bibliographie der Musik-Sammelwerke*, 1560c. Cf. also François (Grudé) de La Croix Du Maine, *Premier Volume de La Bibliothèque* (Paris, 1584), p. 275: 'IOSQUIN DES PRETZ, natif du pays de Haynault en la Gaulle Belgique'; the 1772 reprint of La Croix Du Maine (vol. ii, p. 7) adds supplementary notes, but leaves the statement about Josquin's birthplace unquestioned.

that his Roman benefices should have involved contacts at St. Ghislain, at Soignies and at Condé itself within the County, and at Cambrai and Basse-Ittre just outside its borders. But it must be admitted that the description of Josquin as 'picardo' (see Osthoff, i, p. 16) speaks more strongly for the former possibility. The answer may perhaps be that Josquin, born in Picardy or the Vermandois when those territories were under Burgundian control, maintained that allegiance after they had been recovered by the French crown, and that he therefore thought in terms of acquiring benefices in Burgundian (or Hapsburg) rather than French territory.

*   *   *

One further question arises from the Roman bulls regarding Josquin's benefices: did they take effect? For the first, the canonry at St. Omer, the answer may possibly be found in the archives still preserved in that charming town, one of the very few in this corner of France to have escaped the worst ravages of successive wars (cf. note 42). For the second, the chaplaincy at Basse-Ittre, the evidence, if it survives at all, might be in a number of places: Cambrai, Lille, Brussels come immediately to mind, but there are others. For the third, the canonry at St. Géry, Cambrai, some evidence does exist and it is negative. The chapter acts of St. Géry are preserved in the Archives du Nord at Lille, and the volumes for the relevant period (7.G. 577–580) contain a number of lists of the canons in order of their reception. In spite of the fact that these are informally written, with crossings-out and duplications, it is fairly clear that Josquin was not received as a canon of St. Géry, though a number of his colleagues in the Papal Chapel were: Johannes Monstreul, Innocent Cossée (who was appointed as Provost), and Anthoine Baneston. A certain Egidius (= Gilles) Despres or Desprez was also among the canons of this period; he may have been a relation of the composer, but the family name is a common one. Further examination of the chapter acts themselves might reveal whether Josquin's claim was ever presented, and if so why it was not accepted.

In fact there is one circumstance that tends to suggest that all of these benefices granted to Josquin in Rome may have been ineffective. It is well known, of course, that towards the end of the Middle Ages many national rulers took action to curb the use, and abuse, of papal provisions within their borders. Charles VIII's revival in the 1490s of his grandfather Charles VII's Pragmatic Sanction is the most famous example, but in the *Placcaert-boecken van Vlaanderen*[77] we find similar measures already being taken by the Burgundian rulers in the previous decade. An edict promulgated at

[77] Thirteen folio volumes were published at Ghent and Brussels between 1639 and 1786. The edicts which concern us are all contained in the first of these, of which I have used the second, enlarged edition: *Tweeden Druck van den eersten Bouck der Ordonnancien...* (Ghent, 1639).

Brussels on 1 September 1484 by Maximilian and his son Philip (the heir to the Burgundian territories, but at this date still a minor) details at considerable length the inconvenience, the expense, and the juridical encroachments caused by the over-use of papal provisions during the reign of the late Pope (Sixtus IV), and goes on:

SCAVOIR FAISONS, que nous. . .avons en tant que en nous est. . .ordonné & déclairé, & de nostre certaine science ordonnons & déclairons, que d'oresnavant lesdictes bulles, graces expectatives & aultres provisions queles qu'elles soyent ou aulcuns d'icelles, sur la collation desdictz bénéfices de nosdictz pays & seigneuries, n'auront cours & ne seront admises ou receuës en iceulx nos pays & seigneuries. Et deffendant par ces mesmes présentes à toutes personnes tant d'Eglise que aultres, & tant de nostredict pays que estrangiers qu'ilz n'apportent, admettent ou recoipvent aulcunes desdictes bulles, lettres expectatives ou aultres telles provisions en iceulx nos pays: sur peine de perdre le fruict d'icelles & d'estre puniz & corrigez par nous & nos officiers, comme infracteurs de nosdictes ordonnances à l'exemple d'aultres: avec ce d'estre déclairées inhabiles de non jamais pouvoir tenir & posséder aucunes bénéfices en nosdicts pays & seigneuries: & ce jusques à ce, qu'aultre & meilleur ordre soit mis sur le faict desdicts bénéfices, & que par nous aultrement en soit ordonné. . . .[78]

In view of the fact that this edict had been neither published nor observed in the county of Flanders, it was reiterated with particular respect to that province on 12 September of the following year, 1485.[79]

It might be thought that so sweeping a measure left no doubt that Josquin must be completely debarred from making use of the three bulls or rescripts which we have presented in this paper, but the mere fact that Philip, having achieved his majority, was compelled to reiterate the edict once more on 20 May 1497 is sufficient indication that it had not been entirely effective. The preamble to the 1497 edict confirms as much:

Et pour ce, que depuis aucuns s'avanchoyent de plus en plus (en contrevenant directement à nosdictes deffenses) obtenir semblables bulles & rescrit & certains monitoires pénaulx de ladicte Cour [i.e., the court of Rome], & aultres contenans grandes peynes & censures à l'encontre de nos subjectz, les aucuns non ouyz en leurs deffences & aultres adjournez, hors nosdictz pays en première instance: contre les droictz, haulteur & prérogatives, franchises & libertéz, de nous & de nosdictz pays, & à la grand' foulle de nosdictz subjectz. . .[80]

A jurisdictional trial of strength was being carried on, throughout the period that concerns us, between Rome on the one hand and the rulers of both France and the Low Countries on the other. True, the edict of 1497 does leave a loophole for the approval of certain papal provisions:

. . .Et jusques à ce que lesdictes provisions & bulles auront esté veües en nostredict grand Conseil, & que pour exécution d'icelles aurons accordé nos lettres patentes de consentement en forme deüe. . .[81]

[78] Ibid., i, p. 207.   [79] Ibid., i, pp. 205, 208.   [80] Ibid., i, p. 209.   [81] Ibid., i, p. 210.

But whether or not Josquin was able to profit by this loophole can probably not be decided without further work on unpublished archival material. What can be said, however, is that the provostship at Condé was not the first benefice to be conferred on Josquin in the ex-Burgundian, now Hapsburg, dominions, but rather the culmination of a whole series of them.[82]

Appendix A

(In this and the three following documents the frequent contractions have been resolved, paragraphing and additional punctuation introduced, and capitalization and word-division—though not spelling—to some extent standardized in the interests of legibility.)

Rome, Archivio di Stato, Camerale I, vol. 1099, fols. 297–9[83]

Innocentius etc. [= episcopus servus servorum dei]

Dilecto filio Judoco de Pratis Canonico ecclesie sancti Audomari de Sancto Audomaro Morinensis diocesis familiari nostro Salutem etc. [= et apostolicam benedictionem:]

Grata familiaritatis obsequia que nobis hactenus impendisti et adhuc solicitis studiis impendere non desistis, necnon vite ac morum honestas aliaque laudabilia probitatis et virtutum merita quibus personam tuam tam familiari experientia quam etiam fidedignorum testimoniis juvari percepimus, nos inducunt ut tibi reddamur ad gratiam liberales:

Hinc est quod nos tibi, qui etiam continuus commensalis noster et in Capella nostra Cantor Capellanus existis, premissorum obsequiorum et meritorum tuorum intuitu specialem gratiam facere, et presentes ac si sub datis Kalendis Novembris Pontificatus nostri Anno Tertio concesse forent litteras valere volentes,

teque a quibusvis excommunicationis suspensionis et interdicti aliisque ecclesiasticis sententiis censuris et penis a iure vel ab homine quavis occasione vel causa latis, si quibus quomodolibet innodatus existis, ad effectum presentium duntaxat consequendum harum serie absolventes et absolutum fore censentes,

motu proprio, non ad tuam vel alterius pro te nobis super hoc oblate

---

[82] This paper was written before I was aware of Prof. Herbert Kellman's important archival discoveries at Condé, suggesting that Josquin was born 'beyond the *Noir Eauwe*' and thus just outside the borders of Hainaut (see below, p. 208). I have decided to let it stand as written, however, since it does at least demonstrate, I think, his close connection with the region.

[83] I should like to thank Professor Rosalind Hill of Westfield College, University of London, for her kind help in interpreting the three papal documents.

petitionis instantiam sed de nostra mera liberalitate, Canonicatum ecclesie sancti Audomari de Sancto Audomaro Morinensis diocesis cum plenitudine iuris canonici apostolica tibi auctoritate conferimus et de illo etiam providemus, prebendam vero ac dignitatem personatum administrationem vel offitium eiusdem ecclesie, etiam si ad illam illam [should read 'illum'] vel illud consueverit quis per electionem assumi eique cura imineat animarum, dummodo dignitas ipsa in eadem ecclesia principalis non existat,

necnon benefitium ecclesiasticum cum cura vel sine cura consuetum clericis secularibus assignari, cuiusquidem benefitii fructus redditus et proventus si cum cura quadraginta si vero sine cura fuerit triginta librarum turonensium parvorum secundum taxationem decime valorem annuum non excedant, ad collationem provisionem presentationem seu quamvis aliam dispositionem dilectorum filiorum Abbatis et Conventus monasterii sancti Gisleni ordinis sancti Benedicti Cameracensis diocesis communiter vel divisim pertinens,

si que vacant ad presens aut cum simul vel successive vacaverint, que tu per te vel procuratorem tuum ad hoc legitime constitutum infra unius mensis spatium postquam tibi vel eidem procuratori vacatio illorum innotuerit duxeris acceptanda, conferenda tibi post acceptationem huiusmodi cum omnibus iuribus et pertinentiis suis donationi apostolice reservamus;

districtius inhibentes venerabili fratri nostro Episcopo Morinensi ac dilectis filiis Capitulo dicte ecclesie ac illi vel illis ad quem seu ad quos in ipsa ecclesia prebendarum ac dignitatum personatuum administrationum vel offitiorum collatio provisio presentatio electio seu quevis alia dispositio communiter vel divisim pertinet, ne de prebenda ac dignitate personatu administratione vel offitio inibi, necnon Abbati et Conventui prefatis ne de beneficio huiusmodi, interim etiam ante acceptationem eandem, nisi postquam eis constiterit quod tu vel procurator predictus illa nolueritis acceptare, disponere quoquomodo presumant; ac decernentes ex nunc irritum et inane si secus super hiis a quoquam quavis auctoritate scienter vel ignoranter contigerit attemptari:

Et nichilominus venerabili fratri Episcopo Tornacensi et dilectis filiis Nicolao Rombert Canonico ecclesie Cameracensis ac Offitiali Morinensi motu simili per apostolica scripta mandamus, quatenus ipsi vel duo aut unus eorum per se vel alium seu alios te vel procuratorem tuum nomine tuo in dicta ecclesia in Canonicum recipi faciant et in fratrem, stallo tibi in choro et loco in capitulo ipsius ecclesie cum dicti iuris plenitudine assignatis, prebendam vero et dignitatem personatum administrationem vel offitium dicte ecclesie necnon benefitium huiusmodi, si vacant aut cum vacaverint ut prefertur, tibi post acceptationem predictam cum omnibus iuribus et pertinentiis supradictis auctoritate nostra conferant et assignent,

inducentes te vel dictum procuratorem pro te in corporalem possessionem canonicatus et prebende ac dignitatis personatus administrationis vel offitii necnon benefitii iuriumque et pertinentiarum predictorum, et defendentes inductum, ac facientes te vel dictum procuratorem pro te ad dignitatem personatum administrationem vel offitium necnon benefitium huiusmodi ut moris est admitti, tibique de illorum ac canonicatus collati et prebende reservate predictorum fructibus redditibus proventibus iuribus obventionibus universis integre responderi;

Contradictores auctoritate nostra appellatione postposita compescendo; ... [There follows a series of formal 'non obstantibus' clauses, designed to provide against various legal circumstances which might hinder or prevent the bull's taking effect.]

... Et insuper ut ex litteris et gratia huiusmodi celeriorem consequaris effectum, motu simili volumus et apostolica tibi auctoritate concedimus quod in canonicatus et prebende ac dignitatis personatus administrationis vel offitii necnon benefitii huiusmodi assecutione omnibus et singulis ac illis prorsus similibus antelationum prerogativis decretis declarationibus favoribus gratiis privilegiis et indultis quibus nonnulli familiares nostri continui commensales in quibusdem litteris nostris descripti in simili assecutione canonicatuum et prebendarum ac dignitatum personatuum administrationum vel offitiorum necnon benefitiorum ecclesiasticorum que vigore gratiarum expectativarum per nos eis concessarum expectant utuntur potiuntur et gaudent, ac uti potiri et gaudere poterunt quomodolibet in futurum, ad instar dictorum familiarium descriptorum pariformiter et absque ulla differentia sine tamen eorum preiuditio uti potiri et gaudere valeas, in omnibus et per omnia perinde ac si unus ex dictis familiaribus et in prefatis litteris descriptus existeres,

quodque tam predictis descriptis quam quibuscunque aliis cuiuscunque dignitatis status gradus ordinis vel conditionis existentibus quascunque secundas gratias aut primarum gratiarum revalidationes habentibus, quoad huiusmodi secundas gratias et primarum revalidationes, duntaxat in canonicatus et prebende dignitatis personatus administrationis vel offitii seu etiam benefitii huiusmodi assecutione possis et debeas omnino anteferri pariter et preferri: ... [Further clauses, formal and general, designed to strengthen the bull's effect]

Datum Rome apud Sanctum Petrum Anno etc. [= incarnationis dominice] Millesimoquadringentesimooctuagesimonono, Quinto Idus Septembris, Pontificatus nostri Anno Quinto.

Appendix B

Archivio Segreto Vaticano, Reg. Vat. 782, fols. 33ᵛ-35 (see Pls. 5-7).

Alexander etc.

Dilectis filiis Sonegiensis et Condatensis Cameracensis diocesis Decanis et Johanni de Porta Canonico Cameracensis ecclesiarum Salutem etc.

Grata familiaritatis obsequia que dilectus filius Indocus [sic] de Pratis clericus Cameracensis diocesis cantor capellanus et familiaris noster nobis hactenus impendit ad adhuc solicitis studiis impendere non desistit, necnon vite ac morum honestas aliaque laudabilia probitatis et virtutum merita quibus personam suam tam familiari experientia quam etiam fidedignorum testimoniis iuvari percepimus, nos inducunt ut sibi reddamur ad gratiam liberales:

ad audientiam siquidem nostram, dicto Indoco referente, pervenit quod dilectus filius Emericus de Honstat, qui se gerit pro clerico ad perpetuam capellaniam ad altare sancti Theobaldi situm in parrochiali ecclesia de Bassaytea [sic] dicte diocesis, simoniace aspirans cum dilecto filio Martino Kegels, tunc ad dictum altare perpetuo capellano, pepigit et convenit quod si dictus Martinus capellaniam huiusmodi ad hoc ut de illa ipsi Emerico provideretur resignare vellet et dictus Emericus illam ex huiusmodi resignatione assequeretur, ipse Emericus eidem Martino certam tunc expressam pecunie quantitatem persolveret, et deinde pacto et conventione predictis sic precedentibus prefatus Martinus capellaniam huiusmodi quem tunc obtinebat in manibus tunc domini temporalis loci de Bassaytea et de Famel [?] dicte diocesis extra Romanam Curiam resignavit, ipseque dominus dicti loci, cum ad illius dominum pro tempore existentem resignationis dicte capellanie que pro tempore fit admissio illiusque dum vacat collatio et provisio ex spetiali privilegio apostolico, cum non est actenus [sic] in aliquo derogatum, pertinere noscatur, pacti et conventionis huiusmodi forsan ignarus, resignatione huiusmodi per eum extra dictam Curiam ordinaria auctoritate admissa, capellaniam predictam tamquam per resignationem huiusmodi tunc vacantem prefato Emerico dicta auctoritate contulit et providit etiam de eadem, quamvis de facto ac prefatus Emericus collationis et provisionis earundem pretexta capellanie predicte possessionem apphrehendit [sic], similiter de facto ac pecunie quantitatem predictam eidem Martino realiter et cum effectu persolvit, simonie labem ac excommunicationis aliasque sententias censuras et penas in simoniacos latas damnabiliter incurrendo, in anime sue periculum ac perniciosum exemplum et scandalum plurimorum:

Cum autem secundum premissa collatio et provisio predicte iuribus non subsistant, dictaque capellania adhuc ut prefertur vacare noscatur, Nos prefato Indoco, qui etiam continuus commensalis noster existit, premissorum obsequiorum et meritorum suorum intuitu specialem gratiam facere volentes,

ipsumque Indocum a quibusvis excommunicationis . . . sententiis . . . absolventes et absolutum fore censentes, [absolution clause as in App. A]

necnon omnia et singula beneficia ecclesiastica cum cura et sine cura que dictus Indocus etiam ex quibusvis dispensationibus apostolicis obtinet et expectat ac in quibus et ad ['quem' deleted] que ius sibi quomo[do]libet competit, quecunque quotcunque et qualiacunque sint, eorumque fructuum reddituum et proventuum veros annuos valores ac huiusmodi dispensationum tenores, presentibus pro expressis habentes,

discretioni vestre per apostolica scripta mandamus quatinus vos vel duo aut unus vestrum, si dictus Indocus eundem Emericum super eisdem relatis coram vobis accusare seque in forma iuris inscribere voluerit, postquam illum accusaverit et se inscripserit ut prefertur, vocatis dicto Emerico et aliis qui fuerint evocandi, super eisdem relatis inquiratis auctoritate vestra [nostra?] diligentius veritatem, et si per inquisitionem huiusmodi relata ipsa repereritis veritate subniti, collationem et provis[i]onem predictas et indesecuta quecunque nulla et invalida nulliusque roboris vel momenti fuisse et esse eadem auctoritate vestra [nostra?] declaretis, ipsumque Emericum a detentione dicte capellanie realiter amoveritis, prout de iure fuerit faciendum:

Et nichilominus, si declarationem et amotionem huiusmodi per vos vigore presentium fieri contigerit ut prefertur, capellaniam predictam, que sine cura est et cuius fructus redditus et proventus quindecim librarum Turonentium parvorum secundum communem extimationem valorem annuum, ut dictus Indocus asserit, non excedunt, sive ut premictitur sive alias quovismodo aut ex alterius cuiuscunque persona seu per similem resignationem dicti Martini vel alterius de illa extra dictam curiam etiam coram notario publico et testibus sponte factam vacet, etiam si tanto tempore vacaverit quod eius collatio iuxta Lateranensis statuta Concilii ad sedem apostolicam legitime devoluta ipsaque capellania dispositioni apostolice spetialiter reservata existat, et super ea inter aliquos lis cuius statum presentibus haberi volumus pro expresso penderit indecisa, dummodo tempore dictorum presentium non sit in ea alicui specialiter ius quesitum, cum omnibus iuribus et pertinentiis suis eidem Indoco auctoritate nostra conferre et assignare curetis,

inducentes per vos vel alium seu alios eundem Indocum vel procuratorem suum eius nomine in corporalem possessionem capellanie iuriumque et pertinentiarum predictorum, et defendentes inductum, amoto etiam exinde quolibet alio illicito detentore, ac facientes Indocum vel pro eo procuratorem predictum ad capellaniam huiusmodi ut est moris admitti, sibique de illius fructibus redditibus et proventibus iuribus et obventionibus universis integre responderi;

Contradictores auctoritate nostra appellatione postposita compescendo. . . [The document concludes with the 'non obstantibus' clauses.]

Datum Corneti Anno etc. Mcccclxxxxiij, Sexto Idus Novembris, Pontificatus nostri Anno Secundo.

Appendix C

Archivio Segreto Vaticano, Reg. Vat. 787, fols. 285^v–287

Alexander etc.

Dilectis filiis Cameracensis et Nivellensis Leodiensis diocesis ecclesiarum Decanis ac Officiali Cameracensi Salutem:

Grata familiaritatis obsequia que dilectus filius Indocus [sic] de Pratis clericus Cameracensis diocesis familiaris noster nobis hactenus impendit et adhuc solicitis studiis impendere non desistit, necnon vite ac morum honestas aliaque laudabilia probitatis et virtutum merita quibus personam suam tam familiari experientia quam etiam fidedignorum testimoniis iuvari percepimus, nos inducunt ut sibi reddamur ad gratiam liberales:

cum itaque sicut accepimus canonicatus et prebenda ecclesie sancti Gaugerici Cameracensis quos quondam Nicolaus Menent ipsius ecclesie Canonicus dum viveret obtinebat per obitum eiusdem Nicolai, qui extra Romanam Curiam diem clausit extremum, vacaverint et vacent ad presens,

Nos prefato Indoco, qui etiam continuus commensalis noster et in Capella nostra Cantor capellanus existit, premissorum obsequiorum et meritorum suorum intuitu gratiam facere specialem volentes,

ipsumque ['Nicolaum' has been deleted here and replaced by 'Iudocum', and the following note entered in the margin: 'Correpta/ De mandato domini nostri/ correptis (?) referente (?)/ domino L. Podocatharo/ die xviiii 1495 febr.'] Iudocum a quibuscunque excommunicationis . . . sententiis . . . absolventes et absolutum fore censentes, [absolution clause as in Appendix A]

necnon omnia et singula beneficia ecclesiastica cum cura et sine cura que dictus Indocus etiam ex quibus[vis] dispensationibus apostolicis obtinet et expectat ac in quibus et ad que ius sibi quomodolibet competit, quecunque quotcunque et qualiacunque sint, eorum fructuum reddituum et proventuum veros annuos valores presentibus pro expressis habentes,

discretioni vestre per apostolica scripta mandamus quatenus vos vel duo a[ut] unus vestrum per vos vel alium seu alios canonicatum et prebendam predictos, quorum fructus redditus et proventus xxiiij librarum turonensium parvorum secundum communem extimationem valorem annuum, ut dictus Indocus asserit, non excedunt, sive ut premittitur sive alias quovismodo aut ex alterius cuiuscunque persona seu per liberam resignationem dicti Nicolai vel alterius de illis extra dictam Curiam etiam coram notario publico et testibus sponcte [sic] factam vacent, etiam si tanto tempore vacaverint quod eorum collatio iuxta Lateranensis statuta Concilii ad sedem apostolicam legitime devoluta ipsique canonicatus et prebenda dispensationi apostolice specialiter reservata existant, et super eis inter aliquos lis cuius statum presentibus haberi volumus pro expresso penderit indecisa, dummodo tempore dictorum presentium non sit in eis alicui specialiter ius quesitum, cum plenitudine iuris canonici ac omnibus iuribus et pertinentiis suis eidem Indoco auctoritate nostra conferre et assignare curetis,

inducentes eum vel procuratorem suum eius nomine in corporalem possessionem canonicatus et prebende iuriumque et pertinentiarum predictorum, et defendentes inductum, amoto exinde quolibet illicito detentore, facientes Indocum vel pro eo procuratorem predictum ad prebendam huiusmodi in dicta ecclesia in canonicum recipi et in fratrem, stallo sibi in choro et loco in capitulo ipsius ecclesie cum dicti iuris plenitudine assignatis, sibique de ipsorum canonicatus et prebende fructibus redditibus proventibus iuribus et obventionibus universis integre responderi;

contradictores auctoritate nostra etc. [= appellatione postposita compescendo] [The document concludes with the 'non obstantibus' clauses.]

Datum Rome apud Sanctum Petrum Anno etc. Mcccclxxxxiiij, Quintus Idus Novembris, Pontificatus nostri Anno Tertio.

Appendix D

Paris, Archives Nationales, Reg. JJ 226ᴬ, fol. 144ᵛ (no. 245)[84]
[in margin] Littera naturalitatis magistri Ludovici Compere
   Charles &c.   Savoir faisons &c.
Nous avoir[85] receu humble supplicacion de nostre cher et bien amé chappelain ordinaire et chantre de nostre chappelle maistre Loys Compère, natif du pays de Haynault, contenant que puis aucun temps il s'en est venu demourer en nostre Royaume où il a acquis aucuns biens et encores espère en acquérir d'autres en intencion d'y user et finer le demourant de ses jours, Mais obstant ce qu'il est estrangier et non natif de nostre dit Royaume, il doubte que noz officiers ou autres luy vueillent cy après empescher qu'il n'en puisse disposer, Avis après son décès et trespas les prétendre nous compecter et appartenir par droit d'aubeyne, Et par ce moyen en frustrer

---

[84] The phrases in square brackets have been supplied by comparison with the document immediately following this one in the register, which confers similar favours on another royal chaplain and singer, Jehan Cannet, 'natif de Cambray'.

[85] The infinitive depending on 'Scavoir faisons' is a Latinate accusative-and-infinitive construction in place of the 'que' construction we would expect today.

ses héritiers qu'il a de présent ou pourra avoir cy après, Et avecques ce doubte que à cause de ce qu'il est estrangier comme dit est, on ne le seuffre joyr des bénéfices ou temporel d'iceulx qu'il a ou pourra avoir à nostre moyen en nostre dit Royaume, Se sur tout ce que dit est il n'estoit par nous habilité, humblement requérant noz grace et liberalité luy estre sur ce imparties;

Pourquoy nous, inclinans libérallement à la supplicacion et requeste dudit suppliant, en faveur mesmement &c. Alentour de nous [et espérons que encores face cy après,] Pour ces causes &c. Audit suppliant avons octroyé et octroyons voulons et nous plaist de grace especial par ces présentes qu'il puisse et luy lase tenir en nostre dit Royaume tous telz biens meubles et immeubles qu'il y pourra licitement acquérir, Et d'iceulx et aussi de ceulx qu'il y a ja acquis disposer et ordonner par testament et ordonnance de derrenière voulenté, donnacion faicte entre vifz, et aucunement à son plaisir et voulenté, et que ses héritiers présents et advenir luy puissent succéder en iceulx biens, tout ainsi que s'il estoit natif de nostre dit Royaume, Et avecques ce qu'il puisse et luy lase tenir et possider tous telz bénéfices dont il a esté et pourra estre justement et canonicquement pourveu en nostre dit Royaume, et en joir pareillement tout ainsi que s'il en estoit natif;

Et quant à ce l'avons habilité, et habilitons de nostre grace [especial] &c. Sans ce que à la cause dessusdit on luy puisse en ce mectre ou donner &c. Ne qu'il soit pour ce tenu paier à nous ne aux nostres aucune finance ou indempnité, Et laquelle finance, à quelque somme qu'elle eust peu monter ou estre tauxée, Nous luy avons donnée et quictée, donnons et quictons par cesdites présentes signées de nostre main. Par lesquelles donnons en mandement A noz amez et féaulx gens de noz comptes et trésoriers à Paris Au prévost de Paris Et à tous &c. Que de noz présents grace octroy habilitacion don quitance et choses dessusdits ilz facent &c.

Sans luy faire mectre ou donner &c.

Non obstant [les ordonnances par nous derrainement faictes et quelzconques autres ordonnances,] Et afin &c. Sauf &c.

Donné à Lyon sur le Rosne, au moys d'avril L'an de grace mil cccc iiij^xx et xiiij [1494]

Et de nostre Regne le xj^me

Charles,   Par le Roy.

Robineau Visa Contentor. gratis Budé.

Josquin at Ferrara:
New Documents and Letters

LEWIS LOCKWOOD

In the limited span of this paper I can only hope to hint at the broader background against which the documents presented here must be seen. We face two problems: one is to assess the changing role of Ferrara as a musical centre in the late fifteenth and early sixteenth centuries, about which we still know remarkably little; the other is to establish the precise connection between Josquin and the Ferrarese court, and to relate this to Josquin's career and development as a composer. Vander Straeten first brought to light his relations with Ferrara on the basis of modest documentation presented in 1882 in Volume vi of *La Musique aux Pays-Bas*.[1] In the 1950s new and important material on the background of Josquin's arrival at Ferrara in 1503 was discovered by Professor Helmuth Osthoff.[2] In 1968 I set out to assemble material for a study of music at Ferrara in the period of Josquin—roughly from 1470 to about 1530[3]—with the aim of achieving a more substantial understanding of this musical centre and its European role. I was fortunate enough to turn up new source material on Josquin as well as on other composers of this period, and thus to solve some long-standing problems. My principal work was in the Archivio di Stato in Modena, from which all the documents mentioned here have been drawn;

---

[1] E. Vander Straeten, *La Musique aux Pays-Bas*, vi, pp. 69–124 (a chapter nominally devoted to Josquin des Prez but in fact presenting an unorganized though valuable mass of documents on a number of musicians at Ferrara in addition to Josquin). While the inevitably vague means of reference used by Vander Straeten for his sources (characteristically labelled simply as 'Archives de l'Etat à Modène') may have reflected the general state of organization of the archive at that time, it made further research difficult. Throughout this article, the abbreviation 'ASM' designates Archivio di Stato di Modena. For furthering my research in the archive I am particularly indebted to its director, Dott. Filippo Valenti.

[2] See his article, 'Josquin' in *Die Musik in Geschichte und Gegenwart*, vii (1958), cols. 190–200 (biographical section), and *Josquin Desprez*, i (Tutzing, 1962), pp. 45–6 and 50–60. I must record my indebtedness to Professor Osthoff for his encouragement of my studies on Ferrara and to his archival discoveries for the stimulus they provided to my own research.

[3] A preliminary account is given in my study, 'Music at Ferrara in the Period of Ercole I d'Este', *Studi Musicali*, i (1972), pp. 101–31.

its holdings include the largest surviving proportion of the extant historical records of the Este dynasty at Ferrara.[4]

The historical setting for these documents is the court of Ferrara during the reign of Duke Ercole I d'Este (1471–1505). This period was marked by accelerated cultural growth and by major achievements in painting, architecture, theatre, poetry, literary and philosophical thought.[5] As the milieu of Boiardo, Ariosto, and Tasso, Ferrara was the primary centre of the Italian chivalric epic. The revival of classical drama at the court in the 1480s and 1490s opened the way to a lively tradition of secular theatre that lasted through the sixteenth century and is significant for the pre-history of opera;[6] important too is a tradition of sacred representations under Ercole that deserves to be better known.

During Ercole's reign the architect Biagio Rossetti enlarged the city, built new streets and palazzi, and established Ferrara as one of the first planned cities in Europe.[7] In political affairs Ercole continued the long established control of the Estense dynasty over Ferrara; he negotiated advantageous marriages for his children to members of other dynasties (the Sforzas, Gonzagas, and most conspicuously the Borgias); and he

[4] The most useful brief introduction to the Modena archive is Filippo Valenti, *Panorama dell'Archivio di Stato di Modena* (Modena, 1963), published as No. 1 of a series entitled *Scuola di Paleografia, Diplomatica e Archivistica dell'Archivio di Stato di Modena, Lezioni e Ricerche*; see also F. Valenti, *Archivio di Stato di Modena, Archivio Segreto Estense, Sezione 'Casa e Stato', Inventario* (Rome, 1953), the first volume of a projected three-volume nventory of the Estense archive. A useful introduction to the diplomatic papers in this and related archives is Vincent Ilardi, 'Fifteenth-Century Diplomatic Documents in Western European Archives and Libraries (1450–1494)', *Studies in the Renaissance*, ix (1962), pp. 64–112.

[5] For a recent critical appraisal of earlier studies on the cultural history of the court of Ferrara, see W. Gundersheimer, 'Towards a Reinterpretation of the Renaissance at Ferrara', *Bibliothèque d'Humanisme et Renaissance*, xxx (1968), pp. 267–81, and the same author's recent book, *Ferrara: The Style of a Renaissance Despotism* (Princeton, 1973). A useful survey of the entire Estense dynasty is given in Luciano Chiappini, *Gli Estensi* (Varese, 1967), and still valuable are older works by Giulio Bertoni, *La Biblioteca Estense e la Coltura Ferrarese ai tempi del Duca Ercole I* (Turin, 1903), and Edmund G. Gardner, *Dukes and Poets in Ferrara* (London, 1904).

[6] On the Ferrarese theatre under Ercole, see Alessandro d'Ancona, *Origini del Teatro Italiano*, 2nd ed. (Turin, 1891), ii, pp. 127–35; G. Pardi, 'Il Teatro Classico a Ferrara', *Atti della Deputazione Ferrarese di Storia Patria*, xv (1904), pp. 3–27; and Elena Povoledo, art. 'Ferrara' in *Enciclopedia dello Spettacolo*, v (1958), cols. 173–85. Recent studies of the musical aspects of this phase of theatre at Ferrara are Nino Pirrotta, *Li due Orfei* (Turin, 1969), pp. 57–99, and Wolfgang Osthoff, *Theatergesang und darstellende Musik in der italienischen Renaissance* (2 vols.; Tutzing, 1969), i, pp. 132 ff.

[7] See B. Zevi, *Biagio Rossetti: il primo urbanista europeo* (Turin, 1960). For a late-fifteenth-century map of Ferrara showing the enlargement of the city under Ercole, see the article by W. Gundersheimer cited in note 5; also Michele Catalano, *Vita di Ludovico Ariosto* (Geneva, 1931), i, facing p. 56.

maintained the political leverage of his small but strategic duchy by means
of a close alliance with the court of France. What we may call the politics
of culture at Ferrara under Ercole emerges in part from his carefully calculated dealings with the Papacy on the one hand and the court of France
on the other.[8] When we look at the development of music at Ferrara in his
time, the effects of this dual diplomacy are obvious, and it becomes clear
why Ferrara, as a virtual client state of French political interests in Italy,
should have been able to rise to the level of a musical centre of international
significance during the thirty-five years of Ercole's reign.

Among Italian statesmen of the late fifteenth century, Ercole had unusually strong musical proclivities, perhaps developed during his early years
at the court of Naples.[9] His interest in music is documented in later years
again and again, amounting almost to an obsession and evidently rivalling
his other major preoccupation, namely, a deep and sincere religious devotion.[10] All seven children of Ercole seem to have shared his passion for music

[8] On Ercole's diplomatic role at the time of the French invasions, see Paolo Negri,
'Studi sulla crisi italiana alla fine del secolo XV', *Archivio Storico Lombardo*, Ser. V, Vol. l
(1923) and Ser. VI, Vol. li (1924); also his 'Milano, Ferrara e Impero durante l'impresa di
Carlo VIII in Italia', *Archivio Storico Lombardo*, Ser. V, Vol. xliv (1917); also Chiappini,
Gli Estensi, pp. 184–91. On Ercole's affiliation to France see Ilardi, 'Fifteenth-Century
Diplomatic Documents', p. 103; Luigi Simeoni, *Le Signorie*, ii (Milan, 1950), p. 758 and
especially pp. 961–4. Symptomatic of the connection between diplomatic ties and the
exchange of music is a letter from Ferrante d'Este to Ercole I of October 1494, written from
Casale, where he was attached to the French court, reporting on an attempt to secure
music from Loyset Compère (the full text is given on pp. 129–30 of my study cited in
note 3).

[9] Ercole, aged 14, was sent to the court of Naples in 1445, and remained there despite
brief interruptions until 1463 (aged 33) when he was made governor of Modena by his
half-brother Borso, then Duke of Modena and Marchese of Ferrara; this stay of eighteen
years at Naples must have played a decisive role in Ercole's development, and it reflects a
continuing relationship between Naples and Ferrara that has its own importance for music.
Marriages that strengthened the connection were those of Leonello d'Este to Maria d'Aragona in 1444, and Ercole's own marriage to Eleonora d'Aragona in 1473. On the musical
establishment at the Aragonese court during Ercole's residence there, see Camillo Minieri
Riccio, 'Alcuni fatti di Alfonso I. di Aragona dal 5 Aprile 1437 al 31 di Maggio 1458',
Archivio Storico per le Provincie Napoletane, vi (1881), pp. 1–36, 231–58, 411–61. In 1451, for
example, we find at the court a company of nineteen singers, led by Giacomo Borbo, plus
two organists.

[10] On Ercole's religious tendencies, see particularly Gardner, *Dukes and Poets*, pp. ix,
302ff, 363ff. In his later years he became a devotee of the cult of Saint Catherine of Siena,
was sympathetic to Savonarola's reforms, and sought in various ways to augment the
seriousness of religious observance at Ferrara. In 1497 he brought the mystic Suor Lucia da
Narni to Ferrara and built a convent for her. In a contemporary Deposition of Christ, a
sculpture attributed to Guido Mazzoni, Ercole is represented as Joseph of Arimathea; see
Catalogo della Esposizione della Pittura Ferrarese del Rinascimento (Ferrara, 1933), pp. 209–11.
Evidence of his interest in religious disputation emerges in his middle and last years. In 1480
a disputation on the Immaculate Conception was held in Ferrara and a tract by one of the

with the same intensity with which they ignored his religious one, and all became important patrons of music; they include Alfonso, the succeeding Duke; Ippolito I, the Cardinal; his daughters Beatrice and Isabella d'Este, and the other sons. Ercole's support of music goes far beyond that of his predecessors. His oldest brother, Leonello, had fostered music to some degree during his brilliant short reign, from 1441 to 1450, but under Borso d'Este, from 1450 to 1471, music had played little more than a secondary role. Borso sought his glorification in the acquisition of titles, honours, splendid manuscripts and portraits; his most vivid monument is the series of depictions of himself and his court in the frescoes of the Palazzo Schifanoia. Ercole evidently sought a way of securing his worldly fame that would compete with that of Borso but avoid direct comparison, and this, I suggest, may be the basis for the glorification of his name and rank that is conveyed in an unprecedented way in Josquin's 'Missa Hercules Dux Ferrariae'.

Ercole began to assemble a musical chapel immediately after attaining power on Borso's death in 1471. Within eighteen months of his becoming Duke (on 20 August 1471) he had secured the services of an impressive international corps of singers, plus choirboys, led by Johannes Brebis and Johannes Martini.[11] His main competitor for musicians was then Galeazzo Maria Sforza of Milan, who set about the same task at the same time and tried to hire many of the same singers. A well-known list of Milanese court singers dated 15 July 1474 shows Johannes Martini in Sforza service among the 'Cantori de cappella', together with Josquin and Compère,[12]

---

participants, Fra Vincenzo Bandello, was published in 1485 with a dedication to Ercole; see Paul Oskar Kristeller, 'A Thomist Critique of Marsilio Ficino's Theory of Will and Intellect,' *Harry Austryn Wolfson Jubilee Volume* (Jerusalem, 1965), pp. 463–94. In 1503 or 1504 a disputation was held before Ercole involving a Franciscan, a Dominican and the Jewish savant and scribe Abraham Farisol, who was active at Ferrara for many years; see Cecil Roth, *The Jews in the Renaissance* (Philadelphia, 1959), p. 122, and Alexander Marx, *Studies in Jewish History and Booklore* (New York, 1944), pp. 108f, 269.

[11] The ducal musical forces in 1473 included at least twelve mature singers and a group of eight 'garzoni todeschi'. The former group was composed of Zohanne Martin todescho cantadore compositore; fra Zoane Bribas (= Brebis); don Domenico contrabasso; don Pedros contralto; Jachetto de Marvilla; Niccolo d'Olandia; Bartolomeo Cattalano soprano; don Jeronimo de Ferrara soprano; Piedro de Nantes de Bretagne soprano; Zoane de Bechari de Ferrara; don Marino cappellano; and Zohane Bon todescho, 'maestro de la cappella'; finally a don Bernardo sonadore is found grouped with the singers; see ASM, Archivio della Camera Ducale, Guardaroba, Spesa de lo Ofitio del Sp. Marco de Galeoto, 1473, fols. 37, 40, 42, 45, 48ᵛ, 50. The same register (fol. 76) lists 12 *piffari* and *sonatori*, plus a group of trumpeters.

[12] For this list as well as three others of this period, see Claudio Sartori, 'Josquin des Prés Cantore del Duomo di Milano', *Annales Musicologiques*, iv (1956), p. 64, n. 1. The list of 15 July 1474 includes at least six singers who were also in Estense service at some time during the 1470s: Zorzo Brant; Antonio de Cambrai; Cornelio [de Lillo]; Michele de Feys;

but the evidence shows beyond question that for Martini this was a short interlude of a few months during a career at Ferrara that lasted from at least 1473, if not 1471, until his death some time between late October 1497 and approximately May 1498.[13] The chapel was from the beginning one of the largest in Europe, including a brilliant group of instrumentalists and some twenty-two to thirty singers, or even more. Ercole went to remarkable lengths to attract singers to Ferrara and, to hold them in service, carefully negotiated with the Pope for the right to confer benefices on them himself. The better-known names in the chapel before 1500 include Jean Japart (1477–9, at least), Jachetto of Marvilla, Jean Verbonnet-Ghiselin (1491–3 and informally later on), and of course Jacob Obrecht, who visited in 1487 and was hired in 1504; he died at Ferrara in 1505.

★　★　★

For the entire period from the beginnings of Ercole's chapel in 1471 down to the year 1503 I have found no record of any explicit or formal relationship between Josquin and the court of Ferrara. Since the rosters of paid court musicians are preserved for this period and are largely continuous, it seems safe to say that Josquin was not a member of Ercole's chapel at any time before 1503.[14] Yet the close relations between Ercole and the

---

Johannes Martini; and Jachet de Rohan, also known as Jachetto de Marvilla. In Ferrarese documents this singer is known only by the name Jacheto de Marvilla, while in Milanese records he appears under both of these names. For information on the latter point I am indebted to Professor Lowinsky.

[13] Martini was still alive but apparently near death on 21 October 1497, when Anna Maria Sforza (first wife of Alfonso d'Este) wrote to Cardinal Ippolito I asking that a favourite of hers be given the benefices held by 'Zoanne Martino Cantore quando il caso de la morte sua accadesse...' (ASM, Carteggio tra Principi Estensi, B. 140). On 29 December 1497, Ercole informed Ippolito: 'We wrote to Messer Ludovico di Carissimi asking him to appeal to His Holiness to reserve for us the benefices of Giovanni Martini, our singer, before they would be vacated by his death' ('inanti che vacasseno li beneficij de Zoanne Martino per la morte soa, scrivessimo a messer Ludovico di Carissimi che suplicasse a la Santità de nostro Signore per una reserva de dicti beneficij. La predicta Santità fo contenta di farla...'); ASM, Cart. tra Principi Estensi, B. 69/9, Doc. 1652—XIV/54.

[14] After the rapid exchange of musicians with the Sforza chapel in the 1470s and after the upheaval caused by the war between Ferrara and Venice in 1482–1484, the chapel membership remained relatively stable; many singers maintained their positions in it for a number of years. The years before 1503 for which no payment rosters are available are 1475, 1482, 1483, 1486, 1487, 1489, 1495, 1496, 1498 and 1502. But for some of these years the names of certain singers can be filled in from other sources. Gustave Reese, *Music in the Renaissance* (New York, 1959), p. 229, refers to evidence purporting to show that Josquin was in the service of the Duke of Ferrara in 1499. The sources cited are André Pirro, *Histoire de la Musique de la fin du XIVe siècle à la fin du XVIe* (Paris, 1940), p. 173, and L. Valdrighi, 'Cappelle, concerti e musiche di casa d'Este', *Atti e Memorie delle RR. deputazioni di storia patria per le provincie modenesi* (1884), p. 422. Pirro's statement is based on

Sforzas, in particular his long friendship with Ascanio Sforza, suggest that Josquin may have had informal connections with Ferrara that are not officially documented. Particularly noteworthy is Josquin's departure from Milan in April 1479, after which we have no record of his whereabouts until his first appearance among the singers of the Papal Chapel in 1486. Significantly, the year 1480 marked the beginning of a prolonged visit by Ascanio Sforza to Ferrara, which lasted for eighteen months until September 1481.[15] One chronicler tells us that his retinue was composed of some 200 men, and quite conceivably such an entourage included Josquin.[16] It seems plausible to imagine that the 'Hercules' Mass could have been written during this time.[17]

Valdrighi, Valdrighi's on Canal, 'Della Musica in Mantova', *Memorie del R. Istituto Veneto di Scienze, Lettere ed Arti*, xxi (1879). Canal (p. 668) merely paraphrases a letter sent on 19 December 1499 to the Marquis of Mantua by a singer. The same letter was once again paraphrased by A. Bertolotti, *Musici alla Corte dei Gonzaga in Mantova* (Mantua, 1890), p. 18. Claudio Gallico, in his 'Josquin nell'Archivio Gonzaga', *Rivista Italiana di Musicologia*, vi (1971), pp. 205–10, has published the letter, from which it can be seen that the writer's name was not 'Giovanni Venaysius' but 'Joannes Viuaysius, cantor Ill^mi Ducis Ferrariae' (often called Vivas in the Ferrarese registers), that the letter was not written from Venice, but from Ferrara, and that the 'canto de Ioschino bono per excellentia' which the writer sent to the addressee, the Marquis of Mantua, came from Ferrara. The letter does *not* say that Josquin was in Ferrara at that time.

15 Ascanio had been in Ferrara briefly in June of 1477, exiled from Milan after an unsuccessful *coup d'état* against Duchess Bona di Savoia (regent of the young Gian Galeazzo Sforza, after the murder of Duke Galeazzo Maria Sforza in 1476); see the anonymous author of the *Diario Ferrarese, 1409–1502* in L. A. Muratori, *Rerum italicarum scriptores*, xxiv, Pt. vii/1, p. 94; also the *Diario di Bernardino Zambotti* (1476–1504), ibid., Pt. vii/2, p. 34. In 1480 Ascanio is reported by these chroniclers to have arrived in Ferrara on March 7 and to have remained until 30 September 1481. For particulars on his activities at Ferrara during this period, see especially the diary by Zambotti, op. cit., pp. 77ff. On Ascanio and Josquin see Edward E. Lowinsky's article in these Proceedings, pp. 31–75.

16 The chronicler Ugo Caleffini says that from 26 July 1480 to September 6 of the same year Ascanio was in Naples, returning to Ferrara after this journey; see *Cronaca di Ugo Caleffini, 1471–1494* in Biblioteca Apostolica Vaticana, MS. Chigi J. I. 4, fols. 126, 129, 133^v (complete photocopy and modern transcription in Ferrara, Biblioteca Comunale Ariostea, MS. Cl. I 769). This alleged interruption of forty-five days in Ascanio Sforza's stay in Ferrara in 1480 is not corroborated by other local chroniclers but remains to be verified by other documentary evidence. The text of Caleffini's chronicle was partially published by G. Pardi in two volumes (Ferrara, 1940) but is incomplete. For an evaluation of the Ferrarese chronicles of this period see L. Chiappini, *Indagini attorno a cronache e storie ferraresi del secolo XV* (Rovigo, 1954). In private communication, Professor Lowinsky has informed me that he believes Josquin came to Ferrara with Ascanio.

17 Edward Lowinsky has proposed that the Mass was composed and performed on the occasion of Ercole's state visit to Rome in 1487; see 'Josquin des Prez and Ascanio Sforza', *Congresso internazionale sul Duomo di Milano, Atti*, ed. M. L. Gatti Perer, ii (Milan, 1969), p. 19.

The first documents showing interest in Josquin's music at Ferrara and finally in obtaining his services were published in Osthoff's first volume. Works by Josquin were sent to Ferrara by the Ferrarese ambassador in France, Bartolomeo de' Cavalieri, and by Ghiselin-Verbonnet, 'singer of His Most Christian Majesty' and one-time singer at the court of Ferrara[18] (see Appendix I, Documents 1 and 2).[19] Document 3, a dispatch from Cavalieri of 13 December 1501, reports that while in Blois he met 'a singer named Josquin, whom Your Excellency had sent to Flanders to find

[18] [It may be useful to correct here the interpretation of a document important in the biography of Ghiselin-Verbonnet. In a letter of 1491 by Verbonnet to Ercole published by Clytus Gottwald in his fine study on the composer, *Johannes Ghiselin-Johannes Verbonnet* (Wiesbaden, 1962), p. 11, the former asks the Duke for a recently vacated benefice for his little son. Gottwald is not certain whether the son is a legitimate child, that is, whether Verbonnet was a priest or a layman, but the letter says 'per che essendo mi usorato non seria capace per mi prego Vostra Excellentia se voglia dignare de proverderne ad Hercule mio figliollo. A ciò che ancho lui se possa dare ala virtude per grazia de Vostra Celsitudine...' which means: 'Since I, being married, would not be eligible [for such a benefice] I beseech Your Excellency to deign to provide my little son Hercules with it so that also he can follow the path of virtue thanks to Your Highness....' As Gottwald explained, it was possible at that period for a minor to be provided with a benefice.—Ed.]

[19] In the absence of precise information on the makeup of the French court chapel at this period, we can only speculate about Verbonnet's relationship to it in 1501. Little enough is known at present about his entire career; see Frank A. D'Accone, 'The Singers of San Giovanni in Florence during the 15th Century', *Journal of the American Musicological Society*, xiv (1961), p. 345, and Clytus Gottwald, *Johannes Ghiselin-Johannes Verbonnet*, pp. 7–17. A letter from Verbonnet to Ercole d'Este dated from Reggio on 10 July 1491 (Gottwald, p. 11; see also fn. 18 to the present paper) speaks of a benefice in a manner that can only imply his being already in Ercole's service at this time. In correspondence and payment registers he is usually called 'Verbonetto' or 'Barboneto' (with various spellings). In 1492 'Verbonetto cantore' is a paid singer at Ferrara (ASM, Libri d'Amministrazione di Ercole I, No. 25). In October 1492, thanks to evidence given by D'Accone (see above-mentioned article, p. 345), Verbonnet is known to have joined the chapel of the cathedral of Florence, but this could not have lasted beyond March 1493 at the latest, since the chapel was then disbanded. In April of 1493 Duke Ercole helped Verbonnet gain his freedom at Florence, where he had been imprisoned for a debt he had contracted with Bonaventura di Mosto of Ferrara. After this we lose track of Verbonnet until he reappears in 1501 in the diplomatic correspondence from France. In 1503 he and Coglia are mentioned as accompanying Josquin to Lyons, but thanks to documents published by Gallico (see fn. 14) it is now clear that he did not then travel with them all the way to Ferrara. The name 'Messer Johane fiamengo' on the benefice list of 17 October 1503 at Ferrara has been associated with him, and in all likelihood this refers to the musician who is known as 'Giam de Fiandra', who remains in Estense service from 1503 to 1509. The problem with identifying the two is that in the years 1507 and 1508 a 'Meester Janne Verbonnet' is recorded as a singer in Bergen op Zoom, and if this is Ghiselin-Verbonnet, which appears to be the case, then he is not the same man as the Ferrarese 'Giam de Fiandra'. In any event, it seems likely that between the years 1493 and 1501 Verbonnet must have remained on good terms with Ercole d'Este, though not as a paid singer in his regular service; perhaps he was then mostly in France.

singers'. This implies that Josquin had been in the service of the Duke before 1501, but I have found no corroborating record for such service. It is also curious that Cavalieri should speak in this letter of 'a singer named Josquin' as if he had not known the name before, although three months earlier he had written 'Verbonnet is sending a new work which he says is by Josquin', showing that he did know the name.[20] Possibly Josquin's commission to look for singers was issued through another agent, conceivably Verbonnet. Whatever Josquin's service at this time, France is the area from which his music is sent and from which he himself comes to northern Italy.

Document 5 shows the next phase leading to Josquin's engagement at Ferrara. In May 1502, two months after the celebrations for the wedding of Alfonso d'Este and Lucrezia Borgia, Alfonso made a diplomatic journey to France to visit Louis XII.[21] From there he made his way to Lyons, following the French court on its travels. Document 5 shows his special interest in taking with him a singer named Girolamo; this is Girolamo Beltrandi of Verona, who was then at Ferrara but ten years earlier had been in St. Peter's (later called the Cappella Giulia) at the same time that Josquin was in the Papal Chapel.[22]

The name 'Coglia' has been known as that of the man accompanying Josquin on his journey to Ferrara in April 1503.[23] Document 6 (see Appendix I) shows that he too was travelling to Paris in May 1502. But Coglia's role

---

[20] This passage comes from a postcript to a letter from Bartolomeo de' Cavalieri to Ercole d'Este, dated 25 September 1501: 'Postscriptum[:] Verbonet manda certa cosa nova che dice ha facto Joschin a vostra excellentia come vedera per sue lettere' (Osthoff, i, p. 45; Gottwald, p. 14); I read the name as 'Verbonet', not 'Verbotet'. Later dispatches by Cavalieri mentioning unspecified works acquired for the Duke by 'Breboneto' or 'Brebonet' are dated 13 December 1501 and 23 December 1501. In minutes of 27 December 1501 and 1 February 1502 the Duke thanks Cavalieri for news of the music secured for him by 'Borboneto'.

[21] Letters from Alfonso to his father are preserved from these stations along the way: 3 May 1502 (Lyons); 14 June (Lyons); 26 June (Grenoble); ASM, Carteggio tra Principi Estensi, B. 70/9, Doc. 1653–IV/2–4. Ambassadorial dispatches from France corroborate Alfonso's accounts (ASM, Ambasciatori, Francia, B. 3). Other correspondence makes it clear that in Alfonso's retinue was Girolamo da Sestola, dicto il Coglia; on 30 May 1502 Coglia writes from Lyons to Ercole d'Este.

[22] Alfonso's letter of 2 May 1502 (Document 5) mentions only this singer's first name, Girolamo. But another letter, from the ducal chamberlain Girolamo Gilioli to Ercole I, of 9 May 1502, explicitly names the singer 'Hieronymo Beltrandi cantore' as being in ducal service (ASM, Particolari, 'Gilioli'). Beltrandi evidently joined the chapel early in 1502 and remained until April of 1504, when he departed (coinciding with the departure of Josquin?). By January 1505 he was back in service and stayed until 1510, when the chapel was disbanded due to the extraordinary political and financial difficulties occasioned by Alfonso's alliance with France. The chapel was reconstituted in the following year, but remained smaller than it had been before.

[23] Osthoff, i, p. 53.

was more important. His real name was Girolamo da Sestola. He was a friend of Ariosto's[24] and a vivid court personality, combining the talents of courtier, horseman, dancer, musician, spy, gossip, newsmonger, and man of all occasions.[25] In 1491 he was sent to Isabella at Mantua as musical instructor.[26] He undertook a number of trips to Flanders for Ercole, bringing back what Italian courts especially prized from that region: horses, tapestries, and musicians.[27]

Gian de Artiganova, or Gian Gascon—the 'Gian' of Documents 7–9—was a singer and courtier whose role in affairs and intrigues at court equals that of Coglia. Gian had started out as a young singer in 1491, and by 1502 he had risen to the post of court chamberlain, a highly paid position.[28] Like Coglia, he is a well-known figure in the annals of Ferrara. In 1505 he became enmeshed in a political plot against Alfonso and Ippolito hatched

[24] Michele Catalano, *Vita di Ludovico Ariosto*, Vols. 1 and 2, *passim* (see index for numerous references to 'Girolamo da Sestola detto il Coglia', and several letters from him). Letters from or about Coglia in AMS, Particolari, 'Coia', are found as late as 1543. His association with Ariosto is of importance to the poet's biographers; a letter from Coglia to Isabella d'Este Gonzaga of 7 July 1533 on Ariosto's death (Catalano, Document 621) is crucial for fixing the date of that event.

[25] Letters from Coglia to Ercole, to Isabella (mostly in the Archivio di Stato, Mantova), to Ippolito and Alfonso, as well as numerous entries in Ferrarese payment registers, testify to Coglia's versatile roles in the affairs of the court.

[26] S. Davari, 'La Musica a Mantova', *Rivista Storica Mantovana*, i (1884), p. 15, refers to 'Gerolamo Sextula' as Isabella's music instructor in 1491, just after her removal to Mantua following her marriage to Francesco Gonzaga in 1490. In September of 1490 she had requested and obtained the services of Johannes Martini to instruct her in music, but only for a short time; see Davari, loc. cit. The evidence for the sending of Sestola is found in two letters from Alfonso d'Este to Isabella, one of 26 June 1491 (responding to her request for Sestola) and one of 24 October 1491 (referring to her inability, up to then, to make use of 'hieronymo sextula che haveti là ultra per lo imparare sonare...'); Sestola evidently played keyboard instruments. Source: Archivio di Stato, Mantova, Archivio Gonzaga, B. 1185, Docs. 31 and 58.

[27] In a dispatch to Ercole I of 27 June 1498 from Antwerp, after writing mainly about horses, he adds: 'Your Lordship will be well provided with Masses, since Gian and I will bring you back about twenty of them, and we will also bring a very good soprano...' ('Vostra Signoria serà ben fornita di mese da Gian e mi e ne porteremo una vintina e si meneremo uno bonissimo soverano.... A dì 27 de zugno 1498 data in anversa'); Source: ASM, Amb. Germania, B. 1, Filza 14. In 1510 Coglia went to France for Duke Alfonso and in 1515 to England, where he is said to have sung and played for the royal court; see Catalano, *Vita di Ludovico Ariosto*, i, p. 499.

[28] The name 'messer Giam cantore' is met for the first time in ducal payment registers in 1490; in 1491 it bears the addition 'm. Giam cantore...conduto per soprano'. For 1492 no list is extant; in 1493 the name is given as 'Giam Francese cantore' in a list which also contains 'Verbonetto cantore', showing the two are not identical. I take it that this 'Giam cantore' is the singer who rises to the role of ducal chamberlain in 1500, where in one register he is listed alone, not among musicians, and is called 'Giam Chantore dito Chamerlengo'. His entire service would seem to have extended from 1490 to 1506.

by their younger brothers Ferrante and Don Julio d'Este, and in 1507 he was publicly tortured and executed in Ferrara.[29]

Documents 7–9 show us that in July 1502 Gian had gone to Savoy to look for singers, and had been caught and detained there on charges of luring singers away from the court of Savoy. Within little more than a week after Alfonso's message to his father (Document 7), Ercole receives word that Gian has returned from Savoy with several excellent singers.[30]

In a letter of 4 August 1502 (see Document 10) Coglia writes to Ercole, then in Milan, as follows:

Don Alfonso...informs Your Lordship that Gian has arrived safe and sound, that the singers have at last arrived at Modena, and that by the grace of God they all look well...the singers are truly perfect, and...Don Alfonso can hardly wait for Your Lordship's coming...to let you hear these singers. (See Plate 8.)

Three days later, on 7 August, 'Jan' writes a letter telling Ercole exactly the same thing (Document 12). This letter has been known since Vander Straeten, but without the context of the documents offered here it was not possible to interpret it correctly. Now we can see it as part of an emerging pattern of rivalry between Coglia and Gian, each striving to maintain a favourable position in court affairs, and each anxious, as will be seen, to influence the Duke's choice of a major composer. This post had been open since the death of Johannes Martini five years earlier. In Document 14, of 14 August 1502, ten days after Gian's arrival from Savoy, Coglia once more praises the singers and specifically recommends Josquin.

I must tell Your Lordship that I am already in fear of being bewitched by...the singing of these singers, and I can hardly wait for Your Lordship's arrival, because you will derive such enjoyment and consolation from them...not only in the chapel but in the chamber as well, and in any use you like.

.   .   .

The singer Bartolomeo [de Fiandra] requests Your Lordship's consent to give him a three months' leave to go home....Your Lordship is bound to let him go because he says that Your Lordship promised it to him....[31]

---

[29] On the role of 'Gian cantore' in the plot hatched by Don Julio and Ferrante d'Este against Duke Alfonso and Cardinal Ippolito I in 1506, see Gardner, *Dukes and Poets*, pp. 497ff.; also A. Lazzari, 'Il Dramma di Don Giulio d'Este' in his *Attraverso la Storia di Ferrara* (Rovigo, 1953), pp. 111–28; and above all the comprehensive account, based on most of the known documents, of Riccardo Bacchelli, *La Congiura di Don Giulio d'Este* (Verona, 1931).

[30] In mid-June Ercole left Ferrara for Milan, where he remained for several months with Louis XII; see the *Diario di Bernardino Zambotti*, p. 340. His absence from Ferrara on this diplomatic mission necessitated the letters written in August to inform him of Gian's adventures in Savoy and his subsequent return to Ferrara with the singers.

[31] This request on behalf of Bartolomeo de Fiandra (a singer at court from 1499 until 1505) is corroborated by the letter of 13 August 1502 given here as Document 13.

My Lord, I believe that there is neither lord nor king who will now have a better chapel than yours if Your Lordship sends for Josquin. Don Alfonso wishes to write this to Your Lordship and so does the entire chapel; and by having Josquin in our chapel I want to place a crown upon this chapel of ours. (See Plates 10–11.)

This letter shows first that Josquin had already come up for active consideration; second, that Coglia was strongly in favour of bringing him to Ferrara, and that this is also the wish of Alfonso and the singers. Particularly striking is the reference to Josquin as the potential crowning figure of a chapel that is already strong but will rise beyond that of any lord or king if he is brought to lead it.[32] It must be remembered that the title of 'Duke of Ferrara' had first been obtained by Borso d'Este in 1471 just a few months before his death, and that thus Ercole was the first real Duke of Ferrara. In a legal sense he was a vassal of the Papacy and the Empire, to which he owed his title; politically, of course, he was a vassal of France. The symbol of his rank was not a crown but a beret, which we see in the famous portrait of him by Dosso Dossi. Josquin, then, is portrayed by Coglia as being metaphorically a crowning figure, and the implication is that by hiring him Ercole can aspire to higher status than most dukes can claim. A further implication is that the musician of great reputation can confer upon a patron the same measure of reflected glory that had traditionally been attributed to poets and painters.[33]

The communication from Coglia also shows us for the first time how to interpret that well-known letter written by Gian (Document 17). This is the letter, dated simply 2 September, the year of which has been a matter of contention ever since its first publication by Vander Straeten a century ago.[34] Thanks to new evidence, it can now be definitively assigned to the

[32] An episode of 1494 illustrates the value of maintaining a first-class musical establishment. In November 1494, when Charles VIII of France swept down into Italy with his invading army, he discovered that Ercole's *piffari* were superior to his own, and through Ferrante d'Este, then attached to the French court, he requested the loan of Ercole's best wind players to make his entry into Pisa. From letters sent by Ferrante to Ercole we learn that Charles personally auditioned the players and liked them so much that he kept them with him for his subsequent entry into Florence and wanted to keep them with him all the way to Rome. A year and a half later, in 1496, Ferrante writes several times on the King's behalf from Lyons to ask once more for the Ferrarese 'tromboni e piffari', but this time Ercole found an excuse for failing to send them (ASM, Carteggio tra Principi Estensi, B. 133/10 and 134/10).

[33] On the role of the artist, see E. H. Kantorowicz, 'The Sovereignty of the Artist: A Note on Legal Maxims and Renaissance Theories of Art', in Ernest H. Kantorowicz, *Selected Studies* (Locust Valley, New York, 1965), pp. 352–65.

[34] See Osthoff, op. cit., ii, p. 307, for a rebuttal of an earlier proposal to date the letter 1495. Osthoff (i, p. 211) questions whether the author 'Gian' is identical with Gian de Artiganova, on the grounds that this letter of 2 September is in a hand different from that written 30 November 1498 and signed 'Joannes de ortiganova alias giam'. While it is true that these letters are in different hands, I believe that the one of 1498 may well have been

year 1502, and it fits exactly into this chain of events.[35] This is the letter on Josquin and Isaac containing the famous description of Isaac's trip to Ferrara, his writing of a motet on the motif 'La mi la sol la sol la mi' in only two days, and the offer to Isaac to join the chapel. I quote its best known passage:

To me he [Isaac] seems well suited to serve Your Lordship, more so than Josquin, because he is more good-natured and companionable, and he will compose new works more often. It is true that Josquin composes better, but he composes when he wants to, and not when one wants him to, and he is asking 200 ducats in salary while Isaac will come for 120—but Your Lordship will decide.

There is a second part to this letter that has never been discussed since it was published by Vander Straeten, but which is crucial for fixing its date. It reads in part:

Don Alfonso has told me that Your Lordship has written to say that those two sopranos are to be dismissed. May I advise you that one [of them] is good and very suitable, and today another one named Coletta arrived from the Kingdom of Naples . . . we will try out this Coletta and one of the two singers mentioned before, and we beg Your Lordship to tell us what you want done. I believe news has reached Your Lordship that Fra Giovanni, the soprano, is on his deathbed, and if the Lord takes him, it would be well to put one of these in his place. . . .

The mortal illness of Fra Giovanni and the arrival of Coletta are facts that can be exactly corroborated by other letters; see Documents 16 and 18, written the day before and the day after the letter of Gian, which in turn is written less than three weeks after Coglia's letter in favour of Josquin. So Coglia and Gian were opposed to each other, one in favour of Isaac (or perhaps against Josquin), the other in favour of Josquin; within several more months it must have become clear that Josquin's services could be obtained, and the stage was set for Coglia himself to bring Josquin from Paris to Ferrara in April 1503.

* * *

In mid-April 1503 Josquin was established as 'maestro di cappella'.[36] His entire tenure at Ferrara lasted from the end of April 1503 to April 1504,

---

written by a court scribe or secretary, as were an enormous number of letters of the court, whether or not by high officials. There is no other reason to question the assumption that 'Gian', 'Gian Cantore', and 'Gian de Artiganova' are one and the same individual.

[35] The new corroborative evidence for the year 1502 confirms the hypotheses of Vander Straeten, vi, p. 89, and Osthoff, i, p. 51.

[36] In the early years of Ercole's chapel, the principal musician, Johannes Martini, had normally been called 'cantadore compositore' in the records, whereas the term 'maestro de la cappella' was assigned to a person who had charge of the choirboys. Later, at least for a number of years, there seems to have been no attempt to designate any singer as 'maestro di cappella', a fact perhaps associated with the decline in the use of boy sopranos,

about a calendar year.[37] His name was set at the head of the other singers in the payment registers, and if one examines the monthly payments made to him and the annual tabulations of payments, it becomes clear that his total salary was 200 ducats a year.[38] This is exactly the figure mentioned by Gian in his famous letter of the previous September; from this we see that Gian was well informed on Josquin's terms as well as on his character. Perhaps he had found out these things in Savoy.

Osthoff published a valuable list of benefices held by the court singers, dated 17 October 1503; curiously, the list contains no benefices next to

---

due to the war with Venice in 1482; see Werner L. Gundersheimer, ed., *Art and Life at the Court of Ercole I d'Este: The 'De triumphis religionis' of Giovanni Sabadino degli Arienti* (Geneva, 1972), p. 89 (see my review in *Renaissance Quarterly*, xxvi (1973), pp. 494–7). Martini nevertheless seems to have exercised the role of leader among the singers. But by 1503, its application to Josquin, at least in the benefice list if not in payment records, suggests that the term had changed its implications and reflects Josquin's stature.

[37] The exact dates of Josquin's arrival and departure from Ferrara are based on the following evidence. On 13 April Cavalieri reported to Ercole that Josquin and Coglia were at Lyons (Doc. 20); on 17 April (Doc. 21) he added that Coglia had left Lyons that day for Ferrara. On 28 April (Doc. 22) Ercole replied that Josquin had not yet arrived but was expected at any hour. The first payments to Josquin are entered into the registers under the date 13 June, but they include payments retroactive to March. Probably he was given an advance payment by Coglia or another ducal representative. The summary of payments for 1503 stipulates that Josquin was paid for ten months of that year at a salary of 200 ducats a year. In 1504 the last recorded payment to Josquin is made on 22 April, and the annual summary reports payment to 'messer Juschino Cantore' for 'his salary for four months of the present year at a salary of 200 ducats a year.' On 13 April 1504 Alfonso left Ferrara on another trip to France to visit Louis XII, while a few days earlier (9 April) Cardinal Ippolito I had gone off to Mantua; see *Diario di Bernardino Zambotti*, pp. 357f. We have no knowledge of Josquin's destination on his departure from the Ferrarese chapel in April 1504. [However, see Kellman, below, p. 207.—Ed.]

[38] The normal Ferrarese currency of the period were the standard *lire*, *soldi* and *denari* (1 lira = 20 soldi = 240 denari). The usual value of the ducat was 3.2 lire (= 64 soldi); see E. Martinori, *La Moneta* (Rome, 1915). In 1503, while Josquin was being paid L.51.13.4 per month (= 620 lire annually) the next most highly paid singers, fra Zoanne Francesco da Padova, Antonio da Venexia, Girolamo Beltrandi, and Nicolo Fiorentino, were each receiving L.216.0.0 annually, slightly more than a third of Josquin's stipend. The other salaries ranged from a low L.36.0.0 for several of the 'cappellani' (who were either expected to live frugally or had income from benefices) to L.144 for long-time members of the chapel. In addition, a number of singers could count on income from benefices. The *piffari* and *trombetti* enjoyed much higher average salaries than the singers (L.214 and 183 respectively, as compared to L.145 in 1503), and their respective leaders, Messer Piero Trombone (as he is known) and Raganello, the leading trumpeter, were each paid more than any singer except Josquin. For example, in 1503, Piero received L.288 and Raganello L.252 (ASM, Archivio della Camera Ducale, Memoriale del Soldo, 1503, fols. 152ᵛ–53). Obrecht, on the other hand, was hired in the fall of 1504, after Josquin's departure, for 100 ducats, exactly half of Josquin's salary; see note 49.

Josquin's name.[39] This list is only a small part of an extensive documentation concerning benefices for singers, a matter that was one of Ercole's ruling passions. But even if Josquin had received no benefices, he left Ferrara in April 1504 as the highest paid singer in the history of its chapel.

The evidence of his activity at Ferrara is limited, and comes largely from outside sources. No family correspondence between the Duke and his children mentions him. But we can be quite sure that word of his arrival at Ferrara spread quickly. In January 1504 the ducal ambassador in Venice sent a work to Ferrara by an unnamed composer 'to have it looked over by that singer of yours named messer Josquino, the most excellent composer, to see if it is praiseworthy'[40] (see Plate 12 and Document 23). Three months later the same ambassador sent more music, this time identifying the composer as a twenty-year-old Dominican friar named 'Fra Iordano de Venezia' (Document 24). This is none other than Giordano Paseto, who in 1520 became chapelmaster at the Cathedral of Padua[41] and is the scribe and compiler of the important motet manuscript A 17 of the Capitular Library in Padua, written in 1522.[42]

These letters from Venice support what ought to be inferred in any case—that strong musical links existed between Ferrara and Venice at this period, the more so as Venice became increasingly the vital centre of music printing. Josquin's stay at Ferrara falls just between Petrucci's publications of his first and second books of Masses, and it coincides with a period of increasing expansion and rapidity of output of new music from Petrucci's shop. Other connections between Venice and Ferrara along these lines remain to be explored.

The character of musical life at court in Josquin's year must have been strongly mixed, reflecting the tastes of the ducal family. The Duke's preference was for sacred music, that of Alfonso and Ippolito for secular music and exchange of poetry, music, and musicians with Mantua. The sparse documentation suggests that Josquin principally furnished Masses and motets. The Duke was still receiving Mass settings from his agents abroad, including a Mass promised him by Louis XII and given his ambassador

39 Osthoff, i, plate 12 and pp. 212–15. [Josquin enjoyed substantial benefices granted him by Innocent VIII and Alexander VI; see Jeremy Noble's article in these Proceedings, pp. 76–102.—Ed.]

40 See Document 23.

41 On Paseto's later career at Padua, see R. Casimiri, 'Musica e Musicisti nella Cattedrale di Padova', *Note d'Archivio*, xviii (1941), pp. 101–4. Thanks to this letter, Paseto's birth can be assigned to the year 1484.

42 [That Paseto's admiration for Josquin continued undiminished may be deduced from the choirbook that he wrote in the year 1522 for the cathedral of Padua, which opens with two works by Josquin and includes six more; see Walter Rubsamen's catalogue of Padua, Biblioteca del Duomo, MS. A 17 in 'Music Research in Italian Libraries', *Notes*, second ser., Vol. viii (1950), pp. 80–6.—Ed.]

by Prioris, then master of the King's chapel.[43] A copyist at Ferrara was paid
for the copying of a Mass by Josquin in August 1504; unfortunately, the
Mass is not named (see Appendix III). In the years 1503 and 1504 sacred
dramas were lavishly mounted. On 28 March 1504, for example, a representation of the life of St. Joseph was staged, and a chronicler describes it as
follows:

it was performed in the cathedral on great platforms, with scenery painted to
depict castles; and on the roof of the cathedral, before the great altar, was constructed a heaven that opened and disclosed the glory of Paradise; and one saw
and heard angels playing and singing various melodies, and these were the singers
and players of our Duke....[44]

We may wonder whether Josquin was among the singers, or if the music
performed could have been his, a point on which at present we can only
speculate. Outside evidence enables us to attribute two motets to the
Ferrarese period with considerable confidence: the 'Miserere mei Deus'
and the motet 'Virgo salutiferi'. Folengo tells us that the 'Miserere' was
written at the express request of the Duke of Ferrara; this is further corroborated by an added sixth voice part written by the famous singer Bidon,
who was among the singers Gian brought from Savoy; he was a member of
the chapel at Ferrara under Josquin.[45] Another work assignable to this stay
is the five-voice 'Virgo salutiferi' (*Werken*, Motetten, Bundel vii, no. 35).
Until a few years ago, this text had been known only from a late sixteenth-
century anthology of metrical prayers; Edward Lowinsky found it to be
by the Ferrarese court poet Ercole Strozzi and published in 1513.[46] Ercole

[43] ASM, Archivio Segreto Estense, Cancelleria, Estero, Ambasciatori, Francia, B. 2,
letter of Bartolomeo de' Cavalieri to Ercole, dated 8 June 1503 and sent from Lyons:
'Most Illustrious and Excellent Lord: ...by means of Alberto da Canossa, who [is] with
the Most Reverend and Illustrious Monsignor Ascanio [Sforza], who is coming home, I
am sending Your Excellency the Mass that the Most Christian Majesty promised Your
Excellency at Pavia. He has had it given to me by Prioris, his chapelmaster, who commends
himself to Your Excellency; I have asked him [Alberto] to give it at Reggio to Antonio
Cordetta who will bring it quickly to Your Excellency...' ('Illustrissimo et Excellentissimo
Signore mio, per m. Alberto da Canossa che [è] con il Reverendissimo et Illustrissimo
monsignore Ascanio, il quale vene a casa sua, mando ha [sic] vostra excellentia la messa
quale promisse la Maestà Christianissima a vostra Excellentia a Pavia; me l'ha facta dare
da Prioris suo maystro de capella, il quale se recomanda a vostra Excellentia; l'o pregato la
dia a Regio ad Antonio Cordetta che subito la mandi a vostra Excellentia...'). The title
and authorship of the Mass are not mentioned, but it is possible that it was a work by
Prioris himself.

[44] *Diario di B. Zambotti*, p. 357.

[45] For the passage from Folengo, see especially A. W. Ambros, *Geschichte der Musik*,
iii, p. 12; it is from Folengo's *Opus...macaronicum*, 1521. The voice-part by Bidon for the
'Miserere' is preserved in St. Gall, Stiftsbibliothek, MS. 463; see *Werken*, Motetten, Bundel
viii, no. 37, where it is printed as an additional voice.

[46] Edward E. Lowinsky, *The Medici Codex of 1518* (*Monuments of Renaissance Music*,
iii; Chicago, 1968), pp. 87 and 199–200.

Strozzi was active at Ferrara both as literary man and as administrator during the whole year of Josquin's residence. Osthoff assigns the 'Hercules' Mass to this period as well, and whatever the date of its composition, the Mass must have seemed, when published by Petrucci in the very year of Ercole's death, a tribute by a great composer to a famous patron.

Josquin's departure from Ferrara could have been purely a prudent gesture. Chroniclers and letter-writers tell us that in July 1503 plague broke out at Ferrara and lasted throughout the summer and fall; by September Ercole and his entire court were ensconced at Comacchio, on the coast; two-thirds of the citizens of Ferrara had fled the city, where many lay dying.[47] Correspondence about the plague between Ercole Strozzi and the Duke was carried on until January 1504.[48] After Josquin's departure, his place was taken by Obrecht, and he did fall victim to the plague early in 1505.[49]

After Ercole's death in 1505, music at Ferrara had two chief patrons: Duke Alfonso I and his remarkable brother, Cardinal Ippolito I. Each maintained a separate musical establishment of considerable size. Perhaps the greatest surprise to have turned up in this study is that from 1516,

---

[47] *Diario di B. Zambotti*, pp. 351ff (beginning of plague in September of 1503); also the Chronicle of Paolo de' Zerbinati, valuable excerpts from which are preserved in a sixteenth-century copy at Ferrara, Biblioteca Comunale Ariostea, MS. Cl. I 337, fol. 16ᵛ.

[48] Correspondence of 1503–4 from the Duke to Ercole Strozzi on the plague is found in ASM, Archivio per Materia, Letterati: Strozzi, Ercole (letters of 1502–5, largely to Ercole, including several of November and December 1503 on the plague); also Ferrara, Biblioteca Comunale Ariostea, MS. Cl. I 210 (includes two minutes of letters from Ercole to Strozzi dated 11 October 1503 and 10 January 1504 concerning measures to be taken to end the plague).

[49] See Bain Murray, 'New Light on Jacob Obrecht's Development—A Biographical Study', *The Musical Quarterly*, xliii (1957), pp. 500–516. Although Murray reported no evidence of Obrecht's having been paid at Ferrara after 31 December 1504, I can mention two further archival references to Obrecht from early in 1505. The first is dated 10 February 1505 and involves payment of taxes for several members of the Ferrarese court entourage: 'li Infrascripti deno [= devono] dare a dì X de febraro la Infrascripta quantità de dinari che per loro se fanno buoni a Simon dal Bambaxo exatore de le tasse de Rezo per tanti li a pagati contanti in ferrara e posto a credito a dicto Simone: ...messer Ubreto Compositore de canto a li[bro]...[fol.] 167...[L.] 23.5.0' (ASM, Memoriale del Soldo, 1505 = Reg. 4911/97, fol. 17).

The second is dated two days later, 12 February 1505, and shows a payment for Obrecht to the Ferrarese bankers Jacomo and Baldissera Machiavelli: 'messer Ubreto compositore de Canto sino a dì 12 del presente a li[bro]...c. 167...[L.] 2.11.8' (ASM, Memoriale del Soldo, 1505, fol. 20ᵛ). No further mention of Obrecht is found in this register. The epitaphs by Gasparo Sardi quoted by Murray and presented in facsimile by L. G. van Hoorn, *Jacob Obrecht* (The Hague, 1968), opp. p. 106, bear the date 'Anno d. 1505. die trigesimo Augustj', but this date refers to the death of the person to whom the first epitaph is addressed On this point I am indebted to Edward Lowinsky. The absence of any further mention of Obrecht in the registers after 12 February 1505 may indicate that his death took place between mid-February and the middle of the year 1505.

Ippolito's chapel included Adrian Willaert.[50] Thus Willaert's career in Italy began not in 1522, as formerly believed, but six years earlier; one document even suggests that he may have joined the Cardinal's service as early as the middle of 1515.[51] In addition, 'Adriano' went with the Cardinal

[50] The account books of Cardinal Ippolito I show numerous references to 'Adriano Cantore' in the years 1516 and 1517 (to be published in another study). The *Mandato* officially taking him into the Cardinal's service is dated 6 April 1516 and shows a salary of 9 lire per month. The source is ASM, Carteggio tra Principi Estensi, B. 139/10 (Letters of Cardinal Ippolito I), Filza 1688–XXVII/33, No. 20.

[51] The many *libri d'amministrazione* of Cardinal Ippolito I include a small packet (= Register 823) containing two small payment books of 1517, the first of which is entitled 'Compendio de Salariati che sono in Ungaria/facto per tutto Ottobre 1517' (Ippolito left Ferrara for Hungary in October 1517 for an extended stay). The register contains these entries on folio 4v:

Adriano Cantore debe dare como al/memoriale f c. 64: 1. 0.0
E debe dare como al memoriale f c. 167 .... 9.12.0
E debe dare como al dcto. Zornale 169 .... 9.12.0
E debe dare como al dcto. Zornale 168 .... 0. 6.0
E debe dare como a Libro e de Salariati 15. 8.0
E a dì 17 Gienaro 1517 ali Salariati 18.12.0
E a dì 9 de marzo 1517 ali Salariati..................... 9. 0.0
E a dì 10 de aprile 1517 ali Salariati 9. 4.0
E a dì 29 de magio 1517 ali Salariati..................... 9. 4.0
E a dì 25 de septembre 1517 ali Salariati 18. 0.0
E debe dare como a Libro f de Salariati 5 ....49. 1.0
                                                    ──────────
                                                    148.19.0

and in the adjacent column:

Adriano cum provixione de L. 9 marchesane el mese/che
  principiò el suo Salario a dì 6 de Aprile 1516 per tutto
  dexembre...79.10.0
E debe havere a dì primo Giennaro 1517 per tutto Ottobre ..90. 0.0
E debe havere a dì primo Giennaro 1516 per tutto dì 5 Aprile a
  ragione de L. 3 & mezo 9.10.0
E debe haver per suo Resto a Libro de roma tenuto per
  Jacomo Botoxo [fol.] 64 ....14. 0.0
E debe haver da dì 8 de luio 1515 per tutto dexembre 17. 6.0
                                                    ──────────
                                                    197. 0.0
                                                    148.19.0

Resto Creditore per tutto ottobre   48. 1.0

The entry on fol. 5 for the Libro de Roma and for 8 July 1515 shows that Willaert was carried on the books of Cardinal Ippolito as early as mid-1515, even though he became a formal member of his entourage only in April 1516. According to this register, the other musicians accompanying Ippolito to Hungary in October 1517 were Jam Jacomo de Vicenza musico, Francesco Zoppo musico, Zoane Lourdel (= Lourdault) Cantore, Alvise Podriglia Cantore, and Alberto Piffaro. This is about half the normal complement of twelve to fourteen musicians whom he had kept regularly in his employment in Ferrara in the years 1516 and the first ten months of 1517. His company of musicians is quite distinct from the group of singers employed simultaneously by his brother, Duke Alfonso I.

to Hungary in October 1517, returning to Italy about August 1519.[52] It need hardly be said that this new discovery of the young Willaert's relationship with Ferrara and Hungary has substantial implications.

But even more remarkable is another figure in the Cardinal's account books in these years. Side by side with 'Adriano cantore' we find, for the years 1516 and 1517, the name 'Josquino Cantore'. This musician is never called by any other name; sometimes the spelling is 'Jusquino' and sometimes 'Josquino', but there is no doubt that he is a highly regarded musician, to judge from the number and quality of his payments in kind.[53] He served the Cardinal all through 1516 and most of 1517, but did not go with him to Hungary. Still, when Ippolito travelled back from Budapest to Ferrara by slow stages in the spring of 1520, we find 'Josquin' with him once more; in June 1520 he is given a gift by the Cardinal, perhaps on his departure.[54]

I do not know if this can be Josquin des Prez, and I am inclined to doubt it. More likely he is one of the musicians named Josquin who can be partially traced from the fragmentary records known so far, and quite possibly he is the one named 'Josquin Doro' who is found as a papal singer in 1520 and 1522.[55] Nevertheless, the music of the great Josquin continued to have importance for Ferrara precisely during these years. In 1517 the Cardinal

[52] Willaert returned to Ferrara from Hungary in August 1519, seven months before the Cardinal's own return to Ferrara in March 1520.

[53] ASM, Guardaroba, Memoriale 'D', 1516 (from internal evidence clearly originating from Cardinal Ippolito's books), contains numerous entries for 'Jusquino Cantore' as well as 'Adriano Cantore', along with other musicians.

[54] No. 818 of the *Libri d'amministrazione di Card. Ippolito I* is a remarkable document: it is a travel diary labelled '1520—Card. Ippolito I—Viaggio di Ungheria', a small volume of 106 written leaves bound in red leather, consisting of a travel diary for Ippolito's long journey from Hungary to Ferrara, with his retinue, in early 1520. Fol. 87, recording expenses in Budapest of 21 February 1520, contains this item: 'Item dinari dodese a Josquino per comprarsi paro uno de scarpe.....d.12'. On 17 March 1520 in Treviso, this item appears: 'Item craici quatordese a Josquino per uno capello comprato per il Signore.....cr. 14'. (*Craici* were Hungarian monetary units.) Fair copies of these entries in the diary are found in Register 797 of the *Libri d'Amm. di Card. Ippolito I*, fols. 138–48. Several months later, on 18 June 1520, the Cardinal is reported to have bought a lute and lute-case and to have given them to 'Jusquino Cantore', perhaps as a parting gift: Reg. 821, Zornale de Ussita K, 1520, fol. 43: 'Luni a dì xviii de Zugno/a lo Illustrissimo Signore Nostro Cardinale per conto de dinari donati L. nove marchesane e per sua Signoria contati a maestro Scotto sonatore de liuto per lo pretio de uno liuto cum la sua Cassa comprato da lui, per donarlo a Jusquino Cantore.....L. VIIII.-.-.' On 26 July 1520 the same register shows a payment 'a Jusquino Cantore L. sei marchesane', after which he no longer appears in the Cardinal's employment.

[55] The disappearance of Josquino Cantore from the Cardinal's books after 26 July 1520 fits in well with the theory that he is identical to the 'Josquin' who was paid as a singer in the private service of Pope Leo X in September of the same year. Afterwards, 'Josquin Dor' or 'Josquino Doro' is found as a papal singer in September of 1522, after the death of Pope Leo. A portion of a 'Missa de nostra Domina' (*Kyrie* and *Gloria*) is attributed to him in Rome, Biblioteca Apostolica Vaticana, MS. Capp. Sist. 55.

purchased music which included a full set of the three volumes of published Masses of Josquin.[56] In 1519 the Ferrarese ambassador at Rome took the trouble to inform the Duke that a 'Salve Regina' which he attributes to a certain 'Joasquin' was performed by the papal singers,[57] but this does not seem to refer to any known work by Josquin. The situation is puzzling and difficult, and it suggests how little we really know about the movements and affairs of the last years of Josquin's life—and not only the last years. It suggests that further explorations of various archival resources might well yield a more concrete and comprehensive account of his biography than is yet to hand. The possible consequences of such an undertaking for the dating of his works, and thus for our understanding of his development as a composer, can hardly be overestimated.

[56] ASM, Guardaroba, Memoriale 'E', 1517 (stemming from Cardinal Ippolito), fol. 35, dated 9 February 1517, shows the following expenses 'a maestro Zoane Maria Caraffa cartolaro per lo amontare de li infrascripti libri di canti comperati da lui...

       Messe diciasette di Josquin in tri libri
       Messe cinque de Zoanne gislin in un libro
       Messe cinque de Alexandro Agricola in un libro
       Messe cinque de Orto in uno libro
       Messe cinque de Obreth in uno libro
       Messe cinque de Diversij Autori in uno libro
       Messe Fragmenta Missarum in un libro'

[57] ASM, Ambasciatori, Italia, Roma, B. 25, Doc. 170–VI/26: Dispatch of the Ferrarese ambassador in Rome, Antonio Pauluzzi, to the court, dated Rome, 14 February 1520: 'Pransato fui [sic] in castello, et trovasi Nostro Signore ancor in mensa con musica de una salve regina per Joasquin, et fu molto bello, che vi intervenoro alcuno Duo, che molto satisfecero' ('Dinner took place in the castle, and His Holiness is still at the table, listening to the music of a "Salve Regina" by Josquin which was very beautiful; it included several duos, which were very pleasing.') The two 'Salve Regina' settings of Josquin for four voices (*Werken*, Motetten, Bundel xxv, no. 95) and for five (Bundel xi, no. 48) contain no duos.

Appendix I

Josquin and the Court of Ferrara: A Summary of Documents

I 1501–2

No.	Date	Writer	Recipient	Main content	Publication
1	21 July 1501	B. de' Cavalieri	Ercole I d'Este	Verbonnet, a singer at French court, sends music to Ercole.	Osthoff, i, p. 45 (reference only); Gottwald, p. 14[58]
2	25 September 1501	B. de' Cavalieri	Ercole I	Verbonnet sending a new work by Josquin.	Osthoff, i, p. 45
3	13 December 1501	B. de' Cavalieri	Ercole I	Cavalieri, in Blois, has met 'Joschin' who is looking for singers for Duke Ercole.	Osthoff, i, p. 51. [See also Stevenson, these Proceedings, p. 217. —Ed.]
4	24 February 1502	S. Cantelmo	Ercole I	Cantelmo sends 'Salve Regina' by Josquin to Ercole.	Osthoff, i, pp. 51 and 211
5	2 May 1502	Alfonso d'Este	Ercole I	Alfonso wishes to take the singer Girolamo [Beltrandi] with him to France.	Published below, Doc. 5
6	30 May 1502	Girolamo da Sestola, 'il Coglia' (in Lyons)	Ercole I	Don Alfonso will send Coglia to Paris 'tomorrow'.	Published below, Doc. 7
7	27 July 1502	Alfonso d'Este	Ercole I	News received that 'Gian' has been detained in Savoy on charge of luring away singers.	Published below, Doc. 7
8	31 July 1502	Alfonso d'Este	Ercole I	Gian apparently still detained.	Published below, Doc. 8
9	4 August 1502	Alfonso d'Este	Ercole I	Alfonso is glad to hear that Ercole has sent a rider to Savoy to look after Gian.	Published below, Doc. 9
10	4 August 1502	Girolamo da Sestola, 'il Coglia'	Ercole I	Gian has arrived at Modena with excellent singers; Don Alfonso wants Ercole to come and hear them.	Published below, Doc. 10
11	4 August 1502	Girolamo da Sestola, 'il Coglia' 'Jan'	Ercole I	Essentially the same message as No. 10.	Published below, Doc. 11
12	7 August 1502	'Jan'	Ercole I	Jan has arrived safely at Ferrara with three excellent singers.	Vander Straeten, vi, p. 89
13	13 August 1502	Bartolomeo de Fiandra, Cantore	Ercole I	Bartolomeo asks for three months' leave to go home.	Published below, Doc. 13
14	14 August 1502	Girolamo da Sestola, 'il Coglia'	Ercole I	The new singers are magnificent, and Ercole should come at once to hear them; the chapel members have never heard better singing. Bartolomeo wants leave to go home, and Ercole should give permission. *Urges Ercole strongly to bring Josquin to the chapel.*	Published below, Doc. 14

new music.

No.	Date	Writer	Recipient	Main content	Publication
16	1 September 1502	Alfonso d'Este	Ercole I	Fra Giovanni, a court singer, is ill.	Published below, Doc. 16
17	2 September [1502]	'Gian'	Ercole I	Isaac has been at Ferrara. Alfonso has asked Gian to sound him out on his willingness to join the chapel. Gian's comparison between Josquin and Isaac. The singer Coletta has arrived; illness of the singer Fra Giovanni.	Published below, Doc. 17; Vander Straeten, vi, p. 87; Osthoff, MGG, vii, col. 194 (facs.); Osthoff, i, p. 211
18	3 September 1502	Ferrante d'Este	Ercole I	More on Coletta, who has arrived in Ferrara.	Published below, Doc. 18

II 1503
(Josquin's tenure at Ferrara: April 1503–April 1504)

No.	Date	Writer	Recipient	Main content	Publication
19	12 April 1503	G. d'Adria (Lyons)	Marchese Fr. Gonzaga, Mantua	Reports that Coglia is at Lyons with Josquin and Verbonnet; Josquin is on his way to Ferrara.	Osthoff, i, p. 53
20	13 April 1503	B. de' Cavalieri	Ercole I	Coglia is at Lyons with Josquin.	Osthoff, i, p. 53
21	17 April 1503	B. de' Cavalieri	Ercole I	Coglia departed today for Ferrara.	Osthoff, i, p. 53
22	28 April 1503	Ercole I	B. de' Cavalieri	Josquin has not yet arrived but is expected at any hour.	Published below, Doc. 22
23	27 January 1504	Bartolomeo Cartari (Venice)	Ercole I	A composition ('Patrem') by a Venetian singer is sent to the Duke to be sung and to be judged by Josquin.	Published below, Doc. 23
24	29 April 1504	Bartolomeo Cartari (Venice)	Ercole I	Ercole likes the 'Patrem' and wants the entire Mass; Cartari obliges him and identifies the composer as Fra Giordano de Venezia.	Published below, Doc. 24
25	17 May 1504	Ercole I	Alfonso d'Este (in France)	The Ferrarese chapel needs more singers. Alfonso goes on a trip and receives precise instructions from his father on the hiring of new singers.	L. van Hoorn, *Jacob Obrecht*, p. 98 (reference only); published below, Doc. 25

Appendix II

Documents

With the exception of Documents 12 and 17, this Appendix provides original texts and translations only of those documents previously unpublished. For a full listing of relevant documents on Josquin known thus far see Appendix I, where references are also given to the earlier studies in which some of them have been published. Punctuation, accents, and apostrophes have been added and words written together have been separated where necessary. Abbreviations have been resolved and *u* and *v* have been interchanged in accordance with modern usage. Perfunctory words of greetings at the end of many of the letters have been replaced by 'Greetings, etc.'

Doc. 5   (ASM, Carteggio tra Principi
                                           Estensi, Ramo Ducale, Principi
                                           Regnanti: B. 70/9, Doc. 1653–IV/1)
Letter from Alfonso d'Este to Duke Ercole I d'Este, dated Ferrara, 2 May
1502 (to Duke at Codigoro).
Illustrissimo Signore mio. Hieronymo cantore presente exhibitor ritorna
a vostra excellentia, La quale prego non existimi che lo haverlo electo per
condure cum epso me in francia sia stato per fare cosa che dispiaqua
a quella, ma solamente per mia delectatione & piacere. Imperò vostra
signoria serà contenta che cussì la supplico ad darli licentia che'l possa
venire cum epso me, che la me ne fara singulare gratia. . . . Ferrarie ij
Maij 1502.
    Eiusdem Excellentie Vestre Filius & Servitor   Alfonsus Estensis

———————

Most Illustrious Lord: The singer Girolamo, the bearer of this letter, is
returning to Your Excellency [in Codigoro]. I ask you not to think that I
have chosen him to accompany me to France to cause you displeasure, but
solely for my entertainment and gratification. I beg Your Lordship to be
kind enough to grant my request that he be given permission to accompany
me since you will do me a singular favour. Greetings, etc. Ferrara, 2 May
1502.
                    Your Son and Servant Alfonso d'Este

Doc. 7
                        (ASM, Carteggio tra Principi Estensi, Ramo
                        Ducale, Principi Regnanti, B. 70/9, Doc. 1653–IV/11)
Letter from Alfonso d'Este to Duke Ercole I d'Este, dated Ferrara, 27
July 1502.
Illustrissime princeps: et excellentissime Domine: Pater: & Domine mi

observandissime: è venuta qui fama che Giam sia stato retenuto in le terre del signore Duca de Savoia per imputatione de havere desviati cantori a sua Signoria. Et perchè io non voria, che per questa causa Il patisse alcuno sinistro: prego vostra Excellentia, se voglia dignare ó cum mandare uno cavallaro ó altra persona chiarisse del caso: & ritrovando che'l sia impedito, per detta casone, fare tale provisione, che'l sia relaxato: come mi persuado, che vostra excellentia per la prudentia sua sapera ordinare. . . . Ferrarie 27 Julij 1502.

Celsitudinis Vestre Filius & Servitor Alfonsus

Most Illustrious Prince and Lord, Father, and most honoured Master: News has reached here that Gian has been detained in the lands of the Duke of Savoy on the charge of having lured away singers from the service of his Lordship. And since I would not wish him to suffer any harm on this account, I ask Your Excellency whether you would consent to send either one of your riders or some other person to clear up the matter; and if the emissary finds that he has been confined for that reason, he ought to take steps to have him set free. I am sure that Your Excellency, with your customary prudence, will know how to take care of the matter. Greetings, etc. Ferrara, 27 July 1502.

Your Grace's Son and Servant   Alfonsus

Doc. 8   (ASM, Carteggio tra Principi Estensi, Ramo
                Ducale, Principi Regnanti, B. 70/9, Doc. 1653–IV/14)
Letter from Alfonso d'Este to Duke Ercole I d'Este, dated Ferrara, 31 July 1502.

Illustrissimo signore mio. Non mi occure de presente che significare a vostra Excellentia [cose] digne de lei. Ma solo mi pare racordargli, che non ho sentito nova alcuna de Jan Cantore; havendone noticia vostra signoria, la serà contenta advisarmene. Et quando [?] sino a quest'hora la non ni havesse presentito alcuna cosa, non seria male, che essendo là ultra vostra excellentia, La facesse qualche provigione per intender nova del facto suo, adciò che quando li fusse Intravenuto alcuno sinistro, el si possa adiutare, ad fine che'l non se perda. . . . Ferrarie ultimo Julij 1502.

Eiusdem Excellentie vestre Filius & Servitor   Alfonsus/Estensis

---

Most Illustrious Lord: At this moment there is nothing especially noteworthy to report to Your Excellency. I should only like to remind you that I have not heard anything of the singer Jan. If Your Lordship receives any news of him I hope you will be good enough to send it to me. And if up to this moment nothing further has been heard about him, it would not be a bad thing if Your Excellency, while you are up there, took some steps to find out what has happened to him, in order to help him should he have fallen into some mishap, lest he come to grief. Greetings, etc. Ferrara, the last day of July 1502.

Your Excellency's Son and Servant   Alfonsus/Estensis

Doc. 9   (ASM, Carteggio tra Principi Estensi, Ramo
              Ducale, Principi Regnanti, B. 70/9, Doc. 1653–IV/15)
Excerpt from letter from Alfonso d'Este to Duke Ercole I d'Este, dated Ferrara, 4 August 1502 (to the Duke at Milan).
... La quale ha facta bona provisione per intender quello sia de Jan Cantore, essendosi mandato quello Cavallaro Regio in Savoia. Havendo vostra Signoria notitia di Lui, La se degnarà advisarme. ...

———

Your Excellency has made good provision for finding out what has become of the singer Jan, by sending that royal messenger to Savoy. If Your Lordship receives news of him, I pray you to let me know.

Doc. 10   (ASM, Particolari, 'Coia, Girolamo')
Letter from Girolamo da Sestola ('il Coglia') to Duke Ercole I d'Este, dated Modena, 4 August 1502. (See Plate 8.)
[Verso:] a lo Illustrissimo signore patron mio el signore ducha di ferara.
[at side:] a dj 5 de agosto 1502. [below:] ... cito/cito/cito/cito
[Recto:]
   Illustrissimo signore mio: scrivo questa letra in nome del signore don Alfonso; sua Signoria avisa vostra Signoria como gia[n] è venuto sano e salvo, como li chantori, li quali sono al fine zonti a modena e fano una bona ciera per la gracia di dio, e no dirò altro a la Signoria vostra se non che li chantori sono perfeti, e don Alfonso non vede l'ora che vostra Signoria vegna per ogni cosa e tanto più quanto per farve sentire quisti chantori; e desiti a Tommaso che voio che'l se spauri a oldirli. A vostra Signoria di continuo se ricomanda el signore don Alfonso, el socio, e mi e Gian, el quale io li o dito per parte di vostra Signoria como quela li a perdonato. A dì 4 di agosto 1502 data in modena.
   il vostro servitore   geronimo/da sestola dito Coia/in nome del signore
                   don Alfonso

———

Most Illustrious Master: I am writing this letter on behalf of Don Alfonso. His Lordship informs Your Lordship that Gian has arrived safe and sound, that the singers have at last arrived at Modena, and that by the grace of God they all look well. And I will only say to Your Lordship that the singers are truly perfect, and that Don Alfonso can hardly wait for Your Lordship's coming, for many reasons but all the more to let you hear these singers. And tell Tommaso that I want him to listen to them with fear and awe.[59] To Your Lordship Signor Don Alfonso commends himself, and so do Il Socio[60] and I and Gian, to whom I have said, on behalf of Your Lordship, that he is pardoned. Written in Modena on the 4th of August 1502.

    Your servant/Geronimo da Sestola called Coia

              In the name of My Lord Don Alfonso

Doc. 11   (ASM, Particolari, 'Coia, Girolamo')
Letter of Girolamo da Sestola ('il Coglia') to Duke Ercole I d'Este, dated Modena, 4 August 1502. (See Plate 9.)[61]
[Verso:] a lo Illustrissimo Signore Patron mio el Signore ducha di ferara/a dì 5 de agosto 1502 [Below:] cito/cito/cito/cito in milano
[Recto:]
Illustrissimo Signore patron mio: aviso vostra Signoria como Io vi domando nonciatura como gia[n] e li chantori sono arivati a modena sani e salvi tuti & si che Io ve aviso che voio la nonciatura e no la voio perdere perchè io la merito. Vostra signoria a inteso el tuto. Non vi voio dire altro se no[n] che mai sentisti meio chantare a la vita vostra tri compagni soprani. A vostra signoria di continuo m'aricomando. Apreso el signore don Alfonso acompagnato el signore Ducha di romagna fino a l'Enza e li avemo fato onore a ferara e modena e rezo compagnatolo fino a l'Enza como o dito di sopra a vostra Signoria.

                . . .

data In modena/a dì 4 di agosto 1502.
   el vostro servitore   Geronimo/da sestola dito Coia

Most Illustrious Master: This is to notify Your Lordship that I am asking you for a reward since Gian and the singers have all arrived at Modena safe and sound, and therefore I inform you that I want the reward,[62] and do not want to lose it, because I deserve it. Your Lordship has understood everything, and I only want to tell you that you have never heard better singing

[59] This is perhaps the singer Tommaso de Parixe (also called Tomaso de Fiandra) who was a bass in the chapel from 1499 through 1501 and probably also in 1502, a year for which a full roster is still lacking.

[60] This doubtless refers to a courtier named Socio di Bonlei, a member of the circle of roistering companions that surrounded Alfonso; see Catalano, *Vita di Ludovico Ariosto*, i, pp. 110f.

[61] This letter and the preceding one (Doc. 10) were obviously written on the same day, 4 August, and dispatched on 5 August from Modena. Coglia's evident purpose is to reach the Duke at one destination or another at the earliest possible moment; thus Doc. 10 is sent to wherever the Duke may be found by the courier, while Doc. 11 is sent to Milan.

[62] In old Italian *nunziatura* can mean advantage, gain (see P. Petrocchi, *Novo dizionario universale della lingua Italiana* (Milan, 1917), ii, p. 361).

in your life than from three sopranos like these.[63] And I commend myself to you as ever. As for Don Alfonso, he has accompanied the Duke of Romagna[64] as far as the Enza, and we have shown him honour at Ferrara and at Modena and at Reggio, and accompanied him as far as the Enza, as I have told Your Lordship above.

. . .

Written in Modena the 4th of August 1502.
   Your servant Geronimo/da Sestola called/Coia

Doc. 12   (ASM, Archivio per Materia, Musica e Musicisti B. 1)
Letter of 'Jan' to Duke Ercole I d'Este, dated Ferrara, 7 August 1502.
Original text: E. Vander Straeten, *La Musique aux Pays-bas*, vi, pp. 89–90 (the text as given by Vander Straeten has been compared with the original).
Translation:
To the Most Illustrious and Excellent Lord My Only Lord the Duke of Ferrara.
Most Illustrious and Honoured Lord: I have arrived here safely and have brought with me three singers who are excellent in this art, and they too have arrived safely. And it so happened that on account of this mission I was in great peril of my life, but this I did not mind at all in order to do what would please Your Excellency, as I am sure I have done. And if in any particular I may have displeased you, I beg you humbly to pardon me, for I do ask your forgiveness. I would gladly have come to pay homage to Your Lordship with these singers, but finding two of them to be ill, and knowing the difficulty of the journey and also of those places, it seemed better to come along later with them, and to do this office by means of this letter. Their indisposition was the reason for my lateness in arriving with them,

[63] Although the three sopranos are not named here or in later letters, the name of at least one can be deduced from Ferrarese lists of 1503 and from a list of singers at Savoy in 1502 that was kindly sent to me by Madame Marie-Thérèse Bouquet, of Torino, who has done extensive research on musicians at Savoy. This is Antonio Colombaudi, dicto Bidon, who was to join the Ferrara chapel and became one of the most celebrated vocal virtuosi of the first two decades of the century. From the list of singers at Savoy it is not yet clear who the other two singers were, although strong possibilities are 'Jannes Pezenin' and 'Masino', who are not in the Ferrara chapel in 1501 but do appear with Bidon in 1503.

[64] The Duke of Romagna is of course Cesare Borgia, son of Pope Alexander VI and, as of January 1502, brother-in-law of Alfonso d'Este. 1502 is the year of Cesare's third *impresa*, as his biographers call it: his military campaign of that year against Urbino and Camerino. After the fall of Camerino to his forces on 21 July 1502, Cesare set out for Milan where he was to meet Louis XII of France. His stop at Ferrara along the way is put at 28 July by his biographers, which would indicate in all probability the dates 27–29 July for the portion of his trip described by Coglia. See William Harrison Woodward, *Cesare Borgia* (London, 1913), p. 249, and Gustavo Sacerdote, *Cesare Borgia* (Milan, 1950), p. 514. The river Enza divides the territory of Reggio from that of Parma—the *Reggiano* from the *Parmense*.

having been held up on my journey for ten consecutive days. I have arranged that my lady, the Illustrious Madam Duchess,[65] should hear them sing, and they pleased Her Excellency so much that it is impossible to describe it. Greetings, etc. Ferrara, 7 August 1502.

Your Illustrious Lordship's/Most faithful servant/Jan

Doc. 13 (ASM, Archivio per Materia, Musica e Musicisti, B. 2) Letter of Bartolomeo Cantore (known as Bartolomeo de Fiandra) to Duke Ercole I d'Este, dated Ferrara, 13 August 1502.

Illustrissimo principe & Excellentissimo Signore mio. La excellentia vostra si può racordare che gia fano molti giorni: che Io pregai quella fusse contenta de concederme et darmi licentia, che Io potesse andare sino a Casa mia, per tri mesi, per alcune mie facende quale me importavano molto: per le cagione dixi a vostra Excellentia. Quella mi respose che la capella era male in ordene, & maxime de Contra alti, & che io expectasse che fornita che la fusse, vostra Signoria seria contenta concedermi licentia, che io potesse andare: hora, Illustrissimo signore mio, che la capella sua è meglio fornita che la fusse mai, & maxime de contra alti: di novo prego & supplico la vostra excellentia se voglia dignare concedermi licentia per tri mesi, ch'io possa andare & fare quanto me accade & è bisogno ch'io facia. Perchè piacendo a dio mi trovarò al termine al comspecto de la signoria vostra. ... Ferrarie xiij Augusti 1502.

Eiusdem Excellentie vestre fidelis servus Bartolomeus cantor

Most Illustrious Prince and Most Excellent Lord: Your Excellency may remember that many days ago I asked you to be kind enough to give me leave for three months, so that I could go home to take care of some important affairs of mine, for reasons that I explained to Your Excellency. You replied to me then that the chapel was in a poor state, mainly with regard to contraltos, and that I should wait, for as soon as it would be [better] supplied, Your Lordship would be glad to give me leave so that I could go. Now, Most Illustrious Lord, since the chapel is better staffed than ever before, and especially with contraltos, I ask once again and implore Your Excellency to give me leave for three months so that I can go and take care of my affairs, and it is necessary that I do so, so that, if it please God, at the end I shall once more be in Your Lordship's sight. Greetings, etc. Ferrara, 13 August 1502.

Your Excellency's faithful servant Bartolomeus cantore

[65] This can only refer to Lucrezia Borgia d'Este, who had married Alfonso in January of 1502 and had been in residence in Ferrara from February on. Ercole's wife, Eleonora d'Aragona, former Duchess of Ferrara, had died in 1493 and he had never remarried. Numerous documents show that Lucrezia was called 'la Duchessa' from the time of her marriage to Alfonso, the rightful heir to the Dukedom, even though three more years elapsed before Ercole's death and Alfonso's legal acquisition of the title.

Doc. 14 (ASM, Particolari, 'Coia, Girolamo')
Letter of Girolamo da Sestola to Duke Ercole I d'Este, dated Ferrara, 14 August 1502. (See Plates 10–11.)

Illustrissimo Signore patron mio: Io aviso vostra signoria como Io o gia paura de inspirtarme a oldire chantare quisti chantori e non vedo l'ora che vostra signoria vegna solo per che quela se li golderà in tanta consolatione che nol potria dire et in chapela e in chamara e como vorrà quela. E sono zovenj, de 25 ani el più vechio; li nostri chantori sono remasti stupefati e dichono bortelamio e don piero e li altri che mai non sente meio a la sua vita e che in [sic] ninchacha, merboneto e sandrechino si che per mi non vedo l'ora che vegnati solo per vedere vostra signoria e poi per che vedo el piasere che n'averiti e di continuo a Vostra signoria m'aricomando.

· · ·

Bortelamio chantore prega vostra signoria che sia contenta di darli licentia per tri misi de andare fina a chasa sua per che l'è gran tempo che'l non giè stato e che'l ad a fare asai là e che'l vole menare in za uno suo fratelo a stare a ferara e l'è forza che la signoria vostra gi la dia per che lui dise che la signoria vostra gi l'a promese si che el pare al signore don Alfonso che'l sia meio che vostra signoria gi la dia adeso che aspetare a un'altra volta per che la chapela è ben fornita di contralti e poi la signoria vostra si è fora e se la non si gi dese se[m]pre el seria in suso questa, e non staria mai contento e poi vostra signoria sa che'l a adeso quelo chasale a ferara che'l non giè più pericolo e che'l non staria che'l non tornase, si che la signoria vostra gi la po le dare.[66] Vostra signoria me fazi dare risposta de quelo che'l [h]a a fare perchè lui è in ordene e si s'a comperato za uno chavalo.

[page 2] Signore mio, Io credo che'l non sia Signore ni re che abia adeso la miore chapela di vostra signoria se vostra signoria manda per Ioschino, e don Alfonso el vole scrivere a vostra signoria e tuta la chapela; et abiendo Ioschino in la nostra chapela voio poi fare una corona a la dita nostra chapela. Lè rivato qui li dui soprani che a mandato vostra signoria, e uno altro è rivato chiamato baldisera, che se oldissi adeso la chapela fu uno bon oldire. ... A dì 14 di agosto 1502 data in ferara.

el vostro servitore Geronimo/da sestola dito coia

———

Most Illustrious Master:

I must tell Your Lordship that I am already in fear of being bewitched by hearing the singing of these singers, and I can hardly wait for Your Lordship's arrival because you will derive such enjoyment and consolation from them, not only in the chapel but in the chamber as well, and in any use you like. They are young men; the oldest is only 25 years of age, and

———

[66] For the correct reading of this passage I am indebted to Professor Edward Lowinsky.

our singers are astonished by them. Bartolomeo and Don Piero[67] and the others say that they have never heard better in their lives, not even Ninchacha, Merboneto, and Sandrechino,[68] so that for my part I can hardly wait for you to come here, only to see Your Lordship and then to see the pleasure you will take in them, and as ever I commend myself to you.

. . .

The singer Bartolomeo requests Your Lordship's consent to give him a three months' leave to go home, because he has not been there in a long time and he has a good deal to do there. He wants to bring a brother of his back to stay in Ferrara. Your Lordship is bound to give him permission because he says that Your Lordship promised it to him. Don Alfonso, too, thinks it would be better for Your Lordship to grant him leave now than to wait for another occasion because the chapel is well staffed with contraltos, and then too Your Lordship is now away. Also, if you were not to grant it to him now he would always be resentful about it and would never be content. Besides, Your Lordship knows that he now has that country house at Ferrara and there is no longer any danger that he would stay and not return, so that Your Lordship can indeed give him leave. I pray Your Lordship to give me an answer on what to do about it because he is all ready to go and has already bought a horse.

My Lord, I believe that there is neither lord nor king who will now have a better chapel than yours if Your Lordship sends for Josquin. Don Alfonso wishes to write this to Your Lordship and so does the entire chapel, and by having Josquin in our chapel I want to place a crown upon this chapel of ours.

There have arrived here the two singers sent by Your Lordship, and another one has arrived named Baldisera. If the chapel were to be heard now it would be worth hearing. Greetings, etc. Written in Ferrara the 14th of August 1502.

Your servant

Geronimo/da Sestola called Coia

[67] 'Bortelamio' is Bartolomeo de Fiandra; 'don Piero' is probably Don Piero Cariom, a *cappellano* and long-time singer in the chapel, who served from 1490 to at least 1505.

[68] Coglia's spelling and grammar are so eccentric that to translate even his factual statements is difficult enough; his rendering of names and nicknames is much harder. 'Ninchacha' (?), perhaps an indecorous nickname, is impossible to identify; 'Merboneto' is, I take it, a humorous and scurrilous corruption of 'Verbonneto', who may have been back with the Ferrara musicians at this time, even though he was not then a member of the chapel, as pointed out earlier. 'Sandrechino' is a name met with on more than one occasion; it may well be a diminutive of 'Alessandro', in which case it could refer here to Alexandro Demophonte (= Alexandro de Bologna) who is represented by a piece in Petrucci's Second Book of *Laude* in 1507 and was later a paid member of the retinue of Ippolito I.

Doc. 15   (ASM, Carteggio tra Principi Estensi, Ramo Ducale,
                   Principi Regnanti, B. 70/9, Doc. 1653–IV/24)
Excerpt from Letter of Alfonso d'Este to Duke Ercole d'Este, dated Ferrara,
25 August 1502.
... ho commisso al Coglia et a Gervase Cantore, che vengano a ritrovare
quella portando cum loro qualche canto novo. ...

I have given orders to Coglia and to the singer Gervase[69] to come to join
you, bringing with them some new music.

Doc. 16   (ASM, Carteggio tra Principi Estensi, Ramo Ducale,
                   Principi Regnanti, B. 70/9, Doc. 1653–IV/29)
Excerpt from letter of Alfonso d'Este to Duke Ercole I d'Este, dated
Ferrara, 1 September 1502 (to Duke at Reggio).
... Frate Zoanne soprano: Cantore de vostra signoria sta male; accadendo
il caso de la morte sua, recordo a vostra Excellentia che qua sono cantori
che hano bisogno che'l li sia facto provisione de beneficij. ... Ferrarie primo
Septembre 1502.

Fra Giovanni soprano, Your Lordship's singer, is ill. In the event of his
death, I remind Your Excellency that there are singers here who are in need
of having benefices conferred on them. Greetings, etc. Ferrara, 1 September
1502.

Doc. 17   (ASM, Archivio per Materia, Musica e Musicisti, B. 1)
Letter of 'Gian' to Duke Ercole d'Este, dated Ferrara, 2 September [1502].
Original text: Vander Straeten, op. cit., vi, pp. 87–8 (with a few slight
deviations from the spelling of the original document); the entire letter is
given in facsimile in *Die Musik in Geschichte und Gegenwart*, vii (1958),
Tafel 10, facing col. 194.
Translation of entire letter:
Most Illustrious Lord: I must notify Your Lordship that Isaac the singer has
been in Ferrara, and has written a motet on a fantasy entitled 'La mi la so
la so la mi' which is very good, and he wrote it in two days.[70] From this
one can only judge that he is very rapid in the art of composition; besides,
he is good-natured and easy to get along with, and it seems to me that he
is the right man for Your Lordship. Signor Don Alfonso bade me ask

---

[69] 'Gervase' is a court singer whose full name is 'Zoanne Vivas dito Gervase' who was
in service from at the latest 1493 and stayed until 1510. He is the writer of the 1499 letter
published by Gallico (see footnote 14).

[70] On Isaac's 'La mi la sol' composition, see Martin Just, 'Heinrich Isaacs Motetten in
italienischen Quellen', *Analecta Musicologica*, i (1963), pp. 1–19. Although Just's date for
this letter (1494–6) must be replaced by 1502, his discussion of the 'motet' remains valid.

13. View of Milan, c. 1480–90: in the centre the Cathedral under construction; at the extreme left the Ospedale Maggiore; at the extreme right the Castello Sforzesco. Sgraffito, Chapter Hall, Abbey of Chiaravalle. (p. 138)

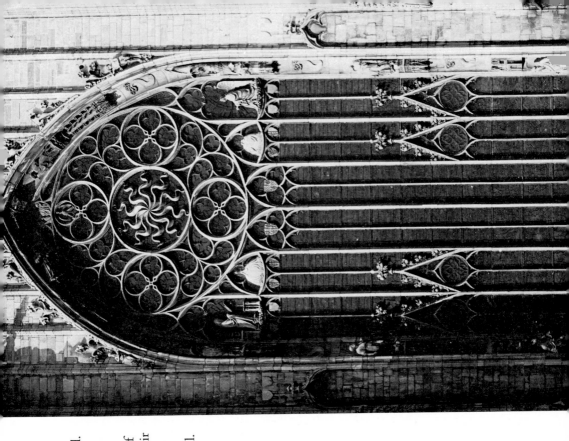

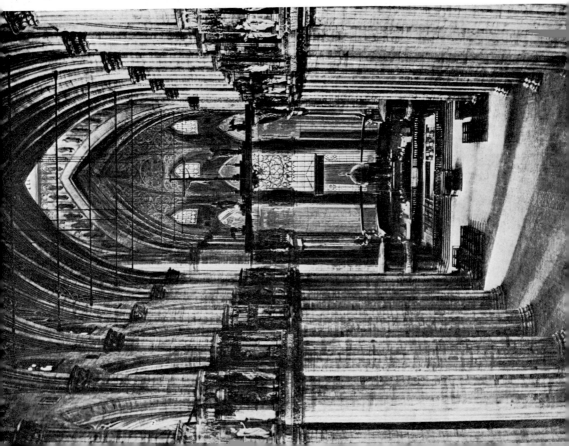

14a Interior, Milan Cathedral. (p. 138)

b. Upper portion of main choir window, Milan Cathedral. (p. 138)

15a. Crossing Tower, Abbey of Chiaravalle. (p. 139)

b. Bergognone: *Crucifixion*; detail showing the Certosa of Pavia under construction. Certosa di Pavia. (p. 139)

17. Workshop of the Zavattari: *Wedding Banquet of Queen Theodolinda*. Monza Cathedral. (p. 140)

16a. *A Ball Game*. Wall painting, Palazzo Borromeo, Milan. (p. 139)

b. *A Game of Tarot*. Wall painting, Palazzo Borromeo, Milan. (p. 139)

18. Masolino: *St. John before Herod*. Baptistry, Castiglione d'Olona. (p. 141)

19a. Masolino: *The Feast of Herod*. Baptistry,
Castiglione d'Olona. (p. 141)

b. Detail of 19a.

20. Bonifacio Bembo and Assistants: Painted Ceiling of the Chapel, Castello
Sforzesco, Milan. (p. 144)

21a. Benedetto Ferrini: The Chapel, Castello
Sforzesco, Milan. (p. 143)

b. Detail of Pl. 20.

22a. Filarete: Ospedale Maggiore, Milan. (p. 143)

b. Filarete and Others: The Cortile della Rocchetta, Castello Sforzesco, Milan. (p. 143)

23a. Portinari
Chapel, S.
Eustorgio,
Milan.
(p. 144)

b. Interior,
Portinari
Chapel, S.
Eustorgio,
Milan.
(p. 144)

25. Detail of Pl. 24b.

4a. Interior View of the Dome, Portinari
Chapel, S. Eustorgio, Milan. (p. 144)

b. Detail of above.

26. Vincenzo Foppa: *St. Peter Martyr and the Miraculous Healing of the Foot.* Portinari Chapel, S. Eustorgio, Milan, with perspective scheme, after Dalai. (p. 144)

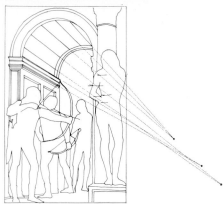

27. Vincenzo Foppa: *The Martyrdom of St. Sebastian*.
Brera Gallery, Milan, with perspective scheme,
after Dalai. (p. 145)

28. Butinone
and Zenale:
*Consecration of
St. Ambrose*
(detail).
Grifi Chapel,
S. Pietro in
Gessate,
Milan.
(p. 145)

him if he would like to join Your Lordship's service, and he replied that he would rather be in your service than in that of any other lord whom he knows, and that he does not reject the proposal; and he has taken the period of one month to reply as to whether he will serve or not. We have accepted that term for taking him into service (only in order to advise you about it) and we have promised him 10 ducats a month, provided that you approve, and we ask you if you will deign to let us know if you approve of this or not. To me he seems well suited to serve Your Lordship, more so than Josquin, because he is of a better disposition among his companions, and he will compose new works more often. It is true that Josquin composes better, but he composes when he wants to, and not when one wants him to, and he is asking 200 ducats in salary while Isaac will come for 120—but Your Lordship will decide.

Signor Don Alfonso has told me that Your Lordship has written to say that those two sopranos are to be dismissed. May I advise you that one [of them] is good and very suitable, and today another one named Coletta arrived from the Kingdom of Naples [de lo reame]. And I hear from him and from others that Your Lordship has sent as far as Naples for a certain Frate Felice, who is not suitable for Your Lordship because he has lost a good deal of his voice in the past few months and doesn't sing accurately.[71] So we will try out this Coletta and one of the two singers mentioned before, and we beg Your Lordship to tell us what you want done. I believe that news has reached Your Lordship that Fra Giovanni, the soprano, is on his deathbed, and if the Lord takes him, it would be well to put one of these in his place. To conclude briefly, Your Lordship is advised that those two whom you sent and this Coletta would be good to keep and suited to your service, when Your Lordship wishes to dismiss those [others] who would be of no use to you. Greetings, etc. Ferrara, 2 September.

Your Illustrious Lordship's Most Humble Servant   Gian

Doc. 22   (ASM, Arch. Segr. Estense, Cancelleria, Estero,
Ambasciatori, Francia, B. 3, Filza IX minute di
Lettere a Bartolomeo Cavalieri, 1500–1505)

Minute of ducal letter to Bartolomeo de' Cavalieri, dated 28 April 1503.
Commendemovi de li libri & farse che haveti date al Coia, se bene anchora non li habiamo havuti, per haverli lui lassati a [lione che siano mandati cum altre robe.] (Joschino cantore che veniva dreto cum piu comodità che non veniva lui, Il quale) [*preceding words in parentheses crossed out in original; preceding words in brackets added in original*]. Joschino cantore non è anchor gionto qua, ma de hora in hora lo expectamo cum desiderio; attento che

---

[71] On Coletta see Document 18; Vander Straeten surmised correctly that 'de lo Reame' meant Naples. Despite Gian's opinion, Fra Felice da Nola was taken into the chapel and remained a member through 1503 and down to 1505.

per la celerità che usate [?] il coglia in venire, il lassete drieto, aciò il venisse più comodamente.

Cussì etiam vi laudemo de la Instantia che fareti per vedere de fare che habiamo quella messa che vi ha promesso la Maestà Christianissima de farne fare. Sollicitati de haverla & mandaticela, che la mi serà gratissima.

We commend you for the books and plays which you have given to Coglia, even if we have not yet received them, since he left them at Lyons to be sent on with other things. Josquin the singer is not yet here, but we are looking forward to his arrival from hour to hour with keen anticipation. Because of the rapidity of Coglia's journey here, he left him behind, so that he might come at a more comfortable pace.

Thus we shall also praise you for your troubles in seeing that we receive that Mass which the Most Christian Majesty has promised you to have made. Hasten to procure it and send it to me, for it will please me very much.

Doc. 23   (ASM, Arch. Segr. Estense, Cancelleria, Estero,
                    Ambasciatori, Venezia, B. 11, Doc. 69–V/20)
Letter of Bartolomeo Cartari, Ferrarese ambassador at Venice, to Duke Ercole I d'Este, dated Venice, 27 January 1504. (See Plate 12.)
... Zo. Carolo da li orlogij, quale sta qui a l'opera de lo orologio che ha facto a questa Signoria, me dice che è uno cantore qui che ha facto questa opera alligata: la quale dice sia[72] tenuta una cosa per excelentia e me ha pregato la mandi a vostra celsitudine aciò e per farla cantare a quelli soi cantori & per farla vedere a quello suo cantore chiamato messer Iosquino excellentissimo compositore veda Se 'l hè cosa che merita laude: per che quando vostra excellentia la Iudichi como vero musicho che la è, essere bona cosa: operirà che quella averà da quello tale compositore o cantore altre digne cose come ciò: Cusì la mando a Vostra Illustrissima aciò pigliandone piacere la ni possa fare quello Iuditio le parerà: E dice che tale non vole nominare che el sia, se prima non intende l'opera essere piaciuta a vostra celsitudine. ... Venecii 27 Jan. 1504.

E. Ill. du. do. V.   Servus Bartolomeus de Cartariis

Giovanni Carolo, the watchmaker, who is operating [or repairing?] the clockwork here that he has made for this Signoria, tells me that a singer here has written the work that is enclosed with this letter. He says that it is considered an excellent work, and has asked me to send it to Your Excellency, both to have it sung by your singers, and to have it looked over by that singer of yours named messer Josquino, the most excellent composer, to see if it is praiseworthy. For if Your Excellency judges it to be a good work, as the true musician that you are, he will undertake to let you have other

[72] The original looks like 'fi'.

worthy compositions like this one by that same composer or singer. For this reason I am sending it to Your Illustrious Lordship so that if it gives you pleasure you can give me your opinion about it. He says that the composer does not wish to reveal his identity until he knows that his work is pleasing to Your Excellency. Greetings, etc. Venice, 27 January 1504.

Your Illustrious Lordship's

Servant Bartolomeo de Cartariis

Doc. 24 (ASM. Arch. Segr. Estense, Cancelleria, Estero, Ambasciatori, Venezia, B. 11, Doc. 69–V/55)

Letter of Bartolomeo Cartari to Duke Ercole I d'Este, dated Venice, 29 April 1504.

Illustrissimo Signor mio: Quello che mandò el patrem a questi zorni passati a vostra excellentia intendendo che quella vostra [signoria] volentera tuta la messa: me n'a dato questo placheto, quale manda a vostra celsitudine per farli cosa che li p[iacerà] et per aquistare la gratia soa: Et hò vogliuto cognoscere questo tale: e trovo che è uno fratello di sam zohane e polo, del ordine de li conventuali de san domenico, zoveneto de XX anni, el quale in queste cose è tenuto uno mirabile zovene, chiamasse fra Iordano da vinexia. Prega vostra excellentia che li mandi uno tenore de che sorte la vole, per che li farà qualche bello canto sopra; l'ho facto tuto mio per el mezo de zoanne carolo da regio: solo per questa cusì bella e degna virtù [?] che la hà: e desidera molto di satisfare in qualche parte a vostra celsitudine. . . .

Venetii penultime aprilis 1504

E. Ill. D. V.

Servus Bartolomeus de Cartariis

Most Illustrious Lord: The person who sent the 'Patrem' to Your Excellency some days ago, on learning that Your Lordship would like to have the entire Mass, has given me this packet which I am sending to Your Lordship, in order to give you pleasure and to obtain your good graces. I have sought to find out who this person is, and I find that he is a friar of San Giovanni e Paolo, a conventual of the Order of San Domenico, a young man of twenty years of age, named Fra Giordano de Venezia, who is considered very gifted in these things.

He requests Your Excellency to send him a tenor of whatever kind you like, and he will write a beautiful counterpoint over it. I have acquired his friendship through Giovanni Carolo da Reggio, solely because of this excellent and fine gift which he has; he greatly desires to please Your Excellency in every way. . . . Venice, the penultimate day of April 1504.

Your Illustrious Lordship's

Servant Bartolomeus de Cartariis

Doc. 25   (ASM, Cancelleria Ducale, Minutario Cronologico, B. 5, 1504)

Ducal Minute of 17 May 1504, addressed to Alfonso d'Este.

...Preterea perchè havemo pur bisogno de Cantori per la capella nostra, & voluntieri voressimo uno bono Tenorista alto, dui contra alti boni, uno contrabasso bono, & dui soprani boni. Et intendendo che in li lochi che vedrite in la Inclusa pollice, ge ne sono, & le nomi gli sono notati, parme che habiati ad usare ogni diligentia per vedere se dicti Cantori sono boni & optimi & quelli che trovareti che siano boni & excellenti, li condureti in qua, ma non volemo cantori che non siano in perfectione. Et questa nota che ve mandamo ce l'ha data bartholomio de fiandra nostro cantore. Siche vedete mo d'usar circa ciò bona diligentia.

Ferrarie 17 Maij 1504.

————

Moreover, since we still have need of singers for our chapel, and we would gladly have a good high tenor, two good contraltos, a good contrabasso, and two good sopranos. And since we understand that there are such singers in the places you will see in the enclosed orders, and since the names are given, you should use every effort to see whether these singers are good and able, and those whom you find really excellent you will bring here. But we do not want singers who are not perfect. And the enclosed note which we send you was given to us by Bartolomeo de Fiandra, our singer.[73] Thus you will use all possible diligence in this matter.

Ferrara, 17 May 1504.

[73] The note of Bartolomeo de Fiandra (published by Vander Straeten, op. cit., vi, pp. 73–4) lists the names of the singers and their places of work. The latter are the Cathedral of Antwerp (6), the Cathedral of Thérouanne (2), and the Church of Notre Dame in Bruges (1). The note is preserved in ASM, Archivio Segr. Est., Archivio per Materia, Musica e Musicisti, B. 2. See my article, 'Messer Gossino and Josquin Desprez' in *Studies in Renaissance and Baroque Music in Honor of Arthur Mendel*, ed. Robert Marshall (Kassel and Hackensack, 1974).

Footnotes to Appendix III

[74] The present and the preceding figures add up to 51.13.4, that is, one month's salary.

[75] Mixi = mesi (months).

[76] Half this amount constitutes Josquin's regular salary; the remainder seems to be a special payment, perhaps a New Year's gift, since it is not included in the yearly summary.

[77] Mese = messa (Mass).

Appendix III

Some Extracts from Ferrarese Court Payment Registers, 1503–4

Payments to Josquin, 1503–4

Source	Date	Recipient	Reason	Amount
ASM, Archivio della Camera Ducale, Memoriale del Soldo, 1503 (= Reg. 4908/97)	fol. 77ᵛ	G. da Sestola dicto Coglia 'Juschino Cantore'	His expenses in France during February [1503]	L. 155.0.0
	77ᵛ		Part of salary, begun as of March 1503 (to repay Coglia)	114.14.0
	85	'Juschino Cantore'	To repay Coglia money advanced to him in Ferrara	40.6.0
	92ᵛ	'm. Juschim Cantore'	'per tanta roba li avea comprato'	7.5.0
	99ᵛ	'm. Juschino mᵒ de capella'	Salary [at head of list of singers]	51.13.0
	112	Girolamo Beltrandi	'per tanto a fato pagare per lui a m. Juschino cantore...'	7.5.0
	119ᵛ	'm. Juschino Cantore'	Salary [at head of list of singers]	44.8.4[74]
	121ᵛ	'm. Juschino',	Salary [at head of list of singers]	51.13.4
	129ᵛ	'm. Juschino',	Salary [at head of list of singers]	51.13.4
	137ᵛ	'm. Juschino',	'm. Juschino porto don Girolimo de la Frassina'	51.13.4
	166ᵛ	'm. Juschino'.	'm. Juschino cantore per mixi[75] 10 in ragione de ducati 200 d'oro Largo l'anno... per deti mixi 10 a L.51.13.4...al mexe'	516.13.4
ASM, Archivio della Camera Ducale, Memoriale del Soldo, 1504 (= Reg. 4910/97)	4ᵛ	'm. Juschino'	Salary [at head of list of singers]	103.6.8[76]
[Murray, MQ 1957, p. 516]	25	'm. Juschino'	Salary [at head of list of singers]	51.13.4
[Murray, MQ 1957, p. 516]	31	'm. Juschino',	Salary [at head of list of singers]	51.13.4
	52ᵛ	'm. Juschino',	Salary [at head of list of singers]	51.13.4
	61	'm. Juschino',	Salary	51.13.4
	212	'm. Juschino'	m. Juschino Cantore per la sua provisione de mixi quatro de l'ano prexente in ragione de doxento ducati Largo l'ano'	206.13.4
ASM, Archivio della Camera Ducale, Libri d'Amministrazione dei Singoli Principi, No. 35 (= Reg. 6715/130)	34ᵛ	'Juschim Francese'	[Payment from Alfonso d'Este to Josquin]	62.0.0
	40ᵛ		'... al Capelano de li frati de li capuzoli per haver notado una mese[77] che feze Juschi[no] cantore'	0.18.0

Art and Architecture in Lombardy at the Time of Josquin des Prez*

MARIA LUISA GATTI PERER

In what kind of artistic environment did Josquin des Prez spend his most impressionable years? In what way might he, as an individual and as a composer, have been influenced, consciously or not, by visual experiences? This is the question I should like to try to answer. As we all know, Josquin lived in Milan from 1459 to at least 1479, and possibly returned there in later years, even as late as 1487–89.[1] We must, then, ask first of all what the condition of the visual arts in Milan was during those decades. And this means, in essence, that we must focus our attention on those works that reflect the spirit of Milanese humanism, a development that began in 1435 with the frescoes of Masolino in Castiglione Olona, continued in the 1450s with Filarete's work on the Ospedale Maggiore and the Castello, and reached a high point in 1468 with the Portinari Chapel by Vincenzo Foppa.

What did Milan look like at that time? A sgraffito in the Abbey of Chiaravalle, dating from the 1480s, may serve to convey a general impression (Pl. 13). The plan of the city as a whole is still medieval. In the centre rises the imposing mass of the Cathedral, still under construction (Pl. 14); the dome over the crossing has already been started. On the left, we see the Castello with Filarete's tower, and on the right, off by itself, the splendid new Ospedale Maggiore.[2] This novel and ambitious structure, referred to in 1463 as 'the hospital, marvellous to behold, now rising in our city', must have given a new aspect to Milan.[3] A few years earlier, its architect had been warmly commended by the Duke to the Fabbrica (i.e., the architectural supervisors) of the Cathedral, but they soon discharged him

---

* Professor H. W. Janson of New York University revised the English text of this paper, planned the distribution of the plates, and, in the absence of the author due to illness, read the paper at the Conference. Author and Editor are deeply indebted to him.

[1] Edward E. Lowinsky, 'Josquin des Prez and Ascanio Sforza', *Congresso Internazionale sul Duomo di Milano' Atti'* ed. M. L. Gatti Perer (Milan, 1877), pp. 17–22, and above, p. 61.

[2] *Annali della Fabbrica del Duomo di Milano*, ii (Milan, 1969), ii pp. 198–9; Papal bull of 28 February 1460, concerning indulgences in the Cathedral and the 'new hospital'.

[3] Ibid., pp. 219–30: Ducal letter of 31 January concerning the publication of the indulgence granted by Pius II.

on the grounds that 'the Fabbrica doesn't need him'.[4] Evidently, not all opinions in Milan approved of the new Renaissance style imported into the city by Filarete.

Josquin, during the early years of his activity at the Cathedral of Milan, must have witnessed the tearing down of the Early Christian church of St. Tecla, in front of the new building, and we wonder whether this demolition struck him as a sign of changing times.[5] Moreover, the whole area around the Cathedral must have resembled a building yard, since the new Archbishop's Palace was also under construction then. A little farther away, much work was being done on the Castello. The Ducal Chapel, built by the Tuscan architect Benedetto Ferrini in 1472 and consecrated a year later (Pl. 21, fig. b), would have been barely finished at the time when Josquin left the choir of the Cathedral and entered the service of the Duke.

Among finished buildings around Milan which Josquin must have seen was the Abbey of Chiaravalle, the product of an earlier era, yet witness to a local tradition that had always tended toward variations of rhythm and space. Its tall crossing tower so impressed the Milanese that it became the model for the crossing tower of the Cathedral (Pl. 15, fig. a).[6] Chiaravalle, furthermore, was linked with Josquin's patron, Cardinal Ascanio Sforza, who in 1465 became one of its prebendaries. Another famous monastery, the Certosa of Pavia, was still under construction in Josquin's day (Pl. 15, fig. b), as was the Certosa of Garegnano.

In Milan proper, the Palace of the Borromeo family to this day bears witness to the life of the aristocracy around the middle years of the fifteenth century. Its frescoes showing a ball game and card players depict the life of a noble family simply and soberly, yet with an air of elegant formality (Pl. 16). These are everyday scenes, but the gestures are slow and deliberate, and each figure is oddly isolated from the rest, so that the game seems less an amusement than a ritual. The painter, whoever he was—possibly Pisanello, according to a recent attribution—was sensitive to everyday life but viewed it in a poetic key, suggesting the contrast between these pleasurable pastimes and the solemnity of the participants.[7] He was, in

[4] Ibid., p. 153, 5 July 1454. Filarete had been engaged as the master architect of the Fabbrica at the repeated urging of the Duke, who had proposed both Filarete and Giovanni da Solari.

[5] On 11 January 1461 a commission was appointed to demolish the church. On 27 May 1462 it decided to have the choir torn down. By 17 October 1462 the building had already disappeared (ibid., pp. 204, 214, and 216).

[6] M. L. Gatti Perer, 'Appunti per l'attribuzione di un disegno della Raccolta Ferrari. Giovannino de' Grassi e il Duomo di Milano', *Arte Lombarda*, x (1965), pp. 49–64. As late as the eighteenth century the tower of Chiaravalle was still recommended as the model for the spire of the Cathedral; cf. M. L. Gatti Perer, *Carlo Giuseppe Merlo architetto* (Milan, 1966), pp. 375–6, documents 114 and 118.

[7] See Giuseppe Consoli, *I Giuochi Borromeo ed il Pisanello* (Milan, 1966), who dates them prior to 1444.

any event, a modern artist, if by 'modern' we mean not only the conquest of pictorial space but also of man's psychological essence, his varying response to the challenges of life, the subtle melancholy engendered in him by the evanescent quality of all experience. Thus, in Milan, the Borromeo frescoes stand on the borderline of Gothic and Renaissance; they set a precedent for capturing the existential reality of human life with an accent on its secret sorrows rather than its heroic aspects.

Nearby, in the Cathedral of Monza, Josquin must have seen the fresco cycle in the Chapel of Queen Theodolinda, commissioned by Filippo Maria Visconti, as has recently been shown (Pl. 17).[8] That Filippo was the patron confirms my conviction that the real purpose of the cycle was to pay homage to the court of the Visconti by recounting, in fairytale style, the legend of Theodolinda, as if the whole were a kind of stage production dedicated to the early Lombard queen. Hence the frail architectural frame of the various scenes, which recalls the workshop of Milan Cathedral (and let us not forget that the Cathedral, too, was closely linked with the Duke's family). One scene, the wedding banquet of Theodolinda and Agilulf, is of particular interest for students of music. We have here, I believe, a rare view of an instrumental and vocal ensemble like those that enlivened the banquets of Filippo Maria Visconti. In the upper left-hand corner, we see a trumpet player (perhaps the maestro), and nearby a group of boys playing a trumpet, a vielle, and a portative organ. Music historians will be able to give a more precise definition of these instruments. Three other boys, although without instruments, form part of the same ensemble, as indicated by the fact that all the boys wear the same costume and have wreaths on their heads. They are approaching the table in order to help themselves to the sweetmeats (the boy on the right is putting one in his mouth). They are probably singers, and the scene shows a pause between two musical numbers. The old woman whom we see peeping in on the extreme left is supervising the boys. Evidently, then, we have here a group of choirboys playing and singing under the direction of a music master. The solemn wedding banquet thus assumes a more domestic flavour, with affectionate attention paid to the boys and their taste for sweets.

Further on, the Queen is shown supervising the building of the new basilica. As in the banquet scene, her presence does not interrupt the action; masons and goldsmiths go right on with their labours, and the painter seems more interested in their work than in the Queen. If I may return for a moment to my comparison with the stage, everyone participates in the show.

[8] Franco Mazzini, *Affreschi lombardi del Quattrocento* (Milan, 1955), p. 432. It was Augusto Merati who identified the monograms 'fi' and 'ma' flanking the Visconti arms above and below the windows of the Chapel as referring to Filippo Maria Visconti, Duke of Milan from 1412 to 1447.

Perhaps Josquin, during his stay in Milan, visited Castiglione Olona, not far distant. Cardinal Branda had wanted to transform that place into a kind of ideal town, and had brought Masolino with him from Rome for that purpose in 1435. A recent study by Dr. Wakayama has shown that Masolino had full command of the rules of linear perspective and applied them in his Baptistry frescoes with certain deliberate modifications in order to enlarge the space at his disposal (Pls. 18–19).[9] Dr. Wakayama also suggests that Masolino may have known Alberti's treatise on painting and applied some of its rules in the Baptistry frescoes. Moreover, according to the same author, some of the figures in these frescoes represent members of the Cardinal's entourage or individuals with whom the Cardinal had diplomatic dealings. All this leads us to the conclusion that the Baptistry frescoes are indeed the earliest instance of Renaissance art on Lombard soil. But the new style achieves a distinctly different flavour here; the rules of linear perspective are not applied in the abstract but adjusted to the demands of the specific space—that of a small chapel—in which the artist had to work, as well as to his desire to have the *dramatis personae* move freely in the various scenes depicted. This is true especially of the *Feast of Herod*; but even in the badly damaged *Naming of St. John the Baptist* the figures are distributed within the perspective scheme in such a way as to emphasize their rhythmic movements rather than in conformity with a unified conception of pictorial space.

In Masolino's frescoes in the Collegiata at Castiglione Olona, which I regard as later than those in the Baptistry, the architectural setting is again subordinate to the figure composition.[10] In the *Betrothal of the Virgin*, there is a harmonious relationship among the arcades on the first and second floors of the fantastic temple behind the figures; the upward thrust culminating in a pointed pinnacle recalls the tower of Chiaravalle and its significance as a symbol of the Virgin's virtues—the *turris davidica*.[11]

[9] Maria Lucia Eiko Wakayama, '"Novità" di Masolino a Castiglione Olona', *Arte Lombarda*, xvi (1971), pp. 1–16.

[10] See note 9 and the same author's doctoral thesis, 'Nuovi apporti all'iconografia nella Lombardia del primo Quattrocento—Masolino da Panicale a Castiglione Olona' (Università Cattolica, Milan, 1969–70).

[11] For this interpretation, which needs to be further documented, see Maria Luisa Gatti Perer, 'Abbazia di Chiaravalle', *Studi e ricerche nel territorio della Provincia di Milano* (Milan, 1967), pp. 122–8. An interesting passage from St. Bernard of Clairvaux, the founder of the Abbey, for which I am indebted to Dr. Laura Gavazzoli, also has a bearing on our problem: '...Aut si id magis probas, dicemus has cavernas a studiosis et piis mentibus non inveniri, sed fieri. Quonam, inquis? Cogitatione et aviditate. Cedit nempe in modum materiale mollioris pia maceries desiderio animae, cedit purae contemplationi, cedit crebrae orationi. Denique *ORATIO JUSTI PENETRAT CAELOS*. Non utique aeris huius corporei spatiosas altitudines, veluti quodam remigio alarum suarum instar volucris volantis scindet, aut *quasi gladius acutus ipsius firmamenti solidum celsumque verticem perforabit* [italics added]; sed sunt caeli sancti, vivi, rationabiles, qui enarrant gloriam Dei, qui favorabili quadam

Castiglione Olona to this day retains an Early Renaissance flavour such as Milan must also have had in Josquin's time. The palaces—especially the Branda Palace—the courtyards, the streets have a sense of measure that is hard to find anywhere else in Lombardy. The Chiesa di Villa, and especially its façade portal, are very classical in style, recalling the Pazzi Chapel by Brunelleschi. The wall surfaces, however, are subdivided by pilaster strips that are spaced differently on the facade and on the flank, so as to provide a harmonious view of the structure from any angle (the façade faces a small square while the flank faces a narrow street).

This same church also contains some fine Early Renaissance sculpture: an *Annunciation* accompanied by the *Four Latin Fathers*, Augustine, Jerome, Gregory, and Ambrose, suggesting a kind of *Sacra Conversazione*. They, too, might have been seen by Josquin. These figures bring to mind the far more ambitious series of saints and prophets that was started at Milan Cathedral during the latter half of the fifteenth century, in accordance with an iconographic program laid down at the time the building was founded; the plan was tampered with so often that no trace of it remains today.[12] The Early Renaissance, then, appears at Castiglione Olona—as often happens in a small town dominated by a single enlightened patron (one thinks of Pienza and Pope Pius II)—without the difficulties and contradictions that delayed the birth of the new art in Milan proper, where the large and conservative Cathedral workshop was surely an inhibiting factor. Yet Milan, too, had houses of classic design articulated by cornices and reliefs in moulded brick, as evidenced by some architectural remains preserved in the Castello Sforzesco, by some courtyards such as that on Via Sant'Antonio and others that still exist in the neighbourhood of Via Torino, and by the Palazzo Silvestri, which, however, dates from the last decades of the fifteenth century. Unfortunately, the rebuilding of the city, which began under Napoleon in the heyday of Neoclassicism, was carried forward with little regard for Early Renaissance structures. Almost everything of the kind was torn down, such as the so-called 'coperto dei Figini', a covered arcade, which had to give way to the present entrances of the Cathedral Square, and the arcade of the Pozzobonella, sacrificed not long ago because it blocked the present Via Andrea Doria beside the Central Railway Station. It was through the construction of the Ospedale Maggiore, on which

---

pietate nostris se votis libenter inclinant, et sinuatis ad tactum nostrae devotionis affectibus in sua nos recipiunt viscera, quoties digna ad eos intentione pulsamus', *Sermones super Cantica Canticorum*, lxii, ii 2; *S. Bernardi Opera*, ii, ed. J. Leclercq, C. H. Talbot, H. M. Rochais (Rome, 1958), p. 155. Bernard's verbal image of prayer as a sharp sword piercing the zenith—see the passages in italics—suggests that the symbolic meaning of the tower of Chiaravalle to which I have referred is entirely within the realm of possibility.

12 M. L. Gatti Perer, 'Ipotesi iconografiche per il Duomo di Milano', *Congresso Internazionale sul Duomo di Milano*, i, pp. 1–29.

Filarete worked from 1457 to 1465, that Francesco Sforza introduced the new architectural style in Milan. The same realistic attitude that is reflected in the sober dimensions of Milanese private houses here produced a structure of extraordinary complexity to serve the citizenry as a whole. The functionalism of the Ospedale Maggiore is unique in all Italy for its time. It was so well planned, in fact, that it could be used as a hospital almost until today.[13] Although it took two centuries to complete the building, the original plan was followed throughout. In the portion actually built by Filarete, facing toward the apse of the church of S. Nazaro, the architect's classicism is evidenced by the colonnade, which rests on a tall basement (Pl. 22, fig. a). Filarete's treatise on architecture, written during these years, may well reflect the conversations and arguments between the architect and his patron, the Duke.[14] And the citizens, too, probably found architecture an exciting topic to talk about at this time when most of Milan, from the Cathedral to the Castello, resembled one huge construction site. Perhaps they tried to imagine the new look their city would have once the scaffoldings came down.

While the Ospedale Maggiore is Filarete's main achievement in Milan, it is not his only one. To the Castello Sforzesco he added the great tower, strikingly illustrated in another sgraffito at Chiaravalle; and I believe that he may well have had a share in executing the large and finely proportioned Cortile della Rocchetta in the Castello, which so far has not received the attention it deserves as one of the most important Early Renaissance monuments in Milan (Pl. 22, fig. b).

Among the more recent works which Josquin would have had occasion to admire was the Ducal Chapel, which Galeazzo Maria Sforza decided to erect in 1472 at the end of the long hall that occupied the ground floor on the northwest side of the Ducal courtyard (Pl. 21, fig. a). Its design, by the Tuscan architect Benedetto Ferrini, has a vaulted ceiling with groins resting on graceful corbels. The decoration was entrusted to a team of painters headed by Bonifacio Bembo, who completed it between 1473 and

---

[13] See Philip Foster, 'Per il disegno dell' Ospedale di Milano', *Arte Lombarda*, xviii (1973), pp. 1–22. Only after World War II did the Ospedale Maggiore cease to serve as a hospital. Today it houses the State University. For the changes necessitated by its new purpose, and the early steps in the process of restoration (which is still going on), see Liliana Grassi, 'Aspetti nuovi dell'antico Ospedale Maggiore sistemato ad uso dell'Università di Milano', *Arte Lombarda*, i (1955–6), pp. 136–45.

[14] For the date of the treatise see John R. Spencer, 'La datazione del trattato del Filarete desunta dal suo esame interno', *Rivista d'arte*, xxxi (1956; published 1958), pp. 93–103. The text is now available in Spencer's beautiful facsimile edition, *Filarete's Treatise on Architecture* (Yale Publications in the History of Art, 16; New Haven and London, 1965). More recently, the text has been published in a sumptuous two-volume work by Anna Maria Finoli and Liliana Grassi, *Antonio Averlino detto Il Filarete, Trattato di Architettura* (Milan, 1972).

1474.[15] These are the years when Josquin was in the service of the Duke. The walls of the chapel are covered with a long series of saints, starting about five feet above the floor, while the ceiling shows the Resurrection and God the Father surrounded by music-making angels (Pls. 20–21).

During those years Pigello Portinari, the manager of the Medici Bank in Milan, built an impressive palazzo for himself. One richly carved portal, now in the Museum of the Castello Sforzesco, survives today of this splendid structure. An even more important achievement of Portinari as an art patron is the Chapel of St. Peter Martyr in S. Eustorgio, commonly known as the Portinari Chapel, which he had built in 1462–6. Two years later, the Chapel was finished, including the rich interior decoration—surely a topic of unending conversation among the Milanese citizenry (Pl. 23, fig. a). By a miracle, it has survived completely intact. Whoever designed it, the Portinari Chapel, with its complete harmony of interior and exterior, its integration of architecture, sculpture, and painting, is the most striking example of an Early Renaissance monument of specifically Milanese character.[16]

The fresco decoration, by Vincenzo Foppa, is a perfect match for the delicately carved pilasters, arches, and window frames of the interior (Pl. 23, fig. b). Let us note especially how the abstract geometric relationship between the dome and the space cube beneath is transformed and given life by the frieze of dancing angels, who perform their rhythmic movements against a background of arches—arches that are an integral part of both the angel frieze and the architecture of the chapel (Pls. 24–25).

Let us now have a look at the frescoes showing events from the life of St. Peter Martyr. Their wealth of perspective vistas in every scene is carefully calculated to relate each miraculous event to the familiar reality of everyday life—a style of pictorial narrative found at that time only in Milan. In the scene of *St. Peter Martyr Preaching*, for instance, there is a large arched opening in the middle ground that lets us see the full length of the street outside and at the same time admits light and air into the church. The listening crowd is partly indoors, partly outdoors. As the ecstatic Saint raises his eyes heavenward, two merchants in the lower left-hand corner are engaged in a lively conversation of their own, and a woman in the audience suddenly turns her head in alarm because somebody is stepping on her dress. A similar perspective view linking indoors and outdoors may be seen in the *Miraculous Healing of the Foot* (Pl. 26); a child on a staircase overlooking the scene gazes at the drama below as if it were an everyday event. Much the same approach may be found in Foppa's

[15] Stella Matalon and Franco Mazzini, *Affreschi del Trecento e Quattrocento in Lombardia* (Milan, 1958).

[16] Recent scholarship has been unable to agree on the problem of attribution; cf. R. Cipriani, *La Cappella Portinari in Sant' Eustorgio a Milano* (Milan, 1963).

other works, such as the *Martyrdom of St. Sebastian* in the Castello Sforzesco or the fresco of the same subject in the Brera (Pl. 27).

Among the most interesting followers of Foppa is the painter and architect Zenale, who collaborated with Butinone on several important works such as the Treviglio Altar of 1485. Here he demonstrates not only his delicate sense of light and colour but a highly individual and flexible way of relating the figures to their architectural surroundings. *St. Martin Dividing his Cloak*, where the figures are squeezed into the narrow space of a receding arcade, is a good example. So is the *Consecration of St. Ambrose* among the frescoes in the Grifi Chapel of S. Pietro in Gessate, painted between 1489 and 1493, where the church in the background—an ideal Renaissance structure of vast size—serves both to balance the procession in the foreground and to stress the symbolic importance of the consecration of the great Milanese bishop (Pl. 28). Finally, in *St. Ambrose at the Battle of Parabiago*, the Saint dressed in white on his white charger, weightlessly galloping through the clouds, has all the qualities of a sudden, miraculous vision.[17]

Foppa and Zenale confirm our earlier claim that pictorial perspective in Lombard painting has a distinctive character that differentiates it from its Florentine antecedents.[18] What used to be considered 'perspective errors', even in the work of Foppa, has now come to be recognized as 'sensitive departures from perspective theory for the sake of optical realism—a respect for direct visual experience that remained undiminished throughout the development of Lombard Renaissance painting'.[19] Foppa's realism led him to avoid the central vanishing point demanded by the ideal space of scientific perspective. Yet this does not obstruct his pictorial space but rather modulates it in terms of depth, modelling, and light.

Foppa may well have learned the rules of geometric perspective directly from Filarete at the time when both were employed on the same sites—first the Cathedral, then the Ospedale Maggiore—but if so, he interpreted them

[17] For the iconography, see my book, *La chiesa e il convento di S. Ambrogio della Vittoria a Parabiago* (Milan, 1966), pp. 1–8.

[18] Critical opinion of Renaissance perspective has undergone a considerable process of revision in recent years, thanks to the pioneer work of Panofsky, which shows that throughout the Quattrocento the development of perspective must be viewed as 'work in progress' determined as much by pragmatic as by theoretical considerations. See Erwin Panofsky, 'Die Perspektive als symbolische Form', *Vorträge der Bibliothek Warburg, 1924–1925* (Leipzig and Berlin, 1927); *The Codex Huygens and Leonardo da Vinci's Art Theory* (*Studies of the Warburg Institute*, xiii; London, 1940); *Early Netherlandish Painting* (Cambridge, Mass., 1953), pp. 1–20; *Renaissance and Renascences in Western Art* (Stockholm, 1960), pp. 118–45.

[19] Marisa Dalai Emiliani, 'Per la prospettiva "padana": Foppa rivisitato', *Arte Lombarda*, xvi (1971), pp. 117–36.

in a free and independent way.[20] To him, perspective no longer means an ideal space of absolute precision and clarity but a means for extending pictorial reality beyond the confines of the actual space at his disposal. His illusionism, unlike that of Mantegna, aims at truth rather than grandeur, and he does not hesitate to break the rules if this serves his purpose. Thus pictorial space ceases to be a geometric abstraction and becomes personalized and flexible, responding as it were to the human events that take place within it. In his most luminous works, the frescoes of the Portinari Chapel, Foppa struggles to overcome the theoretical assumptions of scientific perspective and to project a reality that is more flexible and for that very reason more interesting. Multiple vanishing points endow this reality with qualities of surprise and novelty, charging it with unforeseen currents of feeling.[21]

I like to think that Josquin spent long hours before the frescoes of the Portinari Chapel, meditating on their vivid, truthful reality. Perhaps Foppa's way of using the rules of perspective without being overpowered by them encouraged Josquin to give freer rein to his own inventive powers, to overcome whatever residual fears he may have had of interpreting the rules of musical composition too freely, and to opt for a style more in keeping with the direct expression of experience. If it is true that the Renaissance analogy between audible harmony and visual proportions was more than theoretical speculation but a statement of deep faith in the harmonious mathematical structure of the universe,[22] as attested by the writings of Alberti,[23] then we must assume that Josquin was as responsive to the innovative qualities of Foppa's work as were the painters and architects of the Milanese Quattrocento, and that he cherished the lesson he found there. In any event, we may be sure that the intense activities of architects, sculptors, and painters in Milan during the 1460s and 1470s had a stimulating effect on anyone who, like Josquin, had something new to say in his own field.

That all these endeavours in the visual arts were to achieve even greater scope in the years to come is well known. Suffice it to recall that it was Josquin's patron, Ascanio Sforza, who initiated the building of the rectory

20 The link between Filarete and Foppa is stressed in Dalai Emiliani, ibid. At the Ospedale Maggiore, Foppa's subject for the lost frescoes in the entrance hall in 1457 was the Laying of the Cornerstone; in the Cathedral, Foppa may have been working on the stained glass windows of the New Testament when Filarete was the chief architect in 1452–4.

21 See the diagrams showing the vanishing points in some of Foppa's most important works in Dalai Emiliani, ibid., pp. 121, 125, 127, 130–31, 133.

22 Rudolf Wittkower, *Architectural Principles in the Age of Humanism* (Columbia University Studies in Art History and Archaeology, i; New York, 1965), p. 117.

23 I have discussed this problem in 'Musica ed arti figurative nel Rinascimento', *Humanitas* (1951), pp. 895–908.

and the cloister of S. Ambrogio, designed and in part executed by Bramante; and that it was he who called upon Bramante to plan the Cathedral of Pavia. According to a recent study, the Milanese architect Cesare Cesariano spent the years 1500 to 1502 in Ferrara at the court of Ercole d'Este.[24] Cesariano states in his autobiography that he was involved with the production of comedies for the Duke.[25] These were elaborate theatrical performances, enlivened by music, song, and dance, which the Duke loved and in which Josquin, too, must have had a share when he came to Ferrara in 1503.[26] But a further discussion of this subject would lead me too far away from my original goal: to give you a picture of the state of the visual arts in Milan during Josquin's most protracted stay in that city.

[24] Sergio Gatti, 'Cesare Cesariano e la cultura classica in Lombardia agli inizi del XVI secolo' (Ph.D. diss., Università Cattolica, Milan, 1969–70), p. 18. See also, by the same author, 'L'attività milanese del Cesariano dal 1512–13 al 1519', *Arte Lombarda*, xvi (1971), pp. 219–30.

[25] Cf. Giulio Bertoni, *La biblioteca estense e la coltura ferrarese ai tempi del Duca Ercole I* (Turin, 1903); A. Piromalli, *La cultura a Ferrara al tempo di Ludovico Ariosto* (Florence, 1954); E. Scoglio, *Il teatro alla Corte Estense* (Lodi, 1965).

[26] [On the date of Josquin's arrival in Ferrara, see Lewis Lockwood, above, p. 114.—Ed.]

Burney and Ambros as Editors of Josquin's Music

DON HARRÁN

At one point in his *History*, Charles Burney paused to reflect on the great composers of ages past: 'As none but the highest mountains and most lofty promontories of a country are visible at a great distance, so none but the most towering and exalted characters of a remote age are prominent to posterity.'[1] For Burney and Ambros Josquin was, indeed, such a 'towering and exalted' figure, to judge from the amount of space they allotted him in their histories and the enthusiasm with which they approached their subject. Burney calls him 'the Giant of his time', arriving at a 'universal monarchy and dominion over the affections and passions of the musical part of mankind';[2] for Ambros he marks 'the first appearance in music history of a composer that strikes one, predominantly, with the impression of genius'.[3] In the discussion that follows, the two historians—the one standing at the threshold of modern musical historiography, the other ushering in the era of historical musicology—will be considered from a single point of view: as editors of Josquin's music. Yet to set the discussion in its proper frame, I have endeavoured to reconstruct their editorial policy at large, to the extent that a statement of policy may be distilled from a perusal of their histories and transcriptions. For its application to the works of Josquin, I refer to the transcriptions of Burney housed in the British Museum, Department of Manuscripts, and those of Ambros in the Music Collection of the Oesterreichische Nationalbibliothek in Vienna. Neither

---

[1] *General History of Music*, 4 vols. (1776–89), in the chapter on 'The Progress of Music in England from the Time of King Henry VIII to the Death of Queen Elizabeth', ii, p. 61. References here are to the modern edition by Frank Mercer in two volumes, printed in 1935 and republished by Dover Press, New York, in 1957.

[2] Ibid., i, p. 738.

[3] *Geschichte der Musik*, iii (1868), 3rd ed. by Otto Kade (Leipzig, 1891), p. 203. (All further references to Vols. ii (1864, 3rd ed. by Heinrich Reimann, 1891) and iii are to the same edition, repr. Georg Olms (Hildesheim, 1968).) Discussed by Bernhard Meier in 'Zur Musikhistoriographie des 19. Jahrhunderts', *Die Ausbreitung des Historismus über die Musik*, ed. Walter Wiora (*Studien zur Musikgeschichte des 19. Jahrhunderts*, xiv; Regensburg, 1969), p. 200.

body of materials, as far as may be determined, has been subject to previous scholarly inquiry.

Burney leads us to his Josquin transcriptions with the remark that he was so fascinated by the writing in the 'Missa L'homme armé [super voces musicales]' that he scored the whole Mass and several others by the composer.[4] He transcribed wholly from primary sources available to him in the British Museum: Petrucci's first and third books of Josquin's Masses; two of Susato's anthologies of chansons for five and six voices: *Le cincquiesme livre contenant trente et deux chansons a cincq et a six parties* (RISM 1544[13]) and *Le septiesme livre contenant vingt et quatre chansons a cincq et a six parties* (RISM 1545[15]); Petrucci's third and fourth books of motets for four and five voices, the so-called *Motetti de la corona* (RISM 1519[2] and 1519[3]); a manuscript of chansons whose signature is MS. Royal 20 A XVI;[5] and the musical examples of Glareanus' *Dodekachordon*. All in all, three Masses and portions of eight others, seven motets and the first part of three others, and five chansons were scored (see Appendix). Of these, two motets ('La Deploration de Jehan Okenheim', as Burney spelled it,[6] and 'Misericordias Domini', Part I) and fragments from four Masses (*Pleni sunt* from 'Missa Mater Patris', *Agnus* II from 'Missa Sine nomine', *Pleni sunt* and two canons from the *Benedictus* of 'Missa L'homme armé super voces musicales', and *Osanna* and *Benedictus* from 'Missa Faysans regrets') were inserted as examples in the *History*.[7] Along with two works in John Hawkins' *General History of the Science and Practice of Music* (1776),[8] these examples are the first by the composer to be printed in a modern history of music.

The transcriptions, numbering 132 pages, were bound (with music of

---

[4] *History of Music*, i, p. 738. Elsewhere he writes: 'I have never seen, *among all his productions that I have scored*, a single movement which is not stamped with some mark of the great master' (italics mine), i, p. 751.

[5] Burney refers to the manuscript with the words: 'In a very beautiful MS. at the British Museum, consisting of French Songs of the 15th century, in three and four parts, there are likewise many of Josquin's compositions' (i, p. 738).

[6] Surprisingly, Burney's score of the 'Déploration' is absent from his other scores of Josquin. This is unfortunate, for Burney confesses to having had difficulties in transcribing the work (cf. i, p. 731). (Pamela Willetts, Assistant Keeper of the Department of Manuscripts in the British Museum, tried, at my request, to trace a copy of the 'Déploration' among the corpus of Burney's transcriptions. Although the results of her search were negative, she did suggest that further volumes may be preserved in other British libraries. The matter is deserving of investigation.)

[7] The printed version of the *Pleni sunt* from 'Missa Mater Patris' (i, p. 739) is erroneously identified as a canon 'un ton plus haut' from the 'Missa Sine nomine', a point that escaped the attention of the editor of the *History*. The *Benedictus* canons from 'L'homme armé' were fully resolved in the manuscript copy, yet printed as one line for didactic purposes ('I shall present him [i.e., 'the musical student'] with these short movements in the same manner as they appear in the printed copy, and leave the rest to his sagacity', i, p. 742).

[8] The 'vox regis' canon, i, p. 324, and the motet 'O Jesu fili David' (= 'Comment peult avoir joye'), i, p. 336. Both are copied from Glareanus.

other composers of the period or later) in four manuscripts whose signatures are Add. 11581 (the Josquin works covering 11 ff.), 11582 (45 ff.), 11585 (9 ff.), and 11588 (1 fol.).[9] They date, according to Hughes-Hughes' catalogue (as in n. 9), from '*ca.* 1780' or 'before 1782'. Inasmuch as Book ii of the *History* was printed in 1782, I would suggest a more likely period for these copies being the later 1770s. They show signs of having been executed in haste;[10] as editions, moreover, they are incomplete, for *musica ficta* and sizable portions of text are invariably lacking. For complete editions of Burney's one might turn to a few of the musical examples in the *History*. Though the latter have the advantage of full text underlay and the marking of extra sharps and flats, they omit ligatures and coloration, copied into the manuscripts exactly as they appear in the source. The reason for their omission seems to be that Burney viewed the finished score as destined for the general musical public, hence to be prepared in the form of a practical edition. In some of the music printed in the *History* not only did Burney add more text and *musica ficta*, change one or more of the original clefs,[11] and discard ligatures and coloration, but where in the transcriptions a note syncopated over two measures is usually centred on the barline between them and the dot of a dotted note (prolonged into a new measure) deferred till after the barline (see Pl. 29), in the prints these features are replaced by simple ties.[12]

We shall now turn to Burney's editorial principles on scoring (barring, clefs, note values), text underlay, and *musica ficta*. Reference will be made to Burney's statements in the *History*, a procedure the more justified since

[9] The transcriptions were originally paginated, and only afterwards provided with foliation (with many of the page numbers cancelled). Augustus Hughes-Hughes, *Catalogue of Manuscript Music in the British Museum*, 3 vols. (London, 1906–9), catalogues the works with folio numbers only, even though the pagination is often the more legible of the two.

[10] In answer to my queries about the ink used in the transcriptions, Miss Willetts kindly informed me that all details of the music were copied in black ink (fading to brown), with red ink appearing on occasion in figuration of the bass. Pencil markings turn up infrequently for sketching in voices, as in Add. 11581, fol. 30.

[11] As in the *Pleni sunt* (*a* 2) from 'Missa Mater Patris'. Where the transcription (Add. 11581, fol. 22ᵛ) retained the alto and tenor clefs of the source, it was rewritten, for the *History*, for two treble clefs in octave transposition (cf. first edition, ii, pp. 490–92; Mercer's edition, i, p. 739). (I owe thanks to Mrs. Ann Basart of the Music Library of the University of California, Berkeley, for information about the clef arrangements of the music printed in the *editio princeps* (1782) of the *History*.) This is one example, though, out of the large majority where Burney, as a rule, does *not* introduce changes of clefs from transcription to print.

[12] The prints teem with errors (in pitches, rhythms), which might lead one to conclude that they were based on careless transcriptions. This is not the case, however, for the transcriptions are, on the whole, very reliable. If anything, Burney (or his editor, Frank Mercer?) should be accused of careless proofreading! (I have been unable to compare the first and later editions with respect to the accuracy of the printed examples. Such a comparison may well clear Burney's name of undeserved suspicions.)

many of the annotations in the transcriptions were carried over into the printed work.[13]

I. Scoring

The purpose of the score, Burney acknowledges, is to allow a rapid comparison of the voices and their relations (i, p. 705). Such a comparison is prerequisite to forming critical judgements about the music. To facilitate the reading, bars are drawn, consistently, across the staves of each system (cf. i, p. 713).[14] A few cases of irregular barring warrant attention: in the *Pleni sunt* of the 'Missa Ad fugam', measure 15 is extended by a semibreve to allow the resolution of a cadence to fall on the first beat of the next measure, which situates the resolution of the final cadence on a first beat too (Add. 11582, fol. 15ᵛ). At the words '[consubstantialem Patri]' in the 'Missa Sine nomine', Burney introduces a change of barring to place the beginnings and endings of phrases on strong beats (ibid., fol. 28).[15] Yet these are exceptions to the rule.

Original clefs and note values are retained.[16] Reduced note values would deprive the music 'of its venerable appearance' and the more 'learned reader' would never know whether it had been copied 'with care and fidelity' (i, p. 713).

Burney's scoring, in short, rests on three fundaments: regular barring, original clefs, and *integer valor*.

II. Text underlay

Burney set great store by the proper adaptation of words to music. He realized that a change of style affects the relationship between them. In discussing inaccuracies in the text setting of Byrd's *Psalms, Songs, and Sonnets* (1611), he remarks: 'After pointing out . . . the *general* inattention at

[13] Examples: Add. 11582, fol. 2, comments on *musica ficta* (cf. i, p. 729, n. z; ii, pp. 253–4); ibid., fol. 16ᵛ, on 'Missa Di dadi' (cf. i, p. 745); ibid., fol. 72ᵛ, on 'Miserere mei Deus' (cf. i, pp. 749–50); ibid., fol. 85, on the meaning of canon as a 'mystery w.ᶜʰ the performer is to unfold' (cf. i, p. 731); Add. 11585, fol. 30, on 'Misericordias Domini' (cf. footnotes a and b to the print of the work in ii, pp. 748–9); etc.

[14] He notes (as his precedent?) that Morley, though he fails to bar editions of his music, does, however, bar the musical examples he inserts in his treatise (i, p. 705, n. a). The former, of course, are part-books. In the second and third parts of his treatise he uses scores.

[15] Another kind of barring occurs in the first part of the motet 'Huc me sydereo', written in triple mensuration (Add. 11582): there the tenor *cantus firmus* is divided into measures three times as long as those of the other voices, a division that does justice to the larger rhythmic values of the tenor.

[16] The examples printed in the modern edition of the *History* do not always hold to the original clefs. Frank Mercer has altered 'the unusual ones'—which, as he explains in the Introduction (p. 6), means all clefs beyond the treble, alto, tenor, and bass—to conform to present usage.

this time to prosody, accent, and quantity ... it would be more candid to others, and, perhaps, kind to ourselves, to examine the compositions of old masters by such rules as were at that period established, than by *ex post facto* laws' (ii, p. 75, n. g). In practice, however, he insists on observing the niceties of prosody, failing which 'it frequently happens that the finest sentiments and most polished verses of modern languages are injured and rendered unintelligible ... ' (i, p. 84).

Burney advocated a resetting of the texts of older music to cleanse them of inaccurate accentuations. He confined his efforts to English music, and there to mere changes of rhythm and occasional division or contraction of notes[17] 'to obviate the objections that are justly made to the want of attention ... to accent and syllabic quantity'.[18]

Burney's ideas about text underlay may be summarized as follows:

1. *Attention must be paid to verbal accent and the quantity of syllables.* He refers to the 'simple and plain rules of giving a short note to a short syllable, a long to a long; and of accentuating the music by the measure and natural cadence of the verse ... ' (i, p. 84). Insignificant words ('expletives, particles, and words of small importance') should not be located in positions of prominence (ibid.). Accented syllables should fall on accented beats of the measure (see also ii, p. 125).

2. *In homophonic passages, all voices should sing the same words in the same rhythm.* Such a setting, Burney writes, 'would greatly facilitate to the congregation the intelligence of what is sung' (ii, p. 125, n. l).

3. *Notes in ligature are sung to one syllable only, to be placed on the first note.*[19] Burney saw ligatures as playing the same part in early music as 'the semi-circular marks, called binding-notes and slurs' in the music of his own day (i, p. 715). Though he does not mark ligatures in his printed examples, the transcriptions do, with few exceptions, retain them in their original form.

4. *One must strive throughout for 'a clear, distinct, and articulate pronunciation of the words'* (ii, p. 127). Addressing himself to the modern composer, Burney recommends note-against-note writing as the best way to highlight the text.[20] Once the words have been clearly delivered, the composer may, for variety's sake, resort to fugal procedures.

17 [The means used by Burney are the same ones employed by sixteenth-century editors bent on improving the text setting of a piece. See, for instance, the collations discussed in Edward E. Lowinsky, *The Medici Codex of 1518* (*Monuments of Renaissance Music*, iii; Chicago, 1968), pp. 88, 133–4, 138, 144–5, 151, 153, 173, 193, 205, 226–7, and 231–2.—Ed.]

18 Volume ii, p. 92, n. c. Though the quotation concerns, in particular, Morley's setting of the *Burial Service* (in the English Prayer Book), Burney includes older music in general: 'And in this manner the words of many of our old and venerable compositions for the church might be adjusted'.

19 Burney speaks of ligatures in Gregorian chant in Vol. i, p. 539, and in the vocal music of the 'early Contrapuntists', ibid., p. 715.

20 Elsewhere he condemned 'figurative Counterpoint' for having 'utterly diverted the

A few of Burney's transcriptions of Josquin's works have text underlaid in all parts: 'Inviolata, integra, et casta es', 5v. (Add. 11585); 'Misericordias Domini', 4v. (ibid.; printed with few changes in the *History*, i, pp. 747–9); and 'Douleur me bat', 5v. (Add. 11588). Still others ('Huc me sydereo', 6v., in Add. 11582; 'Miserere mei, Deus', 5v., and the 'Stabat Mater', 5v., ibid.; 'Domine ne in furore tuo', 4v., ibid.) are supplied with a full (or nearly full) text, though no thoroughgoing attempt is made to line up notes and syllables. In the majority of cases, however, the text is either omitted entirely or only sparsely provided. Yet it is not by the majority that Burney's abilities should be judged, but rather by the examples where obvious care was taken in setting the text. While Burney falls short of meeting the demands of Zarlino or, unknown to him, Stocker, his text underlay is nonetheless singable and reflective of a musical mind.

III. Musica ficta

Burney takes it for granted that *musica ficta* is to be added to older music. In reference to a chanson by Cornelius Canis (ii, p. 248), he notes that the accidentals were omitted from the original, 'as usual with the old masters', and that it was left to the singers to provide them. Burney appends sharps and flats to his transcriptions without further ado,[21] though we would fault him for his failure to distinguish between printed signs and his own. He based his usage on the precepts of the theorists Philippe de Vitry, Marchetto of Padua, Prosdocimus de Beldemandis, Tinctoris, and Gafurius, to whose names and definitions he refers in his *History*.[22]

He recognized *musica ficta* as a deviation from the diatonic scale for the purpose of obtaining semitones not included within the Guidonian gamut.[23] He acknowledges the following rules:[24]

---

attention of the composer, performer, and public, from poetry, propriety, and syllabic laws' (i, p. 528). To the evils of fugue he adds the muddying effect of accompanying vocal music in the church with the organ (ibid.).

[21] At times he felt he owed the reader an explanation, as in the footnotes to the *Osanna* from Josquin's 'Missa Faysans regres' ('No accidental Flats or Sharps occur in the ancient Copy; and perhaps those which are inserted in this, will not satisfy every Musical Reader', i, p. 743, n. a) and to Isaac's motets 'Anima mea' and 'De testimoniis tuis' ('None of the Chromatic Semitones are marked in the printed Copy of either of the Compositions of Henry Isaac; nor indeed would the Puritans in Church Music, at the time they were written, have suffered the Lydian or Mixolydian mode to be contaminated by altered intervals', i, p. 760, n. a).

[22] In Book II, 'The State of Music to 1450', i, p. 646.

[23] *Musica ficta* is 'another name for Transposition from the natural scale into such keys as required sounds different from those which the three hexachords furnished', i, p. 672. His reading of the theorists had made him familiar with variations in terminology (*falsa, ficta, colorata, conjuncta, alterata*, etc.; cf. ibid., n. z).

[24] In the large bulk of transcriptions Burney never got to the stage of inserting accidentals.

1. *The prohibition of tritones and false fifths* (which he more often corrects through the addition of sharps than flats[25]). The old masters are said to have 'held the sharp 4th and flat 5th in such abhorrence, that, to avoid them, they frequently made the 7th of a key flat, even before a close' (i, p. 719, n. ‡). Burney does not advocate diatonic cadences in the manner of a Maurice Cauchie; he merely confirms the presence, in many examples, of double leading notes. Corrections of *mi contra fa* abound, so much so that Burney suggests that the fifth and sixth modes, where the flattening of B imparts tonal definition, be rewritten in F or G major (*sic*).[26]

2. *The 'subsemitonium modi'.* Burney provided *musica ficta* at cadences on D, G, and A as a matter of course.[27] He distinguishes further between a Phrygian cadence form and a Dorian-Mixolydian type.[28]

3. *The raised third at the final cadence.* Burney does not refer to this convention in the *History*. Yet it is confirmed by several examples in the transcriptions. One of them, the chanson 'L'eure est venue' (see Appendix for source and attribution), has a 'Picardy third' supplied, obliquely, by the

[25] He refers as a precedent to the fifth tract, beginning 'Sequitur de Sineminis', of the Cotton MSS. [once belonging to the library of Sir Robert Cotton (1571–1631), now in the British Museum] where the author 'speaks of a cross being put to F to obviate the false fifth between that sound and B.... *Marchetto da Padua* 200 years before had used the same expedient', i, p. 672. Burney relates that the MSS. were destroyed by a fire in 1731; however, Dr. Pepusch managed to have copies made, 'now lodged in the British Museum', i, p. 670. Miss Willetts kindly informed me that the Cotton collection was acquired in 1753, and that the fifth tract was probably in Cotton MS. Tiberius B.IX, of which only burnt fragments remain. The transcript made by Pepusch is included in Add. 4909, ff. 93–94v.

[26] '...but all the compositions of this period, in the fifth or sixth ecclesiastical mode, which we should now write in F and G major, are the more pleasing to modern ears, on account of the key being ascertained', in reference to a work by Josquin Baston, ii, p. 250.

[27] Discussing the enharmonic genus proposed by Vicentino, Burney admits he has no idea to what use it was put in the music of the sixteenth century. He does know, though, that 'whenever other sounds are used than those of the scale, strictly diatonic, by introducing F, C, or G sharp, or any flat, except that of B..., the diatonic is mixed with the chromatic; and to this licence the first contrapuntists were reduced, at a cadence in D and A minor, as well as G major', ii, p. 137.

[28] In speaking about Benedictus Appenzeller's setting of 'Musae Jovis ter maximi', he notes with wonderment an unusual cadence on E where D is to be sharpened as a leading tone and an F♯ is required (in the tenor) 'to prevent a false 5th with B in the *Base*'. It is depicted as an E cadence 'in the modern style': 'Here is a very beautiful and unexpected close in E minor, *alla moderna*, which I never saw, in Music of this early period, before, and of which I should have doubted, as no accidental Flats or Sharps are marked in the printed copy', i, p. 758. Burney's sensitivity to unaccustomed traits of harmony and voice leading comes to the fore also in his previous remarks on this piece (on p. 757) as elsewhere in his *History*. [Frank Mercer errs in changing Burney's attribution from Appenzeller to Ducis; the former is the correct author, according to Dénes Bartha, *Benedictus Ducis und Appenzeller* (Wolfenbüttel-Berlin, 1930), p. 61. Appenzeller's *naenia* on Josquin is edited in the *Werken*, Klaagliederen, pp. 4–7. The cadence in question occurs at mm. 104–5. —Ed.]

figuration of the bass in the last measures. (This is the only instance of continuo figuration in the Josquin copies. It does appear elsewhere, and sometimes plentifully, e.g., in the transcription of Isaac's motet 'Anima mea' [Add. 11585, ff. 39–39ᵛ].)

4. *The retention of the original shape of motives (or a 'cantus firmus') when moved through imitation or transposition or both from one hexachord to another* (cf. i, p. 723).[29] Here Burney invokes Padre Martini as his authority.[30] He mentions, hypothetically, any series of notes in the C hexachord whose imitation in the F or G hexachords must perforce hold to the same intervals, the same *musica ficta* ('. . . no accident of ♭, ♯, or ♮, should have admission in the answer, which does not occur in the subject'), and, hence, the same 'syllables', i.e., solmization syllables (i, p. 724, n. n). Burney draws a distinction, however, between 'answers' at the octave, fifth, or fourth and those at other intervals: where imitations of the first category must abide by the original solmization, those of the second may deviate therefrom. He draws a further distinction between sacred and secular music: secular music, tending to modal ambiguity and freer motivic formation, allows greater latitude in shaping its imitations.[31] Burney says about the rule of real imitations and, in fact, about rules in general that those who follow them with 'rigour and pedantry' are deserving of reprobation. The court of appeals must ever be the ear, for 'rules in music, deduced from any other principle than *effect on the ear*, are absurd' (i, p. 724, n. o).

These four rules held for as long as the practice of inserting accidentals was entrusted to the singer. In the course of time more and more accidentals were placed in prints and manuscripts and the practice of *musica ficta* began to lose ground on the continent. Here it should be kept in mind that *musica ficta*, part and parcel of the old system of solmization and mutation, was incapable, as was the system as a whole, of producing a direct chromatic step such as from F to F♯ or from B♭ to B♮. The writing of accidentals to produce such a chromatic alteration was necessary to supplement the observance of *musica ficta* rules by the practical musician. But in due course —it was a slow development—the frequent writing of accidentals led to

---

[29] Burney's comments in this regard anticipate a trend of present thought. About real imitations in the music of Josquin's generation, see Edward E. Lowinsky, *Tonality and Atonality in Sixteenth-Century Music* (Berkeley & Los Angeles, 1962), p. 31.

[30] *Esemplare o sia Saggio Fondamentale Pratico di Contrappunto Fugato* (Bologna, 1774), ii, p. xxviii. The passage occurs in a section entitled 'Della Fuga del Tuono'. The practice of real answers began, Martini observes, when composers took to imitating fragments of a *cantus firmus* in the upper parts. Care was taken to have 'the imitation and its transposition, especially as regards the [hexachordal] syllables *do re mi fa* etc., resemble the *cantus firmus* almost throughout as a real answer to its subject'.

[31] '. . . for in secular music, composed upon subjects of invention [i.e., not *cantus firmi* or *cantus prius facti*], where the ecclesiastical scales have been abandoned, more latitude, both of subject and reply, has been taken by the greatest masters of the art', i, p. 724, n. o.

the practice of signing most, and finally all, accidentals in the score. This development was preceded and accompanied by the demand of some theorists for specifying all accidentals.[32] Interestingly enough, Burney viewed Orlando di Lasso's collection of 1555 [*Le quatorzième livre à quatre parties contenant dix-huit chansons italiennes, six chansons françaises et six motets*] written 'à la nouvelle composition d'aucuns d'Italie' as marking a turning point in this development:[33] here 'chromatic accidental semitones are expressed by a sharp, and no longer left to the mercy and sagacity of the singer, as was before the constant custom.... Orlando seems the first who, in spite of ancient prejudice and pedantry, when he wished to alter a note, dared to express his intentions in writing' (ii, pp. 253–4).[34]

*   *   *

In the Foreword to the third book of his *Geschichte der Musik*, Ambros defines his approach to historical criticism as building on a comprehension of the developmental process in art: 'I understand an art that is fully grown only when I have understood its previous stages and its gradual formation.'[35] Ambros was the first historian to place Josquin's works in a broad musico-historical context. Not only that, he discussed more works of the composer, and these in greater detail, than any other writer up to his time. His Josquin portrait was so brilliant and original, as Helmuth Osthoff remarked in his monograph on the composer,[36] that all music historical writing, down to the present, has remained indebted to it.

Ambros arrived at his unique estimate of Josquin by way of extensive transcriptions of his works as part of the approximately eight hundred works of Netherlandish music copied over the years in Munich, Vienna,

[32] [See Pietro Aron's condemnation of the use of conflicting key signatures and of the whole practice of *musica ficta* as early as 1523 in his *Toscanello* (cf. Edward E. Lowinsky, 'The Function of Conflicting Key Signatures in Early Polyphonic Music', *The Musical Quarterly*, xxxi (1945), pp. 227–60; esp. 258–9).—Ed.]

[33] The collection, one of the landmarks in music of the Cinquecento, has been linked in recent research with the issue of *musica reservata*. With the insistence in its title on a 'new manner of writing', it conforms to Jean Taisnier's definition of *musica reservata* as having to do with new trends in composition around the mid-century: cf. Claude Palisca, 'A Clarification of "Musica Reservata" in Jean Taisnier's "Astrologiae"', 1559', *Acta Musicologica*, xxxi (1959), p. 149.

[34] The quotation ought to be compared with the original annotation from which it ostensibly derives. On the first page of his transcription of 'Missa L'homme armé' Burney writes: 'Orlando di Lasso, when a very young man ventured to express these Chromatic semitones in print...Perhaps Cipriano di Rore who was born 14 yrs. before Orlando, had done it first' (Add. 11582, fol. 2). In other words, he sensed the important role played by Italy in the development of chromaticism.

[35] *Geschichte der Musik*, ii, p. vi (*Vorrede*).

[36] *Josquin Desprez* (Tutzing, 1962), i, p. 95.

and Italy, to which country he made four trips (in 1861, 1865–6, 1866, and 1868) in preparation for the later volumes of his *Geschichte*.[37] Upon his death the collection was bequeathed, as part of the Ambros Estate, to what is now the Oesterreichische Nationalbibliothek in Vienna. Of some thirty-five volumes, Josquin's works occupy three, and bear the signatures MSS. Supp. mus. 1556 (*Motetten und Lieder*, 102 ff.), 1578 (*sämmtliche Messen*, 202 ff.), and 1579 (*Motetten und Psalmen*, 49 ff.). Separate folios, most of them rough copies, are scattered in seven other volumes (see Appendix). Ambros provided a handwritten catalogue, seventy-eight pages long, to the whole collection,[38] though it must be corrected and supplemented, in Josquin's case, by comparison with the transcriptions themselves.[39]

For some time, apparently, Ambros entertained the idea of bringing out

---

[37] Ambros explains the circumstances attendant upon the collection of his materials in the Foreword (*Vorrede*), signed Prague, 4 March 1868, to his third volume (pp. iii–v). Further information is contained in Otto Kade's Foreword (*Vorwort*) to Volume v (pp. v–xiv), from which we learn that the idea of issuing a volume of musical examples to illustrate Volume iii existed prior to the publication of the latter in 1868. As early as 1862 Kade had been asked by the publisher of the *Geschichte* for his opinion about a number of transcriptions that Ambros assembled and laid out for this purpose. They were copied, in large part, from the collection of scores that belonged to Kiesewetter, Ambros' father-in-law. Kade faulted these scores for their unreliability and for the numerous changes that had been introduced into the original in the name of practicability. He advised the publisher that the only thing for Ambros to do was to visit Italy and gather his materials on his own from the primary sources. Eventually, twenty-six of Ambros' scores were printed as part of the anthology in the fifth volume, the remainder of the eighty-five pieces having been transcribed by Kade. Of the six works by Josquin, only two were drawn from Ambros' collection, though he had scored them all. Kade gave as reason his use of a source unknown to Ambros. That Ambros readied more pieces for publication may be deduced from Kade's remark that the fifth volume 'absorbed a part of the scores that had already been prepared by Ambros'; *Geschichte*, v, p. vi. Originally, Ambros alone was to have furnished the examples for this volume. Kade reports, however, that after several years had elapsed and Ambros was unable to find the time and leisure to rework his materials, it was decided in a meeting held in 1871 between Ambros, Kade, and the publisher (Constantin Sander) to entrust the preparation of the fifth volume to Kade.

[38] MS. Supp. mus. 2472. The title, in another hand, reads: *Alphabetischer-Catalog der Sammlung von Compositionen alter Meister (Italiaener, Niederländer) aus dem Nachlasse des Dr. A. W. Ambros. Sämmtliche Compositionen sind zum grösten Theile durch Dr. A. Ambros aus der Originalnotierung in moderne Schreibweise übertragen.—Alles Handschrift von Dr. A. W. Ambros*. Josquin's works are listed on pp. 55–60. Among them appears a motet, 'Et ecce terrae motus', for six voices. It may be identified as the motet 'In illo tempore stetit Jesus' in MS. Supp. mus. 1556 (see Appendix), listed by Ambros according to the *cantus firmus* 'Et ecce terraemotus' carried by the *sexta pars* (hence the absence of the incipit 'In illo tempore' proper from the *Alphabetischer-Catalog*).

[39] In this catalogue, for example, no mention is made of the volume of Masses (Supp. mus. 1578), the hymn 'Pange lingua', the chansons 'A l'eure que ie vous p.x.', 'N'esse point un grand deplaisir', and three instrumental canons, including 'Vive le roy', altogether twenty-five works.

the music he transcribed in a series of 'Denkmäler'. He negotiated to this end with the publishing house Schreiber-Cranz of Vienna, but at a certain point the dealings seem to have broken down.[40] Ambros' scores of Josquin offer evidence—overlooked so far—of the specific works he intended to publish. In Supp. mus. 1578, three Masses are marked throughout with numbers that bear, presumably, on the division of the musical text for engraving. Two parallel series are to be distinguished: large-size Arabic numerals, running in 'Missa La sol fa re mi' (ff. 15^v–25^v) from 47 to 66, in 'Missa Malheur me bat' (ff. 80–92^v) from 136 to 163, and in 'Missa Pange lingua' (ff. 189–202) from 26 to 46, undoubtedly referring to page numbers; and smaller fractions (usually placed on a lower staff than the previous figures), running in the first Mass from 1/46 to 5/65, in the second from 1/135 to 1/162, and in the third from 1/25 to 4/45, and indicating division of each page into systems. Some of the numbers mark off pages with forty measures or more (though in 'Missa La sol fa re mi', as an example, the average number of measures is thirty-one); and as noted from the fractions above, the systems extend to a total of five per page (though, otherwise, the upward limit is four), some of them containing as many as ten or eleven measures. The large number of measures or systems per page suggests the ample format (folio size) of a 'Denkmäler'-type publication. The two sets of figures seem to have been pencilled in by different hands. Perhaps Schreiber-Cranz had asked two engravers for a cost estimate.[41]

The Josquin pieces in the 'Nachlass' were copied out in large part between the years 1862 and 1865, to judge from the number of instances where dates are inscribed on them.[42] (There is no relation between their grouping in the three volumes and the chronological order of their transcription.) Altogether, they comprise nineteen Masses, forty-eight motets, fifteen French chansons, three Italian secular works, and two instrumental canons. In terms of the total output of the composer, Ambros scored all but one Mass ('Allez regretz'), half the motets, and roughly a quarter of the known secular pieces. One cannot but marvel at the number of transcriptions and the indefatigable energies of the transcriber. True, sometimes, in the essay on Josquin, reference is made to works not represented among his scores. Yet of these several may be accounted for through their availability in

---

[40] See Friedrich Blume's article on Ambros in *MGG*, i, col. 409.

[41] I wish to thank Prof. Othmar Wessely of the Musicological Institute of the University of Graz for his kind help in rechecking the original manuscript (Supp. mus. 1578). Prof. Wessely described to me the numeral systems of the three Masses in detail, confirming my suspicions about their relevance to the dealings with Schreiber-Cranz. I drew from his communication for my own description of the Masses above.

[42] Specifically, fourteen Masses, the earliest being 'Pange lingua', transcribed in 1862 from a manuscript (MS. 4809) in the Hofbibliothek (now Nationalbibliothek) in Vienna, twelve others scored in 1865; four motets (1863–5); and one chanson (1864).

collections by Commer[43] and Kiesewetter,[44] not to mention the examples printed in Glareanus' treatise (*Dodekachordon*) and the histories of Burney and Forkel;[45] the remainder (thirty-one chansons, thirty-three motets) is mentioned but in passing.[46] Whether one agrees with Ambros or not, one must admire his resolve to speak only about music which he himself had transcribed or inspected.

Ambros as editor: here the information yielded by the transcriptions will be supplemented, as was the case with Burney, by comments of his in the body of his *Geschichte*. First, some general remarks on the transcriptions. Although not readied for publication, they show the hallmarks of a critical approach to editing: ligatures are marked by slurs; blackened notes appear as in the original, though lined up with the other parts; *musica ficta* is added above the notes to which it applies (an improvement over Kiesewetter's habit of placing it, in coloured ink, alongside notes); parallel fifths, octaves, and unisons are frequently signalled.[47] When the music is based on pre-existent materials, the fact is noted, and the relationship between the two

[43] *Collectio operum musicorum Batavorum saeculi XVI*, 12 vols. (1844–58). Fourteen works of Josquin are printed in Vols. vi, vii, viii, and xii. Ambros expressed the opinion that Commer's transcriptions offered 'characteristic' examples of Josquin's art, not the anecdotal items usually transmitted (ii, p. xx).

[44] Kiesewetter's transcriptions of Josquin, gathered for the most part in his *Galerie der alten Contrapunctisten*, are a motley group of complete works and fragments copied from Hawkins, Forkel, Burney, Gregor Faber's treatise of 1553, and more. (Many are printed in the musical supplement to his *Die Verdienste der Niederländer um die Tonkunst*, 1829.) Among the few which seem to have been transcribed from primary sources are 'Missa La sol fa re mi' (*Kyrie*), 'Missa Gaudeamus' (*Kyrie, Gloria*), and 'La Bernardina' (for a full listing, cf. *Galerie der alten Contrapunctisten...Eine Zugabe zu seinem Haupt-Catalog* [Vienna, 1847], p. 4). About Kiesewetter's collections of old music in general, see Herfrid Kier, *Raphael Georg Kiesewetter (1773–1850), Wegbereiter des musikalischen Historismus* (*Studien zur Musikgeschichte des 19. Jahrhunderts*, xiii; Regensburg, 1968), pp. 47–56.

[45] Proske's *Musica divina* (8 vols.) contains nothing by Josquin. The several works of his in Maldeghem's *Trésor musical* (1865–93), with the exception of 'Ave Maria' in Vol. ii (1866), p. 12, were published after the appearance of Ambros' Vol. iii (see Gustave Reese, 'Maldeghem and His Buried Treasure', *Notes*, vi (1948), p. 97).

[46] The only two works which Ambros discusses at some length, and for which I cannot find a later printed source, are the twenty-four-part canon, 'Qui habitat in adjutorio' (iii, pp. 210, 223–4) and 'Ut Phoebi radiis' (iii, pp. 210–11, 229). Yet primary sources for the first (Petreius, *Tomus tertius psalmorum selectorum* [RISM 1542⁶], no. 1) and for the second (Petrucci, *Motetti de la corona. Libro quarto* [RISM 1519³], fol. 6) were available in copies in the Vienna court library (*Motetti de la corona*, iv, was consulted, furthermore, for 'Misericordias Domini'). The transcription of 'Stabat Mater', discussed in Vol. iii, p. 227, and printed as no. 13 in Vol. v, is lacking. It was apparently turned over to the press, and once printed, may have been destroyed.

[47] In 'Ave verum corpus' (*a 5*), for example, he notes parallel fifths (Supp. mus. 1579, fol. 32ᵛ) with the exclamation 'So! So!' Ambros was the author of a monograph *Zur Lehre vom Quinten-Verbote* (Leipzig, 1859), discussed by Guido Adler, 'August Wilhelm Ambros', trans. by W. O. Strunk, *The Musical Quarterly*, xvii (1931), pp. 360–73, on p. 366.

sometimes plotted in great detail (as in Ockeghem's chanson 'Malheur me
bat', analyzed to show its reworking in the Masses that Obrecht and Josquin
composed upon it[48]). Misprints are indicated, curious titles (e.g., 'Missa Di
dadi') elucidated, puzzle canons deciphered and resolved (among them,
'Canon. Et sic de singulis' in the chanson 'L'homme armé' that opens
Canti B[49] and *Agnus* III of 'Missa Da pacem'[50]). Directions for dynamics
and general expression are, on principle, not included.[51] As a matter of
interest, perfections in triple mensuration are designated by check marks.
When the historians or theorists have something to say about a particular
work (its origins, mode, canonic devices, or notation), their words are
copied into the transcription: this is especially true of the volume of Masses,
where quotations are drawn from Aron, Burney, Glareanus, Sebald Hey-
den, Giovanni Battista Rossi,[52] and Zarlino. *Cantus firmi* and motto canons

[48] In the Foreword to Vol. iii (p. iv) Ambros thanks the various institutions in Munich
and Vienna that lent their financial support to his Italian journeys, adding that without
such help it would have been impossible to track down the relationship, among other things,
between Ockeghem's 'Malheur me bat' and the Masses by the same name by Josquin and
Obrecht. He checked the Ockeghem piece in Bologna, the Obrecht Mass in Munich, and
the Josquin Mass in Vienna!

[49] Ambros' transcription (in Supp. mus. 1556, fol. 86ᵛ) reads correctly from beginning
to end, thus anticipating by a century Helen Hewitt's solution of the canon as printed in
her edition of *Canti B* (*Monuments of Renaissance Music*, ii; Chicago, 1967), no. 1. Hewitt
sensed that Ambros was on the right track: 'We possess no published score of this work by
Ambros, but we know he was familiar with it, for he has left us his interpretation of the
canon [in the *Geschichte*]...III, 57 n. 1' (ibid., commentary to the work, p. 24).

[50] The baffling instructions for the tenor canon ('Agnus secundum in superacuta voce
sic incipit') have been variously construed in our time: Friedrich Blume transfers the canon
(derived from Cantus I) to the higher octave (cf. 'Missa Da pacem' [*Das Chorwerk*, no. 20;
Wolfenbüttel, 1932], pp. 33–5), whereas Smijers places it in its natural register (cf. *Werken*,
Missen, xix, pp. 55–8). Ambros' solution agrees with that of Smijers and refutes thereby
Blume's assertion (Foreword to his edition, p. 4) that Ambros (*Geschichte*, iii, p. 222)
regarded *Agnus* III as calling for five instead of for six voices. Blume's argument is restated
by Osthoff (*Josquin Desprez*, i, p. 187). Ambros' transcription (in Supp. mus. 1578, ff.
188–188ᵛ) is scored for the full complement of six voices, with the one difference compared
to the later editions that the Bassus II canon is assigned to the tenor, an octave higher.

[On the unauthenticity of the 'Missa Da pacem', see Edgar H. Sparks, *The Music of Noel
Bauldeweyn* (American Musicological Society, Studies and Documents, no. 6; New York,
1972), pp. 34–98.—Ed.]

[51] In one instance, the motet 'Domine ne in furore tuo' (Supp. mus. 1556, ff. 9–11),
Ambros added dynamic markings. The piece may have been edited with a particular
performance in mind. (Ambros seems to have copied it from Commer's *Collectio operum
musicorum Batavorum saeculi XVI*, vi: the two transcriptions correspond even in minor
details. Yet Commer here, as elsewhere, refrains from dynamic indications. The one who
does suggest dynamics on occasion is Kiesewetter; see Kier, *Kiesewetter*, p. 79.)

[52] Rossi was an Italian monk associated with Genoa. He completed his *Organo dei Cantori
per intendere da sè stesso ogni passo difficile che si trova nella musica* about 1585 (it was printed
in 1618).

are reproduced, along with the transcription, in their original notation;[53] wherever Gregorian models, folk melodies (e.g., 'Scaramella'[54]), and *cantus prius facti* of other kinds can be traced or reconstructed, these are provided too. A few works elicit special words of praise from Ambros: 'Ecce tu pulchra es' is described as 'summa tantae pulcritudinis, quo nil majus sol optet, admiratione' (Supp. mus. 1556, fol. 75), the 'Missa Gaudeamus' as 'diese merkwürdige Missa...' (Supp. mus. 1578, fol. 26). The comments he appends to 'Absalon fili mi' are especially interesting: 'This composition, remarkable for the intensity of its expression, is instructive for the following reasons: 1) the use of *chiavette*... [see below]; 2) the application of the rule 'una nota super la semper est canendum fa' [NB. This second point was later cancelled. See Pl. 30]; 3) the explicit indication by Josquin of accidentals unprecedented for their time; these lead, in turn, to modulations of a kind, again, unprecedented for the time' (Supp. mus. 1556, fol. 7).[55] (None of these comments is to be encountered in the *Geschichte*.)

Generally, Ambros lists the sources from which he copied (this is the case for sixty-three of the transcriptions); when he does not, they can be supplied by their mention (in footnote) in the *Geschichte*. Where several sources are given, the main one may often be inferred by checking the one-source listings in Ambros' own catalogue.[56] It might be noted that as far as Josquin is concerned, Ambros, like Burney, drew on local materials for the sources of his transcriptions: with few exceptions, they were available in the holdings of the imperial library (Vienna). (For a listing of primary sources, see the Appendix.)

Several annotations, mostly in the volume of Masses, testify to a collation of sources, though such work is still in a rudimentary state. Ambros seems to have consulted different sources when he ran up against problems in the course of transcription (notational errors, changing mensural signs, dissonances, awkward voice leading, etc.), though here and there he compares

---

[53] The problematical chanson 'L'homme armé', for example, was copied out *in toto* (see n. 49 above).

[54] He remarks here on Josquin's ingenious treatment of the folk-song in these words: 'Dieses ingeniöse höchst geistvolle Stück zeigt, was ein Genie, wie Josquin, aus der verachteten Form der "frottola" ["the disdained frottola form"] zu machen im Stande war!' (Supp. mus. 1556, fol. 6).

[55] 'Diese durch die Stärke des Ausdrucks bewundernswerthe Composition ist auch lehrreich: 1) für die Anwendung der Chiavette...; 2) für die Anwendung der Regel "una nota super la, semper est canendum fa"; 3) wegen der von Josquin ausdrücklich beigesetzten, für die Zeit unerhörten Accidentalen, wodurch Modulationen—für die Zeit abermals unerhörter Art—entstehen'. Ambros was the first to underline the unusual chromatic features of this work, thus anticipating their by now standard discussion in Edward Lowinsky's *Secret Chromatic Art in the Netherlands Motet* (New York, 1946), pp. 24ff.

[56] Whenever Ambros transcribes from a secondary source, he does not say. In a few instances, though, such copies may be traced clearly to Commer or Kiesewetter (cf. n. 51 above).

them for discrepancies in notation as well. Had he set out to prepare a critical edition of Josquin's works, he would probably have done a responsible job of it. One conjectures this, at any rate, from a passage in the 'Missa Ave maris stella' (Supp. mus. 1578, fol. 69) where he notes a 'better reading' of two, or from the comment regarding the readings in the Petrucci and Junta prints of *Kyrie* II from 'Missa Ad fugam': 'the small deviations are noteworthy' (ibid., fol. 138).

I. Scoring

Just as the music is transcribed from the sources in *integer valor*, so its original clefs are, almost without exception, retained.[57] With regard to *chiavette* Ambros followed the precedent set by Kiesewetter[58] and proposed a reading up or down by thirds or fifths in a number of works, among them 'Missa L'homme armé sexti toni', 'O Jesu fili David' [= 'Comment peult avoir ioye'], 'De profundis clamavi ad te' (*a 4*), 'Absalon fili mi', and 'Ecce tu pulchra es'. In 'De profundis', for example, the unusual arrangement of clefs M–T–Bar–SubB is replaced by S–A–T–B (with three flats), though, as Reese pointed out,[59] Ambros' version contradicts Glareanus' explicit directions against changes of register: 'Here indeed I should like everyone to observe carefully how the beginning of this song is composed, with how much dignity he has brought in the phrase *De profundis*; indeed, he has not moved these modes upwards from their natural position, as otherwise usually happens to them.. . .'[60] In 'Absalon fili mi' (transcribed from Kriesstein's anthology of 1540, no. 23), Ambros suggests substituting the clefs S–A–T–B (with two flats) for the combination high G-clef–S–M–T (all with one flat), thus moving the piece down a fifth. He writes in the transcription: "It [i.e., the piece] is undoubtedly calculated to be sung exactly a fifth lower. For the soprano the composer used the high G-clef (French violin clef)'.[61] Such a transposition is still a fifth higher than the

---

[57] In one passage in 'Missa Mater Patris' ('et resurrexit', Supp. mus. 1578, fol. 123), though, Ambros seems to have taken a more realistic view of the problems of score reading by suggesting that the two upper voices (in parallel thirds) in the tenor and mezzo-soprano clefs be read according to the alto clef. Similarly, in 'Ave Christe immolate' (Supp. mus. 1579, fol. 35ᵛ) he substitutes a bass clef for the original baritone.

[58] 'Über die Nothwendigkeit viele Compositionen der alten Meister für unsere Zeit in andere Tonlagen zu versetzen', *Cäcilia*, xxvii (1848), pp. 65ff.; originally printed as the Foreword to his catalogue of the *Galerie der alten Contrapunctisten*, pp. v–xvi.

[59] *Music in the Renaissance*, rev. ed. (New York, 1959), p. 249.

[60] *Dodekachordon*, trans. by Clement A. Miller (American Institute of Musicology, *Musicological Studies & Documents*, vi, 1965), ii, p. 266. See also Oliver Strunk, *Source Readings in Music History* (New York, 1950), p. 222.

[61] 'Sie ist durchaus berechnet, gerade um eine Quinte tiefer gesungen zu werden. Der Componist wendet für den Sopran den hohen G-Schlüssel (französischen Violinschlüssel) an' (Supp. mus. 1556, fol. 7).

arrangement of clefs in British Museum MS. Royal 8 G VII, which Lowinsky considers as offering 'the most reliable reading'.[62]

As for the barring of the transcriptions, Ambros, like Burney, drew lines across the staves of each system according to equal units of measure (breves). The two historians were thus spared the controversies surrounding regular barring, *Mensurstrich*, irregular barring, etc., all of which sprang up in our own century. Regular barring was, for them, the most natural way of dividing and organizing the voices of an ensemble, nor did they attempt to rationalize this usage.[63]

II. Text underlay

Ambros was not as text- or word-conscious as was Burney. In his brief comments on text underlay in the *Geschichte* (iii, pp. 140–41), he acknowledges Zarlino's role in bringing order into the practice. He says, on the authority of Coclico, that Josquin lay great stress on the proper adaptation of words to music.[64] Yet his other utterances testify that Ambros followed no clear set of guidelines in this matter. In the last analysis, he writes, the composer seems to have relied on the singers to figure out the proper distribution of text. The main concern of the Netherlanders was writing music, not observing 'exactly and carefully the grammatical and syntactical construction of words' (p. 141), and with this remark he dismisses the subject from further consideration. His seeming indifference to the difficulties in reaching a satisfactory coordination of text and music is reflected in the transcriptions. He copied the text, for the most part, as it appeared in the original, if he copied text at all. Indeed, large sections of the Masses are devoid of text or only sparsely provided with key words here and there. Sometimes the beginnings of pieces are fully underlaid with text, whereas the pages following remain textless.[65] Considering the large number of Josquin's works that Ambros transcribed, it is not surprising that the problems in achieving a good text underlay received but scant attention from

---

[62] *Secret Chromatic Art*, p. 24.

[63] Lowinsky speaks in a similar vein about early barring in his article on 'Early Scores in Manuscript', *Journal of the American Musicological Society*, xiii (1960), p. 156.

[64] 'Josquin machte sie [i.e., Textunterlegung] beim Unterrichte zu einem Hauptgegenstande, auf den er grosses Gewicht legte', iii, p. 140.

[65] One may infer acquaintance with Zarlino's rule proscribing the setting of text to seminimims from the exclamation of surprise at its infraction at 'lumen de lumine' in 'Missa L'homme armé super voces musicales' (Supp. mus. 1578, fol. 6) and at 'miserere' (m. 15) in the *Agnus* of 'Missa Dung aultre amer' (ibid., fol. 118). There are, to be sure, some fairly good (and complete) examples of text setting (e.g., 'Missa Pange lingua', 'Benedicta es coelorum regina', 'Magnus es tu Domine', 'Planxit autem David'). Needless to say, the more declamatory the style, the more satisfactory the alignment of syllables and tones.

him: had he tried to work them out carefully, he would have transcribed far less.[66]

III. Musica ficta

If the issue of text underlay was not crucial enough to Ambros to command his full interest, the matter was quite otherwise with *musica ficta*. In Volume iii of his *Geschichte*, he devotes a whole section of the chapter on music theory (*Die Musiklehre*, section b: 'Die Accidentalen', pp. 100–11) to this question, not to speak of the many references to *musica ficta* in the chapter entitled 'Guido von Arezzo und die Solmisation' in Volume ii (see especially pp. 171–2). To realize the extent to which Ambros knew and applied the rules of *musica ficta*, it is enough to open the third volume to the excerpt from the four-voice chanson 'Una musque de Biscaya' (p. 233). There the canon *a 2*, printed as one line by Petrucci (in *Canti C*, fol. 192ᵛ), is resolved, and (1) the new voice (derived from the contra at the upper fourth) is made to preserve the solmization of the *dux*; (2) accidentals are added at the cadence; and (3) a tritone is corrected by flattening B. Ambros harboured no doubts about *musica ficta* forming an integral part of the music of earlier times, and he expressed himself categorically on the subject, as in the following passage:

As long as Gregorian chant was sung in unison, the strictest diatonicism could be retained with stubborn consistency. In polyphonic music, this was not possible without lending intolerable offence to the ear by harsh combinations of chords. As a way out, one turned to the expedient of *musica ficta*, which was customarily employed by the masters of the first Netherlandish school, as is proven by the few, though as yet infrequent accidentals explicitly indicated wherever, in the course of a composition, doubts about its usage arise.[67]

---

[66] For Kade's ideas on text underlay, see the Foreword to Volume v, pp. x–xii. Ambros discoursed on the general relationship between word and tone in his *Die Grenzen der Musik und Poesie* (1856), inspired by the aesthetic writings of Hanslick (*Vom Musikalisch-Schönen*, 1854) and A. B. Marx (*Die Musik des 19. Jahrhunderts und ihre Pflege*, 1855).

[67] Vol. ii, p. 455. Or again: 'Polyphonic works can hardly be performed consistently within one specific mode and must, as the whole tremendous repertory of music of that period demonstrates, be remodelled and modified, so that an approximation to our tonal system is more or less the result' (iii, p. 98). For Ambros, greater approximation to the major–minor modes is a by-product of supplying *musica ficta*, not the motivating cause for it. Indeed, he warns the reader of the danger of forcing harmonic-tonal thinking on modes (ibid.).

Bernhard Meier suggests that one reason why Ambros was so attracted to *musica ficta* is that it corresponded to a basic trait in the romantic psyche, the urge for freedom. He defines *musica ficta* as the means by which music was liberated from the bonds of modal diatonicism or, more succinctly, as the means for breaking away from a system. See 'Zur Musikhistoriographie des 19. Jahrhunderts' (cf. n. 3 above), pp. 200–201. Be this as it may, one must acknowledge that the system that is being abandoned is replaced by another system with laws of its own.

Regarding the addition of accidentals at cadences and for the avoidance of tritones, he writes that in these situations they are so obvious as to be self-evident. To back up his statements, he refers to the writings of Aron, Cotton, Finck, Gafurius, Hothby, Listenius, Ornithoparchus, Regino of Prüm, Tinctoris, and others,[68] yet goes on to suggest that the singers resorted to accidentals far beyond what the circumspect theorists taught.[69] Quoting from Tinctoris,[70] he relates that it is the very absence of what the singers condemned as 'signa asinina'[71] that makes the proper usage of sharps and flats 'perhaps the most difficult aspect of the revival of older music'.[72] That Ambros was not deterred by these difficulties is evident from the attempt to lay down, in his *Geschichte*, a systematic body of principles governing *musica ficta* and to apply these principles in his transcriptions of Netherlandish music. The rules Ambros acknowledged may be summarized as follows:

1. *The prohibition of 'mi contra fa'.*[73] Here Ambros rightly understands formations not only of tritones, but of diminished fifths and diminished and augmented octaves as well. He shows by examples that the rule holds for both melodic and harmonic progressions.[74]

2. *The 'subsemitonium modi.'*[75] All cadence formulas are subject to this rule. He traces its origins to the avoidance of *mi contra fa* at cadences (on G) (iii, pp. 105–6), and quotes Zarlino to the effect that its application is so widespread among learned musicians (*die gebildeten Musiker*) and peasants (*Landleute*) as to constitute a natural law (iii, p. 105).[76] The Phrygian cadence

---

[68] See, in particular, ii, pp. 171ff.

[69] See iii, pp. 109–10, n. 4. Ambros makes the statement in connection with the 1545 edition of Willaert's 'Pater noster', thus anticipating *in nuce* Lewis Lockwood's study, 'A Sample Problem of *Musica Ficta*: Willaert's *Pater Noster*', in *Studies in Music History: Essays for Oliver Strunk* (Princeton, 1968), pp. 161–82.

[70] *Liber de natura et proprietate tonorum*, ch. VIII; printed in E. de Coussemaker, *Scriptorum de musica medii aevi*, iv (Paris, 1876), p. 22.

[71] See iii, p. 108. On this passage from Tinctoris, see the Foreword by Edward E. Lowinsky to H. Colin Slim, ed., *Musica nova* (*Monuments of Renaissance Music*, i; Chicago, 1964), p. viii.

[72] Vol. iii, p. 109, n. 2. Here he criticizes Kiesewetter for applying *musica ficta* 'arbitrarily, immoderately, and by analogy with modern music', yet warns about going to the opposite extreme, that is, imposing a fictitious diatonicism on music. For a statement of Kiesewetter's principles with regard to *musica ficta*, the reader is referred to an extract from the 'Vorrede' to his catalogue of the *Galerie der alten Contrapunctisten* (pp. xv–xvi) printed in Kier, *Kiesewetter*, p. 76.

[73] See ii, pp. 168, 198, 432; iii, pp. 101–2.   [74] See ii, p. 198.

[75] See ii, pp. 171, 456f.; iii, pp. 97–8, 105–6.

[76] Zarlino's passage occurs in *Le Institutioni Harmoniche* (Venice, 1558), Part III, ch. 53, p. 222. It reads: 'Ma la Natura hà provisto in simil cosa: percioche non solamente li periti della Musica: ma anco li contadini, che cantano senza alcuna arte, procedeno per l'intervallo del Semituono'.

is recognized as a form unto itself: its final chord (on E) may be approached by triads on the second [= II or VII⁶] or fourth degrees of the scale, but not by way of the dominant. The reason he gives is that the subsemitone D♯ necessitates a chord with F♯ (i.e., B–D♯–F♯), and such a chord does violence to the distinctive F-sound of the Phrygian mode (ii, p. 456).[77] Ambros distinguishes between the natural sevenths of the Lydian, Ionian, and Phrygian modes on the one hand, and the altered sevenths at cadences in the Mixolydian, Dorian, and Aeolian modes on the other. Such alterations, however, do not change the mode, or to put it differently, the addition of *musica ficta* at the cadence does not entail a change of solmization ('it does not affect any of the notes that are characteristic of the fourth- and fifth-species and, hence, of the mode itself').[78]

3. '*Una nota supra la semper est canendum fa*'.[79] Invoking Hermann Finck as his authority, Ambros writes that the rule is always to be applied, unless specific accidentals indicate otherwise.[80] He quotes Tinctoris' remark in the *Liber de natura et proprietate tonorum*, ch. VIII[81]—Ambros refers erroneously to chapter VII—that 'when, in any mode, the melodic line following the ascent to B *fa* ♮ *mi* descends more quickly to F *fa ut* than it rises to C *sol fa ut*, then the B must generally be flattened' (which may perhaps be related to the old rule stated by Marchetto that ascending motion calls for B♮, descending motion for B♭) (iii, p. 103). If the tritone in ascending melody calls for correction by means of a flat, so must a descending melody likewise be purged of this interval, this time through the sign of a sharp (iii, p. 104). (For his authority he refers to Aron's 'Aggiunta' to *Il Toscanello*.)

4. *Approaching a perfect consonance by the closest imperfect consonance*.[82] Aron, Gafurius, Marchetto, Jean de Muris, Ugolino d'Orvieto, and Zarlino are Ambros' crown witnesses for the claim that 'only through application [of this rule] do numerous passages receive their true sound and colouring' (iii, pp. 107–8). Jean de Muris' precepts of intervallic motion from the *Ars contrapuncti* are followed by the comment that though composers observed them well into the fifteenth century, 'the really great composers of those times, led by Josquin des Prez, sought ways of circumventing the rigid mandates, leading the way to a freer, less hampered practice' (ii, p. 433).

---

[77] Ambros links up the subsemitone rule with that prescribing an approach to a perfect consonance through the nearest imperfect consonance. He quotes Zarlino that 'in a close at the unison the next-to-last harmony of the cadence ought to be a minor third, in accord with the rule that a perfect consonance must be approached from the nearest imperfect consonance'.

[78] See iii, pp. 97 and 98.   [79] See ii, pp. 199, 457; iii, pp. 102–4.   [80] See ii, p. 199.

[81] 'Unde regula haec generaliter traditur, quod in quolibet tono si post ascensum ad B *fa* ♮ *mi* acutum citius in FF *fa ut* gravem descendatur quam ad C *sol fa ut* ascendatur, indistincte per *b* molle canetur' (Coussemaker, *Scriptorum*, iv, p. 22).

[82] See ii, pp. 430–3; iii, pp. 106–7.

Here Ambros took his cue from Coclico's remark, 'but Josquin did not observe these [rules]'.[83]

5. *'Tierce de Picardie'*.[84] Ambros notes that while the initial and final consonances of a composition may lack the third, intermediate cadences often contain them; he traces this usage to the rule, which Tinctoris considered pre-eminent, that all music should begin and end with perfect consonances.[85] When a third does appear in the final chord, however, it should be a major one, though Ambros is quick to add that the precept was not always strictly observed in practice.

Concerning *fa fictum*, Ambros writes[86] that it occurs as a warning sign lest the singer affix a sharp to f'' (as if the note f'' were generally to be sharpened). The true nature of *fa fictum* as designating an extension of the Guidonian gamut had to await the writings of Edward Lowinsky for its elucidation.[87]

The question remains to what extent Ambros abided by these principles in scoring the music of Josquin. As one might expect, his additions of *musica ficta* vary in quantity: some pieces are heavily laden with extra signs, others are moderately or sparsely provided with them, while a number are devoid of them entirely. To the first variety belong the *Gloria* of the 'Missa L'homme armé super voces musicales' with sixty-one indications of *musica ficta*, the *Kyrie* of 'Missa Da pacem' with forty-six, the motet 'In exitu Israel' with sixty-eight in its first two *partes* (the third *pars* is left untouched), and 'Domine ne in furore tuo' with fifty-seven. Among those rather sparsely provided are the 'Liber generationis' with five accidentals, 'Responde mihi' with three, 'Veni Sancte Spiritus' with six, and so forth. (As was the case with full text underlay, sometimes only the first page or pages carry the full complement of editorial accidentals.) Ambros seems to have treated his transcriptions of Josquin as an experimental ground for testing the principles of *musica ficta*. Not only does he mark a number of pages with figures denoting intervals,[88] he covers the works with annotations concerning *fa fictum* ('Missa Gaudeamus', Supp. mus. 1578, fol. 30ᵛ), conflicting signatures (in the *Credo* of 'Missa Sine nomine'), the rule of the closest approach ('Missa Dung aultre amer', ibid., fol. 114ᵛ), noteworthy examples of *musica ficta*, tricky passages with regard to its usage (*Et incarnatus est* from the 'Missa Una musque de Biscaya', ibid., fol. 108), Aron's warning

---

[83] *Compendium musices* (Nuremberg, 1552), facs. ed. by Manfred F. Bukofzer (*Documenat musicologica*, ix; Kassel, 1954), fol. L4ᵛ. Coclico does not refer here to the rule in question. Rather, he makes a general statement on compositional practice.

[84] See iii, p. 115.

[85] From *Liber de arte contrapuncti*, Bk. III, ch. 1 (in Coussemaker, *Scriptorum*, iv, p. 147).

[86] See ii, p. 454; iii, p. 87.

[87] Cf. 'The Function of Conflicting Signatures', pp. 254–5.

[88] 'Missa L'homme armé super voces musicales', Supp. mus. 1578, fol. 2; 'Missa Una musque de Biscaya', ibid., fol. 103ᵛ; 'Pater noster', Supp. mus. 1556, ff. 39ᵛ–40; etc.

in his *De institutione harmonica* against the use of F♯ at cadences in the fourth mode (the hymn 'Pange lingua', Supp. mus. 1556, fol. 16ᵛ), and more. Many signs are pencilled in, many later cancelled. 'Missa Sine nomine' (Supp. mus. 1578, fol. 173ᵛ) and 'Propter peccata' (Supp. mus. 1556, fol. 71) provide a graphic demonstration of the transcriber grappling with the complexities of *musica ficta*; in the 'Missa de Beata Virgine' (Supp. mus. 1578, fol. 164) he appears wavering between the application of one rule or another. The problems of *musica ficta*, as he himself stresses, are extremely difficult. That they must be solved, however, is clear from his study of contemporaneous theory (cf. ii, p. 455) and from the overwhelming evidence of the scores themselves.[89]

Burney's and Ambros' merits with regard to Josquin are manifest: the two historians viewed him as one of the greatest composers of all time; they took it upon themselves to delve into the aspects of this greatness from historical and editorial points of view. Whatever qualitative differences separate the two may be explained by the change of times, the gradual increase in knowledge about older music, the refining of historical methods, and the sharpening of the faculties of critical appraisal. Great as these differences are, both historians showed equal enthusiasm for their subject; both based their discussion of music on works they themselves had transcribed—Burney wrote, for example: '[I am] determined to speak of no music with which I am unacquainted, or of which I am unable to furnish specimens';[90] both recognized the stylistic dissimilarities between the motets and Masses of Josquin; and both approached the problems of musical editing undeterred by the immense obstacles in their path. Their merits have not remained unrecognized.[91] Burney likened the great composers of

---

[89] At this juncture it is well to cite the words of Kiesewetter's in a preface to the Palestrina hymn 'Jesu corona virginum' (Oesterreich. Nationalbibl., MS. SA 67F 33): '...often the conscientious editor is embarrassed and uncertain about his editorial additions, yet he must make his decisions in order to provide the music lover with a practicable score'. (See Kier, *Kiesewetter*, p. 76, for the full quotation.)

[90] See i, p. 705.

[91] Osthoff, who is the only scholar to have surveyed modern Josquin research from Burney on (*Josquin Desprez*, i, pp. 94–100), acknowledged the tremendous influence Ambros' essay on Josquin has had in shaping the thinking of later historians. Blume described the third volume of his *Geschichte* as 'the brilliant climax of Ambros' life work, serving even today as the classical groundwork for all musical research on the Renaissance' (*MGG*, i, col. 411) and on the section dealing with Josquin he wrote: 'It was Ambros who opened the eyes of his generation to the older composer and, with the penetrating vision of a born historian, as remarkable now as then, first recognized the greatness of Josquin. He already understood and formulated the main features of the decisive transformation from the late Gothic style of Ockeghem to a new approach to artistic expression and formation. That he dared to present Josquin not as a forerunner of the deified Palestrina, but as a master of a rank and value all his own will go down as an historic achievement' (Foreword to his first edition of Josquin's 'Missa Pange lingua' (*Das Chorwerk*, no. 1; Wolfenbüttel,

the past to 'the highest mountains and most lofty promontories of a country
... visible at a great distance', a simile that may be turned around to refer
to the great historians of the past as well. Burney goes on to say: 'In proportion as we recede from any period of time, inferior actors, however they
may have distinguished themselves to their cotemporaries, are rendered
invisible.... In Musical History, therefore, it is only a few protuberant
and gigantic characters that the general eye can see stalking at a distance'.[92]
The passage may serve as an epitaph to Burney and Ambros, and to the
few historians in ages past that merit being placed in their company.

Appendix

Burney's and Ambros' Transcriptions of Josquin[93]

Sigla and Abbreviations:

Commer VI, VII, VIII	*Collectio operum musicorum Batavorum saeculi XVI*, 12 vols. (1844–58).
Glareanus	*Dodekachordon* (Basel, 1547).
Hawkins	*General History of the Science and Practice of Music* (1776).
incompl.	incomplete copy.
Osthoff	*Josquin Desprez* (Tutzing, 1962–5).
Petrucci Bk I	O. Petrucci, ed., *Liber primus Missarum Josquin*, 1502.
Bk I³	Idem, 3rd ed., 1516.
Bk II	*Missarum Josquin Liber secundus*, 1505.
Bk III	*Missarum Josquin Liber tertius*, 1514.
RISM 1501	*Harmonice musices Odhecaton A*. Venice: O. Petrucci.
1502¹	*Motetti A. numero trentatre*. Venice: O. Petrucci.
1502²	*Canti B. numero cinquanta*. Venice: O. Petrucci.
1503¹	*Motetti De passione De cruce De sacramento De beata virgine et huius modi. B.* Venice: O. Petrucci.
1504¹	*Motetti C*. Venice: O. Petrucci.
1504³	*Canti C. Nº cento cinquanta*. Venice: O. Petrucci.
1505²	*Motetti libro quarto*. Venice: O. Petrucci.
1505⁴	*Frottole Libro tertio*. Venice: O. Petrucci.
1519²	*Motetti de la corona. Libro tertio*. Venice: O. Petrucci.
1519³	*Motetti de la corona. Libro quarto*. Venice: O. Petrucci.
1520⁴	*Liber selectarum cantionum quas vulgo Mutetas appellant*. Augsburg: Grimm & Wyrsung.
1521³	*Motetti libro primo*. Venice: A. Antico.

1929), p. 2). For a general study of Ambros and his *Geschichte* as set in the frame of the
literary-intellectual currents of nineteenth-century Germany, the reader is referred to
Philipp Otto Naegele, 'August Wilhelm Ambros: His Historical and Critical Thought'
(Ph.D. diss., Princeton University, 1955; a résumé of its contents occurs in *Dissertation
Abstracts*, xvii/6 (1957), pp. 1351–2).

[92] See ii, p. 61.

[93] I wish to express my gratitude to Prof. Helmuth Osthoff, who kindly advised me with
regard to a number of the works listed below whose ascription to Josquin is not easily
ascertained.

1537¹	*Novum et insigne opus musicum, sex, quinque, et quatuor vocum.* Nuremberg: H. Grapheus (Formschneider).
1538³	*Secundus tomus novi operis musici, sex, quinque et quatuor vocum.* Nuremberg: H. Grapheus.
1538⁷	*Modulationes aliquot quatuor vocum selectissimae, quas vulgo modetas* [*sic*] *vocant.* Nuremberg: J. Petreius.
1538⁸	*Symphoniae iucundae atque adeo breves quatuor vocum.* Wittenberg: G. Rhau.
1539²	*Missae tredecim quatuor vocum a praestantiss. artificib. compositae.* Nuremberg: H. Grapheus.
1539⁹	*Tomus secundus psalmorum selectorum quatuor et quinque vocum.* Nuremberg: J. Petreius.
1540⁷	*Selectissimae necnon familiarissimae cantiones.* Augsburg: M. Kriesstein.
1542¹²	*Sacrorum hymnorum liber primus.* Wittenberg: G. Rhau.
1544¹³	*Le cincquiesme livre contenant trente et deux chansons a cincq et a six parties.* Antwerp: T. Susato.
1545²	*Concentus octo, sex, quinque & quatuor vocum.* Augsburg: P. Ulhard.
1545³	*Cantiones septem, sex et quinque vocum.* Augsburg: M. Kriesstein.
1545¹⁵	*Le septiesme livre contenant vingt et quatre chansons a cincq et a six parties.* Antwerp: T. Susato.
1558⁴	*Novum et insigne opus musicum, sex, quinque, et quatuor vocum.* Nuremberg: J. von Berg & U. Neuber.
1559¹	*Secunda pars magni operis musici.* Nuremberg: J. von Berg & U. Neuber.
1559²	*Tertia pars magni operis musici.* Nuremberg: J. Montanus & U. Neuber.
Vienna	Vienna, Oesterreichische Nationalbibliothek.
Werken	*Werken van Josquin des Prés,* ed. A. Smijers et al. (Amsterdam, 1921–69).
Missen	Masses
Motetten	Motets
W.W.	Wereldlijke Werken (Secular Works)
Supp.	Supplement (fasc. no. 55).

I. Burney's Transcriptions of Josquin
(in London, British Museum, Department of Manuscripts)

	Title and number of voices⁹⁴	Source	Modern edition and remarks
Add. 11581			
ff. 22ᵛ–27	'Missa Pater [*sic*] Patris': *Pleni* (= *History,* i, p. 739), *Osanna, Benedictus, Agnus*	Petrucci Bk III	*Werken,* Missen, xii
27ᵛ–28ᵛ	'Missa La sol fa re mi': *Kyrie*	Petrucci Bk I³	*Werken,* Missen, ii
29–30ᵛ	'Missa super Gaudeamus': *Kyrie* I-*Christe, Benedictus, Agnus* II	Petrucci Bk I³	*Werken,* Missen, iii
31–34	'Missa Per [*sic*] fortuna desperata': *Kyrie, Qui tollis*	Petrucci Bk I³	*Werken,* Missen, iv
Add. 11582			
ff. 2ᵛ–11ᵛ	'Missa L'omme armé super voces musicales' (NB. *Agnus* II mensuration canon *a 3* is copied as single voice; Burney refers to the realization by Glareanus); *Pleni* = *History,* i, p. 741; *Benedictus* = ibid., p. 742 [the 3 canons are unrealized in the *History*])	Petrucci Bk I³	*Werken,* Missen, i

⁹⁴ The spelling of titles follows that of the two transcribers; the number of voices is given for motets and secular works only.

	Title and number of voices	Source	Modern edition and remarks
12	Subjects of Josquin's Masses in the first book: 'Missa La sol fa re mi' (*Kyrie I–Christe* [= 1st 11 mm.]) 'Missa super Gaudeamus' (*Kyrie I* [= 1st 6 1/2 mm.]) 'Missa Fortuna' (*Kyrie I*)	Petrucci Bk I[3]	*Werken*, Missen, ii, iii, iv
12ᵛ–15	'Ex Missa Faysans regres': *Kyrie I–Christe, Et incarnatus est...non erit finis, Sanctus* (*Osanna* = History, i, p. 743, *Benedictus* = ibid., pp. 744–5)	Petrucci Bk III	*Werken*, Missen, xiii
15ᵛ–16ᵛ	'Ex Missa Ad fugam': *Pleni, Osanna, Agnus II*	Petrucci Bk III	*Werken*, Missen, xiv
16ᵛ–17ᵛ	'Missa Didadi (Di dadi supra naragie): *Kyrie I, Sanctus, Benedictus*	Petrucci Bk III	*Werken*, Missen, xv
18–25	'Missa De beata Virgine': complete except for *Kyrie II* and *Qui tollis*	Petrucci Bk III	*Werken*, Missen, xvi
25ᵛ–31ᵛ	'Missa Sine nomine' (*Benedictus* canons unresolved; *Agnus II* = History, i, p. 739)	Petrucci Bk III	*Werken*, Missen, xvii
62ᵛ–65	'Huc me sydereo' (6)	RISM 1519[2]	*Werken*, Motetten, no. 32
65ᵛ–66	'Praeter rerum seriem', Pt. I (6): incompl. (only 1st 10 dotted long mm. are scored for all voices)	RISM 1519[2]	*Werken*, Motetten, no. 33
66ᵛ–68ᵛ	'Stabat Mater' (5)	RISM 1519[2]	*Werken*, Motetten, no. 36
69–72ᵛ	'Miserere mei Deus' (5)	RISM 1519[2]	*Werken*, Motetten, no. 37
73–74	'Alma Redemptoris Mater' (4)	RISM 1519[2]	*Werken*, Motetten, no. 38
78ᵛ–80ᵛ	'Domine ne in furore tuo' (4)	RISM 1519[2]	*Werken*, Motetten, no. 39
81 (last 2 mm. on 80ᵛ)	'Nesse pas ung grant desplaisir' (5)	RISM 1544[13]	*Werken*, W.W., no. 8
85	'En non saichant' (5)	RISM 1545[15]	*Werken*, W.W., no. 9
93	'Ave verum corpus' (3): incompl. (1st 2 sections only)	[Glareanus]	*Werken*, Motetten, no. 12
Add. 11585 ff. 23ᵛ–24	'Leure est venue' (3)	London, British Museum, MS. Royal 20 A XVI	Odhecaton, no. 81: Agricola. Burney attributes it to Josquin; Osthoff (ii, p. 184): '...gehört ohne Zweifel Alexander Agricola'.
25ᵛ	'[Que vous Madame]' (3): incompl. (1st 4 mm. only)	London 20 A XVI	*Werken*, W.W., no. 47
26ᵛ–27	'Mes pensées' (3)	London 20 A XVI	Odhecaton, no. 59: Compère

	Title and number of voices	Source	Modern edition and remarks
29–30	'Misericordias Domini', Pt. I (4) (= *History*, i, pp. 746–9)	RISM 1519[3]	*Werken*, Motetten, no. 43
30[v]–33[v]	'Inviolata integra et casta es' (5)	RISM 1519[3]	*Werken*, Motetten, no. 42
38	'Monados in Hypodorio prius Exemplum ex Hercule Jodici [*sic*] Pratensis' [= 'Missa Hercules Dux Ferrariae': *Pleni*]	Glareanus	*Werken*, Missen, vii
	'Agnus Dei, ex Iusquini Missa Hercules. Trium vocum ex una cum resolutione' [= idem, *Agnus* II]	Glareanus	*Werken*, Missen, vii

Add. 11588

ff. 63–63[v]	'Douleur me bat' (5)	[RISM 1545[15]]	*Werken*, W. W., no. 18

II. Ambros' Transcriptions of Josquin
(in Vienna, Oesterreichische Nationalbibliothek, Musiksammlung)

Supp. mus. 1556

	Title and number of voices	Source	Modern edition and remarks
ff. 1–1[v]	'Gloria laus et honor' (4): incompl. (1st 39 mm. of tenor only)	RISM 1538[3]	Ascribed to Brumel in RISM 1505[2].
1[v]–4[v]	'Requiem aeternam' (4) [= 'Mille quingentis' by Obrecht]	RISM 1504[1]	Printed in *Jakob Obrecht, Werken*, ed. J. Wolf, Motetten, pp. 179–81.[95]
4[v]–5	'Ergo Sancti Martyres' (4): incompl. (1st 45 mm. only)	RISM 1504[1]	Cf. Osthoff (ii, p. 7) about ascription to Josquin.
6–6[v]	'Scaramella va alla guerra' (4)	Florence, Bibl. Naz., MS. Magl. XIX, 59	*Werken*, W.W., no. 54
7–8[v]	'Absalon fili mi' (4)	RISM 1540[7]	*Werken*, Supp., no. 5
9–11	'Domine ne in furore tuo' (4)	[Commer VI][96]	*Werken*, Motetten, no. 59
11[v]–12[v]	'Misericordias Domini', Pt. I (4)	RISM 1519[3]	*Werken*, Motetten, no. 43
13–16[v]	'De profundis clamavi ad te' (4)	RISM 1520[4] (1521[3], 1539[9], Glareanus)[97]	*Werken*, Motetten, no. 47

[95] Ambros, together with other earlier writers such as Anton Schmid, the first cataloguer of Petrucci's music, claimed that the copy of Petrucci's *Motetti C* in the Oesterreichische Nationalbibliothek ascribed this piece, as well as *Ergo sancti martyres*, to Josquin. This copy now belongs to the Biblioteca Marciana, Venice, but the tenor part-book is missing. Neither piece carries an ascription in the remaining part-books (see Osthoff, i, pp. 199–200).

[96] Commer's edition is the apparent source of this and several other transcriptions; see above, n. 51.

[97] Primary sources listed in parentheses seem to have been consulted by Ambros (see above, introductory comments on Ambros' transcriptions).

Title and number of voices	Source	Modern edition and remarks
16ᵛ–17ᵛ 'Pange lingua gloriosi' (4)	RISM 1542¹²	*Das Erbe deutscher Musik*, Reichsdenkmale, xxii, ed. Rudolf Gerber, no. 62 (pp. 81–3); cf. Osthoff (ii, p. 15) about ascription to Josquin.
18–20ᵛ 'Sic Deus dilexit' (6)	[Commer VIII]	*Werken*, Motetten, no. 86
21–26ᵛ 'Factum est autem' (4) (28 July 1865; completed 'Nachmittag 6 Uhr bei Sturm, Blitz und Donner')	RISM 1504¹	*Werken*, Motetten, no. 16
27–30 'In principio erat verbum' (4)	RISM 1538³ (Vienna, MS. 15941)	*Werken*, Motetten, no. 56
'Josquini Antiphonae quinque':	RISM 1521³	*Werken*, Motetten,
30ᵛ–31ᵛ 'O admirabile commertium' (4)	(1538³)	nos. 5–9
32–33 'Quando natus est' (4)		
33–34 'Rubum quem viderat Moyses' (4)		
34–34ᵛ 'Germinavit radix Jesse' (4)		
35–35ᵛ 'Ecce Maria genuit' (4)		
36–38ᵛ 'O virgo prudentissima' (6)	RISM 1520⁴ (1538³, 1559²)	*Werken*, Motetten, no. 45
39–46ᵛ 'Pater noster' (6) (Unterdöbling, 16 July 1863)	RISM 1537¹	*Werken*, Motetten, no. 50
47–53 'Veni Sancte Spiritus' (6)	RISM 1537¹	*Werken*, Motetten, no. 49
53–55 'Victimae paschali laudes' (4)	RISM 1502¹ (Glareanus)	*Werken*, Motetten, no. 26
55ᵛ–57ᵛ 'Magnus es tu Domine' (4)	Glareanus (RISM 1504¹, 1538³: H. Finck)	*Werken*, Motetten, no. 19
58–59 'Ave Maria gratia plena...benedicta tu' (4)	RISM 1504¹	*Werken*, Motetten, no. 2
59–61 'Missus est Gabriel' (4)	RISM 1504¹	*Werken*, Motetten, no. 17
61–63ᵛ 'Ave Maria gratia plena...virgo serena' (4)	RISM 1502¹ (Glareanus)	*Werken*, Motetten, no. 1
64–70ᵛ 'Praeter rerum seriem' (6)	RISM 1537¹	*Werken*, Motetten, no. 33
70ᵛ 'O dulcis amica (Fuga sex vocum cuiusvis toni)' (1 voice only)	RISM 1540⁷	Cf. Osthoff, i, p. 8.
70ᵛ 'Ave sanctissima virgo (Fuga quinque vocum)' (1 voice only)	RISM 1540⁷	Cf. ibid., ii, p. 268.
71–73ᵛ 'Propter peccata quae peccastis' (5) [*contrafactum* of instrumental piece 'La Spagna']	RISM 1537¹	*Werken*, W.W., no. 52 [= 'La Spagna']
74–75 'Ecce tu pulchra es' (4) (28 July 1865)	Petrucci Bk I: Appendix	*Werken*, Motetten, no. 30
75ᵛ 'Dilectus Deo et hominibus' (4):	RISM 1538⁷	Anon. in RISM

	Title and number of voices	Source	Modern edition and remarks
	incompl. (1st 40 mm. only)		1519[8]; ascribed to Févin in RISM1538[8]. Osthoff (ii, p. 13): 'sehr zweifelhaft'.
76–76[v]	'Je sey bien dire' (4)	RISM 1504[3]	*Werken, W. W.*, no. 38
77–77[v]	'Una musque de Buscaya' (4) (27 December 1863)	RISM 1504[3]	*Werken, W. W.*, no. 37
78–78[v]	'Vive le roy' (4)	RISM 1504[3]	*Werken, W. W.*, no. 40
78[v]–79[v]	'A leure que ie vous p.x.' (4)	RISM 1504[3]	*Werken, W. W.*, no. 41
79[v]–80	'En lombre dung bissonet' (4)	RISM 1504[3]	*Werken, W. W.*, no. 59
80[v]	'La Bernardina' (3)	RISM 1504[3]	*Werken, W. W.*, no. 42
81–81[v]	'Petite Camusette' (6)	RISM 1545[15] (Commer VII)	*Werken, W. W.*, no. 17
82–83	'Plus nultz regretz' (4)	RISM 1540[7]	*Werken, W. W.*, no. 29
83–84	'J'ai bien cause' (6)	RISM 1540[7]	*Werken, W. W.*, no. 33
84–85	'Mi lares vous' (5)	RISM 1540[7]	*Werken, W. W.*, no. 34
85[v]	'Ave sanctissima virgo (Fuga quinque vocum)' [same as above, fol. 70[v]]	RISM 1540[7]	See above, fol. 70[v].
85[v]–86	'Nesse point un grand desplaisir' (5)	RISM 1540[7] (1544[13], 1545[15])	*Werken, W. W.*, no. 8
86[v]	'Lomme arme ("Canon . Et sic de singulis")' (4)	RISM 1502[2]	*Werken, W. W.*, no. 55
87	'[Adieu mes amours]' (4): incompl. (1 system for 3 upper voices only, written in faint pencil)	RISM 1501	*Werken, W. W.*, no. 35
88–91[v]	'Planxit autem David' (4) (1st page missing)	RISM 1504[1] (Glareanus)	*Werken*, Motetten, no. 20
92–93	'Stetit autem Salomon' (4): incompl. (ff. 92–92[v]: 54 mm.; f. 93 written out in soprano for another 27 mm.)	RISM 1538[7]	*Werken*, Motetten, no. 58
94–95	'Memor esto verbi tui' (4): incompl. (1st 63 mm. only)	RISM 1539[9]	*Werken*, Motetten, no. 31
96	'De profundis clamavi ad te' (4) [same as ff. 13–16[v] above]: incompl. (8 mm. in soprano only)	See above	*Werken*, Motetten, no. 47
97–98	'De profundis clamavi ad te' (4): incompl. (1st 51 mm. only)	RISM 1539[9]	*Werken*, Motetten, no. 91
99–99[v]	'Miserere mei Deus' (5): incompl. (1st 48 mm. only)	RISM 1538[3]	*Werken*, Motetten, no. 37
100	'Inviolata integra et casta es' (5): incompl. (1st 33 mm. only)	RISM 1519[3]	*Werken*, Motetten, no. 42
101	'In illo tempore stetit Jesus' (6): incompl. (1st 22 mm. only)	RISM 1538[3] (1559[1])	*Werken*, Motetten, no. 55

	Title and number of voices	Source	Modern edition and remarks
101ᵛ–102	[End of Isaac's 'Rogamus te', *1.p.*] *2.p.*: 'O Maria o regina' (4)	RISM 1504¹	Cf. Ambros, iii, p. 394.
102	'Requiem aeternam' (4) [same as above, ff. 1ᵛ–4ᵛ]: incompl. (1st 8 mm., crossed out)	RISM 1504¹	See above, ff. 1ᵛ–4ᵛ.

Supp. mus. 1563

no. 44	Iosquin Dascanio: 'El grillo' (4)	RISM 1505⁴	*Werken*, W.W., no. 53

Supp. mus. 1570

no. 10	Ein Ungenannter, vermuthlich kein geringerer als Josquin de Près: 'Forseulement' (4)	RISM 1504³	Cf. Osthoff, ii, p. 172; Ambros was convinced of Josquin's authorship on stylistic grounds.⁹⁸

Supp. mus. 1574

no. 6	'La Bernardina' (3)	RISM 1504³	*Werken*, W.W., no. 42; at the end of the transcription, Ambros writes: 'Josquins Bernardina und Ghiselins Alfonsina sind unverkennbar eine der anderen nachgebildet; es frägt sich welche von beiden das Muster war'.

Supp. mus. 1578

ff. 2–15	'Missa Lomme arme super voces musicales' (Prague, 21 September 1863)	Petrucci Bk I	*Werken*, Missen, i
15ᵛ–25ᵛ	'Missa La sol fa re mi'	Petrucci Bk I	*Werken*, Missen, ii
26–36ᵛ	'Missa Gaudeamus' (13 May 1865)	Petrucci Bk I (Vienna, MS. 11.778)	*Werken*, Missen, iii
37–49ᵛ	'Missa super Fortuna desperata' (23 May 1865)	Petrucci Bk I	*Werken*, Missen, iv
50–61ᵛ	'Missa Lomme armé sexti toni'	Petrucci Bk I	*Werken*, Missen, v
62–69ᵛ	'Missa Ave maris stella' (27 July 1865)	Petrucci Bk II	*Werken*, Missen, vi
70–78ᵛ	'Missa Hercules dux Ferrarie' (7 May 1865)	Petrucci Bk II	*Werken*, Missen vii

⁹⁸ He remarks at the end of the transcription: 'Ex ungue leonem! Diese Bearbeitung voll geistreicher und kühner Züge, voll "Josquinismen", mit dem nachtönenden Schluss im Bass, mit dem Stempel der Originalität und Genialität bezeichnet, und neben Hobrechts meisterhafter, aber entschieden archaischerer Behandlung die beste unter allen, kann kaum jemandes anderen sein als Josquins! Dass Petrucci den berühmten Namen nicht nennt? In den Motetti C verschweigt er bei den Motetten *Planxit autem David* und *Magnus es tu Domine* gleichfalls Josquins Autorschaft, welche doch nach Glarean (: Dodecach. S. 272 u. 367) hier zweifellos ist!'

	Title and number of voices	Source	Modern edition and remarks
79–79ᵛ	Joannes Ockeghem: 'Malheur me bat' (3)	RISM 1501	Odhecaton, ff. 68ᵛ–69; *Werken, Missen,* viii: App.
80–92ᵛ	'Missa Malheur me bat'	Petrucci Bk II	*Werken, Missen,* viii
93–102ᵛ	'Missa super Lami baudichon' (11 July 1865)	Petrucci Bk II	*Werken, Missen,* ix
103–112ᵛ	'Missa Una Musque de Biscaya'	Petrucci Bk II	*Werken, Missen,* x
113–118ᵛ	'Missa super Dung aultre amer' (5 May 1865)	Petrucci Bk II	*Werken, Missen,* xi
119–128ᵛ	'Missa Mater Patris' (19 August 1865)	Petrucci Bk III	*Werken, Missen,* xii
129–136ᵛ	'Missa Faysans regres' (13 July 1865)	Petrucci Bk III	*Werken, Missen,* xiii
137–146ᵛ	'Missa ad Fugam'	Petrucci Bk III	*Werken, Missen,* xiv
147–156ᵛ	'Missa Didadi' (19 July 1865)	Petrucci Bk III	*Werken, Missen,* xv
157–170ᵛ	'Missa de Beata Virgine' (1 August 1865)	Petrucci Bk III	*Werken, Missen,* xvi
171–178ᵛ	'Missa sine nomine' (16 August 1865)	Petrucci Bk III	*Werken, Missen,* xvii
179–188ᵛ	'Missa da pacem' (16 July 1865)	RISM 1539²	*Werken, Missen,* xix
189–202	'Missa de venerabili Sacramento (super Pange lingua)' (23 August 1862)	Vienna, MS. 4809 (RISM 1539²)	*Werken, Missen,* xviii

Supp. mus. 1579			
ff. 2–6	'Huc me sidereo' (6) (9 August 1864)	RISM 1519² (1538³)	*Werken, Motetten,* no. 32
6ᵛ–7ᵛ	'O Jesu fili David' (4) [*contrafactum* by Glareanus of the chanson 'Comment peult avoir ioye' from *Canti B*]	Glareanus (Hawkins)	*Werken, W.W.,* no. 56 (= chanson)
8–12	'Responsum acceperat Simeon' (6)	RISM 1545³	*Werken, Motetten,* no. 85
12–14ᵛ	'Nesciens mater virgo' (5)	RISM 1545³	*Werken, Motetten,* no. 71
15–20ᵛ	'Liber generationis' (4)	RISM 1558⁴ (1504¹, 1538³, Glareanus)	*Werken, Motetten,* no. 15
21–26ᵛ	'Benedicta es coelorum regina' (6)	RISM 1537¹	*Werken, Motetten,* no. 46
27–30ᵛ	'Responde mihi' (4)	RISM 1545²	*Werken, Motetten,* no. 75
31–33ᵛ	'Ave verum corpus' (5)	RISM 1545²	*Werken, Motetten,* no. 80
34–34ᵛ	'Ave verum corpus' (3): incompl. (the 'Cujus latus' section *a 2* omitted)	RISM 1503¹	*Werken, Motetten,* no. 12
35	'Ave verum corpus' (3): same as above, but only 1st 2 sections	Glareanus	*Werken, Motetten,* no. 12
35ᵛ–37ᵛ	'Ave Christe immolate' (4)	[Commer, VIII]	*Werken, Motetten,* no. 76
38–39	'Tribulatio et angustia' (4)	RISM 1537¹	*Werken, Motetten,* no. 54

	Title and number of voices	Source	Modern edition and remarks
39–41^v	'Quam pulchra es' (4)	RISM 1537[1] (1519[2]: Mouton)	Ambros notes conflicting ascription; the motet is now thought to be by Mouton (cf. Osthoff, ii, p. 11).[99]
41^v–49^v	'In exitu Israel' (4)	RISM 1537[1]	*Werken*, Motetten, no. 51

Supp. mus. 1595

no. 11	'Adieu mes amours' (4): cantus and tenor only, copied consecutively	[RISM 1501]	*Werken*, W.W., no. 35

Supp. mus. 1597

no. 1	'Lome arme (Canon Et sic de singulis)' (4): the 4 parts are written out consecutively [cf. Supp. mus. 1556, fol. 86^v]	RISM 1502[2]	*Werken*, W.W., no. 55
no. 2	'Esto nobis (Schluss des Josquinischen Ave verum)' (3): the 3 parts are written out consecutively [cf. Supp. mus. 1579, ff. 34–35]	RISM 1503[1]	*Werken*, Motetten, no. 12

Supp. mus. 1598

no. 12	'Bergerette savoyenne' (4): cantus and tenor parts only, written out consecutively (the word 'unvollendet' is pencilled in at end, and the page cancelled by a diagonal line)	[RISM 1501]	*Werken*, W.W., no. 36

Supp. mus. 1599

no. 16	'Je sey bien dire' (4): the 4 parts written out consecutively	[RISM 1504[3]]	*Werken*, W.W., no. 38
no. 18	'Absalon fili mi' (4): the 4 parts are written out consecutively [cf. Supp. mus. 1556, ff. 7–8^v]	RISM 1540[7]	*Werken*, Supp., no. 5

Supp. mus. 1604

no. 2	'Scaramella va alla guerra' (4): the 4 parts are written out consecutively	[Florence, Bibl. Naz., MS. Magl. XIX, 59]	*Werken*, W.W., no. 54

[99] About Ambros' confusion of the styles of Josquin and Mouton, see Edward E. Lowinsky, *The Medici Codex*, iii, pp. 180–81. For a general discussion of the styles of the two composers, see ibid., pp. 219–28.

II Source Studies

Josquin and the Courts of the Netherlands and France: The Evidence of the Sources

HERBERT KELLMAN

The relationship of Josquin to the courts of the Netherlands and France remains one of the most vexing problems in our efforts to understand the composer's life and works. The purpose of this study is not to attempt to resolve the problem, but rather to pose it anew by showing that even the little we claim to know and to be able to surmise about Josquin in the last decades of his life—especially in regard to his relationship to the Nether-lands—needs to be restated. Toward this end I should like both to review some well known evidence and to examine in a new light a group of musical sources.

A scant body of documents alluding to Josquin's connections with the Netherlands and French courts has come down to us. Fétis, Vander Straeten, and Ambros already knew a sufficient number of these to be able to conclude that Josquin was at the court of Louis XII at some time in his life and that he was held in esteem by the house of Hapsburg. But in more recent scholarship, and especially in the work of Helmuth Osthoff,[1] specific instances of contact with the northern courts have been inferred from four compositions and two archival records. These inferences appear quickly to have become established facts in Josquin's *vita*; and they have been variously, and for the most part uncritically, repeated in the literature, down to the summary biography in the festival programme.[2] I believe that they are based on a number of invalid premises, however, and offer the following critiques and conclusions, taking the liberty of presenting these in summary form. If it is mainly Professor Osthoff's interpretations which are at issue, it ought to be self-evident that this in no sense diminishes the extent of our indebtedness to his wide-ranging work.

[1] 'Josquin Desprez', in *MGG*, vii (1958), col. 195; *Josquin Desprez*, 2 vols. (Tutzing, 1962–5). All references hereafter will be to the latter work.

[2] I do not mean by this to impugn the work of Frank Tirro, the author, who has simply passed on the transmitted canon, very skilfully condensed.

Three compositions and one letter are advanced as evidence of Josquin's close relationship to Margaret of Austria and one record of payment is believed to connect Josquin with Charles V. One composition is allegedly on the death of Louis XII.

'Plus nulz regretz'[3]

Argument: Jean Lemaire wrote the text of this chanson in connection with a peace treaty between the Empire and England, one provision of which was the engagement of the archduke Charles and Mary Tudor. The treaty was signed in Calais on 21 December 1507 and proclaimed and celebrated in Malines on 1 January 1508. Josquin composed the chanson for the celebration. Therefore the chanson was composed in December 1507, and since only a few days were available, Josquin must have been at the court in Malines or nearby.

Critique: The earliest source of Lemaire's text is a print dated 15 February 1508, in which the poem, with a preamble, appears together with two other commemorative works by Lemaire.[4] The preamble explains the genesis of the poem and the chronology of its writing:[5] 'After the successful return from Calais of my lords the ambassadors [on 29 December 1507] ... and after these had given a full report of their very happy achievement, ... on New Year's day ... my lord the Archduke, Madam his aunt, and ... his sisters went in great triumph to hear Mass in the church of St. Rombaut. ... And that very day bonfires were lit throughout Malines to mark the proclamation of this very honourable, beneficial, and necessary union [of Charles and Mary]. And then this new poem was written'.[6] Lemaire thus indicates that his work was written on, or after, 1 January 1508.

[3] 'Plus nulz regretz', 'Plaine de dueil', and 'Parfons regretz' were first interpreted by Osthoff, *Josquin Desprez*, i, pp. 67–9.

[4] *La pompe funeralle des obseques du feu Roy dom Phelippes. Ung chant nouvel touchant aliance dangleterre. Lepitaphe de feux messire george chastelain et maitre Jehan molinet* (Antwerp: Guillaume Vosterman). *La pompe funeralle* is dedicated to Margaret of Austria and *Lepitaphe* to Charles Le Clerc (see Appendix II, Brussels 215/216).

[5] The chronology of Lemaire's writing of the poem, and, consequently, of Josquin's composition of the music, has been misunderstood partly because of the corrupt reading of the preamble (a nineteenth-century translation into French of a Flemish translation of the Vosterman text) transmitted in J. Stecher's *Oeuvres de Jean Lemaire de Belges*, iv (Louvain, 1891), pp. 267–8.

[6] 'Apres le Retour prospere de calais de messeigneurs les embassadeurs,...Et quilz eurent fait ample Rapport de leur tresheureux exploit,...Le premier Jour de lan...Mondit seigneur Larchiduc Madame sa tante, et...ses seurs Alerent en grant triumphe, ouyr messe en leglise saint Rombault,...Et ce iour mesmes, furent faictz les feux de Joye par my malines, pour la publication de ladicte tresnoble aliance, tresUtille et tresnecessaire. Et lors fut mis sus ce chant nouvel'. The last phrase, referring to the poem which imme-

Conclusion: Josquin composed the chanson between 1508 and 1511, the year in which the earliest known source of the work was copied.[7] We cannot from this infer Josquin's presence in Malines, nor can we be certain that the chanson was the result of direct contact with Margaret or Maximilian.[8] Four years earlier Lemaire himself had evidently stimulated Josquin to compose a topical chanson,[9] and he might have done so again in this case.

'Plaine de dueil'

Argument: The text of this chanson begins with the same words as does the rondeau 'Plaine de dueil et loing de bonne voye', which Strelka considers a work of Margaret's.[10] It also has the rhyme and syllable structure of the latter, as well as of 'Cest pour james', of which Margaret's authorship is undisputed. Therefore it is most probably by Margaret too.

Critique: The borrowing of opening refrain phrases (*rentrements*) and the rhyme and syllable structure in question are common in French poetry of

---

diately follows (under the title 'Chant Nouvel'), needs especially to be understood correctly. For the adverb 'lors' see Edmond Huguet, *Dictionnaire de la langue française du seizième siècle*, v (Paris, 1961), p. 45. Like the English 'then', the word may mean 'after that', as in Huguet's first definition, or 'at that time'. I believe that Lemaire uses it in the former sense, though either meaning would lead to the conclusion that the poem was not written before New Year's day, 1508. For the verb 'mettre sus' see Frédéric Godefroy, *Dictionnaire de l'ancienne langue française*, v (Paris, 1888), p. 316. (Osthoff, i, p. 67, omits the crucial 'sus'.) 'Chant' is used figuratively here, as in 'chant royal', a contemporary poetic genre. I am most grateful to Professor Barbara Bowen of the University of Illinois for frequent advice in matters of translation from Middle French.

[7] The part-books Tournai, Bibliothèque de la Ville, Cod. 94, and Brussels, Bibliothèque royale, MS. IV 90. The date 1511 is written in a contemporary hand within the opening initial of fol. 21 of the Tournai book. See Charles van den Borren, 'Inventaire des manuscrits de musique polyphonique qui se trouvent en Belgique', *Acta musicologica*, vi (1934), pp. 119–21.

[8] For new and more definitive evidence regarding this point, see Postscript, (3), below, p. 207.

[9] 'Cueurs desolez' for the death of Louis of Luxembourg (Osthoff, i, pp. 65–67). However, Martin Picker has recently pointed out that while the composer whom Lemaire addresses in *La Plainte du Desiré* is Josquin in the poem's printed version of 1509, it is 'Hilaire' in the manuscript version of 1503 ('Josquin and Jean Lemaire: Four Chansons Re-examined', paper read at the Symposium in Honor of Gustave Reese, New York University, 1 June 1974). This suggests that Lemaire and Josquin may not have been in contact in 1503, after all.

[10] Josef Strelka, *Der burgundische Renaissancehof Margarethes von Österreich und seine literarhistorische Bedeutung* (Vienna, 1957), p. 55.

this period.[11] No student of the poetry of Margaret's court has attributed a work to her on the basis of these criteria.

Conclusion: Margaret's authorship of 'Plaine de dueil' is at best only a possibility.

'Parfons regretz'

Argument: The bass of this chanson appears in a part-book of Vienna, Nationalbibliothek, MS. 18746 below the inscription, 'Chanson de monsieur Bouton. A moy seulle'. Bouton, one of Margaret's courtiers, is known as a poet. Therefore he is the author of the text of 'Parfons regretz'.

Critique: The first word in the inscription is clearly 'Chansons' (Plate 31, fig. a). 'A moy seulle' is the title of an anonymous chanson that appears earlier in the manuscript, separated from 'Parfons regretz' by twenty-four pieces. Therefore the inscription refers to two or more pieces, probably among these twenty-six. Bouton's poetic activity is not documented; his name appears in Margaret's 'Livre des ballades', but this by no means makes it certain that he was a poet. On the other hand, he is known to have had contact with musicians, he was with Philip the Fair in Blois in 1501 and could have met Josquin there, and it was his father for whom the Chigi codex was prepared, perhaps on his orders. The Vienna manuscript was copied in Malines and completed in May 1523.[12] Shortly thereafter Bouton was also in Malines.[13]

Conclusion: It is far more likely that 'Chansons' refers to pieces of music in the manuscript than to texts, the more so since only text incipits occur. Bouton's connection with these could have been as courier or recipient. It is not certain, in any case, that 'Parfons regretz' is one of the pieces to which the inscription alludes.

[11] Marcel Françon, *Albums poétiques de Marguerite d'Autriche* (Cambridge, Mass., 1934), pp. 40–41. In the 'albums poétiques' (Brussels, Bibliothèque royale, MSS. 10572, 228, and 11239) there are seven pairs of poems that begin with the same phrase, and thirty-four poems with the stanza structure of 'Plaine de dueil'.

[12] On fol. 52 of the superius part-book appears the inscription 'clare van diest heft hier gheweest' ('Clare van Diest was here'). The van Diest family is found in the town registers of Malines from 1438 on; it is known that a Claire van Diest married an official of the town, and died in 1530. See M. De Vegiano, Sr. D'Hovel, J. De Herckenrode, *Nobiliaire des Pays-Bas et du Comté de Bourgogne*, ii (Ghent, 1865), p. 650. Petrus Alamire has signed and dated the tenor part-book on fol. 53.

[13] For details of Bouton's life, see M. E. Beauvois, *Un agent politique de Charles-Quint: le Bourguignon Claude Bouton, seigneur de Corberon* (Paris, 1882). Regarding his arrival in Malines, see Wilhelm Bauer, ed., *Die Korrespondenz Ferdinands I* (Vienna, 1912), i, pp. 62–7. The Chigi codex is discussed below.

Letter from the chapter of Notre-Dame in Condé replying to a letter from Margaret[14]

Argument: From the chapter's reply it can be inferred that Margaret had heard that Josquin was ill (the chapter could inform her that he was in very good health), and had offered the services of a certain Doctor Collerab to attend him.

Critique: Doctor Collerab ('le docteur Collerab') could not be a physician. In the sixteenth century the elliptical title 'docteur' was reserved as a prefix for a teacher of, or one learned in, law or theology. A physician, even one with a doctorate in medicine, was identified by the formula 'maistre [name], médecin' or 'maistre . . . physicien' or 'maistre . . . chirurgien'.[15] Margaret's correspondence and court records are completely consistent in this usage: a large number of physicians are mentioned many times by name, but not one is given the prefix 'docteur'. It is, however, given to several other men in her correspondence, and these are ambassadors, court officials, and ecclesiastics.[16] Apart from this, the phrase 'la requeste que il vous a pleut faire pour le docteur Collerab' indicates that Margaret had made a request *on behalf of* Doctor Collerab.[17] Requests on behalf of someone, coupled with references to the illness of another person, occur very frequently in Margaret's correspondence, and always under the same circumstances: Margaret (or Maximilian) has heard of the illness and likely resignation or death of an incumbent of an office or benefice, and requests the position for a particular candidate, should it

---

[14] Lille, Archives départementales du Nord, B. 18829, no. 25216. This document was first published by J. Delporte, 'Un document inédit sur Josquin Desprez', *Musique et liturgie*, xxii (1938), pp. 54–6. It is discussed by Osthoff (i, pp. 69–70), who also gives its full text. A facsimile appears in *MGG*, vii (1958), Plate 11.

[15] See 'docteur' in the following: Edmond Huguet, *Dictionnaire de la langue française*, iii (Paris, 1933); Paul Robert, *Dictionnaire alphabétique et analogique de la langue française*, ii (Paris, 1966); Albert Dauzat, Jean Dubois, Henri Mitterand, *Nouveau Dictionnaire étymologique et historique* (Paris, 1964); Jacqueline Picoche, *Nouveau dictionnaire étymologique du français* (Paris, 1971). See also Georges van Doorslaer, 'Aperçu historique sur la médecine et les médecins à Malines avant le XIXe siècle', *Bulletin du cercle archéologique, littéraire et artistique de Malines*, x (1900), pp. 121–300.

[16] M. Le Glay, *Correspondance de l'empereur Maximilien Ier et de Marguerite d'Autriche*, 2 vols. (Paris, 1839). 'Docteurs' are mentioned in letters nos. 23, 48, 50, 163, 180, 210, 243, 400, 547; physicians ('médecins') are mentioned in letters nos. 109, 129, 130, 153, 287, 291, 330, 382, 485, 538, 546, 573, 574. See also *Archives départementales du Nord, Série B, Répertoire numérique* (Lille, 1921), pp. 437, 440, 442, 443, 447.

[17] A summary of the document appears in the *Inventaire sommaire des archives départementales. Nord. Archives civiles—Série B*, Tome I, 2e partie (Lille, 1906), p. 405. Regarding this phrase, the summary says: 'requête en faveur du docteur Collerab'. Various forms of 'faire une requête pour' appear in Margaret's correspondence, always with the meaning 'to request on behalf of'. See Le Glay, *Correspondance*, letters nos. 32, 33, 58.

become vacant.[18] In June 1508, Maximilian instructed Margaret to find a suitable benefice for one of his secretaries, a Doctor Collauer. Margaret had already found Collauer a curacy, but he had declined it, apparently in hopes of something better. Only in December 1509 was he finally accommodated with the provostship of Louvain.[19]

Conclusion:[20] We cannot possibly infer from the reply of the chapter of Condé that Margaret's letter was one of solicitude for Josquin. In common with many of her other letters, it is much more likely to have stated that she had heard that Josquin des Prez was ill and the provostship might become vacant, and that she was requesting the chapter to approve her candidate. We have a model for precisely such a request on her part in a letter brought by messengers to the chapter of the collegiate church of Saint-Just in Lyons asking for a benefice for Jean Lemaire.[21] If 'Collerab' is a transformation of 'Collauer'—and it is one which could easily have occurred[22]—Margaret wrote to Condé in May 1508 or May 1509. It should be noted that archivists in Lille in the nineteenth century tentatively dated the chapter's letter 1508. The catalogue offers no reason for the dating, but it was probably the result of comparisons with other documents.[23]

Entry in the 1520 account book of Charles V's treasurer[24]

Argument: Josquin came to Brussels or Malines in September 1520 and presented new chansons to the Emperor Charles V. *Prima facie* evidence for this is an entry in an account book of that year, which states that on orders of Charles the sum of 51 *livres*, 15 *solz* was given 'to two singers from the town of Condé of whom one was called Joskin, as a gift which

18 Ibid., letters nos. 14, 22, 32, 303, 309, 388, 506.

19 Ibid., letters nos. 48, 50, 163, 180.

20 New evidence completely clarifies the contents and date of Margaret's letter and the significance of the chapter's reply. See Postscript, (3), below, p. 207.

21 Archives départementales du Rhône, Chapitre de Saint-Just, Actes Capitulaires, vol. X, ff. 269–70, published in Pierre Champion, *Le canonicat pour Jean Lemaire de Belges à Lyon* (Lyons, 1926). I am indebted to Professor Anthony Newcomb of the University of California at Berkeley for obtaining a photocopy of this rare publication for me.

22 The transformation requires only a simple metathesis (in this case -auer to -erau), of which there are several examples in Margaret's correspondence, and the u, v, b exchange common in French orthography. This could well have occurred in the copying process, from Margaret's or the chapter's protocols. Osthoff (i, p. 218, n. 31) noticed the similarity of the two names, but did not pursue its implications.

23 *Inventaire sommaire*, Tome I, 2e partie, p. 405. For the history of the classification of documents see also Tome I (1er partie), pp. XX–XXIV.

24 Lille, Archives départementales du Nord, Régistre B. 2294, f. 279ᵛ. This document was first mentioned by Noel Dupire in his *Les Faictz et Dictz de Jean Molinet*, iii (Paris, 1939), p. 1005.

he had made them in equal portions for some new songs ['aucunes chanssons nouvelles'] which they had presented to him, to help them to live and return to their home'. The second singer was perhaps a pupil of Josquin's. The sum in question was considerably in excess of the usual payments for musical services.[25]

Critique: The entry actually records a reimbursement to the treasurer for the total amount of four payments, the payment to the two singers from Condé being the first; the others are 'to a courier from the town of Antwerp', 'to Katherine, widow of the late Josse van Steelant, in his life-time a singer of the King', and 'to a messenger and three poor women'. It is the total reimbursement that amounts to 51 *livres*, 15 *solz*, whereas the sum paid to Joskin and his companion was, in fact, 37 *livres*, 10 *solz*.[26] In the absence of comparable records of rewards for music presented under similar circumstances, the significance of the latter amount cannot be reliably judged.[27] It may be noted, however, that precisely 37 *livres*, 10 *solz* was given by Philip the Fair, in 1501, to two sackbut players who 'had played before my lord, for his pleasure'.[28] The name Josse (Jodocus) was not an uncommon one, as the reference to Josse van Steelant in the same entry confirms.[29] Since the choir at Notre-Dame in Condé must have been relatively large—it included six choirboys and was capable of singing six-part polyphony[30]—one of its members might well have had this name.[31]

[25] Osthoff, i, pp. 73–4.

[26] Osthoff (ibid., i, p. 73) is apparently not aware of this. He offers an incomplete transcription of only the first portion of the document, producing a reading that appears to make the total reimbursement applicable to the two musicians. The actual amount paid immediately follows this transcribed portion.

[27] The only roughly analogous reward I have been able to find in published extracts of the account books of this period is one from Margaret of Austria: '20 *livres* to Jehan Augier called le Petit Breton, to buy a fur robe, being in reward for, and in consideration of, some epitaphs and other compositions written by him in rhyme and in prose, which he has presented to her' (Lille, Archives départementales du Nord, Régistre B. 2339: 1er janvier–31 décembre 1527; *Inventaire sommaire*, Tome V (Lille, 1885), p. 3). This amount is, of course, slightly more than each of the two musicians received.

[28] Edmond vander Straeten, *La Musique aux Pays-Bas*, vii (Brussels, 1885), p. 272. The two were Hans Nagle and Hans Broen, called 'sackbut players of the king of England'.

[29] In the retinue of Philip the Fair in 1506, besides Josse van Steelant, were Josse d'Isenghien, Josse de Conflans, and Josse Denys; in that of Charles V in 1521 were Josse Weert and Josse Laurens (Lille, Archives départementales du Nord, B. 3463 and B. 3473; *Inventaire sommaire*, Tome VIII (Lille, 1895), pp. 100–2, 121). In 1501, among less than twenty resident canons of the church of Sainte-Gudule in Brussels were Judocus Cloet, Judocus Leenheere, and Judocus de Palude (Brussels, Archives du Royaume, Archives ecclésiastiques no. 388, Roll for 1501).

[30] See Postscript, (6), below, p. 208.

[31] In 1504, one of the contributors to a fund to pay for a new spire for the church was 'Josse Stienne, clerc' (Paris, Bibliothèque Nationale, MS. lat. 9917, f. 2v; see Postscript, (1), below, p. 207).

That there was such a musician who also used the diminutive form of the name is less probable, but not out of the question.[32] Furthermore, there is a noticeable difference between the cryptic reference to 'Joskin', and the usual provision in the court registers of full names and titles of payees of any status but the lowest, certainly of churchmen as high in rank as was Josquin des Prez;[33] the disparity is evident within the entry, in the precise identification of Josse van Steelant, a deceased, relatively minor musician, whose service in the chapel had ended eight years earlier.[34] Both the implication that the named musician was more important than his anonymous companion and the likelihood that he was the latter's master must be countered by the fact that the two were paid equal amounts. And that a functionary's ignorance might have led to the omission of such identifying information as the name Des Prez, or the designation 'prévôt de Condé', is not consistent with the precise terms in which the payment is otherwise described, a precision no doubt attributable to the copying of this entry—in accordance with the usual practise at the Netherlands court—directly from a *mandement* or *lettre de don* issued by the emperor.[35]

Conclusion: We cannot be certain that the musician in question is Josquin des Prez. If this document does record a visit of Josquin to the court, however, it offers evidence that his standing and familiarity there were not what it has been imagined they were, for, without a hint of the vener-

[32] See the concluding section of Lewis Lockwood's article in these Proceedings, pp. 120–21. Traces of at least one other composer named Josquin can be found in Italy at this time, and it must remain a possibility that some of the men who in documents are named 'Josse', would also have been called 'Josquin'. In this respect it may be observed that Des Prez's first name appears as 'Josse' in at least five documents drawn up in Condé between 1504 and 1523.

[33] This may be verified from transcripts of hundreds of documents recording payments, published in the *Inventaire sommaire*, Tome IV (Lille, 1881). Payments made to provosts, between 1500 and 1518, can be found on pp. 296, 308, 310, 311, 336, 339, 341, 355, 358. A receipt of 1518 for money paid to Henry Bredeniers calls this musician: 'Henri de Bredeniers, prévôt de Namur, organiste du Roi' (ibid., p. 359). The following is a representative entry for a payment to a member of a collegiate chapter: 'A messire Franchois Desmons, presbtre, channoine de l'église collégiale de Saint-Piat à Seclin, en la chastellenie de Lille, la somme de dix huyt livres du pris de XL gros, pour don que l'empereur lui en a fait pour aucunes causes..., meismement pour luy ayder à payer certaine amende dont il avoit lors naguerre esté condempné ou siège de la gouvernance à Lille' (1522; ibid., p. 371).

[34] Georges Van Doorslaer, 'La chapelle musicale de Philippe le Beau', *Revue belge d'archéologie et d'histoire de l'art*, iv (1934), p. 157.

[35] For a brief history of the accounting procedures at the Netherlands court, see *Archives départementales...Répertoire numérique*, pp. I–VIII. Many *mandements* and *lettres de don* have survived; when one of these is matched with the appropriate record of payment it can be seen that the two documents have virtually identical wording.

able composer, well known among men of letters, 'princeps omnium' among musicians, head of a major collegiate chapter, 'Sire Josse des Prez' at Notre-Dame, he is described only as a singer from Condé who 'was called ['se nommoit'] Joskin'. I have found no other document in which the identity of a person of comparable stature, supposedly admired by Charles or Margaret, remains so undifferentiated as in this case, or in which such a person's name is introduced by 'called'.

'*De profundis clamavi*'[36]

Argument: The five-voice 'De profundis' is found in Cappella Sistina MS. 38 (dated 1563) with the canon formula: 'Les trois estas sont assembles/Pour le soulas des trespasses'. These words stem from the composer. In the context of a funeral motet they must refer to a French king. The estates-general had a significant role only under Louis XII, to whom they gave the title 'Père du peuple' in 1506. Therefore this motet was composed for the funeral of Louis XII in January 1515.

Critique: The social structure of the three estates and the estates-general ('les états généraux') as a constitutional body existed in the Netherlands as well as in France.[37] Proof that the three estates participated officially in the funeral of a sovereign of the Netherlands comes from Jean Lemaire, who relates that funeral services for Philip the Fair were celebrated in Malines on 18 and 19 July 1507 by 'Monsr larchiduc Charles . . . ma tres redoubtée dame . . . et les trois estatz des pays . . . le lendemain . . . les deputez des trois estatz . . . furent convocquez . . . en la grant salle . . . toute tendue de noir'.[38]

Conclusion: As the only state funeral of a sovereign of France or the Netherlands for which the participation and assembly of the three estates is documented, the funeral of Philip the Fair in 1507 ought to take precedence as a possible occasion for the composition of 'De profundis', if the canon formula is indeed from Josquin's time. But as a formalized social structure the three estates were probably represented officially at every state funeral in both countries in the sixteenth century. Thus the funeral of Louis XII remains a possible occasion for the motet, and the funerals of Anne of Brittany in 1514 and Maximilian in 1519 must also be taken into

[36] Helmuth Osthoff first proposed the connection between this motet and Louis XII in *Josquin Desprez*, *Drei Motetten* (Das Chorwerk, Heft 57; Wolfenbüttel, 1956), pp. III–IV. See also *Josquin Desprez*, i, pp. 48–9.

[37] Henri Pirenne, *Histoire de Belgique*, iii (Brussels, 1912), pp. 195–206: 'Les États Généraux'.

[38] *Chronique annale*; Stecher, *Oeuvres de Jean Lemaire*, iv, p. 515.

consideration.[39] Without further evidence, however, we cannot assign 'De profundis' to any one of these occasions with certainty.

*   *   *

Since these hitherto unquestioned connections of Josquin with the northern courts upon close examination become only possibilities, it is useful to be able to turn to a large group of musical documents which provide a different kind of evidence for Josquin's role in court music in the last decades of his life.

I am referring to the Netherlands court manuscripts listed in Appendix I,[40] a complex of fifty books of polyphony with which I have been occupied for some years.[41] All of these were copied by court scribes in Brussels or Malines, many were illuminated by the Ghent and Bruges workshops, and most were made up as gifts to be sent out to other courts within the Empire or to courts whose favours the Empire sought. Roediger was able to delineate the beginnings of the complex on the basis of the Jena manuscripts, and other scholars have written on others of the books.[42] I have been able to enlarge the complex to its present size, and on the basis of external and internal evidence, to date each within a decade, to establish relationships among the manuscripts, and to arrange them in chronological groups. At the same time it has seemed fruitful to treat the more than 150 Masses, 200 motets, and 170 chansons in these sources as a self-contained repertory, and indeed a repertory to be associated with the Netherlands chapel over a thirty-year period. I shall focus only on the Josquin manu-

[39] The appearance of the work in the print *Altus, Liber secundus* (RISM [1521]⁴), of which half the contents are written by composers primarily associated with France, may point toward a connection with the French court.

[40] This is a revised version of Table 4 in my article, 'The Origins of the Chigi Codex: The Date, Provenance, and Original Ownership of Rome, Biblioteca Vaticana, Chigiana C VIII 234', *Journal of the American Musicological Society*, xi (1958), pp. 6–19.

[41] I have reported on this work in three papers read at annual meetings of the American Musicological Society: 'Illuminated Choirbooks and the Manuscript Tradition in Flanders in the Early Sixteenth Century' (1962), 'The Role of the Empire in the Radiation of the Northern Repertory, 1500–1530' (1965), 'Musical Links between France and the Empire, 1500–1530' (1970). More of the results will soon appear in print.

[42] Bibliography for the manuscripts containing music by Josquin will be found in conjunction with Appendix II. Other studies that pertain to manuscripts in Appendix I are: Georges Van Doorslaer, 'Calligraphes de musique à Malines au XVIᵉ siècle', *Bulletin du Cercle archéologique, littéraire et artistique de Malines*, xxxiii (1928), p. 91; idem, 'La chapelle musicale de Philippe le Beau', *Revue belge d'archéologie et d'histoire de l'art*, iv (1934), pp. 21, 139; René B. Lenaerts, 'Niederländische polyphone Musik in der Bibliothek von Montserrat', in *Festschrift Joseph Schmidt-Görg* (Bonn, 1957), p. 196; Dom David Pujol, 'Manuscritos de música neerlandesa conservados en la Biblioteca del Monasterio de Montserrat', in *Atti del Congresso Internazionale di Musica Sacra, 1950* (Tournai, 1952), pp. 319–26; Albert Smijers, 'Meerstemmige muziek van de illustre Lieve Vrouwe Broederschap te 's-Hertogenbosch', in *Tijdschrift der Vereeniging voor Nederlandsche Muziekgeschiedenis*, xvi (1940), p. 1.

scripts, but provide Appendix I to show the derivation of the repertory in which Josquin's place will be examined.

Twenty of the Netherlands court manuscripts contain works by Josquin. These sources, and the Josquin works in them, are listed in Appendix II, to which the reader will wish to refer throughout the discussion. The manuscripts fall into three chronological groups, indicated by roman numerals. Group I extends from about 1495 to 1508. The sources in this group were copied by scribe B (though Vienna 1783 may be an exception) and generally represent the period in which Philip the Fair controlled the chapel. Group II extends from about 1508 to 1520, a period ending just after the death of Maximilian and just before the death of Josquin, during which the chapel was under the control of Margaret and Charles. Group III comprises posthumous Josquin sources. The date of 1521 is in most cases derived from indications in the manuscript that Josquin is no longer alive, and all instances of it in my list might have to be amended to 1524, should the alleged Josquin copy of Erasmus's *Exomologesis* ever materialize.[43] The group is closed off in 1534, as is the whole complex, with the retirement of Alamire, its main scribe.

I believe we can assume that all of this music by Josquin was known to the chapels of Brussels and Malines, at least in the sense that members of the chapel knew of its existence and its availability for performance. It was, after all, copied into the books by scribes who were themselves musicians and members of the chapel.[44] Perhaps we can go further and assume that the Masses and motets were actually sung in the Netherlands chapel, the secular pieces in the court. Since most of the manuscripts were sent to recipients in other countries, however, this assumption raises fundamental questions regarding their relationship to models or exemplars, and the performing function of the latter, which cannot now be explored.[45] Nevertheless, the chronological distribution of the Netherlands sources allows us to observe the appearance of Josquin's works in the

---

[43] But see Postscript, (4), below, p. 208.   [44] Van Doorslaer, 'Calligraphes', pp. 92–5.

[45] To the extent that the question arose in the older literature it was generally assumed that books of polyphony—or pieces in them—were copied from other bound and complete books, an assumption still encountered occasionally today. In the case of the dispersed Netherlands court sources this was obviously impossible, and as a highly impractical method of producing an anthology it is not likely to have occurred often elsewhere. In my paper, 'Illuminated Choirbooks' (see fn. 41), I suggested that the court scribes may have copied from models kept in stock, which I termed 'master sheets'. However, study of the stemmatic relationships among the court sources reveals that in certain cases different models were apparently used even for chronologically close copies of the same work (see below, p. 203). Thus, the models may not have been kept for long. Perhaps they circulated in the manner of the 'fascicle-manuscripts' posited for the mid-fifteenth century by Charles Hamm ('Manuscript Structure in the Dufay Era', *Acta musicologica*, xxxiv (1962), p. 166).

repertory in the very period for which our biographical information is so scant.

Of course, all conclusions on the basis of these sources will be tentative, as such conclusions must always be. The evidence is largely statistical, and it is very difficult to know if our data are really representative. Many manuscripts must have been lost in 450 years, nor do we know what prints the chapel might have possessed. Yet fifty manuscripts might actually represent a very substantial portion of a chapel collection of the time. When Marie of Hungary had an inventory of her library drawn up in 1559—and this included most of Margaret of Austria's collection of thirty years, as well as her own of thirty more years—it contained some eighty manuscripts of vocal polyphony;[46] and by comparison with Marie's books, our extant Netherlands court sources also appear to give us a fairly reliable weighting of the main composers in the repertory, as will be shown below.

I should like to come immediately to this crucial question: do these sources give independent evidence of a close or consistent relationship of Josquin with the Netherlands court during the last decades of his life? In my opinion they do not.

Two related observations lead to this conclusion. The first concerns Josquin's representation in the total repertory, as compared with that of Pierre de la Rue, the most prestigious of the chapel composers. La Rue overwhelmingly dominates the repertory. His thirty-two Masses are all present and they make 107 appearances, amounting to 40% of all Mass appearances in the manuscripts. Furthermore, with only one or two exceptions, court manuscripts are the earliest sources of these works. Nearly all of La Rue's motets and chansons are found, each appearing at least once, and some motets considerably more often. This composer then —who, to be sure, served the court for over twenty-five years—is represented by virtually his entire output, and his Masses constitute by far the largest element of the repertory that is disseminated from the Netherlands throughout Europe. Josquin, on the other hand, is represented by less than a sixth of his motets and less than a fifth of his chansons, and though fifteen of his Masses are in the repertory, for only eight of these at most is a court manuscript perhaps (in no case definitely) the earliest source. Table I, column 1 demonstrates that in number of appearances in all court sources, La Rue outweighs Josquin almost 4 to 1 in Masses, 3 to 2 in motets, and 2 to 1 in chansons.[47] When the posthumous sources of both composers are omitted, the disparity is even greater, as may be seen in

[46] Vander Straeten, *La Musique aux Pays-Bas*, vii, pp. 471–93.

[47] The statistics in Table I are offered in the belief that the frequency with which the works of a given composer are copied is likely to be indicative of the relative importance of the composer in the repertory.

TABLE I

Comparison of La Rue and Josquin Appearances in All Netherlands Court Sources, and by Groups

	TOTAL 1495–1534 (50 MSS.)		TOTAL without posthumous MSS.		I 1495–1508 (7 MSS.)		II 1508–1520 (23 MSS.)		III 1521–1534 (20 MSS.)	
	La Rue	Josquin	La Rue	Josquin	La Rue	Josquin	La Rue	Josquin	La Rue	Josquin
Masses	107 (32 works)	33 (15 works)	79	14	21	5	58	9	28	19
Motets	33 (25 works)	22 (15 works)	18	11	7	5	11	6	15	11
Chansons	28 (21 works)	14 (11 works)	25	7	12	3	13	4	3	7

TABLE II

Josquin Mass Appearances in Netherlands Court Sources by Groups

	I 1495–1508	II 1508–1520	III 1521–1534	Petrucci
1 L'homme armé 6.t.	Chigi / Vienna 1783		Vienna 11778	1502
2 Ave maris stella	Brussels 9126	Vienna 4809	↑ Vienna 11778	1505
3 Hercules	Brussels 9126	Vienna 4809	↑ Vienna 11778	1505
4 Malheur me bat	Brussels 9126	Vienna 4809		1505
5 Faisant regretz		Vienna 4809		1514
6 Una musque de Buscaya				1505
7 De Beata Virgine		Vienna 4809		1514
8 Sine nomine		Vienna 4809		1514
9 Pange lingua				
10 Allez regretz				
11 L'homme armé s.v.m.	Jena 3	Vienna SM 15495	Jena 21 / Vienna 11778	1502
12 Gaudeamus	Jena 3	Vienna SM 15495	Jena 21 / Vienna 11778	1502
13 Fortuna desperata	Jena 3		Vienna 11778	1502
14 La sol fa re mi	Jena 3		Vienna 11778	1502
15 L'ami Baudichon	Sistina 160		Vienna 11778	1505
Credo Ciaschun me crie	Jena 3		Vienna 11778	1505
Credo Vilayge II (of doubtful authenticity)	Jena 7		Brussels IV 922	1505
Bicinia from:				
M. Pange lingua			Vienna 18832	
M. La sol fa re mi			Vienna 18832	
M. Gaudeamus			Vienna 18832	

Table I, column 2, with almost six times as many Mass appearances by La Rue as by Josquin. Most of La Rue's works enter the repertory in his lifetime; in contrast, Josquin has an altogether minor share while he is alive.

Another way of contrasting the two composers is to note that six Mass manuscripts are devoted entirely to La Rue, and only two to Josquin. It is here that the inventory of Marie's library again appears to corroborate the present statistics, for in that collection there were five manuscripts entirely of La Rue works and two of Josquin's.[48]

In view of the dramatic reflection in the sources of La Rue's presence in the chapel, it is difficult to refrain from the conclusion that had Josquin also maintained a close relationship with the chapel or the court—had he been, for instance, 'Kapellmeister von Haus aus', as has been suggested[49]— his works, and newly composed pieces in particular, would have had a larger place in these sources than they have.

This conclusion is reinforced by the second observation, which concerns Josquin's appearances in each of the three chronological groups of sources. When these groups, and the special character of their most important sources, are examined closely—and this will occupy the remainder of our discussion—not only is the disparity with La Rue revealed far more distinctly, but, even more significantly, we find that Josquin's presence can to a large extent be linked to circumstances other than service for the Netherlands court.

In Group I La Rue's Mass and chanson representation again outweighs Josquin's by 4 to 1, as shown in Table I, column 3. It might be added that Agricola also overshadows Josquin in these two genres, with nine Masses and twenty-two chansons. This is not surprising, in view of La Rue's membership in the chapel for the full period encompassed by the group, and Agricola's membership of six years. Josquin, as we know, was in France for periods of time in 1501 and 1503, and in Ferrara from April 1503 to April 1504.[50]

More significant perhaps is the presence of only four Josquin Masses (one appears twice) in a period in which Petrucci published eleven (see Table II, p. 193). Is this evidence of Josquin's secondary role in the repertory, or is it an indication that the court owned Petrucci's editions? The latter is certainly a possibility; but it may be noted that the nine Masses of La Rue published in his lifetime all occur in the court manuscripts *after* their appearance in print, and thirteen Josquin Masses appear twenty times in the later sources after their publication by Petrucci.[51]

---

[48] Vander Straeten, *La Musique aux Pays-Bas*, vii, pp. 471–93.

[49] Osthoff, i, p. 71.   [50] See Lewis Lockwood's article, above, p. 114.

[51] Not enough information about the relative roles of prints and manuscripts in chapel repertories exists to enable us to deduce the presence or absence of one or the other kind

Josquin's secondary position in the repertory of the first period is reflected in three of the four sources in which his works are found. In Vienna 1783 he is represented by one work among twenty-one, in Florence 2439 by three works among eighty-seven. In contrast, La Rue is given a large share of the contents of both sources, Agricola of the Florence manuscript. In the Chigi codex too, only two of the thirty-three works of the original layer are by Josquin.

But I believe Josquin's appearance in the latter source as well as in Brussels 9126 may be linked to his presence at the French court and his meeting at Blois with Philip the Fair. In writing about the origins of the Chigi codex, I showed this manuscript to be very closely related to Brussels 9126, and suggested that it was in some way connected with the chapel of Philip the Fair, reflecting Philip's contacts with the French court in the choice of its contents.[52] Subsequently I found evidence in the manuscript that resolves the question of its original and later ownership, and indeed strengthens the case for the French orientation of its contents.

An examination of the codex with special lighting reveals that all but one of the coats of arms were overpainted, hiding the first owner's escutcheon. One, however, remains untouched (Plate 31, fig. b), and this can be identified as belonging to the Burgundian family Bouton, of which Claude Bouton, previously mentioned, was a member. The identification is confirmed by the motto 'Ung Soeul Boutton' found towards the end of the manuscript; 'Bouttoň was overpainted with the word 'Dieu', but it is clearly visible with appropriate lighting (Plate 31, fig. c). It is my belief that the Chigi codex was made for Claude Bouton's father, Philippe, for there are many visual allusions to him in the manuscript, including several instances of a dragon, attribute of the apostle Philip, and a donor portrait with St. Catherine, patron saint of his wife, Catherine Di Dio.[53]

Philippe Bouton, an extremely interesting man, a poet of vulgar verse, and, like his son, a courtier, lived in French Burgundy and vacillated in his allegiance and service between the Burgundian Netherlands and

---

of source from statistical evidence. We do know, however, that the publication of a work in print did not necessarily lead to a decrease in manuscript copies of it. On the contrary, publication appears very often to have been followed by, perhaps even to have stimulated, a large body of handwritten copies (for example, Josquin's 'Ave Maria...Virgo serena'), a situation that is not surprising when one considers that prints, because of their smaller size, were not ideal for use by a choir; on the other hand, they were undoubtedly ideal exemplars for scribes. Were it not for the variants between printed editions and manuscripts one might even argue that absence of works in a manuscript repertory after their publication in print suggests that the print was *not* available.

[52] Kellman, 'The Chigi Codex', pp. 10–12.

[53] The author is preparing a comprehensive study of the manuscript's history, in which will be found documentation for the information given here.

France. From 1488 until his death in 1515, he appears to have been loyal
to Charles VIII and Louis XII, both of whom granted him prestigious
offices. There can be little doubt that his links with the French court and
perhaps his consequent taste in music account for the large role of
Ockeghem in the Chigi codex. It is likely that other music in the manuscript would also have come from the French court repertory, and
Josquin's pieces may have been among these. Unless the manuscript was
ordered directly by Philippe Bouton, the person most likely to have had it
prepared was his son Claude, who was in the service of Philip the Fair well
before 1500. As pointed out earlier, Claude accompanied Philip to the
French court in 1501 and could have met Josquin there. However, the
manuscript might have been made up prior to that date.

MS. Brussels 9126, on the other hand, was definitely written after the
meetings of the French and Netherlands chapels at Blois (1501) and Lyons
(1503), and it is striking that the proportion of Josquin's works is substantially larger in this manuscript (seven of twenty-two works) than in
the other sources in the group. Since Brussels 9126 is the only extant
source produced specifically for Philip the Fair,[54] and since it was certainly
copied after Philip's meeting with Josquin and only one and a half years
after the French and Netherlands chapels had last sung together, the
increase in Josquin's representation may well be the result of those contacts.[55]

With the 'Missa Ave maris stella' as the opening work, and the tenor of
the 'Hercules' Mass now entitled 'Philippus rex Castilie', one might be
tempted to see this source as indicative of an even closer relationship of
Josquin to the Netherlands court at the time of its compilation. But a
glance at the arrangement of the contents[56] shows that after the opening
Mass, Josquin's works are interspersed among blocks of works by La Rue
and Agricola, who thus assume the dominant place in this manuscript, as
in the other sources in the group.

[54] Osthoff (i, p. 61) feels that the manuscript 'wurde wohl auf persönliche Initiative von
Philipp hergestellt', following Van Doorslaer who writes that it was 'constitué à l'intention
de Philippe le Beau, et probablement aussi, à son initiative, ce dont semblent attester son
portrait et celui de son épouse, Jeanne la Folle, qui ornent la page de titre . . .' ('La chapelle',
p. 37). Portraits in the court manuscripts, almost without exception, point to recipients,
and thus the book was unquestionably intended for Philip, but there is no evidence that
it was prepared at his request.

[55] It should be noted, however, that the three Josquin Masses in Brussels 9126 are, in
the same order, the first three Masses of Petrucci's *Missarum Josquin Liber secundus* (see the
recently published facsimile of the latter in the series *Monumenta Musica Typographica
Vetustiora Italica*). Although Petrucci's edition was issued on 30 June 1505, it is not likely
that either source directly affected the other. There are considerable variants between them,
and Brussels 9126 was probably assembled throughout the year 1505, since Philip had been
proclaimed king of Castile in December 1504, and left for Spain in January 1506. Nevertheless, the correspondence seems more than a coincidence.

[56] *Werken*, Motetten, Bundel iii, p. v.

Nor is there reason to think that the new title for the 'Hercules' Mass had to be suggested by Josquin himself, for we can find many instances of such alterations in the court manuscripts, clearly conceived by someone other than the composer.[57] Confirmation that Josquin did not enter Philip's employ, either after he was asked to join the chapel in 1501, or after he left Ferrara in 1504, comes from the eighty extant chapel registers dating from 1502 to the dissolution of the chapel in 1506, in which he is not mentioned once.[58]

Group II is of considerable interest because it encompasses the period when Josquin is most likely to have worked for the Netherlands court, if he did so.

Twenty-three manuscripts—or almost half of the whole complex—can be assigned to this period. Only seven of these contain works of his. Table I, column 4 shows that appearances of La Rue's Masses in this group outnumber Josquin's by more than 6 to 1. The nine appearances of Josquin Masses, moreover, include only four cycles that are new to the repertory (see Table II), and three of these appear in sources probably copied after the works were printed by Petrucci. Similarly, in a period in which Josquin's output must have been considerable, only five motets are new to the repertory. In view of the inclusion in this group of Brussels 228, Margaret of Austria's chanson album of fifty-eight pieces, Josquin's chanson representation must be considered particularly small. His four chansons in Brussels 228 include 'Plus nulz regretz', however, and it has been suggested that he is the composer of the anonymous 'Proch dolor', a funeral motet for Maximilian.[59] If he wrote the former as a conscious gesture of honour to the imperial family, and if he is indeed the composer of the latter, this source would provide us with the only works that can definitely be associated with the house of Hapsburg—two compositions written approximately a decade apart and dedicated as much to Maximilian as to Margaret. Yet his role in the source is still distinctly different

[57] In two Alamire manuscripts, state and personal motets by Agricola, Févin, and Mouton are adapted to new recipients, long after the composers' deaths. See below, p. 200.

[58] Van Doorslaer, 'La chapelle', pp. 56–7. In any case, in August 1502 began the Ferrarese correspondence in regard to obtaining his services for the duke of Ferrara (Lockwood, above, p. 113). For his whereabouts after leaving Ferrara, see Postscript, (1), below, p. 207.

[59] Martin Picker makes this suggestion in his excellent edition of Brussels MSS. 228 and 11239 (*The Chanson Albums of Marguerite of Austria* (Berkeley and Los Angeles, 1965), pp. 89–90) and in an earlier article ('The Chanson Albums of Marguerite of Austria', *Annales musicologiques*, vi (1958–63), pp. 174–5). He also cites a passage in the work that speaks against the attribution. Willem Elders (*Studien zur Symbolik in der Musik der alten Niederländer* (Bilthoven, 1968), pp. 22–4) accepts the suggestion, finding no difficulty in the cited passage, and offers further sylistic evidence, worked out by M. Antonowycz, which leads him to conclude that Josquin definitely composed the work. The editors of the *Werken van Josquin des Prés* have included the work in the *Supplement* (Amsterdam, 1969). Not finding the evidence convincing, I believe that the question still remains open.

from that of La Rue, who is represented by fifteen compositions, who opens each section of the manuscript with a block of works, and who bespeaks the personal nature of the source with such chansons as 'A vous non autre' and 'Pour ung jamais'.[60]

Indeed, it is this group of sources that most distinctly reflects a close relationship between court and composer. La Rue appears in virtually every manuscript: whether for reasons of pride, proprietary right, accessibility, or love of his music, his works were copied again and again and distributed to every court with which the Netherlands court had contact. Four manuscripts in this group are devoted exclusively to his Masses, and in three others all Masses but one are his.

Only one book presents Josquin in a similar light. This is Jena 3, which was written between 1518 and 1520 and contains five Josquin Masses, together with three Masses by other composers. It seems significant that two of Josquin's Masses are used as dedicatory pieces for Frederick the Wise of Saxony, to whom the book was sent by Margaret.

The opening work is the 'Missa Faisant regretz', but with the designation of the tenor changed to 'Elizabeth faisant regrets'. The first folio is decorated with a Visitation miniature—the meeting of the two cousins who have conceived, Mary bearing Jesus and Elizabeth bearing John the Baptist (Plate 32). The allusion to Elizabeth in sacred scene and sacred music was doubtless meant as a compliment to Frederick. St. Elizabeth of Hungary was the patron saint of Thuringia, Elizabeth was the name of his mother (to whom he was especially devoted, remaining a bachelor all his life), and a series of associations beginning with the Visitation might have led him ultimately to compare himself with John the Baptist.

Beyond this, there is an even more subtle association, probably unrecognized by Frederick, linking the Visitation with Josquin's Mass. It is dependent on the rondeau 'Tout a par moy', Frye's setting of which[61] the Mass paraphrases. The second part of the refrain begins with the words 'Faisans regrets', and Frye's tenor for these words becomes the main motive of the Mass. In the final Agnus, however, Josquin turns to Frye's setting of the first part of the refrain, especially to his tenor for the opening words, 'Tout a par moy'—words that Petrucci prints at the beginning of

---

[60] 'A vous non autre' has a revised text in Brussels 228, and opens with the lines 'A vous non autre, servir habandoné,/Bien quatorze ans me suis en toute place'. The same version of the text appears in the earlier manuscript Florence 2439 (see Appendix II), and it is most likely that the service referred to is La Rue's own. The text of 'Pour ung jamais' was written by Margaret herself. See Picker, Chanson Albums, pp. 15, 30, 36-8, 53-4, 139-40.

[61] Edited by Dragan Plamenac in 'A Reconstruction of the French Chansonnier in the Biblioteca Colombina, Seville', The Musical Quarterly, xxxvii (1951), pp. 530-31; also in Walter Frye, Collected Works, ed. Sylvia W. Kenney (American Institute of Musicology, 1960), p. 1.

the alto, in his edition of the Mass. Not only these words but the entire first section of the refrain concern a lover's seclusion:

> Tout a par moy afin qu'on ne me voye,
> Si tresdolent que plus je ne parraie,
> Je me tiengs seul comme une ame esbahie...
> (I remain quite apart so that I shall not be seen,
> I shall not appear again, so mournful am I,
> I keep to myself like a numbed soul . . .)

Herein lies the link to the Visitation, for an essential element of the biblical account is the seclusion of Elizabeth:

> And after those days his wife Elisabeth
> conceived, and hid herself five months . . .
> (Luke I: 24. King James Version)[62]

It was only Mary's visit that brought her solitude to an end.

It is difficult to believe that no awareness of this parallel entered into the choice of music and illustration. Normally, sacred pieces in the court manuscripts were illustrated in the most direct manner, and it would certainly not have been difficult for the illuminator to obtain a stock miniature of St. Elizabeth of Hungary. That he used a miniature otherwise found exclusively in a liturgical context quite unrelated to the Mass[63] seems to indicate a special intention. But even if Frederick was unaware of this, he could not have failed to recognize that the presentation of the Mass embodied a tribute to him from at least the court scribes and illuminators, if not Margaret herself. Upon turning to the next Mass in the manuscript he would have found the tribute repeated more overtly, for here the tenor of the 'Hercules' Mass is inscribed, 'Fridericus dux Saxsonie'[64] (Plate 33).

The use of these Masses as dedicatory pieces to open the manuscript gives the impression that they were highly valued by Margaret's court and perhaps even considered as belonging to the court, like the music of La Rue. This impression is reinforced by the appearance of the earlier dedication of the 'Hercules' Mass in Philip's personal manuscript, Brussels 9126, and of the 'Missa Faisant regretz' in Vienna SM 15495, a manuscript made

[62] 'After this his wife Elizabeth conceived, and for five months she lived in seclusion', *The New English Bible*.

[63] The Visitation is most commonly found as an illustration in Books of Hours in connection with Lauds in Hours of the Virgin.

[64] Those who suspect that 'Elizabeth' may be a substitution analogous to 'Fridericus' might wish to note that the 'Elizabeth' or 'Faisant regretz' motive, fa-re-mi-re, is a subject nicely carved out of 'Marguerite'. It can be added that the third stanza of the poem 'Me fauldra-il', often attributed to Margaret, begins with the line 'Parquoy conclus, seullette et a par moy' ('why closed away, alone and apart'), and that in the anonymous setting of this text in Brussels 228, the words 'a par moy' in the tenor fall on the motive fa-re-mi-re, in my text underlay.

up for Maximilian not long after he was proclaimed Emperor, and at least three years before Petrucci's *Liber tertius*.[65] Brussels 9126 shares also the Masses 'Ave maris stella' and 'Malheur me bat' with the Jena manuscript, while Vienna SM 15495 contains two of the three Jena Masses by other composers. With its large Josquin content and its relationship to books of Philip and Maximilian, Jena 3 has the appearance of a source in which Josquin is anthologized as if he were close to the court.

The source may be interpreted differently, however, when the remainder of its contents is taken into account: three Masses by Mouton, Févin, and Compère, the last two of which have concordances in Vienna SM 15495. Beginning with the second group of sources, there is an influx into the Netherlands repertory of music by composers working at the French court, or elsewhere in France, and among these Mouton and Févin are particularly prominent, appearing approximately with the same frequency as Josquin. We do not know by what route this music came to the court, but it is very likely that in part, at least, it was brought back by the court scribes from their travels.[66]

The character of some manuscripts is largely determined by this French component. The motet manuscript London, Royal 8 G VII is a good example of such a source, for of its twenty-one identified compositions, ten are by Mouton, Févin, Lebrun, Thérache, and Verbonnet, and the book opens with Mouton's 'Celeste beneficium' in honor of St. Anne, followed by Févin's 'Adjutorium nostrum' for Louis XII and Anne of Brittany. The French court repertory also served the Netherlands scribes as a prime source of state and personal motets which were produced by changing the names of the French sovereigns in the original texts. Thus Févin's 'Adjutorium nostrum' is turned into a motet for Henry VIII and Catherine of Aragon in the London manuscript, and in the motet collection Vatican, Pal. lat. 1976–79 (Group III) five motets by Agricola, Mouton, Févin, Gascongne, and Richafort,[67] originally for Louis and

---

[65] Osthoff (i, p. 61) believes that Vienna SM 15495 (*olim* Kunsthistorisches Museum, MS. 5248) is the earliest manuscript from an imperial court to contain works by Josquin. His dating of the manuscript is incorrect, however, as was the present author's in 'The Origins of the Chigi Codex'. The distinction of the first Josquin source falls either to the Chigi codex, or to Vienna 1783. Only in the case of 'Faisant regretz' in the Vienna manuscript can we be certain that a Josquin Mass printed by Petrucci appeared earlier in a court source.

[66] The scribe Alamire travelled a great deal, and over a dozen trips are documented from 1515 to 1520. Between 1516 and 1518 he visited France twice, remaining at least five months the second time (J. S. Brewer, *Letters and Papers, Foreign and Domestic, of the Reign of Henry VIII*, ii (London, 1864), nos. 2672, 4117). It would be surprising indeed if this musician who accepted orders for manuscripts wherever he went, and who apparently was an opportunist by nature, had not attempted to obtain new music during his travels.

[67] Respectively, the motets 'Transit Anna timor', 'Non nobis Domine', 'Adjutorium nostrum', 'Christus vincit', 'Exaudiat te Dominus'.

Anne of France, or Francis I, are adapted for Ferdinand and Anne of Hungary, for whom the manuscript was prepared.[68] When Josquin is represented in sources in which the French component is strong, the possibility that his work comes to the Netherlands as part of that repertory, or is considered by the scribes to be a part of it, cannot be overlooked. In this light Jena 3 becomes ambiguous. Even the two central court sources from which it appears to draw its contents are not without French associations. Brussels 9126, as has been pointed out, very likely reflects the musical results of the meetings of the two courts in 1501 and 1503, and Vienna SM 15495 contains Masses by Févin, Compère, and Thérache.

Group III is quite different from the two previous groups. Table I, column 5 shows that in these posthumous manuscripts, the occurrence of Josquin's works increases substantially, both in comparison with La Rue's works and with his own earlier representation. But it will also be observed that five of the nine sources were sent to Raimund Fugger the Elder (1489–1535).[69] These five manuscripts contain every Josquin work in the group, the other four sources having concordances of two Masses and three motets.[70] Among the Fugger manuscripts are also the only books in

---

[68] Walter H. Rubsamen ('Music Research in Italian Libraries', *Notes*, viii (1950), p. 72) identified the recipient as Marie of Hungary, on the basis of the coats of arms and the index title, 'Registrum dive Regine hungarie'. The arms are those of the Empire, however, and the manuscript is dedicated to Queen Anne of Hungary, as becomes apparent from the frequency with which her name, coupled with Ferdinand's, appears throughout the manuscript—an observation first made some years ago by Professor Lewis Lockwood, and kindly brought to my attention.

[69] Leopold Nowak, 'Die Musikhandschriften aus Fuggerschem Besitz in der Österreichischen Nationalbibliothek', in *Die Österreichische Nationalbibliothek. Festschrift...Josef Bick* (Vienna, 1948), pp. 505–15. Four other sources in the complex belong to this group: Vienna MSS. 4810, 9814 (ff. 132–152ᵛ), 11883 (several fascicles), 18825. Nowak has demonstrated that all of these books were part of the Fugger collection purchased for the imperial library in 1656. While several of the manuscripts carry the Fugger coats of arms, only the arms in Vienna 15941 include the initials R. F. Nevertheless, all nine manuscripts undoubtedly stem from the library of Raimund Fugger the Elder. They are all Alamire copies, thus establishing their close relationship, and they were written in a period when Raimund was the only serious collector of books in the family, and certainly the only one known to have possessed a large collection of music and instruments. See Paul Lehmann, *Eine Geschichte der alten Fuggerbibliotheken*, 2 vols. (Tübingen, 1956–60), i, chs. 1 and 2; also Ernst Schmid, 'Fugger', *MGG*, iv (1955), col. 1119.

[70] Three of the other four sources are related to the Fugger manuscripts, however, making this the most homogeneous of the groups: the physical characteristics of Jena 21 (type of paper, size of folios, height and length of staves, distance between staves, style of initials, binding design) duplicate those of Vienna 4809, 4810, 11778; Munich 34 appears to resemble very closely a Magnificat manuscript that was in Raimund's possession (see fn. 72 below), and William of Bavaria maintained close ties with the Fuggers in neighbouring Augsburg; Pal. lat. 1976–79 is physically very similar to Vienna 15941, has twelve concordances with it, and eventually became the property of Ulrich Fugger.

the complex devoted entirely to Josquin, Vienna 4809 and 11778.

In no other instance in the complex is such a large body of works by one composer sent exclusively to one recipient. Furthermore, half of the Masses (Table II, nos. 9–15) and all but one motet and one chanson appear here for the first time. We must conclude that special circumstances not operative elsewhere in the complex determined this emphasis in Raimund Fugger's manuscripts.

While we cannot know what those circumstances were, a document that has come down to us suggests one possibility. An inventory of the music collection of Raimund's son Raimund the Younger, drawn up in 1566,[71] begins with a section listing manuscripts and prints inherited by the latter from his father. The prints are described in enough detail for us to see that Raimund the Elder had owned a substantial portion of Petrucci's production, from the *Odhecaton* to the *Musica de meser Bernardo Pisano*. At least eighteen and probably as many as twenty-six of the listed items are Petrucci editions, including his major motet, chanson, and frottola collections. Raimund's holdings in Mass prints were particularly strong, with the editions of Ghiselin, La Rue, Agricola, Gaspar, Mouton, and Févin all present, as well as the *Fragmenta missarum* and *Missarum diversorum auctorum Liber primus*. Conspicuously missing, however, are Petrucci's three books of Josquin Masses. While the manuscript list is less specific, and Franco-Flemish composers are named in connection with only five of thirty-four manuscripts of polyphony,[72] Josquin is mentioned only among composers of a book of 'Salve Regina' settings. However, Raimund's court manuscripts—absent from the inventory because they were inherited by another son[73]—must have been part of the original collection, and they supply the missing Josquin component. The possibility arises that Raimund expressly ordered books of Josquin Masses and

---

[71] Richard Schaal, 'Die Musikbibliothek von Raimund Fugger d.J.', *Acta musicologica*, xxix (1957), pp. 126–37.

[72] As stated in the inventory, the contents of the five manuscripts are, respectively: six Masses by Ockeghem, seven by Agricola, eight for three voices by Févin, Verbonnet, Pipelare, Prioris, Brumel; 'Salve Regina' settings by Josquin, Noel, Paulus [Hofhaimer?], 'and others'; twenty-two Magnificat settings by R. Févin, Mouton, Lebrun, Rue, Divitis, Pipelare, Prioris, Obrecht, Thérache, Loyset [Compère], Reingot. The last two books may have been counterparts of two manuscripts in the Netherlands complex, Munich 34 containing twenty-nine settings of the 'Salve Regina', and Jena 20 containing nineteen of the Magnificat. Taken together, the composers in these manuscripts and the Fugger books are virtually the same.

[73] Georg Fugger (1517–69). He is known to have inherited a small portion of his father's library, probably works on mathematics, astronomy, and astrology, which were his main interests. His lute tablature (Vienna MS. 18790), thought to be in his own hand, attests also to his interest in music. The collection bought by the Vienna library in 1656 consisted mainly of the surviving portions of the substantial libraries of Georg and his sons. See Lehmann, *Geschichte*, i, pp. 193–208; ii, pp. 552–94, and Nowak, 'Die Musikhandschriften'.

large groups of motets and chansons[74] soon after the composer's death to fill the lacunae in his holdings. A test of this hypothesis must await a more detailed reconstruction of his collection, however.[75]

The route by which Raimund obtained these manuscripts may also have been an unusual one, circumventing the court contacts which normally determined such transmission. It is true that the Fugger family maintained close financial connections with the Netherlands court, but Raimund's role in the affairs of the firm was minimal, and his contacts with members of the imperial family were infrequent. As far as is known, he never visited the Netherlands.[76] Until the Reichstag of 1530 he would not have heard the Netherlands chapel in Augsburg, where he resided, but only Maximilian's *Hofkapelle*. But Petrus Alamire, the copyist of all of these books, is known to have been in Augsburg in February and early March of 1519 to assist in the campaign to obtain the imperial crown for Charles.[77] In that capacity he would certainly have had contact with the Fuggers, who were financing Charles's election. It must therefore be considered a very strong possibility that Raimund ordered the manuscripts directly from the scribe.

If an editor at the Netherlands court was responsible for the choice of music in the manuscripts, it might appear that the emphasis on Josquin's works reflects closer ties between the composer and the court shortly before his death. That such ties probably did not exist even then is suggested by the relationships of sources indicated by arrows in Table II. Recensions of the sources of the 'Ave maris stella' and 'Hercules' Masses[78]

[74] Vienna 15941 opens with a group of five Josquin motets, and three more appear further on in the manuscript. Vienna 18746 contains at least seven, and perhaps as many as eleven of his five-part chansons (see Appendix II, fn. 126).

[75] This may eventually be achieved. See the reconstructions of various Fugger collections in Lehmann, *Geschichte*, and Otto Hartig, *Die Gründung der Münchener Hofbibliothek durch Albrecht V und Johann Jakob Fugger* (Munich, 1917).

[76] The best summary of what is known of Raimund's life is given by Norbert Lieb, *Die Fugger und die Kunst im Zeitalter der hohen Renaissance* (Munich, 1958), pp. 23–64. Raimund appears to have been sickly and to have withdrawn early from an active role in the firm to devote himself to his large collections of antiquities, paintings, medals, books, music, and musical instruments. In 1526, however, he was given the title of Imperial Councillor.

[77] *Deutsche Reichstagsakten. Jüngere Reihe*, i (Gotha, 1893), pp. 414–16. Apparently Alamire was not too busy in Augsburg. On 12 March 1519 Jean Marnix writes to Margaret that on his advice Alamire, who was unoccupied, had been sent to Frederick of Saxony with whom he was in good standing, to ascertain Frederick's position on the election.

[78] I use the term 'recension' as it is used in textual criticism, particularly of classical literature, to denote the process of establishing the relationships of sources to each other, and producing a stemma, or family tree, to express these relationships (see L. D. Reynolds and N. G. Wilson, *Scribes and Scholars* (Oxford, 1968), ch. 5). The work in question was carried out in a seminar at the University of Illinois in 1971. The 'Hercules' recension was

reveal that the Vienna 4809 readings of these two works are closer to Petrucci than to either the Jena or Brussels readings, and the Jena readings are closer to Brussels than to Vienna. Although the relationships among the various sources of the works are more complex than might be suggested by the affinities of these four sources, the Jena and Brussels versions appear to belong to one branch of the stemma,[79] the Vienna and Petrucci versions to another—or to other closely related branches. We may conclude then that Vienna 4809 is dependent on considerably earlier and perhaps not court-related models. That this appears to be so also for its companion volume, Vienna 11778, follows from consideration of this manuscript's curious attribution of Josquin's 'Missa Gaudeamus' to Ockeghem. The presence of this Mass in a two-volume set otherwise devoted entirely to Josquin Masses[80] seems to indicate that the editor of the set considered the work to be Josquin's. This is corroborated by the appearance of three duos from the Mass within a larger group of Josquin duos in another of Raimund Fugger's books, the *bicinia* manuscript Vienna 18832. Thus, the most plausible explanation for the Ockeghem attribution is that through ignorance or oversight the name was copied directly from a misattributed model or master sheet. It would be difficult indeed to conceive of such a model as a late one, or to associate it with Josquin's presence at court.

Finally, it must be noted that much of the other music sent to Raimund Fugger[81] is the work of the French court composers mentioned in connection with Group II. In Vienna 4810, which belongs to the Vienna 4809–11778 set by virtue of its physical characteristics, three of the four identified Masses are by Mouton and Févin. Mouton, Févin, Richafort, and Thérache are responsible for fifteen motets in Vienna 15941; and seven of the eight motets that make up the entire manuscript Vienna 18825 are by Mouton, Févin, Richafort, Lebrun, and Agricola.

* * *

There can be no question that many of Josquin's works were known and admired at the court of the Netherlands. But on the basis of the evidence presented here, I suggest that we have been too eager to make the master himself an intimate of the court. Philip the Fair did not, after all,

---

undertaken as a group project, and valuable individual contributions were also made by Sister Bertha Fox and Susan Hoeksema.

[79] [On the methods of filiation and the drawing up of a stemma, see Lothar Hoffmann-Erbrecht's article in these Proceedings, pp. 285–93.—Ed.]

[80] Vienna 4809 and 11778 are virtually identical in their physical characteristics (see fn. 70), and because of their unified contents can be regarded as one manuscript in two volumes.

[81] See fn. 69.

secure his services. There is no evidence of contact with Margaret, nor can we any longer maintain that Margaret took a personal interest in him. Maximilian had to approve his succession to the provostship at Condé, but his candidacy could have been submitted by the incumbent (presumably Pierre Duwez) or by the chapter itself.[82] If it was Josquin who brought music to Charles in 1520, he hardly appears to have come as a court habitué. Josquin might have composed 'De profundis' on the occasion of Philip's death and 'Plus nulz regretz' in honor of the engagement of Charles and Mary Tudor; he is perhaps the composer of Maximilian's funeral motet. But even if these were certainties—and they are not—they need represent no more than intermittent gestures of respect, and I believe it would be rash to infer from them Josquin's service or attachment to the court, without further evidence.

The Netherlands court manuscripts do not, in my opinion, supply that evidence. In them Josquin's role is at first minor, and later, in those sources produced in his lifetime, it is only slightly more prominent than that of Mouton. To propose then that 'Josquin was closely attached to the Netherlands courts of Marguerite of Austria and Charles V toward the end of his life'[83] and to rank him among 'Composers Active at the Netherlands Courts'[84] is to be too sanguine. And the thought that the composer '[dürfte] sicher oft in dem nicht weit entfernten Mecheln bei der Regentin geweilt haben',[85] while an appealing fancy, runs counter to all that is known of the place of musicians—even provosts—in court circles in this period.[86] One is also tempted to add Vander Straeten's wise reminder, 'Ne faisons pas trop voyager imaginairement nos anciens musiciens: leurs déplacements réels sont déjà assez nombreux'.[87]

We may make progress in other directions, however. The tradition that makes of Josquin a composer of Louis XII is more explicit and may be more reliable than the Netherlands evidence. It is perhaps to the French documents then that we should now turn, beginning with an intense effort to assemble a representative group of French sources from which repertory statistics may be drawn.[88] In this respect, investigation of the

---

[82] But see Postscript, (2), below, p. 207.   [83] Picker, 'The Chanson Albums', p. 163.
[84] Idem, *The Chanson Albums*, p. 36.   [85] Osthoff, i, p. 70.
[86] See Henry Guy, *Histoire de la poésie française au XVIe siècle*, i (Paris, 1910), pp. 46–8: 'Quelle était, auprès des rois, la situation réelle des artistes?'; Nanie Bridgman, 'Mécénat et musique', *International Musicological Society. Report of the Eighth Congress, New York, 1961*, ii (Kassel, 1962), p. 19.
[87] Vander Straeten, *La Musique aux Pays-Bas*, vi, p. 397.
[88] Osthoff, following Jeanne Marix ('Hayne van Ghizeghem', *The Musical Quarterly*, xxviii (1942), pp. 282–3), believes that the manuscript Paris, Bibliothèque nationale, f. fr. 2245 is one of three manuscripts which the singer-copyist Crespières prepared for Louis d'Orléans (later Louis XII) some time before 1498 (i, p. 48; ii, pp. 164, 340). However, this manuscript does not contain Crespières' signature, as alleged by Marix, nor is the number

transmission of the French repertory in Petrucci's collections, particularly in the *Motetti de la Corona*,[89] could be of great value.

'Déplorations' and other poems by such writers as Crétin, Eloy d'Amerval, and Jean Daniel, in which Josquin is named together with French court composers, have been seen as indications of his service for the French court. But we cannot be certain of their meaning until we know more of their literary tradition, and they deserve study as a special genre.[90] Indeed, further study of the poets themselves, and of manuscripts and early prints of poetry, is surely warranted. If we remember, for instance, that both Molinet and Lemaire were probably present at the 1501 Blois meeting; that Molinet was a friend of Compère, Busnois, and Ockeghem, and Lemaire served successively Pierre de Bourbon, Louis of Luxembourg, Margaret of Austria, and Anne of Brittany, we will recognize paths that could yield valuable new insights into the genesis of such works as 'Plus nulz regretz' and 'Cueurs desolez', and more importantly, into the operation of artistic relationships and displacements characteristic of the north.

Finally, on the model of the many scholars who in recent years have brought new Italian documents to light, we must begin, or renew, a systematic search of the archives of both France and the Netherlands. I have no doubt that there lurks in these considerable evidence toward the clarification of many of the problems raised in this inquiry.

POSTSCRIPT

Since this article was first written, the author has found documents in French and Belgian archives and libraries that indeed clarify a number of the issues discussed above and suggest, moreover, an entirely new view of Josquin's activities in the north, after his return from Italy. The following is a summary of the information and conclusions that the documents afford.[91]

1496 on the first leaf its date. The number is written in an eighteenth-century hand, and it is also found in Paris, Bibliothèque nationale, f. fr. 1596, a later book of polyphony which appears to have belonged to Marguerite d'Orléans, sister of Francis I. Paris 2245 contains the Orléans coat of arms, but without further study it cannot be definitely associated with Louis.

[89] Daniel Heartz persuasively suggests that this collection might have originated as a compliment from Urbino to the French court (*Pierre Attaingnant, Royal Printer of Music* (Berkeley and Los Angeles, 1970), p. 40). [David Maulsby Gehrenbeck, in 'Motetti de la Corona, A Study of Ottaviano Petrucci's Four Last-Known Motet Prints' (Ph.D. diss., Union Theological Seminary, 1970), pp. 340–1, concurs.—Ed.]

[90] An excellent beginning has been made by Conrad Douglas in chapter 1 of his 'The Motets of Johannes Prioris' (Master's Thesis, University of Illinois, 1969).

[91] For a more extensive discussion of this material, with transcripts of all the documents, see my study, 'Josquin in Condé: Discoveries and Revisions', forthcoming.

1. Josquin was in Condé, as provost of Notre-Dame, by 3 May 150
A statement of monies collected and spent for the erection of a new spir
on the church, bearing that date, mentions the admission of four canons
to the chapter, among them 'messire Josse des pres'; there is also in the
document a reference to 'monsieur le prevost messire Josse des pres'.[92]
Since the final entry for salary paid to Josquin in the Ferrarese registers is
dated 22 April 1504,[93] the gap between Ferrara and Condé is now closed.
It is also clear that the provostship of Condé was not a benefice to provide
for Josquin's retirement at the very end of his life, but a post which he
held for a full seventeen years before his death, years in which he undoubtedly composed a portion of his opus, and which saw the appearance
of the greater part of his works in manuscripts and prints.

2. At the time Josquin obtained the office, the provostship of Condé
was not at the collation of Maximilian or Philip the Fair, but was bestowed
by election of the chapter.[94] Maximilian was therefore not necessarily
instrumental in the appointment, as it has long been assumed he was. He
cannot be excluded as a possible sponsor of the composer, but if one of the
northern sovereigns was indeed involved, it is more likely to have been
Philip the Fair, who, as count of Hainaut, had the collation of half of the
canonicates in Notre-Dame. However, since the two feudal lords of
Condé shared the collation of the other half, one or the other of these may
have played a role in bringing Josquin to Condé.[95] It is also possible that
Josquin's move was the result of an arrangement among musicians: Pierre
Duwez, Josquin's predecessor and a former member of the Burgundian
chapel, may well have resigned from Condé in exchange for the provostship of the collegiate church of Saint-Pierre in Douai, which he obtained in
1503 or 1504, that post having been resigned, in turn, by Loyset Compère,
who had held it since 1500.[96]

3. The letter from Josquin and the chapter of Notre-Dame to Margaret
of Austria can be dated 23 May 1508. On 20 May 1508 Pierre Duwez had
died in Braine-le-Comte. One of Margaret's counselors, in the belief that
Duwez still held the provostship of Condé at his death, asked Margaret to
try to obtain the benefice for Doctor Collauer, Maximilian's secretary, and
Margaret wrote to the chapter accordingly, requesting that Collauer be
elected. The chapter's reply was intended to inform her that the provost
was not Duwez but someone who was alive and present.[97] Thus, not

---

[92] Paris, Bibliothèque nationale, MS. lat. 9917, ff. 2–2bis^v.

[93] Lockwood, above, p. 137.

[94] Letters of Mercurino de Gattinara; Lille, Archives départementales du Nord, B. 18829,
nos. 25210, 25218.

[95] Brussels, Archives générales du Royaume, Papiers d'État et de l'Audience, no. 1190/4.

[96] Douai, Bibliothèque municipale, MS. 893, vol. i, f. 35.

[97] Letters of Mercurino de Gattinara, cited above.

only was Margaret unaware of Josquin's presence in Condé when she wrote to the chapter, but, to judge from the phrase, 'nostre prevost est en tres bonne sancté appellé Josquin Desprez', it was assumed at Condé—or known, if Josquin helped to formulate the answer—that she was not acquainted with him. In any case, the possibility that Josquin had been in Malines to write 'Plus nulz regretz', or had composed the piece as a result of direct contact with the court, prior to May 1508, can now be eliminated.

4. Josquin was dead by 19 September 1521, the date of a deposition by two aldermen of Condé who, together with the mayor and other aldermen, had visited him on 23 August 1521, in order to legitimize his claim for bequeathal rights. In this document Josquin is called a priest.[98] There is now no reason to doubt that Josquin's death occurred—as his epitaph is said to have stated—on 27 August 1521; and his alleged ex-libris in Coussemaker's copy of Erasmus's 1524 *Exomologesis* can be dismissed as a fiction. The question of his priesthood is also settled, though it cannot be said when he actually took orders.

5. In the above-mentioned deposition, Josquin is quoted as having declared himself *aubain* ('foreigner'), a legal term reserved for one born outside the Empire. He must therefore have been a native of France. He stated further that he was born 'beyond the *Noir Eauwe* [*Eau*].'[99] He may have been referring to the river in the Ardennes now called the 'Eau Noire', which in the fifteenth century delineated the border between the Empire and France for part of its course. It is much more likely, however, that he was using the colloquial but now obsolete name of a larger frontier river, closer to Condé, such as the Escaut. Thus, his precise birthplace remains unidentified.

6. At his death, Josquin bequeathed his house and land to the church of Notre-Dame in Condé, to endow regular commemorations for himself. These were to consist of the celebration of the *Salve* service every evening during Marian feasts and every Saturday of the year, and the singing of his 'Pater noster' and 'Ave Maria', in front of his house, during all general processions.[100] Thus we learn that the choir of Notre-Dame could sing polyphony, and even in six parts. That polyphony was a custom at Notre-Dame is also implied in a document of 1523 which reveals that the church had a larger ecclesiastical establishment than any other collegiate church in Hainaut (provost, dean, treasurer, 25 canons, 18 chaplains, 16 vicars, 6 choirboys, and non-beneficed priests), and that daily services were carried out there with much greater ceremony than in neighbouring churches of that rank.[101] The services were celebrated mainly by the

---

[98] Condé-sur-l'Escaut, Archives communales FF.19 78, September, 1521.
[99] Ibid.　　[100] Ibid., 9 September 1522; 22 June 1523.
[101] Lille, Archives départementales du Nord, B. 19456, ff. 87ᵛ–88.

vicars;[102] therefore these, with the boys, may have formed a choir of as many as twenty-two singers. A slightly later chronicler declares that in Hainaut and neighbouring parts, Notre-Dame is outranked for the renown of its music only by the cathedral of Cambrai and the collegiate church of Saint-Vincent in Soignies.[103] Although we cannot be certain that Josquin resided uninterruptedly in Condé during his seventeen-year tenure as provost, it must be considered a distinct possibility that a portion of his production was written for, or at least was first sung by, the choir of Notre-Dame.

Appendix I

Manuscripts Produced at the Court of the Netherlands, *c.* 1495–1534

(A), (B), and (C) designate, respectively, Scribe A (Petrus Alamire), Scribe B (probably Martin Bourgeois), and Scribe C, in each case the main scribe of the manuscript. Italicized scribe attributions are the author's; the rest were made or suggested by other scholars and have been confirmed by the author. An asterisk indicates part-books.

Brussels, Bibliothèque royale, MSS. 215/216(A), 228(*C*?),[104] 6428(A), 9126(B), 15075(A), IV 922(A).

Florence, Biblioteca del Conservatorio, MS. Basevi 2439(*B*).

's-Hertogenbosch, Bibliotheek van de Illustre Lieve Vrouwe Broederschap, MSS. 72A(A), 72B(A), 72C(A).

Jena, Universitätsbibliothek, MSS. 2(A), 3(C), 4(A), 5(A), 7(A), 8(A), 9(A), 12(C), 20(A), 21(A), 22(B?).[105]

London, British Museum, MS. Royal 8 G VII(*A*).

Malines, Archives de la Ville, Livre de choeur (A).

Montserrat, Biblioteca del Monasterio, MSS. 766(*A*), 773(*A*).

Munich, Bayerische Staatsbibliothek, MSS. 6(*A*), 7(*A*), 34(*A*), F(*A*).

Oxford, Bodleian Library, MS. Ashmole 831(*B*).

Subiaco, Biblioteca del Monasterio, MS. 248(*A*).

Vatican, Biblioteca Apostolica Vaticana, MSS. Chigiana C VIII 234(*B*), Pal. lat. 1976–79(A)*, Cappella Sistina 34(A), 36(*A*), 160(*A*).

Verona, Biblioteca Capitolare, MS. 756(*B*).

Vienna, Oesterreichische Nationalbibliothek, MSS. 1783(*B*?), 4809(A), 4810(A), 11778(A), 15941(A)*, 18746(A & *C*?)*, 18825(A)*, 18832(A)*, 9814 ff. 132–152ᵛ(A), 11883 several fascicles (A), SM 15495(C), SM 15496(*A*), SM 15497 (*A* & *C*).

[102] Brussels, Archives générales du Royaume, Archives ecclésiastiques, no. 16682.

[103] Jacobus Lessabeus, *Hannoniae Urbium et Nominatiorum Locorum ac Coenobiorum* (Antwerp, 1534); in *Collection de Chroniques Belges inédits*, i (Brussels, 1844).

[104] Identical with second hand of Vienna 18746, but not positively scribe C.

[105] Identical with hand of Vienna 1783, but not positively scribe B.

Appendix II

Works by Josquin in Netherlands Court Manuscripts

The names appearing immediately below the sigla are those of the intended recipients of the manuscripts, usually identified through coats of arms. Then follow terminal dates for the production of the manuscript, with reasons for these dates. Where two sets of dates are given, the first set indicates outside limits, the second set the probable period of origin. As study of the complex continues, the latter may be modified.

GROUP I (1495–1508)

Vatican, Chigi C VIII 234[106]

For Philippe Bouton

1495–1505 Philip the Fair assumes control of Burgundian chapel—Philip leaves for Spain January 1506, probably taking MS. along.

1498–1503 First appearance in registers of scribe Bourgeois; death of Ockeghem in 1497—MS. is model for Brussels 9126.

33 Masses and motets (before additions): Josquin, Ockeghem, Barbireau, Agricola, La Rue, Brumel, Busnois, Compère, Gaspar, Isaac, Regis, Anon.

> Missa L'homme armé sexti toni
> Stabat Mater

Vienna 1783[107]

For Manuel of Portugal and Marie of Spain

1500–1505 Wedding of Manuel and Marie—Philip (mottoes in MS.) leaves for Spain January 1506.

1500   MS. probably wedding gift.

21 Masses: Josquin, Barbireau, Gaspar, La Rue, Agricola, De Orto, Verbonnet, Brumel, Isaac.

> Missa Ave maris stella

Brussels 9126[108]

For Philip the Fair and Juana of Spain

1505   Philip becomes king of Castile December 1504—leaves for Spain January 1506.

22 Masses and motets: Josquin, La Rue, Agricola, De Orto. Barbireau.

> Missa Ave maris stella
> Missa Hercules ('Philippus rex Castilie')
> Missa Malheur me bat
> Stabat Mater
> Huc me sydereo
> Missus est Gabriel
> Gaude Virgo Mater Christi

[106] Herbert Kellman, 'The Origins of the Chigi Codex'.

[107] *Bibliothèque nationale d'Autriche: Manuscrits et livres imprimés concernant l'histoire des Pays-Bas, 1475–1600.* Exhibition catalogue, Brussels, Bibliothèque royale (Brussels, 1962). Includes descriptions of Vienna MSS. 4809 (p. 71) and 11778 (p. 70). Helen M. Dixon, 'The Manuscript Vienna, National Library, 1783', *Musica disciplina*, xxiii (1969), pp. 105–16. [See also Walter H. Rubsamen, these Proceedings, p. 370, n. 4.—Ed.]

[108] Georges Van Doorslaer, 'La chapelle musicale de Philippe le Beau', pp. 37–8.

Florence 2439[109]

For an Italian recipient

1506–1514 Earliest date of La Rue's 'A vous non autre'[110]—scribe Bourgeois no longer on payroll after 1514.

c. 1508 'A vous non autre' probably written c. 1507, in MS. soon thereafter.

87 chansons and motets: Josquin, Le Petit, Lannoy, Agricola, La Rue, Compère, Ghiselin, Brumel, Pipelare, De Orto, Obrecht, Prioris, Busnois, Ockeghem, Isaac, Rego de Bergis, Gaspar, Anon.

Entré je suis en grant pensée ('Par vous je suis')
A la mort/Monstra te esse Matrem
Ce pauvre mendiant/Pauper sum ego ('Fortune d'estrange plumaige')

GROUP II (1508–1520)

Vienna SM 15495[111]

For Maximilian I and Bianca Maria Sforza

1508–11 Maximilian confirmed emperor (double eagle)—Bianca Sforza dies 31 December 1511.

7 Masses: Josquin, Obrecht, A. Févin, Compère, Bruhier, Thérache.

Missa Faisant regretz
Missa Una musque de Buscaya

Brussels 215/216[112]

For Charles Le Clerc[113]

[109] Martin Staehelin, 'Quellenkundliche Beiträge zum Werk von Johannes Ghiselin-Verbonnet', *Archiv für Musikwissenschaft*, xxiv (1967), pp. 120–32; Paul G. Newton, 'Florence, Biblioteca del Conservatorio di Musica Luigi Cherubini, Manuscript Basevi 2439: Critical Edition and Commentary' (Ph.D. diss., North Texas State University, 1968). Staehelin points out the close scribal relationship between this manuscript and Verona 756, and discusses the significance of both manuscripts as complementary sources of Ghiselin's works. He also states that the arms in Florence 2439 are those of the family Conte Agostini della Seta of Pisa, but gives no evidence for the identification. The present author finds considerable discrepancies between the arms of the above counts, as described in Rietstap's *Armorial général* (New York, 1965; reprint of 1884 edition), i, p. 15, and those in the Florence manuscript. The simple Agostini-Pisa arms (ibid., Supplément, p. 1177) are much closer to the Florence arms, but still do not match them precisely, for the latter appear to be *coupé*. Confirmation of this identification, therefore, awaits further evidence. Newton does not deal with this problem.

[110] See fn. 60 above. The text refers to fourteen years of service, most likely La Rue's own; he entered the chapel in 1492.

[111] *Maximilian I. 1459–1519. Ausstellung. Österreichische Nationalbibliothek* (Vienna, 1959), p. 47, no. 146. See also fn. 65 above.

[112] Jozef Robijns, 'Eine Musikhandschrift des frühen 16. Jahrhunderts im Zeichen der Verehrung Unserer Lieben Frau der Sieben Schmerzen', *Kirchenmusikalisches Jahrbuch*, xliv (1960), pp. 28–43.

[113] Charles Le Clerc was a nobleman who held a series of high-ranking posts at the Netherlands court. It was to him that Lemaire dedicated the epitaphs of George Chastelain and Jean Molinet, published with 'Plus nulz regretz' in 1508 (see fn. 4 above), explaining that he was doing so because Le Clerc loved and revered the works of these writers, and had offered to have the epitaphs engraved in copper or marble, or made part of a splendid painting, and placed near their tombs.

1508–18   Reestablishment of chapel; Alamire probably begins regular employment—
           La Rue still alive.
1512–16   MS. collateral with Jena 20.
4 Masses and motets (and plainchant): Josquin, La Rue, Pipelare, Anon.

    Stabat Mater

Jena 7[114]
For Maximilian; sent to Frederick of Saxony
1508–19   Maximilian confirmed emperor—Maximilian dies.
c. 1516   MS. collateral with Vienna SM 15496 (can be dated 1515/16).[115]
7 Masses: Josquin, La Rue, Févin, Prioris, Divitis.

    Missa de Beata Virgine

Vatican, Cappella Sistina 160[116]
For Pope Leo X
1513–21   Reign of Leo X.
1518–19   MS. probably sent as gift in connection with imperial election.
9 Masses: Josquin, Barbireau, Obrecht, Mouton, Isaac, Vorda, Mouton/Forestier, Anon.

    Missa de Beata Virgine

London, Royal 8 G VII[117]
For Henry VIII and Catherine of Aragon
1513–25   Motet reference to Charles V[118]; first meeting of Charles and Henry at
           Tournai—break between Charles and Henry.[119]
1516–22   Charles receives own chapel 1515; Alamire in England 1516—Charles in
           London in 1522 with full chapel.
34 motets: Josquin, Mouton, Févin, La Rue, Strus, Lebrun, Thérache, Verbonnet, Isaac,
Anon.

    Descendi in hortum meum
    Fama malum
    Missus est Gabriel
    Dulces exuviae
    Absalon fili mi

---

[114] Karl E. Roediger, *Die geistlichen Musikhandschriften der Universitäts-Bibliothek Jena*,
2 vols. (Jena, 1935), deals with all Netherlands court manuscripts in Jena. On MS. Jena 7,
see *Textband*, esp. pp. 11, 47–8. See also Lothar Hoffmann-Erbrecht, 'Jenaer Musikhandschriften', *MGG*, vi (1957), cols. 1872–6.

[115] Coats of arms indicate that the manuscript was made up after Hungary and Bohemia
were joined to the empire in 1515; an inscription calls Charles V 'Prince of Castile', a
title he gave up when proclaimed king of Spain in March 1516.

[116] Joseph M. Llorens, *Capellae Sixtinae codices musicis notis instructi* (Vatican City, 1960),
pp. 187–9.

[117] Augustus Hughes-Hughes, *Catalogue of Manuscript Music in the British Museum*, i
(London, 1906), pp. 140, 259; ii (London, 1908), p. 193.

[118] Ff. 28ᵛ–30 (anon.): 'Sancta Maria Virgo virginum...Cerne piisima famuli tui
Caroli omne suum desiderium [periculum]'.

[119] Political relations between Charles and Henry deteriorated rapidly in 1525 when
Charles refused Henry's proposal to invade France, and asked to be released from his
earlier promise to marry Princess Mary.

Brussels 228[120]

For Margaret of Austria

1516–23   (main contents) MS. not in 1516 inventory—present in 1523 inventory.
c. 1519   (additions) Maximilian's funeral motet included.
58 chansons and motets: Josquin, La Rue, Ockeghem, Pipelare, Brumel, Agricola, Prioris, Strus, De Orto, Gaspar, Compère, Anon.

> Plus nulz regretz
> Entré je suis en grant pensée ('Entrée suis en pensée')
> Plaine de dueil (addition)
> Ce pauvre mendiant/Pauper sum ego

Jena 3[121]

For Frederick of Saxony

1518–25   MS. indicates Compère deceased—death of Frederick.
1518–20   MS. contains corrections by Adam Rener (died 1520).
8 Masses: Josquin, Févin, Compère, Mouton.

> Missa Faisant regretz ('Elizabeth faisant regretz')
> Missa Hercules ('Fridericus dux Saxsonie')
> Missa Ave maris stella
> Missa Malheur me bat
> Missa Sine nomine

GROUP III (1521–1534)

Jena 21[122]

Sent to Frederick of Saxony[123]

1521–25   MS. indicates Josquin deceased—death of Frederick.
8 Masses: Josquin, Pipelare, La Rue, Gaspar, Anon.

> Missa Pange lingua
> Missa Allez regretz

Vienna 4809[124]

For Raimund Fugger the Elder

1521–34   MS. indicates Josquin deceased—retirement of Alamire.
1521–c. 1525 MS. collateral with Jena 21.
7 Masses: Josquin.

> Missa Pange lingua
> Missa de Beata Virgine
> Missa Hercules Dux Ferrariae
> Missa Malheur me bat
> Missa Faisant regretz
> Missa Sine nomine
> Missa Ave maris stella

[120] Martin Picker, *The Chanson Albums*. Dating of the manuscript worked out by Picker.
[121] Roediger, *Die geistlichen Musikhandschriften, Textband*, pp. 40–41.
[122] Ibid., p. 52.
[123] There is no evidence that this manuscript was prepared specifically for Frederick, but it is clearly a part of the collection sent to him from the Netherlands court.
[124] Leopold Nowak, 'Die Musikhandschriften aus Fuggerschem Besitz', pp. 505–15, deals with all the Vienna manuscripts in Group III; see fn. 69 above.

Vienna 11778[125]

For Raimund Fugger the Elder
Companion volume to Vienna 4809.
6 Masses, 2 *Credos:* Josquin

  Missa L'homme armé super voces musicales
  Missa L'homme armé sexti toni
  Missa Gaudeamus
  Missa Fortuna desperata
  Missa La sol fa re mi
  Missa L'ami Baudichon
  Credo Ciaschun me crie
  Credo Vilayge II (Josquin?)

Vienna 18746[126]

Sent to Raimund Fugger the Elder[127]
1523   Dated and signed by Alamire.
56 chansons and motets: Josquin, La Rue, Richafort, Mouton, Bauldewijn, Prioris, Lebrun,
Brumel, Anon.

  Plusieurs regretz
  Je me complains
  Douleur me bat
  Plaine de dueil
  Parfons regretz
  Du mien amant
  Incessament livré suis

Vienna 18832[128]

For Raimund Fugger the Elder
1515–34   Raimund Fugger settles in Augsburg—retirement of Alamire.
c.1521–c.1525   MS. probably related to Vienna 4809 and 11778 (see above, p. 204).
89 *bicinia*: Josquin, Agricola, La Rue, Obrecht, Févin, Isaac, Brumel, Mouton, Anon.

  Bicinia from: Missa Pange lingua
             Missa La sol fa re mi
             Missa Gaudeamus

Vienna 15941[129]

For Raimund Fugger the Elder
1515–34   See previous MS.
c.1521–c.1531 MS. probably made up after death of Josquin—collateral with Pal. lat.
1976–79 (see below).

[125] Ibid.
[126] Jaap van Benthem, 'Einige wiedererkannte Josquin-Chansons im Codex 18746 der
Österreichischen Nationalbibliothek', *Tijdschrift van de Vereniging voor Nederlandse
Muziekgeschiedenis*, xxii (1971), pp. 18–42. Van Benthem argues for the attribution of
'Sans vous veoir', 'Saillies avant', 'Dame donuer', and 'Consideres mes incessantes plaintes'
to Josquin on stylistic grounds.
[127] This conclusion is based on grounds similar to those stated in fn. 123 above.
[128] Leopold Nowak, 'Eine Bicinienhandschrift der Wiener Nationalbibliothek',
Zeitschrift für Musikwissenschaft, xiv (1931/32), pp. 99–102.
[129] Nowak, 'Die Musikhandschriften'.

32 motets: Josquin, Bauldewijn, Mouton, La Rue, Richafort, Vorda, Forestier, Champion, Févin, Thérache, De Orto, Anon.

In principio erat verbum
In exitu Israel de Egypto
Qui habitat *a 4*
Salve Regina *a 5*
Descendi in hortum meum
Ave mundi, spes Maria
Ave Christe immolate ('Ave caro Christi cara'[130])
De profundis clamavi *a 4*[131]

Munich 34[132]

For William IV of Bavaria

1521–34   MS. indicates Josquin deceased—retirement of Alamire.

1521–*c*.1530 Sent by Margaret or Charles (Charles's last visit to Munich before return to Spain took place in 1530).

29 'Salve Regina' settings: Josquin, La Rue, Divitis, Richafort, Rener, Pipelare, Molumet, Vinders, Bauldewijn, Obrecht, Lebrun, Reingot, Vorda, Craen, Verbonnet, Anon.

Salve Regina *a 5*

Vatican, Pal. lat. 1976–79[133]

For Ferdinand and Anne of Hungary and Bohemia

1528–34   Ferdinand and Anne receive Hungarian crown November 1527—retirement of Alamire.

1528–*c*.1531 MS. contains motet reference to Margaret,[134] completed shortly before or after her death.

37 motets: Josquin, Willaert, Agricola, Mouton, Gascongne, La Rue, Richafort, Bauldewijn, Thérache, Févin, Isaac, Anon.

Ave Christe immolate ('Ave caro Christi cara')
Descendi in hortum meum

Brussels IV 922[135]

For Pompeius Occo of Amsterdam

c.1526–34   MS. indicates Divitis deceased—retirement of Alamire.

[130] Edgar H. Sparks, *The Music of Noel Bauldeweyn* (American Musicological Society, Studies and Documents, no. 6; New York, 1972), pp. 98–103.

[131] I am indebted to Professor Edward Lowinsky for bringing the presence of this work in the manuscript, misattributed to Champion, to my attention.

[132] Jul. Jos. Maier, *Die musikalischen Handschriften der k. Hof- und Staatsbibliothek in Muenchen* (Munich, 1879), pp. 58–9.

[133] Walter H. Rubsamen, 'Music Research in Italian Libraries', *Notes*, viii (1950), pp. 72–4. See fn. 68 above.

[134] No. 10 (La Rue): 'Salve Mater salvatoris...Salve viae gubernatrix/Salve sancta legislatrix...Gaude soror insignita...Gaude sacra Margarita'.

[135] This manuscript was acquired by the Bibliothèque royale in the summer of 1973; I was able to examine it briefly, while it was still in the process of acquisition, thanks to the courtesy of Bernard Huys, head of the library's Music Section. Mr. Huys, who was responsible for the purchase of the book, has since published a study of it, 'An Unknown Alamire-Choirbook ("Occo Codex") Recently Acquired by the Royal Library of Belgium', *Tijdschrift van de Vereniging voor Nederlandse Muziekgeschiedenis*, xxiv (1974), pp. 1–19.

*c.*1530–34   Apparently collateral with 's-Hertogenbosch 72A, 72B, 72C.[136]
7 motets, 8 Masses, 2 *Kyries:* La Rue, Barra, Josquin, Mouton, Gascongne, Forestier,
Isaac, Vorda, Divitis, Anon.

Missa Pange lingua (with *Benedictus* from Matheus Gascongne's Mass 'Es hat ein Sin')

[136] Dated 1530–1, Alamire's last productions of which the commissions are documented.
Like the 's-Hertogenbosch books, the Brussels manuscript has several concordances with
Cambrai, Bibliothèque municipale, MSS. 3 and 4, and it may likewise reflect transmission
of music from the French chapel to the Netherlands chapel at the Franco-Imperial peace
negotiations in Cambrai in 1529.

Josquin in the Music of Spain and Portugal

ROBERT STEVENSON

Josquin's contacts with Peninsular music and musicians

In contrast with Beethoven, who to this day is more honoured on paper than in performances throughout the Peninsula, Josquin completely captivated Spain and Portugal from the moment Petrucci's prints first began circulating abroad. His immediate overwhelming and lasting conquest is all the more notable because unlike Ockeghem, La Rue, and Agricola, he himself seems never to have visited Spain. Not that he lacked an invitation. In a letter to Ercole I dated 13 December 1501, the Ferrara envoy at the French court wrote as follows from Blois:

I have found here a singer named Josquin whom Your Excellency dispatched to Flanders in search of singers. He says that he has left the money in the bank at Bruges, that the singers have been found, and that the Archduke [Philip the Fair (1478–1506)] has invited him to go along to Spain and has written Your Excellency asking to borrow him for the trip.[1]

But if this letter tells us no more than that Josquin stood high in the list of musicians whom Philip wished to recruit for his first Spanish tour, he did lure others, among them La Rue and Josquin's erstwhile companion in Galeazzo Maria Sforza's ducal choir, Agricola, both of whom followed Philip and Joanna to Spain in 1501–2 and 1506. Before these two came Ockeghem, who crossed the Pyrenees in January of 1470; and after them Gombert, who travelled the length and breadth of Spain in Charles V's retinue from 2 October 1526, when he is first heard of at Granada,[2] until about 1540. To commemorate his visit, Ockeghem left us his soulful arrangement of Johannes Cornago's 'Qu'es mi vida preguntays'.[3] La Rue's 'Missa Nunqua fue pena mayor' pays tribute to the most celebrated song of the epoch in Spanish.

[1] Helmuth Osthoff, *Josquin Desprez*, i (Tutzing, 1962), p. 51, quotes the original document.

[2] Joseph Schmidt-Görg, *Nicolas Gombert, Kapellmeister Kaiser Karls V.* (Bonn, 1938), pp. 73–4.

[3] Robert Stevenson, *Spanish Music in the Age of Columbus* (The Hague, 1960), pp. 220–23; Isabel Pope [Conant], 'The Secular Compositions of Johannes Cornago', *Miscelánea en homenaje a Monseñor Higinio Anglés*, ii (Barcelona, 1958–61), pp. 691, 703–5; Gertraut

Nothing so overtly Spanish survives from Josquin. But André Pirro did postulate a Basque origin for the tune of Josquin's 'Una musque de Buscaya', found in the so-called French chansonnier purchased by Ferdinand Columbus in September of 1515.[4] The same tune, whether or not of Basque origin, inspired the one Mass by Josquin in which the *Agnus* repeats the *Kyrie* note-for-note and every movement has four voices, 'Missa Una musque de Buscaya'.

Whence the tune? To believe Pirro, Josquin learned the pretty 'Basque girl' tune from a pilgrim who had visited St. James's shrine in Galicia or from a Spanish colleague in the papal choir.[5] While searching for such a colleague, Pirro might also have cited such Spaniards at Galeazzo Maria Sforza's court as Filipello spagnolo, rewarded for his fine singing in 1468 with a velvet suit; Antonio spagnolo 'nostro cantor', recommended 15 June 1472 to the duke's sister Ippolita, duchess of Calabria; Iohanne Andrea spagnolo 'suonatore d'organo', authorized in January of 1476 to examine some postulant singers; or 'Li dui Spagnoli' who follow Josquin in a list of ducal singers dated 30 March 1475.[6] Should still more names be needed to play a Spanish guessing game, the second most senior singer at the Ferrara court chapel conducted by Josquin was Messer Bartholomio Spagnolo.[7]

According to José Antonio de Donostia, 'Une mousse de Bisquaye' fails to survive among Basque peasantry as a living folk tune.[8] However, in publishing a facsimile of the monophonic ballade,[9] he did class it as the oldest musical setting of any Basque text. In so doing, he echoed Gaston Paris, who in editing Paris, Bibliothèque Nationale, MS. fr. 12744 (this includes not only 'Une mousse', but also source melodies for Josquin's 'Bergerette savoyenne', 'Mon mari m'a diffamée', 'Se congié prens de mes

---

Haberkamp, *Die weltliche Vokalmusik in Spanien um 1500. Der "Cancionero musical de Colombina" von Sevilla und ausserspanische Handschriften* (Tutzing, 1968), pp. 145–7. Ockeghem's rondeau *a 4*, 'Petite camusette/S'elle m'amera je ne sçay', turns up in the same Colombina cancionero (Haberkamp, pp. 256–8).

[4] Seville, Biblioteca Colombina, MS. 5-I-43; see Dragan Plamenac, 'A Reconstruction of the French Chansonnier in the Biblioteca Colombina, Seville—III', *The Musical Quarterly*, xxxviii (1952), pp. 266–7. Petrucci published Josquin's chanson in his *Canti C* (1503).

[5] *Histoire de la musique de la fin du XIVᵉ siècle à la fin du XVIᵉ* (Paris, 1940), p. 185.

[6] Emilio Motta, 'Musici alla Corte degli Sforza', *Archivio Storico Lombardo*, 2d ser., iv (1887), pp. 298 (Filipello), 541 (Antonio), 292 (Ioanne Andrea), 541 (Li dui Spagnoli).

[7] Osthoff, *Josquin Desprez*, i, p. 212. See also plate 12 after p. 48.

[8] Art. 'Basken', *MGG*, i (1949–51), col. 1379.

[9] Ibid., cols. 1375–8. Osthoff, *Josquin Desprez*, ii, p. 312, calls the facsimile of the monophonic 'Une mousse' at cols. 1375–8 'A reproduction of a thus far unnoted old source'. However, the source is the well-known Bibliothèque Nationale MS. fr. 12744, fols. 5ᵛ–6.

belles amours', and 'Se j'ay perdu mon amy') identified *mousse* in the first line of the ballade as Spanish *moza* ('young girl') and the refrain line 'soaz soaz ordonarequin' at the close of each strophe as her whispered Basque advice to her lover.[10]

Josquin in extant Spanish Renaissance manuscripts

The best known Renaissance composer of Basque background, Juan de Anchieta (*c.* 1462–1523), recalled 'Une mousse de Bisquaye' in the *Et exultavit* of his Magnificat *a 3*.[11] The same work occurs on folios 146–147ᵛ of the unnumbered 228-folio manuscript in the Segovia Cathedral,[12] which is also the unique source of a Josquin Magnificat. Osthoff regarded the four-verse Magnificat as an adaptation of a work originally for instruments,[13] analogous to 'Propter peccata quae peccastis'—a motet *a 5* with 'La Spagna' for its tenor. Antonowycz and Elders class the Segovia Magnificat as an original Josquin work, albeit incomplete.[14]

Barcelona, Biblioteca Central, MS. 454[15] contains a four-voice Dorian motet 'Sancta Mater istud agas' ascribed to 'Juisquin'.[16] It supplies suitably emotion-wrought music for the exact four strophes (11–14) that Josquin abstained from including in his 'Stabat Mater', printed eight times between 1519 and 1559. The two motets following 'Sancta Mater istud agas' are correctly ascribed to the chief Castilian composer of the epoch, Francisco de Peñalosa (*c.* 1470–1528).[17] 'Sancta Mater istud agas' turns up in three other Spanish manuscripts—each time, however, with Peñalosa, not Josquin, as the designated composer. As long ago as 1869, Hilarión Eslava published a transcription of this same 'Sancta Mater istud agas', ascribed to Peñalosa

[10] *Chansons du XVᵉ siècle publiées d'après le manuscrit de la Bibliothèque nationale de Paris* (Paris, 1875), pp. 7–9. Paris left it to Basque experts to translate the line in which the 'young girl' urges her fumbling lover to 'get on with it'.

[11] Illustrated in facsimile in *MGG*, i, cols. 1383–4, from Tarazona, Cathedral, MS. 2, fols. 24ᵛ–25.

[12] Higinio Anglés, 'Un manuscrit inconnu avec polyphonie du XVᵉ siècle conservé à la cathédrale de Ségovie (Espagne)', *Acta musicologica*, viii (1936), p. 11.

[13] Helmuth Osthoff, 'Das Magnificat bei Josquin Desprez', *Archiv für Musikwissenschaft*, xvi (1959), pp. 228–30.

[14] *Werken*, Supplement, pp. x and 30–5.

[15] Description in *Monumentos de la Música Española*, i (Madrid, 1941), pp. 112–15. Pedro de Escobar's celebrated 'Clamabat autem mulier Chananea' (fols. 161ᵛ–162) was copied in '1532'. Other dates of copying jotted down here and there throughout this 180-leaf codex range from 20 February 1525 for Francisco de Peñalosa's motet 'In passione positus' to February 1532 for Gaspar van Weerbecke's 'O beate Sebastiane'.

[16] *Werken*, Supplement, pp. 41–4. On p. 44, measure 83 (bass), change E to D.

[17] Stevenson, *Spanish Music in the Age of Columbus*, pp. 151–3, lists his repertory. Barcelona 454 includes three other correctly ascribed Peñalosa motets, but also an 'O bone Jhesu' (fols. 135ᵛ–136) that is actually Loyset Compère's (ibid., p. 136, note 130).

in Toledo Cathedral, MS. 21.[18] Eighty-four years later, Juan Bautista de Elústiza edited the same Peñalosa motet, this time from the Seville source.[19] Still another sixteenth-century codex credits the same 'Sancta Mater istud agas' to Peñalosa (Tarazona MS. 2, fols. 254ᵛ–255). With three manuscripts giving the work to him, not Josquin, and with Barcelona 454 less than infallible in its attributions, Peñalosa's better claim can scarcely be contested.

Although Barcelona 454 must yield to Seville 5-5-20, Tarazona 2, and Toledo 21, so far as 'Sancta Mater' is concerned, it does contain Josquin's 'O intemerata Virgo' (fols. 128ᵛ–129) and 'O Maria nullam' (129ᵛ–130)— third and fourth *partes* of 'Vultum tuum deprecabuntur'. Classed as anonymous works in all previous indexes, these two *partes* join Josquin's 'Ave Maria gratia plena... Virgo serena' (fols. 124ᵛ–126) in having escaped Smijers' notice. Also at Barcelona, Orfeó Català MS. 5 contains the latter motet, a truncated 'Domine non secundum peccata', and two Josquin Masses, the 'Fortuna desperata' (fols. 1ᵛ–10) and 'L'homme armé super voces musicales' (52ᵛ–55).

A still richer Josquin Mass repertory—eleven Masses all told, two of which have gone unrecognized until now—survives in four luxurious parchment choirbooks at Toledo Cathedral copied between 1542 and 1557: MSS. 9, 16, 19, and 27. The 147-folio MS. 9 bearing the arms of the cardinal-archbishop and arithmetician who taught Philip II, Juan Martínez Siliceo (1486–1557), contains five Masses, 'L'homme armé super voces musicales' (4ᵛ–35), 'Ave maris stella' (35ᵛ–54), 'Malheur me bat' (54ᵛ–83), 'Faysant regretz' (83ᵛ–103), and 'Ad fugam' (103ᵛ–127).[20] The 107-folio MS. 16 copied in 1542 (fol. 9ᵛ) and corrected by the Toledo chapelmaster Andrés de Torrentes[21] opens with Josquin's 'De Beata Virgine' (1ᵛ–20) and 'Pange lingua' (20ᵛ–38). The parchment 96-folio MS. 19 copied in 1543 (fols. 25ᵛ and 48ᵛ) adds his 'La sol fa re mi' (71ᵛ–92) and a truncated 'Da

[18] Hilarión Eslava, *Lira sacro-hispana, I/1, siglo xvi* (Madrid, n.d.), pp. 29–33.

[19] Biblioteca Colombina, MS. 5-5-20, fol. 12ᵛ; Juan Bautista de Elústiza, *Antología musical: Siglo de oro de la música litúrgica de España* (Barcelona, 1933), pp. 16–19.

[20] Felipe Rubio Piqueras, *Códices Polifónicos Toledanos. Estudio crítico* (Toledo, 1925), p. 25. For a brief description of the Toledo choirbooks, see René Lenaerts, 'Les manuscrits polyphoniques de la Bibliothèque Capitulaire de Tolède', *Kongress-Bericht, Internationale Gesellschaft für Musikwissenschaft, Utrecht 1952* (Amsterdam, 1953), pp. 276–81.

[21] Rubio Piqueras, *Códices Polifónicos*, p. 33. Torrentes' 'Missa Super Nisi Dominus' *a* 4 (62ᵛ–84), Mouton's 'Missa Dictes moy toutes vos pensées' (38ᵛ–62), and Bauldeweyn's 'Missa En douleur et tristesse' *a* 5 (84ᵛ–106) complete the volume. At the bottom of folio 106ᵛ appears this curious autograph: 'digo yo andres torrentes maeso de capilla desta sancta yglesia de toledo que este quaderno esta corregido por my mano y por ques verdad lo firme mi nonbre digo este cuerpo de livro todo andres de torrentes'. Torrentes's eighteen years as Toledo chapelmaster embraced three terms: 9 December 1539 to 1 September 1545, 16 December 1547 to 27 July 1553, and 9 February 1571 to 4 September 1580 (on which latter date he died). See Rubio Piqueras, *Música y Músicos Toledanos: Contribución a su estudio* (Toledo, 1923), p. 58.

pacem' (92ᵛ–96; the leaves after 'propter magnam' are lost). MS. 27, copied in 1550, contains a total of five Masses, two of which have until now resisted identification as Josquin's—'Gaudeamus' (fols. 85ᵛ–114) and the 'Hercules Dux Ferrariae' (26ᵛ–45).[22]

The Toledo choirbooks also rank highest among surviving Spanish manuscript sources for Josquin's motets. MS. 10, despite having been vandalized of several parchment leaves after 101 and despoiled throughout of its illuminated capitals, still boasts three or four Josquin motets.[23] In Toledo MS. 13, 'Sancti Dei omnes' *a 4* (fols. 1ᵛ–10) should be ascribed to Mouton rather than to Josquin;[24] but 'In illo tempore assumpsit' (29ᵛ–39) and 'Ave nobilissima creatura' (89ᵛ–96) belong to the Josquin canon. MSS. 17[25] and 21 each contain one Josquin motet. The bitextual funeral motet 'Absolve quesumus Domine/Requiem aeternam' *a 6* copied through- out in funereal black at folios 118ᵛ–121 of Toledo 21 (shades of his *Déplora- tion*) is the one Josquin *unicum* at Toledo unreservedly accepted by Osthoff, who argues that the blank three-syllable name accented on the second syllable must originally have been Philippus and that Josquin composed the work for a Brussels or Malines commemoration shortly after Philip the Fair's sudden death at Burgos on 25 September 1506.[26] Immediately before 'Absolve quesumus' in Toledo 21, a manuscript copied in 1549 (see this date in initials of bass on fol. 54, superius on fol. 56ᵛ), comes Morales's five-voice Requiem (97ᵛ–118). The manuscript—which contains the last *Agnus* from Josquin's 'Missa L'homme armé super voces musicales' (fols. 43ᵛ–47, headed 'Clama ne cesses') and Loyset Compère's 'Ave Maria . . . Virgo serena' (58ᵛ–62)—also includes unique copies of Morales's 'Juicio fuerte será dado', 'Circumdederunt me', and 'Salva nos stella'.[27]

While chapelmaster at Toledo in 1545–7, Morales earned an annual base pay of 100 ducats, plus a 6.25 percent bonus added because of his

[22] Two of the five Masses in Toledo 27 are by Morales, the 'De Beata Virgine' *a 4* (1ᵛ–24) and 'Vulnerasti cor meum' (58ᵛ–85). The fifth, which like Josquin's two Masses in this source has up to now been catalogued as anonymous, is Pierre Colin's 'Tant plus de bien'. So far as this last one is concerned, a snipper threw sleuths off the trail when he cut the top of folio 45ᵛ, leaving only 'lus de bien'. However, this Mass can now be identified from the printed concordance in Colin's *Liber octo missarum* (Lyons: Jacques Moderne, 1541).

[23] 'Stabat Mater' *a 5* (fols. 11ᵛ–22), 'Missus est' *a 4* (21ᵛ–34), 'Inviolata, integra et casta es' *a 5* (53ᵛ–60), 'Victimae paschali laudes' *a 6* (60ᵛ–71). [Edgar H. Sparks ascribes the latter to Jo. Brunet (see below, pp. 347–9).—Ed.]

[24] Osthoff, *Josquin Desprez*, ii, p. 22.

[25] 'In principio erat', fols. 1ᵛ–10.

[26] Osthoff, *Josquin Desprez*, ii, p. 59.

[27] Stevenson, *Spanish Cathedral Music in the Golden Age* (Berkeley and Los Angeles, 1961), pp. 32, 108–9. The 'Domine Jesu Christe' on fol. 56ᵛ listed by Anglés (*Monumentos de la Música Española*, i, p. 130) is actually Escobar's 'Clamabat autem mulier Cananea'; the superius begins with the words 'Domine Jesu Christe'.

international reputation.[28] Torrentes, who both preceded and followed him, earned only base pay.[29] How does this 100-ducat salary compare with what it cost to have Josquin's works copied during the epoch of these two *maestros de capilla*? Toledo MS. 9, the 127-folio codex mentioned above that contains five Josquin Masses, cost the cathedral over 34 ducats[30]—more than a third of either chapelmaster's entire annual pay. Another, now lost, Toledo choirbook[31] starting with Josquin's 'Liber generationis' (see Pl. 34)[32] was rated in 1925 as the costliest polyphonic choirbook then still surviving in any Spanish cathedral archive. This choirbook contained six Masses—three by Mouton ('Benedictus Dominus Deus', 'Tua est potentia', 'Verbum bonum') and one each by Févin ('Missa de Feria') and Gascongne ('Missa Nigra sum')—and several motets.[33]

Two of Josquin's motets in this manuscript, 'In principio erat' *a 4* (fols. 52[v]–57) and 'Praeter rerum seriem' *a 6* (85[v]–89) were intabulated in 1552 and 1554, the first by the wealthy Josquin fanatic who was majordomo of Salamanca, Diego Pisador, the second by the blind court favourite, Miguel de Fuenllana.[34] Either by coincidence or because in Spain certain works by Josquin were definitely preferred to others, the Toledo repertory of Masses and motets by Josquin closely matches Pisador's intabulated repertory. No less notable is the fact that between him, the other vihuelists active from 1538 to 1554, and Antonio de Cabezón, nearly the whole Josquin corpus still extant in manuscripts at Barcelona, Seville, Toledo, and Valladolid

[28] Ibid., p. 29.   [29] Ibid., p. 31.

[30] Edmond Vander Straeten, *La Musique aux Pays-Bas*, vii (1885), p. 124, ascribed the copying to 1558, a year in which both Cardinal Siliceo and the copyist Martín Pérez were dead. However, Martín Pérez's heir did sign a receipt in 1558 for what was still owing of the original 12,954 maravedís agreed upon as the copying price. The receipt as given by Vander Straeten ('Relacion de la verificacion de cuento de lo que escribio y punto Martin Perez, difunto, y su official...año 1558') reads thus [one ducat = 375 maravedís; one real = 34 maravedís]:

> Se escrivio y punto un libro de çinco missas de Xusquin, en el qual entran de canto de organo, puntado y escrito CXXVII hojas en pergamino, que por el asiento que se concerto con el dicho Martin Perez, es cada hoja de pergamino escrita y puntada a toda costa de tres reales, que suman XIIUDCCCCLIIII [12,954] mrs, y dellos tiene rescibidos por librança para començar el dicho libro, XIUCCL [11,250] mrs, y alcança por IUDCCIIII [1704] mrs.

[31] Rubio Piqueras, *Música y Músicos Toledanos*, pp. 28–9; *Códices Polifónicos*, pp. 61–2. Schmidt-Görg, *Nicolas Gombert*, p. 68, erroneously cites it as Codex 34. The number of the lost manuscript is Codex 22.

[32] Facsimile of the first opening between pp. 32–3 of *Códices Polifónicos*.

[33] A six-voice 'Ascendens Christus in altum' by Févin, apparently an *unicum* of this manuscript, has not been lost; Hilarión Eslava edited it in *Lira sacro-hispana*, i/1, siglo xvi, pp. 21–8. [The motet occurs anonymously in Florence, Duomo, MS. 11, fol. 105[v].—Ed.]

[34] The 'Liber generationis' manuscript also included Josquin's frequently intabulated 'Pater noster' *a 6* and two psalm motets, 'Qui habitat in adiutorio' and 'In exitu Israel de Egypto'.

found intabulators. On the other hand, those six Masses not now extant in Spanish ecclesiastical archives—'Allez regretz', 'Di dadi', 'D'ung aultre amer', 'L'ami Baudichon', 'Mater Patris', and 'Una musque de Buscaya'— attracted no intabulators whatsoever, either in whole or in part.[35]

So far as correlation between the Spanish intabulated repertory and motets at Seville and Valladolid Cathedrals is concerned, every one, including 'Ecce tu pulchra es' *a 4* at folios 84^v–85 in a 99-folio parchment choirbook of Lady motets at Seville,[36] turns up in Pisador (1552), Fuenllana (1554), or Cabezón (1578). Pisador intabulated 'Ecce tu pulchra' and the 'Salve Regina' *a 5* with which the Seville sixteenth-century choirbook I commences, Fuenllana the 'Praeter rerum seriem' and 'Benedicta es caelorum Regina' *a 6*, and Valderrábano the 'Ave Maria' *a 6* and 'Inviolata, integra et casta' *a 5*.[37] Cabezón's 1578 *Obras de música* includes two different glosses of the *prima pars* of 'Stabat Mater' *a 5*, 'Inviolata, integra et casta' *a 5*, and 'Benedicta es' *a 6*.[38] In Cabezón's 'paraphrase-parody' of Josquin's 'Ave Maria' *a 6*, he continues authorizing the usual thick Spanish *ficta* overlay, but here 'improves' upon the canonic original with numerous fugitive imitative points of his own contriving. The Valladolid Cathedral MS. 17 (= 225)[39] contains 'Stabat Mater' (fols. 116^v–117) and 'Benedicta es caelorum Regina' (182^v–184) plus an extensive mixed sacred and secular repertory by Animuccia, Arcadelt, Rodrigo Ceballos, Clemens non Papa, Crecquillon, Francisco Guerrero, Jachet of Mantua, Lassus, Rinaldo del Mel, Monte, Juan Navarro, Palestrina, Bernardino de Ribera, Melchor

---

[35] Howard Mayer Brown, *Instrumental Music Printed Before 1600: A Bibliography* (Cambridge, Mass., 1965), p. 533. See also Kwee Him Yong, 'Sixteenth-Century Printed Instrumental Arrangements of Works by Josquin des Prez: An Inventory', *Tijdschrift van de Vereniging voor Nederlandse Muziekgeschiedenis*, xxii (1971), pp. 43–65.

[36] Contents indexed by Higinio Anglés, 'La música conservada en la Biblioteca Colombina y en la Catedral de Sevilla', *Anuario musical*, ii (1947), pp. 31–2. 'Ecce tu pulchra es amica mea', the one motet added as a 'coda' to Book I of Josquin's Masses (1502), appears in Pisador retitled 'Tota pulchra' (fol. 78).

[37] Brown, *Instrumental Music*, pp. 100 (no. 26) and 102 (no. 87). Anglés classed the 'Ave Maria' (*secunda pars* of 'Pater noster') as for five instead of six voices because he failed to note the unison canon prescribed between tenor and alto in the Seville choirbook.

[38] In general, accidentals agree in both versions of each *prima pars*. Examples of Cabezón's disagreeing *ficta*: 'Stabat' I, measure 168, B♮, II, 169, B♭; I, 171, B♮, II, 172, B♭; 'Inviolata' I, 80, C♯, II, 81, C♮; I, 97, C♮, II, 98, C♯; I, 105, C♮, II, 106, C♯; 'Benedicta' I, 125, C♮, II, 125, C♯. For discussion and transcriptions, see Charles Jacobs, 'The Transcription Technique and Style of Antonio de Cabezón as shown in his thirteen intabulations of music by Josquin des Prez' (M.A. thesis, New York University, 1957). In addition to the Marian motets, Cabezón intabulated four excerpts from the 'Missa L'homme armé super voces musicales' and the 'Missa de Beata Virgine', *Cum Sancto Spiritu*.

[39] Higinio Anglés, 'El Archivo Musical de la Catedral de Valladolid', *Anuario musical*, iii (1948), p. 85 (no. 71). Josquin's 'Ave Maria' *a 6* (*secunda pars* of 'Pater noster') is also found in Valladolid MSS. 6 and 15 (ibid., pp. 67 [= no. 5] and 82).

Robledo, Alessandro Striggio, Gérard de Turnhout, Verdelot, Vicentino, Willaert, and eight other less well known composers.

The unnumbered Segovia Cathedral manuscript referred to above as the unique source of a truncated even-verse Magnificat in Tone III is a much earlier source than the Valladolid miscellany. Josquin's contributions, apart from the Magnificat, include the 'Missa L'homme armé sexti toni', the motet 'Ave Maria...Virgo serena', '[O] intemerata Virgo', which is the *tertia pars* of the motet in seven *partes*, 'Vultum tuum deprecabuntur', the *Odhecaton* ballade 'Verginorette savosienne' = 'Bergerette savoyenne', and the bitextual tricinium 'Que vous ma dame/In pace'. [40]

Josquin's macaronic 'In te Domine speravi' belongs to a group of seven frottolas copied into Madrid, Biblioteca Real, MS. 2-I-5 (Cancionero Musical de Palacio) at spots left vacant by the first scribe. Although the Petrucci print (*Frottole libro primo*, 1504) must have served as source, the Italian text is corrupt.

As far as Spanish circulation of Petrucci frottola prints is concerned, Ferdinand Columbus bought for his library at Seville the entire eleven-book series, including the now missing tenth book (the eleventh book proved a particularly lucky purchase, since it now survives uniquely at Seville). Among nineteen Antico imprints bought by him, the alto of the Venetian *Motetti libro primo* (1521) is still extant at the Colombina[41] to show Josquin's currency in publications by Petrucci's competitor. Also, Columbus owned Josquin's three books of Masses in the Jacopo Giunta Roman editions of 1526.

In his brilliant article on the Colombina chansonnier,[42] Dragan Plamenac pioneered in calling attention to the present whereabouts of the 42 folios that had been ripped out of it: the present MS. Paris, Bibliothèque Nationale, nouv. acq. fr. 4379 (acquired in 1885). It contains Josquin's 'Helas madame' and 'Une mousse de Bisquaye' (without text).

One of the manuscripts copied in Alamire's workshop, now in Vienna, Oesterreichische Nationalbibliothek (MS. 1783), was probably at one time in Spain. It was ordered by Philip the Fair as a gift for Manuel the Fortunate of Portugal and his Spanish wife Maria. Among its 21 Masses is Josquin's 'Missa Ave maris stella'.[43]

---

[40] Segovia also contains a tricinium ascribed to Josquin (fol. 182ᵛ) of which two voices duplicate Busnois's 'Fortuna desperata' in the same manuscript (fol. 174). Osthoff considers it of doubtful authenticity, but Antonowycz and Elders publish it in *Werken*, Wereldlijke Werken, Bundel iv, no. 48b.

[41] Catherine Weeks Chapman, 'Printed Collections of Polyphonic Music Owned by Ferdinand Columbus', *Journal of the American Musicological Society*, xxi (1968), p. 40.

[42] Dragan Plamenac, 'A Reconstruction of the French Chansonnier in the Biblioteca Colombina, Seville', *Musical Quarterly*, xxxvii (1951), pp. 501–42.

[43] See Herbert Kellman, these Proceedings, p. 210.

Other proofs of frequent Peninsular performance

Among Petrucci Mass collections, the founder of the Colombina owned the 1503 Obrecht, Ghiselin, and La Rue, the 1504 Agricola, 1505 De Orto, 1506 Isaac and Weerbecke, the 1508 *Missarum diversorum auctorum liber primus*, and the 1515 Mouton and Févin.[44] But Catherine Weeks Chapman was not able to discover that Columbus owned any of the *Petrucci* books of Josquin's Masses. Her study summarizes the riches of his library by saying that 'Ferdinand Columbus owned a copy of nearly every now known music book published up to and including 1535.'[45] Why then no Petrucci issues of Josquin's Masses, only Giunta's? During his earliest book-collecting trip to Rome, in February of 1513, Columbus paid 247 quatrines for Petrucci's 1504 *Motetti C*, more than twice what he gave for any other music purchased during the trip,[46] and in *Regestrum B* carefully noted that this collection of forty-seven motets *a 4* and two *a 3* begins with Josquin's 'Ave Maria' *a 4*.[47] He also obtained the Petrucci *Fragmenta missarum* of 1505, in which Josquin, with nine items, easily eclipses Weerbecke with three, Agricola and Compère with two. One must presume that Obrecht, Ghiselin, La Rue, Agricola, and every other composer of individual Mass books published by Petrucci sold so slowly that copies could still be had of dealers a decade and more after first issue. Only Josquin's Masses leaped to such immediate popularity that every Petrucci edition was sold out by the time Ferdinand Columbus arrived in Rome.

The more notable then is the fact not registered by either Smijers or Sartori that the Biblioteca Nacional in Lisbon owns both Superius and Tenor part-books of the 27 September 1502 *Missae Josquin*. No late import but a contemporary purchase, the Portuguese part-books belonged before the suppression of the monasteries in 1834 to the Cistercian royal abbey at Alcobaça (near Leiria), founded in 1148. When sacked by French troops during the Napoleonic wars, the library of 25,000 early imprints and 500 codices rated among the foremost in Portugal. Only two or three Portuguese religious houses could compare with it in pre-1600 musical treasure. It was from the collections of Santa Cruz in Coimbra that the Municipal Library at Oporto obtained its famous fifteenth-century chansonnier (Porto 714).[48]

[44] Chapman, 'Printed Collections', pp. 59–65 (items 2, 4, 6, 8, 13, 20, 21, 34, 42, 43).

[45] Ibid., p. 32.

[46] Ibid., pp. 51 (Motetti 'A' should read 'C'); 60 (item 10).

[47] Entry transcribed by Dragan Plamenac, '*Excerpta Colombiniana*: Items of Musical Interest in Fernando Colón's "Regestrum",' *Miscelánea en homenaje a Monseñor Higinio Anglés*, ii, p. 681 (item 2895).

[48] Music in Porto MS. 714 runs from fols. 51ᵛ to 79 (fifteen songs). Details in *Catalogo da Bibliotheca Publica Municipal do Porto. Indice preparatorio. 1º Fasciculo* (Oporto, c. 1886), pp. 39–40. See also Bernhard Meier, 'Die Handschrift Porto 714 als Quelle zur Tonartenlehre des 15. Jahrhunderts', *Musica Disciplina*, vii (1953), pp. 175–97.

Because printed editions of Josquin's Masses sold out and wore out, it became more and more the custom from 1540 onward for the governors of both Spanish cathedrals and Portuguese monasteries to commission expensive manuscript copies. An inventory dated 'about 1540' of such music at Ávila Cathedral begins with 'a book of Josquin's Masses'. Next came 'another book containing two Masses by Bauldeweyn' and a third book of 'three Masses, the last *a 4* by Morales'.[49] On 23 December 1575 the Ávila Cathedral chapter ordered that two polyphonic books—one of Josquin's works—be repaired so that his music could still be sung.[50] No such Josquin book now survives there, perhaps because it was copied on paper rather than the costlier vellum used for the still extant Toledo MSS. 9, 16, 19, and 27 that include eleven Josquin Masses copied between 1542 and 1557. When the sumptuous royal monastery of Thomar[51] (= Tomar, Portugal, slightly east of the now world-famous Fatima) paid 25,000 reis for six polyphonic choirbooks in 1564, a collection of eight Josquin Masses again headed the list.[52] But these Thomar choirbooks seem also to have perished in the shipwreck of time, thus preventing our knowing whether any of the eight Masses broke out of the charmed circle of favourites.

The earliest extant Portuguese source for any instrumental arrangement of a Josquin work is MS. Mus. n.º 48 at Coimbra University. This 128-leaf codex, an early manuscript in score, contains motets by Arcadelt, Clemens non Papa, Crecquillon, Gombert, L'Héritier, Lupus Hellinck, Mouton, Richafort, Sermisy, Verdelot, and various Peninsular worthies and was

[49] Rafael Mitjana, 'Nuevas noticias referentes a la vida y las obras de Cristóbal de Morales', *Música sacro-hispana*, xii/2 (1919), p. 16. The Spanish reads: 'Un libro de misas de Jusquin/ Otro de dos misas de Baudin/Otro de tres misas: la postrera de Morales de a cuatro'.

[50] Ávila Cathedral, *Actas Capitulares*, 1572-5, fol. 247: 'que adereço dos libros de canto de organo uno de Jusquin'. See Stevenson, *Spanish Cathedral Music*, pp. 340-1, note 150.

[51] Concerning Thomar (= Tomar) in the sixteenth century, see *Grande Enciclopédia Portuguesa e Brasileira*, xxxi, p. 910a. 'The choirbooks were among the most notable in any of our cathedrals, monasteries, or convents', wrote the historian of Thomar music, Francisco Marques de Sousa Viterbo in *A Ordem de Christo e a música sagrada* (Coimbra, 1911), p. 5.

[52] Francisco Marques de Sousa Viterbo, 'Curiosidades musicaes', *A Arte Musical*, xii/267 (1910), p. 16: 'Pagou mais o dito Rev. Antonio Tavares vinte e cinco mil rs. a Fernão Lopez, vigario de Nossa Senhora da Conceição de Lisboa por seis livros de canto dorgão um de Jusquim de biij missas por biij rs e outro de diversas missas por bj rs. e um de motetes por iiij rs. e outros de motetes e magnificas por iiij rs. e dous de missas de forma eguaes iij rs, o qual dinheiro pagou por mandado do padre dom Prior conforme a provisão de sua Alteza.' ('The said Reverend Antonio Tavares paid in addition 25,000 réis to Fernão Lopez, vicar of Our Lady of the Conception at Lisbon, for six polyphonic books, for one of Josquin with 8 Masses 8[000] réis, for another of various Masses 6[000] réis, for a book of motets 4[000] réis, for two of Masses of the same type 3[000] réis, said money paid at the order of the Father Prior and provision of His Highness.') The Portuguese text as quoted from Sousa Viterbo resolves all abbreviations except rs = réis. Original in Torre do Tombo, L.º [*livro*] *de Thomar 103*, fol. 179 (expenses in 1564).

copied at Coimbra around 1559 for the use of Santa Cruz monastery organists. Josquin's 'Salve Regina' *a* 5 (all three *partes*) takes up folios 30ᵛ–33 of this source.[53]

From 17 July 1536 to April 1574 the chapelmaster of Santiago de Compostela Cathedral was Francisco Logroño.[54] Already famous enough to be listed in Cristóbal de Villalón's *Ingeniosa comparacion entre lo antiguo y lo presente* of 1539 as one of the four best chapelmasters then active in Spain,[55] Logroño capped his composing career with twelve Masses presented to his cathedral chapter in September 1566. His reward reached the respectable sum of thirty ducats.[56] Even so, the chapter three years later (21 June 1569) ordered him to stop conducting nothing but his own works, and instead to perform 'works by Josquin and Morales and other notable composers of the past'.[57]

From Morales's death in 1553 to Victoria's appointment at Madrid in 1587, the acknowledged prince of Spanish composers was Francisco Guerrero, the Sevillian maestro whose two books of Masses were published at Paris and Rome in 1566 and 1582. Though far more talented than Logroño, he needed no prodding to keep Josquin in the active repertory. As late as 1586, four years after the publication of his own *Missarum liber secundus*, he persuaded the Sevillian cathedral officials to pay for the copying of Josquin's works anew.[58]

At prestigious Saragossa, cathedral officials esteemed Josquin Masses so highly that in 1587 the chief test piece in conducting assigned the two candidates for the vacant post of Seo chapelmaster was still a Josquin Mass, picked at random by the judges on 15 June. Two days later, on Friday afternoon at the close of the try-out week, each candidate was asked to sing at sight a third voice against a duo from another Josquin Mass selected by the

[53] Santiago Kastner, 'Los manuscritos musicales n.ˢ 48 y 242 de la Biblioteca General de la Universidad de Coimbra', *Anuario Musical*, v (1950), p. 81 (nos. 17–18). Kastner did not recognize the identity of these *partes*.

[54] Santiago Tafall, 'La Capilla de Música de la Catedral de Santiago. Notas históricas', *Boletín de la Real Academia Gallega*, xxvi/232 (1931), pp. 75, 79.

[55] *Ingeniosa comparación* (Madrid, 1898), p. 176. The original edition was printed at Valladolid.

[56] Tafall, 'La Capilla de Música', p. 78.

[57] José López Calo, 'El Archivo de Música de la Catedral de Santiago de Compostela', *Compostellanum*, iii (1958), p. 290: 'Y haga [el maestro de capilla] que tambien [además de las suyas propias] se canten otras cosas compuestas de otros musicos, como de Jusquin y de Morales y de otros musicos notables que a havido.'

[58] Seville Cathedral, *Actas Capitulares*, XXXIIIa (1586–7), fol. 23ᵛ (20 March 1586): 'Este dicho dia llamados cometieron a los señores don Antonio pimentel chantre y don francisco enrriquez Maestroescuela vean lo que aya cerca de lo que el maestro Guerrero propuso sobre el puntar el libro de Jusquin y la neçesidad que de ello ay y Refieran.' See Robert Stevenson, *La Música en la Catedral de Sevilla 1478–1606: Documentos para su Estudio* (Los Angeles, 1954), p. 52a.

judges. After the two candidates failed to do so to the contentment of either the judges or the large assembled audience, they were both awarded twenty ducats for travel expenses home, there to await further word from the chapter appointments committee. At length José Gay of Valencia got the chapter's nod, but by a 4–3 vote.[59]

Parody Masses based on Josquin

Morales paid Josquin his most ambitious tribute in the six-voice parody Mass, 'Mille regretz', that survives in Cappella Sistina MS. 17. The *Sanctus* and *Agnus* I and III differ radically from the corresponding movements in his *Missarum liber primus* (Rome: Valerio & Luigi Dorico, 1544).[60] The archaic movements of this Mass parodying 'the Emperor's song', as Luys de Narváez dubbed 'Mille regretz',[61] differ from the movements in the 1544 published version in several salient ways: (1) only in the archaic movements does he fetter Josquin's superius in bands of breves, slowing the motion of the top voice in *Sanctus* and *Agnus* I to half speed or breves and longs; (2) Morales justifies the slow motion by verbal canons[62] that bear an anagogical interpretation; (3) in the archaic *Sanctus* and *Agnus* movements, the sunlight of rests rarely penetrates to the caged voices; (4) obligatory naturals in the nether voices of the archaic version prevent the other voices

---

[59] Pascual de Mandura, 'Libro de Memorias de las cosas que en la Iglesia del Asseo de Çaragoça se han offrecido tocantes a ella desde el Agosto del año 1579 hasta el año 1601 inclusive', Biblioteca Nacional, Madrid, MS. 14047 (entered in this alphabetically ordered legajo under 'Zaragoza'; copied from the original in the capitular archive of La Seo at Saragossa). The pertinent passages occur at pages 8–11 of the Madrid copy (folios 185–6 of the Saragossa original document): 'Al otro dia se les examino en una missa despues de la conventual...y assi despues de la conventual se les dio una missa de Jusquin.... Miercoles de mañana despues de la missa mayor se dixo una missa de Jusquin y regio la capilla Martin Perez [chapelmaster from Badajoz Cathedral competing against José Gay, a native of Valencia who had been conducting the choir at Gandía].... Viernes a la tarde a 19 de dicho mes y año fue el ultimo examen de ciertas habilidades el Juez [Juan Arnal, chapelmaster of Tarazona Cathedral] propuso y tambien de cantar sobre un duo que compuso dicho Juez para que en el echassen una tercera voz y lo mesmo sobre una missa de Jusquin....' Gay died 10 September 1587 after only a few weeks in office. Further details in Stevenson, *Spanish Cathedral Music in the Golden Age*, p. 472.

[60] Cf. *Monumentos de la Música Española*, xi (1952), pp. 261–73 with xxiv (1964), pp. 121–32.

[61] See *Los seys libros del Delphin de música de cifras para tañer Vihuela* (Valladolid, 1538), ed. Emilio Pujol (*Monumentos de la Música Española*, iii; Barcelona, 1945), p. 56, no. 20.

[62] *Multiplicatis intercessoribus* (first half of Josquin's superius slowed to half speed (*MME*, xxiv, 121)); *Duplicatam vestem fecit sibi* (second half slowed to half speed (xxiv, 124)); *Breves dies hominis sunt* (chanson superius reduced to breves and longs (xxiv, 128)). Job 14:5 is the scriptural source of Morales's last rubric.

from indulging in any *ficta*, except at final chords.[63] The *Sanctus* rewritten in 1544 forgoes any canon, changes metre at the *Osanna*, eschews the long notes, lets in liberal sunlight with rests, and offers opportunity for twenty sharps. Not only are the new *Sanctus* and *Agnus* movements more of a piece with the Josquin chanson, considered a late work by Osthoff,[64] but also Morales's decision to deny himself any display of learning accords more with Josquin's own later Mass style.[65]

Morales's consummate skill in weaving motifs from every voice of the chanson into both versions of his 'Missa Mille regretz' can scarcely be overpraised. He also contrives a *Benedictus* for his 'Benedicta es coelorum Regina' Mass that incorporates motifs from both Mouton's motet *a 4* of that name and Josquin's setting of the same sequence text *a 6*.[66] Although in the main based on Mouton, Morales quotes Josquin in the *Benedictus* so unequivocally that the Mass becomes a prototype for later Spanish parody Masses based on two motets.[67]

In 1578, the year that Cabezón's posthumously published *Obras de musica para tecla arpa y vihuela* paid Josquin's 'Benedicta es' the homage of two alternate intabulated versions, George de La Hêle (1547–87) dedicated his *Octo Missae, quinque, sex, et septem vocum* to the same monarch who received the dedication of Cabezón's book, Philip II.[68] For the climactic final two Masses *a 7* the composer chose as models Josquin's variation-chain sequences 'Praeter rerum seriem' and 'Benedicta es coelorum Regina'. Only one year before publication of La Hêle's *Octo Missae*, Francisco Salinas had explained why these two works remained so popular in Spain.[69] La Hêle, lauded by

[63] When Narváez intabulated Josquin's chanson in 1538, he prescribed 21 sharps in 79 bars of transparent music that never exceeds the four-voice texture of the original. On the other hand, Morales's 81 bars of 'archaic' *Sanctus* six-voice music permit intrusion of only five sharps at most—and these can be inserted only at the final cadences. For Narváez's transcription, see Pujol, *Los seys libros*, pp. 37–8, and these Proceedings, pp. 464–6.

[64] *Josquin Desprez*, ii, p. 202.

[65] See Gustave Reese, *Music in the Renaissance* (New York, 1959), p. 236.

[66] Compare *Monumentos de la Música Española*, xv, pp. 24–6, with Mouton's motet at pp. 185–92 of the same volume and Josquin's at pp. 11–16 of the *Werken*, Motteten, Bundel xi (1954).

[67] See Stevenson, *Spanish Cathedral Music*, pp. 177, 374.

[68] Philip II patronized the most sumptuous Mass publications of the era—for example, Palestrina's books of 1567 and 1570 and Victoria's *Missarum libri duo* of 1583. Vander Straeten, *La Musique aux Pays-Bas*, viii (1888), pp. 365–83, published the Spanish text of the inventory taken of Philip II's choral library (13 September 1598, Escorial Palace). Both La Rue and Josquin were well represented. The inventory mentions one large vellum choirbook containing ten Josquin Masses and another smaller parchment choirbook including seven. Two other choirbooks contained such works as 'Praeter rerum seriem', 'Salve Regina', and Marian motets.

[69] Francisco Salinas, *De musica libri septem* (Salamanca, 1577), pp. 288–9. See below, p. 236.

Antonowycz as a 'master of parody technique who knew how to exploit [Josquin's] smallest and apparently least significant motive',[70] lavished especially loving care on his two last Masses, to judge by the canonic contrivance. In the final *Agnus* of his 'Benedicta es' he devises a canon 'Trinitas in unitate' (superius II answered at the octave and fifth by tenor I and alto II),[71] carrying it through even when he changes metre from duple to ₵3. Within the *Sanctus* he embeds another canon in long note values (tenor followed by superius II at the octave). In both parody Masses he inserts at times several bars of the polyphonic complex into the middle of a *Christe*, *Gloria*, or *Credo*.[72]

Spanish intabulations

The Spanish intabulators active throughout Philip II's reign distinguished themselves from their foreign counterparts by harping on the Masses of Josquin. Only in Spain did a sixteenth-century intabulator attempt ciphering whole Masses by Josquin.[73] Diego Pisador prefaced his 1552 *Libro de musica de vihuela* with an explanation:

Because those who to date have intabulated Josquin have contented themselves with only a few of their favourite excerpts, I have also devoted two books [among the seven comprising this volume] to eight Masses by him. I wished to intabulate eight Masses so that any user of my volume could make his own choices; for this was so fine a composer that nothing by him deserves to be cast aside. Moreover, I beg the user to note that throughout Josquin's Masses, as throughout all else in this volume, I have made every effort to conform exactly with the original and to avoid the confusion of ornaments, so that the player can at once divine the voice movements of the original and can sing any one of the several original voice parts.[74]

[70] *Die Motette Benedicta es von Josquin des Prez und die Messen super Benedicta von Willaert, Palestrina, de la Hêle und de Monte* (Utrecht, 1951), p. 29.

[71] Lavern J. Wagner, 'The *Octo Missae* of George de La Hele' (Ph.D. diss., University of Wisconsin, 1957), ii, pp. 506–13.

[72] Ibid., i, p. 125.

[73] Kwee, 'Sixteenth-Century Printed Instrumental Arrangements', pp. 54–7, lists 44 Spanish intabulations of Josquin's Masses, in whole or in part, as against thirteen German intabulations; no French or Italian printed arrangements are known.

[74] *Prologo al lector prefacio* (fol. A ij): 'Puse tambien dos libros, en los quales se contienen ocho missas de Iusquin porque los que hasta aqui han escripto no pusieron deste autor, sino muy pocas cosas escogiendo ellos lo que les parescia[;] yo quise poner ocho missas para el que quisiesse escogiesse conforme a su voluntad porque el musico fue tan bueno que no tiene cosa que desechar, y juntamente con esto quiero que sepa el lector que en esto y en todo lo que se contiene en el libro puse muy gran diligencia y trabajo para que fuesse verdadero y con gran claridad sin confusion de glosas para que el que tañe: pueda conoscer mas facilmente las bozes como van en la vihuela y las pueda cantar'.

The eight Masses intabulated by Pisador seem to be taken from Petrucci's prints: three Masses come from the 1502 edition ('Gaudeamus', 'La sol fa re mi', 'L'homme armé super voces musicales'), two from the 1505 ('Ave maris stella', 'Hercules'), and three from the 1514 ('Ad fugam', 'De Beata Virgine', 'Faisant regretz').[75] For good measure Pisador adds another four Josquin items.[76] Not surprisingly, Pisador dedicated his extremely handsome imprint to Philip II.

There is reason to suspect that some of Pisador's own personal fortune went for the costs of printing this 112-folio tablature, priced at 629 maravedís (considerably higher per page than Fuenllana's *Orphénica lyra*[77] published only two years later). Just who was this exceptionally ardent Josquin devotee, Diego Pisador? Born at Salamanca in 1509 or 1510, Diego Pisador took minor orders in 1526. Six years later his father, who owned property in Galicia, forsook Pisador's mother, Isabel Ortiz, in order to take an accountant's post with the Count of Monterrey. Diego remained behind to look after her and his younger brother and to collect rents. The paralyzed mother died in September 1550 from a fall. Diego thereupon inherited the considerable bulk of her personal property.[78]

With these biographical data in mind. Diego Pisador's devotion to Josquin takes on added significance. He alone of Spanish vihuelists could afford to consult naught but his own taste.

The larger questions raised by the Josquin repertory intabulated by Spanish musicians have been so magisterially handled by John Ward that no further discussion is needed here. Commenting on Fuenllana's intabulations, Ward remarked that only Josquin inspired the blind vihuelist to add much ornamentation[79] (certainly more than he lavished on Gombert or Morales); the *Credo* of Josquin's 'De Beata Virgine' Mass serves as a good example of this prodigality (*Orphénica lyra*, fols. 73ᵛ–77). Valderrábano's sharps prescribed for the *Cum Sancto Spiritu* of the same Mass agree with the sharps later added by Cabezón (who, however, introduces running ornaments foreign to Valderrábano's style). Inasmuch as the source of Valderrábano's passages frequently stumped even his editor Emilio Pujol, Ward's

---

[75] Brown specifies the missing movements—which are always a *Benedictus*, a *Pleni*, an *Osanna*, or a section of the *Agnus* (*Instrumental Music*, p. 142). As if to compensate, Pisador appends to each 'book' of Josquin Mass intabulations a movement from the 'Missa Fortuna desperata': *Benedictus* to Libro Quarto, *Pleni* to Libro Quinto.

[76] Concerning the motet *a 8*, 'Tulerunt dominum meum', ascribed by Pisador at folio 85 to 'Gombert', see Osthoff, *Josquin Desprez*, ii, pp. 110–11. For the other items, see Brown, *Instrumental Music*, p. 141.

[77] Fuenllana's 10+175 folio tablature was priced at 28 reales = 952 maravedís.

[78] On Pisador, see Narciso Alfonso Cortés, 'Diego Pisador: Algunos datos biográficos', *Boletín de la Biblioteca Menéndez y Pelayo*, iii (1921).

[79] John Ward, 'The *Vihuela de Mano*, and its Music (1536–1576)' (Ph.D. diss., New York University, 1953), p. 217.

identifications are especially welcome. The fantasia alternately called 'remedando a algunos pasos de la misa de Josquin de Ave maris stella' or 'acomposturada de cierta parte de la missa', 'draws very slightly on the second Kyrie and, perhaps, bits of the Credo'.[80] In this instance, Valderrábano may have been merely sheltering himself behind a great name.

In two articles on Spanish intabulations, John Ward uncovered some of the unnamed source material used by the intabulators in their fantasies.[81] Thus Narváez's 'Fantasia del primer tono por ge sol re ut'[82] turns out to be a secret parody of Josquin's 'Adieu mes amours' and of Gombert's 'Tu pers ton temps', 'though no hint of these borrowings is given in the three 16th-century prints in which the piece appears'.[83] Moreover, Albert de Rippe (died 1551), the Mantuan lutenist serving Francis I, in turn parodied Narváez's secret parody.[84]

According to Ward, Smijers verified as Josquin's the 'Fecit potentiam' at folio 4 in Fuenllana's *Orphénica lyra*.[85] Osthoff knows of no Josquin original for this 'Fecit' *a 2* but is encouraged to accept it because Fuenllana's other Josquin ascriptions pass muster.[86] Like Pisador, Fuenllana dedicated his tablature to the future Philip II. Like Antonio de Cabezón, he was a blind virtuoso enjoying the highest court favours.[87] The two Josquin motets in *Orphénica lyra* happen to be precisely the two parodied in La Hêle's *Octo Missae*, also dedicated to Philip II. Against two motets, Fuenllana included eight Josquin Mass sections—further evidence for our thesis that Spain adored Josquin's Masses. As far as the two motets are concerned, Ward deplored Fuenllana's 'inability to indicate the voice-complex clearly'.

---

[80] John Ward, 'Parody Technique in 16th-Century Instrumental Music', *The Commonwealth of Music*, ed. Gustave Reese and Rose Brandel (New York, 1965), p. 226, n. 18.

[81] Ibid.; see also his article, 'The Use of Borrowed Material in 16th-Century Instrumental Music', *Journal of the American Musicological Society*, v (1952), pp. 92–5.

[82] First item in *Los seys libros del Delphin*.

[83] 'Parody Technique', pp. 222, 224–5.   [84] Ibid., p. 222.

[85] 'The *Vihuela de Mano* and its Music', p. 446: 'Prof. Albert Smijers' offer of a copy of Josquin's Magnificat, in which this verse appears, did not materialize in time for inclusion here; however, he had identified the piece as Josquin's.' If so, it nowhere enters the Register that concludes the 1969 Supplement. The source of Fuenllana's 'Fecit potentiam' also remained unknown to Winfried Kirsch, *Die Quellen der mehrstimmigen Magnificat- und Te Deum-Vertonungen bis zur Mitte des 16. Jahrhunderts* (Tutzing, 1966), p. 310.

[86] *Josquin Desprez*, ii, pp. 23, 67. See also his 'Das Magnificat bei Josquin Desprez', pp. 230–31.

[87] Higinio Anglés, 'Per la Història de la Musica Hispànica. Dades desconegudes sobre Miguel de Fuenllana, vihuelista', *Revista Musical Catalana*, xxxiii (1936), pp. 140–43. Further important biographical data in Mercedes Agulló y Cobo, 'Documentos para las biografías de músicos de los siglos XVI y XVII', *Anuario Musical*, xxiv (1969), pp. 220–1, and especially in Francisco Marques de Sousa Viterbo, 'Subsídios para a história da música em Portugal' *O Instituto*, lxxviii (1929), pp. 116–17, identifying him as a chamber musician at the court of the ill-starred King Sebastian in 1574.

According to him, this 'has resulted in a series of parallel octaves and fifths totally absent'[88] from Josquin's original six voices. However, in the very measures from 'Praeter rerum seriem' chosen by Ward to illustrate his point (Ex. 23), Josquin himself prescribes two parallel perfect fifths that no *ficta* can palliate.[89]

Just as Ward and Brown have cleared pathways for all to follow in the study of the Josquin repertory intabulated for vihuela, so Charles Jacobs,[90] Elinore Louise Barber, and Almonte C. Howell, Jr. have amply studied Josquin's part in Cabezón's posthumously published keyboard versions. Barber thus summarized her findings: 'Intabulations from the works of Josquin far outnumber those selected from the compositions of any other composer. It seems highly possible that Josquin's works represent the most important single influence on Cabezón the composer. Cabezón's conception of melodic line, his manner of employing sequence, and his delight in using the technique of voice-pairing reflect what must have been a deep and highly sympathetic knowledge of the works of Josquin'.[91] To confirm her conclusions, she appended four of Cabezón's thirteen Josquin intabulations considered most characteristic by her and by the late Professor Hans T. David, her thesis adviser.[92]

Almonte Howell argued that Josquin's sovereign sway over sixteenth-century Spanish keyboard music sets this national literature apart from every other national keyboard literature of the period. According to him, the hallmark of Josquin's style—paired imitation—is indelibly stamped on the whole repertory of Luys Venegas de Henestrosa (1557), Tomás de Sancta María (1565), and Cabezón.[93] Only in the versets of the Neapolitan Antonio Valente (*c.* 1520–*c.* 1600) did paired imitation outside the peninsula become so 'systematic or pervasive a feature of early keyboard style'.[94] Howell accounts for this pervasive feature of sixteenth-century Spanish keyboard

---

[88] 'The *Vihuela de Mano*', p. 220.

[89] *Werken*, Motetten, Bundel vii, p. 22, mm. 16–18. The consecutives C–G, D–A follow each other (alto and superius) in both measures, 162–3 and 17–18. [For Fuenllana's intabulation of measures 15–17, see Howard Mayer Brown, these Proceedings, pp. 493–4.—Ed.]

[90] 'The Transcription Technique and Style of Antonio de Cabezón as shown in his thirteen intabulations of music by Josquin des Prez' (M.A. thesis, New York University, 1957). See note 38 above.

[91] 'Antonio de Cabezón's Cantus-Firmus Compositions and Transcriptions' (Ph.D. diss., University of Michigan), i, p. 174.

[92] *Clama ne cesses* (*Agnus* from 'Missa L'homme armé super voces musicales'), iii, 179–88; *Osanna* (from same Mass), 190–94; *Benedictus* (= *Pleni* from same), 196–7; 'Ave Maria', 199–211. Cabezón's keyboard versions do not blanch at parallel octaves, accented dissonances on strong beats, downward tenths in eighth-note motion, simultaneous false relations, and other bravados.

[93] 'Paired Imitation in 16th-Century Spanish Keyboard Music', *The Musical Quarterly*, liii (1967), pp. 377–96.

[94] Ibid., p. 394.

style by the extraordinary reverence for Josquin's music in the Iberian peninsula throughout the period and the frequency of Josquin intabulations. Although the keyboard works of Francisco Correa de Arauxo[95] published at Alcalá in 1626 finally did forsake the paired-imitation mold and, in contrast with Cabezón's *Obras*, included only one snippet attributed to Josquin, still so daring a proponent of dissonances as Correa de Arauxo wished to barricade himself behind the walls of Josquin's hallowed name when firing off anything as bold as simultaneous B♭–B♮.[96]

Literary allusions (including theory texts), 1532–1737

Literary allusions to Josquin abound not only in Peninsular theorists from Juan Bermudo[97] to João Álvares Frouvo (1602–82) but also in the writings of cultivated amateurs. João de Barros (1496–1570), the famous historian of the Far East, published a dialogue on spiritual gifts, *Ropica pnefma*, in 1532 in which he divided music into three national camps: French, Italian, and Spanish. While the interlocutor in this dialogue, named Understanding, confesses to preferring Spanish style, 'because it is the most soulful', he readily acknowledges that in French style Ockeghem and Josquin long ago vanquished all rivals.[98] When Cristóbal de Villalón, a tutor of logic at the University of Valladolid, published there in 1539 his 'Ingenious Comparison of the Ancient and the Modern', he listed a total of ten Spanish 'moderns' but only one foreign 'modern' whose ability to stir men's souls entitled them to rank with the fabled Greeks of old, Terpander and Timotheus. Villalón begins his Spanish list with Ferdinand V's chapelmaster, Francisco

[95] Concerning him, see Robert Stevenson, 'Francisco Correa de Arauxo: New Light on his Career', *Revista Musical Chilena*, xxii (1968), pp. 9–42.

[96] *Libro de tientos y discursos de musica practica, y theorica de organo, intitulado Facultad organica* (Alcalá, 1626), ed. Santiago Kastner (*Monumentos de la Música Española*, vi; Barcelona, 1948), p. 50: 'El mismo intervalo de semitono menor simultaneo comete Iosquin de Prest autor antiguo y grave en un tercio que dize: Pleni sunt.' Correa concludes: 'Y porque con Iosquin, Gombert, Montanos, y Hernando de Cabeçon, testigos tan calificados, tengo provado mi intento, baste para dar fin a este tratado.' The *Pleni* to which Correa de Arauxo refers has so far resisted identification.

[97] *Comiença el libro llamado declaracion de instrumentos musicales* (Osuna, 1555), fol. lx: 'Despues poned musica de Iosquin, de Adriano [Willaert], de Iachet mantuano....' Only Josquin escapes his bias against the antique. Because of Bermudo's close association with Morales (whose commendation dated at Marchena, 20 October 1550, prefaces Bermudo's Book V) Bermudo's ideas can usually be taken as an echo of Morales's.

[98] *Ropica pnefma* (Lisbon, 1532), fol. Diij (= 24). After classifying intervals, Intendimento (= Understanding) boasts that with the right intervals, 'faço obras e composturas mais exçelentes que as dokeghem e Josquim: porque elles compõem somente ao modo frances, i eu, Frances, Italiano e Espanhol que ee mais saudoso.' Barros again mentions Ockeghem and Josquin in his 1540 *Dialogo em louvor da nossa linguagem* (2d ed., p. 221).

de Peñalosa (died 1528), whom he calls the Apollo of modern times.[99] He also names a composer who only began to publish in 1539, Cristóbal de Morales, and concludes with the then only 29-year-old Antonio de Cabezón. But so far as power to move men's passions is concerned, Villalón ignores Ockeghem, whom Barros had coupled with Josquin only seven years earlier in a Lisbon publication. Now, Josquin alone among foreigners remains worthy of comparison with the fabled ancients.

How widely the idea that Josquin alone among foreigners had the power to move stones gained ground throughout the entire peninsula during the next few years comes to light in a play by the one Portuguese playwright who worthily rivalled Gil Vicente, António Prestes, a native of Torres Novas. In 1587 seven of his plays were published at Lisbon in a collection that also contains two by the supreme poet of the age, Camões (1524–80).[100] The twenty-four characters in the first of Prestes's plays include the Devil, Sensuality, other Vices, three angels (Michael, Gabriel, Raphael), Three [Heavenly] Powers, two philosophers (Heraclitus laments Reason's overthrow, but Democritus laughs at Sensuality's victory), and a Knight whom in the end Michael rescues, despite his evil deeds while in the Devil's clutches. When Reason describes the Three [Heavenly] Powers coming from afar to try to win back the Knight from his evil course, Reason describes all three of the Powers as 'learned musicians of Josquin's stripe'.[101] The Powers enter singing a three-part cantiga. When they finish Reason murmurs, 'Oh, sweet song'—a sentiment at once echoed by an attendant who says, 'Sweet enough to make stones weep!'[102]

Prestes again refers to Josquin in his play of 'the bewitched Moor'. Wife and husband spar. She rants at everything, especially at him whom she despises as no better than a lowlife drummer. At last in desperation he cries

---

[99] See note 55. In the 1539 original, Villalón's much-quoted assessment of 'modern' musicians begins thus (fol. Cij): 'Muy poco ha que murio aquel famoso varon don Francisco de Peñalosa maestro de capilla del catholico Rey don Fernando: el qual en la musica en arte y boz excedio a Apolo su inventor. Ribafrecha fue deste tiempo, de gran sufficiencia y abilidad. E Jusquin d'l mesmo tiempo y saber. Agora bive matheo ferdandez maestro d' capilla de nuestra señora la Emperatriz: varon de gran sentido, y admirable composicion. Bive en Roma un español que se llama Morales maestro de las obras del Papa, unico en la composicion y boz.'

[100] *Primeira parte dos autos e comedias portuguezas Feitas por Antonio Prestes, & por Luis de Camões, & por outros Autores Portuguezes* (Lisbon, Andrés Lobato, 1587). For references to this 179-folio quarto, from which Tito de Noronha extracted the seven *Autos de Antonio Prestes 2.ª edição* that remains the sole modern reprint available (Oporto, 1871), see António Joaquim Anselmo, *Bibliografia das obras impressas em Portugal no século XVI* (Lisbon, 1926), p. 226 (item 786). Aubrey F. G. Bell, *Portuguese Literature* (Oxford, 1922), p. 160, summarizes the plot of the *Ave Maria* auto, which he dates after 1563.

[101] In the original, the passage reads (fol. 7, col. 1): 'musicos são/As mais graves,/mais jusquinas, mais suaves;/ & na solfa que nos dão/consistem nossos conclaves.'

[102] In the 1587 original: [Rasão] 'ho cantar doce' [Moço] 'de doçar/as pedras fara chorar.'

out, 'Oh my Josquin, oh my Morales, what vile tunes hate conjures up!'
Unimpressed, she advises him 'not to beat any big drums'.[103] In still a
third Prestes play, that of 'the jealous woman', the wife is so paranoid that
she will not allow her husband off the premises even to get a haircut. Instead,
the barber must attend at their house, where she can watch her husband's
every move. The husband asks the barber not to cut off too much hair.
The barber assures him that he knows his job. The wife demands the
scissors, whereupon the husband suggests her acting instead as 'mirror'.
This is too much for the barber—first husband, then wife. But with exquisite
tact the abused barber pleads: 'Sir, as Josquin once said, *la sol fa re mi*, for
I am an old dog at this.' Husband cuts the barber short, 'More care and a
little less old [razor] blade would do better.'[104]

On the title page of the 1587 edition of Prestes's plays, not he, but a
member of the royal chapel named Afonso Lopes, claims credit for having
'now newly gathered together and emended [them] in this first printing'.
Could Prestes, before his marriage, have also been a member of the Portuguese royal chapel choir? At any rate, Prestes's allusions prove that even
before Spain and Portugal were united under one crown, Josquin was
enough of a household word in Lisbon for audiences there to savour a
Josquin joke.

The general Spanish admiration for Josquin is also found in theoretical
treatises. Salinas rates Josquin as 'easily the chief composer of his time'.[105]
Displaying his familiarity with Josquin's works, Salinas cites the 'Missa
L'homme armé sexti toni', *Et resurrexit*, first sounding interval (alto and
bass), as an example of an unprepared and highly exposed fourth.[106] He
returns to Josquin at pages 288–9 with a passage explaining why motets on
familiar chant melodies outdistance other motets in popularity:

And Aristotle in his *Problems* [Bk. XIX, sec. 5], inquiring why we tend to listen
with greater pleasure to a song that we already know than to one that is unknown
to us, among other reasons gives these: that when we know what is sung, it is
more obvious that the singer is performing what the composer intended; just
as the familiar attracts the eye with more pleasure, so also the familiar is sweeter
to the ear than the unfamiliar. Furthermore, when a familiar song is heard, we
more pleasurably perceive in its sounds the various modes which the good writer
of music uses. Wherefore, those highly celebrated motets of Josquin des Prez,

[103] Ibid., fol. 127, col. 2: [Fernam] 'A meu josquin, meu morales,/quantos males/solfais
a me querer mal' [Grimaneza] 'Não se tocam atabales...' According to Bell, *Portuguese
Literature*, p. 160, this auto postdates 1554.

[104] Ibid., fol. 125, col. 1: [Barbeiro] 'Direy como diz josquin/señor, la so fa re mi/porque
ja sou perro velho'. [Casado] 'Mas cuido que ferro velho'. [On the precedents of *la sol fa re mi*
in Italian literature, see James Haar's article in these Proceedings, pp. 564–74.—Ed.]

[105] 'Iodocus Pratensis, inter Symphonetas sui temporis facilè princeps'; *De musica libri
septem* (Salamanca, 1577), p. 56.

[106] *Werken*, Missen, v, p. 118, measure 82.

'Inviolata', 'Benedicta es coelorum Regina', and 'Praeter rerum seriem', are held in greater esteem than those of which he himself was entirely the composer, since to the songs that have been used for centuries in the church and are familiar to all, the intertwining of many parts was added.

The paramount Portuguese musical authority of the sixteenth century, at least in international circles, was of course Vicente Lusitano, whom I have tentatively identified as the writer of the treatise in Paris, Bibliothèque Nationale, fonds espagnols, MS. 219 (*olim* 7817) that had reached the royal library there no later than 1682.[107] Like Despuig[108] and Salinas, Lusitano classes the fourth as a consonance, albeit a less perfect consonance than the octave and fifth.[109] Lusitano cites Josquin's practices in four Masses to settle moot points of notation: the 'L'homme armé super voces musicales' (*Osanna*,[110] last *Agnus*[111]), 'Di dadi' (*Domine Deus rex*,[112] *Credo*[113]), 'Malheur me bat' (*Osanna*[114]), and the 'De Beata Virgine' (*Credo*[115]). Lusitano also cites two motets ('Stabat Mater'[116] and 'Mente tota'[117]). Some Mass move-

[107] Henri Collet, ed., *Un tratado de Canto de Organo (Siglo XVI) Manuscrito en la Biblioteca Nacional de Paris, Edición y Comentarios* (Madrid, 1913), p. 13. See Robert Stevenson, 'Vicente Lusitano: New Light on his Career', *Journal of the American Musicological Society*, xv (1962), pp. 76–7.

[108] Concerning Guillermo Despuig, see Stevenson, *Spanish Music in the Age of Columbus*, pp. 75–6.

[109] *Un tratado*, p. 64, line 3.

[110] Ibid., pp. 48 (tenor, *gaudet cum gaudentibus*, ⊙ ℭ ⊙ = 9/4, 6/4, 9/4, against C3 = 6/4 (not 3/2) in other parts); 104 (in imperfect prolation, two minims should equal semibreve (not three)).

[111] Ibid., p. 54 (for superius of *clama ne cesses*, Josquin's mensuration sign was two vertical lines covering three spaces; these are not to be confused with rests (cf. Willi Apel, *The Notation of Polyphonic Music*, 5th ed., 1953, p. 124)).

[112] Ibid., p. 77 (in measures 58–64, Josquin pitted threes against twos—6 against 4).

[113] Ibid., pp. 57, 58 (first breve in superius escapes alteration, despite semibreve value that follows, because shapes of the first and second notes (second note begins ligature *cum opposita proprietate*) are the same), 62 (in bass, an unaltered white note mixes in with blacks).

[114] Ibid., p. 104 (rest extending three spaces (not two) = two bars of C3 music).

[115] Ibid., p. 60 (at *Qui cum Patre*, Josquin specifies three black breves in the superius against two white breves in the remaining voices (mm. 184–9)).

[116] Ibid., p. 60 (since all voices, except *cantus firmus*, shift simultaneously from binary to triple at measure 160, some would like Josquin to have inserted a new mensuration sign here instead of using black notes).

[117] Ibid., p. 56 (in 'Mente tota', the *quinta pars* of 'Vultum tuum deprecabuntur', Josquin writes some 9–8 suspensions (mm. 311, 316–17); whatever Josquin permits himself, even if only in 'Mente tota', is equally allowable in counterpoint exercises). Not mentioned by Lusitano is the impossibility of applying consistent *musica ficta* in measures 317 and 318. To avoid an unprepared diminished fifth (only two voices are sounding) at the start of measure 319, Smijers flats the bass. Reading backward, he opts for a *ficta* flat in the alto that condemns the performer to an equally offensive diminished fifth at the beginning of measure 318.

ments he refers to more than once. Without naming any specific work, on one occasion he specifies Josquin's orthography as a model for placement of rests on lines.[118] However, Lusitano does object to Josquin's sometimes using $\odot$ and $\mathbb{C}$ instead of $\odot^{3}_{2}\ \mathbb{C}^{3}_{1}$ or $\odot^{3}_{1}\ \mathbb{C}^{3}_{2}$ to indicate proportions.[119]

All nine of Lusitano's allusions to specific movements from Josquin's Masses are inspired by problems of mensural notation. So is the allusion to the 'Stabat Mater'. Only once does he use a Josquin work—the *quinta pars* of 'Vultum tuum'—to justify unusual counterpoint, in this instance 9/8 suspensions. His predilection for Masses fits the Peninsular syndrome. The emphasis on Masses that inspired Paolo Cortese (1465–1510) in *De cardinalatu libri tres* (1510) to give Josquin 'highest honour as a composer of Masses'[120] rather than of motets (by which so many of his present-day admirers would prefer to remember him) runs like a binding thread through every allusion, every catalogue of his works, and even tablature that came out of the sixteenth-century Spanish peninsula.

Pedro Thalesio, elected professor of music at Coimbra University in 1612,[121] published there in 1618 and 1628 an *Arte de canto chão com huma breve instrucção*. The most historically-minded investigator of plainchant of his time, Thalesio anticipates Urbanus Bomm[122] when he contends that many chants had been transposed a fourth or fifth from their original pitches simply to make them conform to a late, artificially contrived system of eight plainsong modes. He cites as examples of chants that in old chant collections end on *A* the Mass introit 'Gaudeamus omnes'[123] and the Annunciation vespers antiphon 'Ave Maria'.[124] Instead of eight plainsong modes, Thalesio advocates reclassifying the whole plainchant repertory to conform to the system of twelve modes propounded for polyphonic music by Glareanus and Zarlino.[125] Victoria's 'Gaudeamus' Mass conforms

---

[118] *Un tratado*, p. 53.

[119] Ibid., p. 105. According to John H. Lovell, 'The Masses of Josquin des Prez' (Ph.D. diss., University of Michigan, 1959), p. 13, Hermann Finck (1527–1558) was the first to comment adversely on any aspect of Josquin's musical technique (*Practica musica*, Wittenberg, 1556) when he complained that there were too many rests (fol. A 2).

[120] Nino Pirrotta, 'Music and Cultural Tendencies in 15th-Century Italy', *Journal of the American Musicological Society*, xix (1966), pp. 142, 154: 'And so, just for this reason, they say that Iuschinus Gallus was the one who excelled among many, because more science was put by him in the propitiatory genres of singing [= Masses] than it is usually put into it by the unskilled zeal of recent musicians .

[121] Ernesto Vieira, *Diccionario Biographico de Musicos Portuguezes* (Lisbon, 1900), ii, p. 350.

[122] Urbanus Bomm, *Der Wechsel der Modalitätsbestimmung in der Tradition der Messgesänge im IX. bis XIII. Jahrhundert* (Einsiedeln, 1929).

[123] *Liber usualis*, p. 1368; *Arte de canto chão* (2d ed., Coimbra, 1628), p. 64.

[124] *Liber usualis*, p. 1416; *Arte de canto chão*, p. 63.

[125] *Arte*, p. 63. (Glareanus, *Dodekachordon* (Basel, 1547), Book II, ch. 6, 7, and 17, cited in margins of pp. 63–4.)

to the chant editors' revamping of the 'Gaudeamus' introit to begin with c d d a b♭[126] a (and to end on d); this introit, according to Thalesio, should begin: G A A e f e, and end on A. Thus restored to its original pitches, the 'Gaudeamus' introit belongs not to Mode I (Dorian)[127] but to Mode IX (Aeolian), decrees Thalesio. Next he praises 'the great Josquin'—*musicorum lumen*, 'the light of musicians'—for having recognized the source chant as Mode IX when composing his 'Gaudeamus' Mass (third in the 1502 book), with the result that Josquin's *Kyrie*, *Gloria*, *Credo*, *Sanctus*, and *Agnus* all begin with G A, rising thence to e f e, and all close on the A chord.[128] Also Pierre de la Rue deserves praise, according to Thalesio, for having correctly chosen Mode IX for his 'Missa Ave Maria' published in the 1516 collection dedicated to Leo X, *Liber quindecim missarum*.[129] La Rue's movements begin with c G A and end on the A chord approved by Thalesio.[130]

In both the 1618 and 1628 editions of his plainchant book Thalesio claimed to have ready for publication a treatise on polyphony. That the manuscript copy survived him is proved by the following entry in João IV's celebrated catalogue: '*Compendio de Canto de orgão, contrapunto, composição, fugas, & outras cousas. Pedro Thalesio*'.[131] But the support hoped for from his previous patron failed to materialize. As a result, it was not Thalesio but the composer-theorist António Fernandes who in 1626 became the first to broach in print a controversial subject that was to be a favourite topic in Portuguese-language treatises for over a hundred years—namely, the 'three black breves' in the *Et in Spiritum Sanctum* of Josquin's Lady Mass, composed, as Glareanus has it, in friendly competition with Brumel.[132] This *sesquitertia*, and the parallel pitting of three black breves against four white semibreves in the *Christe* of Morales's 'Missa Mille regretz', continued being live topics for debate in Portuguese-language treatises as late as 1761,

---

[126] At page 39 Thalesio lashes out against four prior Peninsular theorists who had dared argue for B♮ (instead of B♭) as the fifth note (see Stevenson, *Spanish Music in the Age of Columbus*, p. 96). The four who advocated B♮ were Guillermo Despuig (= de Podio), Gonzalo Martínez de Bizcargui, Juan de Espinosa, and Juan Martínez.

[127] Bomm, *Der Wechsel*, p. 49: 'Cist [*Graduale Cisterciense*, see p. 16] vertritt ebenfalls die Auffassung, der Intr sei I auth'.

[128] *Arte de canto chão*, p. 64: 'O introito, *Gaudeamus omnes in Domino*, estava antigamente appontado por Gsolreut o primeiro ponto, & acabava em Alamire que vinha a ser do mesmo tono [i.e., nono tono], sobre o qual o grande Iosquin (musicorum lumen) fez hũa Missa....'

[129] Ibid., 'Sobre esta Antiphona [Ave Maria] compos Pierres de Larue, hũa Missa do nono tono'.

[130] *Les Maîtres Musiciens de la Renaissance française*, viii (1898), pp. 77-131.

[131] *Primeira parte do Index da livraria de musica do muyto alto, e poderoso Rey Dom Ioão o IV*. (Lisbon, 1649), p. 121 (item 515). Facsimile reprint issued by Academia Portuguesa da História, 1967.

[132] Glareanus, *Dodekachordon*, p. 366. For the possible symbolism of this *sesquitertia*, see Stevenson, *Spanish Cathedral Music*, p. 49. [On Josquin's 'Missa de Beata Virgine' see Gustave Reese's article in these Proceedings, pp. 589-98.—Ed.]

in which year the mulatto from Recife, Brazil, Luis Álvares Pinto (1719–88), wrote an *Arte de solfejar* that today takes pride of place as the earliest surviving treatise on music by anyone born in the Americas.

According to Fernandes, each black breve sung by the superius in Josquin's 'De Beata Virgine' Mass to the text *Qui cum Patre et Filio* ought theoretically to equal 4/3 of a semibreve. However, interpreters of Josquin's Mass in Fernandes's time often treated the first and second in each group of three black breves as white dotted semibreves, the result being that the last black breve emerged in performance as a white semibreve. But, adds Fernandes—who was himself a practising musician[133]—in the *Christe* of Morales's 'Missa Mille regretz' it is customary to allow the first and last of the three black breves the value of dotted white semibreves, thus leaving no other course but to treat the 'poor middle black breve' as a white undotted semibreve.[134] As if it were not bad enough for both Josquin's and Morales's black breves to be robbed of the equality rightly their due, Fernandes finds it even worse for Josquin's *sesquitertia* to be treated as 3+3+2, whereas Morales's exactly parallel *sesquitertia* is resolved as 3+2+3. How shameful for two such famous composers to appear as if contradicting each other, he concludes.

The next author in Portugal to take a go at Josquin was none other than the most illustrious music collector and amateur composer of the age, João IV (1604–56). The one Peninsular king honoured by a biographical article in all leading music lexicons—but unfortunately never with an article free of notable errors[135]—João IV published at Lisbon in 1649 (the same year that the first part of the catalogue of his music library was printed there) a 'Defense of modern music against the false opinion of Bishop Cirillo

---

[133] On the title page he lists himself as 'mestre de Musica na Igreja de Sancta Catherina de Monte Sinai' and calls himself a native of Souzel (= Sousel, halfway between Évora and Portalegre in Alentejo). Albert Luper analysed Fernandes's treatise in his Eastman School of Music master's thesis, 'Portuguese Music Theory in the Early Seventeenth Century' (1938).

[134] *Arte de musica de canto dorgam, e canto Cham, & Proporçoẽs de Musica* (Lisbon, Pedro Craesbeeck, 1626), fol. 19: 'Porque nos tres breves de Morales se a regra fora boa & certa perdera tanto hum como o outro, mas ao pobre que ficou no meio fazem perder ametade, & nam a quarta parte, & Iosquim faz perder ao derradeiro dos tres breves ametade, & nam a quarta parte: logo falsa he a regra que diz perdem as figuras nem no Binario, nem no Ternario: pois estes dous Authores taõ famosos se encontram hum com o outro sem conta, pezo, nem medida, que he a verdade da Musica'.

[135] *Grove, Fasquelle, Riemann*, and *MGG* credit him with spurious works but fail to mention the only two motets authentically his, 'Anima mea valde turbata est' *a 6* and 'Vivo ego dicit Dominus' *a 6*, both published the year after his death as the last two items in the part-books (pp. 57–60) of João Lourenço Rebello's (= Rabello's) *Psalmi pro vesperis* (Rome, 1657). The copies of Rebello's psalms at the Lisbon Biblioteca Nacional bear the call numbers, Res 2232–2234–2235V (olim E-2-3, E-2-4, E-2-5).

Franco',[136] voiced in a letter written in 1549 and first published in Venice in 1564.[137] Railing against the 'Missa Hercules Dux Ferrariae' and others of its class, Cirillo writes: 'For the love of God, tell me what feelings of devotion can the Duke of Ferrara inspire?'[138] He also objects to Josquin's custom of adhering to the same mode throughout an entire Mass.[139] If each mode, Dorian, Phrygian, Lydian, and the like, inspires a different emotion, then he who hews to the same mode when setting texts so anti-thetic as *Kyrie* and *Gloria* does not take the texts seriously, contends Cirillo. He finds the simultaneous singing of two single words so opposed in mean-ing as *Sanctus* and *Sabaoth* almost equally offensive.[140] In ancient Greece none of these musical corruptions existed.[141]

Answering Cirillo's objections to Josquin's 'Missa Hercules Dux Fer-rariae', João IV likens a *soggetto cavato* to a preacher's text. Just as the pulpit orator must stick to a single text and to one theme if his message is to strike home, so the composer of powerful Masses must stick to one subject and one mode.[142] In order better to defend Josquin, João gives the standard explanation of the derivation of the *re ut re ut re fa mi re cantus firmus*. Next

[136] *Defensa de la musica moderna contra la errada opinion del Obispo Cyrilo Franco*, facs. ed. by Mário de Sampayo Ribeiro (Coimbra, 1965).

[137] *Raccolta Aldina di lettere volgari, libro terzo* (Venice: Manuzio, 1564), fol. 114. João refers to the edition of 1567, fol. 216. Aldo Manuzio erred in identifying Bernardino Cirillo. João followed suit. Bernardino Cirillo was born at Aquila in 1499 and died on 18 June 1575 in Rome.

[138] *Difesa della Musica Moderna... Tradotta di Spagnuolo in Italiano* (Venice, [1667]), p. 18: 'Volete ancora vederlo più chiaro, & onde sia ciò avenuto; diranno, bella Messa si è cantata hoggi in Cappella, domandate, che Messa fù, risponderanno. *L'huomo armato*, ò *Hercules Dux Ferrariae*; che diavolo hà che fare la Musica con l'huomo armato, ò con la filomena, ò col Duca di Ferrara? Veda per l'amor di Dio, che numeri, che toni, che armonie, che muovere d'affetti di devotione si ponno cavare dall'huomo armato, ò dal Duca di Ferrara.'

[139] Ibid.: 'tutte queste cose tanto differenti fra esse, si cantano col medesimo Tono, e di una medesima maniera.'

[140] Ibid., p. 21: 'nel medesimo tempo, che uno dice *Sanctus* dica l'altro *Sabaoth*....'

[141] Ibid., p. 15. In his eagerness to make his point, Cirillo confused Alexander with Timotheus. In the margin João IV also corrects Cirillo's modal confusions.

[142] Ibid., pp. 52–3: 'E rispondendo à quello che riprova dicendo, che hà che fare vedere la Messa con l'huomo armato, ò con *Hercules Dux Ferrariae*, ò altri titoli somiglianti?...Se un Compositore hà fatto molte Messe, come si hà da sapere quale di esse è quella che hà da cantare, ò vedere, se non fosse per il titolo? mà non è questo il principale intento di questi nomi, la cagione è l'ingegno, studio, & habilità del compositore, perche così come il Predicatore piglia un' argomento, e sopra di esso và fondando il suo discorso, & il Poeta fà il medesimo, così ancora il compositore prende un' argomento, sopra del quale và fondando la Messa, sciegliendo sempre soggetto à quello, come fece Ioschino nella Messa *Ferrariae Dux Hercules*, nella quale fà una voce, che alza un canto fermo, e la Musica và dicendo le medesime sillabe della lettera....' For translation of selected excerpts from João's 'defence', see K. G. Fellerer, 'Church Music and the Council of Trent', *Musical Quarterly*, xxxix (1953), pp. 584–5.

the royal defender of Josquin cites a more recent example of just such a Mass, Philippe Rogier's 'Philippus secundus Rex Hispaniae'[143]—this being the tribute to the royal dedicatee with which Rogier's *Missae Sex* of 1598 began. Had he so liked, João IV could have named still other Spanish polytextual tenor Masses that despite rulings by the Council of Trent continued paying patrons such tribute as late as 1631.[144] Manifestly then, what Josquin had started even the Council of Trent could not stop. As far as Portugal was concerned, not only had the Lisbon-based Calced Carmelite whom João particularly favoured, Manuel Cardoso (1566–1650), published a polytextual Mass honouring Philip IV of Spain in 1636,[145] but also João IV's catalogue, printed in 1649, testifies to Cardoso's having composed before then a polytextual tenor Mass in which he paid similar tribute to João IV himself, 'Missa Iohannes quartus Portugaliae Rex', *a 9*.[146]

At last, the relevance in 1649 of Cirillo's 1549 attack on Josquin's 'Hercules' begins to become somewhat clearer. In no other nation did sixteenth-century contrapuntal practice hold on longer than in Portugal, where every chief master until 1640 continued publishing *prima prattica* parody, paraphrase, or tenor Masses. The old masters around whom an aureole still clung when João IV wrote his defence began with Tristano de Sylva (Ramos de Pareja's friend and contemporary), continued with Ockeghem (whom João twice calls Josquin's teacher), and touched next on Isaac.[147] The composers of his own time whom he admired most worked in Spain or Portugal: Mateo Romero, Gabriel Dias, Carlos Patiño, Francisco de Santiago, Manuel Cardoso, and especially João Lourenço Rabello—the composer of polychoral Masses and vespers music to whom the defence itself is dedicated. Among Italians close to his own generation, João favoured Gesualdo and Monteverdi.[148] Their music, and that of their many unpublished compatriots, 'shows how distinct is the power of music in these times to move men's souls, how aptly these composers can set the

---

[143] *Difesa*, pp. 53–4. See also Paul Becquart, *Musiciens néerlandais à la cour de Madrid. Philippe Rogier et son école (1560–1647)* (Académie royale de Belgique. Classe des Beaux-arts. Mémoires, xiii; Brussels, 1967), pp. 50, 55–6.

[144] Stevenson, *Spanish Cathedral Music*, p. 313 (Escobedo's Philip II Mass); José Subirá, 'Músics espanyols del segle XVII: Diego de Pontac', *Revista Musical Catalana*, xxxi (1934), p. 449. Diego Pontac began his 1631 anthology of seven Masses, five motets, and two Salves with a tribute to the archbishop of Granada, 'Missa Cardinalis Espinola' *a 6*. Facsimile of first opening in José Subirá, *Historia de la música española e hispanoamericana* (Barcelona, 1953), p. 383.

[145] Vieira, *Diccionario*, i, pp. 213–14. For full contents of Cardoso's *Missae de Beata Virgine Maria quaternis, quinis, et senis vocibus* (Lisbon, 1636), see Mário de Sampayo Ribeiro, *Frei Manuel Cardoso* (Lisbon, 1961), pp. 26–7.

[146] *Primeira parte do Index*, p. 444 (recte 448).

[147] *Difesa*, pp. 47, 58: 'Giodoco Platense per altro nome Giuschino, Enrico Isac suo contemporaneo...'

[148] Ibid., p. 52.

text, and how well they understand the art and its [deeper] meaning'.[149]

João forbore entering the lists under his royal name, preferring instead to sign himself 'D.B.' (Duke of Bragança).[150] To his librarian João Álvares Frouvo he assigned the 'defence' of another much debated point, the consonance of the perfect fourth.[151] Not only because João as a musician trod in the footsteps of such Peninsulars as Guillermo Despuig (1495), João de Barros (1532), and Francisco Salinas (1577) when he classified the fourth as a perfect consonance, but also because João is spelled with four letters and he was the fourth of that name to occupy the throne, Álvares Frouvo found himself working in a climate where '4' had become an article of faith.[152] Frouvo spent at least eight years assembling his data.[153] Far from stopping with the one consonant fourth that Salinas had spotted in Josquin's 'L'homme armé sexti toni', Álvares Frouvo picks examples from Josquin's 'L'homme armé super voces musicales' and from other authors as varied as La Rue ('Missa de Beata Virgine'), Andreas de Silva ('Missa Malheur me bat'), Mouton ('Missa Tua est potentia'), Sermisy [Verdelot] ('Missa Philomena praevia'), Clemens non Papa ('Mane nobiscum' *a 5*), and Jachet of Mantua ('In illo tempore dixit' *a 4*). Frouvo moved familiarly through the riches of his royal patron's incomparable library—which, if Frouvo's chapter-and-verse citations may be believed, went far beyond what the 1649 catalogue reveals, including manuscript copies of Marchettus of Padua, Philippe de Vitry, Prosdocimus de Beldemandis, and Guillaume de Machaut.[154]

---

[149] Ibid.

[150] In 1654 he published *Respuestas alas dudas Que se pusieron a la Missa Panis quem ego dabo de Palestrina* (published with introduction and notes by Mário de Sampayo Ribeiro as first volume in the series *Rei Musicae Portugaliae Monumenta* [Lisbon, 1958]). An Italian translation of João IV's study was published in Rome by Mauritio Balmonti in 1655.

[151] *Discursos sobre a perfeiçam do Diathesaron, & louvores do numero quaternario em que elle se contem, com hum encomio sobre o papel que mandou imprimir o Serenissimo Senhor elRey D. João IV. Em defensa da moderna musica & reposta sobre os tres breves negros de Christovaõ de Morales* (Lisbon, Antonio Craesbeeck de Mello, 1662), p. 69. Consonant fourths in the 'Missa L'homme armé super voces musicales' (identified here in the 1957 *editio altera*): pp. 4 (63³), 13 (20²). Like any interested party, Frouvo quotes from Josquin and others only what he thinks will prove his point. He says nothing, for instance, of Josquin's parallel fifths in the same Mass (pp. 14, mm. 30–31, and 23, m. 48).

[152] Ibid., p. 19. Álvares Frouvo also cites other examples of the number four, such as the four evangelists, the four seasons, and the four letters of the name of God in Latin and Spanish, *Deus* and *Dios* (compare Durán's praises of the number 7 in his 1498 *Comento sobre Lux bella*; see Stevenson, *Spanish Music in the Age of Columbus*, p. 68). John's famous library contained still another *Discurso de la perfection del Diatesaron* (item 540 of the 1649 catalogue).

[153] Although published in 1662, at least a preliminary *Discurso sobre a perfeição do Diatesaron* was ready in 1649. See *Primeira parte do Index*, p. 124, item 536. At page 56 of the 1662 imprint Frouvo attacks Giovanni d'Avella's *Regole di musica*, which he correctly identifies as having been published in 1657.   [154] Frouvo, *Discursos*, pp. 55, 88.

Frouvo copies at page 92 of his *Discursos* the 'black breve' section from the *Credo* of the 'De Beata Virgine' Mass (the eighth note in the bass, read by Frouvo as a semibreve followed by semibreve rest, is a breve in the 1526 Giunta print). At page 66, Frouvo inserts three snippets from the 'Missa L'homme armé super voces musicales'. How acute his eye was can be appreciated by studying what he has to say concerning an example twice attributed to 'Luys Pratense' in Cerone's *El Melopeo y Maestro*.[155] As printed there, the example purportedly shows a farfetched composer of that name beginning a five-voice unnamed piece with an exposed eleventh between bass and soprano. Bad enough for Cerone to have stolen the example from Glareanus's *Dodekachordon* (pp. 388–9) and to have tried covering up by changing the composer's name, complains Álvares Frouvo, but worse still, Cerone misunderstood the canon given by Glareanus: 'In gradus undenos descendant multiplicantes Consimilique modo crescant Antipodes uno', taking it to mean that the *Resolutio* in the bass clef must be sung simultaneously with the soprano-clef part, above which the word 'canon' is printed. 'This is no five-voice untitled piece', protests Álvares Frouvo in righteous rage, 'but is instead *Agnus Dei* I *a 4* from Josquin's "Fortuna desperata" Mass published at Venice in 1505'. Here Álvares Frouvo gives a welcome indication of the place and date that can now be assigned the lone bass part-book in the Oesterreichische Nationalbibliothek, Vienna, of a hitherto unidentified issue of Josquin's *Liber primus missarum*.[156] Cerone's contempt of Spaniards, whom he never tired of comparing unfavourably with Italians, and more particularly his disdain of Lisbon, ruled by Spanish kings 1580–1640, makes it poetically just that the first man to have detected him in a consequential mistake—a mistake resulting from one of his clumsier thefts—should have been none other than a chapelmaster of Lisbon Cathedral (1647–82).[157]

Portuguese poets were perhaps the latest in the Peninsula to invoke Josquin's name as a household word. The Oporto-born poet Francisco França da Costa (= Francisco de Francia y Acosta in his Spanish publications)[158] mentions Josquin in Romance IX of his *Iardin de Apolo* of 1624.

---

[155] Ibid., pp. 67–8; Cerone, *El Melopeo y Maestro* (Naples, 1613), p. 319.

[156] Smijers lists this as printed source 4 throughout the *Missen*, Deel I, and again in the *editio altera* started in 1957. Petrucci also published the *Missarum Josquin Liber secundus* at Venice on 30 June 1505.

[157] For further biographical detail, see Vieira, *Diccionario*, i, pp. 438–42.

[158] França da Costa belonged to the company of 123 poets published in Pedro de Herrera's *Descripcion de la Capilla de N.ª S.ª del Sagrario, que erigio en la S.ta Iglesia de Toledo el Ill.mo S.or Cardenal D. Bernardo de Sandoval y Rojas* (Madrid, Luis Sánchez, 1617). He again contributed occasional verses to a 1622 anthology. For details of his literary career at Madrid see Julio Cejador y Frauca, *Historia de la Lengua y Literatura Castellana* (Madrid, 1916), v, p. 24. *El Peñasco de las lagrimas*, published at folios 20–29 of the 1658 Coimbra anthology, was first published at Madrid in 1624.

29. Burney's transcription of 'Missa de Beata Virgine'; end of *Credo* and beginning
of *Sanctus*. London, British Museum, Add. MS. 11582, fol. 22. (p. 150)

30. Ambros' transcription of 'Absalon fili mi'; opening. Vienna, Oesterreichische Nationalbibliothek, MS. Supp. mus. 1556, fol. 7. (p. 161)

31a. Inscription 'Chansons de monsieur Bouton. A moy seulle'. Vienna, Oester-reichische Nationalbibliothek, MS. 18746, Bass part-book, fol. 38ᵛ–39. (p. 184)

b. Coat of arms of the Bouton family. Vatican City, Biblioteca Apostolica Vaticana, MS. Chigiana C VIII 234, fol. 249ᵛ (detail). (p. 195)

c. Motto 'Boutton' overpainted with 'Dieu'. Vatican City, Biblioteca Apostolica Vaticana, MS. Chigiana C VIII 234, fol. 282 (detail). (p. 195)

32. Visitation of Mary and Elizabeth. Illumination in Jena, Universitätsbibliothek, MS. 3, fol. 1ᵛ. (p. 198)

33. Josquin, 'Missa Hercules Dux Ferrarie' (title changed to 'Fridericus dux Saxsonie'). Jena, Universitätsbibliothek, MS. 3, fol. 15ᵛ. (p. 199)

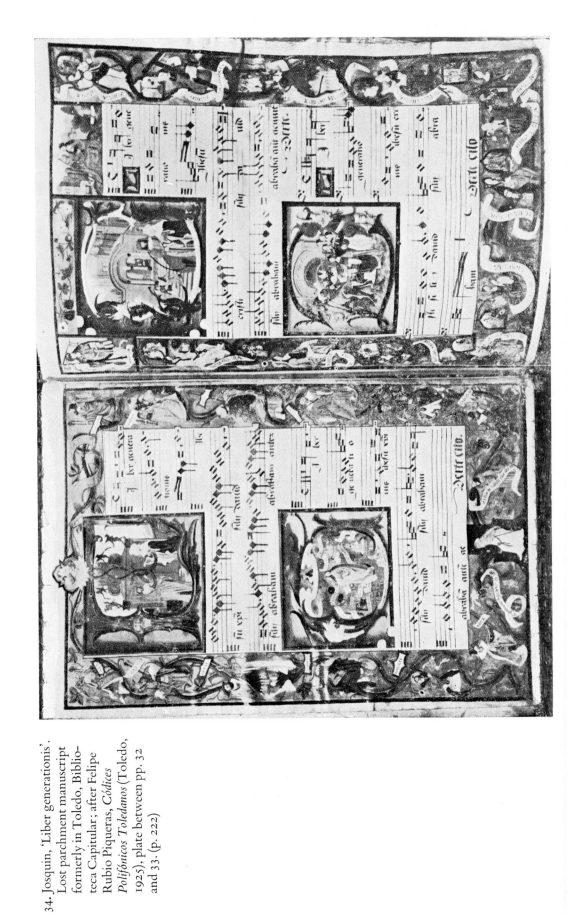

34. Josquin, 'Liber generationis'. Lost parchment manuscript formerly in Toledo, Biblioteca Capitular; after Felipe Rubio Piqueras, *Códices Polifónicos Toledanos* (Toledo, 1925), plate between pp. 32 and 33. (p. 222)

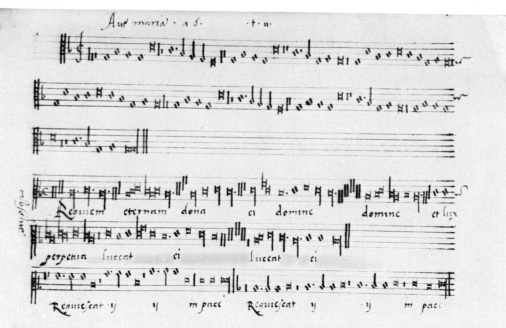

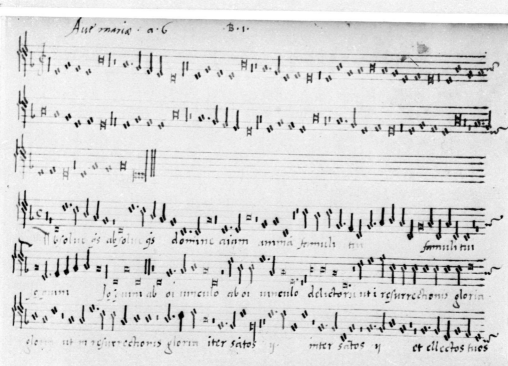

35a. Josquin, 'Ave Maria', and anonymous funeral motet for Josquin, 'Absolve quesumus'. Piacenza, Archivio del Duomo, MS. without signature, Vol. I (Tenor II), fol. 1. (p. 247)

b. 'Ave Maria' and 'Absolve quesumus'. Vol. II (Bass I), fol. 1. (p. 247)

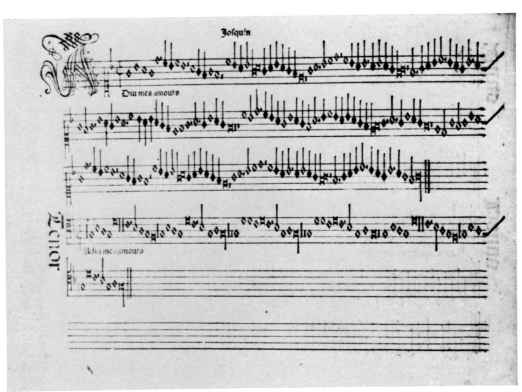

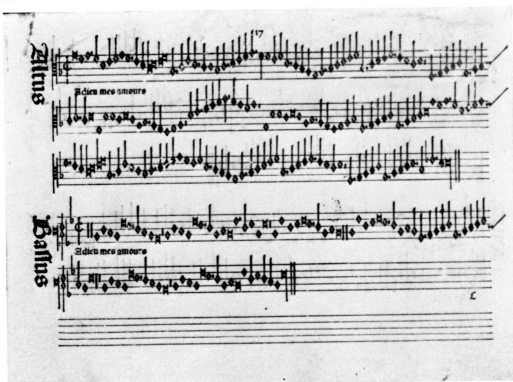

36. Josquin, 'Adieu mes amours'. Petrucci, *Harmonice musices Odhecaton A* (1501), fol. 16ᵛ–17. (p. 248)

37a. Josquin, 'Ave Maria'. Bologna, Civico Museo Bibliografico Musicale, MS. R 142, fol. 33ᵛ. (p. 248)

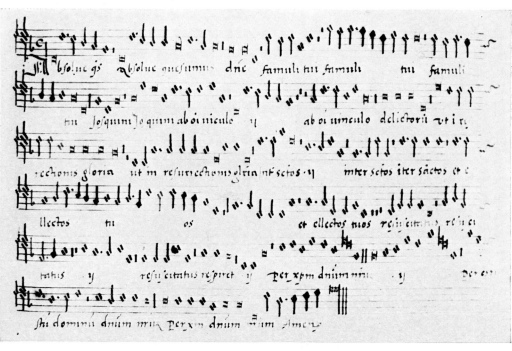

b. 'Absolve quesumus'. Piacenza, Archivio del Duomo, MS. without signature (Bass II), fol. 1ᵛ. (p. 255)

57

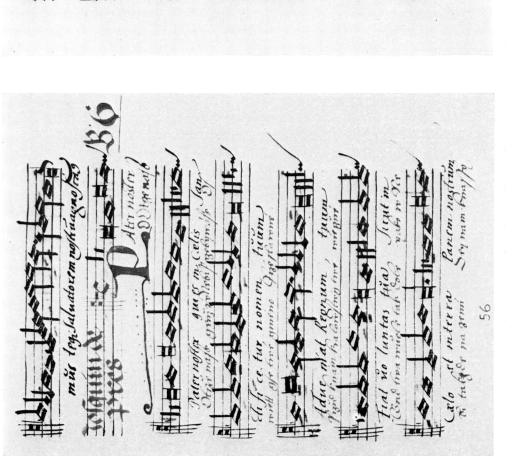

56

38. Josquin, 'Pater noster' with Czech translation. Hradec Králové, Museum, MS. II A 22a, pp. 56–7 (continued on plate 39). (p. 280)

39. Josquin, 'Pater noster', pp. 58–9.

41a. Josquin, 'Missa La sol fa re mi', initial of *Kyrie* in superius. Vatican City, Biblioteca Apostolica Vaticana, Cappella Sistina MS. 41, fol. XXXVIIIᵛ. (p. 567)

b. Initial of *Kyrie* in alto, fol. XXXVIIII. (p. 567)

40. Pavel Spongopeus Jistebnický, Mass on Josquin's 'Praeter rerum seriem'. Klatovy, Museum, MSS. 75–76, no. 43. (p. 281)

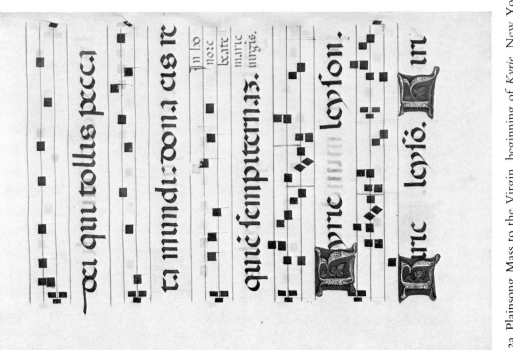

42a. Plainsong Mass to the Virgin, beginning of *Kyrie*. New York, Pierpont Morgan Library, MS. M. 683, fol. 39ᵛ. (p. 591)

b. Same; cross-references to *Sanctus* and *Agnus Dei* melodies. New York, Pierpont Morgan Library, MS. M. 683, fol. 44ᵛ. (p. 591)

43a. Same; beginning of *Sanctus*. New York, Pierpont Morgan Library, MS. M. 683, fol. 16ᵛ. (p. 591)

    b. Same; beginning of *Agnus Dei*. New York, Pierpont Morgan Library, MS. M. 683, fol. 5ᵛ. (p. 591)

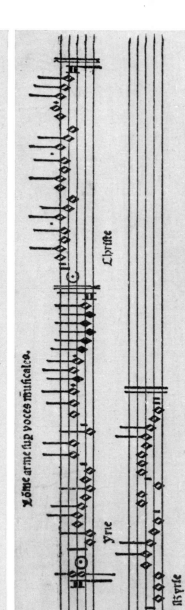

44a. Josquin, 'Missa L'homme armé super voces musicales'; *Agnus Dei II.* Petrucci, *Misse Josquin* (1502). (p. 706)

b. Josquin, 'Missa L'homme armé super voces musicales'; *Kyrie.* Petrucci, *Misse Josquin* (1502). (p. 707)

c. Josquin, 'Veni Sancte Spiritus'; beginning of tenor. Regensburg, Proskesche Musikbibliothek, MS. A.R. 879, fol. 39ᵛ. (p. 732)

d. Josquin, 'Missa L'homme armé super voces musicales'; *Agnus Dei III*; beginning of alto. Regensburg, Proskesche Musikbibliothek, MS. A.R. 879, fol. 67ᵛ. (p. 732)

Complaining of the vices rampant in Madrid, he scores pride so gross that a petty music scribbler of Roldán's stripe can pretend 'that he has written more canons than Josquin or Juan Blas [de Castro]'.[159]

The fame Josquin enjoyed among Spaniards and Portuguese re-echoed in the New World. What seems to be the first American allusion to Josquin turns up in a versified *Historia de Cartagena* antedating 1588 by the soldier-poet Juan de Castellanos (1522–1607)—who in 1554, fifteen years after emigrating to the New World, turned priest. His sponsor at ordination was Juan Pérez Materano, dean of Cartagena Cathedral since 1545 and writer of the earliest documented New World music treatise.[160] Castellanos studied music with Pérez Materano before becoming a priest. Their musical interests were sufficiently kindred for Castellanos to take great pride in having developed a fine polyphonic choir at Tunja, where he resided from 1561 until his death.[161] The highest compliment that Castellanos could pay his master was to call him a 'Josquin in music theory'.[162]

In neighbouring Peru, Josquin's reputation as the supreme master of his epoch lingered on until at least 1737. In that year the rector of San Marcos University, Pedro José Bermúdez de la Torre, published a 179-folio pane-gyric entitled *Triunfos del Santo Oficio Peruano*, in which he catalogued the great names of music history. Josquin des Prez heads his list.[163] His purpose was to supply a musical genealogy for Rocco (= Roque) Ceruti, a native of

---

[159] *Iardin de Apolo* (Coimbra, 1658), fol. 41ᵛ: 'Vereis cierto valenton,/que direis que es un Roldan,/y es tal, que ha hecho mas fugas/que Iusquin, y que Iuan Blas.' The original edition dates from 1624 and has a preface by no less an authority than Lope de Vega. On Roldán, a singer at Toledo and later chapelmaster at Málaga from 1642 to 1645, see Rubio Piqueras, *Música y Músicos Toledanos*, pp. 68 and 47, and Andrés Llordén, 'Notas históricas de los maestros de capilla en la Catedral de Málaga (1641–1799)', *Anuario Musical*, xx (1965), pp. 105–7. According to a letter from Seville dated 22 June 1654, to King John IV of Portugal (who had inquired about various Spanish composers) Pérez Roldán was con-sidered lazy and not above signing his name to works not actually his own (Vasconcellos, *El-Rey D. João o 4.ᵗᵒ*, p. 23). On Juan Blas de Castro, who died in 1631, see Ramón Adolfo Pelinski, 'Die weltliche Musik Spaniens am Anfang des 17. Jhs.' (Ph.D. diss., Ludwig-Maximilian-Universität, Munich, 1969), pp. 58–60.

[160] Robert Stevenson, 'The First New World Composers: Fresh Data from Peninsular Archives', *Journal of the American Musicological Society*, xxiii (1970), pp. 98–9. Pérez Materano reached Cartagena in 1537, was named a cathedral canon there in 1539, and elevated to dean in 1545. In 1555 (August 25) he was offered a canonry in Venezuela diocese but refused. He died at Cartagena on 27 November 1561.

[161] Isaac J. Pardo, *Juan de Castellanos. Estudio de las Elegías de Varones Ilustres de Indias* (Caracas, 1961), p. 301, quoting *Nuevo Reino*, xviiii: 'Ni más autoridad, ni mejor coro,/Ansí de voces como de instrumentos.'

[162] Juan de Castellanos, *Elegías de Varones ilustres de Indias* (Biblioteca de Autores Españoles, iv; Madrid, 1857), p. 366, col. 2: 'venerable persona, docto, santo, y Jusquin en teórica de canto.'

[163] (Lima, 1737), fol. 53. See Robert Stevenson, *The Music of Peru: Aboriginal and Viceroyal Epochs* (Washington, 1960), p. 86.

Milan, who came to Lima in 1708 to conduct the private band of the 24th
Viceroy of Peru, a lavish patron of the arts. Ceruti's 1737 panegyrist had
known him intimately for almost thirty years, and was only echoing the
Milan-born composer's own preferences when he drew up a musical tree
for Ceruti that began with none else but Josquin.

Josquiniana in Some Manuscripts at Piacenza*

MARTIN PICKER

Some sixteenth-century manuscript part-books in the archives of the Cathedral at Piacenza, described in the recently published catalogue of that collection by Francesco Bussi,[1] contain two fragmentary compositions that shed new light on the work and influence of Josquin des Prez. One of these is the initial item in the two part-books remaining of a much larger set, perhaps of six or seven.[2] This composition bears the title 'Ave Maria a 6', and the two voice-parts are marked 'T. II.' (for *Tenor secundus*) and 'B. I.' (for *Bassus primus*). The manuscripts do not supply further text or the composer's name (see Plate 35).

Both voices state, in canon at the octave at the distance of one and a half breves, a melody easily recognized as 'Adieu mes amours', a song found in the early sixteenth-century monophonic chansonnier known as the 'Bayeux' manuscript[3] and incorporated in whole or in part in some eleven polyphonic chanson and Mass settings from about 1500 to 1530.

* I am indebted to the Research Council of Rutgers University and the National Endowment for the Humanities for their generous support of the work leading to the present paper.

[1] *Piacenza, Archivio del Duomo. Catalogo del Fondo Musicale* (Bibliotheca Musicae, v; Milan, 1967). I am grateful to Dr. Bussi for responding to my inquiries and to Don Domenico Ponzini, archivist of the Cathedral, for graciously and promptly answering my request for photographs and permitting me to examine the manuscripts personally. I also wish to express my thanks to Professor Claudio Gallico for his generous assistance.

[2] Bussi, *Catalogo*, pp. 147–51: 'Willaert Adriano e altri—Messe, Inni, Lamentazioni, Motetti (Archivio Vecchio. Nessuna segnatura.)' The two part-books are in oblong-4⁰, and consist of 82 and 88 numbered leaves, plus 22 and 14 unnumbered, respectively. Each contains an alphabetical table of contents on three unnumbered leaves bound in at the beginning. The contents include motets, a madrigal, Masses, lamentations, and hymns, written in various hands. All compositions are anonymous except for the bulk of the hymns, which in Volume I are assigned to 'Adrianus Vuilaert' or 'A.W.' (see n. 27 below). The contents of these manuscripts are described in Jane B. Weidensaul, 'Early 16th-Century Manuscripts at Piacenza: A Progress Report', *Current Musicology*, xvi (1973), pp. 41–8. The two part-books discussed above are listed under number (3) in Ms. Weidensaul's article.

[3] Paris, Bibliothèque nationale, MS. f. fr. 9346, fol. 85ᵛ; modern edition by Théodore Gérold, *Le Manuscrit de Bayeux* (Strasbourg, 1921), p. 100.

Best known of these settings is a four-part chanson by Josquin published
in Petrucci's *Odhecaton* of 1501 (see Plate 36) and preserved in numerous
manuscript and printed sources of the early sixteenth century.[4] In this
famous piece, as in the Piacenza composition, the popular melody is sung
canonically by the tenor and bass.

To the canonic pair of voices in the Piacenza manuscripts we are able to
add a third voice from yet another source: Bologna, Civico Museo Bibliografico Musicale, MS. R 142, a manuscript part-book of the early sixteenth
century that differs in contents and handwriting from the part-books in
Piacenza. Here we find an 'Ave Maria' with complete text inscribed 'Josquin
a 7', which fits perfectly with the canon in the Piacenza part-books and
undoubtedly belongs to the same composition (see Plate 37, fig. a). This
single voice-part is published in the recent Supplement volume of the
Josquin *Werken*.[5] Ex. 1 presents a transcription in score of the three extant
voices of this work.[5a]

Jaap van Benthem, in a recent study of Josquin's five- and six-part
chansons, advances the theory, based on internal evidence and without
reference to the Piacenza source, that the single voice in the Bologna
manuscript is related to and may be contrapuntally combined with the
popular melody 'Adieu mes amours'.[6] This perceptive hypothesis is now
confirmed. Van Benthem also suggests that 'Ave Maria' is not the text on
which this composition was originally written.[7] Even though both sources
give only these words (an incipit in Piacenza, the full text in Bologna), I
believe that his hypothesis is well grounded. By way of justification, Van
Benthem points out that at least three of Josquin's chansons appear in the
Bologna manuscript as Latin *contrafacta*.[8] He also notes that the Bologna

[4] Among the many modern editions of Josquin's chanson, the following give extensive
information concerning the sources: *Werken*, Wereldlijke Werken, iv, pp. vii–ix, and Helen
Hewitt and Isabel Pope, eds., *Harmonice Musices Odhecaton A* (Cambridge, Mass., 1942),
pp. 134–5.   [5] No. 16.

[5a] The text of the 'Ave Maria a 6' is taken from Paris, Bibl. Nat., MS. f. fr. 9346, fol. 85[v].

[6] Jaap van Benthem, 'Zur Struktur und Authentizität der Chansons à 5 & 6 von Josquin
des Prez', *Tijdschrift van de Vereniging voor Nederlandse Muziekgeschiedenis*, xxi (1970),
p. 187, n. 25; cf. *Werken*, Supplement, p. vii.

[7] The first two verses of this text, which is found in full only in the Bologna manuscript,
correspond to those in the sequence 'Ave Maria... Virgo serena' (*Variae Preces* (Solesmes,
1901), p. 46), but the remainder has not been identified.

[8] These are: fols. 2[v]–3, 'Adiuro vos' (= 'Plus nulz regretz', Wereldlijke Werken,
no. 29); fol. 32, 'Vidi speciosam' (= 'Tenez moy en voz bras', ibid., no 13); and fols.
49–50, 'O Maria virgo sanctissima' (identified in the Tabula as 'O maria cioé se conge pres';
= 'Se congié prens', ibid., no. 12). Another possible *contrafactum*, found on fols. 39[v]–40,
is 'Videte omnes populi' (identified in the Tabula as 'Videte cioé nimphes'; = 'Nimphes,
nappés', ibid., no. 21). Helmuth Osthoff, *Josquin Desprez*, ii, p. 94, follows Marcus van
Crevel, *Adrianus Petit Coclico* (The Hague, 1940), pp. 103–10, in considering the Latin to
be the original text and the French the *contrafactum*. However, the Tabula of the Bologna
manuscript indicates that at least the copyist believed the reverse to be the case.

Ex. 1 'Josquin a7' (superius), Bologna MS. R 142, ff. 33ᵛ- 34

'Ave Maria' part (apparently a *contratenor altus*) is heavily dependent on the popular melody for its structure and melodic content. This voice conforms to the virelai-like structure of the Piacenza tenor (which, by assigning a letter to each phrase, may be expressed as: ABCCABB), and it adopts the two motives of the tenor's first phrase, thus participating in the imitation. It seems unlikely that a voice musically so dependent on the tenor would have been written for a text totally independent of that part. Further indication that the Latin text is not the original is the difficulty of matching it to the music in any convincing way. To demonstrate this point the text underlay of the Bologna manuscript has been reproduced as closely as possible in Ex. 1. In its structural dependence on a secular, monophonic *cantus firmus*, this 'Ave Maria' is unlike any known motet by Josquin.[9]

[9] Among the motets, comparison with the well-known 'Stabat Mater' (*Werken*, Motet-ten, Bundel viii, no. 36) is instructive. In that case the *cantus firmus* is also a chanson, but it is a polyphonic tenor, drawn from Binchois's 'Comme femme desconfortée'. It is isolated from the other four voices of the motet, and its identity is disguised, since it is stated in augmentation.

However, it is similar in style and construction to some of his six-voice chansons, particularly those based on popular melodies, such as 'Se congié prens' and 'Petite camusette', both of which also present the borrowed melody in canon.

Until all the voice-parts are found, many questions about this composition must remain unanswered. Nevertheless, some clues are provided by the evidence available. As to the number of voices for which the composition was originally written, the Piacenza part-books indicate six, but the Balogna manuscript specifies seven. Knowing only the Bologna source, Willem Elders has offered the explanation that the seven voices may symbolize the Seven Sorrows of Mary, in connection with the 'Ave Maria' text.[10] This interpretation rests on two premises: (1) that the work is actually for seven voices, and (2) that 'Ave Maria' is the original text. We have already demonstrated the weakness of the latter premise. As for the former: only one seven-voice motet is attributed to Josquin by the editors of the *Werken*,[11] and no seven-voice chansons by Josquin are known to exist. It is noteworthy that the Bologna part-book contains no other seven-voice pieces. It tends to group works for four, five, and six voices together, and this 'Ave Maria' is surrounded by pieces for six voices. Moreover, it is listed in the original table of contents among pieces 'a sei'. Thus, of the two possibilities, it seems far more likely that the composition was originally for six than for seven voices.

A second and more important question is: can we accept the ascription to Josquin that appears in the Bologna manuscript? We have thus far doubted the authenticity of the text given there, as well as the number of voices specified in that source. Should we not also doubt the accuracy of the manuscript in naming Josquin as the composer? The evidence is by no means conclusive, but I believe that it tends to support the attribution to Josquin. Of twenty compositions for which the manuscript names Josquin as the composer, not counting this work, seventeen are confirmed as his from other sources.[12] Two are *unica*,[13] and only one is demonstrably by another composer.[14] A ratio of seventeen correct attributions to one

[10] Willem Elders, 'Das Symbol in der Musik von Josquin des Prez', *Acta Musicologica*, xli (1969), p. 174.

[11] *Werken*, Supplement, no. 14. This motet ('Proch dolor/Pie Jesu') is anonymous in the only source transmitting it. Concerning the likelihood of Josquin's authorship, see the present writer's *The Chanson Albums of Marguerite of Austria* (Berkeley and Los Angeles, 1965), pp. 89–90.

[12] *Werken*, Motetten, nos. 17, 30–34, 46, 49, 55, 83, 84; Wereldlijke Werken, nos. 12, 13, 17, 21, 29; and the *Agnus* of the 'Missa Hercules Dux Ferrariae' (Missen, vii).

[13] Fols. 8v–9, 'Iniquos odio habui' *a 4* (*Werken*, Supplement, no. 17), and fol. 57v, 'Fors seulement' *a 6* (= superius of Ockeghem's rondeau).

[14] Fol. 57, 'Salva nos, Domine', ascribed to both Mouton and Willaert in contemporary sources, but to Josquin only in Bologna MS. R 142 (see Osthoff, *Josquin Desprez*, ii, p.

incorrect one reflects a relatively high standard of accuracy for sixteenth-century sources.

Internal evidence is difficult to adduce on the basis of so fragmentary a work, but there does exist a small but significant musical relationship between Josquin's four-voice 'Adieu mes amours' and our 'Ave Maria' that is shared by no other setting that I have found. It is to be seen in the *cantus firmus* itself. To be sure, the two canons are by no means identical. Josquin's four-part setting is canonic in a loose sense only: the bass follows or anticipates the phrases of the tenor at the fourth below, freely extending some phrases. The 'Ave Maria', on the other hand, presents the melody, in a slightly different form, in strict canon at the octave throughout. Another difference is that the 'Ave Maria' employs the final, repeated phrase of the popular melody that is omitted in the four-part setting; thus the 'Ave Maria' is 69 measures long, as against 60 in the four-part 'Adieu mes amours'. But the versions of the melody in the two settings have one unique feature in common. In the four-part setting, a variant of the melody occurs in the bass while the alto and tenor preserve the original form of the tune. This passage occurs in the middle (C) section of the piece, where the alto initiates the imitation, followed by the quasi-canonic bass and tenor. Alto and tenor have *re la la sol la*, the original form of the melody, but the bass has *re la fa sol la* (see Plate 36 and Ex. 2a). The same melodic variant is adopted in *both* voices of the canon in the 'Ave Maria' (Ex. 2b). This variant is not to be found in any other setting of the popular melody among the eight that I have examined (these include two Mass settings by Obrecht; one Mass each by Festa, de Silva, and Layolle; a motet by Divitis; a chanson by Mouton; and one anonymous chanson).[15] I assume the variant to be Josquin's inven-

---

292). Josquin is also the composer of another work in the Bologna manuscript for which no composer is named: fols. 12–12ᵛ, 'Ave Maria' *a 4* (Motetten, no. 2).

[15] (1) Mouton, chanson, 4 v., double canon (Basel, Univ.-Bibl., MS. F.X.1–4, no. 98; RISM 1520³, anon.). (2) Anon., chanson, 4 v., melody in canon, superius and alto (Florence, Bibl. Naz. Centr., MS. Magl. 164–167, no. 59). (3) Obrecht, 'Missa Adieu mes amours', 4 v. (Jena, Univ.-Bibl., MS. 32, fols. 142ᵛ–158). (4) Obrecht, 'Missa diversorum tenorum', 4 v.: *Et resurrexit* (Milan, Duomo, MS. 2268, fols. 136ᵛ–143). (5) C. Festa, 'Missa carminum', 4 v.: *Osanna* and *Agnus* I (Biblioteca Vaticana, Capp. Giulia MS. XII.2, fols. 192ᵛ–206). (6) F. de Layolle, 'Missa Adieu mes amours' (RISM [1532]⁸; 1539¹). (7) A. de Silva, 'Missa', 4 v.: *Agnus* III (Biblioteca Vaticana, Capp. Sist. MS. 45, fols. 100ᵛ–117). (8) A. Divitis, 'Salve regina/Adieu mes amours', 5 v. (Munich, Bayr. Staatsbibl., MS. 34, no. 8).

In addition, two incompletely preserved settings of the melody lack the phrase in question: (1) Gaspar van Weerbecke, 'Bon temps/Adieu mes amours', 4 v. The tenor quotes the opening only (Florence, Bibl. del Conservatorio, MS. B 2442, pp. 172–74; the bass is lacking).(2) Anon., chanson, 3 v. (?). Only the superius is preserved, but it makes a plausible counterpoint to the melody (Florence, Bibl. Naz. Centr., MS. Magl. XIX, 107bis, fol. 10ᵛ). I have not seen Adam Rener's 'Missa Adieu mes amours', listed in *MGG*, xi, col. 292.

tion, fashioned to meet the contrapuntal needs of his four-part setting, for A instead of F in the bass would produce a fourth with the alto (the note in question is marked with an asterisk in Ex. 2a). I believe that this relationship between the two settings provides forceful evidence of their common authorship.

Ex. 2
a) 'Adieu mes amours' mm. 21-7 (alto, tenor, bass only)

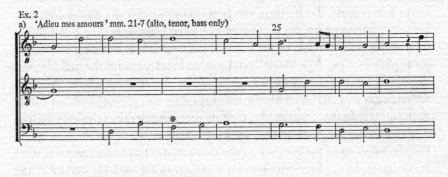

b) 'Ave Maria,' mm. 22-8 (T. II and B. I only)

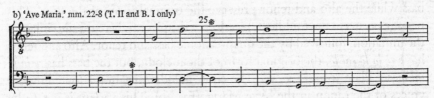

If the 'Ave Maria' were in some sense a 'recomposition' by Josquin of his four-part 'Adieu mes amours', it would not be a unique example of self-parody among Josquin's chansons. At least one of his three-part chansons served as a model for a four-voice work: 'Entré je suis'.[16] Like 'Adieu mes amours', the two settings of 'Entré je suis' apply canonic treatment to a popular melody, which in Josquin's hands exhibits a stronger profile than in settings by other composers, among them Busnois, Isaac, Agricola, and Prioris.[17] Chronologically, the three-part 'Entré je suis' appears to be a very early work with markedly archaic characteristics, while the more mature four-part setting is similar in style to the four-part 'Adieu mes amours', that is, it is composed of a canonic vocal duo accompanied by two voices of a more active, and possibly instrumental, character.

Jaap van Benthem, in his study previously mentioned, discusses some three-part settings of popular songs that may have served as models for

16 See Picker, *The Chanson Albums*, pp. 80–1 and 285–8. See also Josquin des Prez, *Werken*, Wereldlijke Werken, nos. 57 and 58.

17 See Martin Picker, 'Polyphonic Settings *c.* 1500 of the Flemish Tune, "In minen sin"', *Journal of the American Musicological Society*, xii (1959), pp. 94–5. Jaap van Benthem has published a study of this composition: 'Die Chanson *Entré je suis* à 4 von Josquin des Prez und ihre Überlieferung', *Tijdschrift van de Vereniging voor Nederlandse Muziekgeschiedenis*, xxi (1970), pp. 203–10.

five- and six-part chansons by (or attributed to) Josquin, specifically, 'Faulte d'argent' and 'Tenez moy en vos bras'. The three-part settings are anonymous in the sources, but van Benthem suggests that Josquin may be their composer.[18] If this were true, Josquin's fondness for parody procedure in his chansons would appear in a new light. In each case a popular melody underlies the chanson chosen for parody.

The second of the two pieces with which this paper is concerned is an anonymous motet, 'Absolve, quaesumus, Domine', that follows the 'Ave Maria' in the two Piacenza part-books already discussed. According to the original index of the manuscripts, this work is for seven voices.[19] A third part-book in the Piacenza Cathedral archives supplies yet another voice, a *Bassus secundus*, written in the same hand but apparently belonging to a different set than the other two (see Pl. 37, fig. b).[20] The *Bassus primus* (Pl. 35, fig. b) and *Bassus secundus* (Pl. 37, fig. b) carry the principal text, 'Absolve, quaesumus', while the *Tenor secundus* (Pl. 35, fig. a) provides the *cantus firmus*: 'Requiem aeternam', the plainsong Introit of the Mass for the Dead.

'Absolve, quaesumus' is a prayer for absolution that forms part of the Burial Service, and in which the name of the deceased is inserted.[21] In this motet, the text begins as follows: 'Absolve, quaesumus, Domine, animam famuli tui Josquini ab omni vinculo delictorum' (Absolve, we beseech you, Lord, the soul of your servant Josquin from every bond of sin). Josquin had utilized the same absolution text in a six-voice motet based on the same *cantus firmus* (in the only source, the place for the name of the deceased is marked by the letter 'N', as in the liturgical books).[22] Musically, these two works are totally different compositions. Noting that in Josquin's motet the *cantus firmus* is stated in canon at the fifth, one easily discovers that the *Tenor secundus* of the anonymous motet forms the *comes* of a canon, the *dux* of which begins two measures earlier a fifth below, in what would presumably be the *Tenor primus*. Thus four voices are extant of the seven that originally constituted this work. Ex. 3 is a transcription of the first 40 measures (the entire motet is 150 measures long).

[18] 'Zur Struktur und Authentizität', pp. 170 ff. Van Benthem believes, however, that the five-voice 'Faulte d'argent' may not be by Josquin.

[19] See Bussi, *Catalogo*, p. 147.

[20] Ibid., p. 139: 'Passioni, messe, salmi, magnificat, motetti.' Similar in size and appearance to the two part-books described above (see n. 2), it is written on a different type of paper and its contents correspond only partially. It consists of 77 numbered and 18 unnumbered leaves, with an alphabetical table of 3 leaves bound in at the beginning. Fol. 1ʳ is headed 'B.II.' in the same hand as the similar voice designations in the other two books. This page was originally blank, but has been filled in with four voices of a *lauda*, 'Sancta Maria, ora pro nobis', by a different and more careless hand. The table of contents lists an 'Ave Maria a 6', but this has been crossed out. 'Absolve, quaesumus' appears on fol. 1ᵛ. This manuscript is listed under number (1) in the article by Ms. Weidensaul cited in fn. 2 above.

[21] Cf. *Liber Usualis* (Tournai, 1953), p. 1821.

[22] Josquin's motet is published in the *Werken*, Motetten, Bundel xxiii, no. 82.

Despite their use of the same plainsong, the canons in Josquin's motet and in the anonymous work differ in rhythm, in the time interval of their imitation, and in the order in which the voices enter. Nevertheless, the coincidence of texts, *cantus firmus*, and canonic structure provide rather strong evidence that the anonymous composer modelled his work on Josquin's. Thus this motet takes its place among others on Josquin's death, especially those of Vinders and Gombert, which pay homage to him by utilizing *cantus firmi* that Josquin himself had employed in lament compositions.[23] The relationship between the two works places in new perspective

[23] The laments of Vinders and Gombert are published in *Werken*, Klaagliederen op den dood van Josquin, nos. 1 and 3.

the question of the authenticity of Josquin's 'Absolve, quaesumus' raised by
Martin Just in a review of the Josquin edition.[24] Myroslaw Antonowycz,
editor of the work in question, has strongly defended Josquin's authorship.[25]
The apparent fact that Josquin's composition served as a model for a motet
on his death tends to confirm Antonowycz's opinion that the work is
authentic.

Certain musical features of the anonymous motet are of interest in their
own right. The two bass voice-parts engage in close, constant imitation,
suggesting that the texture of the whole work was so conceived. Combined
with this tightly-knit imitation is a starkly syllabic declamation that carefully preserves the natural accentuation of the text. Josquin's name is set
prominently to a three-note motive, giving it special emphasis. All of these
features point to the hand of a skilled progressive follower of Josquin, one
acquainted with both the sophisticated methods of northern polyphony
and the new humanist attitude arising in the sixteenth century of shaping
music to a specific text.

A surprise awaits us at the conclusion of the motet, on the words 'Requies-
cat in pace'. Here each of the three extant voices divides in two (see Pl. 35,
fig. 1). If we continue the tenor in canon (though the plainsong *cantus firmus*
is abandoned), we have a total of seven voices out of a much greater number,

Ex. 4

[24] *Die Musikforschung*, xviii (1965), pp. 109–10.

[25] M. Antonowycz, 'Zur Autorschaftsfrage der Motetten *Absolve, quaesumus, Domine*
und *Inter natos mulierum*', *Tijdschrift van de Vereniging voor Nederlandse Muziekgeschiedenis*,
xx (1966), pp. 154–69.

1) Orig.: G

perhaps as many as fifteen, that originally made up the final section of the work. (Ex. 4 presents a transcription of this section.) We are able at least to imagine the massive climax to this composition which is almost without parallel in early sixteenth-century music.[26] The motet as a whole, and especially its conclusion, seems to reflect the striving for full and spacious sonorities that can be traced above all in the sacred music of the Venetian school throughout the century.

This leads us to the most tantalizing question of all: who might the composer of this motet be? No certain answer can be offered as long as the provenance and repertory of the Piacenza manuscripts remain unexplored, but some suggestive information may be provided. Only one composer is named in these manuscripts: 'Adrianus Vuilaert', whose full name or initials appear in one part-book in connection with a group of hymns.[27] Immediately following 'Absolve, quaesumus' in all three part-books, and in the same hand, is a 'Beata es virgo Maria' for seven voices that is identifiable as a work by Philippe Verdelot.[28] We may speculate that the composer of this motet on the death of Josquin was, like Willaert and Verdelot, a Franco-Netherlander active in northern Italy during the 1520s.

To sum up: The Piacenza manuscripts contain two works that cast new light on Josquin. In one case, they supply two voices that join a single part in Bologna MS. R 142 to form three out of a total of six (or possibly seven) voices of a composition by Josquin based on the popular melody 'Adieu mes amours', bearing the text 'Ave Maria', and related to Josquin's four-part 'Adieu mes amours'. In the second case, they provide four of the seven voices of a heretofore unknown motet, 'Absolve, quaesumus, Domine', on the death of Josquin, which takes as its apparent model a funeral motet on the same text by Josquin himself. Thus, 450 years after his death we continue to discover new evidence of Josquin's creative activity, his influence, and the high esteem in which he was held by the musical world of his time.

[26] Concerning the related practice of multiple choirs, found mainly in the province of Venice in the first few decades of the sixteenth century, see Giovanni d'Alessi, 'Precursors of Adriano Willaert in the Practice of *Coro Spezzato*', *Journal of the American Musicological Society*, v (1952), pp. 187–210; and Norbert Böker-Heil, 'Zu einem frühvenezianischen Motettenrepertoire', *Helmuth Osthoff zu seinem siebzigsten Geburtstag* (Tutzing, 1969), pp. 59–88.

[27] Vol. I, fol. 48ᵛ ff., 54ᵛ, 55ᵛ, and 78ᵛ. See Bussi, *Catalogo*, p. 148.

[28] Fols. 1ᵛ–2ʳ (Bussi, pp. 148 f., 140). This same work is copied again, without text, on fols. 3ᵛ–4ʳ (B.I. and T.II) and 8ʳ–8ᵛ (B.II). See Norbert Böker-Heil, *Die Motetten von Philippe Verdelot* (Cologne, 1967), p. 274.

Josquin's Motets in the German Tradition

WINFRIED KIRSCH

Each work of music has its own history. Composed at a certain time, at a certain place, and perhaps written for a special occasion, it is entered into manuscripts or incorporated into prints together with other compositions; it thus becomes a part of various local traditions, it is heard in different styles and interpretations, it exerts its influence upon composers, it is sometimes updated through modern variants, and finally it is forgotten. Its history becomes an integral part of the musical text and is of prime importance for its critical examination. Manuscripts and prints are the most useful means to clarify this history; they not only transmit the musical text of a work, they are a part of its past.

Research on musical sources, involving historical and aesthetic inter-pretation of diverse traditions in space and time, is one of the main tasks of contemporary musicology. Many misjudgements of older compositions have resulted from the failure to examine them in their historical context. The haphazard survival of musical sources necessarily leaves us in many cases with an incomplete history of the work. But this must not detain us from doing our utmost with the means available.

The present paper is only one step in the systematic investigation of the German reception: at what time do compositions by Josquin begin to appear in German[1] sources? What are the particular centres of the tradi-tion? Does the repertory chosen for the German sources have a special character? Is there any relationship between the literary texts, the musical structure, the circumstances of the compositions, and the German tradition?

The present investigation is confined to the ninety-one motets of religious character by Josquin des Prez that are regarded as authentic by Helmuth Osthoff.[2] Osthoff's book and the lists of sources in the *Werken* provide the statistical basis. Of course, any statements about quantity and quality of musical sources are subject to change, and Josquin research, above all, is currently in a state of flux.[3] Moreover, the complexity of the Josquin

[1] Sources from other German-speaking countries, such as Switzerland, are also included.

[2] Helmuth Osthoff, *Josquin Desprez*, 2 vols. (Tutzing, 1962–5).

[3] The contributions to the present volume by Myroslaw Antonowycz, Edgar H. Sparks, and Herbert Kellman already change the picture presented here.

sources as a whole makes it very difficult to trace clear lines in the various traditions. Nevertheless, I believe that the statements and hypotheses presented in this paper will remain valid in principle, though subject to change in details.

Next to the Italian, the German Josquin tradition is the most important one. German sources alone contain one more motet than all other sources combined. Nearly half of all written and printed copies of Josquin motets are to be found in German manuscripts and prints. In contrast to the situation in Italy, there are only few German sources from Josquin's lifetime in which his motets appear. We can cite no more than four: Berlin, Staatsbibliothek, MS. 40021; St. Gall, Stiftsbibliothek, MS. 463; Munich, Bayerische Staatsbibliothek, Mus. MS. 3154; and Regensburg, Proske-Bibliothek, MS. C 120. Of the remaining fifty-three manuscripts with authentic compositions by Josquin, twenty-four come from the first, eighteen from the second half of the sixteenth century. The dates of eleven manuscripts are unknown. About half of the German manuscripts should be dated after 1550. The situation is similar with regard to printed sources. Fourteen prints were published in the first, thirteen in the second half of the century. With one exception (*Liber selectarum cantionum*, Grimm and Wyrsung, 1520), all German prints are posthumous.

The German Josquin tradition begins about 1520 and grows in the third and fourth decades of the sixteenth century, that is, at the time when German music printing comes into its own and when handwritten sources, too, multiply. Examination of the manuscripts reveals no one particular German centre of the Josquin tradition. The motets are distributed fairly evenly over the repertory of the German sources containing works of both German and foreign composers. The printed Josquin tradition, however, is concentrated in a relatively small group of well-known collections, the publications of Grimm and Wyrsung (1520), Formschneider-Ott (1537 and 1538), Petreius (1538–42), and Montanus and Neuber (1553–64). Only seven manuscripts include more than four authentic Josquin motets.[4] Among the prints, Petreius 1538[6] and Montanus 1559[1] have six motets each; Montanus 1553[4] and 1558[4] have seven each; Grimm and Wyrsung 1520[4], Petreius 1539[9], Montanus 1559[2], and the *Dodekachordon* of Glareanus (1547) have nine motets each; the collections by Formschneider-Ott of 1537[1] and 1538[3] have eleven and thirteen settings, respectively.

Only a small part of the ninety-one authentic motets by Josquin—exactly twenty-one settings—does not appear in German sources. Thus, the greater portion of Josquin's motet oeuvre was known in the sixteenth century in

---

[4] Regensburg, Proske-Bibliothek, MS. C 120 and Nuremberg, Germ. Nationalmuseum, MS. 83795 (Tenor) (5 each); Gotha, Landesbibliothek, MS. Chart. A. 98 (6); Munich, Universitätsbibliothek, MS. 8⁰ 322–325 (7 settings) and MS. 4⁰ Art. 401 (10 settings), Kassel, Landesbibliothek, MS. 4⁰ mus. 24 (13), and St. Gall, Stiftsbibliothek, MS. 463 (15).

Germany, although the popularity of the works varied widely, if the number of their appearances in the sources may be taken as a criterion. Sixty-one motets are found in German prints, fifty-one in German manuscripts. The great majority of settings appears in sources from the first half of the century. In the period before 1550 the prints transmit fifty-one compositions, the manuscripts thirty-seven, including eleven motets not appearing in German printed sources. The prints must be considered as the starting point of the German Josquin tradition. In general, they are more reliable than the manuscripts. They offer five motets[5] of which no other sources exist, fifteen compositions that have not come down in earlier manuscripts and prints, seventy-seven appearances of other motets already known, and fifteen settings, in twenty-two appearances, with dubious or wrong attributions. In comparison, the manuscript sources include no more than two works[6] that are *unica* and two compositions that probably appear for the first time,[7] but they have 136 entries of motets known from earlier sources, and thirty other motets, in thirty-nine appearances, with doubtful or wrong attributions (almost all in sources dated after 1535).[8] The chronological and geographical distance from the point of origin explains the unreliability of many German sources. Moreover, outside Italy Josquin's name was often used to upgrade anonymous settings. Only by considering the exact number of written or printed appearances of each single motet and by comparing the German and the foreign tradition will the real extent of the German Josquin tradition become evident. On the basis of the frequency of appearance, Josquin's motets can be divided into six groups:

Group I (see Table I) contains twenty-two compositions surviving only in German sources, about 25% of the authentic motets (including twelve psalm motets, about half of all psalm settings by Josquin). This seems a peculiar circumstance, because all twenty-two compositions must have been imported. But the base of the German tradition is very small; the twenty-two motets are not widespread in musical sources. Seven motets have one source only, six occur in two sources, seven pieces in three, and only two settings occur in four sources. The prints of Petreius and Montanus and Neuber are the most important sources of this group. However, a large part of the repertory of Montanus and Neuber is taken from the Petreius collections. Most of the German manuscript sources of these *unica* must be considered peripheral to the Josquin tradition. Moreover, all the Josquin motets they transmit belong to this group.[9]

---

[5] 'Christus mortuus est', 'Levavi oculos meos', 'Responde mihi', 'Responsum acceperat', 'Sic Deus dilexit'.

[6] 'Magnificat III. toni', 'Scimus quoniam diligentibus'.

[7] 'De profundis' (no. 47), 'O bone et dulcissime Jesu'.

[8] See the Appendix for a list of the sources used and the Josquin motets contained in them.

[9] Halle, Universitätsbibliothek, MS. Ed. 1147, Appendix; Berlin, Staatsbibliothek, MS.

With the exception of the 'Magnificat III. toni', the works listed in the first group appear relatively late, at the end of the thirties, sometimes not until 1550. This late and peripheral tradition of about a fourth of Josquin's motets may perhaps have something to do with the exceptional character of many of these motets with regard to religious and liturgical practice. The psalm motets are primarily non-liturgical compositions. As to the other pieces—Passion motets, motets for the celebration of the Holy Sacrament and for the Office of the Dead—we must presume that specific circumstances of origin prevented a wider distribution (perhaps they were works with a limited local function). The greater part of this group (16 settings), according to Osthoff, is comprised of late or very late compositions; four are early works,[10] and only two motets date from Josquin's Roman years. Perhaps Josquin's late musical activity, outside Italian musical centres, had an influence on the particular tradition of these motets. How they found their way into German prints and manuscripts is not clear. There must have been Italian, and above all French and Netherlandish, sources that were lost during the political disorders of the third and fourth, and particularly the seventh and eighth decades of the sixteenth century.

Group II (Table II) includes thirteen motets, among them four psalm settings, with a preponderantly German tradition. Generally, the distribution of sources here is more widespread. Outside Germany, almost half of the motets appear in only one source. The number of works from Josquin's middle period is relatively small. Among the non-German sources containing works of this group are Petrucci's early prints of 1502 (*Motetti A*) and 1503 (*Motetti de Passione*) as well as some very late sources from the second half of the century, like the MSS. Cappella Sistina 38 and Leiden 862. MS. Bologna, Civico Museo Bibliografico Musicale, Q 20, which contains several *unica*, shows a strong connection with German sources.[11]

The sixteen motets belonging to Group III (Table III) have an extensive tradition in both German and non-German sources. Among them we find five late and three early works, and eight compositions probably from Josquin's Roman years or shortly thereafter. Four psalm motets belong to this group.

Of the fourteen motets in Group IV (Table IV), all with only a slight

---

40031; Leipzig, Universitätsbibliothek, MS. Thom. 51; Dresden, Sächsische Landesbibliothek, MS. I/D/505 (*olim* Annaberg, St. Annenkirche, MS. 1126); Regensburg, Proske-Bibliothek, MS. A.R. 888.

10 [Edgar Sparks argues that three of these 'early' works are not by Josquin and date from the third or fourth decades of the sixteenth century; see these Proceedings, pp. 353–6. —Ed.]

11 See the discussion of this manuscript in my 'Die Motetten des Andreas de Silva. Studien zur Geschichte der Motette im 16. Jahrhundert' (Habilitations-Schrift, Frankfurt am Main, 1971), in press.

tradition in Germany and most with an extended tradition abroad, a high percentage of ten or eleven settings can be assigned to Josquin's middle period. At most, only three motets are early works, and none dates from Josquin's late period.

Group V (Table V) includes six motets with a slight tradition in general. Here the early works and those from the Roman period predominate. Among the six motets there are two compositions for special occasions: the funeral motet for Louis XII, 'De profundis', and the exceptional 'Absalon fili mi'.

The preponderance of early works is most striking in Group VI (Table VI), which includes twenty-one motets without a German tradition; only two settings seem to have been composed after 1500. With the exception of 'Alma Redemptoris/Ave Regina' and 'Ecce tu pulchra es', these settings appear sparsely even in Italian sources. Again we find motets for special occasions: 'Absolve quaesumus/Requiem' (an *unicum* from a Spanish manuscript), probably composed for the funeral of Philip the Fair, the Marian motet 'Illibata Dei Virgo' with the Josquin acrostic, 'Ut Phoebi radiis', a kind of musical exercise, and the two settings of hymn verses, 'Honor decus', and 'Monstra te esse Matrem', part of the reworking of the Dufay hymn cycle in MS. Cappella Sistina 15, which seems to have had only local use.

The statistical investigation of the German Josquin tradition yields the following conclusions:

1) Aside from some motets for special occasions and the large number of psalm motets in German sources, the type of text set to music is of no particular significance for the German Josquin tradition.

All twenty-three settings of psalm texts appear in German sources, twelve of them exclusively there. The preference for Josquin's psalm motets in German sources results partly from the liturgical reform of German Protestantism. The meaning of the psalm texts and their musical interpretation correspond to the new spiritual orientation of the Protestant service. Martin Luther, a musician and singer himself, had the highest regard for Josquin's music. Moreover, Josquin's motets on psalm texts are mostly late compositions, and Josquin's mature syle, with its emphasis on declamation and on the musical expression of the text, corresponds not only to the ideas that the new religious movement had on the proper relationship between music and the Divine Word, but also to the general musical style of the years in which this repertoire appears in German sources.

2) Aside from the motets in Groups III and V, the number of sources for individual works does not seem to be related to the number of non-German sources. On the other hand, in many cases the German tradition of a single work may be traced to the special character of the first source, from which later copies were made. The interdependence of these sources is a complex

matter and cannot be evaluated until a filiation of all works *and* sources has been carried out. Professor Hoffmann-Erbrecht's paper gives a demonstration of the working methods of filiation.[12]

3) There is a direct correlation between the time of origin of Josquin's motets and their appearance in German sources. Josquin's late compositions (30 of 91) have their most expansive, and frequently their only, tradition in Germany; exactly two-thirds of the sources are of German provenance. The opposite obtains for the early works (28 of 91); here only one-third of the sources comes from Germany. The thirty-three settings of Josquin's middle period tend to be more widely distributed than the early and the late motets, but the non-German sources predominate. It appears that in Germany it was the work of the Roman and above all of the late Josquin that was known and appreciated. There are good reasons for this, some of which we have already hinted at. German editors must have found access to Josquin's later motets easier than to the earlier ones. Moreover, the style developed by Josquin in his late Italian works, with modern harmonies, rhetorical declamation of the text, and simplified polyphonic structure, had become the predominant style throughout Germany. Josquin's motets in German sources usually occur together with a younger repertory, much of which was shaped in emulation of an artist who, in Germany, was considered as the eminent musical innovator, and as a master of the sixteenth century, rather than as a famous but now outmoded Netherlandish composer of the late fifteenth century. At first, German editors of manuscripts and prints seem to have accepted uncritically the available works of the master. Later, however, they concentrated on those late works that exemplified the contemporary style.

Much more work needs to be done to illuminate the history of Josquin's motets. The German reception is not only a very interesting but a substantial part of this history. The Italian sources give us more information about his beginnings as a motet composer; the German sources reflect both the development of his style and the impact of his compositions on the musical life of sixteenth-century Europe.

[12] See these Proceedings, pp. 285–93.

Note to the Tables: The designation of the number of voices is confined to motets set twice, with varying number of parts.

TABLE I

Motets with an exclusively German tradition

		number of sources	date of earliest source	period of composition*
1	Ave verum corpus, 5v. (no. 80)	2	1545	very early
2	Benedicite omnia opera (no. 53)	3	1537	late
3	Caeli enarrant gloriam (no. 61)	3	1538	late
4	Cantate Domino canticum (no. 72)	2	1539	very late
5	Christus mortuus est (no. 87)	1	1564	very late
6	Domine Dominus noster (no. 89)	3	after 1550?	c. 1490
7	Domine exaudi orationem (no. 92)	2	after 1550	last
8	Domine ne projicias me (no. 64)	4	1538	last
9	Dominus regnavit (no. 65)	3	1539	late
10	In Domino confido (no. 73)	3	1538	late?
11	Jubilate Deo (no. 66)	3	1539	last
12	Levavi oculos meos (no. 70)	1	1539	late?
13	Magnificat III. toni (no. 77)	1	c. 1490/1500	early Roman
14	Mirabilia testimonia tua (no. 69)	2	1539	late?
15	Nesciens Mater (no. 71)	2	1545	early
16	Qui habitat in adjutorio, 24v.	4	1542	late?
17	Responde mihi (no. 75)	1	1545	late
18	Responsum acceperat (no. 85)	1	1545	very early
19	Scimus quoniam (unpubl.)	1	c. 1530	early
20	Sic Deus dilexit mundum (no. 86)	1	1564	very late
21	Stetit autem Salomon (no. 58)	2	1538	last
22	Usquequo Domine (no. 60)	3	1538	late?

* 'Early' indicates the years at the court of Milan (1473–9) up to the Roman period (1486 to at least 1494), the years at the Cathedral of Milan (1459–72) not yet having been drawn into the chronology of Josquin's works. 'Late' indicates the time after the year in Ferrara (1503–4).

TABLE II

Motets with a preponderantly German tradition

		German sources	other sources	period of composition
1	Ave verum corpus, 2–3v. (no. 12)	4	1	early Milanese
2	De profundis (no. 47)	7	2	late
3	Domine ne in furore (no. 59)	4	1	late?
4	Domine non secundum (no. 13)	7	3	1486–92?
5	In exitu Israel (no. 51)	4	2	late
6	In illo tempore stetit Jesus (no. 55)	4	2	early
7	Laudate pueri (no. 68)	3	1	late
8	Magnus es tu Domine (no. 19)	6	1	l.p. early; 2.p. somewhat later
9	O Virgo prudentissima (no. 45)	5	2	Roman
10	Veni Sancte Spiritus (no. 49)	11	2	Roman
11	Victimae paschali laudes, 4v. (no. 26)	3	1	early
12	Videte omnes populi (mostly as Haec dicit Dominus)	10	2	last
13	Virgo prudentissima (no. 25)	4	1	1490–1500

TABLE III

Motets with an extended tradition in German and foreign sources

	German sources	other sources	period of composition
1 Ave Maria...Virgo serena (no. 1)	11	5	before 1500?★
2 Benedicta es caelorum Regina (no. 46)	9	13	1500–10
3 Domine ne in furore tuo (no. 39)	6	4	Roman?
4 Huc me sydereo (no. 32)	4	9	late Roman?
5 In principio erat verbum (no. 56)	5	4	last
6 Inviolata, integra et casta (no. 42)	7	11	Roman
7 Liber generationis (no. 15)	5	8	Roman
8 Memor esto (no. 31)	6	7	1498–1503
9 Mente tota (5.p. of Vultum tuum deprecabuntur, no. 24)	4	4	early
10 Miserere mei, Deus (no. 37)	9	7	1501–5
11 Missus est Gabriel, 5v. (no. 40)	3	5	early
12 Pater noster—Ave Maria (no. 50)	10	9	late
13 Planxit autem David (no. 20)	3	4	before 1504 (Roman?)
14 Praeter rerum seriem (no. 33)	12	14	early Roman
15 Qui habitat in adjutorio, 4v. (no. 52)	7	4	late
16 Stabat Mater (no. 36)	9	15	early

★ See also above, pp. 68–9.

TABLE IV

Motets with a comparatively slight German tradition

	German sources	other sources	period of composition
1 Ave Christe immolate (= Ave caro Christi cara) (no. 76)★	1	3	late
2 Ave nobilissima creatura (no. 34)	1	3	early
3 Ecce Maria genuit (no. 9)	1	4	1490–1500
4 Gaude Virgo, Mater Christi (no. 23)	1	3	late Milanese or early Roman
5 Germinavit radix Jesse (no. 8)	1	3	1490–1500
6 Magnificat IV. toni (no. 78)	1	3	early Roman
7 Missus est Gabriel, 4v. (no. 17)	1	12	1490–1500
8 O admirabile commercium (no. 5)	1	5	1490–1500
9 Paratum cor meum (no. 67)	1	3	early or early Roman
10 Quando natus est (no. 6)	1	5	1490–1500
11 Rubum quem viderat (no. 7)	1	5	1490–1500
12 Salve Regina, 5v. (no. 48)	1	10	about 1500
13 Tu solus qui facis (no. 14)	1	11	early
14 Virgo salutiferi (no. 35)	2	7	Roman

★ [See Edgar H. Sparks, *The Music of Noel Bauldeweyn* (New York, 1972), pp. 98–103.—Ed.]

TABLE V

Motets with a generally slight tradition

	German sources	other sources	period of composition
1 Absalon fili mi (Suppl., no. 5)	2	1	1497*
2 De profundis, 5v. (no. 90)	2	2	last (1515)
3 Lectio actuum apostolorum (no. 41)	2	2	early
4 Misericordias Domini (no. 43)	2	3	Roman?
5 O bone et dulcissime Jesu (no. 96)	2	3	before 1500?
6 Regina caeli (Suppl., no. 3)	1	1	early

* This motet has been brought into precise relationship with the assassination of Alexander VI's oldest son in 1497; see Edward E. Lowinsky, 'Josquin des Prez and Ascanio Sforza', *Congresso Internazionale sul Duomo di Milano, Atti*, ed. M. L. Gatti Perer (Milan, 1969), ii, pp. 20–21.

TABLE VI

Motets without a German tradition

	sources	period of composition
1 Absolve quaesumus/Requiem (no. 82)	1	1506?
2 Alma Redemptoris Mater (no. 38)	3	1490–1500
3 Alma Redemptoris/Ave Regina (no. 21)	8	early
4 Ave Maria... benedicta tu (no. 2)	2	early
5 Descendi in ortum meum (Suppl., no. 6)	3	early
6 Ecce tu pulchra es (no. 30)	9	Roman?
7 Factum est autem (no. 16)	2	Roman
8 Homo quidam fecit (no. 28)	3	early Roman or before
9 Honor decus (Suppl., no. 2)	1	Roman
10 Illibata Dei Virgo (no. 27)	2	early*
11 In illo tempore assumpsit (no. 79)	2	late (Ferrara?)
12 Inter natos mulierum (no. 84)	3	early
13 Mittit ad Virginem (no. 3)	3	early
14 Monstra te esse Matrem (Suppl., no. 1)	1	Roman
15 O Domine Jesu Christe (no. 10)	1	early
16 O Virgo virginum (no. 83)	5	early Roman
17 Qui velatus facie fuisti (no. 11)	1	early
18 Salve Regina, 4v. (no. 95)	2	early Roman
19 Ut Phoebi radiis (no. 22)	2	very early
20 Victimae paschali, 6v. (no. 81)	4	early
21 Vultum tuum deprecabuntur (no. 24; cf. Table III, no. 9)	2	early

* [For arguments in favour of a later dating, see Myroslaw Antonowycz's article in these Proceedings, pp. 545–58.—Ed.]

Appendix I

German Sources Containing Motets by Josquin[13]

A. MANUSCRIPTS

Augsburg, Staats- und Stadtbibliothek, MS. 142a (olim 18).
  Missus est Gabriel 4v.
Basel, Universitätsbibliothek, MS. F.X. 22–24; 1547.
  Ave verum corpus 2–3v.
Berlin, Preussische Staatsbibliothek, Mus. MS. 40013 (lost); c. 1540.
  Ave Maria...Virgo serena
  Domine non secundum
  Haec dicit Dominus (= Videte omnes populi)
  Pater noster
Berlin, Staatsbibliothek der Stiftung Preussischer Kulturbesitz, Mus. MS. 40021; 1490/1500.
  Magnificat III. toni
  Mente tota (= 5. p. of Vultum tuum deprecabuntur)
Berlin, Preussische Staatsbibliothek, MS. 40031 (lost).
  Domine, ne projicias me
Budapest, National Széchényi Library, MS. Bártfa 22; completed after 1550.
  Magnificat VII. toni (dubious)
Budapest, National Széchényi Library, MS. Bártfa 23; completed after 1550.
  Date siceram (= Claudin)
Dresden, Sächsische Landesbibliothek, Mus. MS. I/D/3 (olim B. 1270); c. 1548.
  De profundis 5v.
  Miserere mei Deus
  Qui regis Israel (dubious)
Dresden, Sächsische Landesbibliothek, Mus. MS. I/D/6 (olim Oels 529); c. 1560/70.
  De profundis 4v. (no. 47)
  Domine, ne in furore (no. 59)
  In exitu Israel
  Jubilate Deo
  Tribulatio et angustia (= Verdelot)
Dresden, Sächsische Landesbibliothek, MS. I/D/505 (olim Annaberg, St. Annenkirche, Cod. 1126); end of the 1520s.
  Scimus quoniam diligentibus
Dresden, Sächsische Landesbibliothek, MS. I/D/506 (olim Annaberg, St. Annenkirche, Cod. 1248); end of the 1520s.
  Liber generationis
  Planxit autem David
Dresden, Sächsische Landesbibliothek, Cod. Glashütte 5; 1583–8.
  Pater noster

---

[13] The Appendix is based on sources given in the *Werken* and additional sources noted by Osthoff, *Josquin Desprez*, passim. Pieces called 'dubious' are those listed by Osthoff under 'Werke ohne bisher nachgewiesene abweichende Autorangaben' (ii, pp. 294–7); erroneous attributions to Josquin are followed by the name given in other sources ('Werke mit widersprechenden Autorangaben', ibid., pp. 289–93).

Different settings of the same text are identified by reference to the numbers under which they appear in the *Werken*. If a different setting carries no number, it is not published in the Josquin edition, because of attribution to another composer.

Praeter rerum seriem
Veni Sancte Spiritus
Dresden, Sächsische Landesbibliothek, Mus. MS. Grimma 54.
Congratulamini (= Richafort)
Dresden, Sächsische Landesbibliothek, Mus. MS. Grimma 55.
Veni Sancte Spiritus
Dresden, Sächsische Landesbibliothek, MS. Pirna VIII; second half of the sixteenth century.
Veni Sancte Spiritus
Eisenach, Stadtarchiv, Cod. s.s. ('Kantorenbuch'); *c.* 1550.
Sancta Trinitas unus Deus (= Févin)
Gotha, Landesbibliothek, MS. Chart. A. 98; 1545.
Ave Maria... Virgo serena
Haec dicit Dominus (= Videte omnes populi)
Pater noster
Praeter rerum seriem
Qui habitat in adjutorio 4v.
Veni Sancte Spiritus
Halle, Universitätsbibliothek, MS. Ed. 1147, Appendix.
Domine Dominus noster
Heilbronn, Gymnasialbibliothek, MS. IV, 2 and V, 2.
Qui habitat 24v.
Heilbronn, Gymnasialbibliothek, MS. XCII, 3–XCVI, 3.
Domine, ne in furore (no. 59)
Domine, ne in furore (no. 39)
Domine, ne projicias me
Usquequo Domine
Kassel, Murhard'sche und Landesbibliothek, MS. 4⁰ Mus. 24; after 1550.
Beati omnes 6v. (= Champion)
Bonitatem fecisti (= Carpentras)
Caeli enarrant gloriam Dei
Clamavi: Ad Dominum (dubious)
De profundis 4v. (no. 47)
De profundis 4v. (no. 91; dubious)
De profundis 5v.
Deus in adjutorium meum (= Senfl)
Domine Dominus noster
Domine exaudi
Domine, ne in furore (no. 39)
Domine, ne in furore (2. *p.*, Discedite) (= Verdelot)
Domine, quis habitabit (dubious)
Domini est terra (= Vinders or Benedictus)
Illumina oculos meos (dubious)
In Domino confido
In exitu Israel
Lauda Jerusalem (= Maître Jan)
Laudate pueri
Memor esto
Miserere mei Deus
Qui habitat 4v.
Qui habitat 24v.

Kassel, Murhard'sche und Landesbibliothek, MS. 4⁰ Mus. 38; *c.* 1566.
    Inviolata, integra 12v. (dubious)
Königsberg, Staats- und Universitätsbibliothek, MS. 1740 (lost); 1537–43.
    Alleluja. Laudate Dominum (dubious)
    Ite in mundum (dubious)
    Petre, tu es pastor omnium (dubious)
    Regina caeli 4v.
Leipzig, Universitätsbibliothek, MS. Thom. 49; 1558.
    Beati omnes 6v. (= Champion)
    Conserva me (= M. Wolff)
    Laudate Dominum omnes gentes 16v. (dubious)
    Magnificat IV. toni
    Magnificat VII. toni (dubious)
    Pater noster
    Tribulatio et angustia (= Verdelot)
Leipzig, Universitätsbibliothek, MS. Thom. 51.
    Dominus regnavit
Munich, Bayerische Staatsbibliothek, Mus. MS. 10; first half of the sixteenth century.
    In principio erat verbum
    Liber generationis
    Miserere mei Deus
    Qui habitat 4v.
Munich, Bayerische Staatsbibliothek, Mus. MS. 12; first half of the sixteenth century.
    Pater noster
    Stabat Mater
Munich, Bayerische Staatsbibliothek, Mus. MS. 19; first half of the sixteenth century.
    Ave Maria...Virgo serena
    Memor esto
    Mente tota (= 5. *p.* of Vultum tuum deprecabuntur)
Munich, Bayerische Staatsbibliothek. Mus. MS. 34; first half of the sixteenth century.
    Salve Regina 5v.
Munich, Bayerische Staatsbibliothek, Mus. MS. 41.
    Ave Maria...Virgo serena (with 2 added voices)
    O bone et dulcissime Jesu
Munich, Bayerische Staatsbibliothek, Mus. MS. 260.
    Per illud ave (2. *p.* of Benedicta es caelorum Regina)
Munich, Bayerische Staatsbibliothek, Mus. MS. 1536; before 1583.
    Benedicta es caelorum Regina
    In nomine Jesu (= Mouton)
    Lugebat David (dubious)
    O Virgo prudentissima
    Pater noster
    Tulerunt Dominum meum 8v. (= Lugebat David) (dubious)
    Veni Sancte Spiritus
Munich, Bayerische Staatsbibliothek, Mus. MS. 3154; *c.* 1520.
    Ave Maria...Virgo serena
Munich, Universitätsbibliothek, MS. 8⁰ 322–325 (olim Cim. 44ª); 1527.
    Ave Maria...Virgo serena
    Ave verum corpus 2–3v.
    Domine, non secundum
    Magnus es tu, Domine

Memor esto 4v.
Tulerunt Dominum 4v. (= Michael de Verona)
Victimae paschali laudes 4v.
Virgo prudentissima
Munich, Universitätsbibliothek, MS. 326 (olim Cim. 44^b); 1543.
Ave Maria...Virgo serena
Inviolata, integra et casta 5v.
Munich, Universitätsbibliothek, MS. 327 (olim Cim. 44^b); 1543.
Miserere mei Deus
Stabat Mater
Munich, Universitätsbibliothek, 4⁰ Art. 401, MS Appendix (olim Cim. 44^i); 1536–40.
Ave nobilissima creatura
Benedicta es caelorum Regina
Circumdederunt me (= Haec dicit Dominus and Videte omnes populi)
Lectio actuum apostolorum
Missus est Gabriel 5v.
O Virgo prudentissima
Pater noster
Praeter rerum seriem
Stabat Mater
Verbum bonum et suave (dubious)
Virgo salutiferi
Nuremberg, Germanisches Nationalmuseum, MS. 83795 (Tenor); *c.* 1539.
Ave Maria...Virgo serena
Domine non secundum
Haec dicit Dominus (= Videte omnes populi)
Pater noster
Veni Sancte Spiritus
Nuremberg, Germanisches Nationalmuseum, MS. 83795 (Bass); before 1548.
Ave Maria...Virgo serena
Domine non secundum
Haec dicit Dominus (= Videte omnes populi)
Veni Sancte Spiritus
Regensburg, Proske-Bibliothek, MS. A.R. 786/837; 1578.
Lugebat David (dubious)
Regensburg, Proske-Bibliothek, MS. A.R. 840; *c.* 1570.
In principio erat verbum
Regensburg, Proske-Bibliothek, MS. A.R. 852.
Congratulamini (= Richafort)
Regensburg, Proske-Bibliothek, MS. A.R. 863–70; second half of the sixteenth century.
Qui habitat 4v.
Regensburg, Proske-Bibliothek, MS. A.R. 879; 1571.
Veni Sancte Spiritus
Regensburg, Proske-Bibliothek, MS. A.R. 888; 1577.
Stetit autem
Regensburg, Proske-Bibliothek, MS. A.R. 891–92.
Inviolata, integra et casta 5v.
Regensburg, Proske-Bibliothek, MS. A.R. 893.
Huc me sydereo
Regensburg, Proske-Bibliothek, MS. A.R. 940/41; before 1557/60.
In principio erat verbum

Qui habitat 4v.

Regensburg, Proske-Bibliothek, MS. B. 211–15; *c.* 1538.
    Clamavi: Ad Dominum (dubious)
    Haec dicit Dominus (= Videte omnes populi)
    Magnus es tu, Domine

Regensburg, Proske-Bibliothek, MS. B. 220–22; *c.* 1538.
    Per illud ave (= *2. p.* of Benedicta es caelorum Regina)

Regensburg, Proske-Bibliothek, MS. C. 120; before 1522/3.
    De profundis (no. 47)
    Domine, ne in furore (no. 39)
    Inviolata, integra et casta 5v.
    Mente tota (= *5. p.* of Vultum tuum deprecabuntur)
    Praeter rerum seriem

Rostock, Universitätsbibliothek, MS. Mus. Saec. XVI–49; 1566.
    Te Deum (alternatim; dubious)
    Te Deum (= de Silva)

St. Gall, Stiftsbibliothek, MS. 463–464; 1517–20.
    Ave Maria...Virgo serena
    Ave verum corpus 2–3v.
    Bonitatem fecisti (= Carpentras)
    De profundis 4v. (no. 47)
    Domine, non secundum
    Huc me sydereo
    Inviolata, integra et casta 5v.
    Magnus es tu, Domine
    Memor esto
    Miserere mei Deus
    O bone et dulcissime Jesu
    Planxit autem David
    Praeter rerum seriem
    Tu solus qui facis
    Victimae paschali laudes 4v.
    Virgo prudentissima

Stuttgart, Württembergische Landesbibliothek, Cod. mus. 25; *c.* 1542.
    In illo tempore stetit Jesus

Stuttgart, Württembergische Landesbibliothek; Cod. mus. 36; 1548–50.
    Veni Sancte Spiritus

Vienna, Oesterreichische Nationalbibliothek, MS. Suppl. Mus. 15500; 1544.
    Jubilate Deo
    Magnus es tu, Domine

Weimar, Stadtkirchenbibliothek (currently Jena, Universitätsbibliothek), Cod. B; *c.* 1542.
    Haec dicit Dominus (= Videte omnes populi)

Wrocław, Biblioteka Uniwersytecka, MS. Brieg K. 40; second half of the sixteenth century.
    Praeter rerum seriem

Wrocław, Biblioteka Uniwersytecka, MS. Brieg K. 52; second half of the sixteenth century.
    Praeter rerum seriem

Wrocław, City Library, MS. 5; second half of the sixteenth century.
    Congratulamini (= Richafort)

In illo tempore stetit Jesus

Wrocław, City Library, MS. 11; second half of the sixteenth century.

Praeter rerum seriem

Stabat Mater

Zwickau, Ratsschulbibliothek, MS. XXXIII, 34 (Vollhardt, no. 19); end of the sixteenth century.

Stabat Mater

Zwickau, Ratsschulbibliothek, MS. LXXIII (Vollhardt, no. 4); before 1547.

Verbum caro factum est (= Benedictus)

Zwickau, Ratsschulbibliothek, MS. LXXIV, 1 (Vollhardt, no. 11); second half of the sixteenth century.

Ecce Dominus veniet (= Senfl)

Haec dicit Dominus (= Videte omnes populi)

Zwickau, Ratsschulbibliothek, MS. LXXXI, 2 (Vollhardt, no. 16); first half of the sixteenth century.

Domine, ne in furore (no. 39)

Zwickau, Ratsschulbibliothek, MS. XCIV, 1 (Vollhardt, no. 9); 1590.

Praeter rerum seriem

Tulerunt Dominum 8v. (= Lugebat David) (dubious)

B. PRINTED EDITIONS[14]

1520[4] *Liber selectarum cantionum*, Grimm & Wyrsung (Augsburg).

Benedicta es caelorum Regina

De profundis 4v. (no. 47)

Inviolata, integra et casta 5v.

Lectio actuum

Miserere mei Deus

Missus est Gabriel 5v. (attr. to Mouton)

O Virgo prudentissima

Praeter rerum seriem

Stabat Mater

1537[1] *Novum et insigne opus musicum*, Formschneider-Ott (Nuremberg).

Benedicite omnia opera

Benedicta es caelorum Regina

Congratulamini (= Richafort)

Haec dicit Dominus (= Videte omnes populi)

In exitu Israel

Miserere mei Deus

Misericordias Domini

Pater noster

Praeter rerum seriem

Quam pulchra es (= Mouton)

Qui habitat in adjutorio 4v.

Tribulatio et angustia (= Verdelot)

Veni Sancte Spiritus

Virgo prudentissima (attr. to Isaac)

1538[3] *Secundus tomus novi operis musici*, Formschneider-Ott (Nuremberg).

Deus pacis reduxit (= Stoltzer)

[14] The printed publications are listed in chronological order with RISM numbers.

Ecce Maria genuit
Germinavit radix Jesse
Gloria laus et honor (=Brumel)
Huc me sydereo
In illo tempore stetit Jesus
In principio erat verbum
Inviolata, integra et casta 5v.
Liber generationis
Magnus es tu, Domine (attr. to Heinr. Finck)
O admirabile commercium
O Virgo prudentissima
Quando natus est
Rubum quem
Stabat Mater

1538[6] *Tomus primus psalmorum selectorum*, Petreius (Nuremberg).
Beati quorum remissae (dubious)
Caeli enarrant gloriam Dei
Domine ne in furore (no. 39)
Domine ne in furore (no. 59)
Domine ne projicias me
In Domino confido
Judica me Deus (= A. Caen)
Qui regis Israel (dubious)
Usquequo Domine

1538[7] *Modulationes aliquot*, Petreius (Nuremberg).
Dilectus Deo et hominibus (= Ant. Févin)
Stabat Mater
Stetit autem Salomon

1539[9] *Tomus secundus psalmorum selectorum*, Petreius (Nuremberg).
Cantate Domino canticum
De profundis 4v. (no. 47)
De profundis 4v. (no. 91; dubious)
Dominus regnavit
Jubilate Deo
Laudate pueri
Levavi oculos meos
Memor esto
Mirabilia testimonia tua
Paratum cor meum

1540[7] *Selectissimae necnon familiarissimae cantiones*, Kriesstein (Augsburg).
Absalon fili mi

1542[6] *Tomus tertius psalmorum selectorum*, Petreius (Nuremberg).
Qui habitat in adjutorio 24v.

1542[12] *Sacrorum hymnorum liber primus*, Rhau (Wittenberg).
Pange lingua (dubious)

1545[2] *Concentus octo, sex, quinque & quatuor vocum*, Ulhard (Augsburg).
Ave verum corpus 5v.
Responde mihi

1545[3] (= 1546[5]) *Cantiones septem, sex et quinque vocum*, Kriesstein (Augsburg).
Nesciens Mater
Responsum acceperat

1545[6]   *Officiorum . . . Tomus primus*, Rhau (Wittenberg).
      Per illud ave (= *2. p.* of Benedicta es caelorum Regina)

1547[1]   Glareanus, *Dodekachordon* (Basel).
      Ave Maria . . . Virgo serena
      Ave verum corpus 2–3v.
      De profundis 4v. (no. 47)
      Domine non secundum
      Liber generationis
      Magnus es tu, Domine
      Per illud ave (= *2. p.* of Benedicta es caelorum Regina) (attr. to Mouton)
      Planxit autem David
      Victimae paschali laudes 4v.

1549[16]   *Diphona amoena et florida*, Montanus & Neuber (Nuremberg).
      Domine non secundum

1553   G. Faber, *Musices practicae erotematum libri II* (Basel).
      Stabat Mater

1553[4]   *Psalmorum selectorum . . . Tomus primus*, Montanus & Neuber (Nuremberg).
      Beati quorum remissae (dubious)
      Caeli enarrant gloriam Dei
      Domine Dominus noster
      Domine ne in furore (no. 39)
      Domine ne in furore (no. 59)
      In Domino confido
      Judica me Deus (= A. Caen)
      Miserere mei Deus
      Usquequo Domine

1553[5]   *Tomus secundus Psalmorum selectorum*, Montanus & Neuber (Nuremberg).
      Cantate Domino canticum novum
      Deus in nomine tuo (= Carpentras)
      Domine ne projicias me
      Dominus regnavit
      Laudate pueri
      Quam dilecta tabernacula (= Certon; attr. to Josquin in altus only)
      Qui regis Israel (dubious)

1553[6]   *Tomus tertius Psalmorum selectorum*, Montanus & Neuber (Nuremberg).
      Benedicite omnia opera
      Domine exaudi orationem meam
      Mirabilia testimonia tua

1554[10]   *Evangelia dominicorum et festorum dierum*, Montanus & Neuber (Nuremberg).
      In principio erat verbum
      Tulerunt Dominum 8v. (= Lugebat David) (dubious)

1558[4]   *Novum et insigne opus musicum*, Montanus & Neuber (Nuremberg).
      Benedicta es caelorum Regina
      Haec dicit Dominus (= Videte omnes populi)
      Huc me sydereo
      In nomine Jesu (= Mouton)
      O Virgo prudentissima
      Pater noster
      Praeter rerum seriem
      Veni Sancte Spiritus

1559[1]   *Secunda pars magni operis musici*, Montanus & Neuber (Nuremberg).
          In illo tempore stetit Jesus
          Inviolata, integra et casta 5v.
          Miserere mei Deus
          Missus est Gabriel 5v. (attr. to Mouton)
          Stabat Mater
          Virgo salutiferi
1559[2]   *Tertia pars magni operis musici*, Montanus & Neuber (Nuremberg).
          Absalon fili mi
          Benedicite omnia opera
          In exitu Israel
          Liber generationis
          Memor esto
          Mente tota (= 5. *p.* of Vultum tuum deprecabuntur)
          Misericordias Domini
          Quam pulchra es (= Mouton)
          Qui habitat in adjutorio 4v.
          Tribulatio et angustia (= Verdelot)
          Virgo prudentissima (attr. to Isaac)
1563   Wilphlingseder, *Erotemata Musices Practicae* (Nuremberg).
          Gaude Virgo Mater Christi (only a short section)
1564[1]   *Thesaurus musicus*, Montanus & Neuber (Nuremberg).
          Lugebat David (dubious)
1564[3]   *Thesauri musici tomus tertius*, Montanus & Neuber (Nuremberg).
          Christus mortuus est
          In nomine Jesu (= Mouton)
          Sic Deus dilexit mundum
1564[5]   *Thesauri musici tomus quintus*, Montanus & Neuber (Nuremberg).
          Ave Christe immolate (= Ave caro Christi cara)
1568[7]   *Cantiones triginta selectissimae*, Neuber (Nuremberg).
          Ave verum corpus 5v.
          Qui habitat in adjutorio 24v.

Josquin in Czech Sources of the Second Half of the Sixteenth Century

JITKA SNÍŽKOVÁ

Josquin—this 'genius of sparkling musical ideas and overflowing musicality', as the theorist Glareanus[1] put it—had a deeper influence in Bohemia than it would appear at first glance. His music penetrated into Czech church brotherhoods and into the chapels of the Calixtine churches in Hradec Králové, Rokycany, Klatovy, and other Czech towns. His works were copied into Czech manuscripts, together with native compositions.

Josquin's impact on Czech musical culture expressed itself in several ways, both direct and indirect. Direct documentation is provided by the presence of his compositions in Czech sources, most of which survive in fragmentary state. Indirect documentation exists in references to Josquin in Czech musical theory and in his influence on music by Czech authors.

The great majority of polyphonic music in Bohemia has been preserved in part-books that are mere remnants of complete sets; they may contain detailed specification as to the nature of the composition and sometimes the author's name, but we are unable to offer a complete score.[2] However, a few sets of part-books have been preserved complete.[3] Most Czech polyphonic music was destroyed in the following century.[4] The church brotherhoods, who performed this polyphony, were Calixtine in character,[5] and

---

[1] Helmuth Christian Wolff, *Die Musik der alten Niederländer* (Leipzig, 1956), p. 58. Heinrich Glarean, *Dodekachordon* (Basel, 1547), p. 362.

[2] E. Trolda, *Kapitoly o české mensurální hudbě* [Contribution to Czech Mensural Music] (Cyrill, 1933), pp. 27–30. Trolda's scores are housed in the National Museum (Music Department, sign. XXVIII E 54)—Maršálek/Quercertus; for a list of their contents, see Alexandr Buchner, *Hudební sbírka Emiliána Troldy* [The Music Collection of Emilián Troldy] (Prague, 1954), p. 75. K. Konrád, *Dějiny posvátného zpěvu staročeského* [A History of Czech Church Music] (Prague, 1893); J. Pohanka, *Dějiny české hudby v příkladech* [A History of Czech Music in Examples] (Prague, 1958), pp. 52–3.

[3] J. Snížková, *Česká vokální polyfonie* [Czech Vocal Polyphony] (Prague, 1969).

[4] J. Snížková, 'Notovaný zlomek ze Zámrsku' [Fragment from Zámrsk], *Opus musicum* (Brno, 1971), pp. 16–17.

[5] [The Calixtines (from *calix*, chalice), also called Utraquists, were the conservative

in the seventeenth century, when Bohemia was forcibly re-Catholicized, religious books written in Czech and songs to Czech words were banned.

The incompleteness of the surviving sources obstructs our endeavour to draw up a complete catalogue of Josquin's music in Czech sources. However, we can learn much even from the remaining part-books. I present here a survey of those compositions of Josquin that were accessible to me in the museums and archives in Bohemia. At the present time no list exists of these sources or of their contents, with the sole exception of the manuscripts in the Museum of Hradec Králové.[6] Undoubtedly, there are other sources that have not yet come to light.

The great popularity which Josquin enjoyed in Bohemia is documented by a copy of the 'Pater noster', carrying his name, in Hradec Králové, Museum, MS. II A 22a, pp. 56–9. Here we have the extraordinary case of the Latin prayer appearing with a Czech translation beneath it (see Pls. 38–39). The Czech text is written in red ink, as is the title and Josquin's name. The style of the handwriting indicates that the piece was copied in the sixteenth century, the characters being the same as those in other motets in the Czech language. The single voice remaining, the first tenor, is found together with the works of various Czech authors—mostly Jiří Rychnovský and Jan Simonides Montanus—whose motets are written in Latin as well as in Czech.

It is not accidental that only the first part of the motet was translated into Czech. The *secunda pars*, a setting of the prayer 'Ave Maria', does not carry a Czech translation. This corresponds to the Calixtine tendency not to extol the Virgin Mary, as we are informed by the sixteenth-century New-Utraquist Agenda of Benešov.[7]

Two voices of Josquin's 'Stabat Mater' are found in the MS. A V 22a, b of the Rokycany Church Archive. The incipit of the *secunda pars*, 'Christe verbum, fons amoris', indicates that the piece was probably copied from the *Novum et insigne opus musicum*, either the edition by Ott (RISM 1538³) or by Montanus and Neuber (RISM 1559¹).[8] The superius *prima vox* and superius *secunda vox* of the same motet also occur anonymously in the MS. II A 26a, b of Hradec Králové, Museum. The superius *secunda vox*, with the

---

faction of the Hussites in Bohemia. They insisted on communion in both kinds, bread *and* wine (*sub utraque specie*), but otherwise agreed with the chief tenets of Roman Catholic dogma.—Ed.]

[6] J. Černý, *Soupis hudebních rukopisů muzea v Hradci Králové* [Catalogue of the Musical Manuscripts of the Museum at Hradec Kralové] (Prague, 1966), p. 235: Josquin legacies.

[7] F. Hrejsa, 'Z rukopisů muzejních, Benešovská agenda novoutraquistická' [From Museum Manuscripts: New Utraquist Agenda of Benešov], *Časopis Českého Musea* (1918), p. 59.

[8] The voices are the superius and another part in the treble clef, apparently an added sixth part (see the appendix).

original text in the *secunda pars*, 'Eya Mater fons amoris', is to be found in a MS. appendix to the print II A 41 of the Hradec Králové Museum.[9]

'Praeter rerum seriem' also enjoyed a certain popularity in Czech sources. The second bass part is contained in Hradec Králové, Museum, MS. II A 29, p. 424. In the Rokycany Church Archive the superius and first bass are found in MS. A V 22a, b. Josquin's motet was used as model for a six-part Mass by the Czech composer, Pavel Spongopeus Jistebnický. Only two voices, tenor and bass, survive in two part-books of the Museum at Klatovy, where in 1594 it was listed as number 43, sign. 75–76 (see Pl. 40). The Mass has the following title:

Officium super Praeter rerum seriem VI vocum Josquini
Paulus Spongopeus Gistebnicenus

The Mass Ordinary, as was customary in Czech Calixtine Masses, has only the *Kyrie*, *Gloria*, and *Credo* (with a four-part *Crucifixus*). Pavel Spongopeus Jistebnický was a Czech composer born at Jistebnice around 1550; he died at Kutná Hora in 1619.[10] His extensive oeuvre is dispersed in separate part-books. This is the reason why we have not yet found—in contrast to Jiří Rychnovský and Jan Traian Turnovský—any complete work of his, although we know him to have been one of the most productive Czech polyphonic composers. He symbolizes the fate of Czech Renaissance polyphony in its upsurge and its annihilation in the period following the battle of the White Mountain.[11]

Josquin's impact on Czech music cannot be traced to a direct 'school'; his influence, as elsewhere in Europe, was so universal that—as Helmuth Osthoff puts it—it is almost impossible to specify a clear-cut Josquin 'school'.[12]

The admiration for Josquin's work is illustrated by the fact that in 1561 a Czech theorist, probably the composer Jan Facilis Boleslavský, published a theoretical work in Czech, *Muzyka*, under the name of Jan Josquin. It is an important treatise for the development of music in the Unity of Czech Brethren.[13]

[9] This is the *quinta pars* part-book of Ott's *Novum et insigne opus musicum* (RISM 1537[1]).
[10] *Československy hudebni slovník* [The Czechoslovak Musical Dictionary], ii (Prague, 1965), p. 581.
[11] [The White Mountain (Czech, Bílá Hora) was the scene of the battle on 8 November 1620 in which the Catholic forces of Maximilian I, Duke of Bavaria, under the command of the Count of Tilly, defeated the Bohemian Protestants under Frederick IV; Bohemia lost its independence.—Ed.]
[12] Helmuth Osthoff, art. 'Josquin Desprez', *MGG*, vii, col. 200.
[13] Copy in the National Museum, Prague (sign. NM F 24). Facsimile of the title page in Åke Davidsson, *Bibliographie der musiktheoretischen Drucke des 16. Jahrhunderts* (Baden-Baden, 1962), pl. 12. See Otakar Hostinský, *Jan Blahoslav a Jan Josquin* (Prague, 1896). The identification of the author was made by Ivan Vávra; see his essay on 'Autor t.zv.

In contrast to the secular preoccupations of European courts, the intellectual climate in Bohemia was strongly spiritual in character. The religious confraternities included in their repertory works of Western European composers, including those of Josquin, as well as compositions by native composers. The economic basis of the church brotherhoods could not be compared to the professional, financially secure chapels of other European countries. They had no funds to pay their singers; everyone participated voluntarily in the faith that they were serving God.[14] Nowadays we can only wonder at the extensive polyphonic repertory that these choirs performed. To judge from the remaining sources, Josquin's works were much in demand, even at the very end of the sixteenth century, when the singers of Rudolph's chapel performed in Prague (Rudolph was King of Bohemia from 1575 to 1611).[15]

The popularity of Josquin's work in Bohemia dates back to at least 1505, for Josquin's 'Christum ducem' is found in a manuscript bought by Johannes Franus in that year.[16] Josquin's music, intermingling late-Gothic elements[17] with compositional procedures of the Renaissance, must have been dear to the Czech Calixtine soul even in the sixteenth century, for Calixtine culture intentionally clung to the stylistic procedures of the Gothic period. This is characteristic for Bohemian church architecture as well as the primitive polyphony recorded as late as the sixteenth century in Czech cantionals.[18] No wonder, therefore, that even in the second half of the sixteenth century, Czech composers used some of the contrapuntal techniques cultivated by Josquin. The following procedures seem to derive from the music of Josquin and his contemporaries:

1) The syllabic recitation of the text, increasingly favoured by Josquin,

---

Josquinovy Muziky' [The Author of the so-called Josquin-Music], *Miscelanea musicologica*, xi (Prague, 1959), pp. 35–59. Jan Josquin, who can be traced in Mladá Boleslav in Bohemia in 1555, was inscribed at the University of Wittenberg on 30 April 1563 as Johannes Josquinus Boleslavensis. A composition of his for four voices, 'Když jsi v štěstí', is printed in the collection of Václav Dobřenský; see Jitka Snížková, *Musica polyphonica Bohemiae* (Prague, 1958), pp. 86–7.

14 L. F. Miškovský, *The Unitas Fratrum* (Prague, 1928), pp. 3, 4, 5–8.

15 V. Helfert, 'Dvůr Rudolfův' [Rudolph's Court Chapel], *Co daly naše země Evropě* [What Our Lands Gave to Europe] (Prague, 1940), p. 146; Jan Racek, *Kryštof Harant z Polžic a jeho doba* [K. Harant from Polžice and his Time] (Prague, 1970), pp. 69–70.

16 J. Černý, *Hudební rukopisy královéhradeckého muzea a dějiny české hudby 15. a 16. stol.* (Hradec Králové, 1967). *Klenoty starých pergamenů* [Music Manuscripts in the Museum at Hradec Kralové].

[See also Kurt von Fischer, 'Repertorium der Quellen tschechischer Mehrstimmigkeit des 14. bis 16. Jahrhunderts', *Essays in Musicology in Honor of Dragan Plamenac on his 70th Birthday*, ed. Gustave Reese and Robert J. Snow (Pittsburgh, 1969), p. 56.—Ed.]

17 Wolff, *Die Musik der alten Niederländer*, p. 62.

18 J. Snížková, 'Vícehlasé hudební památky našeho kraje' [Polyphonic Musical Relics of Our Region], *Orlické hory a Podorlicko*, 2 (Rychnov nad Kněžnou, 1969), pp. 9–21.

found a well-prepared ground in Bohemia, for the Hussites advocated intelligibility of the text in music, and syllabic setting was a characteristic feature of the Hussite monophonic compositions which, in the sixteenth century, were set polyphonically—contrary to the original Hussite intention.

2) The technique of the 'pes descendens et ascendens', as used by Josquin in his famous 'Miserere mei, Deus', appears in the compositions of Jiří Rychnovský (1545–1616) as well as in some anonymous Czech works and also in a composition of the above-mentioned theorist, Jan Facilis Boleslavský. That Josquin's 'Miserere' was known in Bohemia is documented by the single *Quinta vox* part-book (without title, but belonging to Ott's *Novum et insigne opus musicum* of 1537) preserved in Hradec Králové, Museum, sign. II A 41.

3) The combination of a *cantus firmus* with the new imitative technique found a deep response in Czech music.

4) The 'nota cambiata' encountered frequently in Josquin's music occurs also in the work of Czech polyphonists; this of course was common throughout the sixteenth century.[19]

5) The technique of pervading imitation evidently prevails in the structure of four-, five-, and six-voice compositions not only in Bohemia, but also in the music of other nations.[20] Clear contrapuntal setting in real five-voice compositions is typical for the Czech polyphonists Jiří Rychnovský and Jan Traian Turnovský.

6) The principle of varied imitation was taken over from the Josquin tradition by J. Rychnovský in several parts of his five-voice compositions.[21]

7) Clear formal structure and repetition of sections are regularly found in the motets and Masses by Czech polyphonists; this of course was widespread in sixteenth-century music, generally speaking.

8) Varied vocal scoring, especially the duo writing that is so characteristic of Josquin, can also be found in a series of Czech five-voice compositions— 2 plus 2 plus 1, or 3 plus 2.[22]

9) The equal treatment of voices in pervading imitation found in Josquin was used, among Czech authors, by J. Rychnovský and especially by Kryštof Harant z Polžic, who must have become familiar with Josquin's works at the court of the archduke at Innsbruck.[23]

This brief survey is only a small reflection of the influence that Josquin exercised on Czech music. Nevertheless, it may illustrate that the cultural context of the musical development in Europe in the sixteenth century knew no frontiers, geographical or intellectual.

---

[19] Knud Jeppesen, *Counterpoint* (New York, 1939), pp. 146–7.

[20] Hieronim Feicht, *Polifonia renasancu* (Cracow, 1957), pp. 12–13.

[21] See, for example, his 'Missa super "Et valde mane"', ed. Jitka Snížková (*Das Chorwerk*, 118; Wolfenbüttel, 1973).

[22] See Rychnovský's Mass, ibid.   [23] Jan Racek, *Kryštof Harant*, pp. 30, 111.

A Checklist of Josquin's Music in Czech Sources of the
Second Half of the Sixteenth Century

'Stabat Mater dolorosa'

   1. Rokycany, Church Archive, MS. A V 22a, b, fol. 2 (superius and an
     added sixth voice only). Anon.
     Incipit of sixth voice:

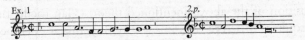

   2. Hradec Králové, Museum, MS. II A 26a, b, p. 11 (superius and superius
     secunda vox only). Anon.

   3. Hradec Králové, Museum, MS. appendix to II A 41, p. 4 (tenor only).
     Anon.

'Pater noster'/'Otče náš'

   1. Hradec Králové, Museum, MS. II A 22a, p. 56 (first tenor only).
     Josquin.

'Praeter rerum seriem'

   1. Rokycany, Church Archive, MS. A V 22a, b, fol. 54ᵛ (superius), fol. 10
     (first bass). Anon.

'Propter peccata quae peccastis' (= 'La Spagna')

   1. Rokycany, Church Archive, MS. A V 22a, fol. 5ᵛ (superius only).
     Anon.

   2. Hradec Králové, Museum, MS. II A 22a, p. 48 (tenor only). Josquin
     de Pres.

'Nesciens Mater Virgo virum'

   1. Hradec Králové, Museum, MS. II A 29, p. 260 (bass only). Josquin de
     pres.

   2. Hradec Králové, Museum, MS. II A 26a, b, p. 68 (*quinta vox*), p. 74
     (superius). Josquin de pres.

'Veni Sancte Spiritus'

   1. Hradec Králové, Museum, MS. II A 22a, p. 45 (*quinta vox* only).
     Josquinus.

I wish to add to this list:

'Missa Praeter rerum seriem' by Pavel Spongopeus Jistebnický

   1. Klatovy, Museum, MSS. 75, 76: 'Officium VI vocum super Praeter
     rerum seriem Josquini—Paulus Spongopeus'.

Problems in the Interdependence of Josquin Sources

LOTHAR HOFFMANN–ERBRECHT

Before the beginning of this century, older composers, unlike older writers, were virtually unknown except to a chosen few, and their works had to be gradually rediscovered. Friedrich Blume[1] is no doubt right in his assumption that we are nowhere near the end of this pioneering work yet. Albert Smijers, succeeded by Myroslaw Antonowycz and Willem Elders, broke new ground in the edition of the Works of Josquin des Prez, which has just now been completed. The rediscovery of manuscripts, composers, and even whole styles has kept us so busy that we musicologists may perhaps be excused for certain failings in our methods of research: we have not yet developed the methods of textual criticism that have been standard in literature for centuries. Georg von Dadelsen[2] has pointed to the existence of two distinct types of editions of old music. Autographs, original performance material, authentic first editions, authorized copies, and similar sources can be arranged in a logical order, making it easy to choose the basis of the text. This method is practical in relatively recent music, but the further we go back in history, the more difficult it becomes to find these primary sources: the scribal copies and posthumous prints, which are often all that is available, can rarely be arranged in an order that has any claim to logic. The editor can either toss a coin to determine the best source on which to base his text (this method has the advantage of saving a long critical report), or he can use his experience and personal opinion in arranging the sources; this is what Smijers did in the Josquin edition, and the writer of this paper admits that he has often followed the same method himself.[3] The chief aim is a sound musical text, free of mistakes, that does not require asking too many questions about the value of each source. Many pages of variants— meticulous lists of slips of the pen, typographical errors, peculiarities of

---

[1] Friedrich Blume, 'Historische Musikforschung in der Gegenwart', International Musicological Society, *Report of the Tenth Congress, Ljubljana 1967* (Kassel, 1970), pp. 13–25.

[2] Georg von Dadelsen, ed., *Editionsrichtlinien musikalischer Denkmäler und Gesamtausgaben* (Kassel, 1967), pp. 7ff.

[3] See my edition of *Heinrich Finck, Ausgewählte Werke*, i: Messen und Motetten zum Proprium Missae (*Das Erbe deutscher Musik*, 57; Frankfurt, 1962).

orthography, ornaments, writing habits, and many more such details—may indeed ease the editor's conscience, but the reader capitulates before such lack of system.

As early as 1958, Franz Krautwurst[4] emphasized the necessity for more painstaking research into the interdependence of sources. He was working on German music of the Reformation era, but his remarks are of general relevance. Study of the interdependence of sources is called filiation, which he defined thus:

> In the study of manuscripts, filiation denotes both the derivation of whole or part of a manuscript from one or several others, and the work of ascertaining and proving this derivation. To affiliate a manuscript means to use the dependence thus discovered in order to consider the manuscript's proper place in history.[5]

Clearly, the filiation of sources is much more than the brilliant mental game for which it has been taken by certain critics who do not see the need for philologically accurate method in establishing a text. It cannot be dispensed with if a piece of music is to be edited *critically*, and if the background and the liturgical significance of a sacred work are to be clarified.

While no serious editor doubted the necessity of source filiation, the way to go about it remained a puzzle until recently, when musicologists began to adapt to their particular field the methods of textual criticism established centuries ago in classical philology.[6] These methods affiliate— that is, establish a genetic relationship among—the sources by a scientific examination of the transmission of an old text.

Textual criticism begins with the *collation* or comparison of all known texts. In Germany, collation is known by the Latin term *recensio*. The derivation is investigated, the filiation is ascertained, and unreliable sources are eliminated. The result of the collation is a *stemma* or family tree of the genetic relationship of the sources, with the help of which the numerous minor sources can be shown to be derived from a small number of major sources; sometimes a lost major source can even be reconstructed with some degree of reliability. Filiation is based on the premise that all scribes and printers make an occasional error that is perpetuated by all succeeding scribes and printers in addition to their own errors. Therefore, all manuscripts deriving from a certain source will contain the *significant* or *indicative errors* (*Leitfehler* in German) and *significant readings* (*Leitvarianten*) of that source, while a

---

[4] Franz Krautwurst, 'Grundsätzliches zu einer Filiation geistlicher Musikhandschriften der Reformationszeit', *Bericht über den siebenten Internationalen Musikwissenschaftlichen Kongress Köln 1958* (Kassel, 1959), pp. 166–9.

[5] Ibid., p. 167.

[6] O. Stähelin, *Editionstechnik* (Leipzig–Berlin, 1914); Hermann Kantorowicz, *Einführung in die Textkritik* (Leipzig, 1921); Paul Maas, *Textkritik* (4th ed., Leipzig, 1960), English translation by Barbara Flower, *Textual Criticism* (Oxford, 1958); Hans Werner Seiffert, *Untersuchungen zur Methode der Herausgabe deutscher Texte* (Berlin, 1963).

different set of significant variants and errors can be taken as proof that the source or sources concerned derive from a different major source.[7] Thus the significant readings and errors serve to group the genealogy into various families. In comparing two or more copies belonging to the same family, the significant variants and errors of that family are referred to as *conjunctive variants* or *errors* (*Bindevarianten* and *Bindefehler*), while in a comparison of two copies from different families, an error occurring in only one is called a *separative error* (*Trennfehler*), to show the independence of the correct source from the one that contains the error. Of course, new errors in a later copy are not separative errors from an earlier source of the same family, since both will contain the same significant variants of that family; such an error only shows which of the two sources is the ancestor of the other.

At best, the collation will show a single source, the *codex unicus*, which is the direct or indirect ancestor of all the others. More often, it will only be possible to trace the genealogy back to the heads of the various families, and in many cases the editor will be able to eliminate only a few copies at the extreme branches of the tree, and the inner genealogy will remain a secret. But the collation is never superfluous. Even if not a single genetic relation can be found among the sources, methodical collation is needed to prove this fact. The editor will then have a clear conscience in choosing the best source; he may list the more important readings in other sources or even all of them in his report, if the value of the music justifies it.

The collation is followed by the *examination* of the *codex unicus* or the best source. This is necessary because even an original, if found, may not be entirely free of errors. The editor's report will list these errors and also all variants in other sources not eliminated by the collation. Since it is the aim of the collation to reduce the sources to as few important ones as possible, it follows that painstaking collation will not only yield a more reliable text but will free the report of all irrelevant readings.

Not all significant variants may be the result of scribal or printer's errors; any work of art may exist in more than one authentic version, and the editor will have to choose between them, for a conflation of several versions will never carry the authority of any one of them. For the same reason it might be advisable to edit the best of several heads of genetic families, even if they do not deserve consideration as different authentic versions, rather than to produce an artificial mixture of the best readings found in all of them. The determination of the best source does not depend on stylistic considerations alone; it is facilitated by knowledge of the reliability of the scribes and their peculiarities. A date in a manuscript may be helpful, but one must discover whether it refers to the time of composition, transcription, dedication,

---

[7] Significant variants are variants that two scribes are unlikely to have made independently. See L. D. Reynolds and N. G. Wilson, *Scribes and Scholars: A Guide to the Transmission of Greek and Latin Literature* (London, 1968), ch. 5, 'Textual Criticism'.

performance, or some other event.[8] Besides, the age of a source is not an unfailing guarantee of its closeness to the *codex unicus*; anyone who has studied the various branches of a transmitted text has seen old sources spoiled by corrupt readings.

Textual criticism of music is harder than that of literature in that a changed note is not simply the equivalent of a changed word. Moreover, the writing of music is much more involved than the writing of words, with all the symbols needed to represent pitch, duration, rests, ligatures, text repetitions, points of division, and so forth; it is therefore inherently more prone to scribal error. Not all the written marks carry the same weight; every scribe follows his own habits when there is a choice among several notational possibilities. Ligatures can be broken up and new ones can be written, division points can be omitted or added, ditto marks can replace a text repetition or vice versa, all without throwing the least light on the genetic derivation. Even a change in the notes may be inadvertent or intended. Experience alone will teach the editor in the end to distinguish between errors and genuine variants, and not even the accumulated experience of a board of editors is sufficient to guarantee their infallibility.[9]

The first musical publication to use the method of source filiation based on classical text criticism was the author's edition of the psalm motets of Thomas Stoltzer for *Das Erbe deutscher Musik*.[10] Georg von Dadelsen, the general editor of this series, stimulated and encouraged this pioneer project in musicology. The subject seemed predestined for genetic research, for some of the motets were widely known in the sixteenth century and exist in numerous sources, all posthumous. The filiation, surprisingly, deflated the hitherto high reputation of a number of them, including the Dresden

---

[8] Lothar Hoffmann-Erbrecht, 'Datierungsprobleme bei Kompositionen in deutschen Musikhandschriften des 16. Jahrhunderts', *Festschrift Helmuth Osthoff zum 65. Geburtstage* (Tutzing, 1961), pp. 47–60.

[9] [For an application of filiation to the late fifteenth-century chanson repertory, see Allan W. Atlas, 'Rome, Biblioteca Apostolica Vaticana, Cappella Giulia XIII. 27, and the Dissemination of the Franco-Netherlandish Chanson in Italy, *c*. 1460–*c*. 1530' (Ph.D. diss., New York University, 1971), esp. Ch. V, 'The Methodology of Relating Sources', pp. 82–103. Atlas lists as significant variants: (1) 'those that involve substantial differences either in the entire polyphonic complex or in the melodic line of an individual voice part'; (2) the presence of a *si placet* part (this can be used only as a conjunctive variant, since a scribe may omit the *si placet* part, knowing it is not original); (3) spellings found in text incipits, especially where garbled readings occur; (4) in the case of a work with conflicting attributions, the ascription to a particular composer; and (5) identical 'breaks for the turn of the page in precisely the same spot in each voice part' (pp. 95–7). As non-significant variants, Atlas includes: (1) different stereotyped cadential formulas; (2) accidentals; (3) coronas; (4) clefs; (5) ligatures; (6) minor color; (7) a sustained note instead of repeated notes, and vice versa; and (8) the filling in of the interval of a third (p. 98).—Ed.]

[10] *Thomas Stoltzer, Ausgewählte Werke*, ii: Sämtliche Psalmmotetten, ed. Lothar Hoffmann-Erbrecht (*Das Erbe deutscher Musik*, 66; Frankfurt, 1969).

manuscripts 1/D/2 and 1/D/3, which were demoted to the rank of secondary if not tertiary Stoltzer sources, while the Heugel manuscript (Kassel MS. Mus. 24) was substantially revalued, at least as far as Stoltzer's psalm motets are concerned. The limitations of the method also became apparent: wherever a sufficient number of important links had been lost, the derivation was hard or impossible to prove. At any rate, the newly gained knowledge about the relative value of the sources eliminated enough of the unimportant ones to reduce the critical report to about half the size of comparable reports.

The transmission of the works of Josquin des Prez is particularly extensive and would constitute a rewarding study in filiation. If carried out consistently, it could establish a priority of sources, eliminating a host of texts that are mere copies of copies. Moreover, the methodical application of philologically accurate textual criticism would render the editor's decision about the best source easier, or even relieve him of it altogether. Under no circumstances can Smijers be blamed for not following a method he cannot be expected to have known; his very great editorial achievement must be judged in the light of the methods available to him. It now behooves us to use these new methods to improve on his edition.

I should like to present a demonstration of the filiation method by studying the transmission of the texts of three of Josquin's motets. Smijers edited Josquin's works, as a rule, on the basis of one single source, presumably the best one. In case of doubt, he also consulted other sources, but he refrained from critical evaluation of variants and errors. The deviations from his main source found in other manuscripts and prints were noted under the rubric 'Aantekeningen'; however, the variants were not covered systematically but selectively, according to his personal judgement. Any attempt at filiation on the basis of Smijers' incomplete critical notes is therefore a risky and problematic undertaking. The following observations can do no more than hint at the method. Nor did we undertake a critical examination of the sources (*examinatio*). Only a new investigation of all errors and variants could produce reliable results. The sources that remained unknown to Smijers at the time of his publications are only summarily noted in the examples of filiation, but they could not be evaluated in the first two examples.

Example 1: 'De profundis clamavi'[11]

Sources:
S *Liber selectarum cantionum*, edited by Senfl and Peutinger (Grimm & Wyrsung, Augsburg; RISM 1520⁴)
A *Motetti libro primo* (Antico, Venice; RISM 1521³)
M [*Motetti et carmina gallica*] (Antico? RISM [*c.* 1521]⁷), Alto only

[11] *Werken*, Motetten, Bundel xi, no. 47.

P   *Psalmorum selectorum*, ii (Petreius, Nuremberg; RISM 1539[9])
G   Glareanus, *Dodekachordon* (Basel, 1547)
D   Dresden, Landesbibliothek, MS. Oels 529, Bass only
SG St. Gall, Stiftsbibliothek, MS. 463, Superius and Alto only
K   Kassel, Landesbibliothek, MS. Mus. 24
R   Regensburg, Proske-Bibliothek, Pernner Codex (MS. C 120)
V   Vienna, Nationalbibliothek, MS. 15941 (attributed to Champion).

The most important sources are the printed editions S and A, namely
Liber selectarum cantionum of 1520 edited by Senfl and Peutinger and the
Antico print of 1521. The former was chosen by Smijers as the primary
source for his edition of the work. The alto part is all that exists of the source
M, *Motetti et carmina gallica*, which is not considered here. MS. Vienna
15941,[12] which Smijers overlooked, is also not considered. The Pernner
codex of Regensburg, R, is the most important manuscript.
Genealogy:

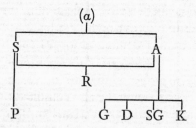

1. The reading characteristic of the A family is soprano, mm. 44–5:
instead of . G, SG, K, and R
share the reading of A.

2. The A and S families provide totally different solutions for mm. 18–21
of the alto. Since the two main branches of the tradition show deviations
so strong in one passage that they clearly point to the uncertainty of the
scribes, we may presume that α is corrupt. Naturally, it is not impossible
that α followed either the reading of the A or the S family. Let us therefore
adopt the cautious formulation: Alto, mm. 18–21: the A family shows a
separative variant from the S family.

3. Near the beginning of the *secunda pars*, A, G, SG, and D read
in the bass of m. 99 instead of
in S, P, R, and K, and the three upper voices enter a half measure later than
in these last sources.

R follows S in bass, m. 95 (2 semibreves D, as against a breve in A, G,
D, and K), and A in soprano, mm. 44–5. This scribe evidently referred to

[12] Dated *c.* 1521–1531 by Herbert Kellman; see his article in these Proceedings, p. 214.

both sources and conflated them. R is therefore close to a and is almost as valuable as S and A: this is the surprising result of the filiation. Its intermediate position between the two families helps confirm the date (about 1522–3) when the two separate parts of the manuscript were put together, as Krautwurst has shown.[13] One of the parts, containing chiefly secular compositions, was finished by one scribe in 1521, while the part in which the sacred works predominate was written by a number of copyists.

Example 2: 'Domine, ne in furore tuo arguas me'[14]

Sources:

P   *Motetti de la corona*, iii (Petrucci, Venice; RISM 1519²)

G   *Motetti de la corona*, iii (Giunta, Rome; RISM 1527)

Pe *Psalmorum selectorum* (Petreius, Nuremberg; RISM 1538⁶)

Mo *Psalmorum selectorum* (Montanus & Neuber, Nuremberg; RISM 1553⁴)

K   Kassel, Landesbibliothek, MS. Mus. 24

L   London, British Museum, Add. MS. 19583,
      Alto only   } two part-books of

M   Modena, Biblioteca Estense, MS. α F 2.29,   the same source[15]
      Bass only

R   Regensburg, Proske-Bibliothek, Pernner Codex (MS. C 120) (not filiated here).

Genealogy:

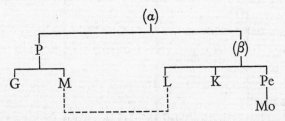

P and G share the erroneous semibreve C in bass, m. 199₃₋₄, which distinguishes their family from the other branch of the tree. Pe, Mo, K, and L share a number of readings and errors: alto, m. 45 has breve G; alto, m. 200₂₋₃ has semibreve A; and tenor, m. 184₁ has semiminim F instead of D (not in L, which lacks this voice). Pe and Mo also have a minim D in superius, m. 88₄, which the scribe of K subsequently corrected in his copy. β is presumably corrupt in bass, mm. 106–7, since K on the one hand and Pe and Mo on the other provide different solutions for this passage, both

---

[13] Franz Krautwurst, art. 'Pernner', *MGG*, x (1962), col. 1075.

[14] *Werken*, Motetten, Bundel viii, no. 39.

[15] See Edward E. Lowinsky, *The Medici Codex of 1518* (*Monuments of Renaissance Music*, iii; Chicago, 1968), pp. 117–18.

of which differ from P. I have shown elsewhere[16] that the first part of K (through no. 59) was written before 1538; therefore K (no. 9) cannot derive from Pe, which was published in 1538.[17] From conjunctive variants we infer a common source β for Pe and K. G and Mo are reprints of no value.

The filiation of L and M illustrates the difficulty of dealing with single part-books. I had originally placed M with the P family and L with β. It was pointed out at the Conference that the part-books belong to the same set. Therefore, L and M possibly form a separate branch of the genealogy, halfway between P and β; in the absence of the remaining two part-books, their position cannot be more precisely defined.

In this example, the genetic relationship can be ascertained with an unusual degree of certainty. The filiation confirms the Petrucci edition, P, used by Smijers, as the best source. The only surprising result is that none of the other sources derives directly from Petrucci; they all belong to a family separate from the Italian one. Genealogical research into other works would be necessary to show whether the German transmission of Josquin's works as a whole derives from sources different from Petrucci.

Example 3: 'Virgo salutiferi'[18]

Sources:

P   *Motetti de la corona*, iii (Petrucci, Venice; RISM 1519²)
G   *Motetti de la corona*, iii (Giunta, Rome; RISM 1527)
A   *Liber quartus. XXIX musicales...modulos habet* (Attaingnant, Paris; RISM 1534⁶)
Mo *Opus musicum*, ii (Montanus & Neuber, Nuremberg; RISM 1559¹)
Me Florence, Biblioteca Mediceo-Laurenziana, Acquisti e Doni 666 (Medici Codex)
L   London, Royal College of Music, MS. 1070 (canonic voices missing in *prima pars*)
Mu Munich, Universitätsbibliothek, Art. 401 App. (tenor missing)
R¹ Rome, Biblioteca Apostolica Vaticana, Capp. Sist. MS. 16
R² Rome, Biblioteca Apostolica Vaticana, Capp. Sist. MS. 42

Smijers placed particular weight on P, R¹, and R², and he collated all the other sources listed except the Medici Codex, which he did not know. The importance of the Medici Codex as a source has been emphasized by Edward Lowinsky in his edition of the whole codex, in which he closely examined the readings of other sources.[19]

---

[16] Hoffmann-Erbrecht, 'Datierungsprobleme', p. 53.
[17] *Stoltzer, Ausgewählte Werke*, ii, pp. 175–6 (nos. 7 and 8).
[18] *Werken*, Motetten, Bundel vii, no. 35; Lowinsky, *The Medici Codex*, iv, no. 42.
[19] Lowinsky, *The Medici Codex*, iii.

Genealogy:

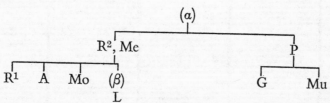

P, G, and Mu share the reading in alto, mm. 70–1 and the erroneous *longa* B♮ (instead of C) in second tenor, m. 171. As in the motet 'Ave nobilissima creatura', Mu is only a transcription of P or G and has no value of its own.

All the other sources except Mo and L share the note-divisions in alto, m. 69 and m. 177_{3-4}. R² and Me have only minor differences; their actual notes are identical. R¹ has dotted minims in alto, m. 30_{2-3} and bass, mm. 191_4–192_1: these are scribal peculiarities distinguishing this copy from R² and Me, but all three derive from a common source. Alto, mm. 344–351, tenor, mm. 384–392, bass, m. 176_{2-4} and mm. 212_4–213_2 prove the direct descent of A and Mo from the source of R² and Me; all four sources agree with each other but not with P. A certain degree of relationship between L on the one hand and R² and Me on the other is proved by alto, mm. 344–351, tenor, mm. 384–392, but L also contains a number of individual readings and errors: minim A in tenor, m. 42_3, semibreve A in alto, m. 61_{3-4}; breve G instead of F in alto, m. 67; semibreve A in bass, m. 67_{3-4} and again in bass, m. 70_{3-4}. Therefore an intermediate source β might be inferred.

Me and R² are the best sources and probably derive directly from the inferred original α. A modern edition should follow them and not the Petrucci edition P used by Smijers. Lowinsky has shown that the words and accidentals are written with even greater care in Me than in R², and this filiation confirms every detail of his remarks on this piece.[20]

I have chosen these three examples out of a number of other filiations I have attempted because they demonstrate a wide range of results. In the first example, the filiation showed that the value of the Pernner Codex had previously been underestimated. Example 2 brought out the independence of the whole German transmission vis-à-vis the Italian sources. Finally, Example 3 confirmed with its filiation the wide-ranging observations that Edward Lowinsky made in his edition of the Medici Codex. In his investigations, Lowinsky took careful note of variants and errors of the various sources and he evaluated them critically. He achieved with the means of his method the same results that the stemma of Example 3 graphically illustrates, underscoring thereby the high value of the Medici Codex already recognized by him.

[20] Ibid., pp. 199–201.

III Style and Analysis

Towards Objective Criteria for Establishing Chronology and Authenticity: What Help can the Computer Give?

ARTHUR MENDEL

Since Professor Lewis Lockwood and I first began our flirtation with the computer some years ago we have more than once been warned by respected colleagues in these discouraging words: 'Any question the computer can answer is not worth asking'. We are still trying to find out whether they were right.

Elements of style are complex entities. One only begins to realize *how* complex when one tries to define them in terms so unambiguous that the computer can identify them. The instructions one gives the computer must cover every single pertinent decision we make, consciously or unconsciously, in hunting for what we seek and differentiating it from everything else. These decisions, especially the unconscious ones—the tacit assumptions on which we proceed—are legion, and the opportunities for overlooking one of them, or for failing to formulate it with complete precision, are similarly legion. Partly for this reason, we have had to begin[1] by asking questions that are musically so simple that to some they may seem irrelevant or inane. The answers—those we finally succeeded in getting—are at most only raw material for stylistic description. If they are impressive

[1] An account of the difficulties that have attended this beginning is contained in my paper, 'Some Preliminary Attempts at Computer-Assisted Style-Analysis in Music', in *Computers and the Humanities*, iv (1969), pp. 41–52. The examples of coding of the musical notation contain errors. The project on which that paper and the present one report has been supported by the Rockefeller Foundation, the Computing Activities Division of the National Science Foundation, and Princeton University. A brief description of our system was given by Professor Lockwood in a paper read at the Ljubljana Congress in 1967 (*Report of the Tenth Congress of the International Musicological Society, Ljubljana, 1967* (Kassel and Ljubljana, 1970), pp. 444–9).

at all, they are so only for the volume of data they describe.

I should preface our discussion by stating that what we have fed into the computer as data is a translation into a computer-acceptable code of all the Masses and some sixty-odd motets as printed in the Smijers edition. The task of eliminating errors from this coding has proved a never-ending one, and since simple errors can wreak havoc with computer operations, we have concentrated our efforts on the Masses numbered 1–18 in the Smijers edition. These are all the Masses generally accepted as genuine, and it is from them (plus a few odd Mass fragments) that we shall have to derive our standards of what constitutes Josquin's Mass style. In what follows, I am referring only to them.

Some of our earliest efforts were to obtain data that would be of help to Professor Lockwood in his studies of *musica ficta*. It seemed likely that those movements containing the most accidentals—both those taken over from the original sources and those suggested by the editor—would be the ones containing the greatest number of situations presenting problems of *musica ficta*. As a convenience, therefore, and as an early exercise in music informa-tion retrieval, Mr. Lockwood obtained a map and count of the accidentals in every movement. He later obtained also maps of all the linear tritones and of all the harmonic intervals of a fourth or a fifth involving B, B♭, E, or E♭. These, I repeat, are only maps (or lists) and counts: to produce them, the computer did a kind of clerical work that human beings should not have to do, and could hardly do on the scale and with the accuracy that the computer can.

Similarly, for a study of Josquin's declamation, I have obtained a list of all the syllabic passages in the Masses as printed in the Smijers edition. Computer programs are in preparation to find out in what proportion accented syllables come on longer notes than unaccented, or on higher notes, or in stronger metric positions.[2]

This brings us to the next step: compiling figures on the comparative frequency of certain features in different Masses, different sections, and different sub-sections. One of the many questions about music of this period to which we have no definite answers is what its tempi were—not only the absolute tempi, but the relations between tempi of different works or sections of the same work. When two voices that are to be performed simultaneously have two different mensuration signs, it is clear what the tempo relation implied by the presence of the two signs is. When C and ℂ occur simultaneously, for example, it is clear that two semibreves of ℂ are equal to one semibreve of C. But is this true when the two signs do not occur simultaneously? Is the semibreve of a whole piece marked ℂ to last only half as long as that of a whole piece in C? Towards finding an answer to

---

[2] For a brief report on our work in this direction, see these Proceedings, pp. 700–3.

such questions, Charles Hamm counted the frequency of the different note values in each of several pieces—a tedious job.[3]

The computer, however, has no taste in jobs. For each mensuration (and for each voice, sub-section, section, or Mass) it can add the durations of all the notes occurring in that mensuration and divide the total duration of all the notes by the total number of notes, thus arriving at the average note-value. If the average note-value in $\mathbb{C}$ turns out to be twice that in C, there will be support for the idea that a breve in $\mathbb{C}$ is intended to have about the same duration as a semibreve in C. If the average note-value in $\mathbb{C}$ is greater than in C but less than twice as great, we may take this as suggesting that a breve in $\mathbb{C}$ is shorter than a breve in C, but longer than a semibreve. A table of the average note-values of all the mensurations used by Josquin will give us some evidence about the relative tempi implied by the different mensuration signs.[4]

Another relatively simple job for the computer was suggested to me by my studies on pitch.[5] For those studies, I examined the voice ranges of all Bach's Weimar Cantatas and of some representative works of the Leipzig period, and found that the average mid-range in the Weimar notation was nearly a tone below the average mid-range in the Leipzig notation. This fitted very well with the other data I had been able to gather to determine at what pitches Bach's vocal music was sung in the two places. Of course, we know a great deal more about the conditions of performance in Weimar and Leipzig in the eighteenth century, the organs that accompanied the singing, the nature of the singers, etc., than we do about those in Milan, Rome, Ferrara, and Paris in the fifteenth and sixteenth centuries. Moreover, the St. Matthew Passion and the B minor Mass each has an overall vocal range of forty-three semitones—three octaves plus a fifth—so there is not

[3] *A Chronology of the Works of Guillaume Dufay Based on a Study of Mensural Practice* (Princeton, 1964).

[4] This paper as read at the Conference included such a table, with the following note: 'A word of caution concerning all the data presented in this paper is in order. Since these techniques are in their infancy, it is possible that errors have crept into our calculations—errors of coding and errors of programming. We should be grateful if any errors discovered or suspected were pointed out to us'. The warning was all too appropriate: the data on which the table was based included the cantus prius facti in their 'Resolutio' form—that is, notated in the mensuration prevailing in the other voices, rather than in their original mensurations—and this distorted the data presented. I discovered the error while these Proceedings were in the publishers' hands, and it has not been possible to revise the table in time for publication. Perhaps it is not altogether unfortunate that so striking a reminder should have been given of the fact that the computer blindly delivers information derived from the data and the instructions it receives, and that the information delivered cannot be any better than the quality of thought that caused its production.

[5] Arthur Mendel, 'On the Pitches in Use in Bach's Time', *The Musical Quarterly*, xli (1955), pp. 332–54 and 466–80; reprinted in A. J. Ellis and Arthur Mendel, *Studies in the History of Musical Pitch* (Amsterdam, 1969).

much room for transposition, while the greatest overall range of any of the Josquin Masses is only thirty-eight semitones—three octaves plus a whole-tone.

For the Bach works, I had calculated the average mid-range by finding the mid-range of the soprano—that is, the central note between the extreme outer notes—and that of the alto and the mid-point between those mid-ranges, doing the same for bass and tenor, and then finding the mid-point between those two mid-points. This procedure tended to minimize the influence of a single exceptionally high or low note in any voice on the average mid-range. It also, of course, left the question of tessitura completely out of account, but I saw no way of gathering data about tessitura without prohibitive amounts of clerical work. Nor had I any idea of how different the results of such an enormous ant-heap would be from those produced by finding the mid-ranges.

For Josquin Masses we have now calculated by computer not only the mid-range, but also the average mean pitch. We numbered each pitch in the total range, from lowest to highest. Then for each voice we multiplied the duration of each occurrence of each pitch by its number, totalled the results, and divided by the total sounding duration of that voice. Finally we averaged the mean pitches of all the voices. It developed that the difference between the average mean pitch and the mid-range was rarely more than a semitone even for one voice in one sub-section, and never more than a semitone for a whole Mass. The results of this program are summarized in Table I.

A program to find large skips—defined as melodic intervals of a major sixth or more, except octaves—was devised for the purpose of checking our data—that is, the computer-coded notation of the Masses. Our method of coding has one big disadvantage, among others, in that it is easy to make a mistake of an octave in the register of the note being coded. This program turned up numerous coding mistakes; it also turned up numbers of large skips. The numbers are presented in Table II in decreasing order because we hypothesized that the number of large skips would be smaller in Josquin's later Masses than in his earlier ones, and indeed the 'Missa Pange lingua' and the 'Missa de Beata Virgine' do appear near the bottom of the list. (It is not our idea that any table of the frequency of occurrence of one such characteristic will be likely to suggest chronological order, but rather that when many such characteristics have been tabulated some helpful correlations among the tables may be found.)

Another stylistic feature relatively easy to identify by our computer programs is the presence of consecutive fifths and octaves, parallel or by contrary motion. The results are given in Table III.

A characteristic that one might well expect would increase with time is the prevalence of full triads. Table IV (which, since it is based on a smaller

TABLE I

Mid-range and Average Mean Pitch of the Josquin Masses

Mid-range		Average mean pitch		Width of range*
g	L'homme armé 6. toni	ab	Ad fugam	30
	Di dadi	a	Mater Patris	31
a	L'homme armé s.v.m.		L'homme armé s.v.m.	33
	D'ung aultre amer		Sine nomine	
	Mater Patris	bb	Pange lingua	
	Una musque		Ave maris stella	
	Faisant regretz		L'homme armé 6. toni	34
	Hercules Dux		Una musque	
bb	Malheur me bat	b	Faisant regretz	
	La sol fa re mi		L'ami Baudichon	
	Sine nomine		Di dadi	
b	Pange lingua	c'	D'ung aultre amer	36
	Fortuna desperata		Malheur me bat	
	Gaudeamus		La sol fa re mi	
c'	De Beata Virgine		Gaudeamus	
	Ad fugam	c#'	De Beata Virgine	38
c#'	Ave maris stella		Hercules Dux	
	L'ami Baudichon		Fortuna desperata	

* Counted in semitones, e.g., 36 = 3 octaves.

TABLE II

Large Skips in the Josquin Masses

	M6 ↑↓	m7 ↑↓	M7	m9	M9 ↑↓	m10 ↑↓	M10 ↑↓	Total
Una musque de Buscaya	3	1	4		2			10
Malheur me bat	1				1	4	2	8
Gaudeamus	3	2			2			7
Hercules Dux Ferrariae	3					3		6
L'homme armé 6. toni	4					1		5
Di dadi	1					4		5
La sol fa re mi	2	1				1		4
L'ami Baudichon	4							4
Sine nomine	3	1						4
Ave maris stella	3							3
Faisant regretz	1	1				1		3
L'homme armé s.v.m.	2	1						3
D'ung aultre amer	1					1		2
Pange lingua	2							2
De Beata Virgine	1*							1
Fortuna desperata								0
Mater Patris								0
Ad fugam								0

* This sixth is major as notated, but the application of *musica ficta* might well make it minor: *Kyrie* II, mm. 104–5, Superius.

TABLE III

Pairs of Consecutive Fifths* and Octaves in the Josquin Masses

	Parallel			Contrary Motion		
	5ths	8ves	Total	5ths	8ves	Total
L'homme armé s.v.m.	5		5	3		3
La sol fa re mi	6	1	7	1		1
Gaudeamus	11	1	12	3		3
Fortuna desperata	13	2	15			
L'homme armé 6. toni	10	1	11	1		1
Ave maris stella	3	1	4	3	1	4
Hercules Dux Ferrariae				4		4
Malheur me bat	13		13	4	1	5
L'ami Baudichon	2	1	3			
Una musque de Buscaya	21	2	23	1	3	4
D'ung aultre amer	3		3	1	1	2
Mater Patris	2	1	3	7		7
Faisant regretz	5		5			
Ad fugam	8	2	10	1		1
Di dadi	4		4	1		1
De Beata Virgine	5		5	3		3
Sine nomine	2		2	2	1	3
Pange lingua				3		3

* All fifths, whether notated as perfect or diminished, are included, since by the application of *musica ficta* some of the diminished fifths might be made perfect. Such a table, then, presents raw data, which could be refined only by examining the context of each occurrence, to see what rules of *musica ficta* might be applied. The computer printout of which this is a summary gives the location of each occurrence.

quantity of data, was not made by computer) lists for each Mass the percentage of all cadences in three or more parts at the ends of sub-sections that close with a complete triad, presented in order of increasing percentage.

TABLE IV

Final Cadences of Sub-sections ending with a Full Triad

	%*
Ad fugam	0
Di dadi	14
Ave maris stella	17
L'ami Baudichon	18
L'homme armé 6. toni	23
Fortuna desperata	27
L'homme armé s.v.m.	29
Una musque de Buscaya	40
D'ung aultre amer	40
Faisant regretz	40
Gaudeamus	43
Pange lingua	46
Sine nomine	50
De Beata Virgine	64
Hercules Dux Ferrariae	69
Mater Patris	71
Malheur me bat	75
La sol fa re mi	75

* Total of sub-section final cadences in each Mass ending in full triads divided by total number of sub-section final cadences in three or more parts.

A program to show the percentage of full triadic sonority not just in cadences but throughout whole Masses is in progress. So far, we have had the computer analyze every sonority in three whole Masses (only three because this program has been difficult and long to develop, and because it uses up large amounts of computer time—about twelve minutes per Mass). It cuts a vertical slice down through the polyphonic texture at every change of pitch in any voice, and classifies the simultaneities it finds at every such point, as unisons or octaves, thirds or sixths, fifths, triads and first inversions, and 'others' (i.e., dissonant combinations). Table V presents the ratio of the total duration of all complete triads to the total duration of all thirds, sixths, and fifths, including doublings.

Only very preliminary conclusions can be drawn from these figures. The highest ratio is in the *Et in Spiritum* of the 'Missa L'homme armé super voces musicales', as one might expect, since this is doubtless a spurious addition to the Mass made many years after Josquin's death. The next highest ratio is in the *Et incarnatus* of the 'Missa Pange lingua'—a section only twenty *tempora* long, and completely chordal throughout.

★　★　★

TABLE V

Ratio of Total Duration of Complete Triads to Total Duration of Other Consonances★

	Three voices			Four or more voices		
	L'homme armé s.v.m.	Ave maris stella	Pange lingua	L'homme armé s.v.m.	Ave maris stella	Pange lingua
Whole Mass	1.0	1.0	0.9	3.6	1.8	2.4
Kyrie 1	1.3	0.9	0.6	5.2	1.5	1.6
Christe	0.7	0.6	0.6	4.4	5.9	2.5
Kyrie 2	1.0	1.1	0.9	5.6	0.5	1.3
Gloria	0.8	1.0	1.3	2.4	1.4	3.0
Qui tollis	1.1	0.8	0.9	4.5	2.2	2.1
Credo	1.0	1.1	0.6	3.8	1.8	2.0
Et incarnatus	} 1.0	} 0.9	—	} 5.6	} 3.1	9.0
Crucifixus			} 1.3			2.7
Et in Spiritum	1.7		} 1.0	9.3		} 3.3
Confiteor	1.2			1.9		
Sanctus	1.3	2.0	1.4	1.7	1.5	3.8
Pleni	0.4	1.8	(2v.)	(3v.)	(3v.)	(2v.)
Hosanna	1.3	1.1	0.6	4.6	2.0	1.6
Benedictus	} (2v.)	} (2v.)	} (2v.)	} (2v.)	} (2v.)	} (2v.)
Qui venit						
In nomine						
Agnus 1	0.7	0.8	1.6	2.9	1.4	2.0
Agnus 2	0.4	(2v.)	(2v.)	(3v.)	(2v.)	(2v.)
Agnus 3	1.4	1.7	0.7	2.9	1.4	1.5

★ Thirds, sixths, and fifths, including doublings; octaves and unisons excluded.

Now, having presented samples of some first moves toward computer-aided style analysis, I should like to step back and reconsider the basic question: Are the questions we are able to ask the computer worth asking? Is the use of the computer appropriate to humanistic research?

Humanists have shown an understandable reluctance to see works of art attacked by machines. It is important to distinguish between what can best be accomplished 'by hand'—that is, by ear and eye—and what best with mechanical means. In the study of individual works, the role of the computer, if any, is likely to be a minor one. Even when one seeks characteristics common to whole groups of works—the characteristics that make up a 'style'—there are many possible conclusions toward which the computer seems to offer little or no help. Consider the following discussions by two eminent musicologists:

Ockeghem's mature style displays a careful polyphonic balance and a judicious alternation of full and divided choir. Strict observance of the ecclesiastic tonalities, and a majestic and dignified musical language following the text with a true and pure musical feeling always in accordance with the liturgic requirements, combine to make him one of the outstanding church musicians of all time. . . .

More important than canonic virtuosity was the systematic development of a technical principle of composition known as 'continuous imitation', in which a voice (or part) repeats a melodic figure previously presented in another voice. Such imitation does not entail literal copying of the first statement, as in strict imitation (canon); it is used rather freely, preserving approximately the rhythm and general outline of the original figure.... Thus the opening words of every line, and significant words through the text, wander, accompanied by the same thematic material, through all parts.... The result of these new principles of composition was a music which in its endless, inexorable flow came close to the contourless mysticism of Catholic liturgy. The same *devotio moderna* that emanates from the works of Thomas à Kempis fills this music; the same gentle piety and unworldliness breathes through the interlaced contrapuntal lines of Ockeghem's Masses that permeates the sturdy Latin of the *Imitatio Christi*. The current of artistic creation, though trained to rational principles of construction and proportion, had still its intuitive side which, fed by Gothic traditions, flowed on along with 'scientific' art, influencing and animating the theory and mitigating its severity.[6]

...Ockeghem's sacred works are characterized by sparseness of imitative entries, and the few that can be found are restricted to motto beginnings, which may not even be Ockeghem's own, or to transitory and sometimes singularly vague imitations without structural function....

Ockeghem's sacred music has been justly associated with the ecstatic fervor of the *devotio moderna*....[I]f the music has the power to evoke or represent mysticism, which is traditionally inarticulate, there must be distinct, palpable, and describable technical features which create that impression. What are these traits—or, to put it bluntly, how does Ockeghem manage to be 'mystical' in music? Looking back on the salient characteristics of his style, we find that he renounces with amazing consistency all customary means of articulating a composition: cadences, profiled motives, symmetrical phrase structure, lucid interrelation of parts, imitation, sequences, prominence of one voice over others, and so forth.... Ockeghem's methods of composition can be rationally analyzed, however irrational their effect may be.[7]

The qualities ascribed to Ockeghem's style by these two eminent writers fall into at least two classes:

1) Characteristics which can presumably be clearly defined, and of which the relative frequency of occurrence can be objectively determined: cadences, profiled motives, symmetrical phrase-structure, imitation, sequences, etc.

2) Qualities not thus susceptible to objective determination of their presence or absence: 'true and pure musical feeling', 'endless, inexorable flow', 'gentle piety and unworldliness', 'ecstatic fervor'—and perhaps even 'careful polyphonic balance', 'judicious alternation', 'lucid interrelation of parts'.

To say that the qualities in the second category are not susceptible to

[6] Paul Henry Lang, *Music in Western Civilization* (New York, 1941), pp. 186, 188, and 189.
[7] Manfred F. Bukofzer, '*Caput:* A Liturgico-Musical Study', *Studies in Medieval and Renaissance Music* (New York, 1950), pp. 281, 291, and 292.

objective determination is not to say that the terms in which they are described are meaningless or futile. It is true that to anyone who does not find these qualities in the music the words may remain meaningless, but others may respond to them and value insights to which the authors have helped them. The fact that intersubjective agreement is not the same thing as objective determination does not make it valueless. Its realm is, at any rate, one into which the computer cannot enter.

Similarly, to say that locating cadences, profiled motives, symmetrical phrase-structure, imitations, sequences, large skips, full triadic sonorities, and all sorts of other objectively identifiable features does not necessarily lead to drawing wise conclusions is true but irrelevant. It is possible to do useless work and to draw stupid conclusions with or without the computer. But when one is attempting to draw conclusions about a large body of works, and when one wishes to base them on facts rather than mere impressions, the computer can gather, sort, and order the data faster and more accurately than one could by hand, and on a scale that would be absurd to attempt by hand.

This is not to underestimate the difficulties that attend its use. First of all there is the problem of converting musical notation into computer input. This is itself a job more suited to machines than to men, and there is some reason to believe that the use of optical-scanning equipment for this purpose may be possible in the not-too-distant future. But after that hurdle has been surmounted, the writing of computer programs for the analysis of the converted data is itself no easy task. The computer can only do what it is told. And it has been our experience that nothing reveals the imprecision of our concepts like the necessity of defining them sharply enough to instruct the computer what to look for.

What is a cadence? What do all cadences have in common that distinguishes them from non-cadences? What is 'good declamation'? 'Increase in tonal feeling'? 'Continuous imitation'? The complexity of the processes by which the human mind identifies the presence of such features is perhaps never so fully revealed as in the attempt to make them explicit so that the computer can imitate them.

But why should the computer imitate them? We identify features, it will be said, in order to appreciate them, and appreciation is *a priori* beyond the capabilities of the computer. The truth is, however, that we identify musical characteristics not only to appreciate them in individual works, but also in order to be able to place individual works in relation to others, to generalize, to group the works that share them and contrast the group with other groups—to create order among the things we know. We do this in the absence of that complete knowledge which alone could completely verify our generalizations, and this will remain true even when we have the aid of the computer.

Once one has accepted a definition of the 'technical principle of composition known as "continuous imitation"', one would not need the computer, perhaps, to determine the degree to which it is present in the known works of Ockeghem, for those works are not a large corpus of material. But if one wishes to be able to make general statements about continuous imitation or any other feature, not just for Ockeghem but for, say, the some 120 volumes of related music edited by some two dozen different scholars for Armen Carapetyan's American Institute of Musicology, then the computer can seek out, compile, and order the data—a task which would otherwise require the combined efforts of teams of scholars for decades.

Computers are widely used nowadays for setting text in type, particularly where it will be desirable to retrieve information contained in the text for indexing, tabulation, and other manipulations. We are all familiar with one example of this: the periodical *RILM* (*International Repertory of Musical Literature*).

Similarly, a system is in an advanced stage of development, by Bauer-Mengelberg and Ferencz, for converting computer-coded music into musical notation—a system designed to replace music-engraving, 'autography', music-typewriting, etc. It seems altogether probable that this or some other system to accomplish the same purpose will be widely used in the not far distant future.

When this occurs, we can foresee the following situation. The musical notation for a complete edition, like that of the works of Josquin, or for a whole series of such editions, like that of the American Institute of Musicology, will be created by computer. The information contained on the magnetic tapes on which the code for the musical symbols has been recorded will then be available for retrieval in all sorts of forms. Every aspect of music that can be read from its notation can be 'read' by the computer from this tape. This does not mean, of course, that one will *have* to use the computer; the musical notation will be available just as it is today for the uses in study and performance that it now serves. But every question that can be answered from looking at the musical notation will be similarly answerable from the tape, for what it contains is, after all, only another form of notation. Framing the questions with the requisite precision will often be slow work, just as it is today—though the framing of one question can often build upon the framing of a previous one. But once the question is framed precisely—once the computer program is perfected—it can be answered for many pieces in as little time as it could be answered by ear-and-eye for one.

Everything we can learn from a computer is based on sorting, combining, or otherwise making use of the answers to two types of question: 'Yes or no?' and 'How many?'. How drastic a limitation this is depends partly on how limited our ability is to break up what may at first seem grey areas into relative frequency and size of tiny black areas and white areas, as in the 'shadings' of an engraving. One can imagine defining the criteria for determining objectively the relative independence of the different voices of a polyphonic web, and applying those criteria to comparisons of different pieces by computer, to determine the nature of their 'polyphonic balance'.

But there would be no way of determining objectively what constitutes a 'careful polyphonic balance': 'careful' means what strikes me, or you, or some number of qualified observers, as careful.[8] It is conceivable that our techniques of question-asking may some day develop to the point where we can program the computer to tell with a high degree of probability Josquin from Pierre de la Rue. But we need not fear that it can ever tell us which is the better composer.

[8] Of course, if anyone gave the computer rigorously defined criteria of what he considered 'careful', it could report whether a given piece met those criteria.

The Structure of Wide-Spanned Melodic Lines in Earlier and Later Works of Josquin

WALTER WIORA

Josquin was a professional singer and obviously an excellent one.[1] He was a singer-composer, whereas the great composers of later times, such as Bach, Mozart, and Beethoven, had their own practical experience primarily in instrumental music. The extended melodies in Josquin's Masses and motets, unless their function is confined to mere contrapuntal accompaniment, are genuine vocal music. A great many of them are appropriate to solo singers and many even to virtuosos. It would be unthinkable that Josquin should not have created music in which singers, excelling in the chapels of the Italian Renaissance courts, could fully develop their vocal capabilities. However, Josquin's virtuoso writing for the voice is also an expression of a mighty personality of deep religious conviction. His enthusiasm in pieces such as 'Pleni sunt coeli et terra gloria tua' springs from the idea that to sing the glory of God in heaven and earth, the voice, too, has to be full of glory, that is of splendour and grandeur.

Wide-spanned melodies I call extended melodic lines with the quality of long breath, of enduring tension. They are more numerous in Josquin's Masses than in his motets, and are seldom found in his chansons. They appear less frequently in later works than in earlier, though their importance is thereby only restricted, not eliminated. To escape the dangers of premature chronology, I prefer to speak about earlier and later rather than about early and late works of Josquin, basing the relative chronology on stylistic investigation.

One method of investigation is to compare works based on the same *cantus firmus*, for example the two versions of the *Gloria* 'de Beata Virgine'.[2] The isolated *Gloria* printed in the *Fragmenta missarum* of 1505 is obviously

---

[1] See Helmuth Osthoff, *Josquin Desprez* (Tutzing, 1962–5), i, pp. 10, 24–5, and ii, p. 258.
[2] *Werken van Josquin des Prez*, Fragmenta Missarum, i, pp. 85–93, and Missen, xvi. In the following examples the text underlay sometimes differs from that of the edition. About the chronology, see Osthoff, i, pp. 105, 130–1, 181–5, and ii, pp. 248–9.

of much earlier origin than the *Gloria* in the 'Missa de Beata Virgine'.
Characteristic is the following passage:

Ex. 1   *Gloria*, mm. 21-8 (tenor)

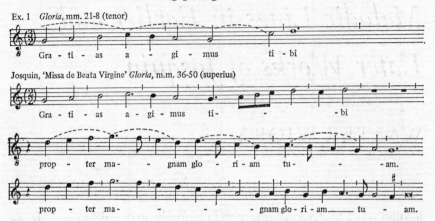

Josquin, 'Missa de Beata Virgine' *Gloria*, m.m. 36-50 (superius)

In both versions a long arch is evident, with the peak in the second half.
But in the second version the movement to the climax is more flowing,
particularly due to the repetition and prolongation of the first motive; the
melodic progression is intensified by the dotted note G and the syncopated
cadence D C D. Both versions are in Mixolydian, but in the earlier one the
fourth is stressed as dominant, as leap, and as framework of a sequential
motive. Thus the earlier version has a more angular effect than the later, in
which the third and the fifth gain greater importance and the fourth
approximates the function of a subdominant. In place of the sequences, a
smooth scale flows down into a long tonic cadence.

In a later passage, one of the tropes of the *Gloria* (see Ex. 2), the change in
direction toward harmonic tonality is remarkable. In the last measures
going toward the cadence, the low and the high F are omitted, and the
major third is used instead of the minor. The older version, composed of
shorter sections, is less even; the use of syncopation produces an irregular,
somewhat jerky line, as though it were rippled.

Ex. 2   *Gloria* de Beata Virgine, mm. 54-9 (alto)

Josquin, 'Missa de Beata Virgine.' *Gloria*, mm. 82-94 (tenor)

Still more obvious is the smoothing of the unevenly broken line at the beginning of Ex. 3. Josquin substitutes for the static motion of only two tones a high swinging gesture with an octave leap. Thus the melody becomes more elastic and almost unrestrained. Of course, in all these examples the balancing effect of the other voices of the contrapuntal setting should be kept in mind.

Ex. 3 *Gloria* de Beata Virgine, mm. 76-80 (tenor)

Similar differences between an earlier and a later style are evident in Josquin's arrangements of the antiphon 'Alma Redemptoris Mater'[3] (see Ex. 4), which, at an earlier time, had mirrored Dufay's and Ockeghem's different musical personalities. The first version, considered a very early

work of Josquin, begins just like Ockeghem's composition and is similar in style. The line is wavy and the rhythm changes from measure to measure. The considerably later version is straighter in line and its rhythm pulsates

---

[3] Motetten, Bundel iv, no. 21, p. 105, and Motetten, Bundel viii, no. 38, p. 77. See Osthoff, i, p. 8, and ii, pp. 41–2, 47–8. The Ockeghem is in Besseler, *Altniederländische Motetten*, p. 5.

more equally. It stresses the octave of the tonic strongly and in contrast to the earlier version sounds the leading note three times shortly after the beginning. By using sequence to achieve symmetry, the melody appears more distinctive and tectonic.

In addition to melodies based upon the same *cantus firmus*, a comparison of others that continue or vary the same motive can be revealing. The duo in the *Agnus Dei* of the 'Missa de Beata Virgine'[4] begins like the duo in the *Sanctus* of the 'Missa L'homme armé super voces musicales':[5]

Ex. 5 'Missa L'homme armé super voces musicales' *Sanctus*, mm. 1-7 (alto)

'Missa de Beata Virgine' *Agnus* II, mm. 28-42 (bass)

Both melodies have an unusually wide span. Once again the later melody unfolds more flexibly, with lighter swing; it flows smoothly and serenely, emphasizing the patterns and functions of the major scale. Indeed, the ascent and descent in the *Sanctus* are balanced; they form an arch of axial symmetry. But in comparison with the later version, the ascent is more turbulent, more laborious, and at the same time more vigorous. Josquin lets the rising sequences begin on different beats of the measure and at different time intervals.

In these and similar cases we can venture a generalization about change of style and relative chronology. In the later works a growing mastery and maturity in melodic writing are evident, as well as the reception of Italian influences. Line, 'tonal order',[6] and rhythm become smoother; angular contours are rounded; the melodies flow more serenely; the voice is more flexible; the division of phrases becomes more transparent; the proportions are more striking. When Martin Luther praises Josquin's music as 'joyous, spontaneous, and overflowing' ('frolich, willig, milde'),[7] he speaks primarily

---

[4] Missen, xvi, p. 162.   [5] Missen, i, p. 20.

[6] See Walter Wiora, 'Der tonale Logos. Zu Jacques Handschins Buch "Der Ton-charakter"', in *Historische und systematische Musikwissenschaft* (Tutzing, 1972), pp. 408–9.

[7] See Walter Wiora, 'Josquin und "des Finken Gesang"', ibid., pp. 229 and 235. According to old German usage, 'milde' means 'liberal', 'generous', 'abundant'; we render it here as 'overflowing'.

of the later style that is determined by his complete 'mastery of the notes' ('der Noten Meister') and by the new Renaissance art.

Comparison between earlier and later versions, however, is only one method of investigation of style and chronology. A more systematic procedure is needed to answer questions of a more fundamental nature: how did Josquin compose melodies that are not only extended, but really wide-spanned? How did he achieve the continuation of the melodic energy? Which devices did he use toward this purpose?

Following the tradition of Ockeghem, many melodies, especially of the younger Josquin, are continued without distinct motives by restless voice movement, kinetic energy, and unstable rhythm. The rhythmic movement presses on through a chain of syncopations, comparable to chains of unresolved dissonances—in this aspect similar to the 'endless melody' of Richard Wagner. Such undifferentiated lines are also to be found in several later works in which motivic organization prevails, for example, the *Kyrie* of the 'Missa Ave maris stella', as opposed to the *Agnus Dei*:[8]

Ex. 6   'Missa Ave maris stella' *Kyrie* I, mm. 2-9 (superius).

'Missa Ave maris stella' *Agnus* I, mm. 2-7 (superius)

In the second melody (Ex. 6b), the wide-spanned curve is motivically organized: a motive in the range of a fourth appears in three sequential patterns, the last time in slightly condensed form. In the first instance (Ex. 6a), however, distinct motives and motivic repetitions are missing; the melody flows as in one continuous breath. Its flow and drive are intensified by the freely changing rhythms (repeated alternation between $\frac{3}{2}$ and $\frac{6}{4}$) and the tonal uncertainty (only toward the end does D maintain itself as tonic against G).

The coherence of wide-spanned melodies often rests on the melodic coherence of the underlying *cantus firmus*. Its shape forms a skeleton that provides a solid contour. In melodic lines without a *cantus firmus* scales and other elementary scaffolding devices assume new importance. Thus melodic

[8] Missen, vi, pp. 1 and 16. On uninterrupted flow and motivic organization as opposite principles of Ockeghem and Busnois respectively, see Edgar H. Sparks, *Cantus Firmus in Mass and Motet, 1420–1520* (Berkeley and Los Angeles, 1963), pp. 226–8, 230, 234–5, 239.

coherence is determined or increased by attaining one and the same high
point in shorter and longer starts and runs:[9]

Ex. 7 'Missa La sol fa re mi' *Gloria*, mm. 100-12 (superius)

The shape of Josquin's wide-spanned melodies is often determined by
gradually rising peaks. Scales are used as swift runs, especially in later works,
such as the 'Missa de Beata Virgine'. In the *Agnus* of the 'Missa La sol fa re
mi'[10] he combines line and point by letting the voice rise repeatedly from
the same starting point to higher and higher degrees of the scale, as did
Beethoven in the finale of his First Symphony:

Ex. 8 'Missa La sol fa re mi' *Agnus* II, mm. 41-50 (superius)

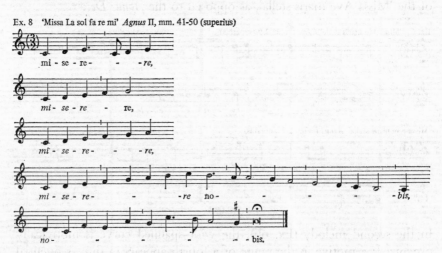

Sometimes he combines line and point with leaps, letting the voice rise
from one and the same starting point by a series of leaps:[11]

Ex. 9 'Missa L'homme armé super voces musicales', *Pleni*, mm. 62-8 (superius)

Scale and leaps are combined in melodic zigzag lines of broken thirds or
fourths in the *Sanctus* of the 'Missa L'ami Baudichon':[12]

[9] Missen, ii, p. 40.   [10] Ibid., p. 56.   [11] Missen, i, p. 22.   [12] Missen, ix, p. 84.

Ex. 10 'Missa L'ami Baudichon' *Sanctus*, mm. 13-17 (superius)

sanc -   -   -   -   -   -   -   -   - tus

In opposition to Tinctoris' dictum and to the Palestrina style, where frequent repetition is not permitted, Josquin made use of the power of reiteration to an astonishing degree and, remarkably, without redundance. Early works, as the Masses 'Ad fugam', 'Di dadi', 'Gaudeamus', but also later compositions, contain numerous extended chains of sequences.

Sequences are frequently used to achieve a climax. In the *Pleni sunt* of the 'Missa Hercules Dux Ferrariae', the climax is intensified through the prolongation of a motive and through rolling and swirling passages, forerunners almost of Handelian coloraturas:[13]

Ex. 11 'Missa Hercules dux Ferrariae' *Pleni*, mm. 47-58 (bass)

glo -   -   -   - ri - a, glo-   -

- ri - a,   glo-   -   -   -   -   ri - a tu - a.

In the Marian motets and in those based upon the Song of Solomon,[14] sequences, often vigorous or turbulent, at other times ecstatic, enlarge an initial space of a sixth to double its size, producing a magnificent climax:

Ex. 12 'Virgo prudentissima', mm. 50-57 (superius)

to -   ta   for-mo -   sa, *for - mo* -   sa et sua -   - vis es,

et sua -   -   -vis es.

Sketchy imitation and imprecise sequence become rare in the course of Josquin's development. Increasingly he modifies reiteration by shifting of accents, by extension and variation. He thus forms melodic lines, for example, in the first *Kyrie* of the 'Missa de Beata Virgine', that are among the most beautiful in the whole history of music. His art of spinning a line by extension and variation is matched by his ability to form a melodic contour through detachment of component motives combined with reiteration and sequence. In this aspect, the ingenious Jodocus Pratensis belongs to the precursors of Joseph Haydn. The following melody is formed by detachment of a motive, which is then augmented, and a further detachment and extension:[15]

[13] Missen, vii, p. 31.   [14] Motetten, Bundel v, no. 25, p. 135.
[15] Missen, ii, p. 48.

Ex. 13 'Missa La sol fa re mi' *Credo*, mm. 226-34 (bass)

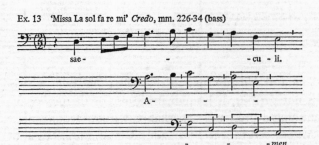

An essential aspect of Josquin's later style is the synthesis of two opposite ideas: wide-spanned melody and expressive declamation. True, even in Josquin's early works wide-spanned melodies are animated by heart and spirit, like religious jubilations according to St. Augustine's conception of absolute music.[16] But now they serve the expression of particular texts, such as the passionate prayers of the psalm motets:[17]

Ex. 14 'Miserere mei, Deus,' 2. *p.*, mm. 1-14 (first tenor)

The history of wide-spanned melodic lines leads from prehistoric origins to graduals and jubilations in plainchant, to organa in the style of St. Martial, through the ages of Dunstable and Ockeghem to the linear counterpoint, long melismatic songs, and far-reaching instrumental themes of Bach, Beethoven, Bruckner, and Bartók. In this kind of musical width and span Josquin is one of the greatest classics.

[16] See Walter Wiora, art. 'Absolute Musik', *MGG*, i, col. 56, and 'Jubilare sine verbis', *In memoriam Jacques Handschin* (Strasbourg, 1962), pp. 56ff and 61ff (reprinted in *Historische und systematische Musikwissenschaft*, pp. 146ff, 150ff).

[17] Motetten, Bundel viii, no. 37, p. 65. The version cited is that of the Medici Codex; see Edward E. Lowinsky, ed., *The Medici Codex of 1518*, iii, p. 198, and iv, no. 41.

Tonal Tendencies in Josquin's Use of Harmony

SAUL NOVACK

The leading-note as a means of intensifying directed tonal motion had fully emerged by the beginning of the Renaissance. The fifteenth century witnessed its enhancement and reinforcement through the fifth relationship, i.e., the dominant-tonic phenomenon. Josquin's use and expansion of this harmonic relationship constitutes an artistic achievement of the highest order. The brief exposition that follows, based on Josquin's sacred music, can only illuminate some of the highlights.

While the problem of the relationship between mode and tonality cannot be considered at this point, even though it is central to the study of harmonic usage, it is significant that Josquin's music already begins to show assimilation of the old modes to modern major and minor. He uses the Ionian mode on both C and F,[1] as well as the related Mixolydian mode, modified through *musica ficta*. There are a number of compositions in Aeolian and many in Dorian on both D and G, modified through both stipulated and unstipulated accidentals to resemble the Aeolian mode. In all of these modes the leading-note punctuates tonal continuity. It is part of the mode in Ionian and is often present through *musica ficta* in the other modes. Only the Phrygian mode remains unaffected. In this mode, which cannot have a dominant on its fifth degree because of the diminished fifth, Josquin relies upon other means to provide tonal continuity. Settings in E Phrygian frequently have extended sections in C and A; sections in C take on the features of C Ionian, and the sections in A, A Aeolian, with frequent use of the appropriate leading-notes.

[1] [Throughout the fifteenth and sixteenth centuries composers set whole Masses, but also motets and other smaller liturgical as well as secular genres, in F with a key signature of one flat in all voices. Theorists called it Lydian, but it was, as Glareanus (*Dodekachordon*, p. 115) rightly insisted, transposed Ionian. This use of Ionian transposed to F was encouraged by such examples of Gregorian chant as the *Kyrie* from the 'Missa VIII (De Angelis)' (L.U., p. 37), in which every B is flatted. And if this example be dismissed, because its origin lies in the fifteenth-sixteenth centuries, as the editors of the *Liber* indicate, then its *Sanctus*, ascribed to the '(XI) XII c.' (L.U., p. 38), or the *Sanctus* and *Agnus Dei* from the 'Missa IX (Cum jubilo)' ascribed to the fourteenth century and '(X) XIII c.', respectively, may serve instead; each of these melodies has many Bs, each one invariably flatted.—Ed.]

While the dominant-tonic relationship was already well established during the fifteenth century, its abundant use by Josquin is neither confined to its position in strategically located cadences nor to the simple V–I progression, which frequently appears in non-cadential situations without the leading-note; it still exercises the force of the relationship of the fifth, but lacks the intensity that the leading-note provides. The V–I progression can dominate the entire setting of a composition.[2]

Various expansions of the V–I progression occur in Josquin's music:

I–II–V–I[3]

I–IV–V–I[4]

I–III–V–I

The last progression assumes great importance in Baroque and Classic forms, representing the motion from the minor tonic to the so-called 'relative major', with eventual return, through the dominant, to the tonic. In Josquin's music there are frequent examples in Dorian and Aeolian settings. The Dorian mode, with its modification of *both* the sixth and seventh degrees, comes closest to the later typical character of the minor mode.[5] A good example of an extended harmonic structure of I–III–V–I is found in 'Vultum tuum deprecabuntur'.[6] At the outset of Part VI, the tonic, G minor, is clearly established. At measure 431 a long extension in B♭ major begins (Ex. 1).[7] This is the III chord of G Dorian, and, as shown in the graph,

---

[2] See, for example, 'O Virgo virginum' (Motetten, Bundel xxiii, no. 83), in G Dorian. Many other examples may be found in Josquin's works.

[3] See 'Descendi in ortum meum' (Supplement, no. 6), where the II chord is prolonged harmonically before moving to V (mm. 61–7).

[4] For example, measures 187–8 and 190–91 in 'Pater noster' (Motetten, Bundel xii, no. 50), in G Dorian. An E♭ is called for in the IV chord, producing a minor IV, characteristic in the minor mode. This is a good example of the assimilation of the Dorian mode to minor.

[5] E.g., Ex. 1, in G Dorian, illustrates the presence of E♭ (stipulated, and through *musica ficta*), E♮, F, and F♯ (through *musica ficta*). In Aeolian compositions the seventh degree is, of course, frequently raised; but the sixth degree, which in the minor mode appears in both forms, is rarely altered.

[6] Motetten, Bundel iv, no. 24.

[7] A brief explanation of the symbols used in the linear analyses in this paper follows: N = neighbouring note; P = passing note; ℕ = neighbouring chord (complete or incomplete), supporting a passing note in the uppermost voice; + = major; — = minor. Arabic numbers have the same significance as in figured bass. The slur (⌒) denotes contexts and their subdivisions; the dotted slur (⌐⌐⌐) and the dotted beam (- - - - -) indicate the return to or retention of a pitch whose structural significance remains the same; the curved arrow (↗) denotes a leading-note chord which resolves to the chord to which the arrow is directed; the straight arrow (——→) shows directed motion from and to chords of structural significance. The beam (———) indicates the structural connection between notes of different pitches; the bracket (⌣) is used to indicate the dominance of a single chord, extended through harmonic progressions and/or contrapuntal motions shown above and within the bracket. Notes do not have durational value; unstemmed

Ex. 1   mm. 430-49

black notes are most 'immediate' in their context, stemmed quarter-notes are 'intermediate' in context and subordinate to the half-note, the most 'remote' and primary symbol. These symbols and terms, derived from the graphing techniques of Heinrich Schenker, are explained in detail in *The Music Forum*, i, ed. William J. Mitchell and Felix Salzer (New York, 1967), pp. 260–8.

it is prolonged with its own harmonic progression of IV (m. 439) moving through II with a passing seventh (m. 441) to V (mm. 442–3), to I (mm. 444–6). E♭ is consistently used within the prolongation of B♭, which acts in effect as the relative major. The tonic, G, is regained at measure 449 through a II⁶–V–I cadence. The shape of the superius, with the same melodic pattern heard once in the dominant and twice in the tonic of B♭ (mm. 442–7), is significant. The first statement of the motive (mm. 442–3) in the dominant of III is balanced by the succeeding statement in the tonic of III, and the reiteration of this last statement builds a climax moving towards the final cadence in the central key, G Dorian-Aeolian. The structural importance of B♭ in the upper voice is revealed in the movement away from it and toward it. This note is not abandoned until the definitive downward motion to the final cadence of the passage.

A further harmonic extension is the termination of a section or composition by the use of successive fifth relationships in the progression I–VI–II–V–I, with its bass moving down a perfect fifth between VI and II, possible only in Ionian and Mixolydian, in the latter with a leading-note in the cadence.

Harmonic progressions are also intensified by the sophisticated use of applied dominants, not only to V but also to other chords.[8]

The motion V–VI as a deceptive cadence is used as a means of extending the V and delaying the resolution to the tonic, particularly at the end of compositions.[9] It may also serve to set off a circuitous path taken in the resolution of the V to the final I, particularly against the final sustained note in the upper voice.[10] The achievement of the tonic releases the tension and enhances the finality of the tonal goal.

There are numerous examples of I moving to IV and returning to I underneath the final sustained tonic, the IV chord acting as a consonant contrapuntal chord against the sustained note. The so-called 'plagal' IV extends the I, serving a coda-like function. If the V–I progression with leading-note intensifies the motion toward the tonic, the IV–I progression at the end serves to sustain and confirm it.

The logical extension of the V–I relationship into motion through the circle of fifths is also found in Josquin's music. Although Josquin is by no

[8] Examples of applied dominants are:

a) to the V chord: 'Benedicite omnia opera Domini Domino' (Motetten, Bundel xiii, no. 53), in F Ionian. This motet contains a number of such examples, e.g. measures 34–5, as well as prolongations of I–V–I in the dominant (mm. 181–7). (For a harmonic analysis of this motet, see Edward E. Lowinsky, *Tonality and Atonality in Sixteenth-Century Music* (Berkeley and Los Angeles, 1962), pp. 20–25).

b) to the III chord: 'Domine, non secundum peccata nostra' (Motetten, Bundel ii, no. 13), measures 213–4, in G Dorian.

c) to the VII chord: ibid., measures 190–92. This applied dominant is possible without *musica ficta* in the Dorian and Mixolydian modes.

[9] An example of movement from V to VI instead of to I is in the concluding section of 'Descendi in ortum meum' (Supplement, no. 6), in which the final V–I is achieved tellingly with fermata.

[10] In 'Paratum cor meum, Deus' (Motetten, Bundel xvii, no. 67), at measures 322–5, V moves to VI, then to IV (preceded by I⁶) as a further delay before resolving to I. These chords are essentially contrapuntal in function, serving as consonant supports of the sustained note above. The VI or the IV, as *harmonic* functions, would operate as such only within the harmonic progressions, such as I–VI–V–I or I–IV–V–I.

Ex. 2   mm. 77-85

means the inventor of this technique, he goes farther than any of decessors and with great imagination sets the stage for the openi the harmonic space in the sixteenth century. The first example is pe boldest of all, the now famous ending of 'Absalon, fili mi'.[11]

The graph in Ex. 2 indicates some important aspects. The uppermost line delineates a motion from the fifth degree of the B♭ tonic to 4, 3, 2, and finally 1, thereby outlining the B♭ minor triad. Meanwhile, the bass moves in perfect fifths alternately via the third of the triad to which it is descending (see graph), in diatonic fashion to B♭ minor, going as far as the VI chord. One cannot go further in the circle of fifths without losing the immediacy of the uppermost line's motion within the tonic triad. At this point Josquin pauses and moves directly to V, the goal of the descending motion. It took more than a century for this progression to become a regularly used harmonic device. The tonal centre of the composition as a whole is B♭. The foregoing excerpt begins in the major and moves into the minor mode, in which it terminates.

Successive fifths are freely used in various parts of compositions. They are frequent in Ionian, Aeolian, and Dorian settings, most often as descending fifths, which may also appear in the form of ascending fourths. They also are used against a *cantus firmus*.[12] Particularly important and fascinating is the fusion of thematic repetitions with root movement by fifth, resulting in perhaps the first genuine examples of so-called 'harmonic sequences'.[13] There are effective settings of as many as four-fold and five-fold repetitions. An unusually extended example is found in the transposed Dorian motet, 'Vultum tuum deprecabuntur',[14] measures 261–83. The first succession has the following repetitions, alternating between bass and tenor:

D to G	melodic figure
G to C	figure repeated, with new counterpoint
C to F	same passage, repeated
F to B♭	same passage, repeated

At the moment the B♭ is attained, the bass enters beneath it with G. A new melodic pattern appears in the following transpositions:

G to D	melodic figure
D to A	figure repeated, with new counterpoint
A to D	original figure, modified, with new counterpoint

[11] Supplement, no. 5.

[12] See 'Ave nobilissima creatura' (Motetten, Bundel vii, no. 34), measures 76–80; also measures 211–15. In both cases the bass moves as follows: D–G–C–F–B♭. The motet is in D Aeolian.

[13] 'O admirabile commercium' (Motetten, Bundel i, no. 5), measures 47–53 (B♭ Ionian). Another example is the repetition in the bass of 'Virgo prudentissima' (Motetten, Bundel v, no. 25), measures 28–39, in which the motive moves up a fourth, the equivalent of down a fifth, in the following order: D–G–C–F, each pattern including the leading-note.

[14] Motetten, Bundel iv, no. 24, Part IV.

> D to G   same passage, repeated
> G to C   same passage, repeated
> C to F   same passage, repeated

'Misericordias Domini',[15] in A Aeolian, has several instances of successive fifths, particularly around C, including a five-fold repetition of a cadential motive. This repetition begins at measure 51 with the first statement of the cadential motive as follows:

Ex. 3   mm 51-3 (superius)

The statements of this motive are:

> m. 51 beginning on E, ending on A
> m. 53 beginning on A, ending on D
> m. 55 beginning on D, ending on G
> m. 59 beginning on G, ending on G (leap of an octave instead of fourth)
> m. 61 beginning on G, ending on C

This is an artful chain of applied dominants and leading-note chords, subtly involving deceptive VI chords to delay resolutions. This technique is used to give relief to the concept 'misericordia Domini'. Almost immediately afterwards the text is repeated and, beginning in measure 70, a new succession of descending fifths with pattern repetition in two phases follows: A–D–G–C–F; D–G–C. Successive fifths are found frequently in compositions set in Phrygian, as though to compensate for the absence of the dominant function in that mode; they frequently move away from E in descending fifths and return in ascending fifths.[16] In 'Factum est autem',[17] in which Part I ends on E, the motion in fifths towards the final E is as follows: from G (m. 88), prolonged at first via C (m. 92), finally to D, then to A, and then to the final E. In the five-part 'De profundis clamavi',[18] the setting of the concluding *Kyrie eleison* begins at measure 104 on C, moves to G (mm. 105–9), then to D (mm. 110–12), to A (mm. 113–15), and then to the concluding E. In the four-part Phrygian setting of 'De profundis clamavi',[19] the shape of the melody at the beginning of the motet, moving down a fifth, results through imitation in the succession E–A–D.

[15] Motetten, Bundel x, no. 43.

[16] See my study of the 'Missa Pange lingua' in 'Fusion of Design and Tonal Order in Mass and Motet: Josquin Desprez and Heinrich Isaac', *The Music Forum*, ii (1970), beginning on p. 206. Of particular interest is the *Osanna* (described on pp. 226 and 228), which involves paired repetition and succession of fifths.

[17] Motetten, Bundel iii, no. 16.

[18] Motetten, Bundel xxiv, no. 90.

[19] Motetten, Bundel xi, no. 47. 'Virgo salutiferi' (Motetten, Bundel vii, no. 35) is an example in which the shape of the melody at the opening outlines an ascending fifth, thereby resulting in the succession, G to D to A.

The succession of fifths may continue into almost a complete diatonic circle of fifths. Thus, in 'Qui velatus facie fuisti'[20] (*secunda pars*, mm. 82–9), ascending fifths, in a prolongation of C Ionian, move as follows: C–G–D–A–E–F–C. Significantly, B is omitted between E and F since B to F would form a diminished fifth. Finally, an example from the 'Missa Fortuna desperata'[21] reveals seven successive descending fifths (Ex. 4). II–V–I of the

Ex. 4 *Credo*, mm. 108-18

[20] Motetten, Bundel ii, no. 11.

[21] Missen, iv. The text to which the descending fifths are applied, quite appropriately, is 'descendit de coelis'. In the motet 'Absalon, fili mi' (see Ex. 2), the descending fifths were applied to the text, 'descendam in infernum plorans'.

Ex. 5   mm. 1-24 (superius and alto)

tonic (F Ionian) in measures 109–10 is succeeded by II–V (without leading-note) –I of G minor, which is the II chord of F Ionian, and is attained at measure 111. The circle of fifths begins with the B♭, the III chord in the G prolongation, includes the augmented fourth between E♭ and A—the direct leap avoided by passing notes—and is extended to the B♭ chord in measure 113. The modernity of this example is obvious; it is a convincing and dynamic part of the total harmonic structure in the conclusion of this section of the *Credo*.

The juxtaposition of old and new in the application of harmonic relation-ships to the *cantus firmus* is a fascinating subject for study. Josquin reveals in his works a whole new view of the *cantus firmus* in its relationship to tonality. The shape and form of the chant melody is exceedingly important. In some motets the Gregorian melody appears in fragments, each of which is treated with harmonic clarity.[22] Josquin's ability to preserve the character of the chant melody while adapting the harmonic treatment to tonality may be shown in a number of cases, among them the two-part opening of 'Mittit ad Virginem',[23] a setting of a so-called 'variation-chain' sequence[24] (Ex. 5). The stanza consists of five lines whose corresponding musical units suggest harmonization in tonic and dominant. Josquin's setting of the Ionian melody reveals his feeling for tonal form; he organizes the five musical units as follows:

1: tonic
2: tonic
3: tonic
4: dominant
5: dominant-tonic (C Ionian)

The penultimate position of the V and its ultimate resolution is most significant. The six-part 'Praeter rerum seriem',[25] one of the most famous motets of Josquin, is marked by considerable division of the chant melody (in G Dorian) into harmonically supported units. 'Planxit autem David',[26] in F Ionian, offers another example of division of text, here separated by rests. The lamentation tone is freely reiterated, sometimes in *cantus firmus* style. Each complete unit of text is prolonged within the tonic. These prolongations appear in various harmonic progressions. Intermediate points are frequently marked by strong cadential figures.

[22] For example, the setting of the *cantus firmus* in 'O Virgo virginum' (Motetten, Bundel xxiii, no. 83), in G Dorian. The small range of the melody, as in the first phrase, G–B♭–A–B♭–G–A–G, leads to strong prolongations of the G tonality and consistent use of the V against the passing and neighbouring notes.

[23] Motetten, Bundel i, no. 3.

[24] On the variation-chain concept, see Oliver Strunk, 'Some Motet-Types of the 16th Century', *Papers Read at the International Congress of Musicology, 1939* (New York, 1944), pp. 155–60.

[25] Motetten, Bundel vii, no. 33.   [26] Motetten, Bundel iii, no. 20.

The *cantus firmus* melodies have each a specific modal character. But Josquin feels free to acknowledge or ignore the modal identity of a melody; occasionally his polyphonic settings will contradict the nature of the mode, the polyphony absorbing the melody within a different tonal centre. Other times he will transpose a melody from one mode to another. The 'Missa L'homme armé super voces musicales' is a prime example. In the case of the Phrygian mode, which has no dominant chord, and therefore no

Ex. 6   mm. 50-58

harmonic motion to its own central note or *finalis*, Josquin sometimes contradicts the mode of the *cantus firmus* in the polyphonic setting. In the 'Missa Pange lingua', the beginning of the Phrygian hymn melody is realized polyphonically in clear-cut C Ionian, with V–I movements in the setting of the text, 'Et incarnatus est'.[27]

Parallel motion between the outer voices, a favourite device of Josquin,[28] is often used in motion directed towards a V–I cadence as a means of intensifying the drive toward the cadence. Such parallel motions are occasionally strengthened through the use of sequence. In the following example from the *Gloria* of the 'Missa Fortuna desperata',[29] measures 50–58, the melodic motion is in descending parallel tenths, while the drive to the cadence is achieved structurally in ascending tenths, as indicated in the graph (Ex. 6). Independent voice-leading is sacrificed to intensify the direction of tonal motion. In such passages the consonant parallel direction terminates on the leading-note, most frequently with a 4–3 suspension, thereby heightening the attainment of the penultimate V.

Clarity of formal design, enhanced by motivic reiterations and contrasts in vocal scoring, is further given depth through renewal of the tonal relationships. An example from 'In exitu Israel de Egypto'[30] is given in Ex. 7. The V, prolonged through measures 210–18, now projects the text, 'et omnes qui confidunt in eis' (m. 218 to end), by a descending line via the dominant triad, supported by its own I–V–I. Immediately afterwards the same text is repeated to the same motive, now prolonged through the tonic triad, the top voice beginning the motion on the third of the tonic, moving down to the leading-note and supported by I–V–I of the tonic. Additional intensity is achieved through use of four voices instead of two, and through the motion of parallel tenths alternating with octaves in the outer voices, as shown in the graph. The parallelism is a striking example of the combination of tonal structure and thematic design to create direction and symmetry.

Some aspects of the direction and function of the upper voice have been considered. The significance of the lowest part in the preceding examples is

---

[27] See Novack, 'Fusion of Design and Tonal Order'; the analysis of *Et incarnatus est* is given on pp. 213 and 218–19. A much later example of the contradiction of linear mode and polyphonic tonality is J. S. Bach's treatment of Hassler's Phrygian melody, 'O Haupt voll Blut und Wunden'. In the 'Passion according to St. Matthew' the first four chorale settings of this melody are in the major, corresponding in their various transpositions to the relationship of C Ionian to E Phrygian. The fifth and final setting, appropriately, is in E Phrygian, terminating on E.

[28] [Remarked on by Gafurius in his *Practica musicae* of 1496, Book III, Ch. 12; see Clement A. Miller, transl., *Franchinus Gaffurius: Practica Musicae* (American Institute of Musicology, 1968), p. 144.—Ed.]

[29] Missen, iv.

[30] Motetten, Bundel xii, no. 51, measures 210–26.

manifest. No longer is the bass exclusively a line like the other voices. Its leaps are often reflections of harmonic motions; its direction, both in step and in leaps, is then conditioned by the tonal goal. As an illustration of the extent of the harmonic orientation of the bass line, the skeletal framework of the lowest voice of an entire motet, 'Levavi oculos meos in montes',[31]

Ex. 7   mm. 210-26

31 Motetten, Bundel xviii, no. 70.

is given in Ex. 8. The bass reiterates, in different ways, motions from I to V and from V to I, frequently with parallel repetitions of design. G Dorian (often turning into Aeolian), as the central note of organization, is realized

through the bass line in a remarkably forward-looking technique. Note-worthy is the parallelism in some repeated units, e.g. at measure 99 and at measure 103. Exact repetition occurs in the bass only, thereby highlighting the importance of the lower voice in the unfolding of the tonic-dominant relationship. Such parallelisms are striking. The beginning of the bass in Part II is quoted exactly to illustrate how thematic material and harmonic function are combined (Ex. 9).

The preceding examples illuminate another important aspect of Josquin's style: all voices share in the thematic material. This is what is known as 'imitative style'. However, the outer voices assume responsibilities that go far beyond those of the middle voices, especially in Josquin's late works. The highest and the lowest lines assert their functions in tonal structure,

Ex. 9   mm. 107-14 (bass)

both individually and together, with a strength and purpose that unequivocally point in the direction of 'polarity of the outer voices'. In this sense Josquin is a great innovator.

The foregoing exposition has been directed to only a few aspects of Josquin's concepts of tonality.[32] Only chordal forms operating within the framework of the dominant-tonic phenomenon and in the fifth relationship have been considered in this brief study. Chords with contrapuntal, voice-leading function also play vital roles in the projection of tonality and must be examined together with the harmonically functioning phenomena.

Needless to say, Josquin's use of harmony cannot be considered solely by examining chords and cadences or by sending the various simultaneities through the computer. The harmonic factors are related to a number of compositional and aesthetic aspects. It is through a study of these inter-relationships that we may realize more exactly the remarkable character of Josquin's concepts of tonality, from which springs a new view not only of musical structure but also of expression of the text.

---

[32] For other aspects, particularly with regard to cadences, the functions of dissonance, harmonic and motivic repetition, see Edward E. Lowinsky's admirable study of the psalm motet, 'Benedicite omnia opera Domini', in his *Tonality and Atonality*, pp. 20–25.

On the Treatment of Dissonance in the Motets of Josquin des Prez

CARL DAHLHAUS

Johannes Tinctoris, humanist and pedant, was given to reproving, in details, composers whom he venerated. Ockeghem, 'optimus compositor', had to endure the reproach of having violated the natural order of dissonance when, in the Mass 'La belle se siet', he arrived at a minim dissonance by the leap of a fourth. 'If such an excellent composer and careful seeker of agreeableness should have done such things I leave to the judgement of those who hear it'.[1] That Hugo Riemann was provoked to contradiction by this petty censoriousness is understandable; questionable, however, is his judgement that Tinctoris thereby proves himself to be a 'conservative schoolmaster'.[2] 'Conservative'—insofar as the word possesses any meaning before the nineteenth century—was Artusi, whose polemics of about 1600 against Monteverdi reveal the indignation of a man for whom an irregular dissonance appeared not only as an artistic, but also as a moral flaw. About 1477, however, the situation was different. In the fifteenth and sixteenth centuries, the epoch of the evolution of the 'reine Satz', composers—at least those in the central tradition culminating in the Palestrina style—rather than striving for a greater wealth of dissonant figures sought the reduction of dissonance and its increasingly rigorous regulation. 'Progressive', then, was the restriction of dissonance, not its emancipation; hence the pedantry of theorists happened to appear 'avant-gardist'. Thus, as Ernst Krenek recognized,[3] it was not Tinctoris but Ockeghem who was the 'conservative'.

The fundamental outlines of the development are unmistakable: From the accidental collision of voices, scarcely controlled by norm, emerged the

---

[1] 'Quod si tamquam optimus compositor ac dulcedinis accuratus exquisitor effecerit cunctis id audientibus judicandum reliquo'; Johannes Tinctoris, *Liber de arte contrapuncti*, end of Book II, ch. 32 (E. de Coussemaker, *Scriptorum de Musica Medii Aevi*, iv, col. 146a).

[2] Hugo Riemann, *History of Music Theory*, transl. Raymond H. Haggh (Lincoln, Nebraska, 1962), p. 266 (p. 316 of the second German edition, Berlin, 1920). The last six notes of Riemann's (and Haggh's) example are transcribed a fifth too high, turning the dissonance of a second into a fourth; the argument, however, is not affected by this error.

[3] E. Krenek, 'A Discussion of the Treatment of Dissonances in Ockeghem's Masses as Compared with the Contrapuntal Theory of Johannes Tinctoris', *Hamline Studies in Musicology*, ii (1947), p. 18.

regulated dissonance of the *prima pratica*, and from this regulated dissonance, the emancipated dissonance of the *seconda pratica*. Indeed, one might roughly distinguish between an archaic, a classical, and a modern stage in the treatment of dissonance. The restriction and standardization in the fifteenth and early sixteenth centuries was a step towards rationalization and total mastery of composition; nothing irregular or accidental was to be tolerated. The transition to the modern counterpoint of the late sixteenth and seventeenth centuries is not to be understood as a reversal but as a development: a deduction from the 'strict style' rather than a relapse into the archaic style. The free counterpoint assumes the strict style as a system of reference: the deviations, if they are to function expressively, must be referred back to the norm which they contravene. In order to perceive, say, the pathetic character of the syncopated dissonance resolved by leap to the lower fifth, one must know the rules of counterpoint so that they become the premise of the way we hear.

The historical reality is of course more complex than the scheme of a straight-line development from accidental through regulated to emancipated dissonance. Moreover, it is debatable to what extent the strict Palestrina style actually constituted the vaunted 'point de la perfection' towards which sixteenth-century counterpoint tended, and whether there did not exist other contemporaneous traditions in which the copiously dissonant older counterpoint was transferred without a break into the free style of the *seconda pratica*. It is not clear how we should understand the deviations from the strict style that Vincenzo Galilei assembled and praised as models: are they an archaism or a modernism, are they remainders of an older obsolete technique of composition, or anticipations and early examples of the free style, which became predominant in the seventeenth century?[4]

Of course, historic and pragmatic aspects are one thing, aesthetic considerations another. Modern counterpoint may at times appear to spring directly from the archaic style, without the intervention of classical counterpoint, but effect and significance differed. The rhetorical, expressive character of the irregular dissonant figures depended upon the relationship to classical counterpoint, which remained as an ever-present background in the listener's consciousness.

* * *

From an historical point of view, in which the Palestrina style forms the culmination of the contrapuntal development of the fifteenth and sixteenth centuries, it would be fairly easy to describe the dissonance treatment in the

---

[4] Claude V. Palisca, 'Vincenzo Galilei's Counterpoint Treatise: A Code for the *Seconda Pratica*', *Journal of the American Musicological Society*, ix (1956), pp. 81–96. Galilei's remark (p. 82) that he examined the works of Josquin, Willaert, and Gombert, among others, to establish the new principles, namely, the principles of the *seconda pratica*, is confusing.

motets of Josquin des Prez and to determine its historical position. If one presumes that Josquin started from the same principles as Palestrina, though less certain and deliberate, then the deviations from 'classical' counterpoint appear as mere imperfections characteristic of a still half-archaic style. Even Knud Jeppesen,[5] who in general takes the attitude of the strict historian and abstains from value judgements, has sometimes described the differences in dissonance treatment as a beclouding of the 'reine Satz', toward which Josquin tended, but which he did not develop with the purity of Palestrina. (Teleological forms of thought, though discredited in methodology, have by no means died out in the writing of history, as they facilitate the historian's task of selecting from the complex mass of facts those that are historically important and of connecting them convincingly.)

The view of Josquin's counterpoint as a Palestrina style with archaic residues and imperfections needs revision. The treatment of dissonance in the period around 1500 must be measured by its own standards. Many dissonant figures that Palestrina banished from the 'reine Satz' appear with great regularity in Josquin's motets, whether late or early. They have the air of self-evidence. Far from forming deviations from a norm that Josquin supposedly shared with Palestrina, they carry their norm in themselves.

The cambiata appears in the motets of Josquin as a self-contained figure of three notes demanding no particular continuation—whether it be through an ascending second or through an ascending third followed by a descending second.[6] In the Palestrina style, according to Jeppesen's psychological explanation, the violation of the rule that demands resolution of the dissonance by stepwise movement is 'only an ostensible one, since the fourth note of the figure was understood as a resolution of the dissonance, which—though belated—finally appears and clears up the situation'.[7] Josquin, however, apparently understood the leap of a third in itself as a satisfactory and regular resolution of the dissonance. And even Tinctoris, otherwise given to restriction, allowed this resolution, next to a stepwise one, although only exceptionally: 'And that same dissonance should immediately be followed by a consonance, one or, very rarely, two steps away.'[8] Therefore, the cambiata has a different motivation in Josquin than in Palestrina.

[5] Knud Jeppesen, *The Style of Palestrina and the Dissonance* (2d ed., Copenhagen and London, 1946), p. 135: 'On the whole great uncertainty prevailed with regard to this relation [the relatively accented passing dissonance] throughout the era of the second Netherlands School.'

[6] Ibid., pp. 210–11; Carl Dahlhaus, 'Die "Nota Cambiata"', *Kirchenmusikalisches Jahrbuch*, 47 (1963), p. 118, Ex. 8b.

[7] Jeppesen, p. 149.

[8] 'Et hanc ipsam discordantiam, concordantia uno gradu vel duobus tantum, quamvis hoc rarissime, distans ab ea immediate sequetur' (Coussemaker, *Scriptorum*, iv, col. 145a).

If one accepts Tinctoris' statement at face value—and historically nothing else is justified—then in the case of dissonance left by a downward leap, a distinction must be made between leaps of a third, which were considered regular, and leaps of a fourth, fifth, and octave, which diverged from the norm:

Ex. 1

The undifferentiated collective term 'dissonance quitted by leap' is too inexact. In fact, the difference in the manner of resolution represents a feature from which a development in Josquin's treatment of dissonance can be deduced. The accumulation of cambiata-like figures resolved by leaps of the fourth, fifth, or octave such as are characteristic in the early motet 'Mittit ad Virginem',[9] presumably dating from the Milanese period (see Ex. 2), would hardly be conceivable in a later period. Not that such figures

Ex. 2 'Mittit ad Virginem'

(a) m. 17
(b) m. 31
(c) m. 58
(d) 2.p., m. 37
(e) 2.p., m. 41

are lacking in the later works—they do, for instance, occur in the motets 'O Virgo prudentissima', 'Benedicta es, caelorum Regina', 'De profundis clamavi', and 'Salve Regina';[10] but the leap of a third appears to have become the accepted resolution, that of the fourth a rare exception, and thus an archaism:

Ex. 3 'De profundis.' m. 160

As Povl Hamburger has shown,[11] the passing dissonance maintained for the duration of a minim is found in Palestrina only under specific conditions.

[9] Motetten, Bundel i, no. 3.
[10] Motetten, Bundel xi, nos. 45, 46, 47, 48.
[11] Povl Hamburger, *Studien zur Vokalpolyphonie* (Copenhagen and Wiesbaden, 1956), pp. 41 ff.

A minim dissonance following a dotted semibreve is usually part of a theme that is imitated and remains unchangeable. In the case of minims following dotted semibreves that are not bound thematically, as well as minims preceded by a minim, we are almost always concerned with a passing dissonance, which, through its relationship to another voice, functions as a preparation for a syncopated dissonance:[12]

Ex. 4

In the motets of Josquin, on the other hand, the passing minim is not subject to restriction; it is available as a technical resource without need of justification. The restriction of the use of dissonance, which constitutes the basic outline of the development of counterpoint from Josquin to Palestrina, in this case manifests less a tendency to suppress than a need for special motivation.

To be sure, one might assume that the regulation of the passing minim later on in the sixteenth century was prompted by a slowing down of tempo, resulting in the dissonance becoming more conspicuous; the same explanation is almost irrefutable when we observe that Palestrina uses the 'sincopa tutta cattiva', the dissonantly introduced syncopated seventh,[13] on a minim, whereas Josquin used it on a semibreve (Ex. 5).[14] However

Ex. 5   'Planxit autem David' mm. 121-2

plausible the hypothesis may appear, it is not conclusive. The motets of both Josquin and Palestrina are written in *tactus alla semibreve*, with the unit of time represented by the minim; the difference in tempo between the tactus of the early and the late sixteenth century, if it existed at all, was negligible. But in Josquin's motets two varieties of beat and tempo can be distinguished; the treatment of dissonance varies accordingly. 'Christum

---

[12] The explanation, which is lacking in Hamburger, is valid for the passing seventh (ibid., p. 57) as well as for the passing fourth (ibid., p. 60).

[13] Jeppesen, p. 239. The syncopated fourth, of which the first section can be defined as a 'quarta consonans', is not considered a 'sincopa tutta cattiva'.

[14] Motetten, Bundel iii, no. 20.

ducem' and 'Qui velatus facie fuisti', for example, are conceived in *tactus alla breve*; minims are consequently treated like semiminims in *tactus alla semibreve*. In 'Christum ducem' (see Ex. 6)[15] one finds an unaccented note-

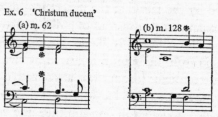

Ex. 6   'Christum ducem'
(a) m. 62   (b) m. 128

against-note minim dissonance (m. 62) and a relatively accented passing minim (m. 128), and in 'Qui velatus'[16] a passing semibreve:

Ex. 7   'Qui velatus' mm. 7-8

In the Palestrina style the relatively accented passing dissonance—defined by Jeppesen as the first semiminim on the second or fourth beat—is subjected to a need for motivation similar to that of the passing minim. Palestrina used it with discrimination: it was permissible without restriction if preceded by a minim (♩♪♪). However, a chain of descending semiminims (♪♪♪♪) was handled as a special case, as Franz Nekes recognized,[17] in that the third semiminim coincides with the preparation of a syncopated dissonance in another voice:

Ex. 8

This dissonant figure, considered antiquated, was justified by the stereotyped character of the clausula, which Palestrina did not wish to dispense with.

In order to explain why Palestrina treated the relatively accented semiminim dissonance following a minim differently than in a chain of semiminims, Jeppesen[18] theorized that the unit of time, in the first instance, must have been perceived as the minim and in the second as the semiminim, and the note has been heard as a dissonant grace note. This hypothesis is psychologically questionable, since the small difference between the

[15] Motetten, Bundel i, no. 4.   [16] Motetten, Bundel ii, no. 11.

[17] Quoted by Jeppesen, p. 120. Jeppesen's arguments against Nekes are inconclusive.

[18] Jeppesen, pp. 140 ff.

two rhythmic figures is not sufficient to justify the feeling of a change in the unit of time. The reason for Palestrina's reserve in the face of the relatively accented passing dissonance as the third note of a chain of semiminims might rather be explained by the fact that the unaccented second note was also nearly always dissonant, so that instead of a dissonance being resolved, it passes into a second dissonance. It is the double dissonance, distinguishing the semiminim chain from the minim followed by two semiminims, that called for different treatment. Josquin was less sensitive to succeeding dissonances in one and the same voice. He does not shrink from stringing three semiminim dissonances together in one and the same voice:[19]

Ex. 9   'Planxit autem David' m. 192

Pietro Aron even formulated a rule that, of the four semiminims, the first and fourth must be consonant while the second and third could be dissonant.[20]

Unaccented note-against-note semiminim dissonances[21]—that is, passing notes that form a dissonance with a note sounded simultaneously in another voice instead of entering inconspicuously over stationary voices—are rare exceptions in the Palestrina style,[22] whereas Josquin used them without restraint. Dissonance resulting from a passing note in one voice and a cambiata in another was almost a stylistic topos around 1500:

Ex. 10

Jeppesen[23] attempted to justify the note-against-note dissonance with the hypothesis that the dissonant voices did not stand in direct relation to each other, but were each related to a stationary voice, a voice that formed the centre of the contrapuntal relationship. However, what must be explained is not only how Palestrina justified the few note-against-note dissonances

---

[19] Motetten, Bundel iii, no. 20.   [20] Quoted by Jeppesen, p. 127.

[21] Jeppesen (pp. 163 ff.) does not differentiate between accented and unaccented note-against-note dissonances. Only the unaccented dissonance is irregular and rare. Relatively accented note-against-note dissonances are frequent and normal.

[22] Jeppesen, pp. 168–9.   [23] Ibid., pp. 167–8.

that he permitted himself, but why, in contrast to Josquin, he almost always avoided this dissonant figure.

The notion of two voices being considered exclusively in relation to a third voice without being related to one another is compatible with the principles of composition in the fifteenth as well as the seventeenth centuries but not with those in the sixteenth century. In the *cantus firmus* style of the fifteenth century it is the tenor, and in the chordal style of the seventeenth century it is the bass that can be considered the centre of the contrapuntal relationship. However, sixteenth-century polyphony, based on systematic imitation, is a complex of voices in which the centre of reference was formed by the themes going from voice to voice, and in which every voice was at all times related to every other voice. Palestrina's relatively rare use of note-against-note dissonance can therefore be understood as a sign of his feeling for the implications of systematic imitation. In contrast, it seems as if Josquin, although tending towards systematic imitation, adhered, in part, to ideas rooted in the *cantus firmus* tradition. At any rate, Jeppesen's hypothesis applies more to Josquin than to Palestrina. Instead of accounting for Palestrina's use of note-against-note dissonance, it offers rather an explanation of why he shies away from this dissonant pattern.

The thesis that the principles that underlie the treatment of dissonance in the fifteenth and sixteenth centuries were realized with the greatest clarity in the Palestrina style is questionable. The restrictions and conditions that Palestrina imposed upon the cambiata, the passing minim, the relatively accented dissonance in a chain of semiminims, and the unaccented semiminim note-against-note dissonance were rather rules governing exceptions through which he fenced in and justified the relics of an older dissonance technique than the means, as Jeppesen thought,[24] that enabled the emergence of the 'true' nature of these particular figures.

*   *   *

Josquin's dissonance technique cannot be codified as strictly and completely as Palestrina's; any attempt to outline a closed system—following the model of the theory of 'classical' counterpoint—would be futile. However, the uncertain chronology of the motets notwithstanding, there are norms emerging in the works of the middle period, coming to ascendancy in the late motets. The deviations from this system found in early works, appearing sporadically and following no recognizable principle, may be viewed as relics of an earlier stage of development in counterpoint, or even as symptoms of uncertainty. Dissonant figures such as the syncopated fourth in the lowest voice that leaps down a third (Ex. 11),[25] the leap from a

[24] Ibid., p. 149.
[25] Motetten, Bundel iv, no. 22.

syncopated dissonance to another dissonance (Ex. 12),[26] the unprepared suspension (Ex. 13),[27] the accented passing minim (Ex. 14),[28] or the un-accented note-against-note dissonance of a minim (Ex. 15)[29]—they are not

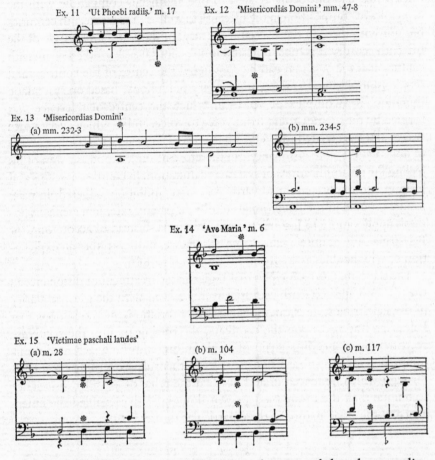

only irregular according to the rules of the Palestrina style but also according to Josquin's criteria.

A tendency toward restraint and rationalization in the use of dissonance

[26] Motetten, Bundel x, no. 43. In measure 66 a syncopated seventh appears to leap to the upper fourth:

But since parallel fifths occur in the same bar—and in two-voice movement—the possibility of a printing error cannot be ruled out. Nevertheless, all six sources agree in this reading.

[27] Motetten, Bundel x, no. 4.

[28] Motetten, Bundel i, no. 2.

[29] Motetten, Bundel v, no. 26. The possibility of a mistake in transmission in the case of

is apparent not only in the development from Josquin to Palestrina but also within Josquin's own work. However, the stricter rules of the Palestrina style must not always be considered an inevitable consequence and extension of the norms that Josquin imposed upon himself.

The development of Josquin's style, moving toward restraint instead of emancipation of dissonance, would appear to contradict the idea that the rhetorical counterpoint of the *musica reservata* was heralded in Josquin's later motets. Musical-rhetorical figures are licences outside the norms of the strict style; they owe their expressive or allegorical substance to their exceptional character. A dissonance technique that moves toward regulation does not lead to the musical rhetoric of *musica reservata* or the *seconda pratica* but draws away from it.

The breaking of norms, however, is not the only means of achieving expressive dissonance; accumulations of regular dissonances may approximate the effect of irregular dissonances. In the motet 'Planxit autem David',[30] whose poignant pathos cannot be missed, dissonances, in some measures, are crowded together. A 'sincopa tutta cattiva' is followed by a passing dissonance coinciding with its note of resolution (Ex. 16a; see also Ex. 5);

Ex. 16 'Planxit autem David'

the semibreve note-against-note dissonance in 'Misericordias Domini', m. 252, cannot be ruled out, although this motet is almost a compendium of irregular dissonance formations:

All six sources have the same reading, however.

[30] Motetten, Bundel iii, no. 20.

two note-against-note dissonances are followed, after a consonance, by a passing note leaping up to the fifth (Ex. 16b); chains of three parallel seconds (Ex. 16c) or sevenths (Ex. 16d) result from the collision of stereotyped melodic formulas; the note of resolution of a syncopated dissonance becomes a passing dissonance against a third voice (Ex. 16e); a note that forms a note-against-note dissonance is arrived at and left by way of a leap of a third (Ex. 16f). These dissonances, although not standing outside of Josquin's norms, nevertheless convey an impression of almost grating harshness. To compose rhetorically Josquin did not depend upon a free style that would have run counter to his tendency towards a more exact regulation of the use of dissonance. He was 'progressive' in his use of expressive means without sacrificing the 'progressive' restriction of dissonance.

Problems of Authenticity in Josquin's Motets

EDGAR H. SPARKS

In his comprehensive monograph on Josquin des Prez, Helmuth Osthoff singles out a group of six motets for special commentary.[1] Osthoff notes —indeed, he emphasizes—that these motets fall below Josquin's usual high standards, that one is attributed to a minor composer as well as to Josquin, and that all appear exclusively in late sources dating from about 1530 to 1573. These features in conjunction—poor quality, conflicting attribution, and late sources—inevitably raise the question of authenticity, and no one is more aware of this than Osthoff himself. One of his greatest contributions to Josquin research, in fact, has been the exposure of numerous false attributions on grounds identical to those listed above. Yet Osthoff accepts these six works as unquestionably genuine.

Osthoff justifies his decisions with a tightly-knit argument that centres on a factor shared by all these motets, but appears in no other work of Josquin: every one of the motets of this group exhibits a particular compositional error, a so-called *Satzfehler*, and Osthoff accepts this common feature as final and unambiguous proof of authenticity.

In the biographical portion of his monograph, Osthoff argues that Josquin's creative career began early and that at forty years of age (1480 or a bit later) a goodly share of his output was already in existence.[2] This would mean that a number of works must have preceded the stylistically important declamation motets, which Osthoff places in the Milanese period,[3] and Osthoff includes among them a group of five- and six-voice motets,

---

[1] Helmuth Osthoff, *Josquin Desprez* (Tutzing, 1962–5), i, p. 19, and ii, p. 28. The motets in question are: 'In illo tempore stetit Jesus in medio discipulorum suorum' (6 v.), 'Nesciens Mater' (5 v.), 'Ave verum corpus' (5 v.), 'Victimae paschali laudes' (6 v.), 'Inter natos mulierum' (6 v.), and 'Responsum acceperat Simeon' (6 v.). All are published in the *Werken*, Motetten, nos. 55, 71, 80, 81, 84, and 85, respectively.

[2] Osthoff, *Josquin Desprez*, i, p. 17.

[3] Edward Lowinsky, in a review of the first volume of Osthoff's Josquin monograph, argues that these works more likely date from the 1490s, since they show the influence of the Italian *lauda* and all known biographic data of *lauda* composers point to the 1490s as the date of origin of the four-part *lauda*; see 'Scholarship in the Renaissance: Music', *Renaissance News*, xvi (1963), pp. 255–62.

obviously beginner's works, that are transmitted by late sources. 'Nesciens
Mater', 'Inter natos mulierum', the five-voice 'Ave verum corpus' (there
is also another setting by Josquin, for 2–3 voices), and 'Responsum acceperat
Simeon' disclose, 'along with a most archaic style, incorrect dominant
cadence formations. Significantly, not a single one of these works was
included in the prints of Petrucci.'[4] Osthoff assigns no specific dates to the
works, but since he assumes that Josquin began composing early, and since,
in his opinion, these motets predate the masterpieces of the Milanese period,
we must assume that he is thinking in terms of the 1460s and early 1470s.

In speaking of the 'Victimae paschali laudes' for six voices, one of the
works in question, Osthoff expands on his argument. He again mentions
the presence of 'a compositional error that is characteristic of an entire
group of five- and six-voice motets: the dominant cadence with leading-
note and leading-note suspension sounding simultaneously in different
voices' (see Examples 1a, b, and c; instances of the *Satzfehler* are marked
with an X). Osthoff proceeds: 'The sources for these motets—Italian

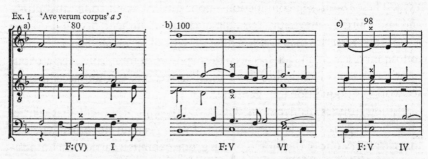

Ex. 1 'Ave verum corpus' *a 5*

manuscripts of about 1530, later German prints, and a Spanish choirbook—
show a wide distribution. Aside from a single manuscript, the attribution of
which must be doubted, Josquin is named as composer throughout. The
antiquated musical style is generally consistent and, along with the stereotyped compositional error, indicates the same hand. Clearly, these are early
works which Josquin, if at all, would certainly never have allowed to
circulate until after revision of the questionable passages. After all, the other
motets, and the numerous five- and six-voice chansons as well, are free of
such crude sonorities.'[5]

Osthoff builds his argument on four interlocking propositions: (1) The
works are attributed to Josquin in a respectable number of sources, and
their antiquated style is generally consistent; (2) the archaic style and many
technical defects indicate that they are apprentice works from the early
part of Josquin's career (it is unthinkable to place them anywhere else, once
Josquin's authorship is accepted); (3) Josquin would never have allowed
them to circulate in the form in which they have come down to us, so that

---

[4] Osthoff, *Josquin Desprez*, i, p. 19.   [5] Ibid., ii, p. 28.

their very inadequacies account for the fact that they appear only in late sources compiled sixty or seventy years after the presumptive date of composition; (4) among the many dubious features, there is one that serves as hallmark (*Indiz*) for the group. This is the *Satzfehler* that Osthoff repeatedly cites as final and conclusive proof of Josquin's authorship, 'the unambiguous characteristic of a very early stratum of motets for five and six voices'.[6] Osthoff argues here for authenticity on the basis of inadequacy, which is unusual for him, but each of his statements seems reasonable enough in itself. However, in such a tight chain of reasoning, the failure of a single proposition is apt to cause the entire argument to collapse.

The 'Victimae paschali laudes' mentioned above is noteworthy because of its extraordinarily dissonant character and because it is attributed to a composer other than Josquin in one source.[7] This is a certain Jo. Brunet, whose music was totally unknown until the recent publication of the Medici Codex, which contains a four-voice motet of his.[8] With reference to this work, Edward Lowinsky comments: 'Astonishing and quite individual is the unconventionality of Brunet's treatment of dissonance'. Lowinsky follows this up with mention of 'a chain of dissonant sevenths and seconds', and a 'tone cluster F–G–A–B♭' sounding simultaneously, and so on.[9]

Since 'Victimae paschali laudes' is more dissonant by far than any work we know by Josquin, it seemed a routine precaution to look further into the music of the contender. One more work of Brunet is known, likewise a sequence, a setting of 'Veni Sancte Spiritus' for five voices.[10] A comparison of the two works makes it apparent at once that 'Victimae paschali laudes' and 'Veni Sancte Spiritus' are, stylistically, identical twins. The helterskelter treatment of the *cantus firmus*, the character of the voice lines, the harmonic idiom with its pervasive dissonance and not infrequent parallel perfect intervals, the imprecise relation of text to music, all point to the same hand—and not to the hand of Josquin.[11] On stylistic grounds, Brunet

[6] Ibid., ii, p. 100.

[7] Rome, Biblioteca Apostolica Vaticana, MS. Capp. Sist. 24 (dated 1545), no. 17, Jo. Brunet. The two sources naming Josquin as composer are Rome, Biblioteca Vallicelliana, MS. San Borromeo E. II. 55–60 (dating from 1530–1), second series, no. 25, Josquin, and Toledo, Catedral Primada, Biblioteca Capitolar, MS. 10 (dating from the 1540s), Josquin. Florence, Biblioteca Nazionale Centrale, MS. Magliabecchi XIX, 125 *bis* (dating after 1529), fol. 9, transmits the work (alto I only) anonymously.

[8] 'Ite in orbem universum', *The Medici Codex of 1518*, ed. Edward E. Lowinsky (*Monuments of Renaissance Music*, iii–v; Chicago, 1968), iv, no. 27, p. 193.

[9] Ibid., iii, p. 169.

[10] Rome, Biblioteca Apostolica Vaticana, MS. Capp. Sist. 46 (dated 1527), no. 23.

[11] In both works the *cantus firmus* is occasionally stated in brief points of imitation involving some or all of the parts; more often, it is presented in relatively long values in one part (often the highest sounding one) and accompanied from time to time by subsidiary, freely imitative statements in faster moving values, wherever they can be fitted in. The statement

would have a formidable claim to the work, were it not for 'an inconspicuous clue which furnishes unequivocal proof of Josquin's authorship [of
'Victimae paschali laudes']; this is the twofold appearance of the *Satzfehler*.... '[12]

Brunet's setting of 'Veni Sancte Spiritus', however, shows that the two
instances of the *Satzfehler* not only do not provide 'unequivocal' proof of
Josquin's authorship of 'Victimae paschali laudes'—they provide no proof
at all. Brunet himself commits the identical compositional error in two
places in his 'Veni Sancte Spiritus' (compare Ex. 2a and b and Ex. 2c and d).

Ex. 2a and b: Brunet, 'Veni Sancte Spiritus'

Ex. 2c and d: Josquin/Brunet, 'Victimae paschali laudes'

It will be shown below that this particular suspension occurs in the works
of many composers other than Brunet. The *Satzfehler* is by no means a
trademark of Josquin, and Osthoff's argument that it points exclusively to
him is not supported by the facts.[13]

For the purposes of this investigation, the invalidation of the argument
concerning the *Satzfehler* is far more important than the establishment of
authorship for 'Victimae paschali laudes'. I myself am convinced that Brunet
is the author. The six motets that have been accepted as genuine chiefly

---

in longer values moves irregularly from part to part at intervals ranging from approximately six to twelve measures. The impressively dissonant nature of the harmony is
illustrated in Ex. 3a, and in Exs. 2c and d. Parallel fifths occur in 'Veni Sancte Spiritus'
at measures 29, 40, and 161; 'Victimae paschali laudes' presents parallel fifths in measure
18 and parallel unisons in measure 85. Parallel perfect intervals are used with good effect
by Josquin, on occasion, so that the mere presence of such intervals forms no proof that
the work is not by him.

[12] Osthoff, ii, pp. 27–8.   [13] See note 20. below.

on the basis of the *Satzfehler* must now be re-examined as critically and severely as the other motets that appear only in late sources.

Concerning the *Satzfehler*, it should be pointed out that the suspension is embedded in a generally dissonant context, in conjunction with other suspensions in which dissonance and resolution are expressed simultaneously (see Exs. 3a and b, and 2a and c, where such occurrences are marked by arrows). The *Satzfehler* appears merely as an extreme instance of a general tendency to pile up dissonance and to thicken the texture.

Ex. 3 Josquin/Brunet, 'Victimae paschali laudes'   Brunet, 'Veni Sancte Spiritus'

Regarding the distribution of sources, it needs to be stressed that only three works, including 'Victimae paschali laudes', occur in from three to six sources, and so have the rather broad base that Osthoff mentions, whereas the remaining motets do not. They each appear only once, in prints of 1545 edited by Sigismund Salblinger.[14]

---

[14] Salblinger edited two collections of motets in 1545: (1) *Cantiones septem, sex, et quinque vocum* (Augsburg: M. Kriesstein, RISM 1545³) containing 'Nesciens Mater' (no. 22) and 'Responsum acceperat Simeon' (no. 7); (2) *Concentus octo, sex, quinque et quatuor vocum* (Augsburg: Ph. Ulhard, RISM 1545²) containing 'Ave verum corpus' (no. 10). 'Nesciens Mater' and 'Responsum acceperat Simeon' are unica, while 'Ave verum corpus' was copied twenty-three years later in a print edited by Cl. Stephan, *Cantiones triginta selectissimae: quinque, sex, septem...vocum* (Nuremberg: U. Neuber, RISM 1568⁷), no. 22. This publication cannot be counted as an independent source. It reproduces the musical text of the edition of 1545 note for note, and in so doing, perpetuates errors that could not escape immediate detection on rehearsal. (In m. 70₃, a semibreve e' in the superius, in error for f', produces a major seventh chord instead of the intended triad, and at m. 40 an imperfect instead of a perfect *longa* rest makes it impossible to perform the canon correctly for the remainder of the *prima pars*.)

We owe a great debt to Salblinger for printing such magnificent works as 'Absalon fili mi' and 'Responde mihi', but we cannot fail to notice that his versions are marred by errors of the crudest sort. (In addition to the two instances mentioned above, I might cite glaring parallel octaves in 'Nesciens Mater', mm. 13₃–14, which would have been apparent to the dullest ear; in the *Werken*, the three notes in the superius have been placed a third lower.) The fact that such errors are perpetuated in later prints indicates how little care went into some sixteenth-century editions. It seems that the music was neither rehearsed nor proofread carefully. (Stephan is not the only offender. Salblinger, in the 1546 reprint of *Cantiones septem...*, repeats all the errors of the original 1545 edition.)

These are errors of a type that occur frequently in the publications of Johannes Ott, and Osthoff has shown that the carelessness in Ott's musical text is paralleled by negligence

Two of the motets in the Salblinger publications, 'Nesciens Mater' and 'Ave verum corpus', show striking similarities to a widely known master-work of Josquin's full maturity, 'Inviolata, integra et casta es, Maria'.[15] The similarities are far-reaching, and were apparently inspired by the identity of the opening notes in the respective Gregorian melodies. As Ex. 4a shows, rhythmic features of 'Nesciens Mater' and 'Inviolata' are very close. Voice entries are at strictly regulated intervals of three measures (marked by brackets at mm. 1, 4, and 7), and each statement of the borrowed melody is given an identical declamatory rhythmic pattern. The sweeping scale-line descent of a tenth in the counterpoint is the same in both motets, although there are differences in rhythmic detail (see Ex. 4a, mm. 4–7). Descending scales in parallel tenths are also similar, down to the staggering of the opening notes in a brief point of imitation (see Ex. 4b, mm. 7–10; there are again differences in rhythmic detail). Furthermore, this descent is repeated in 'Nesciens Mater', just as it is in 'Inviolata'.[16]

After the opening notes, however, the two Gregorian melodies diverge, and it becomes impossible for the counterpoints to maintain their near identity. It is precisely at this moment that the quality of the writing plummets in 'Nesciens Mater'. The sweeping, graceful lines of the beginning are replaced by short-breathed phrases formed on commonplace cadential figures; cadences appear every two measures with monotonous regularity, and so many bald, unprepared suspensions are presented that the editor of the *Werken* felt compelled to rewrite them wherever it was possible to do so.[17]

It is not necessary, in this case, to speculate on the possible degree of inadequacy of Josquin as a youthful composer. The problem is not one of qualitative level, but of disparity in quality. 'Nesciens Mater' reminds one of a paper of an undergraduate student who fails to acknowledge the authors he quotes; the quality fluctuates wildly from primitive doggerel to flowery, sometimes literary English. The unevenness of 'Nesciens Mater' makes it

---

in attribution to composers (see *Josquin Desprez*, ii, pp. 10ff.). Osthoff sees no reason to question Salblinger's three Josquin attributions which he accepts as genuine because of the *Satzfehler*. I find nothing in Salblinger's editorial methods to inspire more confidence in his attributions than in those of Ott.

[15] *Werken*, Motetten, Bundel x, no. 42. Lowinsky, *The Medici Codex*, iv, p. 231 (transcription); iii, p. 180 (commentary).

[16] The repetition is disguised in the *Werken* in an editorial attempt to correct the impossible parallel octaves of the original (mm. 13₃–14) by moving the three notes in the superius down a third.

[17] Each instance of rewriting is carefully documented in the editorial remarks on the motet, so it is possible to reconstruct the original form of the suspensions. See *Werken*, Motetten, Bundel xix, p. V.

very difficult to accept the work as genuine. To do so, one would have to assume that Josquin could show the mastery of his mature style for eighteen or twenty measures, and then, suddenly, lose all his technical skill, worse, his musicality for the remainder of the work. It is simpler and more probable to assume that 'Nesciens Mater' belongs to a large class of works popular at the time—those written in imitation, or as reworkings, of highly regarded masterpieces. Rewriting of this sort was apparently considered a worthy form of musical endeavour, and it was carried out in a great variety of ways, with widely varying degrees of skill.[18]

'Ave verum corpus', in addition to the similarities at the beginning illustrated in Exs. 4a and b, carries out the long-range structural setup of 'Inviolata'. In both works, the *cantus firmus* is presented in canon at the fifth above, and at the time interval of three breves in the *prima pars*, of two breves in the *secunda pars*, and of one in the *tertia pars*. Like 'Nesciens Mater', it is a not very skilful imitation of 'Inviolata', but for different reasons.

We do not find internal contradictions as in 'Nesciens Mater', for 'Ave verum' tends to be stodgy from the beginning. In contrast to the 'peculiar grace' and 'the infinitely subtle rhythms and floating accentuations' of Josquin's 'Inviolata',[19] Ex. 4a shows that the author was a firm believer in expressing the strong beats of the metre (see mm. 4–7); the same attitude toward rhythm and the total straightforwardness in the expression of the parallel tenths of the contrapuntal voices is shown in Ex. 4b (last score).

Can the work be an early one? None of the well-authenticated early works of Josquin compares with it. Whatever weaknesses we may find in 'Ut Phoebi radiis', 'Illibata Dei Virgo nutrix', or the 'Missa L'ami Baudichon', rhythmic bluntness of this sort is not one of them. Furthermore, if we, with Osthoff, account for the defects of 'Ave verum corpus' by dating it early, a serious problem of anachronism arises. The regularity of the formal layout is not characteristic for the tenor motet in the 1460s and early 1470s. The very beginning of the work, with its absolutely regular entries, one voice following the other at intervals of precisely three breves, and every one of the voices presenting the motive in exactly the same form —rhythmically and melodically—is utterly atypical for that time. Tenor motets and tenor Mass movements begin with duets; if there is imitation,

---

[18] Some cases involve merely the addition of voices, an instance of this being the six-voice version of Josquin's 'Ave Maria. . .Virgo serena' (*Werken*, Motetten, Bundel i, no. 1a). In other cases, as in an anonymous reworking of Mouton's motet 'Tua est potentia', there may be 'a free rearrangement of the whole score'. The original motet and the derived one are printed by Lowinsky, *The Medici Codex*, iv, p. 250, and iii, pp. 188–92. Works such as these represent a phase of the general tendency to parody technique, but it seems that, on the whole, these 'parody motets' are less interesting musically than parody Masses.

[19] Lowinsky, *The Medici Codex*, iii, p. 181.

the entries are not regularly spaced, nor are they identically formed; neither is every voice involved in the imitation.

The opening measures of 'Ave verum corpus' totally lack the quality of *varietas* that characterizes important works in the 1460s and 1470s. The canon on the Gregorian melody, with its strictness and with its simple plan of progressively decreasing intervals of entry, bears out the character of the beginning. The work exhibits an almost complete lack of rhythmic intricacy, of organization by sequence, ostinato, or other motivic means that characterize the early period. (The absence of the typical 'under-third' cadence in which the leading-note descends to the sixth degree before proceeding to the tonic is also a suspicious circumstance, but it could be accounted for by later revisions in accordance with changing tastes.)

The soberness of rhythmic movement and the simplicity and consistency of formal design point to Josquin's full maturity. If he wrote the work as a very young man, before he had achieved his characteristic musicality and lively imagination, his clairvoyance is all the more remarkable, for he forecasts in detail aesthetic attitudes that were not to develop for about twenty years. Once again, it is easy and reasonable to interpret the peculiarities of the work by viewing it as an imitation of a model, as a gesture of respect by a not very competent musician, but one who had experienced the consistency and uniformity of the late style of Josquin and his younger followers.

Before proceeding with the motets, let us go back to the *Satzfehler* itself. It occurs, as we have seen, in works for five or more voices of composers other than Josquin. But oddly enough, this form of the cadential suspension appears to be very rare in the early part of the period we are discussing. In the motets for five voices of Regis and Compère, for example, I found not a single instance. This was also true of Obrecht, whereas in the works of Isaac the device does occur, albeit rarely. I was able to locate only two instances in Ockeghem, both in the five-voice 'Missa sine nomine'. This came as a surprise, because Ockeghem uses dissonance much more freely than Josquin. Moving on into the sixteenth century, a few instances could be located in Mouton, but in the third decade, with L'Héritier and Hellinck, examples became much more frequent. The heyday of the device, however, proved to arrive in the 1530s and 1540s. In the works of Clemens non Papa and Gombert—two of the most respected composers of their generation—the *Satzfehler* appears everywhere.[20] The suspension is so much a part of

---

[20] The cadential suspension in which the leading-note and the suspension resolving to the leading-note are sounded simultaneously is possible in scales in which the seventh degree is a leading-note by nature (i.e., in Lydian or Ionian modes on C, F, and B♭). The works cited here all have a signature of one flat and frequent cadences on F or B♭, or are without key signature and have cadences on C or F. The Isaac example occurs in the *Sanctus* of the 'Missa de Beata Virgine, V vocum (I)' as the final cadence of the *Benedictus*;

their complex and generally dissonant contrapuntal style that it seems improper to continue calling it a 'compositional error'. Moreover, the time at which this dissonance becomes a common part of the musical vocabulary coincides with the period in which the sources begin to present the *Satzfehler* motets attributed to Josquin. It seems perfectly logical that this is the time in which some of them originated.

The motet, 'In illo tempore stetit Jesus', is almost certainly a product of the third or fourth decade of the sixteenth century. The continuously dense texture, the invariable overlapping of cadences, the provision of a point of imitation for nearly every clause of the text, the complexity of the points which, in several cases, present more than one entry per voice—all are well known features of the northern style of the 1530s and 1540s, and all make

Ex. 5   mm. 36-48

see *Heinrich Isaac, Messen*, ed. Martin Staehelin (*Musikalische Denkmäler*, vii; Mainz, n.d.), p. 37, m. 108. See also the commentary of Staehelin with reference to the final cadence on G of *Kyrie* I of the same Mass (ibid., *Revisionsbericht*, p. 94), where F♮ in the *vagans* prevents a leading-note in the superius. The two cadences in the 'Missa sine nomine' of Ockeghem occur in measure 66 of the *Gloria* and measure 125 of the *Credo* (*Johannes Ockeghem, Collected Works*, ii, ed. Dragan Plamenac (New York, 1947), pp. 79 and 82). Instances in Mouton may be found in the 'Missa Lo serai' in the final *Agnus*, measures 47 and 72 (*Johannes Mouton, Opera Omnia*, iii, ed. Andrew C. Minor (American Institute of Musicology, 1969), pp. 37 and 39). Examples in L'Héritier are very numerous, but a few may be cited: see *Johannis Lhéritier Opera omnia*, ed. Leeman L. Perkins (American Institute of Musicology, 1969), pp. 151, m. 31 and m. 33, 160, m. 234, 168, m. 53, and 169, m. 58. Examples of the *Satzfehler* abound in Gombert and Clemens and, once again, only a few need be cited: *Jacobus Clemens non Papa, Opera omnia*, ed. K. Ph. Bernet Kempers (American Institute of Musicology, 1951–), i, fasc. 4, pp. 5, m. 15, 9, m. 21, 10, m. 50, 14, m. 69, 18, m. 57, 32, m. 87, and 36, m. 69; *Nicolai Gombert Opera omnia*, ed. Joseph Schmidt-Görg (American Institute of Musicology, 1951–), vii, pp. 108, br. 1, m. 3, and 109, br. 4, m. 3; viii, pp. 107, m. 60, and 124, m. 63.

their appearance to varying degrees in the music of Richafort, L'Héritier, and others writing in the 1520s. Ex. 5 illustrates a rare instance of thinning of texture (from six to four voices), the density of the imitative writing (the figure in the first measure of the example appears 17 times in sixteen measures), and the relation of text to music (note the setting of 'Et dixit eis: quid turbati estis?' in tenor I (the next to lowest voice), mm. 41ff., and superius, mm. 43ff.). These features, along with the prevalence of steady quarter-note motion, would place the work, at best, at the end of Josquin's life, along with such a motet as the 'De profundis' for five voices. This is an unsatisfactory conclusion, not only because of the clumsiness of the writing (the static nature of the harmonies is well illustrated in mm. 9–29, which consist of an almost unrelieved alternation of triads on G and D), but also because the work gives every evidence of being post-Josquinian. It goes without saying that I consider it impossible to make a plausible case for this work as a product of Josquin's Milanese period, or even of the Roman period.[21]

'Responsum acceperat Simeon', the third of the motets published by Salblinger in 1545, is not so advanced in style as the work just discussed and does not depend on points of imitation as the main structural procedure. It does present, however, continuously dense texture with the full complement of voices sounding almost constantly in the *prima* and *tertia partes*. (Even in the *secunda pars*, a trio, all voices sing from beginning to end.) Steady motion, overlapping of cadences, lack of motivic organization of the voices, as well as the continuous two-part canonic *cantus firmus*, argue against accepting this motet as a work originating in the 1460s or 1470s, when Josquin was still a 'beginner'. It reminds one, rather, of works of a composer such as Thomas Stoltzer, who was writing early in the sixteenth century.

The work least easy to fault, it seems, is 'Inter natos mulierum', which Osthoff at one time considered spurious, although he now accepts it as authentic.[22] Here, the irregularity of the points of imitation, when they occur, the constant use of hemiola in triple metre, and other features make

[21] Osthoff is apparently not convinced that this work is very early for, in an earlier article, he classes it with motets standing on the threshold of the middle period, such as 'Domine, Dominus noster', 'O Virgo virginum', 'Praeter rerum seriem', and so on; see 'Josquin Desprez', *MGG*, vii, col. 210.

[22] Osthoff lists 'Inter natos mulierum' among the doubtful and inauthentic works in the article 'Josquin Desprez', *MGG*, vii, col. 203. M. Antonowycz argues for the authenticity of the work, and points out that the opening motive is one often used by Josquin. This is true, but the motive is one of a common fund used by many composers, among them Noël Bauldeweyn (Thomas Stoltzer?) in the psalm motet, 'Benedicam Dominum' (opening of the *quarta pars*, 'Clamaverunt iusti'); see *Thomas Stoltzer, Ausgewählte Werke, 2. Teil: Sämtliche Psalmmotetten*, ed. Lothar Hoffmann-Erbrecht (*Das Erbe deutscher Musik*, 66; Frankfurt, 1969), p. 34, mm. 226–31. Antonowycz, 'Zur Autorschaftsfrage der Motetten *Absolve, quaesumus, Domine* und *Inter natos mulierum*', *Tijdschrift van de Vereniging voor Nederlandse Muziekgeschiedenis*, xx (1966), pp. 154ff., cites other examples of Josquin's use of the subject.

In an earlier article, Antonowycz argues for the authenticity of three other works discussed here ('Nesciens Mater', 'Ave verum corpus', and 'Victimae paschali laudes'). He mentions the use of scale lines extending an octave or more, of repetitions of phrases, of statements of the *cantus firmus* sometimes in long values contrasting with the faster movement of the counterpoints, sometimes in shorter values agreeing with them, and so on. These are features of Josquin's writing, certainly, but they are common features of the writing of his contemporaries as well, and hence seem to me much too general to establish any exclusive connection to a single writer. See Myroslaw Antonowycz, 'Die Josquin-Ausgabe', *Tijdschrift van de Vereniging voor Nederlandse Muziekgeschiedenis*, xix (1960–61), pp. 6–31.

a date of the latter half of the fifteenth century plausible. The smoothness of the writing indicates a musically gifted composer, although he apparently liked the dubious cadential suspension very much, for all four appearances are repetitions of one another.[23] Even though this motet does not present the serious internal contradictions of the others, the thick scoring of the *prima pars*, the numerous suspensions with resolution and dissonance sounding simultaneously, and the lack, despite the great amount of repetition, of symmetrically balanced pairs of phrases (29 out of the 88 measures of the work are repetitions) make the work sound unusual for Josquin. Furthermore, Osthoff's primary evidence for accepting the motet as genuine (the *Satzfehler*) is now shown to be valueless, so that his former rejection of the work takes on renewed importance. I am inclined to agree with his first reaction, and to suggest that it belongs among the *opera dubia*.

Having discussed all works presenting the *Satzfehler*, we are now in a position to review the four propositions, listed above, that summarize Osthoff's reasons for accepting them as genuine. Starting with proposition four, we assert that the *Satzfehler* is not proof positive of Josquin's authorship; it is used by many other composers, particularly in the second quarter of the sixteenth century, and by some very extensively. The device has a definite harmonic significance: it is sharply dissonant in itself and occurs in generally dissonant contexts; it beclouds harmonic issues, mingling elements of suspension and resolution, and it is found in association with other suspensions doing the same. It points away from Josquin who, from the very beginning, stands for harmonic clarity and, certainly in his early style, for reserve in the use of dissonance, as well.

Proposition three explains the total absence of any of these works in the central sources on the grounds that Josquin would not allow them to circulate. However, the *Satzfehler*, now that its historic location is ascertained, justifies dating these works fairly closely to the sources in which they are found. This obviates the necessity of assuming a sixty- or seventy-year-long wait in darkness, arising from Josquin's reluctance to let the youthful experiments out of his hands.

Proposition two accounts for the inadequacies of the works by assigning them to an early period. This is a quick and easy way to explain their peculiarities but, to a large extent, it is a form of self-deception. What is being sought is not an early period as such, but one before Josquin became endowed with the superior musical talent and the vivid imagination for

---

[23] *Werken*, Motetten, Bundel xxiii, no. 84. Compare mm. 14–17 with 36–9, 40–41, and 83–6. These are not structural repetitions, separated from the general flow of the work, nor are they consistently used to underline repetitions of text, since the first is set to 'Johanne Baptista', the others to 'Alleluia'. Another extensive repetition, this time to the same text, is found in mm. 60–68 and 68–77.

which he is so well known, and which shines through in even the earliest well-authenticated works.

It is not good historical practice to relegate a work to a certain period on grounds of inadequacy. It must be demonstrably inadequate in terms of the taste and style of the period to which it is assigned. Four of the six motets show not the faintest influence of the aesthetics of the period 1460–75, nor any trace of its musical techniques. The requirement of *varietas*—respected by all composers of the time, and congenial to Josquin in the highest degree—is totally disregarded in the works in question. Granted, the works are incompetent, but they are so in terms of a period that had other aesthetic ideals. Every element, including the *Satzfehler* itself, points to the turn of the century and to the decades immediately following.

Proposition one concerns the distribution of the sources. This aspect of my investigation is not yet completed—copies of all the documents have not been made available to me—but it has proceeded far enough to show that the situation is somewhat less impressive than it first seemed. Documentary support for three of the works is slight indeed, since in each case it consists of a single, none-too-reliable German print of 1545.

'In illo tempore stetit Jesus' appears in the greatest number of sources; it is transmitted by no less than six, five of which contain an attribution to Josquin. This number is largely illusory, however, for several of the documents are no more than copies of one another. It can be stated at the moment that three, at most, are independent, and it is perfectly possible that these three will shrink to two on further investigation—the Italian tenor part-book Bologna, Civico Museo Bibliografico Musicale, MS. R 142, and the German print of 1538, *Secundus tomus novi operis musici*, edited by Johannes Ott.[24]

'Inter natos mulierum' is supported by two sources naming Josquin, whereas a third transmits it anonymously.[25] 'Victimae paschali laudes' counts four sources, but here the situation is complicated by conflicting attributions, so that a decision will depend heavily on a study of the music of Brunet, the contending composer. Nevertheless, an investigation of the

---

[24] The Breslau manuscripts 2 and 5 (which have been destroyed, according to a communication from the University Library of Wrocław) are copies of one another, the first presenting the work in score, the second in separate part-books; see Emil Bohn, *Die musikalischen Handschriften des XVI. und XVII. Jahrhunderts in der Stadtbibliothek zu Breslau* (Breslau, 1890), pp. 8 and 20. Stuttgart 25 is a copy of Ott's print of 1538, as is the print of Montanus and Neuber of 1559; see Clytus Gottwald, *Die Handschriften der Württembergischen Landesbibliothek Stuttgart. Erste Reihe, erster Band. Codices musici I* (Wiesbaden, 1964), p. 47.

[25] These are Bologna, Civico Museo Bibliografico Musicale, MS. R 142, fol. 30ᵛ, Josquin; Rome, Biblioteca Vallicelliana, San Borromeo E. II. 55–60, second series, no. 6, Josquin; and Rome, Biblioteca Apostolica Vaticana, MS. Capp. Sist. 38 (dated 1563), no. 30, anonymous.

sources is essential in order to gather whatever information they may offer.[26]

Final decisions, however, must be made in most cases on the basis of stylistic evidence—the best evidence and, at the same time, the trickiest to handle. We must take as norms the well-authenticated early works and demand that a suspect work show some resemblance to them. In 'Illibata Dei Virgo nutrix' or the 'Missa L'ami Baudichon', to mention only two of the early productions of Josquin, we do not find a great concentration of dissonance; on the contrary, the trend is all to harmonic smoothness. The ideal of *varietas*, far from being rejected, is an integral feature of their musical idiom. Rhythmic or harmonic dullness, or incompetence in the handling of cadences or voice lines do not occur. In short, the well-authenticated early works point to a high level of musicality, as well as of technical competence.

I am inclined to reject every one of the '*Satzfehler* motets'. I do not find them musically convincing, nor the arguments in their behalf persuasive. True, one can hardly expect Josquin to write a masterpiece every time he sets pen to paper; nor can one expect him to write without stylistic variation. But how dull a work, and how much variation from the norm can one accept? Personal judgement, with its inevitable variability, will always prevent complete agreement on points of authenticity. In those cases, however, where charges of anachronism, of internal contradiction, or of superior force of the claims of another composer can be brought against a work, general agreement as to authenticity or lack of it should be possible to achieve.

[26] Sources are given in note 7.

An Unsolved Riddle—
The Apparent Absence of
Ambrosian Melodies in the
Works of Josquin des Prez

JACQUELYN A. MATTFELD

Claudio Sartori's discovery in the records of the Cathedral of Milan that Josquin was a singer there as early as 1459[1] not only required that we assume a birthdate for him earlier by at least a full decade than previously hypothesized, it has forced us to rethink his place in the 'generations' of Netherlandish composers. We are required to grapple from a new perspective with the chronology and stylistic evolution within the authenticated extant works, all of which must now be considered compositions of the fully mature man and artist. We are confronted, more dramatically than ever before, with a whole series of tantalizing questions about Josquin's development as a composer. One such question is the unsolved riddle in the title of this essay, 'How can we account for the apparent absence of Ambrosian melodies in Josquin's works?' If an answer can be found, we will have new insights into the relationship of the sacred genres in which Josquin wrote, and the melodic materials he drew upon, to the peculiar liturgical and devotional practices of his ecclesiastical and princely employers as well as to the broader traditions and innovations associated with those categories of composition.

We now know that for at least the first twenty years of his adult professional life Josquin was employed as a singer in Milan. If the liturgical jurisdiction of the diocese of Milan was binding upon the city's churches in the second half of the fifteenth century, we may assume that for fourteen of those twenty years Josquin, as a member of the chapel choir of the Cathedral itself, must daily have heard, if not sung,[2] Ambrosian chant in the services according to Ambrosian rite, and not only the Mass and canonical hours but all the special services held at the Cathedral for the major state

---

[1] Claudio Sartori, 'Josquin des Prés Cantore del Duomo di Milano (1459–1472)', *Annales musicologiques*, iv (1956), pp. 55–83.

[2] The singers' statute of 1463 (ibid., p. 71) specifies only polyphonic music.

occasions of the Sforzas. Josquin's name first appears in Cathedral records in 1459, the year of the Congress of Mantua, when Pius II raised the last doomed crusade against the Turks. Between then and December 1472 when his name appears for the last time, a whole range of dramatic life-and-death events in the ruling family must regularly have occasioned special high Masses and processions at the Cathedral. In 1466 Francesco died and was laid in state and his funeral held. In 1469 Bianca Maria died en route to retirement at Cremona; in the same year Galeazzo Maria was solemnly invested as Duke, and his first son and heir, Gian Galeazzo, was christened. For none of these solemn occasions have we evidence—even indirect—of the special works we might expect to have been composed by Josquin or by his colleagues in the Cathedral choir. But then we have unfortunately so far not identified any choir book owned by the Cathedral or even written in Milan datable within the years 1459–79. Except for the Gafori codices (copied after 1484),[3] we have not even found later ones close enough in time to be assumed to contain the polyphonic repertory of the Cathedral before the Duke established his chapel choir in 1472 or immediately there-after. Lacking these, there is as yet no shred of evidence that Josquin composed at all during those years, either for the choir of which he was a member or on commission for any other group. It is of course possible that he did not, but it is very unlikely.

It seems probable that the modest musical resources of the Cathedral—seven singers and three instrumentalists—reflect only moderate musical activity due to limited funds or higher priorities established by the Cathedral's authorities. Under those circumstances the artistic productions of a young resident cleric would surely have been utilized fully by the Cathedral even if he were not recompensed or the works not preserved with care. Certainly the noble worshippers at the Cathedral, and especially the music-loving Galeazzo Maria, would have been quick to recognize his extraordinary gifts, and even before the establishment of the Sforza chapel may well have singled Josquin out to execute commissions for other churches in their realms or for special events. Those presently unexplained absences from the payroll of the Cathedral could well reflect not trips home, 'vacations', or pilgrimages, but time on loan to another church or even a court to compose or sing. The records now known to us are silent. We are faced with a yawning gap in the mosaic of Josquin's biography and works during the Milanese years we would like to reconstruct.

In the absence of works from this key period in Josquin's life, we are left to speculate about another related matter. What actual steps were taken in bringing forth a new work in fifteenth-century Italy? If requested by a

---

[3] See Knud Jeppesen, 'Die 3 Gafurius-Kodizes der Fabbrica del Duomo', *Acta musicologica*, iii (1931), pp. 14–28 and Claudio Sartori, 'Il Quarto Codice di Gaffurio non è del tutto scomparso', *Collectanea historiae musicae*, i (1953), pp. 25–44.

patron or instructed by a religious superior to compose, was the composer given general or specific instructions; if so, of what sort, and by whom? Who chose the text to be set? Under what circumstances did a composer write as his own muse moved him? And specifically, how did Josquin the artist-priest proceed, once having decided to compose a Mass, or a motet for a canonical or votive office? If we may safely infer that Josquin composed during the 1460s, may we expect those lost works to have included Masses and motets based on Ambrosian texts and melodies of the Cathedral's liturgical manuscripts? To this last question we must answer firmly, 'Not necessarily'.

Some of us—this writer included—have assumed that a choir singer of the cloth who was also a composer, if commissioned to write for a particular occasion or to set a specific text, would have turned either instinctively or according to regulation to the chant versions prescribed in the ritual books used in the church or diocese to which the choir or chapel was attached. We do not in fact *know* that this was so, however—either categorically or for particular individuals. In the case of Josquin, whose practice of incorporating the chant associated with each liturgical text he set is so invariable as to be an identifying hallmark,[4] we cannot prove that he did not select the particular chant melody from his own storehouse of remembered variants according to taste or fancy, much as a folk singer who knows some half-dozen variants or alternate melodies of a familiar text sings now one, now another, and sometimes combines and alters them into a version all his own. On the other hand, even in a period of such liturgical licence as the fifteenth century, we may speculate that the probability of the youthful if strong-willed Josquin's drawing upon Ambrosian models when he composed as a member of the Milanese Cathedral choir would have been greater than at any time again in his long life. For this reason alone those hypothetical compositions might have provided a key to Josquin's compositional procedures, to the Cathedral's practices, or both—if only they existed.

But even if we should find Masses and motets datable between 1459 and 1479 we would not necessarily have the answers to all our questions. If the texts or sequences of texts in such a corpus were to be identified in contemporaneous Ambrosian liturgical sources, *and* their Ambrosian chant melodies used as *cantus firmi* of the works, we would have a basis for concluding that Josquin was respectful of the liturgical authority of the Ambrosian rite when composing for churches in the diocese of Milan. If such Masses and motets were observed to use *texts* found in fifteenth-century Ambrosian liturgical books with one group of melodies, but set polyphonically by Josquin using as *cantus firmi* chant variants or

---

[4] See Jacquelyn A. Mattfeld, 'Some Relationships between Texts and Cantus Firmi in the Liturgical Motets of Josquin des Prés', *Journal of the American Musicological Society*, xiv (1961), pp. 177–80.

different chants associated with the same texts in *other* rites, we would have
to seek further evidence to determine whether personal preference on the
part of Josquin, or commonly accepted casualness about such liturgical
niceties, or both, made the phenomenon possible. And, of course, if both
texts and chant on which these hypothesized works were based proved alien
to Ambrosian sources, we would be left to argue whether they had been
commissioned by churches in which other uses were standard or whether
specific other liturgies were approved alternatives to the prescribed Ambrosian one during the second half of the fifteenth century in Milan. The
elaborate conjectural discussions of the contents of the Gafori Codices
suggest that a full study of this latter subject is long overdue in any event.[5]

Sometime between the end of 1472 and September 1473 Josquin became
one of Galeazzo Maria's *cantori de cappella*. As in the Cathedral choir, Josquin
was never the conductor and, to judge by his salary, not considered among
the most distinguished of its number.[6] Yet he must have enjoyed a singular
relationship with the Sforza dynasty, for the traces we have of his life from
his entry as a man of about thirty-five into the ducal choir of Galeazzo
Maria, until the letter of concern for his health as an octogenarian from
Margaret of Austria,[7] all suggest that his destiny was inextricably woven
together with theirs.[8]

Once having become a member of the Sforza household, all probability
of his being tied as a composer to any liturgical strictures of the Ambrosian
rite disappear, and with them much chance of solving our riddle. Membership in the ducal chapel, by definition not under the authority of the local
diocese, would automatically have precluded any restrictions that would
normally be imposed on those responsible for the religious services of
monastic or collegiate church, or cathedral, though predilections of the
choirmaster or even a musically opinionated patron might have been
honoured. It has been recognized for some time now that until the reforms
of Pius V not only every diocese but also every important church and private

[5] Compare Jeppesen, 'Die 3 Gafurius-Kodizes'; Ludwig Finscher, 'Loyset Compère
and His Works—The Motetti Missales', *Musica disciplina*, xiv (1960), pp. 131–57; Edward
E. Lowinsky, 'Scholarship in the Renaissance: Music', *Renaissance News*, xvi (1963), pp.
258–60; Thomas Lee Noblitt, 'The *Motetti Missales* of the Late 15th Century' (Ph.D. diss.,
University of Texas, 1963), and the review of that dissertation by David E. Crawford in
Current Musicology, x (1970), pp. 104–6.

[6] This statement was proved in error by new information revealed by Professor Edward
Lowinsky; see above, pp. 33–6.

[7] [For a different interpretation of this document, see Herbert Kellman, above, pp.
185–6 and 207–8.—Ed.]

[8] A simple place and date line for Josquin, juxtaposed with the places, personages, and
marital and political connections and activities of the Sforzas, already makes the pattern
strikingly clear. Professor Lowinsky's paper, above, pp. 31–75, has given us new detailed
documentation of the years Josquin was in the service of Ascanio.

chapel, and many lesser ones, had their own calendars, their special votive Masses and offices, their own chants and variants of common chants. We shall need all the information a full-scale investigation of the primary sources will yield to learn what rite or rites the Cathedral of Milan and the Sforza chapel followed, and what local conditions and practices affected musical performance, of both chant and polyphony, in their services.[9] It can easily be demonstrated, however, that *whatever* the custom of the ducal chapel, Josquin simultaneously had direct contact throughout the 1470s not only with the liturgical materials sung by it, *and* with the texts and music of the Ambrosian rite as observed in the Cathedral and in the churches of S. Ambrogio and S. Stefano where the Sforzas worshipped on special feasts, but with a variety of other usages.

The Dukes of Milan from Francesco through Ludovico il Moro moved frequently from one of their castles in the Duchy to another and visited the nobility in cities and towns, only some of which were possessions and none of which were obligated to follow the Milanese rite. Towns such as Cremona, dowry city of the first Bianca Maria, and especially Pavia, of which Galeazzo Maria was count and Ascanio bishop before they became Duke of Milan and Cardinal respectively, were the most frequent residences of the ducal family and the site of great entertainments and important ceremonial events involving their state guests. Both lay outside the diocese.[10] On all important trips information provided by the chroniclers assures us that the ducal party was made up of the greater part of the ducal household, which after 1472 included both chapel and court choirs. Clearly Josquin's services as singer and composer involved him in religious ceremonies and secular celebrations well outside the Milanese bishops' diocesan concern. In other words if, as is commonly accepted on the strength of the studies by Osthoff, Graue, and others,[11] a small corpus of Josquin's works composed during the 1470s has indeed come down to us, it would *not* be surprising—in view of the cosmopolitan habits of the Sforzas and the eclectic liturgical taste reflected in what remains of their library—if some of the works he composed in the 1470s while in their service stood outside the Ambrosian

---

[9] For a model of such an investigation see the articles by Frank A. D'Accone: 'The Singers of San Giovanni in Florence During the 15th Century', *Journal of the American Musicological Society*, xiv (1961), pp. 307–58, and 'The Musical Chapels at the Florentine Cathedral and Baptistry During the First Half of the 16th Century', ibid., xxiv (1971), pp. 1–50.

[10] Archdale A. King, *Liturgies of the Primatial Sees* (Milwaukee, 1957), pp. 286 ff.

[11] See Jerald C. Graue, 'The Milanese Motets of Josquin des Prez' (M. Mus. thesis, University of Illinois, 1966), and Helmuth Osthoff, 'Zur Echtheitsfrage und Chronologie bei Josquins Werken', *Internationale Gesellschaft für Musikwissenschaft, Kongressbericht, Utrecht, 1952* (Amsterdam, 1953), pp. 303–9, and *Josquin Desprez* (Tutzing, 1962–5); cf. also Edward Lowinsky's review of Osthoff's book, *Renaissance News*, xvi (1963), pp. 255–62, and the paper of Arthur Mendel in these Proceedings, pp. 297–308.

rite and/or did not draw upon Ambrosian melodies. It is only perplexing that *all* of them seem to.

At least three-quarters of Josquin's motets were written for performance in ritual or votive services, if we may judge by their texts, and at least thirty-five—all those that appear in the liturgy with their own melodies—use the chant in some form as their organizing principle.[12] *Only four texts of the thirty-five in this last group appear in the twelfth- and fifteenth-century Ambrosian manuscripts consulted.*[13] These are:

> O admirabile commercium
> Rubum quem viderat Moyses
> Nesciens Mater Virgo[14]
> O Virgo virginum

(The *modern* (1939) Ambrosian *Liber Vesperalis* also contains 'Alma Redemptoris Mater' and 'Ave coelorum Regina'.) The text of each of these motets is a Marian antiphon, for which the melodic material of the Ambrosian chant associated with the antiphon closely resembles the music assigned the same text in the fifteenth-century Roman and Cistercian sources[15] used for comparison. All of these particular antiphon motets are accepted as 'early' Josquin works probably written before the years in Rome. All draw unmistakably upon one of the three chant versions found, or upon one resembling them as closely as they resemble each other. Significantly, at each point where the motet *cantus* differs from any of the three antiphon melodies, it departs farthest from the Ambrosian line and remains faithful to the Roman or Cistercian source, or it is unlike all three. While the sampling provided by this group of motets is too limited to be conclusive, it is at least suggestive that in the earliest sacred works we have from Josquin's pen he did not select an Ambrosian setting of a text for his *cantus firmus* even when one existed. Lacking works that can be shown to have originated during his years in the Cathedral choir and more certain dating

---

[12] For a discussion of the structure and use of the chant in those motets, see Jacquelyn A. Mattfeld, 'Cantus Firmus in the Liturgical Motets of Josquin des Prez' (Ph.D. diss., Yale University, 1959), pp. 74–134, and the paper of Willem Elders in these Proceedings, pp. 523–42.

[13] These are:

Antiphonarium Ambrosianum, British Museum, Add. MS. 34209 (12th c.); transcription in *Paléographie musicale*, vi (Solesmes, 1900). *Antiphonarium Diurnum Ambrosianum Mediolanum*, executed for the monastery of St. Ambrosius Major at Milan (late 15th c.), Philadelphia Free Library, John F. Lewis Collection.

[14] [Edgar Sparks, however, believes that 'Nesciens Mater' was written by an imitator of Josquin; see these Proceedings, pp. 350–2.—Ed.]

[15] *Missale* (Antiphonarium Romanum) (15th c.), Wellesley College Library MS., unnumbered. *Antiphonarium*, Cistercian use, written in Lombardy (1474–5), Boston Public Library, MS. M. Cab. 2. 51.

of works presumably composed during his employment by Galeazzo Maria, this observation about Josquin's compositional procedures must, however, be considered purely speculative.

If we are to pursue the solution to the riddle of the apparent absence of Ambrosian melody in the chant-based compositions of the greatest musician with long residence in Milan, the task that faces us is clear. An exhaustive study must be undertaken of the rich store of fifteenth-century Ambrosian liturgical materials still preserved at Milan and elsewhere. Ordinals and other ceremonial books and documents in the archives of the churches of Milan and of the city must be given particularly careful scrutiny. The sacred works of other composers employed at the Cathedral or at the Sforza court must be analyzed for the presence or absence of Ambrosian melodies in their works as a whole and in those works believed to have been written while they were living in Milan. Such investigations will then have to be followed by a systematic comparison of texts, melodies, and musical practices ascertained to have been in use by the ducal chapel with those of the Cathedral and affiliated churches of the diocese. Both sets of data must be checked against comparable materials in use in the churches and at the ducal chapels where the Sforzas—especially Galeazzo and Ascanio—are known to have attended services regularly.

Until all this has been done we shall remain as ignorant of the reasons for this presently inexplicable omission as we now are. The solution to our riddle is caught between our fragmentary knowledge of Josquin's compositional habits and our incomplete information about the musical and ecclesiastical practices and activities of church and court in Milan. While no certain success can be guaranteed to those who may decide to search the labyrinthine byways of religious music practice in and around Milan in that splendid period of infinite variety, the study will be worthwhile in itself and is bound to result in unexpected happy discoveries.

IV Studies of Genres

Unifying Techniques in Selected Masses of Josquin and La Rue: A Stylistic Comparison

WALTER H. RUBSAMEN

During the first half of the sixteenth century certain works of Pierre de la Rue were ascribed to Josquin in both manuscript and printed sources; for example, the former's 'Missa Cum jucunditate' is labelled 'Missa Dirige' under the name of Josquin in Mus. MS. E. 46 of the Biblioteca Ambrosiana in Milan, and La Rue's 'Missa Sub tuum praesidium' is falsely attributed to Josquin in three of the four part-books comprising Hieronymus Form-schneider's *Missae Tredecim*, published in 1539. Attaingnant printed a *Trente sixiesme livre contenant XXX chansons... le tout de la composition de feu Josquin des Prez* in 1549, but included in the collection a five-part 'Incessament mon povre cueur lamente', ascribed in three other sources to La Rue,[1] and used by him as the model for a parody Mass, as well as the five-part 'Cent mille regretz', given to La Rue in an earlier source, MS. Pal. lat. 1982 of the Biblioteca Vaticana.[2]

Were the two composers actually so close in style that their Masses and chansons could readily be exchanged, or were La Rue's pieces mislabelled in order to capitalize on Josquin's greater and more enduring fame? In the attempt to shed some light on possible stylistic differences between them, I have undertaken to compare several of their four-voiced Masses from the viewpoint of unifying and cohesive techniques. Obvious candidates for

---

[1] St. Gall, Stiftsbibliothek, MS. 463, no. 197; *Livre de meslanges*, Paris, A. Le Roy et R. Ballard, 1560 (Eitner 1560c), f. 28; *Mellange de chansons*, Paris, A. Le Roy et R. Ballard, 1572 (Eitner 1572a, RISM 1572²), f. 52. Anonymous in Bologna, Civico Museo Biblio-grafico Musicale, R 141, first print (RISM [c. 1521]⁷), f. 18, and four other sources; see article 'La Rue' in *Die Musik in Geschichte und Gegenwart*, viii, col. 232. As a motet, 'Sic Deus dilexit', anonymous in four sources; see ibid. Published as probably by La Rue in Josquin des Prez, *Werken*, Wereldlijke Werken, Bundel iii, no. 27.

[2] See Walter H. Rubsamen, *Music Research in Italian Libraries* (Los Angeles, 1951), p. 49 (repr. from *Notes*, vi (1949), nos. 2 and 4, and viii (1950), no. 1). Anonymous in Vienna, Oesterreichische Nationalbibliothek, MS. 18746, no. 1. Published in Josquin des Prez, *Werken*, Wereldlijke Werken, Bundel iii, no. 26.

comparison are the Masses of Josquin published by Petrucci in 1502 and
1505, the 'Missa Faisant regretz', which appears in manuscript sources of
the turn of the century, and those Masses known to have been composed by
La Rue before 1506,[3] including the five published by Petrucci in 1503
(Masses 'De Beata Virgine', 'Puer natus est', 'Almana' or 'Sexti ut fa',
'L'homme armé', 'Nunqua fué pena maior') and the Mass 'Cum jucunditate', which is contained in Vienna, Oesterreichische Nationalbibliothek,
MS. 1783, datable at 1505.[4] Purposely excluded from consideration, except
for incidental mention, are Josquin's last two Masses, 'De Beata Virgine'
and 'Pange lingua', as well as the five- and six-voiced Masses of La Rue
assignable to the final decade of his life.

Josquin's two 'L'homme armé' Masses and the one based on the same
song by La Rue are eminently comparable; not only do they fit into the
chosen time span, they also make widespread use of canonic devices.

[3] This was a turning point in La Rue's career, the year of the ill-fated second expedition
to Spain by Philip the Fair, King of Castile, accompanied by a large retinue including his
chapel choir, of which the composer was a leading member. After Philip's untimely death
at Burgos, on 25 September 1506, La Rue remained for a short time in the service of Queen
Juana, but his subsequent whereabouts are unknown until he returned to the Netherlands
in 1508.

[4] The manuscript in question must have been commissioned by Philip the Fair before
his second trip to Spain (his mottos, 'Qui vouldra' and 'Moy tout seul', appear on ff.
65ᵛ–66) as a gift for Manuel I, King of Portugal (1469–1521), and his queen, the Infanta
Maria of Castile (1482–1517), who was the sister of Philip's wife. The arms of both
Manuel and Maria appear at the beginning of the codex, as well as on f. 17ᵛ. The manuscript
comprises eighteen complete Masses, two of which contain extraneous *Credos*, as well as
two separate Mass movements. Of these twenty-two compositions seven Masses are by
La Rue, three Masses and a *Credo* by Agricola, two Masses and a separate *Credo* by de Orto,
and one Mass by Gaspar van Weerbecke, all of whom were in the service of Philip the
Fair at various times between 1494 and 1506. A clue to the exact date of the codex is provided
by the presence of works by de Orto, who did not become a member of the chapel until
24 May 1505 (G. van Doorslaer, 'La Chapelle Musicale de Philippe le Beau', *Revue Belge
d'Archéologie de l'Histoire de l'Art*, iv (1934), p. 152), and of later Masses by La Rue, 'Cum
jucunditate' and 'O sacer Anthoni', neither of which had been part of Petrucci's publication
of 1503. Helen M. Dixon, in 'The Manuscript Vienna, National Library, 1783', *Musica
disciplina*, xxiii (1969), pp. 105–16, contends that the manuscript was compiled for the
wedding of Manuel and Maria on 30 October 1500 ('the two "M"s around the shield on
f. 2ʳ allude to this union'), but there is nothing in the manuscript to link it to the actual date
of marriage. Certainly the royal couple remained united for a long time after 1500, as
Maria had nine children by Manuel between 1502 and 1515. Nor can one place much
confidence in Miss Dixon's suggestion (p. 116) of de Orto's first employment by the
Hapsburgs 'at the court of Philip's infant son, later Charles V—being in 1505, the year of
Philip's death'. As stated above, Philip died in September 1506, and the young Archduke
Charles did not take over the reins of government in Flanders until his grandfather,
Maximilian I, declared him of age and had him proclaimed as ruler (5 January 1515). Miss
Dixon also asserts (p. 106, fn. 5) that 'the one Josquin mass—*Ave maris stella*—is in the second
book of *Missae diversorum auctorum quatuor vocibus* (1508)', but no second book of this
collection is known to exist, and the first book does not contain Josquin's Mass.

Similarly, the Masses 'Ave maris stella' and 'Puer natus est' exemplify the *cantus firmus* techniques employed by both composers; the Masses 'Fortuna desperata' and 'Nunqua fué pena maior' illustrate their earlier approaches to the parody Mass; and of the compositions based on a short *cantus firmus* treated as an ostinato, Josquin's Masses 'Faisant regretz', 'Hercules Dux Ferrariae', and 'La sol fa re mi' contrast with the Masses 'Almana' and 'Cum jucunditate' by La Rue.

No great differences exist between the two composers in their treatment of a *cantus firmus*. Both use the borrowed melody literally, in long note values, or weave its phrases into melismatic passages, or freely dissolve its endings. In Josquin's 'Missa L'homme armé super voces musicales', the *cantus firmus* appears on different steps of the hexachord, on *ut* in the *Kyrie*, *re* in the *Gloria*, and so on; similarly, La Rue repeats the *cantus firmus* on descending steps of the hexachord in the *Sanctus* of the 'Missa Cum jucunditate'.

Both composers were masters of canonic techniques. The very title of Josquin's 'Missa Ad fugam', in which a series of canons at the fifth between superius and tenor serves as the framework, confirms his preoccupation with this technique. In his 'Missa Sine nomine' the two canonic voices and the interval of imitation vary from movement to movement throughout the entire work, whereas in the 'Missa La sol fa re mi' canonic imitation between two or three voices occurs sporadically in the *Gloria*, *Credo*, *Osanna* II and *Agnus* I. The *Benedictus* and *Agnus* II of his 'Missa L'homme armé super voces musicales' are examples of the mensuration canon, in two and three voices respectively.

For his part, La Rue, in his 'Missa L'homme armé',[5] writes a two-voiced mensuration canon accompanied by a pair of free voices in each section of the *Kyrie* and caps the whole with a mensuration canon for four voices in the second *Agnus Dei*. From this he progressed to an entirely canonic Mass, 'O salutaris hostia', in which four voices are extracted from a single notated part throughout, except that the *Pleni* and *Benedictus* are duets.

Another method of unification common to both composers is the so-called motto technique, i.e., identical or similar beginnings of the major movements in all voices. Josquin's Masses 'Ave maris stella', 'Ad fugam', 'Di dadi', and 'L'ami Baudichon' can be matched with La Rue's 'Puer natus est' and 'Nunqua fué' in this respect.

Before approximately 1506 both composers approached the parody technique in gingerly fashion, Josquin moving somewhat further towards a complete absorption of the model than La Rue. Not the entire polyphonic complex of the chanson 'Allez regretz' by Hayne van Ghizeghem but its individual voices used separately serve as the framework of Josquin's Mass.

[5] Modern edition by Nigel Davison, *Pierre de la Rue, Missa L'homme armé I* (Das Chorwerk, 114; Wolfenbüttel, 1972).

A slight departure from this method occurs in the 'Missa Malheur me bat', whose model is a three-voiced chanson attributed to Ockeghem in the *Odhecaton*. Here Josquin cites one chanson voice after another until the *Agnus* III, in which he has both superius and tenor of the model appear simultaneously, and in the same intervallic relationship. However, what appears to be a step towards the true parody technique is actually a double *cantus firmus*, and not the elaboration of an entire polyphonic complex, including its points of imitation and its pattern of entrances. In the 'Missa D'ung aultre amer', on the other hand, Osthoff finds 'ein keimhafter Ansatz zur Parodietechnik',[6] because Josquin not only uses the chanson tenor as a *cantus firmus*, but also occasionally quotes fragments of the other chanson voices in the accompaniment. A slight intensification of this process can be observed in La Rue's 'Missa Nunqua fué pena maior',[7] where the composer sometimes (*Kyrie* II and *Osanna*) uses elements of the model's three voices simultaneously, or two of them literally, in the original time values (*Agnus*), but for the most part simply quotes the Spanish tenor or discant in long notes as a *cantus firmus*. Josquin's 'Missa Fortuna desperata' simultaneously employs all three voices of a composition ascribed to Busnois at the beginnings of *Kyrie* I and *Credo*, and two of them in the *Sanctus*, but otherwise works with individual voices in the traditional manner.

A sharp difference exists between the two composers in their later approach to this technique, however. La Rue embraced the full-fledged parody technique in his five-voiced 'Missa Incessament'[8] and six-voiced 'Missa Ave sanctissima Maria',[9] whereas Josquin relied upon liturgical *cantus firmi* in his last two Masses and ignored the burgeoning *Missa parodia*, except for the 'Missa Mater Patris', about whose authenticity there are strong doubts.

In several of his Masses Josquin treats a short *cantus firmus* as an ostinato, that is, as a motive repeated immediately, or after a short pause, either exactly or transposed. In the 'Missa Hercules Dux Ferrariae' he limits this technique to the close of the *Osanna*; in the Masses 'La sol fa re mi' and 'Faisant regretz' the ostinato thoroughly permeates the texture. Josquin repeats ostinato motives exactly or sequentially, varies them rhythmically, and even embellishes them to a marked degree. La Rue, in the Masses

---

[6] Osthoff, *Josquin Desprez* (Tutzing, 1962–5), i, p. 129.

[7] Based upon Johannes Wreede's (Urrede's) villancico in the *Odhecaton*, the *Cancionero de Palacio*, and many other sources; cf. Helen Hewitt, ed., *Harmonice Musices Odhecaton A* (Cambridge, Mass., 1942), pp. 130–1. Hellmuth C. Wolff published the *Kyrie* I in *Die Musik der alten Niederländer* (Leipzig, 1956), p. 259.

[8] The *Kyrie* was published by Smijers in *Van Ockeghem tot Sweelinck*, iv (2d ed., Amsterdam, 1952), no. 36.

[9] Edited by Laurence Feininger in *Documenta polyphoniae liturgicae S. Ecclesiae Romanae*, ser. I. B, no. 1 (Rome, 1950) and by Antonio Tirabassi in *P. de la Rue, Liber Missarum* (Malines, 1941), pp. 135–63.

'Almana' and 'Cum jucunditate', does likewise, but also fills in the intervals for the sake of variety.

Both composers usually treat the motive as a melodic unit, but La Rue also creates a new motive by extracting an interval comprising the ambitus, using it as a separate entity in both ascending and descending fashion. In the *Et in terra* of his 'Missa Cum jucunditate',[10] for example:

Ex. 1 *Gloria*, mm. 29-35

the ostinato *cantus firmus* containing an ascending fourth appears in the tenor, while the reverse, filled-in *descending* fourths, follow one upon the other in discant and bass, measures 31–5, and in the discant, measure 43 to the end:

Ex. 2 mm. 42-7

10 Munich, Bayr. Staatsbibl., Mus. MS. 65, fol. 44ᵛ.

Similar repetition, but also sequential ordering of a filled-in, descending fourth may be heard earlier in the movement as well, in three voice-parts, measures 16 through 18, and of the unadorned fourth moving downwards in the *Qui tollis*, measures 38–47. Also in the *Agnus* I of his 'Missa Almana':[11]

a movement dominated by the ascending fourth, *ut fa*, treated as a sequential ostinato, the same interval, now descending, filled-in and ornamented, is repeated in the alto, measures 5–7, imitated in the discant, measures 8–10, and used sequentially in all voices except the tenor, measures 27–31:

11 Jena, Univ.-Bibl., MS. 22, fol. 152ᵛ.

Ex. 4   mm. 27-32

In general, La Rue thinks more in intervals than does Josquin, varying his repetitions by reversing the interval's direction, or, as in the parody Mass 'Ave sanctissima Maria',[12]

Ex. 5   a) Anon., 'Ave sanctissima Maria' mm. 1–9

[12] Brussels, Bibl. roy., MS. 15075, fol. 84v.

(b) Missa 'Ave sanctissima Maria' *Kyrie*, mm. 1–9

the order of the two intervals comprising the theme. In the anonymous motet (probably also by La Rue) that serves as his model,[13] the theme consists of two motives, a descending triad and a third, the latter starting a whole step below the *initium*. In the Mass, La Rue at first (*Kyrie* and *Gloria*) reverses the order, so that the descending third is followed by the triad a

Ex. 6   mm. 17-34

[13] Published by Attaingnant in *Liber tertius: viginti musicales quinque, sex, vel octo vocum motetos habet* (Paris, 1534), with an ascription to Verdelot; edited by A. Schering in *Geschichte der Musik in Beispielen* (Leipzig, 1931), no. 97; and by Smijers in *Treize livres de motets parus chez Pierre Attaingnant en 1534 et 1535*, iii (Monaco, 1936), pp. 166–72.

whole step higher; then, in the *Credo*, he returns to the motet theme in its original pattern.

The inner architecture of La Rue's melodic lines differs noticeably from that of Josquin. Sometimes the younger composer writes a theme from which he subsequently extracts motives to be used alternately or simultaneously. In the *Pleni sunt* (Ex. 6) of his 'Missa Cum jucunditate', for example, he establishes a point of imitation throughout the parts in measures 17–19, which is followed immediately, in the discant and alto, by two shortened versions of the theme, the second of which is extended. In measures 19–22 all three varieties sound simultaneously, but from

Ex. 7 *Gloria*, mm. 36-49

measures 22 to 34 only the foreshortened ones, to which various extensions have been appended.

Occasionally the reverse procedure takes place: in the *Qui tollis* of the 'Missa Nunqua fué pena maior',[14] for example (Ex. 7), a short theme (discant, mm. 37–9) appears in stretto imitation, a prefix being added to the alto and all subsequent statements. La Rue omits the theme's initial note from the repetitions in alto and bass, but not from those in the discant. These new versions run throughout the participating voices, the final recurrences being marked by variant endings.

Josquin, in a much more open and widely-spaced use of the same technique in the *Pleni sunt* of the 'Missa Faisant regretz',[15] presents the theme in an initial point of imitation, measures 24–30, extracts a motive from it and treats this sequentially to form a new theme, measures 31–7, then extends it in various ways, measures 38–50:

Ex. 8   mm. 24-51

---

[14] Jena, Univ.-Bibl., MS. 22, fol. 54ᵛ.   [15] *Werken*, Missen, xiii.

A similar procedure is followed in the *Pleni* of the 'Missa L'homme armé super voces musicales'. But Josquin handles each version of the motive separately, in distinct, widely-spaced points of imitation, not as in the aforementioned *Pleni* and *Qui tollis* of La Rue, where the texture is tight and the variants appear simultaneously or alternately.

Further enlightenment as to the differences between the two composers with respect to motivic work results from an examination of the long, pauseless melodic lines that occur frequently in La Rue, but somewhat less so in Josquin. The latter's early Mass, 'Una musque de Buscaya',[16] contains many extended, continuous melodic lines in which little or no repetition or sequential treatment of motives occurs, as in the alto part of the *Sanctus* between measures 7 and 20:

16 *Werken*, Missen, x.

Ex. 9   mm. 1-22

Shorter, but still quite long for Josquin's Masses of the middle period, is the discant line of the 'Missa Faisant regretz', *Kyrie* I:

Ex. 10

Here a wide-spanned, flowing theme (mm. 7–9) derived from the Gregorian *Kyrie* (*Orbis factor*) recurs in measures 9–11, and, foreshortened, in measures 11–14. Parallel repetitions of a contrasting theme take place in the bass, and ostinato statements of the *cantus firmus*, set off by rests, appear in the tenor.

Quite different and thoroughly characteristic of La Rue is the discant of his 'Missa Cum jucunditate' at the end of the first *Kyrie*, measures 11–15, constructed by circumscribing and repeating an extension of the *cantus firmus*, a motive in a small ambitus (B, G, A) that lies still as the line spins on in almost constantly changing rhythmic configuration:

Ex. 11   mm. 1-15

The entire *cantus firmus* (or variants of it) appears in both tenor and bass. Two motives, one of which is a simple two-note ostinato (A–D), alternate in the bass of his 'Missa Nunqua fué', *Patrem*, measures 25–9:

Ex. 12 *Credo*, mm. 24-30

whereas only one completely dominates proceedings in the alto and discant of the *Et in terra*, measures 5–9 (Ex. 13), again illustrating La Rue's trademark, the syncopated repetition of a motive in a small ambitus:

Ex. 13 *Gloria*, mm. 1-11

In contrast, Josquin, in the *Sanctus* of his 'Missa L'homme armé super voces musicales',[17] measures 18–22, chooses a longer and more flowing motive in the ambitus of a fifth, without ostinato figures, and treats it in a three-fold sequence beginning on middle C and continuing on B♭, A, and G in the bass, and in two-fold sequence in discant and tenor in close imitation of octave and fourth:

[17] *Werken*, Missen, i.

Ex. 14   mm. 18-22

A further illustration of inner cohesion of La Rue's long melodic lines, as he works with short motives, repeating them at pitch or sequentially, or varying them by means of extensions, but running them into one another without a break, is found in the discant of his 'Missa Puer natus est',[18] *Sanctus*, measures 3–10:

Ex. 15   mm. 1-11

[18] Jena, Univ.-Bibl., MS. 22, fol. 42^v.

Two motives are involved here: a descending, scale-wise pattern of four, then five, notes which appears at first in the discant, measure 3, and sequentially in the bass, measures 3–5; and the descending succession of a half-note and a quarter, which regularly precedes the initial motive in the discant, alto, and bass, at various times between measures 4 and 10. La Rue extends the first motive to six notes from measure 7 in all three voices. A similar technique is used in many other sections of this Mass: for example, at the end of *Agnus* I, where a four-note motive with a distinctive dotted rhythm, but varying second and fourth notes, is treated sequentially or repeated in two or even three voices simultaneously, sometimes with extensions (discant, mm. 23–5; bass, mm. 24–5), or introductions (discant, mm. 25–6; tenor, mm. 26–7):

Ex. 16   mm. 23-8

Josquin normally would have separated these repetitions by rests, as in the *Gloria* of the 'Missa Fortuna desperata',[19] bass, measures 42–6:

Ex. 17   mm. 42-6

the *Qui tollis* of the same Mass, bass, measures 131–43:

[19] *Werken*, Missen, iv.

Ex. 18   *Gloria*, mm. 130-43

and *Agnus* I of the 'Missa L'homme armé sexti toni',[20] bass, measures 12–22:

Ex. 19   mm. 12-27

20 *Werken*, Missen, v.

His sequential passages contain few if any pauses, and his repetitions usually occur in regular succession, without the variable notes or rhythmic displacements resulting from La Rue's insertions into or additions to the motive. Illustrations of this technique may be found in the alto of Josquin's 'Missa Hercules Dux Ferrariae',[21] *Kyrie* II, measures 38–46:

Ex. 20   mm. 38-47

the bass of 'Missa Ave maris stella',[22] *Sanctus*, measures 11–16:

Ex. 21 mm. 12-21

or the *Osanna* of the same Mass, where sequences of a theme made up of ascending, scale-wise motives run through the entire bass and parts of the discant. In addition, the starting points of Josquin's wide-ranging sequences often cover the ambitus of a sixth or fifth, compared to La Rue's more static treatment in the discant of Ex. 15, measures 3–10, where the sequential points of departure are limited in range to a third, or the bass of Ex. 16, measures 24–7, in which the repeated motive lies virtually still. Sequences

[22] *Werken*, Missen, vi.

in the middle voices of this example move further afield, however, and in
so doing correspond more closely to Josquin's technique.

Extending the zone of action even further, Josquin, in the bass of his
'Missa L'homme armé super voces musicales', uses a short motive of three
notes, sometimes extended to four, to organize the bass part over an area of
fifteen measures:

Ex. 22   *Agnus Dei I, mm. 8-23*

The freedom in patterning the sequences (mostly in skips of thirds, at times stepwise), and the large range of close to two octaves (from d' to F) over which the motive plays illustrate the difference of style in Josquin's freer and wider-ranging procedures.

Both Josquin and La Rue use single and double ostinati to effect a climax at the end of a movement. Multiple ostinati occur frequently in the Masses of both composers, but with a difference. Josquin usually leaves more air between repetitions, spacing them widely, while La Rue tends to bunch them in a dense texture without pause. In the second *Kyrie* of the 'Missa Hercules Dux Ferrariae' (Ex. 20), Josquin establishes a double sequence in the discant and alto, measures 38–42, and another in the upper pair and bass, measures 42–6, separating one of the sequential patterns by rests, the other not. A double ostinato using motives from both parts of Agricola's chanson, 'Tout a par moy',[23] runs throughout the alto and tenor voices of 'Missa Faisant regretz', *Agnus* III, in a well-spaced pattern, repetitions of both motives usually being separated by rests.

Although Josquin uses three different motives simultaneously in sequence towards the end of the *Sanctus* in his 'Missa L'homme armé super voces musicales' he releases one in measure 29 (bass), another in measure 31 (discant), and continues that in the tenor only, apparently not desiring a driving climax in the three non-*cantus firmus* voices:

Ex. 23   mm. 25-33

23 In the *Bijlage* of the 'Missa Faisant regretz', *Werken*, Missen, xiii, pp. 56–9.

The repetitive intensity is also mitigated by coloration of a motive (discant, m. 21) and insertions of interludes (discant, mm. 28–9; tenor, mm. 27–9). Only in the tenor are the sequences not separated by pauses; otherwise Josquin's usual airy texture and wide range of voices prevail. In the 'Missa Hercules Dux Ferrariae', *Sanctus*, Josquin again uses a double ostinato, now carrying it through until the end of the movement:

Ex. 24

He prepares for a sequence in the bass by introducing the first motive in the discant (mm. 1, 3), but again prefers variety to the cumulative effect of a second repeated motive in the discant (m. 5) by discontinuous use of it (mm. 8, 13, 16) as it alternates with the initial motive or free material. The alto sings a variant of the second motive, repeating it several times from measure 10, but not without interruptions and variants.

A different procedure may be found in La Rue's 'Missa Almana',[24] *Agnus* III:

[24] Jena, Univ.-Bibl., MS. 22, fol. 152ᵛ.

Ex. 25 mm. 44-60

Varied and extended repetitions of three-measure phrases in the pauseless upper voices, measures 44 (last note) to 53, accompany a two-note ostinato in the tenor, while iterations of the initial discant motive, now separated by rests in Josquin's manner, recur in the bass. Actually, the discant line is continuous from measure 40 until the end (m. 60). From measures 53–60 La Rue simultaneously repeats three different motives distributed among four voices in sequential or ostinato fashion without any break whatsoever, except for a minim pause in the bass.

La Rue's syncopated motivic work, intense and florid, is akin to the late Gothic style in architecture, transferred to music. Excitement and musical climax are achieved through motivic repetition and polyphonic complexity; textual expression is of secondary importance. In such passages La Rue's style is the exact opposite of 'musica reservata', which attempts to paint in tones the meaning of the words.

The Literary Texts of Josquin's Chansons

BRIAN JEFFERY

The French chanson of Josquin's time by definition combined both literature and music, and so it deserves attention from literary scholars as well as
from musicologists. Yet it has seldom received such attention. Of what
kind were the poems that were set to music at that time? And how was the
fusion of the two arts achieved by chanson composers, in particular by the
greatest musical master of the age, Josquin des Prez?

Most of the literary texts of Josquin's chansons are fragmentary in the
musical sources, a well-known fact which presents problems to the editor,
to the performer, and to anyone interested in Josquin as an artist. Some of
them can be completed or at least expanded from other sources, but a host
of textual problems remain. At the end of this paper is a detailed study of
Josquin's chansons from the literary point of view; in the paper itself I
wish to draw certain conclusions which, I hope, will not be invalidated by
future research on details.

We may set aside settings of old texts to melodies by older composers
(such as 'Fors seulement'), and also those pieces which are definitely instrumental. There remain sixty-three secular pieces to French texts certainly or
probably by Josquin, some of which may perhaps likewise be instrumental.
From a literary point of view, some of the texts demonstrate an old-
fashioned form and content, in the style of those poets sometimes called
Rhétoriqueurs or *Grands Rhétoriqueurs*; others are in a more modern 'popular'
or 'volkstümlich' style; and since Josquin lived in an age of transition, still
others, in various ways, come in between.

First, the poems of the *Rhétoriqueurs* or *Grands Rhétoriqueurs*. This name
has frequently been applied in a general fashion to the French poets of the
late fifteenth and early sixteenth centuries. But the name itself has recently
been shown by Pierre Jodogne to be a misinterpretation or sheer mistake
by the nineteenth-century literary historians C. d'Héricault and Petit de
Julleville.[1] A literary revaluation has also taken place in recent years: in

---

[1] Pierre Jodogne, 'Les "Rhétoriqueurs" et l'humanisme', *Humanism in France at the end
of the Middle Ages and in the early Renaissance*, ed. A. H. T. Levi (Manchester, 1970),
pp. 150–75.

1910 Henry Guy applied to the poetry of this period terms such as 'gaucherie laborieuse et. . . complication ridicule' and 'art difforme et stérile',[2] whereas by 1962 Raymond Picard was calling these same poets masters of a highly sophisticated art.[3] This revaluation is doubtless connected with our own artistic preoccupations and growing distance from Romanticism. The literature with which we are concerned here, specifically written for music, is in fact only a small part of a very large body of poetry written at that time, most of it in long, ambitious, complex, and finely wrought poems by writers such as Molinet and Chastellain. Chanson verse, on the other hand, is usually short, unpretentious, and less complex. Its content is generally abstract, its imagery pale. It may be compared to the modest poems often used in nineteenth-century *Lieder*, or to those set in early seventeenth-century England, coexisting with the most complex Metaphysical poetry.

Many of the poems of this kind in Josquin's music are in rondeau form. But only one of them, 'La plus des plus',[4] is known to survive with a full text (another of them, 'Adieu mes amours', also has a full text but, being combined with a bergerette, is a special case). Of eight other poems, while the music is clearly in rondeau form, only the incipit or the refrain of the text survives. More interesting are the cases where Josquin appears to be playing with the rondeau form. A significant example is 'Cueurs desolez', of which a full text of thirteen lines survives; yet Josquin has set only the first five lines, without a firm medial cadence, thus making a performance with the full repetitions of a rondeau unlikely. In 'Douleur me bat', 'Incessament livré suis', and 'Plusieurs regretz' the same may well be true; Josquin provides no medial cadence for what in each case appears to be the refrain of a rondeau (which, it must be remembered, cannot be distinguished with certainty from the first stanza of a strophic poem). If this is true—and it can be demonstrated in 'Cueurs desolez'—we may say that Josquin is using the form in a free way, thereby playing his part in the transition from the *formes fixes* to strophic poems. Similarly, his 'Regretz sans fin' sets a poem very similar to the first eight lines of a thirteen-line rondeau, but in such a way that the old-fashioned repeats would be quite impossible.

Fewer puzzles are presented by the two chansons in which Josquin set poems by the most famous poets of the age, Jean Molinet and Jean Lemaire de Belges. They are 'Nymphes des bois'[5] and 'Plus nulz regretz': despite their

---

[2] *Histoire de la poésie française au XVIe siècle*, i (Paris, 1910), pp. 21 and 377.

[3] Raymond Picard, 'Les grands rhétoriqueurs', in *Tableau de la littérature française*, i (Paris, 1962), pp. 186–95.

[4] For the modern edition or source of all Josquin's chansons cited in this paper, see the Appendix.

[5] It should be noted that the text of 'Nymphes des bois' in the *Werken* needs revision; see the Appendix.

length compared with the ordinary chanson text, they are much shorter than most other compositions by either of these two poets.

Other texts of Josquin's chansons may be described as 'popular' or 'volkstümlich'. In these, as is well known, the rondeau has all but disappeared in favour of strophic poems, while other *formes fixes* remain only in modified form. The imagery becomes more vivid. The virelai adopts a more flexible form; the ballade sheds its envoy and becomes a mere strophic poem with refrain. Sources of the texts of these poems are the Bayeux manuscript (Paris 9346), MS. Paris 12744, manuscripts and prints of polyphonic chansons, and miscellaneous literary sources. A number of printed collections survive without music, including some which have only recently come to light.[6]

This 'popular' verse, so important in Josquin's music, with its wider variety of subject matter, its concrete and picturesque imagery, its 'modern' tone, appeals to our present critical sense. This is the forward-looking Josquin, whose influence on his contemporaries would be hard to deny. The poetry of these chansons owes something to the past; for example, the printed collections already mentioned still contain rondeaux and the older form of ballade with envoy, while the imagery has a long ancestry in medieval literature of all kinds. The genre is thus not totally new; yet precisely because it was taken up by musicians from about 1480, it came to be produced in much greater quantity. Josquin belongs to this period of transition; Ockeghem and Binchois before him set mostly *formes fixes*, his younger contemporary Févin set strophic poems, but Josquin set both kinds. A good example is his chanson 'Se congié prens', a ballade without envoy set in the new musical style, but with the old abstract content and imagery. Previously, musicians borrowed a humble minor genre from literature; now great writers come to music for their material: Rabelais constantly refers to chansons, Marguerite de Navarre composes *contrafacta*, Ronsard uses 'Allegez moy' (a chanson set by many composers, including Josquin) when he desires a particular effect.[7]

The characteristics of this 'popular' kind of chanson verse, with particular reference to Josquin's musical settings of it, are as follows:

1) There is no definitive text. In this respect, the popular verse may be compared to folk-song or to the poems in Professor de Sola Pinto's *The Common Muse*.[8] The text often varies according to the nature and the purpose of the source, and though corruptions were certainly introduced in the course of textual transmission, we should be wary of blaming variants

---

[6] For a complete edition of these poems in printed collections up to 1530, see *Chanson Verse of the Early Renaissance*, ed. Brian Jeffery (London, 1971).

[7] The Ronsard poem is 'Ha, Bel Accueil' (*Amours de Cassandre*, Sonnet 86).

[8] Vivian de Sola Pinto and Allan Edwin Rodway, eds., *The Common Muse, An Anthology of Popular British Ballad Poetry, XVth–XXth Century* (London, 1957).

too often on such corruptions. An example in Josquin is 'En l'ombre d'ung buissonnet', of which three settings of two different texts survive in Josquin's works alone, apart from many other versions. Josquin certainly did not have in mind one or even two fixed texts of 'En l'ombre d'ung buissonnet', but he set a poem that was one among many other possible versions that he might have chosen.[9]

2) With the exception of certain narrative poems, the stanzas are more independent of each other than is usual in purely literary poetry, whether by Ronsard or Malherbe, Rimbaud or Baudelaire. This relative independence, however, is quite usual in musical verse of any period, be it troubadour lyrics, eighteenth-century chansons, or hymns. Where several stanzas survive for a chanson of this kind (as with 'Faulte d'argent', for which seven stanzas are known), the choice of which stanzas to sing lies with the performer. When a poem *is* narrative, all stanzas should be sung.

3) The poems are interrelated in many different ways. There are straightforward relationships such as the use of timbres, 'responces' or quodlibets. Then there are *topoi* in Curtius' sense,[10] associations of imagery, stanza structure, and so on. Often the relationships are more complex. Josquin, for example, set the poem 'Je me complains de mon amy', adding at the end a snatch of the much earlier tune 'La tricotée'.[11] The poem deals with a girl whose lover used to come to her in the early morning but has now not appeared all day; 'La tricotée', as Josquin and his hearers knew, is about a girl who gets up in the early morning and goes off to the woods herself. With the snatch of the gayer 'La tricotée', Josquin has added his own ironic comment. The idea of getting up in the morning to go off to the woods is not merely a *topos*: it was associated at that time with specific poems, specific ideas, and specific tunes, and Josquin has used it economically in this chanson as a concept saturated with associations. (Ninot le Petit's 'Et la la la la' in Petrucci's *Canti B*—'a hit tune of the first order', as Professor Lowinsky has called it—quotes a variant of the 'La tricotée' tune, for precisely the same reasons.[12]) Another example in Josquin is his 'Tant vous aimme, bergeronnette', in which he uses both a tune and a set of images full

---

[9] [Jaap van Benthem, below, pp. 437–42, discusses the various textual versions of 'En l'ombre d'ung buissonnet'.—Ed.]

[10] Ernst Robert Curtius, *European Literature and the Latin Middle Ages*, transl. Willard R. Trask (*Bolligen Series*, xxxvi; New York, 1953); see in particular chapter 5, 'Topics'.

[11] On this piece, see Alan Curtis, 'Josquin and "La belle Tricotée"', *Essays in Musicology in Honor of Dragan Plamenac*, ed. Gustave Reese and Robert J. Snow (Pittsburgh, 1969), pp. 1–8.

[12] Ninot le Petit's chanson is no. 27 in Helen Hewitt's edition of *Ottaviano Petrucci, Canti B* (*Monuments of Renaissance Music*, ii; Chicago, 1967); Professor Lowinsky's comment is on p. xv. The resemblance to 'La tricotée' has to my knowledge not been pointed out before.

of similar associations; a girl gathering flowers in her father's garden was an old theme, familiar to all his contemporaries.

4) Exactness of syllable count or stanza structure was not considered so necessary in this popular musical verse as in purely literary poetry; one should beware of regarding such inexactitudes as necessarily due to textual corruption. The authors of these poems are anonymous, though a clue is afforded by the frequent references to students, petty thieves, and the like, but certainly they were not the artistic sophisticates of the age.

Josquin's chansons on the 'popular' texts fall into certain forms. There are four bergerettes or possible bergerettes. Of the latter, 'Adieu mes amours' is puzzling because it has a second text in rondeau form that is sung simultaneously. Because the words of 'Je sey bien dire' are missing, and those of 'Quant je vous voy' so corrupt, it is impossible to tell for sure whether these poems are bergerettes. In the case of 'Que vous, ma dame', Josquin has combined a bergerette with a Latin text 'In pace in idipsum'; since the first part is the respond and the second the verse, the repetitions involved in the bergerette form are quite possible. Josquin has wedded a bergerette to a responsory with perfect decorum. It seems clear, even from these few examples, that he played with this *forme fixe* just as he did with the rondeau.

None of his ballades has an envoy. Originally, this form had no envoy: it was added in the late fourteenth century, but dropped again in the late fifteenth century, so that we may say that Josquin uses the modern form of the ballade exclusively. Five of his ballades, unfortunately, have only one stanza; since a single-stanza ballade is improbable, it is likely that their texts were once longer. Another of his ballades is the regional 'Una musque de Buscaya', the story of the Basque girl, for which four narrative stanzas are found in MS. Paris 12744. Since they are narrative, they should all be sung to Josquin's music. The subject matter of his ballades is always 'popular' except in the interesting transitional 'Se congié prens', mentioned above.

Some of his chansons are strophic poems with refrain, and again their form is very free.

Outside these formal categories, there remain more modern poems in which stanzas of similar shape follow each other. For five of Josquin's chansons of this kind, various sources provide longer texts than do the actual musical sources: they are 'Faulte d'argent', 'Allegez moy', 'Si j'avois Marion', and two settings of 'En l'ombre d'ung buissonnet'. Because (as we have said) the stanzas of this kind of non-narrative poem are relatively independent of each other, the editor's task is to give the fullest text available, and the performer remains free, now as in Josquin's time, to choose whichever stanzas he wishes. In seven other chansons by Josquin, only one stanza is known to survive, though most probably others once existed. Two others have more than one stanza, but are through-composed. Finally, there remain two special cases. In 'Guillaume se va chauffer', because of the famous *vox regis* on a single note, any repetition to extra stanzas is surely inconceivable. And 'La belle se siet' is unusual in every way, both in Josquin's sonorous setting for three bass voices, and in its most exceptional form of five two-line stanzas; this very old poem is an ancestor of the new popular poetry but not a part of it. The strophic poems in Josquin's chansons show the greatest variety of treatment.

Finally, how does Josquin use his literary texts, and how do his settings of them differ from those of other composers? He was, after all, the greatest musician of his time and he can hardly have been careless of so important a part of his art, due allowance made for the notoriously different attitude of his age towards the relationship between word and note.

Above all, we may point to his sheer musicality, his understanding of the essential possibilities of the texts which he chose, especially of the popular texts with their associated melodies. He set them in complex musical ways, favouring canon above all, and generally chose texts that had already been used by other composers before him, so that not many of Josquin's poems are peculiar to him. This is the attitude of an essentially professional musician, and is different from that of, say, Claude le Jeune, who because of certain philosophical preoccupations of the late sixteenth century subjected his music so thoroughly to words. Josquin did not select the finest poems of his time from the literary point of view. True, he set poems by Lemaire de Belges and by Molinet, but others that he did not choose seem better to us today.

His setting of words is clear in its general outlines, yet to adapt them to the notes is by no means an easy task nor something editors necessarily agree upon. What is universally accepted is his capacity to render the varying texts in a fitting and expressive form. As Glareanus said, he adapts his music to the demands of the subject matter in innumerable masterly ways.[13]

He was catholic in his taste, setting poems of all forms and all types of subject available to a musician of his day. Living in an age of transition, he was able to use fully all the literary and musical possibilities offered by these texts, both new and old. Whereas Compère, for example, preferred satirical and anti-clerical poems, and Févin almost exclusively strophic popular poems, Josquin had no one-sided preference in the choice of texts: he embraced them all.

Josquin had an outstanding sense of humour. Examples abound: 'Guillaume se va chauffer', with its *vox regis* on a single note; 'Que vous, ma dame', a love song set simultaneously with the psalm verse 'I will both lay me down in peace and sleep'; the satirical 'L'amye à tous' in which the tenor ironically sings the old tune 'Je ne vis oncques la pareille'; the comic ballade text 'Una musque de Buscaya', with the story of a Frenchman whose amorous designs

---

[13] Henricus Glareanus, *Dodekachordon* (Basel, 1547), p. 362; *Heinrich Glarean, Dodecachordon*, transl. Clement A. Miller (American Institute of Musicology, 1965), ii, p. 265.

fail through the unintelligibility of the Basque words of the refrain; and the irony of 'Je me complains de mon amy', discussed above.

The most individual feature of his chansons—musically as well as in the treatment of words—is their freedom: they are sublimely oblivious of the honoured tradition of the *formes fixes*. In this Josquin may be compared with Rabelais, and indeed with the whole of French literature of the early sixteenth century, which was so much freer and more willing to experiment than the self-restricted Pléiade and post-Pléiade literature of the later part of the century. Specifically, he may have influenced the development from rondeau to strophic form by setting only the refrains of rondeaux, without medial cadence, and the development of three-part popular settings, taken up after him by so many composers—a field in which he seems to have been an innovator.[14] But the most important feature of Josquin's chansons remains their vitality, exceeding the bounds of conventional literary as well as musical forms by using them in a disciplined but unfettered way.

Appendix

The following list provides notes on all Josquin's chansons from the literary point of view. It is designed to guide the performer and editor in the matter of literary texts and to supplement (and where necessary correct) the modern editions of the chansons. For questions of source material, see the editions cited and Osthoff, ii, pp. 278–84 and 298–301.

A number of abbreviations are used in the list, viz:

Brown, 'Catalogue'	Howard Mayer Brown, 'A Catalogue of Theatrical Chansons', printed as pp. 183–282 of his *Music in the French Secular Theater, 1400–1550* (Cambridge, Mass., 1963).
Canti B	Ottaviano Petrucci, *Canti B*, ed. Helen Hewitt (*Monuments of Renaissance Music*, ii; Chicago, 1967).
Chanson and Madrigal	*Chanson and Madrigal 1480–1530*, ed. James Haar (Cambridge, Mass., 1964).
Chanson Verse	*Chanson Verse of the Early Renaissance*, ed. Brian Jeffery (London, 1971).
MS. Paris 12744	Paris, Bibliothèque Nationale, MS. fr. 12744, cited in the edition by Gaston Paris and Auguste Gevaert, *Chansons du XVᵉ siècle* (Paris, 1875).

[14] On the three-part popular setting at this time, see Howard M. Brown, 'The Genesis of a Style: The Parisian Chanson, 1500–1530', *Chanson and Madrigal 1480–1530*, ed. James Haar (Cambridge, Mass., 1964), pp. 1–50.

Newton   Paul G. Newton, 'Florence, Biblioteca del Conservatorio di Musica Luigi Cherubini, Manuscript Basevi 2439: Critical Edition and Commentary' (unpubl. Ph.D. diss., North Texas State University, 1968).

Odhecaton   *Harmonice musices Odhecaton A*, ed. Helen Hewitt (Cambridge, Mass., 1942).

Osthoff   Helmuth Osthoff, *Josquin Desprez*, ii (Tutzing, 1965).

Picker   *The Chanson Albums of Marguerite of Austria*, ed. Martin Picker (Berkeley and Los Angeles, 1965).

Theatrical Chansons   *Theatrical Chansons of the Fifteenth and Early Sixteenth Centuries*, ed. Howard Mayer Brown (Cambridge, Mass., 1963).

Werken   *Werken van Josquin des Prez: Wereldlijke Werken*, ed. A. Smijers et al. (Amsterdam, 1925–69).

1) 'A la mort/Monstra te esse Matrem'
    Edition: Newton, ii, pp. 229–30. Beginning printed in Osthoff, ii, p. 163.
    The French words are hard to read in the sole source but appear to have four lines. A medial cadence suggests that this is a rondeau quatrain (of which the remaining text is missing) combined with a Latin hymn. It is apparently not a secular love poem, but a sacred poem addressed to the Virgin Mary and as such commenting on the Latin text.

2) 'A l'eure que je vous p.x.'
    Edition: *Werken*, no. 41.
    No further text. Probably instrumental.

'A l'ombre d'ung buissonnet'
    See 'En l'ombre d'ung buissonnet'.

3) 'Adieu mes amours'
    Editions: *Werken*, no. 35; *Odhecaton*, no. 14; these Proceedings, pp. 665–8.
    This chanson has a six-line text underlaid to tenor and bass. In addition, in one source only (MS. Florence 2794), the refrain of a rondeau cinquain is underlaid to the superius, with the remainder of the text written out beneath the chanson. This rondeau text may be inauthentic. But if it is authentic, then the performance possibilities (not discussed in the modern editions) are as follows: (1) The six-line text appears to be a bergerette, and Josquin's setting is in bergerette form (of the 60 measures, mm. 1–20 are the same as mm. 40–60, and

21–30 roughly equal 31–40). The chanson could thus be performed as a bergerette, repeating measures 1–20 at the end, but this would disrupt the rondeau text. (2) It could be performed as a rondeau with full repetitions (though with difficulty, because of a weak medial cadence), but this would break up the bergerette. (3) Remembering that Josquin has scant respect for *formes fixes*, it may be that the chanson should simply be performed once through as it stands; Josquin thus achieves the humorous effect of combining these two similar texts while not concerning himself with the strict form of either. Of the three possibilities I think that (3) is most likely; (1) is less likely, and (2) is least likely (because of the loss of humorous effect that so much repetition would entail).

4) 'Allegez moy'
    Edition: *Werken*, no. 14.
    The text is strophic with refrain. One extra stanza could be added from an anonymous setting printed in *Theatrical Chansons*, no. 1 (though this comes from a source of 1560, and so the extra stanza may be a later addition):

> Si vous tenoy un mois en ma chambrette
> Dessoubz la boudinette,
> Si vous tenoy un mois ou quinze jours,
> Je vous feroy la couleur vermeillette,
> Dessoubz la boudinette.

The chanson was famous enough to be referred to by Ronsard in two poems, 'Ha Bel Accueil' (*Les Amours*, 1552, Sonnet 136), and 'Je vy tes yeulx' (ibid., Sonnet 14), where the whole first line is quoted. Marot and Molinet also mention 'Allegez moy'; see Brown, 'Catalogue', p. 186.

5) 'Basiez moy'
    Editions: *Werken*, no. 20a; *Canti B*, no. 34. (The six-part version is probably inauthentic; see *Canti B*, pp. ix–x and 71–2).
    Perhaps originally strophic, but through-composed by Josquin with some repetitions, though not enough for this chanson to be considered a *forme fixe*.

6) 'Belle, pour l'amour de vous'
    Edition: Picker, pp. 428–9.
    Strophic, but only one stanza survives.

7) 'Bergerette savoyenne'
    Editions: *Werken*, no. 36; *Odhecaton*, no. 10.
    A ballade with two eight-line stanzas, the last line being a refrain. It is possible that there were once more stanzas. The subject is regional

(Savoy) and in this respect, as well as in the ballade form, may be compared to 'Una musque de Buscaya' (q.v.) and such poems as 'Aymez moy, belle Margot' (in *Chanson Verse*, pp. 234–5).

8) 'Ce povre mendiant/Pauper sum ego'
   Editions: *Werken*, no. 46; Osthoff, *Musikbeilagen*, 5; Picker, pp. 389–90.
   This chanson appears in three sources, once with the two texts printed by Picker and Osthoff, once with 'Pauper sum ego' in all voices, and once with the incipit 'Fortune d'estrange plummaige' combined with the Latin 'Pauper sum ego'. Newton, i, pp. 40–41, defends the last possibility with great ingenuity, based on a parallel between Fortune's wheel and the descending ostinato bass, and this may well be correct. There remains the obvious parallel of sense between the Latin and the other French text. The setting has a firm medial cadence, but the descending ostinato bass suggests that this is not a rondeau but a through-composed setting of the texts.

9) 'Cela sans plus'
   Editions: *Werken*, no. 44; *Odhecaton*, no. 61.
   No further text. Neither the four-line poem used in the Obrecht and Lannoy settings in *Canti B*, nor another text suggested in *Odhecaton*, p. 178, can easily be underlaid to Josquin's music. A firm medial cadence does suggest that the original poem was a rondeau.

10) 'Cent mille regretz'
    Edition: *Werken*, no. 26.
    Five lines of text, apparently set as a rondeau. The poem is probably a rondeau cinquain of which only the first five lines remain. The chanson may be by Pierre de la Rue; see Osthoff, ii, p. 185.

11) 'Comment peult avoir joye'
    Editions: *Werken*, no. 56; *Canti B*, no. 19.
    Josquin's setting is through-composed, and the eight lines printed in *Canti B* (recovered from other sources) fit the music. It is a strophic poem of which more stanzas may have existed.

12) 'Cueur langoreulx'
    Edition: *Werken*, no. 1.
    Despite an unusual enjambement from line 3 to line 4, the text appears to be the refrain of a rondeau cinquain of which the remainder is missing. In the *Jardin de Plaisance*, f. 74, is a version in which the poem is made into a complete rondeau quatrain.

13) 'Cueurs desolez/Plorans ploravit' (*a 5*)
    Edition: *Werken*, no. 28.

The text as printed in the *Werken* is corrupt and should read as follows (for a performance, the underlay should be changed accordingly):

> Cueurs desolez par toutes nations,
> Assemblez dueil et lamentations,
> Ne cherchez plus l'armonieuse lyre
> De Orpheus pour vostre joye eslire,
> Mais plongez vous en desolations.

(Attaingnant's text, amended as little as possible, on the basis of poem LXXVI in *Poèmes de Transition, Rondeaux du Ms. 402 de Lille*, i, ed. Marcel Françon (Cambridge and Paris, 1938).) Picker, pp. 330–8, prints another setting of 'Cueurs desolez' in rondeau form in which the third stanza is different; Josquin's setting, however, is through-composed and appears to be an example of his practice of setting no more than the first part of a rondeau, with no interest in the repetitions associated with the rondeau form. (The setting *a 4*, the text of which differs after the first two lines, is probably not by Josquin; see Osthoff, ii, pp. 184–5.)

14) 'De tous biens plaine' (*a 3*)
    Edition: Osthoff, ii, pp. 395–6.
    No further text. Probably instrumental.

15) 'De tous biens plaine' (*a 4*)
    Edition: *Werken*, no. 49b.
    No further text. Probably instrumental.

16) 'Douleur me bat'
    Edition: *Werken*, no. 18.
    The medial cadence is weak indeed; this is probably another example of a poem that was originally a rondeau cinquain.

17) 'Du mien amant'
    Edition: *Werken*, no. 23.
    This and the 'Residuum' are both strophic poems of two stanzas each, in which the second stanza is sung to the same music as the first.

18) 'En l'ombre d'ung buissonnet au matinet' (*a 3*)
    Edition: *Werken*, no. 61.
    Two eight-line stanzas are given in the *Werken*; Josquin's setting, despite many repetitions of musical phrases, is not strophic but through-composed (16 lines).

19) 'En l'ombre d'ung buissonnet au matinet' (*a 4*)
    Edition: *Werken*, no. 59.

The poem is a variant of no. 18 with only six lines. Josquin has set it as two stanzas of three lines each, with a cadential formula or coda at the end.

20) 'En l'ombre d'ung buissonnet tout au long d'une riviere'
Edition: *Werken*, no. 60.

Although the two poems begin alike, the present chanson is a setting of a different text from nos. 18 and 19. The text in the *Werken* is unsatisfactory because only one stanza is given; this is a narrative poem of four stanzas, of which stanzas 2, 3, and 4 may be found in MS. Paris 12744, no. 9. Both poem and musical setting are in ballade form. In performance, the extra stanzas should be sung, if the narrative is not to be left incomplete. They are easily underlaid and may be found in G. Paris' edition, *Chansons du XVe siècle*, no. 9.

21) 'En non saichant'
Edition: *Werken*, no. 9.

The text is evidently corrupt; it consists of six lines, through-composed.

22) 'Entrée suis en grant pensée' (*a 3*)
Editions: *Werken*, no. 58; these Proceedings, pp. 432–4.

The text given in the *Werken* should be emended as follows: in measures 15–17 read *treuve* for *tienne*, in measure 43 read *ce* for *le*. In measures 1–2 the text should be emended to read *Entrée suis*: the sense demands the feminine, rendering 'je' superfluous. Josquin's setting is in AAB form, suggesting the form of an eight-line ballade, but the unsatisfactory underlay in B suggests that the text here is corrupt; experiment with an eight-line text as in the following chanson is hardly more satisfactory.

23) 'Entrée suis en grant pensée' (*a 4*)
Editions: *Werken*, no. 57, Picker, pp. 285–8, Osthoff, *Musikbeilagen*, 7.

The text should be *Entrée suis*, not *Entré je suis* (see above). It is an eight-line ballade, set as such by Josquin. More stanzas may have existed. One source gives an incipit 'Par vous je suis', which may simply be a variant beginning of the same poem. Three others give German words 'In minen zinn' (see Picker, pp. 132–3, and Osthoff, pp. 201–2).

24) 'Faulte d'argent'
Edition: *Werken*, no. 15.

See Brown, 'Catalogue', no. 131, for many references to other versions and settings of this famous chanson. The most reliable literary text is to be found in *S'ensuivent plusieurs belles chansons nouvelles. Et sont en nombre iiii.xx et dix* (Paris, *c.* 1515–20) (see *Chanson Verse*, pp. 55–7) and also *S'ensuivent plusieurs belles chansons nouvelles… qui sont en nombre cinquante et troys* (Paris, *c.* 1515–20) (a slightly different version, printed in *Theatrical Chansons*, p. 69). Josquin's setting is in the form ABA with a coda. Seven stanzas are known. The poem is not narrative; indeed, its seven stanzas are not all related. Stanzas 1, 3, 4 are connected by the 'argent' motif and the consonant rhymes of lines 2 and 8. Further, line 8 in stanza 1 is repeated in line 2 of stanza 3, and lines 4 and 6 of Stanza 1 rhyme with lines 4 and 5 of stanza 2. Stanzas 2, 5, 6, 7 are another poem entirely, a pure love poem. It seems that we have here two separate poems that somehow got mixed up together; but the various stanzas of the two poems are definitely connected with one another. Performers might do well to confine their choice of stanzas to 1, 3, and 4.

25) 'Fors seulement' (*a 4*)

Edition: O. Gombosi, *Jacob Obrecht* (Leipzig, 1925), *Musikbeilagen*, no. 12.

No further text; probably instrumental.[15]

26) 'Fors seulement' (*a 6*)

Edition: none. Beginning printed in Osthoff, ii, p. 177, after the unique source, Bologna, Museo Civico Bibliografico Musicale, MS. R 142, fol. 57ᵛ (one voice only, largely identical with the superius of Ockeghem's setting).

In the absence of the other voices, it is impossible to tell whether this is a vocal or instrumental setting.[16]

27) 'Guillaume se va chauffer'

Edition: *Das Liederbuch des Johannes Heer von Glarus*, ed. Arnold Geering and Hans Trümpy (*Schweizerische Musikdenkmäler*, v; Basel, 1967), p. 92.

Josquin's setting includes a part for one voice on a single note, and the story that he composed this part for Louis XII to sing is quite plausible.[17] Whether he did or not, it is unlikely that extra stanzas were sung to the music; none are known.

28) 'Hélas ma dame'

Edition: *Werken*, Supplement, no. 11.

No further text. A poem with a long stanza and a four-line refrain would fit, but I know of none beginning 'Hélas ma dame'.

---

[15] See Helen Hewitt, '*Fors seulement* and the Cantus Firmus Technique of the Fifteenth Century', *Essays in Musicology in Honor of Dragan Plamenac*, pp. 91–126; p. 114, no. 26.

[16] Ibid., p. 111, no. 11.

[17] Glareanus, *Dodekachordon*, p. 468; Miller, ii, p. 284.

29) 'Incessament livré suis à martire'

    Edition: *Werken*, no. 6.

    The medial cadence is weak. This is apparently a through-composed setting of five lines, probably the first five lines of a rondeau.

30) 'J'ay bien cause de lamenter'

    Edition: *Werken*, no. 33.

    Perhaps instrumental: see Osthoff, ii, pp. 226–7. But if the words are genuine, then this is a through-composed, perhaps strophic chanson. The last word should read *habandonnée* (not *habandonner*, as in the *Werken*).

31) 'J'ay bien nourry sept ans'

    Edition: none. Beginning printed in Osthoff, ii, p. 167. For sources see Osthoff, ii, p. 281.

    The three-part chanson in MS. Florence 178, fol. 32^v, bears the incipit '[J']ay biem norise tans'. Osthoff lists it as 'J'ay bien rise tant', a probable corruption of 'J'ay bien nourry sept ans ung joly gay', a poem in MS. Paris 12744, no. 26. The first stanza fits Josquin's music, if we assume a long coda; the others, having somewhat shorter lines, fit less well. The irregularity of stanzas in MS. Paris 12744 suggests that the text is corrupt. Perhaps Josquin set a version of this or a related poem; Josquin's music, however, is unrelated to that in MS. Paris 12744.

'J'ay bien rise tant'

    See 'J'ay bien nourry sept ans'.

32) 'Je me'

    Edition: none. Beginning printed in Osthoff, ii, p. 167, after MS. Florence 178, fol. 10^v.

    No further text. Josquin's music appears to be in rondeau form, but it is difficult to find a suitable text among the many that begin 'Je me'.

33) 'Je me complains de mon amy'

    Edition: *Werken*, no. 11.

    This chanson is among the most interesting with regard to Josquin's experiments with words. The basic text has six lines, of which Josquin has set lines 4–6 to the same music as lines 1–3 (but with many small differences); he then adds the words 'La tricoton, la belle tricotée', familiar from an earlier text and melody. See above, p. 404.

34) 'Je ne me puis tenir d'aimer'

    Editions: *Werken*, no. 31; these Proceedings, pp. 684–9.

    Eight lines, through-composed. Related to a poem in MS. Paris 12744, no. 102, whose fifth stanza begins thus, but the relationship is distant. There may have been more stanzas in Josquin's poem.

35) 'Je n'ose plus'
Edition: Osthoff, ii, p. 189.
No further text. The medial cadence suggests that the text was a rondeau.

36) 'Je ris et si ay larme à l'oeul'
Edition: *Werken*, Supplement, no. 12.
Only four lines survive (through-composed). The theme is a familiar medieval topos.

37) 'Je sey bien dire'
Edition: *Werken*, no. 38.
No further text. The musical form, in which the opening bars are repeated at the end, shows that it was probably a bergerette or (less likely) a chanson à refrain.

38) 'La belle se siet'
Editions: *Werken*, no. 62; Osthoff, *Musikbeilagen*, 6.
Five two-line stanzas. Ancient popular ballade, already set by Dufay (*Opera omnia*, vi, ed. Heinrich Besseler, no. 12). The story of the girl whose lover is condemned to death survives into our century (see Osthoff, ii, pp. 194–5).

39) 'La plus des plus'
Editions: *Werken*, no. 45; *Odhecaton*, no. 64.
Apparently in rondeau form. The modern editors of the *Odhecaton* underlay a rondeau cinquain from the Rohan manuscript, not very successfully. If it *is* the right text, then this is the only rondeau by Josquin that comes down to us with a complete text.

'La tricotée'
See 'Je me complains de mon amy'.

40) 'L'amye à tous/Je ne vis oncques la pareille'
Edition: *Werken*, no. 25.
Amusing combination of texts. In a through-composed setting, Josquin uses the old tenor 'Je ne vis oncques la pareille', while simultaneously setting another poem, related but totally opposed in sense.

41) 'Le villain'
Edition: none. Beginning printed in Osthoff, ii, p. 171 after Augsburg, Staats- und Stadtbibliothek, MS. 142a, fol. 45.
I have been unable to see the unique source. Osthoff considers it to be instrumental, but one might suspect that it is a setting of the famous chanson 'Hé l'ort vilain jaloux' (many settings known; text from literary sources in *Chanson Verse*, p. 84; see also *Chanson and Madrigal*, p. 13, n. 28).

42) 'Ma bouche rit'
    Edition: *Werken*, no. 19.
    Probably instrumental, for reasons set out in Osthoff, ii, pp. 213–15.

43) 'Ma dame helas'
    Edition: *Odhecaton*, no. 66.
    No further text. The music is clearly in rondeau form.

44) 'Mi larés vous'
    Edition: *Werken*, no. 34.
    A weak medial cadence suggests that this is not a rondeau but a
    four-line strophic poem, through-composed. Only one stanza survives.
    The opening notes *mi la re* echo the first words.

45) 'Mille regretz'
    Editions: *Werken*, no. 24; *Chanson and Madrigal*, Ex. 2, pp. 143–6.
    Four lines of text, through-composed. The piece appears in Attain-
    gnant's *Chansons musicales à quatre parties* of 1533 with the note 'J.
    lemaire'. The poem is not attributed to the poet Jean Lemaire de Belges
    in any literary source, and this note in a relatively late musical source
    does not seem to me to constitute sufficient evidence to justify the
    attribution. More stanzas may have existed.

46) 'Mon mari m'a diffamée'
    Edition: These Proceedings, pp. 444–5.
    There are many settings of this strophic chanson with refrain (see
    Canti B, pp. 37–9); texts without music occur in early printed sources;
    see *Chanson Verse*, p. 85.

47) 'N'esse pas ung grant desplaisir'
    Edition: *Werken*, no. 8.
    A weak medial cadence suggests that this is a strophic poem, not a
    rondeau.

48) 'Nymphes des bois/Requiem aeternam'
    Editions: *Werken*, no. 22; *Medici Codex* (see below).
    The text underlaid in the *Werken*, taken from Susato, is manifestly
    corrupt. Molinet, a perfectionist, could never have written this irregu-
    lar stanza as it stands. Two other versions of the literary text survive.
    One, printed in *Les Faictz et Dictz de Jean Molinet*, ed. Noël Dupire, ii
    (Paris, 1937), p. 833, gives a 14-line text with a clear rhyme-scheme
    ABABCCDDEFEF. The other is found in the Medici Codex; though
    irregular from the literary point of view in that it inserts an extra
    unrhyming line after line 7, the source dates from Josquin's lifetime
    and is probably the poem set by Josquin. The extra line describes
    Ockeghem as 'Doct, elegant de corps et non point trappé', a pleasing

and very credible personal touch. In his edition of *The Medici Codex* (*Monuments of Renaissance Music*, iii–v; Chicago, 1968), Edward Lowinsky fully discusses the question (iii, pp. 66–8), prints the full text (ibid., pp. 213–14) and underlays it to the music (iv, no. 46), superseding the version in the *Werken*.

49) 'Nimphes, nappés/Circumdederunt'
    Edition: *Werken*, no. 21.
    Possibly a secular contrafactum of a sacred text, 'Videte omnes populi' (see Osthoff, ii, pp. 94–5). It is set as a through-composed four-line stanza.

'Par vous je suis'
    See 'Entrée suis'.

50) 'Parfons regretz'
    Edition: *Werken*, no. 3.
    Five-line text; Josquin's setting is in rondeau form, so we may assume that this was a rondeau cinquain of which the remaining text is now missing. The poem is tentatively attributed to Claude Bouton (see Osthoff, i, p. 68, and ii, p. 210).[18]

51) 'Petite camusette, à la mort m'avez mis'
    Edition: *Werken*, no. 17.
    A four-line stanza set by Josquin as a chanson à refrain: A (line 1), B (lines 2–3), A (line 4, which is the same as line 1). More stanzas may have existed. Newton, i, pp. 103–8, relates this chanson to the play *Le jeu de Robin et Marion* by Adam de la Halle.

52) 'Plaine de dueil et de melancolie'
    Editions: *Werken*, no. 4; Picker, pp. 362–7.
    A five-line stanza, through-composed. Two further five-line stanzas are given in one source only (MS. Brussels 228), unfortunately with one line missing; these stanzas are printed in the *Werken*. Without these, the poem would have appeared to be a rondeau cinquain of which Josquin had set only the refrain, through-composed. The text has been tentatively ascribed to Margaret of Austria (Osthoff, i, p. 69, and ii, p. 210).[19]

53) 'Plus n'estes ma maistresse'
    Edition: *Werken*, no. 30.
    Josquin's setting is in ABA form with coda. It is not a bergerette but probably a chanson à refrain of which only one stanza survives.

---

[18] [See also Herbert Kellman, above, p. 184.—Ed.]
[19] [See, however, Kellman, above, pp. 184–5.—Ed.]

54) 'Plus nulz regretz'

Editions: *Werken*, no. 20; Picker, pp. 280–84; these Proceedings, pp. 675–9.

This is a setting of a poem of twenty lines by Jean Lemaire de Belges, a longer poem than usual for Josquin, and the most sophisticated that he is known to have set. He has written music for the first eight lines only, but it is possible to sing lines 9–12 to the same music as lines 1–4, and lines 13–20 to the same music as lines 1–8, a procedure which fits the rhyme scheme of the poem.

55) 'Plusieurs regretz qui sur la terre sont'

Edition: *Werken*, no. 7.

Five lines, through-composed. An anonymous setting of these same five lines from MS. Brussels 228, no. 37 is published by Picker, who points out (p. 136) that another poem, a complete rondeau beginning 'Tous les regretz qui sur la terre sont', is identical after the first line. It can be underlaid to the Brussels version. But Josquin's setting has no medial cadence; once again we find Josquin composing only the refrain of a rondeau without allowing for repetitions.

56) 'Pour souhaitter je ne demande mieulx'

Edition: *Werken*, no. 10.

Because of doubts about the music (see Osthoff, ii, pp. 225–6), this chanson may not be by Josquin.

57) 'Quant je vous voy'

Edition: *Werken*, no. 65.

A poem of twelve very short lines whose form is hard to make out, as indeed is the form of the music. It seems to be a chanson à refrain, but might be a corrupt bergerette.

58) 'Que vous, ma dame, je le jure/In pace'

Editions: *Werken*, no. 47; Picker, pp. 461–3.

The French text is a bergerette; Josquin has combined a love song with the Latin text 'I will both lay me down in peace and sleep'. This is a unique example in Josquin's music of a bergerette composed over a *cantus firmus*, let alone one of this humorous kind. Picker does not indicate the repeats necessary in a performance; they are: repeat measures 43–61 with the words 'Oncques riens mieulx. . . ,' then sing measures 1–42 with the words 'Craindre me soit. . . ,' and finally repeat measures 1–42 with the original words.

59) 'Qui belles amours a'

Edition: none. Beginning printed in Osthoff, ii, p. 173, after Vienna, Oesterreichische Nationalbibliothek, MS. 18810, fol. 23ᵛ.

To judge from Osthoff's discussion of this chanson (I have not seen the unique source), this appears to be a setting of the poem found in a version with three stanzas in MS. Paris 12744, no. 103. It is a chanson à refrain.

60) 'Regretz sans fin'
Edition: *Werken*, no. 5.

The poem, without music, would appear to be a rondeau cinquain lacking the last five lines. But this is not a regular rondeau setting; there is no clear medial cadence after line 3, and lines 6–8 are set to new music, leading back to the beginning, without any musical parallels between lines 1–5 and 6–8. Once again Josquin appears to have set a rondeau or a rondeau-like text in a free fashion.

61) 'Se congié prens'
Edition: *Werken*, no. 12.

Text and music are in ballade form. Four stanzas are found in MS. Paris 12744 and should be underlaid to Josquin's music for the performance of extra stanzas; they are readily available in G. Paris' edition, *Chansons du XVᵉ siècle*, no. 52. The poem is the new form of ballade without envoy, yet the sentiments and imagery are totally abstract and old-fashioned. It is perhaps not surprising that Josquin should have set a poem of this peculiarly transitional nature.

62) 'Se j'avoye Marion'
Edition: *Werken*, no. 63.

Eight lines, through-composed. Five more stanzas are in *S'ensuyvent unze belles chansons nouvelles* (Paris, *c.* 1515–20) (edited in *Chanson Verse*, pp. 163–5), which could be underlaid to Josquin's music.

63) 'Se j'ay perdu mon amy' (*a 3*)
Edition: *Werken*, no. 64.

The poem is a ballade and set by Josquin as such. Three stanzas are in MS. Paris 12744, no. 95 (see notes to no. 64 of the *Werken*); in performance it is best to sing all three. The poem is related to another ballade in MS. Paris 12744, no. 120.

64) 'Se j'ay perdu mon amy' (*a 4*)
Edition: none. Beginning printed in Osthoff, ii, p. 175. For sources, see Osthoff, ii, p. 283.

Ballade form and set by Josquin as such. The remarks to the preceding chanson apply here too.

65) 'Tant vous aimme, bergeronnette'
Edition: none. Beginning printed in Osthoff, ii, p. 176, after Florence, Conservatorio, MS. 2442, no. 6.

This four-line stanza set by Josquin in the form A (line 1), B (lines 2–3), A (line 4, which is the same as line 1) is a chanson à refrain, of which there may have been more stanzas.

66) 'Tenez moy en voz bras'
     Edition: *Werken*, no. 13.
     Lines 1–4 are a refrain repeated at the end of Josquin's setting, with a cadential formula. Lines 5–6 appear to be the first stanza of a strophic poem of which no further words are extant. The music appears also with a Latin text, 'Vidi speciosam', in MS. Bologna R 142 (see Osthoff, ii, p. 215), but the French text is almost certainly the original one. The same melody occurs in other settings of the chanson text.

67) 'Una musque de Buscaya'
     Edition: *Werken*, no. 37.
     A ballade in the new form, of which three further stanzas are in MS. Paris 12744 (see notes to no. 37 in the *Werken*). Josquin's setting observes the ballade form. The poem is narrative; performers should sing all four stanzas if the chanson is to make sense.

68) 'Vivrai je tousjours'
     Edition: none. Beginning printed in Osthoff, ii, p. 180, after Cambrai, Bibliothèque Municipale, MS. 125–128, fol. 15.
     In the absence of an edition, we withhold comment save for the observation that Sermisy's 'Vivray je tousjours' is quite different from the Josquin setting, to judge from the part printed by Osthoff.

69) 'Vous l'arez, s'il vous plaist, madame'
     Edition: *Werken*, no. 16.
     One five-line stanza, through-composed.

70) 'Vous ne l'aurez pas si je puis'
     Edition: *Werken*, no. 2.
     One four-line stanza, through-composed.

Josquin's Three-part 'Chansons rustiques': A Critique of the Readings in Manuscripts and Prints

JAAP VAN BENTHEM

The subject of this paper is Josquin's three-part 'chansons rustiques',[1] with respect to their transmission, their musical structure, and their texts. The purpose is to determine the vocal or instrumental character of the various voice parts on the basis of style and structure and to clarify what aspects in their transmission are of importance in the search for the most authentic version of music and text.

We shall deal with the following subjects:

1) the transmission of the compositions;
2) the transmission of the texts and text underlay;
3) the structure of the chansons as a whole and of each voice;
4) criteria for determining which voice parts carry the text;
5) criteria for determining the best version of the text.

Transmission of the chansons

We know of eight three-part 'chansons rustiques' of Josquin des Prez: 'En l'ombre d'ung buissonnet, au matinet', 'En l'ombre d'ung buissonnet,

---

[1] On the 'chanson rustique' see the following publications by Howard Mayer Brown: *Music in the French Secular Theater, 1400–1550* (Cambridge, Mass., 1963); 'The Genesis of a Style: the Parisian Chanson, 1500–1530', in *Chanson and Madrigal 1480–1530*, ed. James Haar (Cambridge, Mass., 1964), pp. 1–36; 'Critical Years in European Musical History 1500–1530', in *International Musicological Society, Report of the Tenth Congress, Ljubljana 1967* (Kassel, 1970), pp. 78–94; 'The *Chanson rustique*: Popular Elements in the 15th- and 16th-Century Chanson', *Journal of the American Musicological Society*, xii (1959), pp. 16–26. Isabelle Cazeaux, in a review of Howard Brown's book (*Journal of the American Musicological Society*, xviii (1965), pp. 95–6), questions the advisability of applying the literary term 'chanson rustique', from the middle of the sixteenth century, to an earlier musical repertory.

tout au long', 'Entré je suis en grant pensée', 'La belle se siet au pied de la tour', 'Quant je vous voye', 'Si j'ay perdu mon amy', 'Si j'eusse Marion, hélas',[2] and 'Mon mary m'a diffamée'.[3] The anonymous three-part chanson 'Tenez moy', the basis for Josquin's six-part chanson of the same name, may be ascribed to him with a high degree of probability on stylistic and technical grounds.[4] (However, I shall not use this anonymous chanson in formulating analytical conclusions.) These nine works form the subject matter of the present paper.[5]

Seven of these compositions, only three of which carry Josquin's name, have come down to us in eight early sixteenth-century manuscripts:[6]

MS. Bologna Q 17, fol. 45ᵛ	'En lombre du(n)g buisonet...[tout]' Josquin
MS. Brussels IV 90/Tournai 94,	
fol. 11/12	'En lombre...tout'
fol. 13ᵛ/15	'Mon mari ma diffamee'
MS. Florence Ricc. 2794, fol. 69ᵛ	'Entre suis' Josquin des pres
MS. St. Gall 461, p. 34	'Se je p(er)du mo(n) amy' Josqin [sic]
p. 58	'En lombre... [au matinet]'
MS. Gdańsk 4003, part III, no. VIII	'Tenez moy'
MS. Copenhagen 1848, p. 125	'Tenes moy'
MS. London 35087, fol. VIIᵛ	'Quant je vous voye'
fol. XIIᵛ	'En lombre...tout'
fol. XXIᵛ	'Mon mary ma diffamee'

---

[2] *Werken*, Wereldlijke Werken, nos. 61, 60, 58, 62, 65, 64, 63 (the reading 'j'eusse' instead of 'j'avoye' in no. 63 is preferable; see below). The edition is not always reliable with respect to the names given to the voices (in nos. 60 and 65, 'altus' and 'tenor' should be exchanged).

[3] A transcription of 'Mon mary m'a diffamée' may be found at the end of this paper.

[4] See my study, 'Zur Struktur und Authentizität der Chansons à 5 & 6 von Josquin des Prez', *Tijdschrift van de Vereniging voor Nederlandse Muziekgeschiedenis*, xxi (1970), pp. 177–8; the chanson is transcribed in Anhang I. For a correction of my transcription, see *Tijdschrift*, xxii (1971), p. 39.

[5] The three-part chanson 'Hélas ma dame' may also be a 'chanson rustique' (*Werken*, Supplement, no. 11, with an altus part found in two of the four sources). The melody of the chanson, unfortunately textless in all sources, has an affinity with 'Hellas ma dame q(ue) je desire tant' in MS. Paris fonds fr. 9346 ('Bayeux MS.'), no. XLII, fol. 45. This was first pointed out by Dragan Plamenac in 'A Reconstruction of the French Chansonnier in the Biblioteca Colombina', *The Musical Quarterly*, xxxvii (1951), pp. 110–11 (see also note 13, below).

[6] Bologna, Civico Museo Bibliografico Musicale, MS. Q 17; Brussels, Koninklijke Bibliotheek, MS. IV 90/Tournai, Bibliothèque de la Ville, MS. 94 (superius/tenor); Florence, Biblioteca Riccardiana, MS. 2794; St. Gall, Stiftsbibliothek, MS. 461; Gdańsk, Biblioteki Pan, MS. 4003; Copenhagen, Kongelige Bibliotek, MS. 1848/2⁰; London, British Museum, Add. MS. 35087; Paris, Bibliothèque Nationale, MS. f. fr. 1597.

MS. Paris 1597, fol. XLVII^v   'Se iay perdu'
         fol. LXXV^v   'A lombre... au matinet'

The earliest printed source containing one of these compositions, without attribution, is probably the untitled print by Christian Egenolff[7] (RISM [c. 1535][14]), of which only the superius remains. 'En lombre... [tout]' appears as no. 27 of the third part. *La Courone et fleur des chansons à troys*, published in 1536 in Venice by the printers Andrea Antico[8] and Antonio dell'Abbate (RISM 1536[1]), includes six three-part 'chansons rustiques' ascribed to Josquin. The first and last of these are not to be found in earlier sources up to now:

RISM 1536[1], fol. 7^v   'Si ia voye marion' Josquin
    fol. 7^v/8/7^v   'En lombre... tout' Josquin
    fol. 12/12^v/12   'Si iay perdu' Josquin
    fol. 14^v/15^v/14^v 'Quant je vous voy' Josquin
    fol. 17^v/18^v/18 'En lombre... au matinet' Josquin
    fol. 20/21/21   'La belle se siet' Josquin

'Quant je vous voye' was reprinted in Rhau's *Tricinia* (RISM 1542[8]), no. LXXXVII, and 'En l'ombre... tout' in Scotto's *Il terzo libro delle muse a tre voci* (RISM 1562[9]), p. 19, both ascribed to Josquin.[9] Finally, the printers Adrian Le Roy and Robert Ballard, in their *Second livre de chansons a trois parties* of 1578, published four chansons:

RISM 1578[15], fol. 9   'En l'umbre... Tout' Josquin
    fol. 9^v   'A l'umbre... au matinet' Josquin
    fol. 10^v   'Si j'ay perdu' Josquin
    fol. 16^v   'Mon mari m'a diffamée' Josquin

This is the only source to name the composer of 'Mon mary m'a diffamée'; it appears anonymously in two manuscripts, MS. London 35087 and MS. Brussels IV 90/Tournai 94, dating from the early part of the sixteenth century.[10]

---

[7] See Nanie Bridgman, 'Christian Egenolff, imprimeur de musique', *Annales musicologiques*, iii (1955), pp. 77–177; Ernst-Ludwig Berz, *Die Notendrucker und ihre Verleger in Frankfurt am Main von den Anfängen bis etwa 1630* (Catalogus Musicus, v; Kassel, 1970), pp. 12–17 and 148–9.

[8] On Antico's life and publications, see Catherine Weeks Chapman, 'Andrea Antico' (Ph.D. diss., Harvard University, 1964) and Anne-Marie Bautier-Regnier, 'L'édition musicale italienne et les musiciens d'Outremonts au XVIe siècle (1501–1563)', in *La Renaissance dans les Provinces du Nord*, ed. François Lesure (Paris, 1956), p. 31–2, 35–7.

[9] The bass part-book is missing.

[10] See the study cited in note 4, p. 185. The 'Petite camusette' *a 3*, attributed to Josquin in *Tiers livre de chansons a trois parties* (RISM 1578[16]) by the same printers, is in fact a chanson by Févin; see Edward Henry Clinkscale, 'The Complete Works of Antoine de Févin' (Ph.D. diss., New York University, 1965), i, p. 231, who overlooked this source.

Transmission of the text and text underlay[11]

Manuscripts:

1) Several manuscripts provide complete literary texts: Brussels IV 90/Tournai 94, Florence 2794, London 35087, and Paris 1597.

2) In these manuscripts, the beginning of each phrase of text generally corresponds to the beginning of the musical phrase. The relation between text and music is also often recognizable at the end of each staff; apparently the last note on the staff was intended to correspond with the last syllable of the text.

3) Within the phrases the relationship between words and notes remains unclear—save for one or two exceptions.

4) Melismatic extensions and motivic repetitions are only exceptionally provided with text.

Prints:

1) The prints of Antico (1536[1]), Rhau (1542[8]), Scotto (1562[9]), and Le Roy & Ballard (1578[15]) furnish text in all voices (the lost bass part-book of the Scotto edition will hardly have been an exception).

2) The placement of the text in Antico (1536[1]), apart from the beginning of a phrase, has little relationship to the musical structure.

3) The chansons in Rhau (1542[8]) and Scotto (1562[9]), with respect to text and text underlay (save for some deviations in the spelling), have been taken over literally from Antico.

4) The print of Le Roy & Ballard (1578[15]) is independent of Antico; it offers a number of variant readings and shows a more careful text underlay.

It is paradoxical that clearly vocal parts have no text in some sources; in others, in which text underlay poses almost insuperable difficulties, text is provided. For example, in all voices of the chanson 'En l'ombre... au matinet' the text can be fitted to the music with ease. Yet, only the superius of MS. Paris 1597, a primary source for the chanson, has a text (probably incomplete), and the many necessary text repetitions have not been written out. The tenor and bass[12] show only fragments of text. The same manuscript presents 'Si j'ay perdu' with complete text in all voices. Text repetitions have been written out, and the relation between text and music is clarified at the end of the staves. Yet, only the superius and tenor emerge with a

---

[11] On text underlay in general see Edward E. Lowinsky, 'A Treatise on Text Underlay by a German Disciple of Francisco de Salinas', in *Festschrift Heinrich Besseler* (Leipzig, 1961), pp. 231–51, and idem, *The Medici Codex of 1518* (*Monuments of Renaissance Music*, iii; Chicago, 1968), pp. 90–107; on text underlay in French chansons see idem, Introduction to *Ottaviano Petrucci, Canti B*, ed. Helen Hewitt (*Monuments of Renaissance Music*, ii; Chicago, 1967), pp. v–viii. See also Don Harrán, 'New Light on the Question of Text Underlay Prior to Zarlino', *Acta musicologica*, xlv (1973), pp. 24–56.

[12] In the terminology of the fifteenth century we should be speaking of contratenor bassus; for simplicity's sake we shall call the part bass.

convincing text underlay; the structure of the bass argues against vocal performance:

1) immediately before the repetition of measures 1–19 as 21–39, a full measure is placed in the bass, anticipating the beginning of the tenor (see Ex. 1, m. 20);

2) the final note of the musical phrases in measures 11 and 14 (and the repetition in mm. 31 and 34) is also the initial note of the next musical phrase (see Ex. 2). In Le Roy & Ballard (1578[15]) the dotted half note in measure 14 has been split into two separate notes to facilitate the text underlay.

The structure of the compositions

Valuable clues to text underlay may be gained from a study of the structure of the composition as a whole and that of each voice separately.

The chansons with which we deal here are all undoubtedly polyphonic arrangements of well-known songs, some of which have come down to us in the monophonic chansonniers Paris, fonds fr. 9346 ('Bayeux MS.') and fonds fr. 12744 (see below).[13] Josquin employs the *cantus prius factus* in three different ways:

Group I. The *cantus prius factus* is laid out unadorned in the tenor:

> 'Si j'eusse Marion, hélas'
> 'Tenez moy en vos bras'
> 'Entré je suis en grant pensée'
> 'Mon mary m'a diffamée'

Group II. Both superius and tenor employ the *cantus prius factus* and have the same contrapuntal continuations:

> 'Quant je vous voye'
> 'En l'ombre d'ung buissonnet, tout au long'
> 'Si j'ay perdu mon amy'

Group III[a]. All voices make use of the *cantus prius factus*, chains of repeated motives, extended free continuations, and short runs with eighth-notes:

> 'La belle se siet au pied de la tour'

Group III[b]. All voices have the same *cantus prius factus* and the same contrapuntal continuations:

> 'En l'ombre d'ung buissonnet au matinet'

The distinction between vocal and non-vocal parts depends on range, character of the line, and the relationship between the basic melody and its contrapuntal continuations.

There are significant differences between the structure and the function of the contrapuntal continuations in the various voices. In the chansons 'Si j'eusse Marion', 'Tenez moy', and in the first part of the chanson 'Mon mary m'a diffamée', superius and bass combine short motives of the *cantus prius factus* with extended continuations. These phrases may accompany several phrases of the tenor without a break. Between or within these phrases we find runs in eighth-notes. In the chansons 'Entré je suis', 'Mon mary m'a diffamée' (second part), and in the chansons of groups II and III a phrase of the basic melody is often lengthened by short cadential motives such as the following:

---

[13] On these monophonic chansonniers, see Gustave Reese and Theodore Karp, 'Monophony in a Group of Renaissance Chansonniers', *Journal of the American Musicological Society*, v (1952), pp. 4–15. For modern editions, though not very trustworthy, see Théodore Gérold, *Le Manuscrit de Bayeux* (Strasbourg, 1921): 'En l'ombre d'ung buissonet...tout au long' (p. 119); and Gaston Paris, *Chansons du XVᵉ siècle* (Paris, 1875): 'Mon mary m'a diffamée' (no. CXI), and 'Si j'ay perdu mon amy' (no. XCV).

These brief continuations add to the rhythmic tension of the basic melody. Occasionally such continuations take on motivic significance and occur as a counterpoint to a phrase of the basic melody.

There are differences not only in the range of the voices but also in the way the range is used. The superius and bass of 'Si j'eusse Marion' and 'Tenez moy'[14] have a wider range than the tenor; in the former the superius exceeds the range of the tenor by a third, in the latter by a fifth. The superius frequently sinks below the tenor, taking on the function of an alto. Sometimes the superius and bass move swiftly through the whole range of a tenth, more than once leaping up or down an octave.

In the chansons 'Entré je suis', 'Mon mary m'a diffamée', 'En l'ombre... tout', and 'Quant je vous voye', superius and tenor (labelled 'alto' in the Josquin edition in the latter two works) have the range of an octave to a tenth, but the areas emphasized differ. Superius and tenor continually imitate each other. Except for 'Entré je suis', the range of the melodic phrases in these voices is seldom more than a sixth. There are no octave leaps within a phrase in superius and tenor.

In the chansons 'Si j'ay perdu', 'La belle se siet', and 'En l'ombre... au matinet' the range of the melodic phrases in the superius is extended by the transposition of a motive having the range of a fifth (see 'Si j'ay perdu', mm. 42–50, 'La belle se siet', mm. 12–21, and 'En l'ombre... au matinet', mm. 37–44). The upward extension of the tenor range to $b\flat$' in 'En l'ombre ... au matinet', m. 56, is justified by the text, a dialogue between Robin and Bellon, for at this point Bellon replies to Robin's 'Aime moy, je suis Robin', with the forceful '(Robin, par saincte Marie,) Je ne t'ayme pas ung brin!' The tenor functions as a second superius at that moment.

The structure of the bass and its relation to the other voices differ. In most of the chansons in Groups I, II, and III[a] the bass traverses its complete range (or nearly so) in the first phrase.[15] Characteristic of this first phrase are: (a) a brief motive derived from the basic melody, followed by a rapid

[14] In MS. Gdańsk 4003, measures 18²–20¹ and 49²–51 of the superius are transposed up an octave, perhaps to make this voice more suitable for vocal performance.

[15] 'Tenez moy', mm. 1–11, 'Entré je suis', mm. 1–13, 'Mon mary m'a diffamée', mm. 1–9, 'Quant je vous voye', mm. 1–8, 'La belle se siet', mm. 1–7, 'En l'ombre... tout', mm. 5–11, 'Si j'ay perdu mon amy', mm. 7³–18. The same disposition of the bass is also found in Josquin's four-part chansons 'Je ris', 'Comment peult avoir joye', and 'Qui belles amours'.

step-wise descent; (b) one or two large leaps, including syncopated octave leaps; (c) the use of the rhythm ♩. ♫♪ | ♩ , both ascending and descending. In the chansons 'Entré je suis', 'Mon mary m'a diffamée', and in the chansons of Group II the first bass phrase is followed by others whose cadences coincide with one or both of the upper voices. Concerning the treatment of the succeeding phrases, two procedures can be distinguished:

1) When superius and bass perform alone, in the chansons 'Entré je suis' and 'Mon mary m'a diffamée', the bass utilizes its upper range, reaching it abruptly by means of a leap, or by runs of ascending eighth-notes; it changes its function from bass in three-part to tenor in two-part passages with the superius.

2) In the chansons 'Si j'ay perdu' and 'En l'ombre...tout' the bass participates in imitative duos.

In the chanson 'En l'ombre...au matinet' all bass phrases are completely integrated into a three-part imitative structure, using not only the basic melody but also nearly the same contrapuntal continuations as the other voices. In parts of the chanson 'La belle se siet' the superius is accompanied by a duo between tenor and bass. Sometimes there are striking contrasts between the superius and the tenor-bass duos:

measures 1–11. The tenor has the same characteristic structure as the first bass phrase.

measures 69–85. Tenor and bass use brief motives in quasi-canonic imitation at close interval beneath a slow-moving superius—a technique strongly reminiscent of Josquin's four-part instrumental arrangement of 'De tous biens plaine'.

These structural analyses suggest that the following voices were intended to be sung:

'Si j'eusse Marion, hélas'	tenor
'Tenez moy en vos bras'	tenor
'Entré je suis en grant pensée'	tenor (superius)
'Mon mary m'a diffamée'	tenor (superius)
'En l'ombre...tout au long'	superius and tenor
'Quant je vous voye'	superius and tenor
'Si j'ay perdu mon amy'	superius and tenor
'En l'ombre...au matinet'	superius, tenor, bass
'La belle se siet au pied de la tour'	superius

Criteria for determining the best version of the text

The texts of Josquin's chansons come down to us with a variety of different readings. Two of the chansons in Antico (RISM 1536[1])—used as the primary source in the Josquin edition—have a more complete text in other sources:

MS. London 35087	'Quant je vous voye'
MS. Paris 1597	'Si j'ay perdu mon amy'
Le Roy & Ballard (RISM 1578[15])	'Si j'ay perdu mon amy'

Other sources also give different words in the following chansons:

MS. London 35087	'En l'ombre... tout au long'
	'Quant je vous voye'
MS. Brussels IV 90/Tournai 94	'En l'ombre... tout au long'
Le Roy & Ballard (RISM 1578[15])	'En l'ombre... au matinet'

To determine the best text and text underlay in Josquin's 'chansons rustiques', we must consider

1) the relationship between text and melody;

2) the relationship between literary and musical variants in the sources; and

3) early sixteenth-century poetic sources as well as compositions on the same texts by Josquin's contemporaries. The following sources[16] furnish valuable additions to the texts of Josquin's 'chansons rustiques':

MS. Paris 9346 ('Bayeux MS.')
   (monophonic chansonnier)

fol. 92ᵛ, no. LXXXIX	'La belle se siet au pie de la tour'
fol. 104ᵛ, no. C	'A lombre dung buissonnet Tout le long dune riuiere'

MS. Paris 12744
   (monophonic chansonnier)

fol. VIIᵛ	'Aupres dun jolys boucquet loree dune riuiere'
fol. LXIII	'Sy je perdoys mon amy'
fol. LXXVᵛ	'Mon mary ma diffamee'

MS. Cambridge Pepys 1760
   fol. IIII^xxiiii ᵛ (= 84ᵛ)   'Si jeusse marion helas' M. gascongne

MS. Florence Cons. 2442, no. 5[17]   'Se iay perdu mon amy' *a 4* Josqui(n) des pres

---

[16] Cambridge, Magdalene College, MS. Pepys 1760; Florence, Biblioteca del Conservatorio, MS. 2442; Florence, Biblioteca Nazionale Centrale, MS. Magl. XIX, 164-7; London, British Museum, MS. Harley 5242; Seville, Biblioteca Colombina, Cod. 5-I-43; *Motetti novi e chanzoni franciose a quatro sopra doi* (Venice, A. Antico; RISM 1520[3]); *Le septiesme livre contenant vingt et quatre chansons* (Antwerp, T. Susato; RISM 1545[15]).

[17] On this manuscript see Howard Mayer Brown, 'The Music of the Strozzi Chansonnier', *Acta Musicologica*, xl (1968), pp. 115–29, and 'Chansons for the Pleasure of a Florentine

MS. Florence XIX 164–167,	
no. XLVI	'Entre ye suis en grant pensier' *a 4* (= Josquin)
no. LII	'Se jay perdu mon amy' *a 4* (= Josquin)
MS. London Harley 5242, fol. 12ᵛ	'Si jeusse marion du tout a mon plaisir' (anon.)
MS. Paris 1597, fol. XXXIIIᵛ	'En lombre dung buyssonnet tout au long (S)/loree (T) dune riuere' (anon.)
fol. LXIXᵛ	'Mon mary ma diffamee' (anon.)
MS. Seville 5–I–43, fol. 103ᵛ	'Lautrier/Trop suis jonette/En lombre ... au matinet' Busnois
RISM 1520³ (Antico), fol. 37ᵛ	'Mon mary ma diffamee' Adrien (= Willaert)
RISM 1545¹⁵ (Susato), fol. 8ᵛ	'Tenez moy en voz bras' *a 6* Josquin des Pres

The following results emerge from an examination of the texts in these sources:

'Si j'eusse Marion, hélas'

The version in Antico (RISM 1536¹) shows an irregularity in the rhyme scheme:

> Si ia voye marion hellas
> du tout amon playsir
> La belle au corps mignon hellas
> que mon cueur a choisi
> Au bois ie la merroye
> dancer ung tourdion et ho
> et puis la remerroye [S: remeroye]
> tout droit en sa maison

In the manuscripts Cambridge Pepys 1760 and London Harley 5242 the rhyme scheme is regular:

MS. Cambridge (superius):	*MS. London* (tenor):
1. Sy jeusse marion helas	Si jeusse marion
2. du to(u)t a mo(n) plaisir	du tout a mon plaisir
3. La belle au corps migno(n) helas	qui a les yeulx rians
4. q(ue) jay volu choisir	et tresbeau maintenir

Patrician: Florence, Biblioteca del Conservatorio di Musica, MS Basevi 2442', in *Aspects of Medieval and Renaissance Music, A Birthday Offering to Gustave Reese*, ed. Jan LaRue (New York, 1966), pp. 56–66.

5. Au v(er)t boys la me(n)roye	au vert boys la menroye
6. danses ung tourdyon et ho	par dess(oubz) le buisson
7. Et sy la ramerroye	et si la remenroye
8. couche(s) en sa maison	coucher en sa maison
9. et ho voy couches en sa maiso(n)	

Variants in other voices:

1. CT, T, B: si
5. T: la missing
   CT: ma(n)roye
6. CT: dansez; T: dances
   B: dancez
8. CT, T, B: couchez
   B: coucher

The text of the Cambridge manuscript is closest to that in Antico. It may well be regarded as the original text of Josquin's chanson.

'Tenez moy en vos bras'

The text in the manuscripts Gdańsk and Copenhagen is not quite correct. Susato's 1545 print of Josquin chansons (no. 14) seems to preserve a better text.

'Entré je suis en grant pensée'

The text in the superius of MS. Florence Ricc. 2794 is very irregular. Comparison with the text of Josquin's four-part arrangement in MS. Florence XIX 164–167 demonstrates that the last phrase of the poem is missing in Florence 2794. I believe that the text in MS. Florence XIX 164–167 (though with some corrections and adaptations after MS. Florence Ricc. 2794) was intended for both versions.[18]

MS. Florence 2794 (superius):	*MS. Florence XIX 164–167* (tenor):
1. Entre suis en grant pensee	1. Entre ie suis en grant pensier
2. Pour faire ung nouvel amy	2. cest po(ur) faire ung nouvelle [*recte* nouvel] amy
3. mais je me(n) treuve courousee	3. Dont ie me trouve courrousse

---

[18] On arrangements of this popular song, see Martin Picker, 'Polyphonic Settings c. 1500 of the Flemish Tune, "In minen sin"', *Journal of the American Musicological Society*, xii (1959), pp. 94–5, and 'Newly Discovered Sources for *In minen sin*', ibid., xvii (1964), pp. 133–43. For an analysis of the structure and sources of the four-part arrangement, see my study 'Die Chanson *Entré je suis* à 4 von Josquin des Prez und ihre Überlieferung', *Tijdschrift van de Vereniging voor Nederlandse Muziekgeschiedenis*, xxi (1970), pp. 203–10.

4. Le cueur triste doulant et
   marry
5. Mais je ne scay
6. se cela me sera bon
7. en se joly moys de moy
   [*recte* may].

4. e le cuer dolent triste et many [*recte*
   marry]
5. mays ie ne scai
6. si ce soyt amou(r) ou non
7. en ce yoli moys de moy [*recte* may]
8. le sarayge ou non.

Variants in other voices:

1. S, B: ye
2. S, B: po(u)r; S/CT: fayr(e)/fair(e)
   B: fayre; CT: nouvel
3. S: courrosse; B: couruosse
4. S, CT: le cuer dolent; B: et le...
5. S, CT, B: mais, scay
6. CT: Amous
7. S, CT: youli; B: mys de moy
8. S, CT, B: saragie; S/B: serai/yge,
   B: saraygie

Ex. 3

Florence, Bibl. Ricc., MS. 2794, fol 69ᵛ
(text corrected after Florence XIX 164–167)

1) Frédéric Godefroy, *Lexique de l'ancien français* (Paris, 1968) p. 149: *dont*, adv., alors.
2) This line is taken from MS. Florence XIX 164–167; the text of MS. Florence 2794 is given in parentheses.

(The first part of this composition seems to offer a problem in *musica ficta*. The E♮ in the bass at measure 5 and the repetition of measures 5–7 a step higher in measures 11–13 suggest that B♭ should be sung in measures 4 and 5 (superius), E♭ in measure 6 (tenor), and A♭ in measure 6 (bass).)

'Mon mary m'a diffamée'

The reading of the text for the second phrase in MSS. London 35087 and Brussels IV 90/Tournai 94 is confirmed by the text in MS. Paris 12744 and by the Willaert chanson in Antico (RISM 1520[3]).[19] The text repetitions in MS. London 35087 (m. 14[4]) are replaced by the exclamation 'He mon amy' in MSS. Paris 1597 and 12744. The arrangements of this popular song in MS. Paris 1597 and in the Petrucci prints *Canti B* (RISM 1502[2]), fol. 15[v] (De Orto) and *Canti C* (RISM 1504[3]), fol. 44[v] and in Antico (RISM 1520[3]) indicate that flats should be added to the tenor in measures 13[3] and 17[1] and the superius in measure 12[4] (see Appendix).

'Quant je vous voye'

There are striking differences in text underlay between MS. London 35087 and the Antico print (RISM 1536[1]):

MS. *London 35087* (superius):	*Antico* (superius):
1. Quant je vous voye mm. 1–8	Quant ie vous voy

[19] For an analysis of this text, see Helen Hewitt, *Ottaviano Petrucci, Canti B*, pp. 37–8. Miss Hewitt states that a new phrase is inserted in line 7 of MS. Tournai 94. This, however, is a misreading; the MS. only repeats the words 'J' en feray'. See also Brian Jeffery, *Chanson Verse of the Early Renaissance* (London, 1971), p. 32, for a different complete text.

2. Daise transi		doys ie transir
3. Il mest aduis		(doys ie transir)
4. que voy ung roy		
5. Il mest aduis	mm. 9–14	Il mest advis
6. Il mest aduis		(Il mest advis)
7. que voy ung roy		q(ue) ie suis ung roy
8. tout hors dennoy	mm. 15–19	tout hors d(e)smoy
9. tout hors dennoy		(tout hors d(e)smoy)
10. me treuve ne		me trou(v)e myeulx
11. quant je voz voy	mm. 20–21	qua(n)t ie vo(u)s voy
12. oussy je croy	mm. 22^2–23^1	ainsi ie croy
13. et souuent dy	mm. 23^3–24^2	q(ue) nul soucy
14. que nulz soussi	mm. 24^4–25^3	avoir ne doy
15. auoir ne doy	m. 26	qua(n)t ie vo(u)s voi
16. qua(n)t je voz voy	mm. 27^2–28^1	avvoir ne doy
17. qua(n)t je voz voy	mm. 28^3–29^2	(avvoir ne doy)
18. qua(n)t je voz voy	mm. 29^4–31^3	aulcun soucy
19. qua(n)t je vous voy	mm. 32–39	qua(n)t ie vo(u)s voy
20. Daise transi		doy ie transir
21. Il mest aduis		(doy ie transir)
22. que voy ung roy		

Variants in other voices:

1. B: voy	12. T, B: ainsy
10. B: ne missing	13. B: souci
11. T, B: vous	15. T: voy
12. T: aussi; B: ousi	16. T: avoir; B: q(uan)t
14. T, B: soussy	ie vo(u)s voi
16–18. T: vous	17. B: avoir
	20. T, B: doys

Although the text underlay in Antico for measures 20–31^3 is not faultless either, it does suggest that the repetition of 'quant je vous voy(e)' in measures 27–31 of MS. London 35087 is not plausible. A correct text underlay should correspond to the repetitions of the several motives in that phrase:

Ex. 4 mm. 19-31

London, British Museum, Add. MS. 35087, fol. VII^v

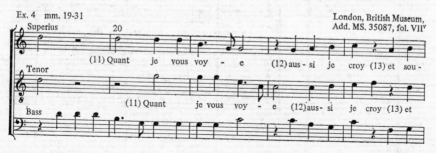

[1)] Orig.: *quant je vous voy*, mm. 27-31 in all voices.

In this way phrases 16–18 show the same rhyme-scheme as phrases 5–7 and 8–10. The repetition of phrases 14–15 in phrases 16–18 also corresponds to the repetition in MS. London 35087 of phrases 3–4 in phrases 5–7, all of which suggests that the London MS. probably has the authentic text underlay for measures 1–8 and 32–9. Superius and tenor (called 'Altus' in the Josquin edition), the two vocal parts, are closely imitative; therefore the version of measures 16⁴–17⁴ of the tenor in MS. London 35087 seems more plausible than the one in Antico:

[1)] Orig.: dennoy, in all voices
[2)] Orig.: ds

'Si j'ay perdu mon amy'

MS. Paris 1597 and Le Roy & Ballard (1578[15]) add two lines (7 and 8) to the text in Antico. The most likely text for the chanson is:

MS. Paris 1597 and Le Roy & Ballard:

1. Si j'ay perdu mon amy

    1. P 1597: Se

2. je n'ay pas cause de rire.

    2. P 1597 S: pas missing; T: point; RISM 1578[15]: point

3. Je l'avoye sur tous choysy;

4. vray dieu, qu'en voulez-vous dire!

    4. P 1597: vous missing

5. Il m'avoyt juré sa foy

    5. RISM 1578[15] S: m'a promis sa foy; T, CT: m'avoit promis

6. de n'aymer aultre que moy

7. tout au long du moys de may;

    6. P 1597 S: d'amer; CT: q(u)'(i)l n(')aymoyt

8. Qu'en voulez-vous dire!

    8. P 1597: vous missing

9. Morte suys si je ne l'ay,

10. et qu'en voulez-vous donc,

    10. P 1597 S: vous missing

11. qu'en voulez-vous dire!

12. Et qu'en voulez-vous donc dire de moy!

Phrases 7 and 8 are underlaid to measures 54–62, replacing the anticipation of phrases 9–10 in Antico's version. Phrases 1–4 are related musically to phrases 7–8 and 9–12 (phrase 10 must be considered an interpolation between phrases 9 and 11; phrase 12 is a repetition of phrase 11 followed by the rhyme word of phrase 6. The musical tension of this chanson is carefully built up by means of the varied repeats, which become shorter and shorter:

	a'	b'	a''	b''	a'''	b'''	b''''
phrases:	1/3	2/4	7	8	9	10–11	12
mm.:	1–7, 20–7	7–20, 27–40	54–8	58–62	62–4	63–7	66–71

'En l'ombre d'ung buissonnet . . . tout au long'

The transmission of the poem for this chanson is very confusing; even in one and the same source the various voices have startling differences in text and syllable structure. Only in the monophonic chansonnier MS. Paris 12744 does the poem have a regular syllable structure: 7878 8787

1. Aupres dun jolys boucquet
2. loree dune riuiere
3. je trouuay le filz marquet

4. qui prioit sa mye chere
5. et disoit en telle maniere
6. je vous ayme fin cueur doulx
7. a donc respond la bergere
8. et comment lentendes vous

In the following manuscripts and prints the third phrase has 8 syllables:
7888

Paris 1597 (tenor)

1. En lombre dung buyssonet
2. loree dune riuere
3. ie re(n)co(n)tray le filz marguet
4. qui p(ri)oit sa dame chere
   2 S: tout au long
   3 S: trouuay le filz marguet
   4 S: qui tenoyt

Paris 9346 (*Bayeux MS.*)

A lombre dung buissonnet
Tout le long dune riuiere
Trouuay robin le filz marquet
Qui prioit sa dame chere

Brussels IV 90/Tournai 94 (tenor)

1. En lombre dun buissonnet
2. to(u)t au loing dune riuiere
3. trouuay robyn le filzs marq(ue)t
4. quy prioyt sa dame chiere

Antico (*Scotto, Le Roy & Ballard*)
              (tenor)

En lombre dung buissonet
tout au loing dunge riuyere
trouay robin le filz marguet
qui prioit sa dame chiere
   2. Antico (S) and Le Roy & Ballard:
      long
   3. Antico (S) and Scotto (S): rubin
      Le Roy & Ballard: Marquet
   4. Le Roy & Ballard: chere

This irregularity seems to be the basis for the use of two quarter-notes instead of a half-note when the opening material is repeated at measure 11.

There are seven readings for the beginning of the fifth phrase; they all can be reduced to two main readings in the Parisian monophonic chansonniers:

Paris 9346: Luy disant
   London 35087: En disant
   RISM 1578[15]: Disant en

Paris 12744: Et disoit
   Brussels IV 90/Tournai 94: et luy dit
   Paris 1597 (S): el me dist
   Paris 1597 (T): luy desoit
   RISM 1536[1] and 1562[9]: Et disoit

All sources, however, agree in the continuation of this phrase: 'en tel[le] maniere', except MS. London 35087: 'par te manire'. Notwithstanding all the conflicting readings, the fifth phrase has eight syllables in all sources.

Instead of 'Je vous ayme d'ung cueur doulx' in the sixth phrase of Antico (RISM 1536[1]), Scotto (1562[9]), and Le Roy & Ballard (1578[15]), the manuscripts agree on the reading '... fin cueur doulx'. The striking correspondence between the melodic phrase on that text in MS. Paris 9346, the anonymous setting in MS. Paris 1597, and the same phrase in the Josquin chanson makes it very likely that 'fin' is the correct version. (The two monophonic melodies are completely different; Josquin uses the one in MS. Paris 9346.)

The seventh and eighth phrases also differ in the number of syllables in the sources; the syllable structure 87 in MS. Paris 12744 is enlarged in the other Parisian manuscripts to 97:

Paris 9346	*Paris 1597* (tenor)
7. Adonc respondit la bergere	Ado[n]c respondi la bergere
8. Et co(m)me lentendez vous	et co[m]ment l'entendez vo(u)s
	7. S: respont

All sources of the Josquin chanson with complete text enlarge this syllable structure to 98:

London 35087 (tenor)	*Brussels IV 90/Tournai 94* (tenor)
7. Adont respondit la bergiere	(missing in the MS.)
8. Robyn co(m)ment latendez vous	Robyn comment lentendes vo(u)s
(CT: lattendez)	
Antico, Scotto (tenor)	*Le Roy & Ballard* (tenor)
7. ado(n)t luy respo(n)d la bergiere	Ado(n)c respondit la bergere
8. Robin co(m)ment lentendes vo(us)	Robi(n) comment l'entendés vous

Thus, the syllable scheme for the text as set by Josquin is 7888, 8798. However, if we interpret the verb 'prier' as 'to invite', MS. London 35087 gives an acceptable alternate reading for the fourth phrase, 'qui prioit à sa dame chère', resulting in an interesting new metric scheme: 7889 8798. The consistent appearance of the ♩. ♪♩ ♩ figuration, which accommodates this extra syllable, in measures 9^4 and 19^4 (superius) and 7^4 and 17^4 (tenor) against ♩ ♩ ♩ in measures 3^2 and 13^2 (superius) and 2^4 and 12^4 (tenor) and the placement of the text in MS. London 35087 support the view that this version also can claim a certain authenticity:

Ex. 6   mm. 5-11 and 15-21   London, British Museum, Add. MS. 35087, fol. XII^v

[1])Orig.: chiere, in all voices

'En l'ombre d'ung buissonnet . . . au matinet'

The text in MS. Paris 1597 has the most regular metric structure: 748 748 8787 748. The prints of Antico and Le Roy & Ballard both enlarge the second syllable group:

Paris 1597 (superius)

A lombre du bissonnet
au matinet
Je trouvay bellon mamye
qui faisoit ung chappelet
de si bon hait
Je luy ditz dieu te begnye

Antico (superius)

En lombre dung buissonnet
au matinet, au matinet
Je trouay bellon mamye
q(ui) faisoit ung chappelet
en lo(m)bre du(n)g buissonet
qui faisoit ung chapelet
de si bon het de si bon et
tout de muguet
Je luy dis dieu te begnie

7. T: het, B: bet

Le Roy & Ballard (superius)

A l'umbre d'un buissonnet
au matinet, au matinet
Ie trouuay Bellot mamye,
Qui faisoit un chappellet
De lauande & de Muguet
A l'umbre d'un buissonnet
au matinet (au matinet)
De si bon hait
Ie luy dit Dieu te benye

The relationship between text and music in mm. 4^3 (S), 6^3 (T), 8^3 (B) and 30^1 (T) demonstrates that the text version in Le Roy & Ballard must have been the basis of the composition:

Ex. 7 mm. 1-14 and 21-35

Paris, MS. f. fr. 1597, fol. LXXVᵛ;
text after Le Roy & Ballard,
Second livre (RISM 1578¹⁵), fol. 9ᵛ

1) Orig.: 𝄽 ♩ ♩ ; see other sources.

In the second part of the chanson text, Antico adds a line not found in the other sources, thus turning the last phrases of the text into a dialogue ended by Robin:

Paris 1597 (tenor, superius)
'Je te prie bellon ma(m)ye
ayme moy je suis Robin,'
'Robin p(ar) saincte marie
ie ne te'ay(m)e pas ung brin'
'Je te donvray de mo(n) pain
ung grant plain poing
de la croste et de la mye'

Antico (tenor, superius)
'Je te prie bellon mamye
ayme moy je suis rubin'
'Robin par saincte marie
je ne taymeray ia grain'
'Je te douuray de mo(n) pain
ung grand plain poing
Dela croute de la mie [T, B: mye]
Se tu veulx estre mamye'

Le Roy & Ballard (tenor, superius)
'Je te prie Bellot m'amie
Ayme moy je suis Robi(n)'
'Robin par sainte marye
Ie ne t'ayme pas un grain'
'Ie te do(n)ray de mo(n) pain
un gros plain poing
De la croute & de la mye'

'La belle se siet au pied de la tour'

The text in Antico differs only slightly from the text of Dufay's composition.[20] Antico gives 'doleur' and 'signeur' (phrases 2 and 4) instead of the older version, 'dolour', 'seignour', which furnish a better rhyme with 'tour', 'jour', 'amours' (phrases 1, 6, 8, 10). The quarter-note was probably divided into two eighth-notes in measures 33 (superius = Bass I), 34 (tenor

[20] See J. F. R. Stainer and C. Stainer, *Dufay and His Contemporaries* (London, 1898), pp. 8–11 and 122–6; *Guillelmi Dufay Opera Omnia*, vi, ed. Heinrich Besseler (Rome, 1964), no. 12; Werner Danckert, *Das europäische Volkslied* (Berlin, 1939), pp. 238–41; Th. Gérold, *Chansons populaires du XVᵉ et XVIᵉ siècles avec leurs melodies* (Strasbourg, 1913), no. I[a,b]; p. 85, Notes.

= Bass II), and 36 (bass = Bass III) to accommodate an extra word of text in the third phrase that is not found in earlier sources:

Dufay	*Josquin*
3. Son père luy demande: (7 syllables)	Son père lui demande: (7)
'Fille, qu'avez vous (5 syllables)	'Ma fille, qu'avez vous? (6)

When the material returns in measure 106, however, the two lines of 7+6 syllables are underlaid without dividing the quarter-note:

7. Et par dieu, belle fille, (7)	Par Dieu, ma belle fille, (7)
a celui faudres vous[21] (6)	a ce la fauldrez vous (6)

Nevertheless, both versions can be fitted to the music without using eighth-notes:

Ex. 8   mm. 32-5

mm. 106-9

[21] Bologna, Biblioteca Universitaria, Cod. 2216, reads 'Par dieu, ma belle fille'; MS. Paris 9346 has 'Ma foy, ma belle fille, a ce la....'

Appendix: 'Mon mary m'a diffamée'

Ex. 9

Brussels, MS. IV 90, fol. 13ᵛ

Text after London, MS. 35087, fol. 21ᵛ

Superius

Tournai, MS. 94, fol. 15

Tenor

London, MS. 35087, fol. 21ᵛ

Bass

¹⁾London MS. 35087 indicates repetition of the previous text; MSS. Paris 12744 and 1597 give 'Hé, mon amy!'.

²⁾RISM 1578¹⁵ :♭

Variant readings:

m. 8³- 9, B.   RISM 1578¹⁵

m. 10¹⁻³, S.   RISM 1578¹⁵

m. 12¹⁻³, S.   RISM 1578¹⁵

m. 16⁴-17³, T.   London, MS. 35087

m. 21⁴-22⁴, S.   London, MS. 35087

m. 26¹⁻⁴, B.   RISM 1578¹⁵

m. 32¹⁻⁴, S.   London, MS. 35087

B.

m. 10⁴, S.   RISM 1578¹⁵
m. 12⁴, S.   Brussels, MS. IV 90,
             RISM 1578¹⁵
m. 16⁴, S.   RISM 1578¹⁵
m. 19⁴, B.   RISM 1578¹⁵
m. 28⁴, B.   RISM 1578¹⁵
m. 30⁴, B.   RISM 1578¹⁵

Josquin's Compositions on Italian Texts and the Frottola

CLAUDIO GALLICO

Frottola is the name of a specific poetic and musical form; at the same time it is the general term for the secular music of the early Italian Renaissance. The convention of calling this repertory, which is varied in itself, by the single name of frottola derives from the title pages of the collections edited by Ottaviano Petrucci between 1504 and 1514; out of the ten books surviving, nine have the general title *Frottole*, even though they include compositions on metrical forms as varied and as different from the frottola as the strambotto, oda, capitolo, sonnet, stanza, Latin metres, and so on.

According to the most recent and authoritative view, the frottola was basically the written tradition and elaboration of musical practices of extemporaneous character widespread by the end of the fifteenth century.[1] These native songs had original Italian stylistic qualities. The development parallels the artistic cultivation of popular music in France during the same period. The frottola enjoyed an extraordinary vogue: the large repertory, the numerous transcriptions for solo lute, for voice and lute, and for keyboard instruments testify to that. With its tunefulness—the melody appearing not in the tenor but in the soprano—with its regular phrasing, its novel and appealing four-part harmony, and its lucid structure, it stimulated the 'oltremontani' to fuse their learned art with the native Italian style, leading to the development of the madrigal.

Notwithstanding recent exhaustive researches,[2] the small number of Josquin's compositions on Italian texts has not increased. The 'Fortuna disperata' attributed to 'Josq(ui)n du pres' in a Spanish manuscript[3] is an

[1] Knud Jeppesen, *La Frottola*, 3 vols. (Copenhagen, 1968–70).

[2] Knud Jeppesen, op. cit.; see also Claudio Gallico, 'Per la compilazione di un inventario di poesia e musica italiana del primo Rinascimento', *Rivista Italiana di Musicologia*, i (1966), pp. 88–93.

[3] Segovia, Catedral, MS. s.s., fol. 182ᵛ. See Higinio Anglés, 'Un manuscrit inconnu avec polyphonie du XVe siècle conservé à la cathédrale de Ségovie', *Acta Musicologica*, viii (1936), pp. 6–17; idem, *La Música en la Corte de los Reyes Católicos*, i, *Polifonía religiosa* (Madrid, 1941), p. 110; and Helmuth Osthoff, *Josquin Desprez*, ii, pp. 166 and 232–3. Osthoff points out (p. 232) that the two upper voices are identical with the version ascribed to Busnois in the same manuscript, which is the basis for Josquin's 'Missa Fortuna desperata'.

instrumental trio of uncertain authenticity on the well-known theme. Other pieces with Italian titles—'La Bernardina', 'Fortuna d'un gran tempo', and perhaps 'La Spagna'—have nothing in common with the style of the frottola and are therefore excluded from consideration.

We are left with three compositions on Italian texts, all very different. Moreover, each of them represents a typical model: 'Scaramella va alla guerra' is the polyphonic elaboration of a popular tune, arranged as an early villota; 'In te Domine speravi' develops a frottola tune ('aer') following the common method; and 'El grillo è buon cantore' is a vivid musical setting of a humorous text, rich in visual and mimic allusions. It is unlikely that other Italian compositions are lost; Josquin's fame was such that the shrewd Petrucci would have incorporated them into his collections.

In his three Italian compositions Josquin avoids the clichés that characterize a large part of the frottola repertory. It seems that the artist deliberately created a single musical essay in each style, making of each a model of its kind.

The lively 'Scaramella'[4] must be considered Josquin's first work on an Italian text. Written in D Dorian and in *proportio tripla* throughout, it has two sections, the first cadencing on the dominant, A major, the second ending on D. It develops the popular tenor in a skilful vocal setting. The *cantus firmus* in the tenor, imitative entrances anticipating the *cantus firmus* melody in the second section, and the simple harmonic texture are all characteristic of the early villota. Josquin's treatment of the popular tune should be compared to Compère's 'Scaramella fa la galla'.[5] The tenor is substantially the same, even if metrically different, and there are a few slight variants in the melody:

Ex. 1
Josquin, 'Scaramella va alla guerra' (tenor)

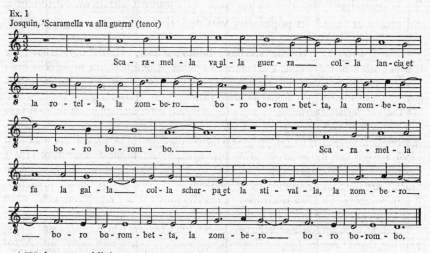

[4] *Werken*, Wereldlijke Werken, Bundel v, no. 54.

[5] Modern edition in *Loyset Compère, Opera Omnia*, ed. Ludwig Finscher, v (Rome, 1972), p. 65. Zürich, Stadtbibliothek, MS. Z. XI. 301, p. 59, has an anonymous instrumental elaboration in three parts related to Compère's version.

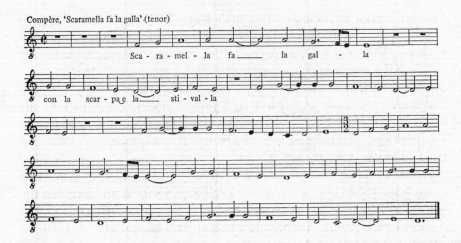

Compère, 'Scaramella fa la galla' (tenor)

Compère's composition is more flexible and airy than Josquin's, due in part to the interesting conflict of rhythm and metre. Compère omits the text of the first stanza, thus disregarding the martial side of the Italian 'homme armé', leaving to the emblematic character only the droll mask of vanity. But even that contrasts with the proverbial description of Scaramella.[6] If the existence of these two settings of 'Scaramella' were to date back to the service of both musicians at the court of Milan,[7] and if they had been written as a musical competition,[8] then we would have to think of a date in the 1470s for their composition.

The popular usage of the Scaramella refrain toward the end of the fifteenth century was almost obsessive, as we know from an elegant epigram, 'In Scaramellam', by the writer and pedagogue Cantalicio, edited in a collection of 1493.[9] Its popularity was such that it appeared in three other

---

[6] 'Un personaggio...povero, vecchio e brutto', a poor, old, and ugly fellow, the laughing stock of the people. Cf. Francesco Novati, 'Contributo alla storia della lirica musicale italiana popolare e popolareggiante dei secoli XV, XVI, XVII', *Scritti varii di erudizione e di critica in onore di Rodolfo Renier* (Turin, 1912), pp. 910–14.

[7] Osthoff, *Josquin Desprez*, ii, p. 203. Josquin served at the Duomo in Milan from 1459 to 1472 (see Claudio Sartori, 'Josquin des Prés Cantore del Duomo di Milano [1459–1472]', *Annales musicologiques*, iv (1956), pp. 55–83) then in the chapel of the Duke (1473 to at least 1479). He was later in the service of Ascanio Maria Sforza. In the documents of 1474–5 'Iuschino' appears together with 'Aloyseto'; see Emilio Motta, 'Musici alla Corte degli Sforza', *Archivio Storico Lombardo*, ser. II, iv (1887), p. 323, and Sartori, op. cit., p. 64, n. 1. It is impossible to establish when they parted company—at any rate before 1486, when Josquin appears for the first time in the account books of the Papal Chapel.

[8] Osthoff, ii, p. 203, compares the two works. On Compère's 'Scaramella', see Ludwig Finscher, *Loyset Compère, Life and Works* (Rome, 1964), p. 243. We may agree with Alfred Einstein, *The Italian Madrigal* (Princeton, 1949), i, p. 341; 'Josquin has treated the "Scaramella" in a similar fashion, though with less art.'

[9] Quoted in its entirety in Novati, 'Contributo', p. 910. It ends in fact: 'Non possum ulterius te, scaramella, pati'.

compositions. The 'Scaramella' tune, with variations, forms the five different 'riprese' of the frottola 'Poi ch'io son in libertate' by Antonio Stringari Patavino (that is, from Padua), published in 1507:[10]

Ex. 2

[10] *Frottole libro octavo* (Venice, RISM 1507⁴), fol. 28ᵛ (no. 31), 'Antonius Pata'. There are interesting textual variants in the 'riprese':

    I. Scaramela fa la galla
       Cu(m) la scarpa e la stivalla
       Lazo(m) beru(m) boru(m) bu(m) beta
       Beru(m) berum bu(m) bu(m) bu(m)

    II. Scaramela se inamora
       Sol per pianger note et hora
       Lazo(m) beru(m) borum &

The incipit of the 'Scaramella' tune is quoted in the superius of Ludovico Fogliano's quodlibet 'cum diversis litteris', 'Fortuna d'un gran tempo', published in 1508:[11]

It is the only known Italian composition of the celebrated Modenese theorist. If it is not an outright musical homage to Josquin, it was possibly written under his influence, because at the beginning of the superius we find joined together two of the tunes elaborated by him, 'Fortuna'[12] and 'Scaramella'. Finally, this same theme appears twice in the quodlibet 'Jam pris amour' attributed to Musicola:[13]

'In te Domine' and 'El grillo' were probably composed when Josquin was in the service of Cardinal Ascanio Maria Sforza (1455–1505), which, for external reasons, can be dated between 1490 and 1493.[14] Petrucci ascribes

> III. Scaramela vase in campo
>   Cu(m) la spada sopra el fianco
>   Lazu(m) beru(m) &
> IV. Scaramela va a la guera
>   Cu(m) la spada e la brochiera
>   Lazu(m) brum &
> V. Scaramela va in galia
>   Per basar una zudia
>   La zum berum &

[11] *Frottole libro nono* (Venice, RISM 1509²), fol. 38ᵛ (no. 48), 'Ludovicus foglianus': S. 'Fortuna du(n) gra(n) te(m)po', A. 'Che fa la ramaci(n)a', T. 'El si son lassame esser', B. 'Dagdu(n) dagdu(n) vetusta'. Modern edition in Fausto Torrefranca, *Il Segreto del Quattrocento* (Milan, 1939), p. 461.

[12] Modern edition of 'Fortuna d'un gran tempo' in *Werken*, Supplement, no. 13.

[13] S, A, T: 'Jam pris amour', B: 'Ma buce rit', Florence, Biblioteca Nazionale Centrale, MS. Magl. XIX, 164–7, no. 40. See Liliana Pannella, 'Le composizioni profane di una raccolta fiorentina del Cinquecento', *Rivista Italiana di Musicologia*, iii (1968), p. 43. The attribution derives from Florence, Biblioteca Nazionale Centrale, MS. B. R. 337, fol. 34ᵛ; see ibid., p. 23, n. 33. Bianca Becherini, 'Tre incatenature del codice fiorentino Magl. XIX. 164–65–66–67', *Collectanea historiae musicae*, i (1953), pp. 85–7, includes a modern edition of the quodlibet.

[14] These are the years when, according to his contemporary biographer, Vincenzo Calmeta, Serafino Aquilano was in the Cardinal's service and must have written the sonnet 'Ad Jusquino suo compagno musico d'Ascanio'; see Osthoff, i, p. 33, and ii, p. 154.

the pieces to 'JOSQUIN DASCANIO'. The plaintive text of 'In te Domine'[15] may have an ambiguous meaning, both spiritual and worldly.[16] I prefer to read it in its direct meaning, rich in positive spirituality, with its expressions of psychic trouble and dilemma, and its cry for divine mercy. The composition follows the customary technique of the frottola: the text is given to the superius, which is a vocal 'aer', and the other parts have instrumental character; the music for ripresa and stanza[17] is the same; the concise four-part setting is regular and clear cut. The basically homorhythmic structure is enlivened by runs of eighth-notes in the lower voices.[18] This is a common and constant 'topos' in the frottola, but here such fiorituras do not achieve an articulated system of imitations.

Ex. 5 mm. 1-6

Edward Lowinsky has found documents in the Archivio di Stato in Milan proving that Serafino had left Ascanio's service by 1490; Josquin, on the other hand, may have stayed on much longer (see above, p. 52).

[15] Modern edition in Rudolf Schwartz, *Ottaviano Petrucci. Frottole, Buch I und IV* (Publikationen älterer Musik, viii; Leipzig, 1935), p. 37, no. 56; Higinio Anglés, *La Música en la Corte de los Reyes Católicos*, ii, *Polifonía profana* (Barcelona, 1947), p. 110, no. 84; *Le Frottole nell'edizione principe di Ottaviano Petrucci*, ed. Gaetano Cesari and Raffaello Monterosso (Cremona, 1954), i, pp. 38 and 19*; Hans Albrecht, ed., *Symphoniae jucundae* (Georg Rhau Musikdrucke, iii; Kassel, 1959), no. 1. To the sources listed by Albrecht should be added: St. Gall, Stiftsbibliothek, MS. 463-4, no. 18 (superius only); Bologna, Civico Museo Bibliografico Musicale, MS. Q 18, fol. 12ᵛ (without text); and Florence, Biblioteca Nazionale Centrale, MS. B.R. 337, fol. 73ᵛ (bass only, without text).

'In te Domine speravi' was also sung as a lauda on a text by Bernardo Giambullari, 'A te, virgo, ognor clamavi'; see *Laudi spirituali di Feo Belcari* (Florence, 1863), no. 384. Osthoff, ii, p. 184, remarks that 'Aus der Frottola, "In te, domine, speravi per trovar pietà" wird zu Luthers Zeit in Wittenberg das Psalmstück "In te, Domine, speravi, non confundar in aeternum"'. This is the version printed in Rhau, *Symphoniae jucundae*. Aside from rhythmic variants to accommodate the text in all voices, his version largely agrees with that of Petrucci.

[16] 'Es ist ein ironisches musikalisches Bittgesuch an einen hohen Herrn'; Osthoff, i, p. 35. This assumption, presumably based on the relations with Ascanio Sforza as described by Serafino Aquilano, is not documented.

[17] There are two stanzas. Osthoff, ii, p. 204, surmises that the poem may be by Serafino Aquilano, who was fond of mixing Latin and Italian words—an assumption supported by the literary style in general.

[18] '"*In te domine speravi*", eine Frottola, deren Begleitstimmen etwas stärker mit Kontrapunkt durchsetzt sind, als es gewöhnlich in den italienischen Tonsätzen der Fall ist'; Walter Rubsamen, art. 'Frottola', *MGG*, iv, col. 1027.

The sources, most of which are fairly late, indicate little or nothing about the date of the composition. The earliest source, MS. Rés. Vm⁷ 676 of the Bibliothèque Nationale, Paris, dated 1502,[19] is already a late one. The appearance of 'In te Domine' in the *Libro primo* printed by Petrucci (1504) and the large number of sources (14) attest to its popularity.

Josquin's 'In te Domine' finds a counterpart in the frottola 'Poi che in te donna speravi' printed in 1507 with the title 'RESPOSTA N. B.'.[20] The author is Niccolò Brocco, a musician about whom we know nothing, but who may be the brother or a relative of the more prolific Giovanni Antonio Brocco from Verona.[21] In the 'answer' of Niccolò, the moral tone—and perhaps the irony—of 'In te Domine' is transformed into a simple love song: literary seriousness turns into banality. The musical relationship between the two frottole is clear. Josquin's tenor becomes the superius of Niccolò's frottola (transposed, and with the addition of an instrumental coda). There are also analogies in the setting of the first three measures of the ripresa:

Ex. 6   mm. 1-6

Poi che in te don-na spe-ra- - - vi

Normally, the chief musical interest of the frottola resides in the superius. Therefore, the transfer of a tenor part to the superius constitutes an anomaly, the more curious since the superius of Josquin's setting is composed of typical melodic patterns after the Italian custom, whereas his tenor is a simple accompaniment part. For this reason, perhaps, Brocco's 'Poi che in te donna' makes a strange effect; its sonority is no match to Josquin's warm harmonious texture.[22]

---

[19] Nanie Bridgman, 'Un manuscrit italien du début du XVIᵉ siècle', *Annales musicologiques*, i (1953), p. 179.

[20] *Frottole libro octavo* (Venice, RISM 1507⁴), fol. 43ᵛ (no. 44).

[21] The piece that precedes 'Poi che in te donna' in the 1507 print begins with the words 'Per servirte perdo i passi' (no. 43) and is attributed in 'N. BROCVS'. This name occurs elsewhere as 'N. Broc.' or 'Nicolo broch.' Only six compositions of Niccolò are known; in addition to three in the *Libro octavo*, three others are edited in Antico's *Canzoni. Sonetti. Strambotti et Frottole. Libro quarto* (Rome, RISM 1517²). All of them are compositions with 'riprese' on popular themes.

[22] Brocco arranges his tenor in an ambitus higher than the alto, contrasting with the usual procedure in the frottola, where the tenor may begin higher, but dips beneath the alto and stays there until the end.

'El grillo'[23] stands out from the common frottola repertory.[24] It is a work entirely *sui generis*, not only for reasons of structure but also for its extraordinary musical quality. The naturalism of the subject sets the text apart from the myriad bloodless love poems of the general repertory. It is related to some contemporary songs in which animals are wittily imitated in onomatopoetic vocal passages.[25] It is closer to literary and musical pieces that have an animal as protagonist: carnival songs,[26] for instance (perhaps to be sung in costume), or songs in the realistic and comic theatrical intermedi. It is quite possible that 'El grillo', like other similar compositions, had a representative purpose.[27]

Josquin's music echoes the text, word for word. The 'imitazione della parola' reaches a plastic sonority, culminating in the onomatopoetic mimesis of the cricket's chirping, with all sorts of vivid visual and gestual implications, choreographic in the section of ripresa, and representative in the stanza. The lively and humorous quality of text and music render it a classically refined, balanced composition: a humanistic scherzo, as it were.[28]

Josquin's agile cricket turns up in a recently discovered source printed in Rome in the year 1526.[29] The last composition in that collection, 'E quando

---

[23] The unique source is *Frottole libro tertio* (Venice, RISM 1505[4]), fol. 61[v] (no. 60), 'IOSQVIN DASCANIO'. Modern edition in Wereldlijke Werken, Bundel v, no. 53.

[24] See the analysis by Osthoff, ii, pp. 204–5.

[25] To quote only from those books in which Josquin appears: the swan (*Frottole libro primo*, no. 13), the crane, with its verse 'gru gru' (ibid., no. 30), the cat, with its verse 'gnao gnao' (*Frottole libro tertio*, no. 11). Elsewhere we find the owl, the bird (also 'gardellin'), numerous variations on the horse, the goat, the sow, and so on (for another cricket, see footnote 28). Like many carnival songs, 'El grillo' seems to have a double meaning, with strong erotic overtones.

[26] Cf. Charles S. Singleton, ed., *Nuovi canti carnascialeschi del Rinascimento* (Modena, 1940), Appendix, nos. 3, 134, 138, 203, 204, 207, 238, 376, 422, 423, 434, 466, 467, 508; and others which cannot be recognized from the first line of the text.

[27] Cf. Nino Pirrotta, *Li due Orfei da Poliziano a Monteverdi* (Turin, 1969), the chapter 'Teatro classicheggiante, intermedi, e musiche frottolistiche', p. 57, where 'el grillo' is quoted, even if in hypothetical form (p. 86); idem, *La Musica, Enciclopedia Storica*, ii, p. 222, where he says about 'El grillo': 'può essere stato un intermedio teatrale'.

[28] Josquin's 'El grillo' evoked another praise of the cricket that appeared at the end of the history of the frottola, 'Leggiadre rime et voi parole accorte' (Bologna, Civico Museo Bibliografico Musicale, MS. Q 21, no. 71); see Claudio Gallico, *Un canzoniere musicale italiano del Cinquecento* (Florence, 1961), pp. 122 and 195–202. In this little poem, of which there exists another setting by Verdelot in *Di Verdelotto tutti li madrigali del primo, et secondo libro a quatro voci. Con la gionta dei madrigali del medesmo auttore, non piu stampati* (Venice, RISM 1540[20]), the erotic implication is clearer.

[29] *Messa motteti Canzonni Novamente stampate Libro Primo* (Rome, 1526). Only the cantus part exists, in the Archivo of the Cathedral of Palma de Mallorca; cf. Jeppesen, *La Frottola*, i, pp. 72–5, and idem, 'An Unknown pre-madrigalian Music Print in relation to other contemporary Italian sources (1520–1530)', *Studies in Musicology: Essays in the History, Style, and Bibliography of Music in Memory of Glen Haydon*, ed. James W. Pruett (Chapel

andaratu al monte' (fol. 16), is a mosaic of various famous incipits. Among
these we find a quotation of the first phrase of Josquin's superius:

Ex. 7   mm. 34-8   (superius)

El   gril - - -lo   el   gril - lo̤ è bon can - tor

proof that his song, although not based on a popular tune, had become
absorbed into the number of Italian popular ditties.[30] In this case, we can
demonstrate the descent from the artistic to the popular culture, the opposite
of 'Scaramella'. Josquin's tune, in a manner exceptional for its time, became
a popular musical theme. Also in this respect, the innovative personality of
Josquin stands in relief as an inventor of models.

Hill, 1969), pp. 3–17. It should be mentioned that Jeppesen (*La Frottola*, iii) quotes a number
of popular tunes as well as melodic correspondences found in the frottola repertory,
including some of the examples cited in the present paper.

[30] Torrefranca, *Il Segreto*, pp. 336–7, hypothesizes instead that Josquin derived the 'nio'
of 'El grillo' from the collection of Italian popular tunes and elaborated it in villota form;
but in that case the migrating tune would have had to be a tenor. (The 'nio' is a term from
the Venetian-Friulian dialect, denoting the more rapid, concluding section of a villotta.)

Instrumental Transcriptions of Josquin's French Chansons

G. THIBAULT

The subject of the present paper was first announced as 'Instrumental Transcriptions of Josquin's Secular Music'. As the work progressed, it became evident that the initial aim had been far too ambitious; I decided to confine my remarks to a survey of the instrumental transcriptions of Josquin's French chansons,[1] leaving aside *frottole*, purely instrumental pieces such as 'La Bernardina', and the like. I have concentrated on such works—be they for lute or for keyboard—as have been chosen by several intabulators; this will allow comparison of different settings of the same piece. I shall try to discover characteristics of style, and to distinguish between general and personal elements in the transcribers' work. Josquin's chansons, with their clear and well-balanced polyphony, are a choice material for adaptation to instruments; in listening to these works, we should be able to find out what changes in taste took place during the first half of the sixteenth century.

I have not had the good fortune to discover any hitherto unknown tablature. I have nothing to add to Howard Mayer Brown's excellent bibliography;[2] however, I shall include a few manuscript keyboard tablatures, such as those of Hans Kotter and Leonhard Kleber. I shall also consider questions of *musica ficta*. Some fifty years ago, there were great hopes that the tablatures, with their precise notation, would help to solve these problems. While there is no doubt as to the use of the *subsemitonium modi* in cadences, there remain many problematical places that are not treated in the same way by all the intabulators. Indeed, there is great latitude in the transcribers' interpretations.[3]

Josquin's chansons met with lasting success for over half a century; secular pieces by his contemporaries—Hayne, Agricola, Brumel—also

---

[1] For a survey of transcriptions of Josquin's works, see Kwee Him Yong, 'Sixteenth-Century Printed Instrumental Arrangements of Works by Josquin des Prez: An Inventory', *Tijdschrift van de Vereniging voor Nederlandse Muziekgeschiedenis*, xxii (1971), pp. 43–66. The chanson intabulations are listed on pp. 60–3.

[2] *Instrumental Music Printed before 1600. A Bibliography* (Cambridge, Mass., 1965), hereafter cited as Brown.

[3] On this problem, see also Howard Mayer Brown, below, pp. 475–522.

tempted many intabulators. But as a rule, the instrumentalists preferred to adapt—even to a lute or a vihuela—Josquin's great religious works, Masses or motets, rather than his secular pieces. The figures speak for themselves: there are only 42 arrangements of secular compositions, compared to the 73 arrangements of motets and 57 arrangements of sections of Masses.

In examining the chansons, I leave aside the dubious 'Fors seulement', which may be by Antoine de Févin,[4] and begin with the most popular among them, 'Adieu mes amours'. Here it is, as it is published in the *Odhecaton*,[5] that is, in its original form, in four parts, three of them bearing words, one—the contratenor—without text, played here by a *viola da braccio*. [A tape recording, made at the Société de Musique d'Autrefois Concert on 8 March 1971, was played.]

What becomes of the long melodic phrase sung by the superius when adapted to the quickly dying sounds of the lute? In Francesco Spinacino's version,[6] the chanson is given almost note for note, with very few 'flores'; at the beginning, an ornament forms a short prelude, and, at the end, a brief coda is added (Ex. 1; cf. pp. 665–8 below for the vocal model):

Ex. 1

1) Orig.: D

[4] See Kwee, pp. 64–5.

[5] Modern edition in *Harmonice Musices Odhecaton A*, ed. Helen Hewitt (Cambridge, Mass., 1946), pp. 249–51.

[6] *Intabulatura de Lauto. Libro primo*, fol. 32ᵛ (Brown 1507₁). The present transcriptions were compared with those obtained by computer, following the method developed by Hélène Charnassé and Henri Ducasse.

Rests and long notes are replaced by little groups or runs of eighth-notes (mm. 3, 5–7, etc.). The two inner voices frequently cross or even merge; the instrumental version is more often written in three than in four parts. Although simpler than the vocal version, the intabulation succeeds in creating the illusion of the original polyphony. [A tape was played of 'Adieu mes amours' in the version by Francesco Spinacino, performed by Guy Robert.]

In Hans Gerle's *Tabulatur auff die Laudten*,[7] published in 1533, the lines of 'Adieu mes amours' become more animated; the melody presents diminutions with series of rapid conjunct notes and short ornaments such as 'mordentes'. (Ex. 2.) The contratenor and tenor are hardly modified and the general ornamentation does not prevent us from hearing the original polyphony. The cadences are decorated in the traditional keyboard style.

In Hans Newsidler's transcription, published three years later,[8] we attain high virtuosity with long runs of sixteenth- and thirty-second-notes and elaborate trills. These animated passages never appear simultaneously in the different parts, and the substance of the chanson remains.

'Adieu mes amours' was adapted to the keyboard by Leonhard Kleber

[7] Fol. 39 (Brown 1533₁).   [8] *Der ander theil des Lautenbuchs*, fol. X3ᵛ (Brown 1536₇).

Ex. 2 Josquin–Gerle, 'Adieu mes amours'

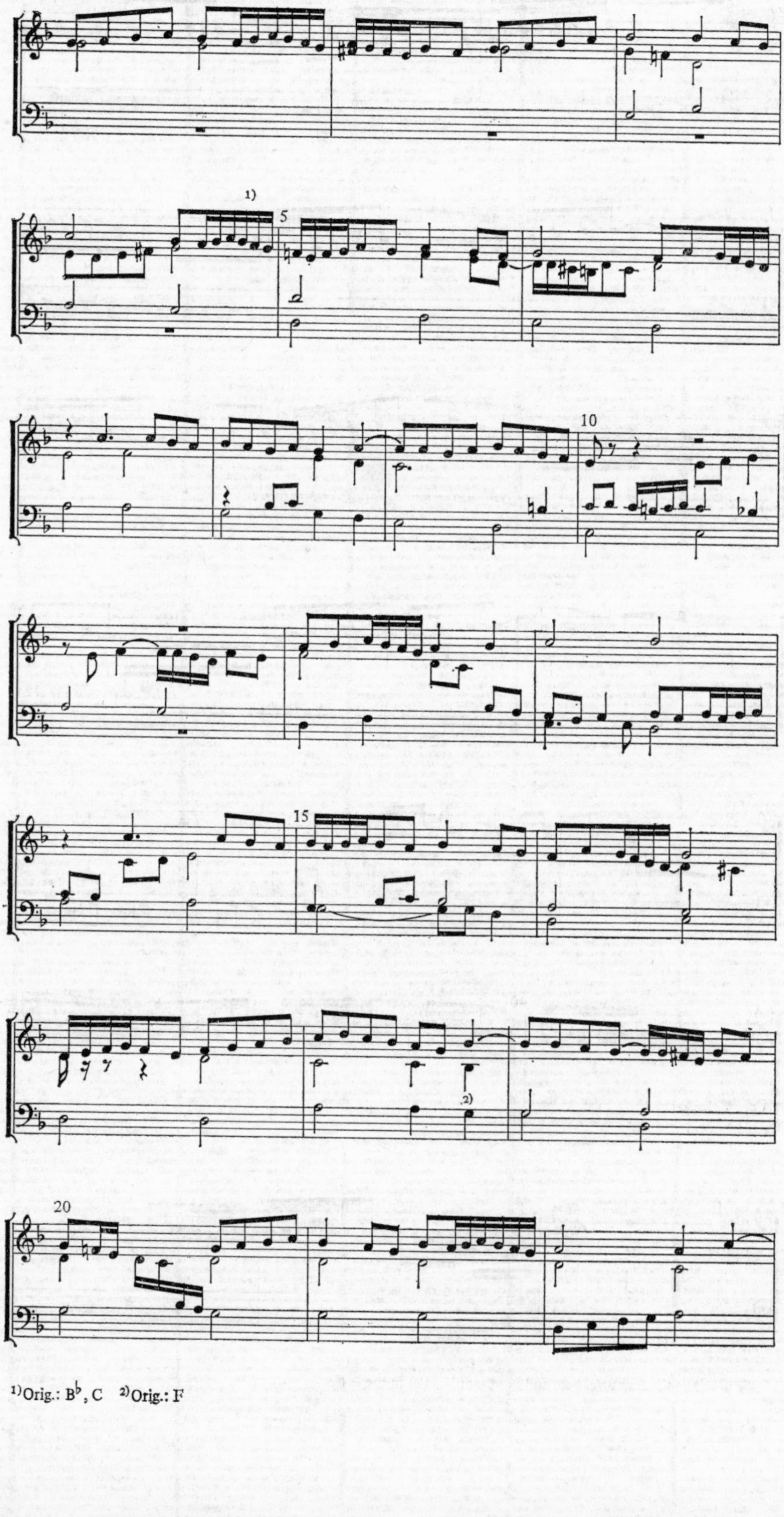

1) Orig.: B♭, C 2) Orig.: F

1) We have left the E natural here and in other places as in the text.

in 1524.[9] It is not a transcription closely following the model, but rather a fantasy written for the organ with pedal (*pedaliter* is marked in the manuscript). The main motif passes through the different voices; in the superius, short ornaments typical of the Hofhaimer school are added, while the pedal repeats the theme of 'Adieu mes amours' several times in long notes. (See Ex. 3, p. 462.)

The version of 'Adieu mes amours' that Hans Kotter, a disciple of the great Paul Hofhaimer, copied into his tablature[10] follows the *Odhecaton* text very closely; there are numerous 'mordentes' in the superius, but very

[9] Berlin, Deutsche Staatsbibliothek, MS. 40026 (olim Z. 26), no. 73.

[10] Modern edition in *Heinrich Isaac, Weltliche Werke*, ed. Johannes Wolf (*Denkmäler der Tonkunst in Oesterreich*, Jahrg. xiv/1), p. 135. The piece is ascribed to Isaac in the tablature.

Ex. 3 Josquin-Kleber, 'Adieu mes amours'

1) Orig.: E
2) Orig.: C

few runs, and trills only in the cadences. The inner voices, particularly the contratenor, are fluid and sinuous. I am presenting Kotter's transcription of 'Adieu mes amours' played on a virginal with a *viola da braccio*, a bass viol, a bass recorder, and a lute. [A tape recording made at the Société de Musique d'Autrefois Concert on 8 March 1971 was played.]

Of the beautiful 'Mille regretz de vous abandonner' eleven transcriptions have come down to us, dating from 1533 to 1563. We need not examine the version attributed to J. Lemaire in the Attaingnant part-books, *Chansons musicales. . . convenables a la fleuste dallemant. . . et la fleuste a neuf trous*,[11] for the superius of the piece (the only part that survives)[12] agrees exactly with that of the Josquin vocal chanson; the ornamentation for flute or recorder is left for the player to improvise. Silvestro Ganassi's *Fontegara* (1535),[13]

[11] Brown 1533₂, fol. 11ᵛ.   [12] Now in M. Jean Cortot's Library, Paris.

[13] Silvestro Ganassi, *Opera intitulata Fontegara* (Venice, 1535); facsimile published by the Bolletino Bibliografico Musicale (Milan, 1934); a German edition by Hildemarie Peter, with English translation by Dorothy Swainson, is also available (Berlin, 1956).

gives us a precise idea of the numerous formulas that a flautist could insert to animate one part or another of the polyphony.

Three intabulations of 'Mille regretz' for lute and one for vihuela were published before 1552: one by Gerle in 1533, one by Newsidler in 1536, one by Narváez in 1538, and one by an anonymous transcriber who worked for Phalèse in Louvain. It is interesting to see how different these pieces are. Those by Gerle[14] and the intabulator of Phalèse's *Hortus musarum*[15] are conscientious transcriptions of the original, moderately ornamented: the recipes for adding 'salt and mustard to season the meat'[16] are well known and employed with a certain sense of variety, but neither of these instrumentalists seems to have felt the beauty of the melodic line that almost disappears under the profusion of runs, scales, and trills. Narváez, on the other hand, enters into the spirit of the chanson; throughout, except for three or four ornamental patterns, the melody is respectfully maintained in its integrity:[17]

Ex. 4 Josquin-Narváez, 'Mille regretz'

[14] *Tabulatur auff die Laudten*, fol. 40ᵛ (Brown 15331).   [15] Fol. 52 (Brown 155211).

[16] Adrian Petit Coclico, *Compendium musices* (Nuremberg, 1552), fol. H IVᵛ: 'caro cum sale et sinapio condita'.

[17] Narváez, *Los seys libros del Delphin* (1538), fol. 40 (tuning in A). Modern edition in *Luys de Narváez, Los seys libros del Delphin*, ed. Emilio Pujol (*Monumentos de la música española*, iii; Barcelona, 1945), pp. 37–8.

Were the words to be sung, they would fall exactly as in the vocal version, and when some embellishments are added, it is not to produce a decorative effect, but with the intention of underlining the sense of a word like 'eslongier'—to send far away—the long stretch of notes evoking the distance between the lover and his beloved one. [A tape was played of the Narváez version, performed by Elizabeth Robert.]

After the intabulation for vihuela, which translates the chanson with such sincerity, it seems almost a pity to hear Newsidler[18] prattling along gaily, dispersing generously the too-well-known ornamental motives, and seeming to enjoy his own virtuosity:

Ex. 5 Josquin-Newsidler, 'Mille regretz'

18 *Der ander theil des Lautenbuchs*, fol. Ee3ᵛ (Brown 1536₇).

1) Orig.: A

2) Orig.: C

It seems difficult to understand today why these mechanical formulas were so lavishly employed. The sense of 'eslongier' is also underlined here—this time with an ascending and a descending scale—but many other passages are ornamented even when the text does not call for such exuberance; perhaps we see here one of the first applications to the lute of a variety of formulas well known to organists, the beginning of the art of 'coloration' or 'diminution' that was to have an immense success throughout the century.

The two intabulations by Hans Gerle[19] and Hans Newsidler[20] of the 'Chant nouvel touchant l'aliance d'Angleterre', 'Plus nulz regretz, grandz, moyens ni menus', written by Josquin in 1508 on a poem by Jean Lemaire de Belges,[21] show the characteristics familiar to us from the previous chansons examined—discretion for the first, virtuosity and brilliance for the latter.

An important aspect of the intabulator's art is how he deals with *musica ficta*. Professor Brown spoke about the applications of the rules of *musica ficta* in motets intabulated for fretted instruments. He remarked that sixteenth-century transcribers 'differed in detail on questions of *musica ficta*', most of them adding more accidentals than do the majority of modern editors: 'since they are not constrained to preserve the original part-writing, lutenists can omit or add a note wherever they wish, change the sonority of a chord, avoid a difficult or impossible position, or alter a note chromatically'.[22] These remarks apply to the chansons as well. When alterations in *musica ficta* originate in the nature of the instrumental embellishments, we must be careful in drawing conclusions concerning the vocal model.

In addition to the chansons already discussed, we have examined with particular care Francesco Spinacino's transcriptions published in 1507 from the point of view of *musica ficta*, bearing in mind Professor Lowinsky's cautionary remark on the use of tablatures in the search for solutions to *musica ficta* problems in vocal music,[23] for tablatures, in addition to the liberties they take with their vocal models, may also have been written too many years after the original, when tastes and conceptions had changed. The Spinacino intabulations, in their simplicity, must not be considered as works of art but as a faithful testimony of the use at a given period; if some pieces—like 'Comment peult avoir joye'[24]—show an abundance of F$\sharp$s, this is simply due to the fact that the chanson has been transposed from C

---

[19] *Tabulatur auff die Laudten*, fol. 41$^\mathrm{v}$ (Brown 1533₁).

[20] *Der ander theil*, fol. Z2 (Brown 1536₇).

[21] See Herbert Kellman, above, pp. 182–3. Professor Kellman sets the date as between 1508 and 1511.

[22] Howard Mayer Brown, these Proceedings, pp. 477 and 479.

[23] See the discussion at the Symposium, this volume, p. 745, and also Edward E. Lowinsky, 'The Function of Conflicting Key Signatures in Early Polyphonic Music', *Musical Quarterly*, xxxi (1945), pp. 229–30.

[24] *Intabulatura de Lauto. Libro secondo*, fol. 19$^\mathrm{v}$ (Brown 1507₂); modern edition of vocal original in *Ottaviano Petrucci, Canti B*, ed. Helen Hewitt (*Monuments of Renaissance Music*, ii; Chicago, 1967), pp. 145–7. The transcription is almost literal.

down to G (G tuning) so as to make use of the best range of the lute; however, it takes away the clarity and transparency of the superius, characteristic of the chanson. On the whole, the accidentals added in the tablature are very few.

We should have liked to focus upon the development from modality to tonality, but this would have entailed numerous comparisons between intabulations of religious and secular music, and such a study would have led us too far afield.

We have not mentioned among the intabulators the great masters of the Golden Age of the lute: Francesco da Milano, Joan Maria da Crema, Melchiore de Barberiis, and others too numerous to mention. However, no secular works of Josquin's are to be found in their books, for in the vogue then (that is, after 1546) were the composers of the Parisian chanson: Janequin, Claudin, Certon, and their colleagues. It is in Germany and in the Netherlands that Josquin's chansons met with lasting success.

Among the chansons transcribed for two lutes, I shall give you now a rendition of 'Alléges moy, doulce plaisant brunette', so beautifully sung and played by the Prague Madrigal Singers in its original version. The transcription for two lutes, published in 1552 in the *Hortus musarum*,[25] while lacking the brilliance of a vocal and instrumental realization, is a clever and refined adaptation of a six-part chanson, with the essential polyphony preserved or delicately evoked. A few discreet ornaments, here and there, give the line more mobility. The search for variety induces the intabulator to transform the initial design, a four-note pattern with F♯ (see Ex. 6), into a version without the F♯ (m. 9). At the end, a surprise awaits us: the first lute finishes in G minor, the second in major. This, evidently, is due to a scribe's mistake! Not knowing which ending to choose, I will let you hear the whole piece with B♭ and then just the last measures with B♮. [A tape was played of 'Alléges-moy', performed by Elizabeth and Guy Robert.]

Ex. 6 Josquin-Phalèse, 'Alléges moy'

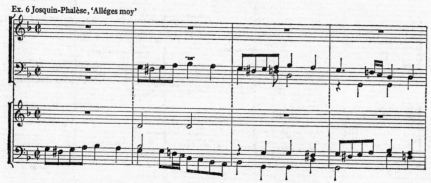

[25] Page 94 (Brown 155211).

1) The four preceding notes (A, B♭, C, A) are in the tablatures.
2) There is a mistake in the tablature; the bass part starts two beats too soon, and the music from here to m. 23 has to be shifted.

3) The two measures between brackets are missing in the tablature.

1) The tablature gives B♭ for the first lute and B♮ for the second.

However brief this survey may have been, pervading all these transcriptions—even Newsidler's elaborate versions—is the beauty of Josquin's original vocal scores that called forth this enormous number of instrumental adaptations, each a homage, as it were, to a universally admired composer.

Accidentals and Ornamentation in Sixteenth-Century Intabulations of Josquin's Motets

HOWARD MAYER BROWN

Sixteenth-century part-books were meant to be used both by singers and by instrumentalists. Title pages often make that point clear by stating that the music is apt for voices or instruments. Not all sixteenth-century instrumentalists, however, could easily play directly from part-books. Musicians whose instruments were capable of reproducing more than one polyphonic line—players of lutes, vihuelas, guitars, harpsichords, organs, and other keyboard and plucked-string instruments—had to write out arrangements of the vocal music they wished to play. When they accompanied one or more singers, or used a vocal composition for an instrumental solo, they had to adapt the music to fit their instruments by combining the separate lines from the various part-books into an intabulation. Plucked strings being tuned to several different pitch levels—lutes in A, G, E, and D were quite common—and beginners not being adept at reading score in staff notation, the most convenient way to notate arrangements for these instruments was in tablature: here letters or numbers indicate where the strings should be stopped.[1]

A number of sixteenth-century instrumental virtuosi have left us memorials of their art in the form of anthologies mixing their own original

---

[1] Johannes Wolf, *Handbuch der Notationskunde*, ii (Leipzig, 1919), is still the best source for descriptions of the various sorts of tablatures in use in the sixteenth century and later. That beginners on the lute were not adept at reading staff notation is suggested by the 'Regola per quelli che non sanno cantare' inserted in many of the volumes of lute music published by Petrucci. These rules are reprinted in Claudio Sartori, *Bibliografia delle opere musicali stampate da Ottaviano Petrucci* (Florence, 1948), pp. 140 and 148, and, in English translation, in Sartori, 'A Little-Known Petrucci Publication: The Second Book of Lute Tablatures by Francesco Bossinensis', *Musical Quarterly*, xxxiv (1948), pp. 234–45. See also the tables in Don Bartholomeo Lieto Panhormitano, *Dialogo quarto di musica* (Naples, 1559), a volume discussed in John Ward, 'Le problème des hauteurs dans la musique pour luth et vihuela au XVIe siècle', in *Le Luth et sa musique*, ed. Jean Jacquot (Paris, 1958), pp. 171–8. The various sizes of lutes in common use in the sixteenth century are discussed in Howard Mayer Brown, *Sixteenth-Century Instrumentation: The Music for the Florentine Intermedii* (American Institute of Musicology, 1973), pp. 29–30.

compositions—fantasias, ricercars, and preludes—with settings of dance tunes and intabulations of vocal music in every genre: Masses, motets, chansons, Lieder, and madrigals.[2] We are fortunate to possess these relics of a past age, for they capture the style and manner of some of the greatest performers of the century as well as the common practices of ordinary hacks. Certain aspects of performance practice emerge more clearly from intabulations than from any other sources. They show the number and types of ornaments added by virtuoso players to vocal compositions transcribed for solo instruments, affording remarkable insight into the taste of an age in which the audience enjoyed the extraordinary freedom taken by the individual performer in his treatment of the model. Intabulations demonstrate with a precision rarely matched in other sources how certain sixteenth-century musicians applied the rules of *musica ficta* in practice. Since lute, vihuela, and guitar tablatures indicate which frets are to be stopped, they notate the precise pitches, with all chromatic inflections. They offer a vast and largely unexplored repertory for the investigation of *musica ficta*.[3] That they were made by a wide variety of musicians—some good and some bad, some early and some late, and some northern and some southern— increases the profit and insight one can draw from their study.

Josquin des Prez was a great favourite of sixteenth-century instrumentalists. Indeed, the first published book of lute music, Francesco Spinacino's *Intabulatura de Lauto, Libro primo* (1507), opens with an arrangement of Josquin's famous 'Ave Maria',[4] and players throughout the century continued to adapt his music to their instruments. From Kwee Him Yong's inventory[5] of the arrangements of Josquin's music for fretted or keyboard instruments printed in the sixteenth century, we learn that players intabulated eight Masses in whole or in part, seventeen motets, fifteen secular compositions, and seven dubious works, for solo lute, vihuela, guitar, and keyboard; for lute or vihuela and solo voice; and for two lutes or vihuelas.

---

[2] All volumes containing tablature printed in the sixteenth century are listed and described in Howard Mayer Brown, *Instrumental Music Printed Before 1600, A Bibliography* (Cambridge, Mass., 1965), referred to hereafter as Brown.

[3] The only previous published investigation of *musica ficta* in tablatures for plucked strings is Charles Warren Fox, 'Accidentals in Vihuela Tablatures', *Bulletin of the American Musicological Society*, No. 4 (1940), pp. 22–4; since this is an abstract, only his general conclusions are presented, without corroborating detail. Willi Apel, *Accidentien und Tonalität in den Musikdenkmälern des 15. und 16. Jahrhunderts* (Berlin, 1936), deals principally with keyboard tablatures, where accidentals are indicated less consistently than in lute and vihuela tablatures. That fact in addition to Apel's failure to consider the musical context in much of his discussion invalidates many of his conclusions.

[4] See Brown 1507[1], no. 1.

[5] Kwee Him Yong, 'Sixteenth-Century Printed Instrumental Arrangements of Works by Josquin des Prez. An Inventory', *Tijdschrift van de Vereniging voor Nederlandse Muziekgeschiedenis*, xxii (1971), pp. 43–66.

I shall confine my remarks here to the printed intabulations of Josquin's motets for fretted instruments. A rapid survey of the nearly seventy examples listed by Kwee reveals the following preliminary conclusions:

1) All instrumentalists applied ornamentation, more or less elaborate, when they transcribed vocal music for instruments; they also liked to embellish their accompaniments for solo singers. One of the rare exceptions, perhaps the only intabulation that contains no embellishments whatever— Hans Newsidler's arrangement, published in 1536, of Josquin's great psalm setting, 'Memor esto verbi tui'—confirms the rule, for the lutenist felt compelled to add an explanation. 'I have not embellished the psalm', he writes at the end of the intabulation; 'it is very good in itself; moreover, a beginner also ought to have something to play in this book'.[6]

2) While the character and extent of disagreement on the practical application of the rules of *musica ficta* on the part of sixteenth-century intabulators differed from that of modern scholars, who do not even agree on the existence and applicability of the rules, there was nevertheless a considerable difference of judgement and taste among the former. To clarify our own views it is important to study what sixteenth-century musicians agreed on and where they differed.

3) However much sixteenth-century instrumentalists may have differed in detail on questions of *musica ficta*, most of them added far more accidentals than do the majority of modern editors. The idea that the musicians of the time were guided by a desire to preserve the purity of the modes must be discarded once and for all. The profusion of accidentals incorporated into intabulations should lead those scholars who still advocate a policy of 'utmost reserve' with respect to *musica ficta* to rethink their positions. Even so well-known a 'radical' in these matters as Edward Lowinsky would never gloss a reading as exuberantly as did some of the sixteenth-century lutenists.[7]

Can the practices of the instrumentalists be applied to vocal music? Do the accidentals added by lutenists really tell us anything about the way singers performed? I would answer both questions affirmatively, for instrumental and vocal music both shared the same theoretical basis in the fifteenth and sixteenth centuries. Writers on counterpoint like Gafurius and Burtius state or imply that their teachings are to be applied both to instruments and

---

[6] The motet (Motetten, Bundel vi, no. 31) is intabulated in Hans Newsidler, *Der ander theil des Lautenbuchs* (Nuremberg, 1536; Brown 1536⁷), no. 29. The note at the end of the intabulation reads: 'Den Psalm hab ich nit colorirt, er ist an ihm selbs ser gut, und das ein ungeübter auch etwas zu schlagen hab in disem buch.'

[7] This is a point he has made himself in his Foreword to H. Colin Slim, ed., *Musica nova* (*Monuments of Renaissance Music*, i; Chicago, 1964), pp. viii–x, where he also discusses the well-known reticence of modern scholars in adding accidentals to scores of fifteenth- and sixteenth-century music.

to voices.[8] Writers on instruments, like Silvestro di Ganassi, insist that players should imitate singers in every way.[9] Lutenists often played with vocal ensembles and with solo singers; they had to fit their parts to music that was sung. All evidence suggests that there was only one theory of *musica ficta*, and it applied equally to vocal compositions and their instrumental arrangements. Of course, the theory could be variously interpreted, depending on local tradition, the fashion of a decade, or, perhaps most important, the ability and temperament of an individual player. Certain it is, it was never ignored.

The rules of *musica ficta* are few and simple. As Lowinsky has formulated them, they are divided into two classes: *causa necessitatis* governs perfect intervals and *causa pulchritudinis* relates to imperfect intervals.[10] The former sees to the perfection of diminished or augmented fourths, fifths, and octaves and accounts for the supplementary rules governing false relations and the well-known *una nota supra la semper est canendum fa*; the latter is responsible for the rules of the subsemitone in cadences, the approach to perfect consonances via the closest imperfect consonance, and the raising of the minor to the major third in final cadences.

Differences about *musica ficta* policy among scholars concern as much the nature and even the validity of the rules as the way in which they are applied to the music.[11] The existence of numerous witnesses from the sixteenth century can be expected to dispel many of our uncertainties. To be sure, these instrumental arrangements must be examined critically: some players were better musicians than others, some were more careful about adding *ficta* notes, some modified their models in ways that affected *musica ficta*.

Chromatically altered notes often appear among the profuse ornaments that lutenists added to the original part-writing. Francesco da Milano's

---

[8] See Keith Polk, 'Flemish Wind Bands in the Late Middle Ages: A Study of Improvisatory Instrumental Practices' (Ph.D. diss., University of California, Berkeley, 1968), pp. 82–3, where he quotes from Gafurius, Burtius, and others. Polk uses the rules of the contrapuntists in an attempt to reconstruct the improvisatory practices of wind bands in the late fifteenth century.

[9] See Silvestro di Ganassi, *Opera intitulata Fontegara* (Venice, 1535; Brown 1535[1]; see there for various modern editions), chap. 1. This point is discussed in Howard Mayer Brown, *Embellishing Sixteenth-Century Music* (London, 1975).

[10] Lowinsky, Foreword to Slim, *Musica nova*, pp. viii–x. A similar summary of the rules of *musica ficta* may be found in Lewis Lockwood, 'A Sample Problem of *Musica ficta*: Willaert's *Pater noster*', in *Studies in Music History, Essays for Oliver Strunk*, ed. Harold Powers (Princeton, 1968), p. 176.

[11] See, for example, Edward E. Lowinsky's reviews of the editions of the works of Gombert in *Musical Quarterly*, xxxviii (1952), pp. 630–40; and of Brumel and Clemens non Papa in *Music Library Association Notes*, x (1953), pp. 312–14, and xiii (1956), pp. 677–8. For the opposite view, see K. Ph. Bernet Kempers, 'Accidenties', *Musicologica Lovaniensia*, i (Louvain, 1969), pp. 51–9.

intabulation of Josquin's 'Pater noster', for example, contains numerous instances of chromatic alterations embedded in the *passaggi* (see Example 18, mm. 4, 5, 8, 10, 11, 12, 13, and so on), but these *ficta* notes do not concern the way a singer would have performed the piece. Sometimes accidentals in the ornamentation conflict with notes in the original vocal lines; some instrumentalists did not hesitate to include both an altered and an unaltered note in close proximity. Thus Hans Gerle—not one of the more musical players, to judge from his intabulations—added E♮s to the flourish shown in Ex. 1 while an E♭ still sounded in a lower voice.[12]

Ex. 1   'Qui habitat' m. 41

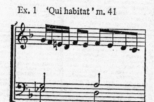

Since they are not constrained to preserve the original part-writing, lutenists can omit or add a note wherever they wish, change the sonority of a chord, avoid a difficult or impossible position, or alter a note chromatically. Sometimes they changed notes of the model for no other purpose than to change the *musica ficta* (see Ex. 2).[13] By doubling the C at the cadence in measure 14 of the 'Stabat Mater' and leading it to F in the inner voice, Josquin indicated that he did not wish it to be raised, and Francesco da Milano, who arranged the motet for solo lute, complied with his wishes. Sebastian Ochsenkun and Simon Gintzler, on the other hand, preferred the sound of the *subsemitonium modi* and either shortened the duration of the C in the tenor (Ochsenkun) or eliminated it altogether (Gintzler).

At times, instrumentalists played embellishments that required some modification of the *musica ficta*. Thus, the long C in the passage from 'Stabat Mater' shown in Ex. 3 cannot be altered by singers, even though it is the seventh in a cadence leading to the *finalis*, because it enters as the top voice

[12] The intabulation of Josquin's 'Qui habitat' (Motetten, Bundel xiii, no. 52) was printed in Hans Gerle, *Tabulatur auff die Laudten* (Nuremberg, 1533; Brown 1533[1]), no. 47.

[13] The intabulations of Josquin's 'Stabat Mater' (Motetten, Bundel viii, no. 36) were printed in Francesco da Milano, *Intabolatura di liuto de diversi* (Venice, 1536; Brown 1536[3]), no. 33 (modern edition in *The Lute Music of Francesco Canova da Milano*, ed. Arthur J. Ness (Cambridge, Mass., 1970) no. 109); Sebastian Ochsenkun, *Tabulaturbuch auff die Lauten* (Heidelberg, 1558; Brown 1558[5]), no. 4; and Simon Gintzler, *Intabolatura de lauto...Libro primo* (Venice, 1547; Brown 1547[3]), no. 13. I have omitted the text in the vocal models except in Examples 15–20. The examples taken from the tablatures have been transcribed in the pitch of the vocal model in order to facilitate comparison.

A.   Ex. 2   'Stabat Mater' mm. 13-15

B.   Francesco

C.   Ochsenkun

D.   Gintzler

of an F major triad and is doubled in a lower voice. But Simon Gintzler breaks up the long note by repeating it several times, and this enables him to decorate it with a conventional flourish and raise it to C♯ at the cadence. Examples such as these reveal how strong the urge was to use leading-notes in cadences; they also confirm that a composer could effectively avoid them by voice-leading and that the intabulators had to change the voice-leading if they wanted to go counter to the composer's intention. These

Ex. 3 'Stabat Mater' mm. 64-7

examples allow us also to form a measure for evaluating the skill and sensitivity of the intabulator: on top stands Francesco da Milano who respects Josquin's original intent; he is followed by Ochsenkun and Gintzler who are musical enough to realize that they have to change voice-leading if they wish to change the whole-tone to a subsemitone cadence.

Although intabulators did take liberties with their vocal models affecting accidentals, and although they hardly ever agree on *musica ficta* throughout a complete piece, there is nevertheless a consensus among them about many passages in each motet. Their agreement is closest in those compositions which present the least problems—motets in so-called F Lydian with the key signature of one flat, for example, where relatively few notes need to be altered chromatically. But even in the most difficult pieces, with a number of ambiguous passages, many of the added accidentals are the same in all of the intabulations, no matter who made them.

Josquin's four-part setting of Psalm 90, 'Qui habitat in adjutorio altissimi',[14] is a particularly instructive example. It is written in that open texture, filled with duets, so characteristic of many of Josquin's compositions, and hence with abundant opportunities for *musica ficta*, especially in cadential

---

[14] Motetten, Bundel xiii, no. 52. Helmuth Osthoff (*Josquin Desprez*, ii, pp. 128-9) questions the authenticity of the piece, not because of a conflicting attribution or stylistic incongruities, but because it makes its first appearance in a relatively late source.

passages. Again, the quality of the intabulations is easy to judge. There are three of them, all for solo lute, one by the German hack, Hans Gerle, one by the very capable lutenist from Heidelberg, Sebastian Ochsenkun, and one by the great Hungarian virtuoso, Valentin Bakfark.[15]

Since the psalm is set in G Dorian, the two main *ficta* notes are F♯, the *subsemitonium modi*, and E♭, used to avoid tritones, to fit the *una nota supra la* rule, and to form transposed Phrygian cadences on D. In addition, there are a few passages in 'Qui habitat' which require C♯s in cadences on D. Happily, opinion is unanimous about the cadences on G in 'Qui habitat'. Smijers, in his edition of the motet in the *Werken*, adds twenty F♯s at cadential points,[16] and all of them without exception are included in the three intabulations. At least in this limited context, then, complete agreement is possible about the rules of *musica ficta* and how they ought to be applied.

On the other hand, the sixteenth-century musicians differ about the way to treat the six cadences on D in 'Qui habitat'. One of them is a V–I cadence (Ex. 4); Gerle and Smijers leave it unaltered, whereas Bakfark and Ochsenkun correctly raise the leading-note to C♯, raising of course B♭ to B♮ as well.

Ex. 4 'Qui habitat,' mm. 28-9 (accidentals after Bakfark and Ochsenkun)

In the five remaining cadences on D,[17] the chord of resolution is preceded not by its dominant, but by a leading-note triad in first inversion, or by the intervals of a sixth, E to C, or a third, C to E. In other words, they all offer a choice between the Dorian form of cadence, with E♮ and C♯, and the transposed Phrygian, with E♭ and C♮. Bakfark considers all but one of them Dorian,[18] and Ochsenkun agrees with him about three of the five.[19] Gerle

15 Gerle, *Tabulatur* (1533), no. 47; Ochsenkun, *Tabulaturbuch* (1558), no. 13; Valentin Bakfark, *Harmoniarum musicarum in usum testudinis factarum, tomus primus* (Cracow, 1565; Brown 1565¹), no. 11. For Bakfark, see Otto Gombosi, *Der Lautenist Valentin Bakfark, Leben und Werke (1507–1576)* (Budapest, 1935).

16 In measures 19, 21, 23, 43, 46, 55, 78, 104, 108, 116, 126, 187, 198, 201, 215, 219, 232, 245, 267, and 269.

17 In measures 98, 112, 224, 228, and 281.

18 The cadence in measure 228 is Phrygian in Bakfark's intabulation (see Ex. 13).

19 The cadences in measures 98 and 228 are both uninflected—that is, they include E♮ and C♮—in Ochsenkun's intabulation.

and Smijers, on the other hand, render two cadences Phrygian, one Dorian, and they disagree about the other two.[20]

One cadence (Ex. 5, m. 98) differs from the rest in that D is preceded by E in the top voice, with C beneath it. The first E in the tenor (m. 98) must

Ex. 5 'Qui habitat' mm. 95-9 (accidentals after Bakfark)

be flatted—Ochsenkun and Bakfark agree, Gerle dissents—since the note preceding would lie a tritone away, were it left unaltered. Perhaps using this as a clue, Smijers has flatted the second E as well to produce a Phrygian cadence. Our three intabulators, though, keep the E in the superius natural, with Bakfark alone requiring a C♯ beneath it. Perhaps the others were reluctant to sanction so chromatic a line in the tenor.[21] Whatever the reason Ochsenkun and Gerle would have given for omitting the C♯, the rule of approaching a perfect consonance through the closest imperfect consonance demands chromatic alteration. The cadence occurs at the end of a duo between superius and tenor, at the moment when bass and alto intone a duo based on the same thematic material, but now cadencing on G. A similar musical procedure follows immediately, with duos in paired imitation ending on D and on G. The sixteenth-century musicians, and Smijers too, agree that the second cadence on D should be Dorian, with E♮ and C♯. Logic suggests that similar passages in close proximity should be treated in similar fashion. If that standard can be applied to sixteenth-century music—and we shall see that there is some evidence to contradict it—then the unison D in measure 99 of 'Qui habitat' is best approached by E♮ and C♯; Bakfark's solution is to be preferred.

In deciding whether the half-cadence on D that concludes the *secunda pars* of 'Qui habitat' (Ex. 6) should be Dorian, as Bakfark and Ochsenkun

[20] The cadences in measures 224 and 281 are Phrygian, that in measure 112 is Dorian, and those in measures 98 and 228 are uninflected in Gerle's intabulation. Smijers reads the cadences in measures 98 and 228 as Phrygian.

[21] Bakfark worked within contemporary musical practice, as may be seen from the chromatic clausula used by Netherlandish composers in the middle of the sixteenth century; see Edward E. Lowinsky, *Secret Chromatic Art in the Netherlands Motet* (New York, 1946; repr. 1967), pp. 11-13.

Ex. 6 'Qui habitat,' mm. 278-82 (accidentals after Ochsenkun)

make it, or Phrygian, as Gerle and Smijers suggest, we face a question different from that raised by the first cadence examined. Whether we are asking which form the composer intended, or which is superior on musical grounds, the answer must be based on purely historical evidence, since both forms make good musical sense, and the context does not clarify the situation. One day, when a sufficient number of intabulations has become available in modern editions, it may be possible to write a history of the way half-cadences concluding a piece in G Dorian were treated by six-teenth-century instrumentalists. Perhaps then one will be able to say which form a composer working in Rome or Milan or Flanders about 1520 or 1540 or 1560 might have preferred. But until the evidence is in, it will be impossible to judge between the two solutions offered here. Both are acceptable, and both were certainly used by performers in the sixteenth century. *Musica ficta*, let us not forget, was a performance technique, and, as with other aspects of performance practice—when, where, and how to add embellishments, for example, and how to mix instruments with voices—performers could make choices among equally legitimate alter-natives.

Like the F♯s, the E♭s required in 'Qui habitat' to avoid tritones or because of the *una nota supra la* rule are often specified by all three sixteenth-century lutenists as well as by Smijers.[22] Passages like those shown in Examples 7a–c need little discussion. Bakfark, Ochsenkun, and Smijers concur in their application of *musica ficta* to Examples 7a and 7c, and they all lower the crucial E in the alto of measure 125 in Example 7b.[23] One is tempted to state categorically that these readings are the only correct ones. Gerle's leaving the Es in Examples 7b–c uninflected confirms the impression

[22] Bakfark and Ochsenkun add the same E♭s as Smijers in measures 13–15, 25, 34, 36, 40–41, 89, 103, 107, 125, 133–7, and 146–7 of the *prima pars* of 'Qui habitat'. Gerle leaves some of these Es natural.

[23] In Example 7b both Bakfark and Ochsenkun leave the E in the alto in measure 123 and in the tenor in measure 126 natural. Gerle simply omits the Es in measures 123 and 126 and leaves those in measure 125 natural.

Ex. 7 (a) 'Qui habitat' mm. 12-15

Ex. 7 (b) 'Qui habitat' mm. 122-26

Ex. 7 (c) 'Qui habitat.' mm. 145-8

that he is the least musical of the three lutenists, a judgement supported by his inconsistent application of E♮s throughout his intabulation of this motet.

The points of difference among the three lutenists concerning the application of E♮s are much more interesting than the points of agreement. For example, a cadence on G introduced by a succession of parallel ⁶₃ chords (Ex. 8) appears in two distinct settings. All three lutenists, along with Smijers, flat the E in the bass in measure 103, since it is *fa* one note above *la*,

Ex. 8   'Qui habitat' mm. 101-5
       (accidentals after Bakfark and Ochsenkun)

and they all raise the F in the alto of measure 104, since it is the leading-note. But Gerle and Smijers also lower the E in the tenor in measure 104, although this follows none of the rules of *musica ficta*, save the unwritten rule of the unity of a phrase,[24] creating thereby a VII⁶ chord. Bakfark and Ochsenkun, on the other hand, offer a better solution by leaving the troublesome E uninflected, thus making all of the triads in first inversion major or minor except for the dominant-functioning VII⁶ chord preceding the resolution. Both versions make sense; ultimately the judgement on the relative merits of specific solutions depends on our knowledge of the conventions of the time. Further investigation may lead to the conclusion that both solutions were equally acceptable. The manner in which eleven sixteenth-century musicians treated a similar succession of $\frac{6}{3}$ chords leading to a cadence on G Mixolydian in Josquin's most widely intabulated motet, 'Benedicta es

Ex. 9   "Benedicta es" mm. 82-5

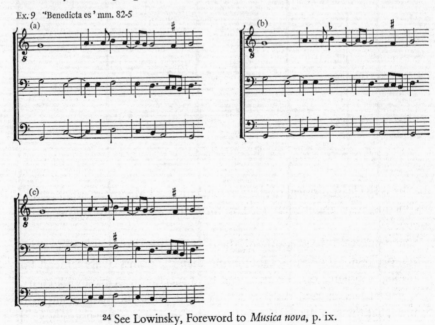

24 See Lowinsky, Foreword to *Musica nova*, p. ix.

caelorum Regina', would seem to support a wide range of choice. Three possible interpretations of the cadence are given in Example 9: the first, proposed by Smijers, I would have thought the correct one. Four of the eleven instrumentalists who intabulated the *prima pars* of this motet—the Gallicized Italians, Alberto da Ripa and Piero di Teghi, the Spaniard Fuenllana, and the German Ochsenkun—agree with Smijers and leave the second of the $\frac{6}{3}$ chords unaltered (Ex. 9a).[25] In four intabulations, two by the Spaniard Cabezón, one by Jakob Paix, and the anonymous version published by Pierre Phalèse in 1553, the arrangers have added a B♭ (Ex. 9b);[26] the remaining three, the Tyrolean Simon Gintzler, the German Melchior Newsidler, and the anonymous one published by Pierre Phalèse in 1571, all raise the F (Ex. 9c).[27] In this case at least, neither local custom, distance in time from Josquin, nor individual temperament and ability seem to have affected the notion that the succession of chords had several possibilities of resolution, all of which are equally suitable. But many more detailed comparisons of similar passages in a wide variety of intabulations would need to be made before more sweeping conclusions could be reached.

In another passage from 'Qui habitat' Gerle and Smijers add *ficta* notes unlike those proposed by Bakfark and Ochsenkun (Ex. 10). All four

Ex. 10 'Qui habitat,' mm. 133-9 (accidentals after Bakfark and Ochsenkun)

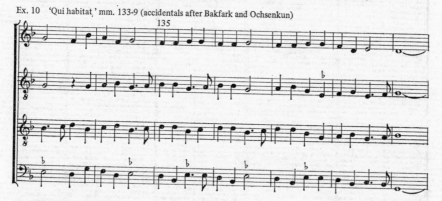

[25] Smijers's version is in Motetten, Bundel xi, no. 46. The intabulations appear in Alberto da Ripa, *Sixiesme livre de tabulature de leut* (Paris, 1558; Brown 1558⁶), no. 3; Piero di Teghi, *Des chansons & motetz reduictz en tabulature de luc...Livre troixiesme* (Louvain, 1547; Brown 1547⁹), no. 19; Miguel de Fuenllana, *Orphenica lyra* (Seville, 1554; Brown 1554³), no. 70; and Ochsenkun, *Tabulaturbuch* (1558), no. 3.

[26] The intabulations appear in Antonio de Cabezón, *Obras de musica para tecla arpa y vihuela* (Madrid, 1578; Brown 1578³), nos. 114 and 115 (for solo keyboard, harp, or vihuela); Jakob Paix, *Thesaurus motetarum* (Strasbourg, 1589; Brown 1589⁶), no. 1 (an intabulation for solo keyboard of the version *a 12* by Jean Castileti); and in *Horti musarum secunda pars* (Louvain, 1553; Brown 1553¹⁰), no. 24. The last-named version uses both F♯ and C♯ to make a double leading-note cadence in measure 84.

[27] The intabulations appear in Gintzler, *Intabolatura...Libro primo* (1547), no. 8; Melchior Newsidler, *Teutsch Lautenbuch* (Strasbourg, 1574; Brown 1574⁵), no. 1; and in *Theatrum musicum* (Louvain and Antwerp, 1571; Brown 1571⁶), no. 159.

authorities agree that E♭s should be added in the bass (mm. 133–7) and in the alto (m. 137). But at the end of this long passage (m. 138), Bakfark and Ochsenkun leave the E in the superius (and alto) natural, whereas Gerle and Smijers flat it, so as to eschew the false relations and to preserve modal unity; also, it appears in a melodic configuration exactly like one heard earlier in the bass (mm. 1334–1351). The earlier Es had to be altered to avoid a tritone, whereas C triads in progressions from C to G are apparently more often major than minor in G Dorian. Evidently neither Bakfark nor Ochsenkun would have sung the passage in question as *la-fa-la* (D-E♭-D in m. 138). Patently, *musica ficta* depends upon the way a passage is analyzed, and therefore some latitude is possible.

Still another problem arises in considering the E♭s Bakfark added to the opening twenty measures of the *secunda pars* of 'Qui habitat'. The first eight measures (Ex. 11) illustrate Bakfark's procedure throughout the passage.

Ex. 11 'Qui habitat,' mm. 156-63

1) Orig.: A♭

In measure 162, and in the following measures wherever the theme is transposed down a fourth, Bakfark alters the E♮ toward the end of the phrase to an E♭. Neither the other intabulators nor Smijers agree with him, although the outline of the bass in measure 162 would be that of a tritone progression without the flat. Bakfark alone departs from the rules in making a series of triads on G major rather than minor (Ex. 12), and in adding a sharp to F in measure 229 (Ex. 13) to create a 'tonal' half-cadence.[28]

[28] That Bakfark regarded this as a half-cadence in G and therefore raised the leading-note to F♯ explains why this is the single cadence on D for which he chose the Phrygian rather than the Dorian form (see n. 18 above).

Ex. 12 'Qui habitat' mm. 46-50

Accidentals added to fast-moving non-harmonic notes—passing notes, neighbouring notes, and the like—also fall into this same category of purely decorative *musica ficta*. Substantial disagreement among sixteenth-century instrumentalists in the treatment of non-harmonic tones shows that these musicians shared our view of them as non-structural notes. Hence there is

Ex. 13 'Qui habitat' mm. 228-30

no reason to expect unanimity. In making these alterations, Bakfark and his contemporaries were guided by their taste and took harmonic liberties that did not necessarily correspond with the composer's intentions. No modern editor could justify so liberal a policy in making a scholarly edition, and yet it is important for the modern performer to realize that such possibilities were available to earlier musicians.[29] Nor can it be mere coincidence that Valentin Bakfark, the most daring of the three sixteenth-century lutenists who intabulated 'Qui habitat', is also the most consistent in his application of obligatory accidentals. Good men live dangerously.

What conclusions can we draw from this brief examination of the way three sixteenth-century musicians arranged Josquin's 'Qui habitat'? In the first place, there is a body of accidentals about which everyone, or nearly everyone, agrees, irrespective of age, nationality, or ability. All F♯s and many E♭s in 'Qui habitat' so clearly follow the rules of *musica ficta* that all three lutenists as well as the modern editor added them in the same places. Some of these passages are entirely unambiguous; only one solution appears to be correct. The inconsistent way in which Gerle adds or omits E♭s reveals him to be an inferior musician. On the other hand, there are passages where the performer may choose between two equally valid possibilities. Whether cadences should be Dorian or Phrygian, for example, can often be deduced from the context, but occasionally either form serves equally well. Finally,

<hr/>

[29] This is what Edward Lowinsky, in the Foreword to *Musica nova*, had in mind when he expressed the belief that 'on the whole, Renaissance musicians interpreted their music, if anything, rather more than less freely than is proposed in this series' and for confirmation pointed to 'the keyboard versions that Venegas de Henestrosa published of several of the ricercari of *Musica nova*' (*Monuments of Renaissance Music*, i, p. x).

performers felt free to add *ficta* notes in accordance with personal taste and their feeling for harmonic colour. Here is an easy test by which to separate the conservatives from the progressives.

Close study of the intabulations of Josquin's motets would deepen our understanding of the way performers of the time interpreted the rules, for every group of arrangements offers new problems as well as further examples of the old.[30] The intabulations of 'Praeter rerum seriem', for example, teach us how sixteenth-century musicians added accidentals to a *cantus firmus*, how they varied literal repetitions, and how their practices can help us in reviewing the application of *musica ficta* in the edition of Josquin's works. 'Praeter rerum seriem', also in G Dorian, is a setting *a 6* of three strophes of a sequence.[31] Four intabulations of it were published in the sixteenth century: those by the Tyrolean lutenist, Simon Gintzler, in 1547; by the Spaniard, Miguel de Fuenllana, who arranged it for solo voice and vihuela, in 1554; by the Gallicized Italian, Alberto da Ripa, in 1555; and by the German, Sebastian Ochsenkun, in 1558.[32]

The four intabulators (and Albert Smijers) often agree about the need to raise F as subsemitone. But there is no agreement on the treatment of the *cantus firmus* between the modern editor and the sixteenth-century musicians. Smijers leaves it completely uninflected, whereas the sixteenth-century musicians do not hesitate to add accidentals to it.[33] In the *prima pars* of 'Praeter rerum seriem' the *cantus firmus* consists of three phrases (Ex. 14).[34] Each phrase is sung both by the first tenor and the superius, and this double exposition of the melody is repeated. Thus in the course of the

Ex. 14

[30] Prof. Thomas Warburton of the University of North Carolina has announced his intention to publish a selection of Josquin's works intabulated for keyboard instruments.

[31] Motetten, Bundel vii, no. 33.

[32] The intabulations appear in Gintzler, *Intabolatura...Libro primo* (1547), no. 10; Fuenllana, *Orphenica lyra* (1554), no. 72; Alberto da Ripa, *Cinquiesme livre de tabulature de leut* (Paris, 1555; Brown 1555⁴), no. 3; and Ochsenkun, *Tabulaturbuch* (1558), no. 2. All intabulations are barred by semibreves. Fuenllana's intabulation is for voice and vihuela, the voice part notated in red ciphers in the tablature and the text given beneath the music. I have omitted the text and any indication of the vocal part in Examples 15–17.

In measure 17 of Ripa's intabulation of 'Praeter rerum seriem' (Ex. 15) the fifth bass note reads D instead of E. In measures 24–5 (Ex. 17) Ripa either made a mistake or rewrote the motet. He omits music to the value of a semibreve at the beginning of measure 24 and adds the following at the end of measure 25: I have aligned his version with the others to faciliate comparison.

[33] See Edward Lowinsky's comment on the modern notion that *musica ficta* must not be applied to a chant melody in the discussions of the Motet Workshop (below, pp. 652–3).

[34] After Osthoff, *Josquin Desprez*, ii, p. 73.

prima pars each phrase is heard four times and there are four opportunities to raise the F at the end of the second phrase to F♯. In its first two appearances, Josquin prevents any chromatic alteration of the F, the first time by harmonizing it with a B♭ major triad, the second time by doubling it in the lower voices (mm. 11 and 14). These clear indications of the composer's intentions notwithstanding, both Gintzler and Ripa add accidentals to the cadences, the latter to both, the former only to the first, not without re-arranging the part-writing and omitting the voices that restrict their choice. Their decisions, based on their changes of voice-leading, do not affect the way the motet ought to be sung. At the third and fourth time the F must be raised to F♯, since it appears in a VII⁶–I or V–I cadential formula. The sixteenth-century intabulators agree in adding the sharps, though Smijers does not. In this case, then, singers should follow the practice of the older musicians, not that of the modern editor.

There are also other passages in the motet where the unanimous judgement of the earlier musicians stands against that of Smijers. Several times a cadence or cadence-like progression on C needs to be approached by a B♮ (mm. 15, 20, and 22). In Example 15, for instance, the intabulators raise the leading-note in measure 15, although they differ about the way the cadence is prepared and about the chord of resolution—whether to leave the Es natural or make them flat. Their unanimity on the B♮ encourages us to correct Smijers, who failed to add it. Similarly, they flat the four Es in the two lowest voices in measures 16–18—notes that Smijers left uninflected, although they fall under the *una nota supra la* rule. Gintzler's and Ripa's F♯s in measure 16 are both obviously impossible in a sung version.

There is complete agreement in the first three measures of the intabulations about the need for E♭ in the motet (see Ex. 16). But in measure 4 Gintzler flats the Es as well; here we have to do with passing notes and we may regard the accidentals as optional rather than obligatory; a certain freedom with regard to non-harmonic tones scarcely threatens the integrity of the system. The V–I cadence at the end of the *prima pars* resolves on a triad on G, left minor by Fuenllana and Ochsenkun, and changed to major by Gintzler and Ripa—similarly, a matter of taste.

How do the intabulators treat literal repetition? The phrase 'Nec vir tangit virginem' (Ex. 17) is immediately repeated an octave higher, and this section is followed by a similar one on the words 'nec prolis originem'. The intabulators vary the ornamentation in the repeats, and most of them change the accidentals in the process. Only Ochsenkun is consistent in his application of *musica ficta* to the two phrases, although Ripa does not make drastic changes. Distinctions can be made between obligatory,[35] optional,[36] and

---

[35] See the B♮s in the lowest voices of measures 20–21.

[36] See the treatment of passing notes, and of the E in the bass at the beginning of measure 21 and in the second highest voice at the beginning of measure 23.

Ex. 15 'Praeter rerum seriem' mm. 15-17 (accidentals after Smijers)

1) F♯ original

Ex. 16   'Praeter rerum seriem' mm. 1-5 (accidentals after Smijers)

Ex. 17 'Praeter rerum seriem' mm. 20-27 (accidentals after Smijers)

arbitrary accidentals,[37] because, manifestly, performers in the Renaissance prized variety and contrast more than structural clarity; the repeats offered them an opportunity to display their ingenuity in the art of variation.

Of all intabulations of Josquin's motets published during the sixteenth century, those of his setting *a 6* of the prayer 'Pater noster'[38] may be the most interesting, for they reveal the greatest range of choice and the most intriguing departures from the vocal model. The printed anthologies contain four intabulations by Francesco da Milano (1536), Piero di Teghi (1547), Simon Gintzler (1547), and Sebastian Ochsenkun (1558).[39] The motet, likewise written in G Dorian, opens with a series of invocations on 'Pater noster', all set syllabically and harmonized as half-cadence formulas, I–V in G and D (Ex. 18). I describe these progressions with Roman numerals since, by a slight extension of the subsemitone rule, the triads on D and A may be read as major, that is, dominant in function. All that stands between F ($\sharp$) and G in measures 3 and 6, and C ($\sharp$) and D in measures 9 and 17, is a pause. In so strong a harmonic context it would seem justified to overlook the pause and raise the seventh to the leading-note. And indeed, three of the four intabulators support such a decision—two at least in part, the other completely. Ochsenkun alone leaves all these chords minor; but he rarely strays beyond the rules, although he is unusually consistent in following them. Francesco da Milano is equally consistent in making all chords major.[40] The lesser musicians, Piero di Teghi and Simon Gintzler, take intermediate positions, and raise only the F in measure 6. Francesco might have justified his chromatic alterations as extensions of the subsemitone rule, which he applied to half as well as full cadences; this practice became quite common in the sixteenth century, to judge from the available intabulations. Indeed, in this same motet, the opportunity to transform a minor into a major third at half cadences presents itself time and again,[41] and the four lutenists each react to these new situations in their characteristic ways: Ochsenkun leaves all of the chords minor, Francesco makes all of them major, and Teghi and Gintzler raise the third in some, keeping it minor in others.

In measure 19 of 'Pater noster' (Ex. 18), the four lutenists agree to add accidentals to the second lowest voice, where the subsemitone rule must be invoked, even though Smijers ignores it. But even there, and in the next

[37] See the C$\sharp$ at the end of measure 21 in Gintzler's intabulation, and the C$\sharp$ in measure 25 in Fuenllana's intabulation.

[38] Motetten, Bundel xii, no. 50.

[39] The intabulations appear in Francesco da Milano, *Intabolatura di liuto* (1536), no. 32 (modern edition in *The Lute Music*, ed. Ness, no. 108); Teghi, *Des chansons…Livre troixiesme* (1547), no. 18; Gintzler, *Intabolatura…Libro primo* (1547), no. 7; and Ochsenkun, *Tabulaturbuch* (1558), no. 1.

[40] At least, C$\sharp$ does appear in the turn in the top voice of measure 9, although the phrase finally comes to rest on C$\natural$.

[41] For instance, in measures 32, 39, 42, 46, and so on.

Ex. 18 'Pater noster' mm. 1-24

Ex. 19   'Pater noster' mm. 31-8

few measures, some details are treated differently in each intabulation. For example, Francesco, always the most liberal of the four, raises several Fs that are passing notes left unaltered by the others, and exploits the sonority of F♯ against B♭; Gintzler, too, places a sharp before F, in a conventional contrapuntal setting, but Teghi and Ochsenkun[42] leave the F in measure 23 uninflected.

In the next section of the motet (Ex. 19), three cadences occur, in measures 31, 35, and 38. All of them offer a choice between Dorian and Phrygian. Ochsenkun and Teghi leave the first two cadences uninflected—a solution justified by the voice-leading, the avoidance of the preceding F (introduced both by Francesco and Gintzler), and of an ornamentation that gives the passage the character of a clausula (like Gintzler) or of a dominant seventh (like Francesco). Both Teghi and Ochsenkun manifestly want a C major sound here. Of the four instrumentalists, Francesco offers the best solution, Dorian cadences with E♮s and C♯s both in measures 31 and 35. Not surprisingly, Francesco, with his strong sense for colour and tonal orientation, instead of treating the harmonic progression in measure 38 as a Phrygian cadence, as do his three colleagues, transforms it into a very modern sounding half cadence (V of V–V), outlining a dominant seventh in his ornamentation (m. 38$_{3-4}$).

The greatest surprise in the *prima pars* of 'Pater noster' comes in measures 56–9 (Ex. 20), where Francesco and Gintzler raise most B♭s to B♮s, transforming the series of triads on G from minor to major. Francesco shows his sense of colour by keeping the E♭ in measure 58, signed in many of the sources of the vocal model,[43] and changing freely between C minor and C major, ending on G major reached via F♯. That two of the four sixteenth-century lutenists thwarted what appears to be the composer's original intentions made me suspect at first that their reading was based on a manuscript tradition different from the mainstream. Perhaps one or more sources preserving the original version of the motet specified at least one B♮ during that phrase. Such is apparently not the case. I have examined all but one source of 'Pater noster': none includes a natural or a sharp before any of the Bs in those measures.[44]

[42] The ornamentation Ochsenkun chose for measure 23 influenced his decision not to raise the F. He also leaves the F in measure 25 natural in contrast to the other instrumentalists.

[43] Gintzler changes it to E♮.

[44] That is, *Novum et insigne Opus Musicum* (Nuremberg, 1537), no. 2; Josquin, *Moduli* (Paris, 1555), fol. 14^v; *Novum et insigne Opus Musicum* (Nuremberg, 1558), no. 2; Berlin, Deutsche Staatsbibliothek, MS. mus. 40043, fol. 34^v; Copenhagen, Kongelige Bibliotek, MS. Gl. kgl. samling 1872, fol. 78^v; Dresden, Landesbibliothek, Sammlung Glashütte, MS. V (superius and sexta vox only); Gotha, Landesbibliothek, Codex A 98, fol. 5^v; Leipzig, Bibliothek der Thomaskirche, MSS. 49–50, no. 7 (superius, tenor, sexta vox, and bass only); Munich, Bayerische Staatsbibliothek, Mus. MS. 12, fol. 20^v; Munich, Bayerische Staatsbibliothek, Mus. MS. 1536, no. 62 (incomplete); Munich, Universitätsbibliothek,

Ex. 20 'Pater noster' mm. 54-60

That 'Pater noster' includes a smaller area of agreement than 'Qui habitat' and 'Praeter rerum seriem' does not alter the general conclusions, but merely identifies that motet as an unusually difficult case. Of its four intabulations, the one by Francesco da Milano is by far the most intriguing, at once more consistent and more daring than those by Ochsenkun, Gintzler, and Teghi. A modern editor, however, would do well to follow the example of Sebastian Ochsenkun rather than Francesco, for the German is exceptionally careful in his application of *musica ficta*. He sticks close to the rules, and seldom indulges in subjectively motivated chromatic alterations. I do not mean to imply, however, that his intabulations support the position of those modern scholars who advocate a policy of utmost reserve in matters of *musica ficta*. On the contrary, even Ochsenkun is usually more daring than most modern editors. His intabulation of 'Absalon fili mi', for example, agrees in all but a few inessential details with the version first proposed in Lowinsky's *Secret Chromatic Art* and most recently printed in Osthoff's biography of Josquin and in the Supplement to his *Werken*.[45] That a sixteenth-century musician, and a conservative one at that, published such a version is impressive confirmation for the validity of Lowinsky's application of the rules of *musica ficta*.

The quality of these intabulations must be judged in the context of the technique of ornamentation brought to bear on the vocal models—a technique that sprang in part at least from necessity. Fast passage work helps to sustain the fragile sounds of the lute and the vihuela that might otherwise die away too quickly to create a likeness of the original polyphonic fabric. Nevertheless, many of these virtuosi added more ornaments than modern musicians think tasteful, especially if the performer's highest goal is understood to be as exact a reproduction as possible of the composer's original intentions. Of course, that ideal must be modified in applying it to past ages, when performers took an active role as collaborators with the composers rather than serving merely as their interpreters. Some aspects of music that have since become an integral part of the compositional process were then conceived to be the prerogative of the performers—instrumentation, for example, and possibly *musica ficta* as well. Moreover, a certain tension evidently existed then—as it exists today—between the performer's

---

Art. 401, App., no. 1 (incomplete); Nuremberg, Germanisches Museum, MS. 83795 (first tenor and bass only); Padua, Biblioteca Capitolare, MS. A 17, fol. 1ᵛ; Rome, Biblioteca Vallicelliana, MS. Vall. S. Borr. E. II. 55–60, second series, no. 9; and Vatican City, Biblioteca Vaticana, MS. Cappella Sistina 55, no. 10. I am grateful to the curator of Isham Memorial Library, Harvard University, for allowing me access to microfilm copies of some of these sources, and to Mr. A. Brian Davenport for checking my work. (I have now been able to examine Toledo, Biblioteca Capitular, MS. 18, which is no exception.)

[45] Edward E. Lowinsky, *Secret Chromatic Art in the Netherlands Motet*, Ex. 23; Osthoff, *Josquin Desprez*, ii, pp. 382–4; and *Werken*, Supplement, no. 5.

wish to express the composer's intentions and his desire to reveal his own personality. Some of the best and most imaginative intabulations from the sixteenth century are those in which the performer has put his own imprint on the music, even at the expense of the original conception.[46]

To be sure, some of the musicians whose arrangements I have discussed scarcely ornamented their models at all, or only enough to sustain the sound. Fuenllana's intabulation of 'Praeter rerum seriem' (see Exs. 15–17) is very close to the original—he does little more than break a number of ties and vary the cadences. Perhaps he felt that the counterpoint in that motet was so dense that he need not complicate it any further. Simon Gintzler's arrangements of 'Pater noster' and 'Praeter rerum' (see Exs. 15–20) include a fair measure of ornamentation without disguising the sound of the original. Gintzler's technique consists mainly of filling in intervals, adding cadential flourishes, and applying a few conventional figuration patterns to the original counterpoint.

Gintzler shares the predilection for using stereotyped runs, turns, and trills with most sixteenth-century instrumentalists. The difference between a good and a bad intabulation often rests on the way this conventional decorative material is used. Piero di Teghi's versions of Josquin's motets (see Exs. 18–20), for instance, are poor not because he uses figures that are different from those used by other lutenists, but because he maintains a steady stream of eighth- or sixteenth-notes from beginning to end, obscuring the contours of his model beneath an avalanche of endless meandering scale figures. Hans Gerle's intabulations are inferior not only because he often leaves out one or more inner voices in order to make the showy diminutions easier to play, but also because he sprinkles ornamental clichés throughout a piece at random, wherever they fit under his fingers.

Heavily ornamented intabulations from the mid-century generally succeed artistically because they restrict the number of stereotyped figures applied to any one section of a composition. Repeated wherever possible, these ornamental clichés form a superstructure, so to speak, over the given vocal piece, a network of motives completely independent of the original conception. Embellishments, in other words, are no help in clarifying the stylistic features of the model—but some instrumentalists have the musical sense to ornament polyphonic imitations in a consistent fashion. Diego Ortiz employs this technique in his arrangements printed in his treatise on the viol,[47] and so does Ochsenkun in his intabulations (see Exs. 15–20). At the beginning of 'Pater noster' (Ex. 18), for instance, Ochsenkun concentrates almost exclusively on a dotted figure (♩♪♫♫) and a scale

[46] These points are discussed more fully in Howard Mayer Brown, *Embellishing Sixteenth-Century Music.*

[47] Diego Ortiz, *Trattado de glosas* (Rome, 1553; Brown 1553[5]), and modern edition by Max Schneider (Kassel, 1936), *passim.*

pattern, and the interplay between these formulas and the structure of the piece adds a new dimension to the instrumental arrangement.

Bakfark (see Exs. 12 and 13), and to a greater extent Francesco da Milano (see Exs. 18–20), go even further than Ochsenkun in ornamenting their vocal models. These virtuosi do not merely sustain the sound, decorate the contrapuntal fabric, or apply a limited number of patterns to the melodic lines; they transform the original motet into an idiomatic and brilliant instrumental piece by means of a profusion of ever-varying runs, turns, and trills. They break up the longer notes of the piece into smaller units; sometimes their embellishments take on motivic significance in the course of a section, but their method is so free and so varied that it cannot be categorized. The original music served them as a basis for comment and elaboration, for a virtuoso display of variation technique. Needless to say, the original composition is often obscured in the process of transformation, but the results can be brilliant, especially in the hands of an imaginative musician like Francesco.[48]

The great virtuosi of the nineteenth century, Liszt above all, proceeded as freely in their transcriptions as did their sixteenth-century predecessors. It may well have been the twentieth-century puritanical attitude toward musicians who tamper with a master's work that has prevented us from looking closely at the plentiful arrangements for fretted and keyboard instruments of some of the greatest masterpieces of the sixteenth century. Whatever the reason, our relative ignorance of this repertoire has kept us from a valuable source of information about the period. Perhaps these intabulations of Josquin's motets do not offer conclusive proof about the way the singers of the time added *musica ficta* in detail, particularly where they change the voice-leading of the original, but the close agreement between intabulators in many situations requiring accidentals, the intimate concordance with the theorists' rules of *musica ficta*, the freedom taken by the greatest musicians of the time, a Francesco da Milano, a Valentin Bakfark, in extending *musica ficta* in the direction of a colourful harmonic palette are eloquent witnesses in favour of a consistent, sensitive, and imaginative application of *musica ficta*, if we are to do justice to the original harmonic concepts of the period.

---

[48] The attitude of the sixteenth-century transcriber agrees with that of the sixteenth-century editor, described by Edward Lowinsky in the following manner: 'They [the collations] show that a sixteenth-century musician copying a piece of music felt entirely free to "edit" that piece according to his own ideas.... The one thing the sixteenth-century "editor" was not interested in, indeed, hardly even dreamed of, was the twentieth-century editor's preoccupation with the "Urtext". It is precisely this situation which makes the establishment of a "definitive" text of the work of a sixteenth-century composer so precarious and the need for various editions of significant works of the period following divergent traditions so urgent' (*The Medici Codex of 1518* (*Monuments of Renaissance Music,* iii; Chicago, 1968), p. 88a).

Plainchant in the Motets, Hymns, and Magnificat of Josquin des Prez*

WILLEM ELDERS

In many of his motets Josquin used traditional Gregorian melodies of the Roman Catholic liturgy. The primary characteristics of a Gregorian chant reside in its monophony and its Latin text, written for a liturgical or ecclesiastical function.[1] Melody and text are integrated to an extent seldom found in the history of music.

The number of motets by Josquin with Gregorian chant adds up to fifty—about half of his output in the genre. This shows how rich a source of inspiration Gregorian chant was for Josquin. To provide an insight into the different procedures used by Josquin in elaborating a chant, it will be helpful to classify the motets in six groups (see the Table).[2]

Groups I and II comprise motets in which the chant is clearly recognizable because its text is different from that of the motet and because it is treated as a *cantus firmus* in long note values. Group I consists of four motets in which the chant appears as a *cantus firmus*; Group II contains seven motets in which the chant is treated canonically.

Groups III–V comprise motets in which the text in all voices is that of the chant. Group III consists of seven motets in which the chant is treated canonically, Group IV consists of five motets in which the chant appears as a migrant *cantus firmus*, and Group V contains twelve motets in which the chant is paraphrased. Group VI, the final category, consists of fifteen motets which do not fit into any of the preceding groups.

Josquin elaborates a chant in a number of different ways: the chant may be quoted whole, or in part, in long or shorter note values; it may be quoted

* I am grateful to Professor Peter Gram Swing of Swarthmore College for his revision of the English text of the present article.

[1] A text is considered liturgical if used in the liturgy of the Roman Catholic Church, ecclesiastical if used in the church in an extra-liturgical context.

[2] In '*Cantus firmus* in the Liturgical Motets of Josquin des Prez' (Ph.D. diss., Yale University, 1959), Jacquelyn A. Mattfeld divides Josquin's liturgical *cantus firmus* motets into no fewer than fourteen categories (see pp. 129–31). The subtlety of the differences between these categories makes it difficult to recognize the composer's fundamental compositional procedures.

TABLE

The Use of Plainchant in the Motets, Hymns, and Magnificat of Josquin des Prez

	number of voices	extent of chant	use of chant	structural technique
GROUP I				
'Ave nobilissima' (no. 34) (c.f. 'Benedicta tu')	6	complete	exact	c.f. 3x in proportional diminution
'Huc me sydereo' (no. 32) (c.f. 'Plangent eum')	6	complete	exact	c.f. 3x in proportional diminution
'Lectio actuum apostolorum' (no. 41) (c.f. 'Dum complerentur')	5	complete	exact	c.f. 3x
'In illo tempore stetit Jesus' (no. 55) (c.f. 'Et ecce terraemotus')	6	complete	exact	c.f. 1x
GROUP II				
'Absolve quaesumus' (no. 82) (c.f. 'Requiem aeternam')	6	complete	exact	c.f. in canon *a 2*
'Proch dolor' (Supplement, no. 14; *opus dubium*) (c.f. 'Pie Jhesu Domine')	7	one phrase	exact	c.f. in canon *a 3*
'Videte omnes populi' (W.W. no. 21)	6	complete	?	
'Christus mortuus est' (no. 87)	6	complete		c.f. in canon *a 2*
'Sic Deus dilexit mundum' (no. 86) (c.f. 'Circumdederunt me')	6	complete	exact/free	
'Virgo salutiferi' (no. 35) (c.f. 'Ave Maria')	5	complete		c.f. in canon *a 2*
'O Virgo prudentissima' (no. 45) (c.f. 'Beata Mater')	6	complete	?	c.f. in canon *a 2*
GROUP III				
'Homo quidam' (no. 28)	5	complete	exact/free	c.f. in canon *a 2*
'Inviolata' (no. 42)	5	complete	exact/free	c.f. in canon *a 2*
'Ave verum' (no. 80)	5	complete	exact/free	c.f. in canon *a 2*
'Alma Redemptoris' (no. 38)	4	complete	coloration/paraphrase	c.f. in canon *a 2*
'Salve Regina' (no. 95)	4	complete	coloration/paraphrase	c.f. in canon *a 2*
'Veni Sancte Spiritus' (no. 49)	6	complete	coloration	c.f. in canon *a 2*
'Benedicta es' (no. 46)	6	complete	coloration/paraphrase	c.f. in canon *a 2* migrans
GROUP IV				
'Praeter rerum seriem' (no. 33)	6	complete	exact?	c.f. migrans
'Victimae paschali' (no. 26)	4	complete	exact/coloration	c.f. migrans
'Victimae paschali' (no. 81)	6	complete	exact/coloration/paraphrase	c.f. migrans
'Mittit ad Virginem' (no. 3)	4	complete	coloration/paraphrase	c.f. migrans
'Ave mundi spes' (Supplement, no. 15)	4	complete	coloration/paraphrase	c.f. migrans
GROUP V				
'Alma Redemptoris/Ave Regina' (no. 21)	4	complete	paraphrase	paraphrase
'Regina caeli' (Supplement, no. 3)	4	complete	paraphrase	paraphrase
'Ave maris stella' (no. 94)	4	complete	paraphrase	paraphrase

	number of voices	extent of chant	use of chant	structural technique
'Ave verum corpus' (no. 12)	2–3	complete	paraphrase	
'Domine non secundum' (no. 13)	2–4	complete	paraphrase	
'O admirabile commercium' (no. 5)	4	complete	paraphrase	
'Quando natus es' (no. 6)	4	complete	paraphrase	
'Rubum quem viderat' (no. 7)	4	complete	paraphrase	
'Germinavit radix Jesse' (no. 8)	4	complete	paraphrase	
'Ecce Maria genuit' (no. 9)	4	complete	paraphrase	
'Ave Maria . . . benedicta tu' (no. 2)	4	one phrase	paraphrase	
'Vultum tuum deprecabuntur' (no. 24)	4	one phrase	paraphrase	
GROUP VI				
'Ave Maria . . . Virgo serena' (no. 1)	4	one phrase	exact	c.f.
'O Virgo virginum' (no. 83)	6	complete	coloration	c.f.
'Nesciens Mater' (no. 71)	5	complete	exact/free	c.f.
'Virgo prudentissima' (no. 25)	4	complete	exact/free	c.f.
'O bone et dulcis Domine Jesu' (no. 18)	4			
(c.f. 'Pater noster')		complete	exact/coloration	c.f.
(c.f. 'Ave Maria')		complete	exact/coloration	c.f.
(c.f. 'Benedicta tu')		complete	exact	c.f.
'Salve Regina' (no. 48)	5	one phrase	paraphrase	c.f. migrans ostinato
'Inviolata' (Supplement, no. 10)	12	partial	exact/coloration/para-phrase	c.f. migrans
(c.f. 'O Maria flos virginum')		one phrase		c.f.
'Ave maris stella' (Supplement, no. 1)	3–4	complete	4th strophe 6th strophe paraphrase 7th strophe coloration	c.f. in canon *a 2*
'Honor decus' (Supplement, no. 2)	4	complete	coloration	c.f.
'Christum ducem' (no. 4)	4	1st phrase	exact	c.f.
		2nd phrase	exact	c.f.
		3rd phrase	exact	c.f.
		4th phrase	exact	c.f.
		5th phrase	exact	c.f.
'Magnificat 3. toni' (no. 77)	4	tonus 3	coloration/paraphrase	c.f. migrans
'Magnificat 4. toni' (no. 78)	4	tonus 4	coloration/paraphrase	c.f. migrans
'Planxit autem David' (no. 20)	4	lamentatio Jeremiae		
'Liber generationis' (no. 15)	4	psalmody	?	
'Factum est autem' (no. 16)	4	psalmody	?	

literally, or with some notes missing, some notes varied, some passing notes added; it may be embellished or paraphrased; if quoted more than once, it may appear in proportional diminution; it may be set in canon, or it may migrate from one voice to another.

When the chant is paraphrased, it is difficult to identify the particular version Josquin may have used. But when the chant appears as *cantus firmus* in long note values, the task is rendered easier. Thanks to Father Hourlier of Solesmes, I was able to consult the monastery's extensive photographic archives. Even though these archives are not complete, they often showed enough versions of a particular chant to facilitate a determination of whether or not Josquin deliberately departed from the version before him.

One result of this study was the discovery that the six-voice motets 'Ave nobilissima creatura' and 'Huc me sydereo' conceivably comprise a motet cycle. Even though both motets are based on a different antiphon,[3] the melodies, with the exception of two repeated notes, are exactly the same:

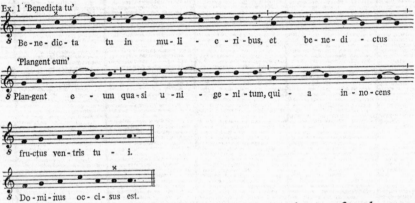

Ex. 1 'Benedicta tu'

Be - ne - dic - ta   tu   in   mu - li - e - ri - bus, et   be - ne - di - ctus

'Plangent eum'

Plan-gent   e - um qua-si   u - ni - ge - ni - tum, qui - a   in - no - cens

fru-ctus ven - tris   tu - i.

Do - mi - nus   oc - ci - sus est.

For a detailed account of this hypothesis, the reader is referred to my article.[4] Here I will confine myself to the relationship between the antiphons and Josquin's *cantus firmi* and that between the two *cantus firmi* themselves. The *cantus firmus* appears three times in strict proportion in each of the motets. The mode of the chant in both motets has been changed by the addition of B♭. The two *cantus firmi* are rhythmically and melodically identical, except for one repeated note in the first phrase:

Ex. 2 'Huc me sydereo'

Plan - gent   e - um   qua - si   u - ni - ge - ni - tum   etc.

'Ave nobilissima creatura'

Be - ne - di - cta   tu   in   mu - li - e - ri - bus   etc.

[3] In *Antiphonale Monasticum* (Paris, Tournai, Rome, 1934), p. 193, and *Antiphonale Romanum* (Paris, Tournai, Rome, 1949), p. 440, respectively.

[4] 'Zusammenhänge zwischen den Motetten *Ave nobilissima creatura* und *Huc me sydereo*

The question is: Are there any deviations from the original Gregorian chant? None of the sources known in Solesmes gives an antiphon melody identical with Josquin's *cantus firmi*. Hence, it appears that it was Josquin himself who omitted a D in the second phrase, introduced a passing note in the fourth phrase, and added a B♭ in the final cadence:

Ex. 3 'Huc me sydereo'

The third motet of Group I is 'Lectio actuum apostolorum' for five parts. The text is the epistle for Pentecost; the antiphon 'Dum complerentur'[5] serves as *cantus firmus*. As in the two preceding motets, the chant appears once in the *prima pars* and twice in the *secunda pars*, this time, however, not in proportion. The three *cantus firmi* are similar to each other melodically, and the only deviation from the version found in the *Antiphonale Romanum* consists of two passing notes.

The fourth and last motet in Group I is the six-voice 'In illo tempore stetit Jesus', based on the gospel for Tuesday after Easter (Luke 24: 36–47). The antiphon 'Et ecce terraemotus' provides the *cantus firmus*. The motet 'In illo tempore' is the only work in this group that does not consist of two *partes*, and in which the *cantus firmus* appears only once. This would hardly be striking were it not that the text of the motet points to the possibility that the work has not been preserved in its entirety. Luke 24 relates the appearance of Christ to the apostles at Emmaeus. In the seven sources we know for the motet,[6] the text ends with Christ's request to have something to eat, whereas the gospel goes on further to describe how Christ was given something to eat.[7] The motet text is incomplete; three other gospel motets

---

von Josquin des Prez', *Tijdschrift van de Vereniging voor Nederlandse Muziekgeschiedenis*, xxii (1971), pp. 67–73.

[5] *Antiphonale Romanum*, p. 503.

[6] To the sources listed in the Josquin edition should be added: Bologna, Civico Museo Bibliografico Musicale, MS. R 142, fol. 31ᵛ (*sexta vox*); Copenhagen, Kongelige Bibliotek, Gl. kgl. Samling 1872, fol. 86ᵛ; and Copenhagen, Kongelige Bibliotek, Gl. kgl. Samling 1873, second series, no. [54].

[7] Luke 24: 36–41: 'Now whilst they were speaking these things, Jesus stood in the midst of them, and saith to them, Peace be to you; it is I, fear not. But they being troubled and affrighted, supposed that they saw a spirit. And he said to them: Why are you troubled, and why do thoughts arise in your hearts? See my hands and my feet, that it is I myself; feel, and see: for a spirit hath not flesh and bones, as you see me to have. And when he had

by Josquin contain the complete text.[8] Possibly, the sources of 'In illo tempore', which are all rather late, provide only a *prima pars*, and the *secunda pars*, which should begin with the text 'At illi obtulerunt ei', is lost. The fact that the *cantus firmus* is stated only once, rather than three times (as in the preceding motets), supports this hypothesis. The antiphon 'Et ecce terraemotus' appears in a large number of medieval antiphonaries, and the versions differ widely. However, MS. 5 of the Chapter Library of Lucca contains a reading (p. 146) almost identical with Josquin's *cantus firmus*:[9]

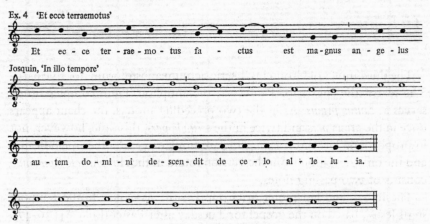

Ex. 4 'Et ecce terraemotus'

Et ec - ce ter - rae - mo - tus fa - ctus est ma - gnus an - ge - lus

Josquin, 'In illo tempore'

au - tem do - mi - ni de - scen - dit de ce - lo al - le - lu - ia.

Group II consists of seven motets in which the chant appears in the form of a canon. The first two motets are lamentations: 'Absolve, quaesumus, Domine', probably on the death of Philip the Fair, set for six voices, and

said this, he showed them his hands and his feet. But while they yet believed not, and wondered for joy, he said: Have you here any thing to eat?' (*The Holy Bible, Translated from the Latin Vulgate* (Boston, 1852)).

[8] 'In illo tempore assumpsit Jesus' (Matt. 20: 17–19), 'In principio erat verbum' (John 1: 1–14), 'Missus est Gabriel angelus' (Luke 1: 26–38).

[9] Manuscript 5 stands out among the manuscripts of this library because it belonged originally to the Order of the Holy Sepulchre of Jerusalem. This order came into existence during the Crusades; monasteries were founded in Italy, Spain, Northern France, Belgium, and Western Germany. As early as 1047 there was a chapel at Cambrai built in imitation of the Holy Sepulchre Chapel at Jerusalem. In 1064 a Monasterium Sancti Sepulchri was founded *extra muros*, and in the same year its church was consecrated. A library was built in 1490, and since a great number of manuscripts belonging to the order have been preserved (in the Municipal Library of Cambrai), it is therefore possible that Josquin knew the musical repertory of the Order of the Holy Sepulchre. For information about the Order of the Holy Sepulchre at Cambrai, see *Gallia Christiana, in provincias ecclesiasticas distributa; qua series et historia Archiepiscoporum, Episcoporum et Abbatum Franciae vicinarumque ditionum ab origine Ecclesiarum ad nostra tempora deducitur, & probatur ex authentis Instrumentis ad calcem appositis. Opera et studio Dom. Dionysii Sammarthani...* Tomus tertius (Paris, 1725), cols. 118–23.

'Proch dolor' (*opus dubium*), probably on the death of Emperor Maximilian, the father of Philip the Fair.[10] In the six-voice 'Absolve, quaesumus, Domine' the introit 'Requiem aeternam Domine'[11] is stated by tenor II and is answered a fifth higher by alto II. Josquin quotes the melody literally. The introit melody, which consists of four phrases (*a*, *b*, *c*, and *d*), is divided into thirteen units. The closing formulas of phrases *a*, *b*, and *d* are melodically similar. The only variant in Josquin's *cantus firmus* appears in the second half of phrase *b*:

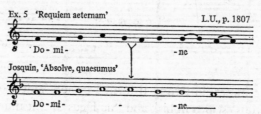

Ex. 5 'Requiem aeternam'   L.U., p. 1807

Do - mi-   - ne

Josquin, 'Absolve, quaesumus'

Do - mi-   -   - ne

This alteration is not required for contrapuntal reasons, because the canon at the fifth also works with the traditional Requiem melody. Since the Requiem melody Josquin used in his lamentation on the death of Ockeghem is identical with the present-day version at this point (although it differs in other places), another reason could have prompted the alteration. Possibly, the small deviation was made to avoid repeating the same closing formula three times. Of course, other considerations, such as text declamation or harmonic development, may also be involved.

The second lamentation, the seven-voice 'Proch dolor', has as a *cantus firmus* the last phrase of the sequence 'Dies irae',[12] 'Pie Jhesu Domine, dona ei requiem. Amen.' The *cantus firmus* is presented as a three-voice canon, as is indicated by the accompanying rubric: 'Celum terra mariaque succurrite pio' (Heaven, Earth, and Seas, succour the pious one). The first voice (Heaven) enters on a', the second (Earth) enters a fourth below, and the third voice (the Seas) an octave below. The phrase 'Pie Jhesu Domine' appears three times. Except for an added note on 'dona' and a note repetition on 'ei', the *cantus firmus* is identical with the sequence:

Ex. 6 'Dies irae'   L.U., p. 1810

(Josquin?), 'Proch dolor'

Pi - e Jhe- su Do - mi - ne,   do - na___ e - i___ Re - qui - em.

[10] The work, anonymous in the unique source, has been attributed to Josquin by Martin Picker; see *The Chanson Albums of Marguerite of Austria* (Berkeley and Los Angeles, 1965), pp. 89–90. See also Willem Elders, *Studien zur Symbolik in der Musik der alten Niederländer* (Bilthoven, 1968), pp. 22–4.

[11] *Liber Usualis* (Tournai, New York, 1961), p. 1807.   [12] Ibid., p. 1810.

These changes had to be made for contrapuntal reasons, since without them the canon could not be worked out. In this setting the canon works perfectly, and the 'dona' of the third voice is joined together with the word 'ei' of the first voice:

Ex. 7

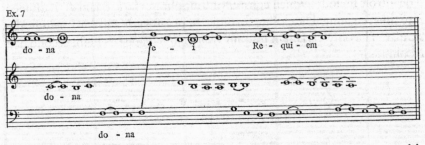

Three of the motets in Group II form a cycle: 'Videte omnes populi', 'Christus mortuus est pro nobis', and 'Sic Deus dilexit mundum'. In each of these six-voice motets, which deal with Christ's sufferings, the chant, 'Circumdederunt me gemitus mortis, dolores inferni circumdederunt me', is presented as a *cantus firmus* in canon. I have not found a source that is precisely like Josquin's *cantus firmus*. The Worcester Antiphonary contains the text of Josquin's *cantus firmus* set to a melody that begins with the same *initium*; there also similarities in the following phrases.[13] The text was also sung on Good Friday as a *responsorium* of the *Improperia*.[13a] This may perhaps be interpreted as a symbolic connection between the texts of the motet and the *cantus firmus*.

The five-voice 'Virgo salutiferi' and the six-voice 'O Virgo prudentissima' remain in Group II. In 'Virgo salutiferi' the antiphon 'Ave Maria'[14] is presented as a *cantus firmus* in canon for two voices. The melody is quoted incompletely in the first two *partes*, completely in the *tertia pars*. Except for the phrase setting 'in mulieribus, alleluia' in the *tertia pars*, Josquin states the antiphon exactly. The *cantus firmus* 'Ave Maria, gratia plena, Dominus tecum' appears three times in the motet.

In 'O Virgo prudentissima', the antiphon 'Beata Mater'[15] is quoted once in the *prima pars* and once in the *secunda pars*. The two *cantus firmi* differ slightly from each other. Thirty manuscripts containing the melody are known at Solesmes. On the strength of these sources, we can ascertain that only the phrase 'Beata Mater et intacta Virgo' is borrowed more or less exactly.

In the motets of Group III, which have the same text in all voices, the chant is treated as a canon for two voices. The first three motets, 'Homo

---

[13] Cf. *Paléographie Musicale*, xii, p. 438. This melody is very similar to the one found by Gustave Reese (*Music in the Renaissance*, p. 255, n. 369) in a Sarum *Manuale* of 1526.

[13a] Cf. *Paléographie Musicale*, xiv, Pl. XLII.

[14] *Liber Usualis*, p. 1679.   [15] Ibid., p. 1476H, and *Antiphonale Monasticum*, p. 713.

quidam', 'Inviolata', and 'Ave verum corpus', are different from the others because they are for five voices, and because their *cantus firmi*, in large measure, have been taken over literally. The melody of the long responsory 'Homo quidam',[16] written at Rouen in the eleventh century for the feast of St. Catherine,[17] is quoted more or less strictly, predominantly in breves and semibreves, except at the final word, 'vobis'. By omitting a few notes of the neumatic chant, Josquin renders the canonic *cantus firmus* more concise. The most conspicuous omission occurs in the long melisma on 'omnia':

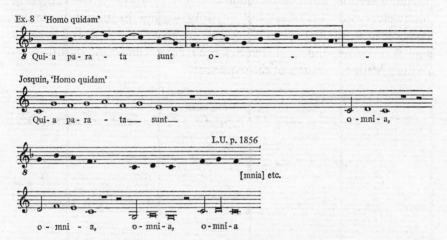

Josquin's *cantus firmus* deviates most noticeably from the version used today at the words 'dicere invitatis'. However, there is a version in a manuscript belonging to the Order of the Dominicans[18] that is very similar to Josquin's *cantus firmus* at this point:

In the motet 'Inviolata' the voice presenting the chant is more integrated, rhythmically, with the other voices of the motet than in 'Homo quidam'. The sequence survives in many sources, but with marked differences in text as well as in melody. A striking melodic difference between the present

---

[16] *Cantus selecti ad benedictionem ss.mi Sacramenti* (Paris, 1957), no. 27.

[17] Cf. ibid., p. 299.

[18] Library of Solesmes, MS. 68, p. 337.

version[19] and Josquin's *cantus firmus* is the second note of the sequence:

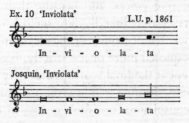

Josquin's version, however, is found in several sources;[20] it also appears in his twelve-voice 'Inviolata' and in many settings by sixteenth-century composers. In the last verse, 'Quae sola inviolata permansisti', I found a significant correspondence between Josquin's *cantus firmus* and the fifteenth-century Milanese version of the sequence:[21]

Here we have a rare example of Josquin's having taken notice, in part at least, of an Ambrosian chant melody.[22]

In 'Ave verum corpus' the chant is treated in the same way as in the motet 'Inviolata'. It is a trope sung during the Elevation as early as the fourteenth century.[23] Josquin also used this trope in another setting of the 'Ave verum' which has a slightly different text. The trope has the structure of a sequence: *aa bb cc d*. In the *prima* and *secunda pars* of the five-voice motet, the repetition of verses *a* and *b* is slightly embellished; in the *tertia pars* not only phrase *c* but also phrase *d* is repeated.

In the four-voice Marian motets 'Alma Redemptoris Mater' and 'Salve Regina' the antiphons of the same name (*tonus solemnior*)[24] are quoted completely. Here we see original and added notes blend into a new melody

---

[19] *Liber Usualis*, p 1861.

[20] *Le Prosaire d'Aix-la-Chapelle* (*Monumenta Musicae Sacrae*, iii; Rouen, 1961), p. 93; 's-Gravenhage, Koninklijke Bibliotheek, MS. 130 G 18 (Northern Netherlands, about 1500; written for the liturgy of the Antonius church of a nunnery).

[21] *Liber Vesperalis Mediolanensis* (Rome, 1939), p. 810. This is the only phrase where the Milanese version differs from the Roman chant.

[22] See Jacquelyn A. Mattfeld's article, above, pp. 360–6.

[23] *Cantus selecti*, no. 11 and p. 298.

[24] *Liber Usualis*, pp. 273 and 276, respectively.

of homogeneous design in a free elaboration of the chant. Nevertheless Josquin preserves the structure of the antiphons. In 'Salve Regina', for instance, the first two phrases are identical, and Josquin emphasizes their correspondence by setting both phrases identically in his motet.[25]

The last two motets remaining in this group are for six voices: 'Veni Sancte Spiritus' and 'Benedicta es'. In 'Veni Sancte Spiritus', a motet for Pentecost, the sequence[26] is elaborated throughout as a two-voice canon. The sequence determines the structure of the entire motet: five large periods, varying in length from fourteen to nineteen measures, are repeated intact. Each of the ten stanzas has three lines of text:

> Veni Sancte Spiritus
> Et emitte caelitus
> Lucis tuae radium
> (etc.)

Josquin separates the three short lines by rests. The canonic voice enters in both *partes* at the time interval of two perfect breves, with the result that the entries overlap only slightly. Consequently, there was little need to alter the *cantus prius factus* in order to make the canon work. The sequence is paraphrased sparingly. Indeed, it might be better to describe the compositional process as embellishment, or coloration, since the written-out ornaments are often stereotyped formulas.

The last composition in Group II, Josquin's famous motet 'Benedicta es', is also based on a sequence.[27] The sequence has six strophes according to the plan *aa bb cc*. In the *prima pars* phrase *a* is elaborated in canonic imitation for two voices, and phrases b^1 and b^2 are quoted freely by the two voices that earlier had presented the canon, i.e., tenor and superius, respectively. The *secunda pars*, scored for two voices, is based on phrase c^1, which is richly paraphrased.[28] In the *tertia pars* one can recognize phrase c^2 in the superius.

[25] I should like to point out that in the Solesmes editions the identity of the first two phrases has been disturbed by the short addition:

ma - ter [misericordiae]

Johannes Maier (*Studien zur Geschichte der Marienantiphon 'Salve regina'* (Regensburg, 1939), p. 30) says that the words 'mater' at the beginning and 'virgo' at the end of the antiphon are trope-like additions; they occur in manuscripts of Gregorian chant as early as the thirteenth and fourteenth centuries and have been sanctioned in the Tridentine version of the Breviary of 1568. Josquin, as Obrecht, Richafort, Senfl, and many of his contemporaries, used the original reading of the text; see the Antiphonaries of St. Gall (*Paléographie Musicale*, 2nd ser., i, p. 10) and Worcester (*Paléographie Musicale*, xii, p. 352).

[26] *Liber Usualis*, p. 880.

[27] *Revue du Chant Grégorien*, xx (1911–12), pp. 3–4; J. Mattfeld, '*Cantus firmus*', plate XXVII.

[28] The duo 'Per illud ave' occurs in numerous sixteenth-century intabulations; cf.

In accord with the sequence structure, Josquin sets the two lines of strophe 3 alike.

Group IV consists of five motets in which the chants—all of the sequence type—migrate from voice to voice. As in the motets of Group III, the chant melody at times is literally quoted, at times coloured, and at times paraphrased.

The six-voice motet 'Praeter rerum seriem' has a regular sequence pattern: *aa bb cc*. The melody appears alternately in superius and tenor I. Only the last phrase of a^2 is sung by tenor II. Although I have not found a version of the sequence that is identical with Josquin's *cantus firmus*,[29] the strict correspondence of stanza pairs within the *cantus firmus* suggests that he borrowed the chant literally. The similarity of two passages, measures 83–98 and 104–19, reflects the correspondence of phrases c^1 and c^2.

Josquin used the sequence 'Victimae paschali laudes'[30] as a *cantus firmus* in two motets, one for four voices, the other for six voices. The sequence has all nine phrases: *a bb c d c d ee*.[31] In the four-voice setting, which adheres more closely to the sequence melody than does the six-voice setting, the chant is stated in the inner voices, for the most part in breves and semibreves. As Osthoff has pointed out, Josquin quotes Ockeghem ('D'ung aultre amer') and Hayne ('De tous biens playne') in the superius of the *prima* and *secunda pars* respectively.[32] Josquin manages to combine the voice parts presenting the sequence with the chanson melodies without having to alter the sequence drastically. The alterations amount to five variant notes and twenty-seven additional notes.

Although the sequence melody 'Victimae paschali laudes' also remains clearly recognizable in the six-voice motet—Josquin leaves out only a few notes—the chant is more freely elaborated. The sequence phrases *a*, b^1, d^1, c^2, and d^2 are set most clearly in the upper voices. The head motives of these phrases, in particular, are quoted literally, and contrast by virtue of their longer note values with the other voices.

The last two sequence motets are four-voice compositions: 'Mittit ad Virginem' and 'Ave mundi spes, Maria'. In these two motets the sequences[33]

Kwee Him Yong, 'Sixteenth-Century Printed Instrumental Arrangements of Works by Josquin des Prez', *Tijdschrift van de Vereniging voor Nederlandse Muziekgeschiedenis*, xxii (1971), pp. 56–9.

[29] Cf. an early polyphonic version in *An Old St. Andrews Music Book*, ed. J. H. Baxter (London, 1931), fol. 194ᵛ; see also J. Mattfeld, '*Cantus firmus*', plate XXX; Alvin H. Johnson, 'The Liturgical Music of Cipriano de Rore' (Ph.D. diss., Yale University, 1954), p. 236.

[30] Peter Wagner, *Gregorianische Formenlehre* (Leipzig, 1921), p. 498; *Liber Usualis*, p. 780.

[31] In the editions of Solesmes the eighth phrase is missing: 'Credendum est magis soli Mariae veraci, quam Judaeorum turbae fallaci'.

[32] Osthoff, *Josquin Desprez* (Tutzing, 1962–5), ii, p. 26.

[33] *Cantus selecti*, nos. 104 and 131, respectively.

are elaborated even more than in the preceding motets of the group. In
'Mittit ad Virginem' the verse pairs *a*, *b*, and *c* appear in the *prima pars*,
d and *e* in the *secunda pars*. The last verse pair of the sequence (*f*) is missing;
it is replaced by the doxology, 'Qui nos salvet per omnia saeculorum saecula.
Amen.' Except for phrase d^2, which appears in the bass, the *cantus firmus* is
sung by superius and tenor.

The sequence 'Ave mundi spes, Maria' has eighteen stanzas and is built
regularly. Unfortunately, Josquin's motet based on this sequence survives
only in one source, and there without superius. As in 'Mittit ad Virginem',
Josquin works with paired voices, with the result that the *cantus firmus*
migrates continuously.

Group V consists of twelve motets in which the chant is paraphrased,
as in Groups III and IV, but not in canon or as a *migrans*.

The first motet in Group V has a double text and double *cantus firmus*:
'Alma Redemptoris Mater' and 'Ave Regina caelorum'. Josquin combines
here two of the great Marian antiphons (*tonus solemnior*)[34] that are sung from
the first Sunday of Advent to Wednesday of Holy Week. The antiphon
'Alma Redemptoris Mater' appears in the two outer voices, the 'Ave
Regina' in the two inner voices. Each antiphon consists of four phrases;
phrases *a* and *b* appear in the *prima pars* and phrases *c* and *d* in the *secunda pars*.
The use of imitation effects an almost continuous statement of both melodies.

The four-part 'Regina caeli' paraphrases the third of the great Marian
antiphons in its *tonus solemnior*.[35] It also illustrates the kind of paraphrase
technique in which the chant is not restricted to only one voice.[36] Josquin
has seldom impregnated his melody with chant as thoroughly as he does in
'Regina caeli', and because of imitation technique—also because the motet
has a structure like a ricercar—we are reminded over and over again of the
antiphon:

Ex. 12   mm. 70-80

[34] *Liber Usualis*, pp. 273 and 274, respectively.   [35] Ibid., p. 275.

[36] It is perhaps not superfluous to state the difference between this technique and that of
the migrant *cantus firmus*. In the latter case the chant melody wanders from one voice to
another in sectional chant passages, in which only one part carries the melody; in the present
case all voices, in general, simultaneously work out the chant motives in imitative counterpoint.

The four-voice motet 'Ave maris stella' is based on a hymn consisting of seven strophes.[37] Notwithstanding the hymn's metric form and the use of all seven strophes of the hymn, the motet is through-composed. To avoid monotony, Josquin varies and paraphrases the hymn melody so thoroughly that its strophic structure is all but obliterated, but he marks the beginning of each strophe by quoting the initial interval of a fifth, *ut-sol*, in all voices. Fragments of the hymn are found in all four voices, but they are not used in a manner that can be called migrant technique.

'Ave verum' is scored for two, then for three voices, 'Domine non secundum peccata nostra' for two, then for four voices. The 'Ave verum' chant, as mentioned above, is a trope with the structure of a sequence. Phrases a^1 and b^1 are first paraphrased in short sections scored for two voices, then the sections are repeated with a third voice added.

'Domine non secundum peccata nostra' is the only motet based on a tract melody.[38] The motet is introduced by the melismatic Gregorian *initium* 'Domine', following which the 'non secundum' is intoned polyphonically. An introductory *initium* like this is uncommon in Josquin's motets; the only other instance I know is in his 'Magnificat quarti toni'. In the *prima* and *secunda pars*, both scored for two voices, the chant appears in the upper voice, i.e., first in superius, then in tenor. In the *tertia* and *quarta pars* it appears in the tenor. Paraphrase is found mainly in the *secunda* and *quarta pars*.

The five motets based on antiphons for the feast of the Circumcision, 'O admirabile commercium', 'Quando natus es', 'Rubum quem viderat', 'Germinavit radix Jesse', and 'Ecce Maria genuit', all scored for four voices, form a cycle unique in the works of Josquin in that their liturgical function is clear.[39] Although the antiphons[40] are occasionally quoted in all four voices, they are paraphrased primarily in the tenor. The Circumcision antiphons survive in numerous medieval antiphonaries. One of the most

[37] *Liber Usualis*, p. 1259.   [38] Ibid., p. 527.
[39] See Edward E. Lowinsky, *The Medici Codex of 1518* (*Monuments of Renaissance Music*, iii–v; Chicago, 1968), iii, pp. 129–34.
[40] *Liber Usualis*, pp. 442–4.

striking variants is found in the *initium* of the first antiphon, 'O ˌ
commercium'. The antiphon begins thus in a number of sources:

Ex. 13   L.U., p. 442

and this version is used at Solesmes. In Josquin's motet we find another
version:

Ex. 14

This *initium* occurs in MS. 5 of the Chapter Library at Lucca, a manuscript
mentioned above in connection with the motet 'In illo tempore stetit
Jesus'.

The remaining two motets in Group V are 'Ave Maria... benedicta tu'
and 'Vultum tuum deprecabuntur', both scored for four voices. In 'Ave
Maria' Josquin paraphrases the antiphon of the same name,[41] but only its
opening phrase, though he retains its entire text. The antiphon text consists
of the archangel Gabriel's salutation to Mary; in the motet this is followed
by a commentary on the salutation.

The Marian motet 'Vultum tuum deprecabuntur' has seven *partes*. Its
text is a compilation of prayers in honour of the Holy Virgin. Because the
opening phrase of text in the *prima pars* is identical with that of the introit
'Vultum tuum deprecabuntur',[42] Josquin paraphrases the introit's melody
for that phrase (it is in the superius), but no further reference to the introit
is made.

In Group VI, containing fifteen motets, there is no common basis for
comparing the motets as far as treatment of a *cantus prius factus* is concerned.
In some motets the chant is elaborated completely, in others partially. Some
treat the chant as a *cantus firmus*, others as a canon or ostinato.

The first motet is Josquin's well-known 'Ave Maria... Virgo serena'
for four voices. The five strophes which form the chief part of the text are
preceded by two lines of the sequence 'Ave Maria'.[43] The sequence offers
Josquin an opportunity to quote the chant, and he does, in fact, quote the
opening, 'Ave Maria, gratia plena, Dominus tecum, Virgo serena' (mm.
1–31). Father Benoit-Castelli of Solesmes has shown in his article on the
motet that Josquin borrowed the sequence phrases a^1 and a^2 and added three
passing notes.[44] He identifies Josquin's bass as the voice stating the sequence.

[41] Ibid., p. 1679.   [42] Ibid., p. 1229.   [43] *Cantus selecti*, no. 128.
[44] G. Benoit-Castelli, 'L'"Ave Maria" de Josquin des Prez et la séquence "Ave Maria...
Virgo serena"', *Études Grégoriennes*, i (1954), pp. 187–94.

While there exist numerous versions of the sequence, there is a German version nearly identical with Josquin's opening points of imitation:

Ex. 15

It is harder to answer the question whether the repeated note instead of the leap of a fourth in phrase a^2 is an authentic reading, as Benoit-Castelli supposes, since the a^1 and a^2 phrases of a sequence rarely differ. An analogous problem exists in the motet 'Ave mundi spes', discussed above. Here too Josquin sets 'Ave' with a leap of a fourth, whereas in the sequence it is set to a repeated note, but in this case the phrases a^1 and a^2 are identical in both sequence and motet. Perhaps Josquin knew a version of this sequence using the initial leap of a fourth. It is just as likely, however, that Josquin introduced the leap of a fourth here, as he may have done in 'Ave Maria', in order to achieve better declamation for the 'Ave'.

Of the next three Marian motets, the six-voice 'O Virgo virginum' has its antiphon melody in the superius, the five-voice 'Nesciens Mater' in the tenor, and the four-voice 'Virgo prudentissima' also in the tenor. The antiphon 'O Virgo virginum'—one of the so-called 'O-antiphons'[45]—opens with the leap of a fourth in several sources. In Josquin's motet the *cantus firmus* opens with a minor third, and there is a version of the chant in MS. lat. 17296 (fol. 4) of the Bibliothèque Nationale in Paris that does likewise. This manuscript belonged to the Abbey of St. Denis, just north of Paris. Josquin presents the chant in long note values, first coloured, later paraphrased.

In the motets 'Nesciens Mater' and 'Virgo prudentissima' the antiphon melodies are less prominent.[46] They are clearly recognizable in some tenor passages but concealed in other voices by paraphrase and freely-composed inserts.

The four-voice motet 'O bone et dulcis Domine Jesu' is the only composition in which different Gregorian chants are presented simultaneously whose texts are unlike that of the motet. One of the more ornamented versions of the 'Pater noster' melody from the Ordinary of the Mass appears in the tenor, whereas two Marian antiphons are used as *cantus prius facti* in the bass. The 'Pater noster' melody has two embellished cadences (mm. 29–30, 47) and some other slight deviations from the version given by Peter Wagner.[47] The first part of the bass (mm. 1–49) quotes the antiphon 'Ave Maria'[48] (also used in Josquin's motet 'Virgo salutiferi'), which ends with the words

[45] Cf. *MGG*, i, col. 534.

[46] *Paléographie Musicale*, ix, p. 39, and *Liber Usualis*, p. 1600², respectively.

[47] See Peter Wagner, *Neumenkunde* (Leipzig, 1912), p. 425, and *Gregorianische Formenlehre* (Leipzig, 1921), p. 67.

[48] *Liber Usualis*, p. 1679.

'benedicta tu in mulieribus'. These words are then repeated, but with a different melody; Josquin has used the last words of the first antiphon as the *initium* of a second antiphon, 'Benedicta tu in mulieribus',[49] which is also cited completely (mm. 56–87). (This antiphon, too, can be found in another Josquin motet, 'Ave nobilissima creatura'.) It is clear that the composer did not simply wish to cite two Marian chants, but rather that he wanted to present the complete prayer 'Hail Mary'. This hypothesis is supported by the fact that at the end of the motet the bass states the word 'Jesus'. This word does not belong to the antiphon 'Benedicta tu', but was first added to the 'Hail Mary' in the fifteenth century.[50] At that time, the 'Hail Mary' is also found in combination with the 'Pater noster'.[51] Josquin has ingeniously used this pair of prayers as a double *cantus firmus* in his setting of a prayer to Christ. As to the elaboration of the two antiphons, the first is cited literally except for an embellished cadence in measures 29–30; the second has a few alterations in measures 75–6; the substitution of E for D in measure 75 was probably made for harmonic reasons; the reading E–F instead of F–E in the following measure may go back to another source of this melody, since the version printed in the *Antiphonale Sacrosanctae Romanae Ecclesiae* (Rome, 1912), p. 194, also has E–F.[52]

A unique composition structurally, and one of Josquin's most beautiful works, is his 'Salve Regina' scored for five voices. It is based on the fourth of the great Marian antiphons (*tonus solemnior*).[53] The chant's head motive: d'-c'-d'-g, is repeated twenty-four times as an ostinato by the *quinta vox*. Since the motive is quoted in long note values, a real *cantus firmus* is produced. I have described elsewhere how the composer has given this dominant part a double symbolic meaning.[54] Josquin not only derives his ostinato from the antiphon but also paraphrases the antiphon *in toto*. It appears most often in the superius, notably in passages where the chant reaches a melodic climax; at other times it migrates to another voice. A striking instance is found in the first measures of the *tertia pars*, where the words 'Et Jesum' are sung in slow-moving homophony. Here the passage of quoted chant contains the chant's lowest pitches, and Josquin gives the passage to the bass, a circumstance as appropriate as it is unusual (Ex. 16).

The sequence 'Inviolata' was also used twice by Josquin. We saw above in the five-voice motet that the chant was treated canonically; in the twelve-voice motet the chant migrates back and forth between discant, alto, and bass voices. The sequence melody ceases to behave like a *cantus firmus* in

---

[49] *Antiphonale Monasticum*, p. 193.
[50] See *Liturgisch Woordenboek*, ii (Roermond, 1965–8), col. 2903.   [51] Ibid.
[52] The text underlay in the *Werken* does not agree with that of the chant.
[53] *Liber Usualis*, p. 276.
[54] 'Das Symbol in der Musik von Josquin des Prez', *Acta Musicologica*, xli (1969), pp. 177–9.

Ex. 16   mm. 118-22

passages where the motet becomes full-voiced; at this point the first tenor enters with a new *cantus firmus*-like phrase, stating in *longae* the words 'O Maria flos virginum' (Ex. 17), so far unidentified.

Ex. 17

'Ave maris stella', scored for three, then for four voices, is totally different from Josquin's other setting of this hymn, a through-composed motet in which all seven strophes can be taken as 'variations on a theme'. Here we deal with an *alternatim* composition. Josquin began with Dufay's three-voice setting of the second strophe, 'Sumens illud ave', and added polyphonic settings for strophes 4, 6, and 7.[55] In these strophes he uses different techniques. The fourth strophe presents the paraphrased hymn melody as a canon at the octave for tenor and superius, the sixth strophe paraphrases the hymn in the superius. In the seventh strophe the hymn melody appears, coloured with a few added notes, simultaneously in superius and bass.

The four-voice 'Honor, decus, imperium' is probably also an *alternatim* composition. Here the superius states an embellished version of the hymn 'Nardi Maria pistici'.[56]

In the four-voice 'Christum ducem', Josquin quotes the opening lines of five different hymns. The motet text, a poem by Bonaventura, consists of five strophes, each ending with the first line of a hymn: 'Exsultet coelum

[55] Ludwig Finscher, in the workshop on the motets (see below, p. 646), questions the authenticity of strophes 6 and 7 not only on stylistic grounds, but also because Josquin's name is attached only to strophe 4, in contradistinction to the procedure used in the same manuscript to repeat the composer's name after an intervening anonymous strophe.

[56] *Monumenta Monodica Medii Aevi*, i, *Hymnen* (I), ed. Bruno Stäblein (Kassel, 1956), p. 443, melody 753.

laudibus', 'Jesu nostra redemptio', 'Aeterna Christi munera', 'Conditor [Creator] alme siderum', and 'Beata nobis gaudia'. In Josquin's motet the chant melodies of all five hymn lines appear in the superius of four-voiced passages, the final chord of which is marked by a fermata. The melodies of the first and third hymns in the motet are identical, as are the accompanying voices; in measures 26 and 88 an E is added.[57] The melody of the second hymn, 'Jesu nostra redemptio', is well known,[58] the only variant being an added E in measure 62. Of the two remaining hymns, 'Conditor alme siderum' and 'Beata nobis gaudia', the first has variant notes, the last is quoted unaltered.[59]

The 'Magnificat tertii toni' and the 'Magnificat quarti toni' are scored for four voices. They are designed for *alternatim* performance. The psalm tones serve in most of the verses as a real *cantus firmus*, sometimes migrating (even within one verse), sometimes coloured and paraphrased.[60]

In the four-voice 'Planxit autem David' Josquin quotes the Gregorian reciting tone for Jeremiah's Lamentations[61] three times as a 'Leitmotiv' in the manner of a *cantus firmus* (in mm. 55, 246, and 312). Possibly the textual similarity between these verses and the first verse of Jeremiah's lamentation, 'Aleph. Quomodo sedet sola', inspired the quotations. Josquin's *cantus firmi* are not identical because he paraphrases the Gregorian reciting tone in a different way each time. Because of their long note values, these three quotations stand out from the other voices, which—at the same time—are melodically influenced by them.

The two last motets of Group VI are 'Liber generationis' and 'Factum est autem'. Both motets deal with the genealogy of Christ, as recorded by St. Matthew and St. Luke, respectively. The *cantus firmi* of these motets

[57] Ibid., p. 100, melody 1142; see also Benjamin Rajeczky, *Melodiarium Hungariae Medii Aevi* (Budapest, 1956), p. 9.

[58] *Processionale monasticum* (Solesmes, 1893), p. 95. The melody may also be found in the *Liber Usualis*, with different texts; see pp. 844, 846, 852, 1590.

[59] *Monumenta Monodica Medii Aevi*, i, p. 255, melody 23, and p. 421, melody 4; the melody of 'Beata nobis gaudia' may be found in *Liber Usualis*, p. 866, with the text 'Jam Christus astra'. 'Christum ducem' was printed in the *Motetti de Passione* (1503) as the *sexta pars* of the cycle 'Qui velatus facie fuisti', but there is some question whether the motet was originally conceived as part of this cycle; see Osthoff, *Josquin Desprez*, ii, p. 30. Hymn lines (some with quotation of the chant) are also interpolated in other *partes* of 'Qui velatus'; the most striking similarity is the appearance of measures 122-9 of 'Christum ducem' as measures 304-11 of the *quarta pars* of 'Qui velatus'—to different texts, however.

[60] For a more detailed study on these motets see Helmuth Osthoff, 'Das Magnificat bei Josquin Desprez', *Archiv für Musikwissenschaft*, xvi (1959), pp. 220-31; R. Lagas, 'Het Magnificat IV toni van Josquin des Prez', *Tijdschrift van de Vereniging voor Nederlandse Muziekgeschiedenis*, xx (1964-5), pp. 20-36; Chris Maas, 'Josquin–Agricola–Brumel–De la Rue. Een authenticiteitsprobleem', *Tijdschrift van de Vereniging voor Nederlandse Muziekgeschiedenis*, xx (1966), pp. 120-39.

[61] *Liber Usualis*, p. 631.

appear in the tenor. It is hard to say to what extent Josquin is quoting the ornamented psalm tones literally. The genealogies were sung in all French churches in Josquin's time, but the melodies differed from church to church, and the ornateness of the melody varied with the degree of solemnity proper to the feast.[62] Although Solesmes has numerous versions of these genealogies, there is not a single one that resembles closely Josquin's tenor parts.[63]

The study of Josquin's use of plainchant and of his selection of the particular versions he worked with is of recent origin. The chants used most often by Josquin are antiphons and sequences. Eighteen different antiphons are found in his antiphon motets, including the four great Marian antiphons. He uses the antiphon 'Ave Maria' three times and the antiphons 'Benedicta tu', 'Alma Redemptoris Mater', and 'Salve Regina' twice. The number of sequences quoted completely or partially adds up to nine, two of them, 'Inviolata' and 'Victimae paschali laudes', being used twice.

The present paper is only a preliminary step in the investigation of structure and musical significance of Josquin's motets, a repertory unequalled for its power and originality in the history of music.

[62] Cf. J. Mattfeld, '*Cantus firmus*', p. 75, n. 1.

[63] Some of these versions come closer to Josquin's melodies than do the versions given by Smijers in the Aanhangsel to Motetten, Bundel v, but the difference remains too great to reach any valid conclusions.

V Individual Works

'Illibata Dei Virgo': A Melodic Self-Portrait of Josquin des Prez

MYROSLAW ANTONOWYCZ

In speaking about self-portraiture in music of the fifteenth and sixteenth centuries, one ventures into the field of metaphor, and enters a realm in which conjecture plays an important role. Still, we have taken this risky road in the hope of making a contribution, be it ever so small, to the understanding of the phenomenon of Josquin des Prez.

The motet 'Illibata Dei Virgo nutrix'[1] has attracted scholars' interest for a long time, chiefly because the text of the motet contains an acrostic. Students of Josquin have used this acrostic not only to derive from it the correct spelling of the composer's name, but also the place of his birth.[2]

Willem Elders reached the conclusion that the name of the composer, beyond the acrostic, is also expressed in its *cantus firmus*, from which it can be retrieved with the aid of numerical symbolism.[3] When the letters of the Latin alphabet are replaced by the corresponding numbers (A equals 1, B equals 2, C equals 3, etc.), one obtains from the name DES PREZ the cipher 88, as follows:

$$D \quad E \quad S \quad \quad P \quad R \quad E \quad Z$$
$$4+5+18+15+17+5+24 = 88$$

The *cantus firmus* of the motet 'Illibata Dei Virgo' has exactly 88 notes.

In an analogous way, the name JOSQUIN can be obtained from the first part of the motet: JOSQUIN = 99; there are nine *cantus firmus* notes in the first part, each ostinato pattern takes up nine breves, and the whole *prima pars* consists of $9 \times 9 = 81$ breves.

---

[1] *Werken*, Motetten, Bundel v, no. 27.

[2] See Albert Smijers, 'Een kleine bijdrage over Josquin en Isaac', *Gedenkboek aangeboden aan Dr. D. F. Scheurleer* (The Hague, 1925), pp. 313–19; Charles van den Borren, 'Une hypothèse concernant le lieu de naissance de Josquin des Prez', *Festschrift Joseph Schmidt-Görg zum 60. Geburtstag* (Bonn, 1957), pp. 21–5; and Caldwell Titcomb, 'The Josquin Acrostic Re-examined', *Journal of the American Musicological Society*, xvi (1963), pp. 47–60.

[3] Willem Elders, 'Josquin des Prez en zijn Motet *Illibata Dei virgo*', *Mens en Melodie*, xxv (1970), pp. 141–4.

In all of this, we must not lose sight of 'Illibata Dei Virgo' as a work of art. In subjecting it to melodic analysis, we are struck by the strong kinship of this work with a number of other works by Josquin. Many melodic phrases from the 'Illibata' motet, especially from its first part, can be recognized in other works of the composer, either unchanged or paraphrased.

The motet opens with two voices in imitation:

Ex. 1   mm. 1-6

The duo is repeated in measures 7–12 by another pair of voices, so that its motive occurs four times in the motet. A melodic variant of it appears in several works of Josquin, especially in the 'Missa Faisant regretz' and in the 'Missa Di dadi'. In the *Kyrie* of the 'Missa Faisant regretz'[4] it appears in the bass:

4 Missen, xiii, p. 33.

Ex. 2   mm. 8-13 (bass)

In the *Pleni sunt*[5] we meet several melodic imitations:

Ex. 3   mm. 24-31

In the *Gloria* of the 'Missa Di dadi'[6] the melody appears in these forms:

At the end of the *Agnus Dei*[7] the following fragment emerges:

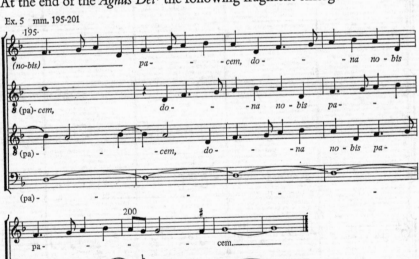

Further examples may be found in the *Kyrie* of the 'Missa L'homme armé super voces musicales':[8]

Ex. 6　mm. 23-5
(superius)　　　　　　　25

e - le-　　　- i - son,_____

mm. 64-6
(superius and alto)　65

Ky-　　-ri - e e-　　　- le-(ison)

Ky-　　　-ri - e_____

In sum, we deal with a phrase that is characteristic for Josquin, especially for a specific period of his creativity, which we shall presently define.

After the extended two-part opening of 'Illibata Dei Virgo', a five-part section ensues, beginning with the following motive:

Ex. 7　mm. 17-21
20

so - la pa - rens　Ver - bi

So - la pa - rens　Ver - -bi　pu - er-(pera)

La_____

ge-　　-ni - trix,　　So - la pa - rens

ge-　　-ni - trix,　So - la pa - rens Ver-(bi)

It is not difficult to recognize here a chief motive of Josquin's 'Missa Faisant regretz', occurring mainly as ostinato in the tenor voice, but also in other parts; see, for example, the beginning of the *Agnus Dei*:[9]

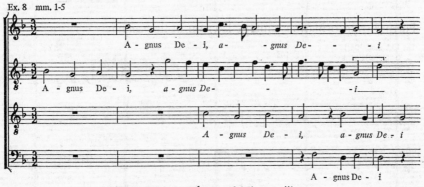

Ex. 8　mm. 1-5

A - gnus De - i, a-　　- gnus De -　　- i

A - gnus De - i,　a - gnus De-　　　- i_____

A - gnus　De - i,　a - gnus De - i

A - gnus De - i

[8] Missen, i, pp. 2 and 3.　　[9] Missen, xiii, p. 52.

After this five-part section of 'Illibata' a duo section with an extensive sequence follows:

Ex. 9   mm. 31-7
(superius and first contratenor)

This sequential melody returns in an abridged, but rhythmically altered, form in the 'Missa Faisant regretz' in the superius of the *Kyrie*:[10]

Ex. 10   mm. 35-41

Variations of it occur in the *Kyrie* of the 'Missa Di dadi':

Ex. 11   mm. 36-40
(superius)

and in the *Gloria* of the same Mass:[11]

Ex. 12   mm. 94-7
(alto)

Further transformations emerge later on in the *Gloria*:

Ex. 13   mm. 104-17
(superius)

[10] Ibid., p. 34.   [11] Missen, xv, pp. 94 and 98.

A similar sequence, but now in three parts, occurs in the 'Missa L'homme armé super voces musicales':[12]

Ex. 14 *Sanctus*, mm. 18-22

About halfway through the *prima pars* the motet contains this phrase, which can also be found in the 'Missa Di dadi':[13]

Ex. 15 'Illibata Dei Virgò' mm. 52-6

[12] Missen, i, pp. 20–21.   [13] Missen, xv, p. 110.

Ex. 16   'Missa Di dadi' *Credo*, mm. 185-91

One motive toward the end of the first part of the 'Illibata' motet recalls a segment of the 'L'homme armé' tune in the version Josquin used in his 'Missa L'homme armé super voces musicales':

Ex. 17a   L'homme armé

Ex. 17b '*Illibata Dei Virgo*' mm. 65-8

In the *Gloria* of the 'Missa La sol fa re mi' the same melodic phrase occurs a number of times, especially in measures 80–90:[14]

Ex. 18 mm. 80-8

Josquin seems to have adopted part of the popular 'L'homme armé' melody and used it on occasion as his own.

The succeeding phrase of the motet offers a new melody, set for three imitating voices:

[14] Missen, ii, pp. 39–40.

Ex. 19   mm. 68-70

The same melodic phrase occurs in the *cantus firmus* of the 'Missa Hercules Dux Ferrariae':

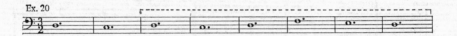

Ex. 20

Finally, the first part of the motet closes with a melody in the bass that is reminiscent of the head motive of the motet 'Memor esto':[15]

Ex. 21   'Illibata Dei Virgo' mm. 79-81

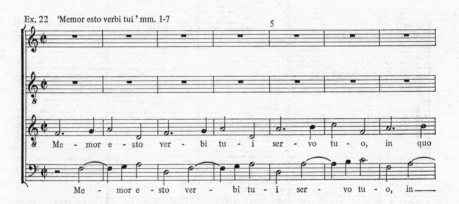

Ex. 22   'Memor esto verbi tui' mm. 1-7

The foregoing examples allow the following conclusions:

---

[15] Motetten, Bundel vi, no. 31.

(1) Various melodic turns and phrases that occupy a prominent position in the motet 'Illibata', whether as a head motive or a theme developed contrapuntally, also have an important place in other works by Josquin.

(2) The works melodically related to the motet 'Illibata' belong to the group generally attributed to Josquin's earlier period.

(3) The term 'earlier period' is to be taken in a relative sense; the style of the motet 'Illibata' covers a long period of Josquin's creative life.

Can these conclusions be validated from the viewpoints of style, *cantus firmus*, and counterpoint?

The motet 'Illibata' offers both wide-spanned melodic lines,[16] strongly differentiated rhythmically, and short, well profiled melodic phrases representing more or less two different phases in the development of Josquin's music. The contrasting melodic types are especially evident in the frequent two-voice passages of the motet.

In the first part of the motet we find long-spanned duos which, as Professor Osthoff rightly observes, are reminiscent of the late Burgundian style.[17] In these extended two-voice passages, use is made first of exact imitation (mm. 1–6 and 6–12), then of free counterpoint (mm. 12–18). In the second two-part section (mm. 28–46) Josquin applies elements of both imitation and free counterpoint, with frequent sequences in the melody (compare Exx. 1 and 9).

The rich and varied use of conservative techniques in melody and counterpoint, in a sudden change of character, is followed by short, sharply drawn melodic phrases holding a lively dialogue in imitation between higher and lower voices:

Ex. 23   mm. 57-65

16 [See Walter Wiora, above, pp. 309–16.—Ed.]
17 Helmuth Osthoff, *Josquin Desprez* (Tutzing, 1962–5), ii, p. 78.

The *secunda pars* opens with a new form of part-writing: short duos are answered in three- and four-part sections, pointing ahead to the dawn of double-choir writing:

Ex. 24   mm. 83-96

The *cantus firmus* of 'Illibata Dei Virgo', although not related melodically to the *cantus firmus* in any other work of Josquin, shows a connection with other works in its conception, form, and use. Characteristic is the construction of the *cantus firmus* melody from the solmization syllables *la mi la*. Josquin used similar techniques in the 'Missa Hercules Dux Ferrariae' and in the 'Missa La sol fa re mi'. These three works show a clear relationship, even though the *cantus firmus* melodies of the first two works and the theme of the last one greatly differ from each other.

The *cantus firmus* of the motet is repeated in the tenor on two different degrees (D–A–D, G–D–G). Ostinato-like treatment of the *cantus firmus* occurs in numerous works of Josquin, but most characteristically in the Masses 'La sol fa re mi', 'Faisant regretz', and 'Hercules Dux Ferrariae'—in short, in the same works that show the greatest likeness in melodic substance. One gains the impression that the composer was experimenting in these works to see what artistic results ostinato technique might yield. Ostinato returns in later works, but by then it is transformed from a compositional device to an expressive means, as in the motet 'Miserere mei, Deus'.

The relation between the *cantus firmus* melody and the other voices of 'Illibata Dei Virgo' changes in the course of the work. In the *prima pars* of the motet, the *cantus firmus* melody is set in large rhythmic values, and in this respect distinguishes itself clearly from other contrapuntal voices. In the *secunda pars* the proportional diminution of the rhythmic values of the *cantus firmus* causes the tenor to become more equivalent to the contrapuntal voices, losing thereby its isolated position.

We witness a process of melodic equalization. This process is occasionally underscored by the use in other voices of the interval of a fourth, prominent in the *cantus firmus* (mm. 132–6, where *la mi la* appears in the text of the other voices) and by occasional leaps of fourths (superius, mm. 158–9, bass, mm. 160–1, 172–3, 179–80, 184–5) and by diatonically filled-in motives outlining a fourth (mm. 61–70, 78–81).

Thus, the *cantus firmus* of the motet 'Illibata' shows a traditional treatment in its first part and the onset of newer techniques in its second part.

The question is: are these resemblances to other works in melody, in *cantus firmus*, and in contrapuntal technique a product of chance, or have they been deliberately incorporated by Josquin? In connection with this question, the chronological position of this work is crucial.

Are we to assume with Professor Osthoff that the motet 'Illibata' belongs to Josquin's earlier works?[18] In that case, it precedes the Masses 'Di dadi', 'Faisant regretz', 'Hercules', and 'La sol fa re mi', with each of which it shares remarkable similarities. I cannot imagine that Josquin, in writing those later and larger works, is quoting consciously from this small motet 'Illibata'. He would hardly say to himself each time: 'Here I am quoting

18 Ibid.

from that old motet of mine'. But if those quotations are accidental, how does one explain the fact that this one motet is such a source of quotations?

Or is 'Illibata Dei Virgo' one of the later works of that period? In that case it was written at the same time as, or later than, the works mentioned above. Now it is very hard to suppose that Josquin would be quoting by accident in writing this motet. It would point to a very limited musical imagination, and as far as we know lack of musical invention was not one of Josquin's shortcomings.

I personally do not believe that the motet 'Illibata' is one of the earliest works or that the similarity with various other works occurs by accident. In this composition, in which Josquin's name is hidden by an acrostic in the text and by numbers of the *cantus firmus*, Josquin has deliberately brought together many elements from other works in order to give us a survey of his melodic, *cantus-firmus*, and contrapuntal techniques. This work may be taken as an exhibition, a display of his style.

Certainly in this sense it is a musical self-portrait by Josquin; in each stroke of the melody and in the tonal colour of each chord we recognize the rich creativity of this mind that belongs among the greatest of the great in the cultural history of Europe.

Editor's Note

With Professor Antonowycz's consent, and with the authors' permission, I am adding the English rendering of 'Illibata Dei Virgo' that keeps the acrostic intact. Professors William S. Heckscher and Virginia W. Callahan are responsible for the *prima pars*, Professor Callahan alone for the *secunda pars*. I wish to thank them both for their kindness in making their ingenious translation available to a wider public and to Professor Antonowycz for allowing me to put it at the most logical place in these Proceedings.

I ncomparable Virgin, nurse of God,
O thou Mother of the Olympian King,
S ole parent and conceiver of the Word,
Q uickening Redeemer thou wast of EVA's Fall,
V ouchsafing Mediator of man's sin,
I n radiant light the Scriptures this reveal.
N urturing womb—child of your Child—
DES ign thou that the joyous melody, the Muses'
P aean, shall prevail and be an AVE,
R everberating sounds wherewith our throats
E ntreat thee and, with pure praise and
Z ealous art, proclaim thee our AVE.

A VE of virgins, adornment of men,
C elestial portal,
A VE of lilies (flower of the humble),
V irgin of beauty,
V ALE now, thou wholly fair as the Moon,
E lect as the Sun, O brightest, rejoice.
S ALVE to thee, thou only beloved,
C omfort those singing, Maria, in thy praise.
A VE Maria, mother of Virtues,
V ein of forgiveness, AVE Maria,
G race-imbued, the Lord is with thee,
A VE Maria, mother of Virtues.
      Amen.

'Ut Phoebi radiis': The Riddle of the Text Resolved*

VIRGINIA WOODS CALLAHAN

The Latin text:

Ut Phoebi radiis soror obvia sidera luna,
Ut reges Salomon sapientis nomine cunctos,
Ut remi pontum quaerentum velleris aurum,
Ut remi faber instar habens super aera pennas,
Ut remi fas solvaces traducere merces,
Ut remi fas sola Petri currere prora,
Sic super omne quod est regnas, o Virgo Maria.

Latius in numerum canit id quoque coelica turba,
Lasso lege ferens aeterna munera mundo
La sol fa ta mi na clara praelustris in umbra,
La sol fa mi ta na de matre recentior ortus,
La sol fa mi re ta quidem na non violata,
La sol fa mi re ut rore ta na Gedeon quo,
Rex o Christe Jesu, nostri Deus alte memento.

English version:

As the Moon, sister of Phoebus, rules with her rays the stars in her path,
As Solomon rules all kings in the name of the wise,
As the oars of those in quest of the Golden Fleece rule the sea,
As the artificer [Daedalus], having wings instead of an oar, rules the upper air,
As it is the task of the oar to convey perishable wares,
As it is the destiny of the oar of Peter to navigate by means of one Ship,
So thou, O Virgin Mary, rulest over all that is.

Everywhere the heavenly host in verse sings this also,
Bringing gifts to a tired world according to Law Eternal:

* The development of my commentary on this motet has been made possible by the generous assistance of William S. Heckscher, the helpful suggestions of Warren Kirkendale, and the patient persistence of Edward E. Lowinsky.

A radiant blossom[Jesus Christ] in shelter [Mary's womb] quickened bright,
A blossom born within memory from a Mother, from moistened fleece,
A blossom, Thou, from fleece truly without blemish,
A blossom, Thou, from fleece (penetrated) like Gideon's by the dew [the
    Holy Spirit].
O Christ Jesus, King, God on high, remember us.

Commentary:

The text of this motet is a charming illustration of the virtuosity of the
Renaissance lyricist. The similes employed in Part One to extol the Virgin
Mary as the Queen of all creation are drawn in quick succession from
classical and biblical sources. The pre-eminence among the stars of Apollo's
sister, the goddess of the Moon, is an echo of a fragment of Sappho.[1]
Solomon's superiority in wisdom to all other rulers is a paraphrase of the
Lord's promise to that king that no one should be his equal.[2] Jason, the
captain of the Argonauts, who secured the Golden Fleece by sailing to
distant Colchis, was the Greek hero *par excellence*.[3] The reference to Daedalus, whose craftsmanship allowed him to fly by the 'oarage of his wings',
is a Virgilian reminiscence.[4] The Church as the bark of Peter, which alone
insures the salvation of its fragile cargo, the souls of men, was among the
earliest Christian symbols.[5]

For the second line in Part Two, 'Bringing gifts to a tired world according
to Law Eternal', Warren Kirkendale (in private correspondence) has
proposed a highly interesting hypothesis. Plato in the *Laws* (653 C-D)
writes:

So the gods, in pity for the human race born to toil, have ordained as respite for
our labour the alternation of feasts celebrated in their honour. As companions in
these festivities they have granted the muses, Apollo Musagetes, and Dionysos....

---

[1] Sappho fr. 3. in J. M. Edmonds, *Lyra Graeca*, i, p. 188 (Loeb Classical Library; London,
1922): 'Around the fair Moon the bright beauty of the stars is lost when her silver light
illuminates the earth.'

[2] Cf. I Kings 3:12: 'Behold I have given you a wise and discerning heart, so that none
like you has been before you and none like you shall arise after you.'

[3] The exploits of Jason and his crew are narrated at length in the Hellenistic epic *The
Argonautica* by Apollonius of Rhodes.

[4] Cf. Virgil *Aeneid* Bk. VI. 14 ff. Daedalus having entrusted himself to the sky 'on swift
wings' (*praepetibus pinnis*), arrives safely in Cumae where he dedicates to Phoebus Apollo
the 'oarage' of those wings (*remigium alarum*). The phrase became proverbial and reappeared
among the *Adages* of Erasmus as *Daedaleum remigium*; see *Desiderii Erasmi Opera omnia*, ii
(Leyden, 1703), col. 1185E.

[5] For early references to the ship as the symbol of the Church, see the extended nautical
metaphor in *The Apostolic Constitutions*, Bk. II, Ch. LVII; Tertullian's 'navicula illa figuram
Ecclesiae', *On Baptism* XII. 6–7, *P.L.* I. 1214; Clement of Alexandria's 'Let our seals be
a dove, or a fish, or a ship flying before the wind', *Paedagogus* Bk. III, Ch. XI, *P.G.* VIII. 633.

But to us men the gods, of whom we have spoken, who were given to celebrate with us, have granted the pleasurable sensation of rhythm and harmony, with which we move and lead our chorus, linked together in song and dance.

Kirkendale suggests that the poet of 'Ut Phoebi radiis', aware of Plato's myth on the origin of the arts, cleverly points to this passage in the *Laws* with the words 'by Law Eternal'.[6]

The 'gifts' heralded here by the heavenly choir are Christ and his Virgin Mother, Mary being likened to the fleece of Gideon, with which that Old Testament hero twice tested and proved the power of the Lord.[7] To discover and to bring to mind prefigurations of Mary's perpetual virginity was one of the delights of the theologians and artists of the Middle Ages.[8] William S. Heckscher, in an iconological study of the myth of Danae,[9] has indicated that the source of inspiration for the later use of such pendants to the Annunciation story would have been not the Old Testament or the classical texts themselves, but a book of prefigurations such as the *Defensorium inviolatae virginitatis beatae Mariae* composed at the end of the fourteenth century by the Dominican Franciscus de Retza.[10] On folio 4 of the block-book edition of that work Gideon is depicted in full armour, kneeling before an extended white fleece, while a winged figure gazes down from heaven. Below the picture is written:

> Psalmista—Descendet sicut pluvia in vellus
> Et sicut stillicidia stillantia super terram.[11]
> (He shall come down like rain upon the mown grass:
> as showers that water the earth.)

[6] For the use of Plato's myth in the sixteenth and seventeenth centuries, see Kirkendale's recently published work, *L'Aria di Fiorenza* (Florence, 1972), pp. 44–5. On the use of well-known concepts in the games of the Renaissance, Kirkendale cites Innocenzio Ringhieri, *Cento giuochi liberali, et d'ingegno* (Bologna, 1551), fols. 143–144ᵛ.

[7] Cf. Judges 6: 36–40. Gideon was seeking assurance that it was God's intention to use him as the instrument of Israel's deliverance from the enemy. His fleece (*vellus lanae*) was first moistened by dew from on high, and in the second test was not penetrated by the earthly dew.

[8] For a general discussion of the miraculous proofs (including the *vellus Gedeonis*) of Mary's virginity, see Friedrich Zoepfl's article, 'Defensorium', in *Reallexicon zur deutschen Kunstgeschichte*, iii (1954), cols. 1206–18. Louis Réau, in his *Iconographie de l'art Chrétien*, ii (Paris, 1956), pp. 231–3, gives an extensive list of the literary and artistic usages of the *Miracle de la Toison* as a symbol of Mary's virginal maternity from the thirteenth century on.

[9] 'Recorded from Dark Recollection', *De artibus opuscula XL: Essays in Honor of Erwin Panofsky*, ed. Millard Meiss (New York, 1961), i, pp. 187–200.

[10] An alternate title of De Retza's work is *De generatione Christi*; a facsimile edition of the block-book version of 1470 was published by Kurt Pfister (Leipzig, 1925).

[11] This is Psalm 71:6 (= Psalm 72 in the King James version). The same verse occurs with similar intent in another of Josquin's motets, 'O admirabile commercium'; cf. Edward E. Lowinsky, *The Medici Codex of 1518*, iii (Monuments of Renaissance Music, iii–v;

An intriguing aspect of 'Ut Phoebi radiis' is the use of solmization puns, in which the syllables *ut, ut re, ut re mi*, etc., are included as part of the text to produce what Gustave Reese has called 'meaningful Latin'.[12] In Part One the solmization is straightforward and there is no problem in translation, but in Part Two, where the order of the solmization syllables is reversed, the meaning does not become clear until each line of solmization and enigmatic syllables is written backwards: *La sol fa ta mi na* thus reads *Animata flos*, '*la*' always becoming part of the next line. The text then reads:

> Animata flos clara praelustris in umbra,
> A lana tima[13] flos de matre recentior ortus,
> A lana te rima flos quidem non violata,
> A lana te rima flos ut rore Gedeon quo.

Chicago, 1968), p. 129. The application of this same biblical reference to Danae in the fourteenth-century *Ovide moralisé* (line 5581), and in Pierre Bersuire's *Repertorium* article 'Pluvia' is noted by Heckscher, 'Recorded from Dark Recollection', p. 197.

[12] Gustave Reese, *Music in the Renaissance* (New York, 1959), p. 256.

[13] For the puzzling *tima* I have resorted, unhappily, to the Procrustean measure of translating it as 'moistened' (*tincta*).

Some Remarks on the 'Missa La sol fa re mi'

JAMES HAAR

The Origin of the Ostinato

One of the best-known anecdotes about Josquin is Glareanus' story of the origin of this Mass, which may be translated as follows:

Josquin, when he asked a favour of some influential person whose name I don't know, and this procrastinator repeatedly answered, in that broken tongue of the French, 'Laise faire moy', that is, 'leave it to me', then without delay wrote a whole Mass, an exceedingly elegant work, based on these same words, thus: La sol fa re mi.[1]

Glareanus having neither dated this anecdote nor given the name of the 'magnate', there has been much speculation about both. The discovery of an anonymous *barzelletta* with the refrain 'Lassa far[e] a mi', printed in several late fifteenth-century *opuscoli*,[2] has given a possible Italian source for Josquin's subject, one corresponding more closely to the solmization syllables used by the composer and chosen by Petrucci for a title when the Mass was published in 1502. In one print the *barzelletta* follows immediately upon a poem by Serafino Aquilano, and although this is no evidence for Serafino's having written 'Lassa far a mi' the poem has often been attributed to him.[3] Serafino, like Josquin, is known to have been in the service of

---

[1] *Dodekachordon* (Basel, 1547), p. 440: 'Idem Iodocus, cum ab nescio quo Magnate beneficium ambiret, ac ille procrastinator identidem diceret mutila illa Francorum lingua, Laise faire moy, hoc est, sine me facere, haud cunctanter ad eadem verba totam composuit Missam oppidò elegantem La sol fa re mi.'

[2] See Mario Menghini, ed., *Le rime di Serafino de' Ciminelli dall' Aquila* (Bologna, 1894), pp. xiv-xvi, for a list and discussion of these prints. The poem is also found in *No expetto giamai: con molte altre canzone*... (Venice: Francesco Bindoni, 1524); see Emilio Picot, 'La raccolta di poemetti italiani della biblioteca di Chantilly', *Rassegna bibliografica della letteratura italiana*, ii (1894), pp. 157-8.

[3] Menghini, *Le rime di Serafino*, says (p. xiv) that there is no proof for 'Lassa far a mi' having been written by Serafino; earlier he says that in ascribing poems to Serafino he has proceeded very warily, 'co' piè di piombo'; at a later point, however (pp. 35-6), Menghini discusses the *barzelletta* as if it could indeed be the work of Serafino. Serafino did make use elsewhere of word-play on solmization syllables. The sonnet 'La vita ormai resolvi e mi

Cardinal Ascanio Sforza, a service that has been said to have been neither altogether agreeable nor highly remunerative; and among Serafino's occasional poems is a sonnet addressed to Josquin, in which the composer is urged to think, despite his poverty, of his true worth, not of the tawdry trappings with which lesser men are undeservingly clothed.[4]

These bits and pieces have been fitted together to form a convincing enough picture: Josquin's requests for money or advancement from his patron Ascanio Sforza were answered by empty promises; he made his plight known to his friend Serafino, who wrote a poem with the Cardinal's words as refrain, while Josquin was busy writing his Mass.[5] All this is thought to have taken place during the period when Josquin, Serafino, and their patron Ascanio were in Rome, at the papal court, that is between 1490 and 1493.

Though this picture is a neat one, there is no solid proof for any part of it, and it may be formed from pieces that belong to entirely different puzzles.[6] Some of its inconsistencies and improbabilities were pointed out over thirty years ago by Fausto Torrefranca, who constructed a new hypothesis,

---

fa degno', contained in a number of printed collections of Serafino's verse, is full of these syllables; every line in fact begins with one. In one edition (Rome, Besicken, 1503, lacking title page) the sonnet is printed with the following remark: 'Artificioso sopra la musica, dove più volte è inserto Ut, Re, Mi, Fa, Sol, La. Alla Nostra Donna.' The sonnet may be found on p. 140 of Menghini's edition and in this volume, p. 57.

In a letter from one Filippo, 'Commendatorio del Monastero di S. Bassiano', to Giacomo D'Adria, dated 3 June 1495, there is a request for 'Quello artificioso sonetto del nostro Seraphino. Dico quello che comprhende [sic] tutta la musica....' This may be the sonnet just referred to; see Claudio Gallico, *Un libro di poesie per musica all'epoca d'Isabella d'Este* (Mantua, 1961), pp. 42–3.

[4] This sonnet has frequently been reprinted in scholarly literature on Josquin. See, for example, Helmuth Osthoff, *Josquin Desprez* (Tutzing, 1962–5), i, pp. 34–5. On Serafino's relationship to Ascanio Sforza, see Vincentio Calmeta, *Vita del facondo poeta vulgare Seraphino Aquilano*, in Menghini, *Le rime*, p. 2. Calmeta says (p. 7) that at a later point Serafino rejoined the Cardinal's services on altogether better terms.

[5] See Walter H. Rubsamen, *Literary Sources of Secular Music in Italy (ca. 1500)* (Berkeley and Los Angeles, 1943), p. 13: 'Perhaps the story [of Glareanus] is true, but there is reason to believe that the theme of Josquin's mass was the result of an inspiration from another source, the popular *barzelletta* beginning: *Lassa far a mi....* To speculate further and thus link both hypotheses, it is entirely possible that Serafino himself became aware of his friend Josquin's plight and wrote the *barzelletta* as a literary barb aimed at Ascanio'.

[6] For instance, the often-repeated accounts of Serafino's relationship to Ascanio Sforza may not be altogether true. Professor Edward Lowinsky has discovered a letter showing that in 1490 Serafino had already left the Cardinal's service and, presumably, Rome; see p. 52 in this volume. The legend of Ascanio's stinginess toward his retainers may also be greatly exaggerated; see Edward E. Lowinsky, 'Josquin des Prez and Ascanio Sforza', *Atti del Congresso Internazionale sul Duomo di Milano*, ed. M. L. Gatti Perer, ii (Milan, 1969), p. 21, and above, p. 42.

according to which both Josquin and the author of the *barzelletta* made use of a popular villotistic refrain.[7] For Torrefranca, the story told by Glareanus was a late invention, made up long after the true origin of Josquin's ostinato had been forgotten.

Although Glareanus, whose admiration for the work of Josquin is well known, seems not to have been personally acquainted with the composer, there is no reason to dismiss his story as sheer fancy. He could have heard it on his Italian trip of 1515, during which he spent some time in Milan, or in the next few years during his stay in Paris—both in Josquin's lifetime and years before the writing of the *Dodekachordon*.[8] Whether the 'magnate' was French, or of some other nationality, and whether he spoke to Josquin in his native language, cannot be determined.[9]

Some oddities about this story remain, no matter how one tries to interpret it. Yet this does not mean it was entirely false. A bit of evidence that may confirm Glareanus' account is provided by what appears to be the oldest manuscript copy of the Mass, that in Codex 41 of the Sistine Chapel manuscripts. A choirbook thought to have been compiled in the last decade of the fifteenth century,[10] Codex 41 is an assemblage of pieces written in different hands on different paper.[11] Here only the section containing the 'Missa La sol fa re mi' is of concern.

---

[7] *Il Segreto del Quattrocento* (Milan, 1939), pp. 62–8.

[8] See Hans Albrecht, art. 'Glareanus', *MGG*, v, col. 216; Clement A. Miller, 'The *Dodekachordon*: Its Origins and Influence on Renaissance Musical Thought', *Musica Disciplina*, xv (1961), pp. 158, 162. In the *Dodekachordon* (p. 91), Glareanus mentions having been in Milan at a time when Gafori was still there.

[9] At the time of the Josquin Festival-Conference, I interpreted Glareanus' words, 'mutila illa Francorum lingua', to mean that the magnate spoke poor French. Since then my attention has been drawn to a passage in Glareanus' treatise that highlights the Swiss humanist's low opinion of the French language. In speaking about Josquin's well-known chanson 'Guillaume s'en va', with the *vox regis* (*Dodekachordon*, p. 468), he says: 'The text was in the Romance tongue, in that imperfect language that France now, having given up the old tongue of the Gauls, stutters rather than speaks' ('Verba erant linguae Romanae, illius mutilae, qua nunc, derelicta uetere Gallorum lingua Gallia balbutit uerius quam loquitur'). This proves that the above-quoted words have to be rendered as 'in that broken tongue of the French'.

[10] See Heinrich Besseler, art. 'Chorbuch', *MGG*, ii, col. 1346: 'Die Musikbestände der Cappella Sistina beginnen erst kurz vor 1500....Nur 6 dieser Papier-Chorbücher, im Grossfolioformat von durchschnittlich 55 × 42 cm, gehören dem Ausgang des 15. Jh. an.' Among these six is Codex 41.

The paper on which the 'Missa La sol fa re mi' was written has a watermark, a siren within a circle, found on paper in Rome and Naples in the closing years of the fifteenth century (see C. M. Briquet, *Les Filigranes*, 4 vols. (Geneva, 1907), nos. 13880–13884).

[11] For a general description of Codex 41, see J. M. Llorens, *Capellae Sixtinae Codices musicis notis instructi* (Vatican City, 1960), pp. 81–2. The watermarks in various sections of the manuscript are quite different. Certainly the handwriting changes from one piece to another.

The facing pages on which the Mass begins are ornamented with miniatures (Pl. 41), one of which appears to be an illustration of the anecdote later told by Glareanus. In Plate 41, fig. 1, 'Ihen Gipon' is, one assumes, the name of the illuminator. Nothing is known about him; the only lead I have found so far is a reference of payment to a copyist named 'Joannes' in the records of the Papal Chapel, dated 1 February 1501.[12] The figure on the facing page (Pl. 41, fig. 2), seated amid a hoard of coins and frozen in the act of saying 'Lesse faire a mi', a kind of Franco-Italian compromise,[13] looks as if he might be the potentate of Glareanus' story—or at least that man's man. The turban is an intriguing rather than helpful detail. There seems no reason to think here of Ascanio Sforza depicted as costumed *alla turchesca*; indeed, his brother Ludovico, known as 'il Moro', would be a more likely candidate, although the portrait does not look like him. If this manuscript is correctly dated in the 1490s, its copying fell into a period in which things Turkish were very fashionable.

Just who this figure may represent I do not know.[14] Its presence in the manuscript and the inscription are evidence that Glareanus did not make up the anecdote he reports; it was in circulation during the period when the Mass was becoming famous. The coins in the figure's lap are almost certainly French; the one in the centre, with three *fleurs-de-lis* under a *couronne*, is an *écu* of the type used from the time of Charles VII into the sixteenth century. What appears to be its reverse is to the right (a large cross). The single large *fleur-de-lis* to the left is more fanciful, or perhaps ironic; only coins of very small value, such as the *demi-niquet*, used the single *fleur-de-lis*.[15] One other possibility is that the coins represent money issued by Charles VIII during his brief sojourn in Naples in 1495.[16]

[12] See F. X. Haberl, *Die römische 'schola cantorum' und die päpstlichen Kapellsänger bis zur Mitte des 16. Jahrhunderts* (*Bausteine für Musikgeschichte*, iii; Leipzig, 1888), p. 59. If Ihen Gipon was indeed the illustrator, he may also have been responsible for at least the text in Josquin's Mass, and for several other pieces in Sistine manuscripts of the same period. This is the opinion of Mr. Richard Sherr of Princeton University, who is engaged in a study of some of these manuscripts and has most kindly communicated to me his findings. Mr. Sherr also brought to my attention two manuscript sources of the Mass not known to Smijers: Rome, Santa Maria Maggiore MS. J.J. III. 4, fols 62ᵛ–77 (this manuscript is now in the Vatican Library), and Bologna, San Petronio, Archivio Musicale, MS. A 31, fols. 7ᵛ–14 (lacking parts of the *Sanctus* and the second *Agnus Dei*).

[13] In the table of contents of the manuscript the title is given as 'Lasse fare amy'.

[14] By no stretch of the imagination could it be said to resemble any of the known portraits of Ascanio Sforza.

[15] See A. Dieudonné, *Les monnaies capétiennes ou royales françaises*, 2ᵉ section (Paris, 1932), pp. 281, 337, 353; cf. Jean Lafaurie, *Les monnaies des rois de France, Hughes Capet à Louis XII* (Paris, 1951). The *écu au soleil du Dauphiné* of the reign of Charles VIII has a *croisette* on the reverse that is very similar to the cross on the coins in Pl. 2 above.

The *fleur-de-lis* appears on Milanese coins after 1500, during the reigns of the French kings Louis XII and Francis I, but its design does not resemble that in Pl. 2.

[16] See Giovan Vincenzo Fusco, *Intorno alle zecche ed alle monete battute nel reame di*

Petrucci did not use 'laise faire moy' or 'lassa far a mi' as a title, but Josquin's Mass was widely known by this name; Teofilo Folengo, for example, refers to it as 'lassaque far mi' in the 1521 edition of his *Maccheronee*.[17] Translated, or rather adapted, into German as 'lass sie fahren', the phrase appears, together with the solmization-theme used by Josquin, throughout the bass of Mathias Greiter's setting of 'Ich stund an einem Morgen' (Ex. 1).[18] The piece is dated 1521 in a reliable source.[19]

Ex. 1   mm. 1-4

As for the *barzelletta* 'Lassa far a mi', its text has often been cited, although in the musical literature only the last stanza is usually given. This is unfortunate, since the obsessive repetition of the ostinato pattern in Josquin's

Napoli da re Carlo VIII di Francia (Naples, 1846). The plates in this volume show coins roughly similar to the *écu*, but none with a single large *fleur-de-lis*. Coins bearing the three *fleurs-de-lis* and crown of the royal arms were minted in Pisa, Solmona, and Aquila, as well as in Naples, according to H.-François Delaborde, *L'Expédition de Charles VIII en Italie* (Paris, 1888).

[17] *Opus Merlini Cocaii Poete Mantuani Macaronicorum*... (Tusculani, 1521), fol. 90. A few lines before the citation of various Masses by Josquin, Folengo addresses another group of musicians: 'O felix Bido, Carpentras, Silvaque, Broier,/Vosque Leoninae cantorum squadra capellae.' Since Andreas de Silva entered the chapel of Leo X in January of 1519, Folengo's verses must have been written between then and the end of 1520 (the print is dated 5 January 1521).

The 23-line passage on Josquin and his contemporaries is cited in A. W. Ambros, *Geschichte der Musik*, 3rd ed., iii (Leipzig, 1891), pp. 12–13, and has since often been referred to. The passage was omitted from later editions of Folengo's work; see *Merlin Cocai, Le Maccheronee*, ed. Alessandro Luzio, ii (Bari, 1928), p. 308.

[18] See André Pirro, *Histoire de la musique de la fin du XIVe siècle à la fin du XVIe* (Paris, 1940), p. 275; Hans Theodore David, 'Themes from Words and Names', *A Birthday Offering to Carl Engel* (New York, 1943), p. 70 n. The piece is printed, without the ostinato text and hence without reference to Josquin, in Ambros, *Geschichte*, v, pp. 361–2.

[19] See *Mathias Greiter, Sämtliche weltliche Lieder*, ed. Hans-Christian Müller (*Das Chorwerk*, Heft 87; Wolfenbüttel, 1962), pp. iv–v.

For Greiter's interest in musical symbolism, see Edward E. Lowinsky, 'Matthaeus Greiter's *Fortuna*: An Experiment in Chromaticism and in Musical Iconography', *The Musical Quarterly*, xlii (1956), pp. 500–519; xliii (1957), pp. 68–85, esp. pp. 81–5.

Mass could be taken as a setting of the poem's endless repetition of the opening phrase. The text as given by Serafino's modern editor is as follows:[20]

Lassa far a mi, lassa far a mi
Non ti curare, lassa far a mi.

Questo lassa far a mi
M'ha tenuto un tempo a bada;
El dir: lassa far a mi
Tanto poco sì m'agrada,
Che m'è al cor pungente spada
Questo lassa far a mi.

Tanto lassa far a mi
Che sarà, de, dimmi un poco,
Per dir lassa far a mi;
Dentro l'acqua starà il foco,
Prima ch'abbia fine o loco
El tuo lassa far a mi.

Lassa, lassa far a mi,
Giorno & nocte mai non manca;
Con dir: lassa far a mi
La tua lingua al mentir franca,
Sarà morta pria che stanca
Con dir: lassa far a mi.

Con dir: lassa far a mi
Quanto gente tradita hai;
Questo lassa far a mi
A che tempo lo farai?
Prima il mondo lasserai
Che dir: lassa far a mi.

Per dir: lassa far a mi
Tu ti credi sia servito;
El dir lassa far a mi
Molte volte m'ha tradito;
Così priego sia exaudito
Tu con lassa far a mi.

Al tuo lassa far a mi
Non si presta or mai più fede;
Col tuo lassa far a mi
Quel che l'ochio certo vede
Affatica l'uom te'l crede
Non che lassa far a mi.

[20] Menghini, *Le rime*, pp. 36–8. The last line in Menghini's edition reads 'Dicon *la, re, fa, sol, mi*'.

Dir pur: lassa far a mi
Poi non far ch'è gran vitio;
Forse il lassa far a mi
Fia al dì del gran giuditio,
  & laggiù nel precipitio
Finir lassa far a mi.

Se'l dir: lassa far a mi
Contentasse ogni persona,
El dir: lassa far a mi
Sare' cosa sancta & buona;
Quel non val, nè fa nè dona
Che dir: lassa far a mi.

Forse al lassa far a mi
Sì s'intende all' altro mondo,
Per dir: lassa far a mi
Muorti presto & va al profondo;
A finir laggiù nel mondo
Questo lassa far a mi.

Quanti son che per dilecto
Non observan mai la fede!
  & dapoi han gran dispecto
Che la gente se n'avede;
Che nessun [da]poi gli crede
Al lor lassa far a mi.

Oggi regna questa usanza
  & pagar di ben faremo,
Qual aspecta e sta a speranza
Si consuma & viensi a meno;
Oggi tucto il mondo è pieno
Di dir: lassa far a mi.

Questo lassa far a mi
Non contenta gli amatori;
Di dir: lassa far a mi
Son le note di cantori;
  . . .
Dicon *la sol fa re mi.*

In the form given by Menghini, the poem's last stanza is defective; its fifth line is missing. Two versions of the missing line may be found among the poem's sources. In one manuscript copy of the *barzelletta* the line reads, 'Che cantando lor amori'.[21] The other version, though made public in an

---

[21] See L. Zambra, 'La barzelletta *Lassa far a mi* in un codice della Biblioteca Comunale di Budapest', *La Bibliofilia*, xv (1913–14), pp. 410–13. This version is cited by Torrefranca, *Il Segreto*, p. 68.

Italian periodical a century ago, has not to my knowledge received any attention. Here the last two lines read, 'Che cantando in lor tenori/Dicon: la sol fa re mi'.[22]

These lines are a quite accurate description of the tenor in Josquin's Mass, and provide suggestive evidence that the 'Missa La sol fa re mi' might well have to be connected with the poem 'Lassa far a mi'.[23] No copy of the book in which the poem appeared is extant; the page or pages containing the poem survived by being pasted onto the inside covers of a work by Poliziano, printed in Florence in 1492.[24] Since the binding has been described as contemporary with the book, the poem in this form may help toward dating the Mass; Josquin's work may have been well known by the early 1490s, hence composed at least a few years earlier.[25]

For Torrefranca, Josquin's 'La sol fa re mi' was derived neither from punning use of a French phrase nor from the *barzelletta*, but from the *nio* (the more rapid, concluding section) of a *villota*, a piece beginning with another solmization pun, 'La mi fa sol fare'.[26] Without accepting Torrefranca's thesis, one may note that 'lassa far a mi' in the piece he discusses is set to a melody similar to Josquin's theme:

Ex. 2   mm. 59-67

[22] Achille Monti, 'Due poesie del secolo xv', *Il Buonarroti di Benvenuto Gasparoni*, ser. ii, vol. viii (1873), pp. 83-7. The poem, which lacks the first two lines of the version printed by Menghini and has a number of minor variants in the text, is given on pp. 85-6.

[23] Josquin would appear to have known the poem in a version including the opening lines as given above; in the Mass the ostinato is very often given in double statements, thus seeming to declaim the opening 'Lassa far a mi, lassa far a mi'; this is particularly noticeable in the *Kyrie*.

[24] Monti, 'Due poesie', p. 84.

[25] The *barzelletta* itself may of course be older yet, with the substitute line the result of the printer or editor's acquaintance with Josquin's work.

[26] The piece is transcribed by Torrefranca from the MS. Venice, Biblioteca Marciana, ital. cl. IV, 1795-1798, on pp. 471-5 of *Il Segreto del Quattrocento*. It is discussed on pp. 62ff. and elsewhere in the book.

Another citation of 'lassa far a mi' occurs in a *centone*, its tenor beginning 'Non dormite, o cacciatori':[27]

Ex. 3 mm. 47-53 (tenor)

This fragment was noticed by Jeppesen as well as Torrefranca. Whether these pieces antedate Josquin's Mass—and I think they do not[28]—is less important than their suggestion that the solmization melody was in common use with the text 'lassa far a mi', as a setting of the *barzelletta* or of another secular text. In other words, Josquin may have drawn the subject for his Mass from a song fragment—text and music—popular at the time.[29] This is not to deny some element of truth to the anecdote told by Glareanus; but the latter is only anecdote, whereas 'lassa far a mi' has a real if not altogether satisfactorily documented existence.

What may have happened is that the popularity of the 'Missa La sol fa re mi' eclipsed the more ephemeral 'lassa far a mi'. In the same manuscript that contains 'Non dormite, o cacciatori' is a dialogue-madrigal, 'Cantiano,

[27] The piece is found in Bologna, Civico Museo Bibliografico Musicale, MS. Q 21, no. 47. See Claudio Gallico, *Un canzoniere musicale italiano del cinquecento* (Florence, 1961), p. 100. Cf. Torrefranca, *Il Segreto*, pp. 141ff, 503–6, and Knud Jeppesen, 'Venetian Folk-Songs of the Renaissance', *Papers of the American Musicological Society*, 1939 (1944), pp. 72–3.

[28] If the 'Mº Rofino' given in the Venice MS. as the composer of 'La mi fa sol fare' is Ruffino d'Assisi, active in the first third of the sixteenth century, his piece is certainly later than Josquin's Mass. Torrefranca, *Il Segreto*, p. 64, rejects this identification since he thinks (p. 66) that the piece must have been written 'intorno al 1480', but his dating of the whole literature he discusses is much too early. On Ruffino d'Assisi see Giovanni D'Alessi in *MGG*, xi, cols. 1075–6, and Knud Jeppesen, *La Frottola*, i (Copenhagen, 1968), p. 161.

[29] Cf. Carl Dahlhaus, 'Studien zu den Messen Josquins des Pres' (Inaugural-Dissertation, Göttingen, 1952), p. 52: 'Der Tenor "la sol fa re mi" ist vielleicht der Beginn einer Volksweise, die in einem Centone in der Hs. Q 21 des Liceo Musicale in Bologna und in einer Villotta von Ruffino d'Assisi...zitiert wird.'

horsù cantiano',[30] an amusing piece in which the singers talk about what they should perform. After trying a madrigal incipit or two they decide to sing 'qualche buona messa', proceeding to do so as in Ex. 4:

Ex. 4   mm. 49-59

Choosing the mode by defining its species of fifth, *la-re*, they then commence an imitative series on *la sol fa re mi*; while not a direct quotation from Josquin's Mass, it is nonetheless an unmistakable reference to the work.

One generation after Josquin's death 'Lassa far a mi' and the 'Missa La sol fa re mi' are fused into one conceit. Thus Perissone Cambio's *villanesca*, 'Madonne, l'arte nostra è di cantare',[31] treats *la sol fa re mi* in a way similar to both the *villota* and the dialogue of some twenty years earlier (cf. Exx. 2, 4):

[30] Bologna MS. Q 21, no. 1. See Gallico, *Un canzoniere*, p. 82. The piece is also in Florence, Biblioteca del Conservatorio, Cod. B 2440, fols. 81ᵛ–83. It has been attributed, on stylistic grounds and by reason of its location among works of Pisano in the Florentine manuscript, to Bernardo Pisano. See Frank A. D'Accone, 'Bernardo Pisano, an Introduction to his Life and Works, *Musica disciplina*, xvii (1963), p. 131. The piece is printed in *Bernardo Pisano, Collected Works*, ed. Frank A. D'Accone (*Music of the Florentine Renaissance*, i; American Institute of Musicology, 1966), pp. 83–5.

[31] *Canzone villanesche alla napoletana a quatro voci* (Venice, 1545), no. 5. The full text of this piece is given below.

Ex. 5 mm. 15-21

'Lassa far a mi' was not forgotten, however; the phrase turns up a century later in a ricercar by Froberger, the successor to a whole series of *la sol fa re mi* fantasias written during the sixteenth and early seventeenth centuries.[32]

Use of the Ostinato in the Mass

In a late sixteenth-century manuscript copy of the 'Missa La sol fa re mi', the work is prefaced and followed by the epigram 'facile est inventis a[d]dere'—'it is easy to add on to things [already] discovered'.[33] As we have seen, it is possible that the hexachord theme itself was not Josquin's invention. Nevertheless this remark seems unjust—no fairer than Dr. Johnson's celebrated judgement on *Gulliver's Travels*, that 'when once you have thought of big men and little men, it is very easy to do all the rest'.[34] Finding

[32] See below for a list of these pieces.

[33] Paris, Bibliothèque nationale, Rés. Vma. MS. 851 (the Bourdeney MS.), p. 376: 'Seguita la Messa de la. sol. fa. re. mi. del detto Josquin de Pres. Facile est inventis adere'; p.383: 'Finis. La.sol. fa.re. mi. facile est inventis adere.' For a description of this manuscript, the relevant contents of which were called to my attention by Professor Alvin H. Johnson, see Nanie Bridgman and François Lesure, 'Une anthologie "historique" de la fin du XVIe siècle: le manuscrit Bourdeney', *Miscelanea en homenaje a Monseñor Higinio Anglés*, i (Barcelona, 1958–61), pp. 161–74.

[34] *Boswell's Life of Johnson*, ed. George Birkbeck Hill, rev. L. F. Powell, ii (Oxford, 1934), p. 319.

a suitable ostinato pattern is perhaps easy; but no one who studies the work would deny the resourcefulness, ingenuity, and wit Josquin expended upon the figure *la sol fa re mi*.

Use of ostinato figures was widespread in the music of the late fifteenth century, and the derivation of musical figures from syllables of the hexachord, with the weight of Ockeghem's great prestige behind it, had become popular as well.[35] Many examples could be cited here, but tabulating them would serve no particular purpose, for Josquin's Mass is quite different from the rest. *La sol fa re mi* is indeed a *cantus prius factus*, but only at times is it a *cantus firmus*—unlike the sober treatment of the Guidonian *Ut re mi fa sol la* in Brumel's Mass, perhaps the first of its name,[36] or the *soggetto cavato* of Josquin's own 'Missa Hercules Dux Ferrariae'.

In its whimsical use of a four-note ostinato pattern—*fa re mi re*—Josquin's 'Missa Faisant regretz' is closer in spirit to 'La sol fa re mi' than any of his other works,[37] but in one respect it is different; in 'Faisant regretz' Josquin transposes the ostinato pattern up and down by step so that its hexachord structure is necessarily altered, a device used by contemporaries such as Obrecht and Isaac as well.[38] In the 'Missa La sol fa re mi' there is none of this; in more than two hundred full repetitions of the subject, the hexachord structure remains intact.

[35] See David, 'Themes from Words and Names', pp. 68–73. David cites Ockeghem's 'Ut heremita solus', with its puzzle-canon tenor making use of solmization syllables, as the earliest such example known to him.

[36] *Antonii Brumel Opera Omnia*, ed. Barton Hudson, i (American Institute of Musicology, 1969), p. xvii: the work uses 'the entire Guidonian system through disposition of the various mutations of the hexachord in ascending order', and does so in very regular *cantus-firmus* fashion.

[37] Perhaps mention should be made here of 'Ut Phoebi radiis' (*Werken*, Motetten, Bundel iv, no. 22), a work described as among the composer's earliest motets (Osthoff, *Josquin Desprez*, ii, pp. 79–80). In this piece an ascending and descending hexachord is heard by degrees, its syllables corresponding to the text in a way that is reminiscent of 'Ut queant laxis'.

[38] This kind of transposition may be seen in a celebrated hexachord piece by Isaac, 'La mi la sol la sol la mi', a work existing in textless form, as a motet with the text 'Rogamus te, piissima Virgo', and—used in its entirety—in the 'Missa O praeclara'. See Gustave Reese, *Music in the Renaissance* (New York, 1954), pp. 215, 648. It is in the Mass that the hexachord figure *la mi la sol la sol la mi* (the significance of which is unknown to me) is heard at various pitch levels involving altered hexachord relationships. I am grateful to Professor William Mahrt for letting me see his transcription of this as yet unpublished Mass. (For other examples of pieces using ostinato figures in the form of *pes ascendens* and *descendens* see M. van Crevel, 'Verwante Sequensmodulaties bij Obrecht, Josquin en Coclico', *Tijdschrift der Vereeniging voor Nederlandsche Muziekgeschiedenis*, xvi [1941], pp. 107–24.)

'La mi la sol' is the work referred to in the famous letter of a certain 'Gian' to Ercole d'Este, comparing the merits of Isaac and Josquin. The letter is given in various places; see Osthoff, *Josquin Desprez*, i, pp. 211–12, and above, p. 132. There are several opinions as to the meaning of the phrase '[Isaac] ha facto uno moteto sopra una fantasia nomata la mi la so[l] la so[l] la mi, lo qualle e molto bono, et hallo facto in dui jorni'; see Osthoff, ii,

Except for one section, the *Christe*, in which the ostinato is heard in all
three hexachords in succession, Josquin uses *la sol fa re mi* beginning either
on E (*hexachordum durum*) or A (*hexachordum naturale*) throughout the Mass.
The resultant tonal monotony is lessened by refreshingly varied harmoniza-
tions of the ostinato figure and by the rhythmic variation that he brings to
bear on it: note values range from longs and breves in the *cantus firmus* to a
flippant mini-repetition in semiminims, and rhythmic accentuations change
kaleidescopically, as if the intended victim were exposed to an endless echo
of his 'lassa far a mi' spoken in every conceivable variety of cadence and
pronunciation.[39] The combination of unchanging pitch with declamatory
variety is surely intended for effect, and if one accepts 'lassa far a mi' as
inspiration for the Mass, it is programmatic in character.

The Mass has often been written about and need not be described in
detail here.[40] Several aspects of the work have received less attention than
they deserve, however, and may be briefly mentioned at this point. First is
the distribution of the ostinato melody among the voices. After a *Kyrie*
in which *la sol fa re mi* is shared by all the voices, with the bass having the
most important statements, the work settles into the traditional framework
of the tenor Mass. Parts of the *Sanctus* and *Agnus Dei* I (= III) again show
further use of the ostinato by all voices. This scheme is not unusual for
Josquin, and the use of plainchant in both *Gloria* and *Credo* results naturally
in reduced use of the ostinato.[41] Nonetheless the work seems to me less
unified in technique and style than Josquin's late Masses. It is almost as if
the composer had begun with the idea of writing a tenor *cantus-firmus* Mass

---

307–8, and David, 'Themes from Words', p. 69 n. It seems to me that by *fantasia* the writer
meant not a textless piece—it would not be an impressive feat to take two days to add text
to a completed piece—but the solmization figure, a conceit or 'fancy' on which Isaac wrote
a composition that became known both as a motet and as an instrumental piece.

Professor Lewis Lockwood has shown (see p. 114 in this volume) that the letter in
question was written in September 1502. Later that same month Petrucci issued the *Misse
Josquin* containing the 'Missa La sol fa re mi'. Perhaps in writing a solmization piece on a
figure similar to that used by Josquin, and at some point expanding it into an entire Mass,
Isaac was indeed entering into competition with his great rival. For a general discussion
of Isaac's motet, differing in many details from that just given, see Martin Just, 'Heinrich
Isaacs Motetten in italienischen Quellen', *Analecta Musicologica*, i (1963), pp. 6, 10–15.

[39] This sensation is felt, and most aptly expressed, by Ambros in his discussion of the
Mass (*Geschichte der Musik*, iii, p. 213): 'Weiss man das Histörchen [of Glareanus], so macht
das *La sol fa re mi* in der Messe freilich einen Effect, wie ein in ein Spiegelzimmer gehängter
Medusenkopf'.

[40] See, for example, Ambros, *Geschichte*, iii, pp. 213, 217f.; Peter Wagner, *Geschichte
der Messe* (Leipzig, 1913), pp. 162–5; Reese, *Music in the Renaissance*, pp. 238–9; Osthoff,
Josquin Desprez, i, pp. 166–71.

[41] Wagner, *Geschichte*, pp. 163–5, stresses the use of plainchant in the *Gloria* and *Credo*
of the Mass. On Josquin's occasional fusion of chant and ostinato figure, see below.

on his chosen figure, ornamented with four-voice imitation at its beginning and end, then, in the course of refining and polishing the work, he introduced more statements of the ostinato outside the tenor, some of them almost certainly afterthoughts, if amusing ones, as in Ex. 6:

It seems perfectly possible to me that the 'Missa La sol fa re mi', in its original form, may have been a relatively early work,[42] and that Josquin, whose habit of keeping back his work in order to refine it was well known in his own time, could have gradually altered the character of the music by infusing more of the ostinato into its substance.[43]

A second distinguishing feature of this Mass, one that adds to its playfulness of tone, is Josquin's use of whimsical hexachord mutations in the ostinato figure. This is seen at many points in the Mass but is most pronounced in the *Pleni sunt coeli*, in which *la sol fa re mi* changes hexachords midway

[42] Dahlhaus, 'Studien', p. 546n, assigns the Mass to the years 1475–79. Osthoff, i, pp. 166–7, believes the Mass belongs to the period 1490–93; but immediately afterwards he adds 'Wenn das Werk auch nachweislich früh in das Repertoire der päpstlichen Kapelle Eingang fand, so spricht die relativ hohe Klanglage (Superius: g–f") doch eher dafür, dass es ursprünglich für eine ausserrömische Kantorei bestimmt war'. By this he presumably means that Josquin while in the Papal Chapel wrote the Mass for another patron.

[43] See the statement of Glareanus, *Dodekachordon*, p. 363, that Josquin, unlike Obrecht, continually corrected and revised his work, cited by Osthoff, i, p. 82.

through the figure, in two different ways, as can be seen in Ex. 7, the complete alto line of this section:[44]

Ex. 7 mm. 33-51 (alto) (1)   35   (2)

[la sol fa re mi la sol fa re mi=la …

—— sol fa re mi … re fa sol …la]

To a generation that knew Ockeghem's 'Missa Mi mi', and one that delighted in verbal and musical puns on solmization syllables,[45] this was but another way to play the game. By the end of the sixteenth century this practice had acquired a name, *inganno* (= trick), applied to it by the theorist Artusi.[46] Josquin may not have been the first to employ such *inganni*, but the fame of his work surely contributed to their continuing use. Several *villote* show this playful adaptation of the principle of mutation, a principle dealt with at solemn length by theorists of the time:[47]

Ex. 8(a) 'La mi fa fa la re'   (?)   (?)

S. La mi fa fa la re, la mi fa fa la re
         La   mi fa fa la re
B. A.
La mi fa fa la re

[44] In Ex. 7 the figures marked (1) show a shift from the natural to hard, or soft to natural hexachords; those marked (2) go from hard to natural. Notice the interlocking statements, and also the ornamented retrograde of the ostinato—itself including hints of mutation—at the end. On Josquin's use of retrograde in this work, see below. The figure A–G–C–A–B has been noticed by others, including Dahlhaus, Osthoff, and Reese.

[45] The *frottole* and *villote* made so much of by Torrefranca are full of such puns, which were clearly much in vogue at the end of the fifteenth century.

[46] *Seconda parte dell'Artusi overo delle imperfettioni della moderna musica* (Venice, 1603), pp. 45-6: 'Lo inganno si fa ogni volta, che una parte incominciando un soggietto il consequente, la seguita non per gl'istessi gradi; ma si bene per gl'istessi nomi di sillabe, ò de suoni….' For a discussion of this passage see Roland Jackson, 'The *Inganni* and the Keyboard Music of Trabaci', *Journal of the American Musicological Society*, xxi (1968), pp. 204–8. I know of no theorist before Artusi who uses the word *inganno* in this sense. For Vicentino it meant a musical trick or surprise of a general nature, an example being a downbeat motive being imitated on the upbeat; see *L'Antica musica ridotta alla moderna prattica* (Rome, 1555; facs. ed. by Edward E. Lowinsky, Kassel, 1959), fol. 78ᵛ.

[47] See Torrefranca, *Il Segreto*, p. 467 ('La mi fa falare'), p. 471 ('La mi fa sol fare'), p. 507

(b) 'La mi fa sol fa re'

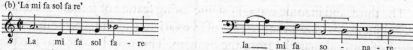

La mi fa sol fa - re   la — mi fa so - na - re

In Ex. 2 above there is an *inganno* in the quotation of *la sol fa re mi* (*mi* is in a different hexachord; see m. 64, tenor and bass, m. 66, alto, m. 67, superius) on which Torrefranca lays stress. Perissone Cambio's refrain (see Ex. 5) shows the survival of *inganni* to the mid-sixteenth century—a conspicuous instance occurs in the bass (mm. 19–20).[48] How widespread this device was is not certain, but examples of it occur in late sixteenth-century music; an attractive one is the opening of Marenzio's 'Mi fa lasso languire':[49]

Ex. 9   mm. 1-8

('O dolce farfarela'). For the sources of 'La mi fa fa la re', see Gallico, *Un canzoniere*, p. 105. The two queried *fa* in Ex. 8a should probably be regarded not as *inganni* but as the result of contrapuntal exigencies displacing the solmization game. For 'La mi fa sol fare', see above, fn. 26.

[48] Another *villanesca* by Perissone, 'Va voglio dire donne' (*Canzone villanesche*, 1545, no. 15), contains some playful treatment of *ut re mi fa sol la*, given at one point as C–A–D–E♭–F–D.

[49] For a modern edition of this piece, see Alfred Einstein, ed., *Luca Marenzio, Sämtliche*

The third, and in some ways most interesting feature of Josquin's ostinato technique in this Mass is the presence of free variation technique, the development of musical material from the ostinato. This may be allied to the use of *inganni*, as in Ex. 10, where the ostinato finally emerges in its original

Ex. 10   *Credo*, mm. 197-214 (alto)

form after a series of statements using both hexachord play and melodic decoration. It may also be the result of the composer's drawing a paraphrased chant melody into the 'magnetic field' of the ostinato, as in Ex. 11:[50]

Ex. 11   *Gloria*, mm. 5-8 (superius and alto)

In many instances it seems to be Josquin's creative imagination working freely, though probably consciously, with the material of the ostinato, in several ways: (1) *la sol fa re mi* may emerge from what at first seems freely composed material:

Ex. 12   *Qui venit*, mm. 34-48 (superius)

Werke, i (*Publikationen älterer Musik*, iv/1; Leipzig, 1929), pp. 80–81. Marenzio's *mi fa la sol la mi re* series is full of *inganni*. The editorial sharp in measure 7 seems called for by the solmization puns. The use of *sol* on notes that have been chromatically altered is not so unusual as it might first appear; on this aspect of solmization, see Lewis Lockwood, 'A Sample Problem of *Musica ficta*: Willaert's *Pater noster*', *Studies in Music History: Essays for Oliver Strunk*, ed. Harold Powers (Princeton, 1968), p. 164 n.

[50] In Ex. 11 the notes marked with asterisks are derived from plainchant (Mass XV; cf. *Liber Usualis*, p. 57), of which the top voice is a paraphrase through much of the *Gloria*.

(2) the ostinato may be stated exactly, then progressively broken down:

Ex. 13 *Sanctus*, mm. 1-11 (superius)

or (3) new thematic material may be created from elements of the ostinato figure:

Ex. 14 *Kyrie*, mm. 47-61 (bass)

The culmination of all these devices is found, not unexpectedly, in *Agnus Dei* I, repeated after a duo as the final movement of the Mass:

Ex. 15

Here distribution of ostinato material in all the voices is accompanied by retrograde statement, use of *inganni*, and free variation so extensive that in this section the work might almost be called a 'Missa quasi fantasia'.

La sol fa re mi *after Josquin*

The following is a list of Masses, secular vocal pieces, and instrumental works based on *la sol fa re mi*, and in many instances showing direct influence of Josquin's Mass.

Masses

1) Jacquet of Mantua, Missa La sol fa re mi', 5 v.
   Sources: Treviso, Biblioteca Capitolare, MS. 23, fols. 29ᵛ–42; Treviso, Biblioteca Capitolare, MS. 9, fols. 36ᵛ–46 (incomplete); Modena, Archivio Capitolare, MS. VI (superius only, incomplete).[51]
   In this work Josquin's tenor is used as a *cantus firmus*; Jacquet's tenor corresponds movement by movement to that of Josquin (some foreshortenings and rhythmic adjustments are made from time to time). The tenor has no text. Motto openings derived from Josquin are used in the first three movements. Totally different from Josquin's work in style and character, this Mass borrows the structural outlines from its model, even to the point of ending on A rather than E.

2) Costanzo Porta, 'Missa La sol fa re mi', 6 v.
   Source: *Costantii Portae...Missarum Liber Primus* (Venice, 1578).[52]
   Likewise a tenor Mass, this work uses Josquin's ostinato in long–note *cantus-firmus* style throughout (including a triple canon in the final *Agnus Dei*).

[51] The MS. Treviso 23 is dated 1563; MS. 9 is dated 1564. The Mass was of course composed much earlier. My thanks are due to Professor Philip Jackson for giving me a copy of his transcription of this unpublished Mass, and to Prof. George Nugent for information about the Treviso MSS. and about the contents of the Modena MS. Treviso MS. 23 contains eight Masses by Jacquet, all of which, except for 'La sol fa re mi', were printed by Scotto in collections of 1554, 1555, and 1561. It might be noted here that in the Modena manuscript Jacquet's 'La sol fa re mi' is followed by another solmization Mass, Pietro Vinci's 'Missa La sol fa mi re ut'.

[52] Modern edition in *Das Chorwerk*, Heft 93, ed. Oscar Mischiati (Wolfenbüttel, 1965).

The ostinato figure is accompanied by imitative counterpoint. Occasionally, hexachord *inganni* may be seen, including an instance in the *Pleni sunt coeli* (*Sanctus*, mm. 60–63), that is clearly derived from Josquin. Otherwise the piece is not very close to its model, and Porta chooses to end the Mass on E rather than A.

3) Pietro Pontio, 'Missa La sol fa re mi', 6 v.

Source: *Missarum*...(Venice, 1590)[?]

I have not been able to find a copy of this work. The authority for its existence is Pontio himself, in a context making clear its connection with Josquin's Mass.[53]

Secular vocal pieces

1) M⁰ Rofino, 'La mi fa sol fare'.

Source: Venice, Biblioteca Marciana, MS. Cl. IV, 1795–98, no. 103.[54]

This and the next two pieces have already been briefly discussed above.

2) 'Non dormite, o cacciatori'.

Source: Bologna, Civico Museo Bibliografico Musicale, MS. Q 21, no. 47.[55]

3) Bernardo Pisano (?), 'Cantiano, horsù cantiano'.

Sources: Bologna, MS. Q 21, no. 1; Florence, Biblioteca del Conservatorio, Cod. B 2440, fols. 81ᵛ–83. (On the attribution of this piece to Bernardo Pisano, see fn. 30).

4) Mathias Greiter, 'Ich stund an einem Morgen'.

Sources: Basel, Universitätsbibliothek, MS. F.X. 1–4, no. 20; Wolfenbüttel, Herzog-August Bibliothek, MS. 292, fol. 21; RISM [*c.* 1535]¹⁵, no. 6; RISM [*c.* 1535]¹³, no. 15.[56]

The text 'lass sie fahren' accompanying the bass ostinato (see Ex. 1 above), and its imitative correspondence in the alto, is missing in RISM [*c.* 1535]¹³.

5) Perissone Cambio, 'Madonne, l'arte nostra è di cantare'.

Source: *Canzone Villanesche...a 4v. di Perissone* (Venice, 1545, 1551), no. 5.

---

[53] *Dialogo del R. M. Don Pietro Parmigiano* (Parma, 1595), p. 60: in discussing various techniques of composition, Pontio says, 'Over si trovarà obligatione di figure, come fece Iusquino nella Missa Hercules Dux Ferrariae, nel secondo libro delle sue Messe à quattro, & altrove nel primo libro di dette Messe, pigliando per soggetto queste figure la sol fa re mi. Et di tali figure si servì anco il Pontio nel primo libro delle sue Messe à sei, le quali hanno per titolo Missa la sol fa re mi....' F. J. Fétis, *Biographie universelle*, vii (2d ed., Paris, 1864), p. 96, lists a volume by Pontio of *Missae 6, 8 voc.*' printed in Venice in 1590, but no copy of this print has as yet come to my attention.

In another work, the *Ragionamento di Musica del Reverendo M. Don Pietro Pontio* (Parma, 1588), pp. 90–91, Pontio discusses the writing of ostinato figures and gives an example consisting of *la sol fa re mi* used in repetitive, sequential fashion over a *cantus firmus*. Of this he says, 'Questo modo di contrapunto si chiama fugato; benche più presto io lo chiamarei obligato, over capriccioso....'

[54] See the inventory of the manuscript in Knud Jeppesen, *La Frottola*, ii, pp. 202–3; modern edition in Torrefranca, *Il Segreto*, pp. 471–5 (facsimile on pp. 362–7).

[55] Modern edition ibid., pp. 503–6.

[56] Modern edition in *Das Chorwerk*, Heft 87, ed. Hans-Christian Müller (Wolfenbüttel, 1962). no. 8 (see also the bibliography in Francis Muller, art. 'Greiter', *MGG*, v, col. 802).

In this piece Josquin's ostinato is introduced (see Ex. 5 above) as part of the word-play of the text, which is as follows:

> Madonne, l'arte nostra è di cantare
> le villanell', e dar la letione.
> Manco d'un hora t'imparò la mano
> con quelle note: *la sol far a mi,*
> Ch'io saccio molto bene l'arte fare.
> Da gamaut voglio cominciare
> passar natura con perfetione,
> Manco d'un hora...
> Poi lo be quadro ti farò provare
> a poco poco senza passione.
> Manco d'un hora...
> Se lo be molle dolce puoi gustare
> più di tre volte mi vuoi nominare.
> Manco d'un hora...

Instrumental pieces

1) Vihuela intabulations[57]

   a) Alonso Mudarra, 'Glosa sobre un Benedictus de una missa de Josquin que va sobre la sol fa re mi'.

   Source: *Tres libros de musica en cifras para vihuela* (Brown 1546[14]), *libro segundo*, no. 35.[58]

   In the introductory bars of this piece the ostinato occurs in transposed form, losing its hexachord significance.

   b) Diego Pisador, 'Fantasia sobre la, sol, fa, re, mi, a tres bozes'.

   Source: *Libro de musica de vihuela* (Brown 1552[7]), no. 13.

   A simple, repetitive piece based on continuous imitative entries of the ostinato, this fantasy is written for beginners ('para los que comiençan a tañer').

   c) Pisador, 'Fantasia del quarto tono sobre la sol fa re mi'.

   Source: Ibid., *Libro tercero*, no. 37.

   The ostinato is here sung by a solo voice against a counterpoint similar to that in the *Benedictus* of Josquin's Mass.

   d) Pisador, 'Missa sobre la sol fa re mi'.

   Source: Ibid., *Libro quinto con otras quatro missas de Jusquin*, no. 63.

   A nearly complete intabulation of the Mass (cf. Brown, p. 142, n. 19).

   e) Miguel de Fuenllana, 'Qui tollis peccata. Segunda parte de la gloria de la

---

[57] Professor John Ward kindly lent me photostats of all these intabulations. Bibliographical information on the collections in which they are found is in Howard Mayer Brown, *Instrumental Music Printed before 1600: A Bibliography* (Cambridge, Mass., 1965). See also Kwee Him Yong, 'Sixteenth-Century Printed Instrumental Arrangements of Works by Josquin des Prez. An Inventory', *Tijdschrift van de Vereniging voor Nederlandse Muziekgeschiedenis*, xxii (1971), pp. 49–50, 56–7.

[58] Modern edition in *Monumentos de la música española*, vii, ed. Emilio Pujol (Barcelona, 1949), pp. 47–8.

sol fa re mi de Josquin'; 'Primero kyrie de la missa de la sol fa re mi; Christe...; Postrero kyrie.'

Source: *Libro de musica para vihuela, intitulado Orphenica lyra* (Brown 1554[3]), *Libro quarto*, nos. 73, 76.

This is also for solo voice with a highly ornamented intabulation of Josquin's lower voices.

2) Giaches organista, 'Recercar sopra la sol fa re mi'.

Source: Rome, Biblioteca Apostolica Vaticana, MS. Chigi VIII, fasc. 41, no. 4 (in score); a lute intabulation is in Uppsala, Universitetsbiblioteket, Vokalmusik MS. 87, fol. 60[v].[59]

Use of the ostinato figure in this work includes entries in the F and B♭ hexachords as well as the customary ones in C and G. The identity of the author is not certain, though it may be Jacques Brumel (or Brunel), organist at Ferrara from 1532 to 1564.[60]

3) Giuliano Tiburtino, '[Ricercare] La sol fa re mi.'

Source: *Fantasie, et recerchari a tre voci* (Brown 1549[7]), no. 12.

This three-voice setting of the ostinato figure comes close to Josquin's Mass in its obsessive repetition, using only the C and G hexachords. The opening, with its quick statement set against a slower-moving one, looks like an obvious reference to the Mass (cf. Josquin, *Kyrie*, m. 9; *Agnus Dei*, m. 15):

Ex. 16   mm. 1-3

4) Giovanni Battista Conforti, 'Ricercar del Quarto tono'.

Source: *Il primo libro de ricercari a quattro voci* (Brown 1558[1]), no. 8.

This piece is similar in technique to that of Tiburtino. A new theme introduced near the end bears a strong resemblance to the opening countersubject in the second *Agnus Dei* of Josquin's Mass.

5) Vincenzo Ruffo, '[Capriccio] La sol fa re mi'.

Source: *Capricci in musica a tre voci* (Brown 1564[8]), no. 1.

Somewhat more elaborate in texture than Tiburtino's piece, this *capriccio* is especially interesting since it may have been meant for vocal as well as

---

[59] Modern edition of the latter in *Codex carminum gallicorum*, ed. Bengt Hambraeus (Uppsala, 1961), pp. 133–7.

[60] See Edward E. Lowinsky, 'Early Scores in Manuscript', *Journal of the American Musicological Society*, xiii (1960), pp. 135–6. The identification of 'Giaches' as Jacques Brumel was made by Knud Jeppesen, *Die italienische Orgelmusik am Anfang des Cinquecento*, i (2d ed., Copenhagen, 1960), pp. 116–17; cf. H. Colin Slim, ed., *Musica nova* (*Monuments of Renaissance Music*, i; Chicago, 1964), pp. xxxviii–xxxix.

instrumental performance, calling for plenty of agility in the technique of
hexachord mutation if it were sung in solmization syllables.[61]

6) [Fantasia *a 4* on *la sol fa re mi*].

Source: Paris, Bibliothèque Nationale, Rés. Vma. MS. 851 (the Bourdeney
MS.), p. 415.

This piece, whose composer is as yet unknown to me,[62] makes use of *la sol
fa re mi* in all three Guidonian hexachords, using long-note *cantus-firmus*
treatment, a large variety of rhythmic contortions of the subject, an occasional
use of the figure in retrograde, and some *inganni*. Among the *inganni* is one
(A–G–C–A–B) used by Josquin in the *Pleni sunt coeli* of the Mass. It is given
such prominence in this fantasia that reference to Josquin seems unmistakable.

7) John Bull, 'Fantasia'.

Source: London, British Museum, Royal Music Library, MS. 23.1.4 (Cosyn
Virginal Book), fol. 69v.[63]

After an opening section in which *la sol fa re mi* is heard in the F, C, and B♭
hexachords, the figure is dropped.

8) Girolamo Frescobaldi, 'Capriccio Quarto, la, sol, fa, re, mi'.[64]

Source: *Il Primo Libro di Capricci* (Rome, 1624), no. 4.

9) Adriano Banchieri, duo on *la sol fa re mi*.

Source: *Il Principiante fanciullo* (Venice, 1625).[65]

The subject is used throughout the piece in a close network of imitative
entries; a second and third subject are introduced but the first theme remains
an *obbligo* throughout. The solmization syllables are at first carefully written
out; some *ij*'s are introduced for later repetitions, but at the occurrence of
an *inganno* the syllables reappear to alert the student that a mutation has taken
place. Banchieri's piece has as *didascalia* the phrase 'Orlando Lasso Imitato e
variato'; and indeed one of Lasso's textless—and untitled—duos, first published in the *Novae aliquot et ante hac non ita usitatae ad duas voces cantiones
suavissimae* of 1577,[66] does begin with *la sol fa re mi* as subject. Unlike
Banchieri's 'imitation', Lasso drops this subject as he introduces others.

[61] In his dedicatory letter, Ruffo says 'poi che ho udito quella [V.S.] cantargli cosi
leggiadramente....' On singing of ricercari, see Slim, *Musica nova*, p. xxxvii.

[62] M. François Lesure wrote me that he and Mme. Bridgman have identified many of
the anonymous pieces in the Bourdeney manuscript, but 'entre les pages 415 et 421, il y a
6 pièces sans textes dont nous n'avons pu trouver l'auteur'.

[63] Modern edition in *Musica Britannica*, xiv, ed. J. Steele and F. Cameron (London,
1960), p. 33.

[64] Modern edition in Girolamo Frescobaldi, *Orgel- und Klavierwerke*, ed. Pierre Pidoux,
ii (Kassel, 1949), pp. 21–5. Carlo Mosso, art. 'Frescobaldi', *La Musica*, parte prima (Turin,
1966), ii, p. 489, describes this capriccio as based on a fragment of the plainchant *Kyrie
Cunctipotens* (= *Kyrie* IV, *L.U.*, p. 25). There is indeed a 'la sol fa re mi' in the first Kyrie
of this chant; the resemblance of Josquin's ostinato to it would seem, however, to be a
matter of sheer coincidence.

[65] On this work see Oscar Mischiati, 'Adriano Banchieri (1568–1634). Profilo biografico
e bibliografia delle opere', *Conservatorio di Musica 'G. B. Martini'*, Bologna. *Annuario
1965–1970* (Bologna, 1971), pp. 118–19.

[66] The duo is printed in *Orlando di Lasso. Sämtliche Werke*, i, ed. F. X. Haberl (Leipzig,
1894), no. 14, p. 9.

10) J. J. Froberger, 'Fantasia Sopra Sol, La, Re'.[67]
The subject of this work is made up of *sol la re*, followed by *la sol fa re mi*,
under which 'lascia fare mi' is written every time the subject occurs. How
Froberger came to know this phrase, and whether it means he also knew
Josquin's Mass, is not certain.[68]

Textless *carmina* with imitative counterpoint were being written at the
time of Josquin, but rarely on solmization themes. Isaac's 'La mi la sol', if
it was originally an instrumental piece, was something of an exception.[69]
The 'Missa La sol fa re mi', which may have taken its subject from a very
concrete source, ended by becoming a sort of abstract fantasia upon its
theme; as such, its influence on the development of this genre may have been
a considerable one, another example of the profit sixteenth-century composers derived from the study of Josquin's music.

★　★　★

Since writing this study I have been informed by Professor Lowinsky
of the existence of two further works clearly related to Josquin's 'Missa La
sol fa re mi'. Their discovery is his, and I acknowledge with gratitude his
sharing it with me. The works are as follows:

1) A four-voice 'Missa La sol fa re mi', anonymous and untitled, may
be found in incomplete form (*Kyrie*, *Gloria*, and part of the *Credo*) in
Dresden, Sächsische Landesbibliothek, MS. I/D/505 (formerly Annaberg/
Buchholz, Kantoreiarchiv St. Annen, MS. 1126), pp. 144–53. The work,
evidently dating from the early sixteenth century, uses Josquin's subject
with great frequency but in a somewhat offhand, almost arbitrary manner.
Other melodic figures, such as the bass ostinato *mi re mi fa mi* in the *Christe*
and *la sol la mi*, prominent in *Kyrie* II, may be found as well.

2) A 'Missa quatuor vocum supra. la sol. mi fa. re' is in Munich, Bayerische Staatsbibliothek, Mus. MS. 7, fols. 77ᵛ–89. On fol. 78ᵛ the work is
ascribed to 'Robertus de fevin pie memorie'. This Mass is close in general
structure and technique to that of Josquin: the tenor uses its subject in much
the same way throughout, employing the figure in the C and G hexachords
and occasionally showing an *inganno*; the other voices share in use of the
subject much as they do in Josquin's Mass; the Credo uses chant paraphrase
as does Josquin's, etc. Professor Lowinsky suggests that Févin's subject, and
hence the whole Mass, might be considered to be a *risposta* to that of Josquin.

[67] For the manuscript sources of this piece, see *Johann Jakob Froberger, Orgel- und
Klavierwerke*, ed. Guido Adler (*Denkmäler der Tonkunst in Oesterreich*, iv/1; Vienna, 1897),
Revisionsbericht. The fantasia is printed on pp. 44–6 of this volume.
[68] Cf. David, 'Themes from Words', p. 74, who thinks it unlikely that Josquin's Mass
could have been known to Froberger, but that 'the story of its origin may still have been
remembered in Froberger's days'. I do not see why Froberger should not have seen
Josquin's music as well.
[69] See fn. 38 above.

The Polyphonic 'Missa de Beata Virgine' as a Genre: The Background of Josquin's Lady Mass

GUSTAVE REESE

In the last two decades, more or less, many isolated bits of information have come to light that bear upon the polyphonic 'Missa de Beata Virgine'[1] of the Renaissance which, in combination, make it possible to single it out with increasing clarity as a musical genre of its own. The purpose of this paper is to bring the various bits together and to add a few that are new.

That the polyphonic Masses in question should bear a relationship to plainsong Masses to the Virgin is to be expected. It is only since the 1950s that we have become aware that early chant books did not, as consistently as modern scholars once thought, group all *Kyries* together, all *Glorias* together, etc. Peter Wagner, in his *Gregorianische Formenlehre*,[2] recognized that, beginning in the eleventh century, manuscripts might, exceptionally, link a *Kyrie* with a *Gloria*, or a *Sanctus* with an *Agnus Dei*. But he understood the grouping together of sections of the plainsong Ordinary into cycles to be a recent development—one, moreover, that came about in imitation of the organization of polyphonic Masses. Now, however, we know that the grouping of plainchant sections for the Ordinary into Mass cycles can be traced back as far as the twelfth century and that polyphonic cycles were written in imitation of them rather than the other way round. The first comprehensive published contributions on this subject were made by Leo Schrade,[3] and additional information has been added by Bruno Stäblein,[4]

[1] By the term 'Missa de Beata Virgine' I am referring to the Continental species; the English Lady Masses of Ludford belong to a different tradition.

[2] *Einführung in die gregorianischen Melodien*, iii: *Gregorianische Formenlehre* (Leipzig, 1921), pp. 436–40.

[3] 'The Mass of Toulouse', *Revue belge de musicologie*, viii (1954), pp. 84–96; idem, 'News on the Chant Cycle of the *Ordinarium* Missae' (abstract), *Journal of the American Musicological Society*, viii (1955), pp. 66–9; and especially idem, 'The Cycle of the Ordinarium Missae', *In Memoriam Jacques Handschin* (Strasbourg, 1962), pp. 87–96.

[4] In the article 'Messe' in *MGG*, ix, especially cols. 151–8; see also examples 2–9.

Dom Dominique Catta,[5] and Kurt von Fischer,[6] the last of whom offered a table dealing with Mass cycles, mostly consisting of *Kyrie, Gloria, Sanctus, Agnus Dei,* and *Ite,* appearing in manuscripts dating from the fourteenth and fifteenth centuries.[7] An unpublished Ph.D. dissertation of 1956 by Martin Joseph Burne is a special study of Mass cycles appearing in chant sources belonging to American libraries.[8]

[5] His comprehensive and informative article, 'Aux origines du Kyriale', has appeared in *Revue grégorienne,* 34 (1955), pp. 175–82.

[6] See his valuable 'Neue Quellen zum einstimmigen Ordinariumszyklus des 14. und 15. Jahrhunderts aus Italien', *Liber amicorum Charles van den Borren* (Antwerp, 1964), pp. 60–68.

[7] The table can, however, be augmented from other sources, some of which are close to our meeting place: Cycles appear in New York Public Library, *Antiphonale* ★MRD (Rome?, 1636); M. 685 at the Pierpont Morgan Library is apparently a copy of that Library's M. 683 (included by Professor von Fischer) and therefore contains cycles like its model. See also note 8.

[8] This dissertation—'Mass Cycles in Early Graduals: A Study of the Ordinary of the Mass Cycles Found in Medieval and Renaissance Graduals in Libraries in the United States' (New York University, School of Education)—, besides containing relevant data on certain items owned by the Pierpont Morgan Library other than M. 683, offers information concerning various manuscript and printed sources dating from the thirteenth century to the eighteenth. The following is a small selection of manuscript sources mentioned by Burne, each of which contains four or more cycles (almost all without a *Credo*); each source listed (except the one at Washington) includes a Marian Mass. From the thirteenth century: Rochester, New York, Sibley Music Library, Eastman School of Music, University of Rochester, M 2147; from the fourteenth century: Cambridge, Massachusetts, Fogg Museum (but now in the Houghton Library), Harvard University, Ms Typ 79; from the fifteenth century: Chicago, Newberry Library, 23864 II; Washington, D.C., Smithsonian Institution, Barney 6862; Chicago, The Scriptorium, Ricketts Choir Book. The chant holdings in American libraries should receive more widespread attention.

Shortly after the Josquin Festival-Conference, Mr. Edward Kovarik of the University of Windsor, Windsor, Ontario, called my attention to several early sources of Ordinary cycles that had apparently not been reported in the relevant literature: Chicago, Newberry Library, +74; Cleveland, Museum of Art, 21.140; Parma, Cathedral, unnumbered manuscript; Paris, Bibl. Nat., Graduale printed by Giunta in 1499 or 1500. Mr. Kovarik commented also upon ten additional sources of such cycles that he had identified by piecing together information contained in the studies by Margareta Melnicki on the *Kyrie* (cf. note 31 below), Detlev Bosse on the *Gloria* (cf. note 32 below), Peter J. Thannabaur on the *Sanctus* (cf. note 33 below), and Martin Schildbach, *Das einstimmige Agnus Dei* (1967). Recently Mr. Kovarik has received his Ph.D. degree from Harvard; his dissertation, 'Mid-15th-Century Polyphonic Elaborations of the Plainchant Ordinarium Missae' (1973), includes information about the various monophonic sources referred to above as having been noted by him. Mention should perhaps be made here likewise of Turin, Biblioteca Nazionale, MS. J. II. 9, which contains five cycles for the Ordinary, but whose chants are not in the Vatican edition. Concerning these cycles, see Manfred F. Bukofzer, *Studies in Medieval and Renaissance Music* (New York, 1950), p. 225; Heinrich Besseler, 'Studien zur Musik des Mittelalters I', *Archiv für Musikwissenschaft,* vii, (1925), p. 212, and Richard H. Hoppin, *Cypriot Plainchant of the Manuscript Torino, Biblioteca Nazionale J. II. 9* (American Institute of Musicology, 1968).

The cycles were intended to serve various liturgical functions. There are Masses *in dominicis, in festis duplicibus, in festis semiduplicibus, in festis simplicibus*, and so forth. Of particular interest to us is the fact that examples of the *Missa in festis Beatae Mariae Virginis* are included. In what ultimately became the standard Vatican edition, there are two Masses bearing this designation—that is, Masses IX and X.[8a] Mass X may be disregarded for present purposes, but the relationship between the earliest Marian cycles and the standard Mass IX is close. Indeed, we find that *Kyrie* IX and *Gloria* IX immediately became standard in Marian cycles, *Gloria* IX characteristically including the six Marian tropes that were to be removed from the liturgy after the Council of Trent. Thus *Kyrie* IX and *Gloria* IX are portions of the incomplete Marian Mass that is one of the ten Ordinary cycles contained in the fourteenth-century source, Toulouse, Bibl. Mun., MS. 94.[9] Of special pertinence to the subject that we are investigating is the fact that, while certain sources already present *Sanctus* IX and *Agnus* IX, these are with some frequency replaced by *Sanctus* XVII and *Agnus* XVII. This does not mean that *Sanctus* and *Agnus* XVII, when they appear, always replace their Mass IX equivalents as a pair. As was pointed out in *Music in the Renaissance* in 1954, an Italian fifteenth-century manuscript in the Pierpont Morgan Library in New York contains a Mass headed *In honorem beate Marie Virginis*, and this Mass includes (through cross-references to other portions of the manuscript) *Sanctus* XVII and *Agnus* IX.[10] The Pierpont Morgan manuscript bears the number M. 683 and is one of a series made for Carlo Pallavicino, Bishop of Lodi (1456–97). It figures in an important way with regard to all ten of the Mass cycles included in Professor von Fischer's table and was mentioned by Schrade.[11] The main bulk of the Pallavicino series is now divided between the Morgan Library (six volumes) and the Library of the Hispanic Society of America in New York (seven; without call number). The latter group contains mostly chant for the Proper, but, among the few sections for the Ordinary, there occurs *Gloria* XV with the Marian tropes (fols. 139v–142v in the Society's sixth volume).

Plate 42, fig. a, reproducing folio 39v of Morgan 683, shows the beginning of *Kyrie* IX. The *Gloria* begins on folio 40v and includes the Marian tropes (see Ex. 1). Plate 42, fig. b shows folio 44v, which includes the first few notes of the *Sanctus* and *Agnus* melodies that are to be used, as well as the cross-references we have mentioned. The beginning of the *Sanctus* melody is found on folio 16v (see Pl. 43, fig. a) and the beginning of the *Agnus* melody on folio 5 (see Pl. 43, fig. b).

[8a] *Liber Usualis* (Tournai, 1961), pp. 40–43 and 43–5.

[9] Schrade, 'The Mass of Toulouse', p. 86.

[10] Gustave Reese, *Music in the Renaissance* (New York, 1954), pp. 242–3.

[11] See the article mentioned earlier, 'The Cycle of the Ordinarium Missae', p. 95. The manuscript has been mentioned, in passing, in notes 7 and 8 above.

Ex. 1 The six Marian tropes shown within the context of Gloria IX

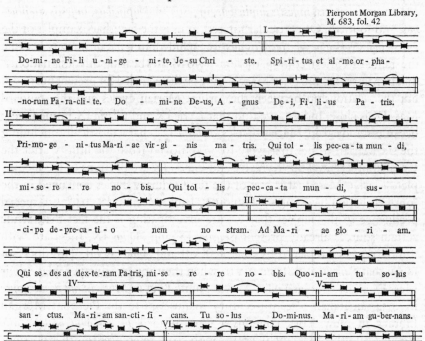

Pierpont Morgan Library,
M. 683, fol. 42

Do-mi-ne Fi-li u-ni-ge-ni-te, Je-su Chri - ste. Spi-ri-tus et al-me or-pha-

-no-rum Pa-ra-cli-te. Do - mi-ne De-us, A - gnus De-i, Fi-li-us Pa - tris.

Pri-mo-ge - ni-tus Ma-ri-ae vir-gi - nis ma - tris. Qui tol - lis pec-ca-ta mun - di,

mi-se-re - re no - bis. Qui tol - lis pec-ca-ta mun - di, sus-

-ci-pe de-pre-ca-ti-o - nem no - stram. Ad Ma-ri - ae glo - ri - am.

Qui se-des ad dex-te-ram Pa-tris, mi-se - re - re no - bis. Quo-ni-am tu so-lus

san - ctus. Ma-ri-am san-cti-fi - cans. Tu so-lus Do-mi-nus. Ma-ri-am gu-ber-nans.

Tu so-lus al - tis - si-mus. Ma-ri-am co - ro - nans. Je-su Chri - ste.

Additional plainsong manuscripts contain further deviations from the selection that has thus far stood forth as normal in our discussion. *Sanctus* IV and *Agnus* IV (not always as a pair) take on a certain prominence. Both are included in the Marian cycles in Vercelli, Archivio Capitolare, MS. 97, an Italian manuscript of the fourteenth century, and in Paris, Bibliothèque Nationale, MS. lat. 842, a fourteenth-century *Missale* from Châlons-sur-Marne. *Sanctus* IV appears in the Marian cycle in Paris, Bibliothèque Nationale, MS. lat. 10506, a fifteenth-century *Graduale* from Paris.[12] The last-named manuscript pairs *Sanctus* IV and *Agnus* XV. This is the only instance that has come to my attention thus far in which *Agnus* XV appears in a Marian Mass. Other rarities are *Sanctus* II, which appears in Cividale, Museo Archeologico, MS. 56, a fourteenth-century *Graduale* that originated in the town where it still remains, and *Sanctus* XVI, which appears in Lambach, Stiftsbibliothek, MS. 242, a German sixteenth-century source. These rare occurrences with regard to the *Sanctus* and *Agnus* have their counterpart with respect to the *Kyrie* also—for example, *Kyrie* II, provided with tropes, appears in Paris, Bibliothèque Nationale, MS. lat. 842, and

[12] It is my particular pleasure to thank Prof. Bruno Stäblein of the University of Erlangen, and his assistant, Frau Helma Hofmann, for their generosity in calling to my attention ten relevant manuscripts reproduced in the Mikrofilm-Archiv at the Universität Erlangen-Nürnberg, including the three just mentioned.

Kyrie IV, likewise troped, supplies the relevant chant melody in Aosta, Seminario maggiore, MS. 9–E–17, a fourteenth-century source. This last *Kyrie*, as we shall see, was to gain currency in polyphonic Marian Masses.

Our hasty survey shows that early chant cycles for the 'Missa de Beata Virgine' normally included *Kyrie* IX, *Gloria* IX (with the six Marian tropes), *Sanctus* IX or XVII or IV, and one of the *Agnus Dei* settings that bear the same numbers. As for the *Credo*: Specific provision is not always made for it. The *Credo* settings included in MS. 683 at the Pierpont Morgan Library are grouped separately, as in current chant books, and this was the norm. The Aosta manuscript draws upon *Credo* II for its Marian Mass, and there are other occasional abnormalities. But from all the evidence (monophonic and polyphonic, old and new), it is safe to accept the probability that *Credo* I was normally employed in the rendition of the Marian Mass in plainsong.

Turning now to the polyphonic 'Missa de Beata Virgine', we find that a *Credo* setting is very often included. As for the chant melodies chosen as *cantus prius facti*, a distinct preference emerges—certainly in the sixteenth century—for the following as the underlying chants:

Kyrie IX, *Gloria* IX, *Credo* I, *Sanctus* XVII, *Agnus* XVII

This selection may be regarded as the one that was finally to crystallize as the normal basis of polyphonic settings—the choice toward which earlier ones were heading. It is, for example, the selection upon which the polyphony is based in the Marian Masses of Arcadelt,[13] Morales,[14] Kerle,[15] and Victoria.[16] Morales has two Marian Masses—one for four voices and one for five—and the selection is virtually the same for both. I use the qualifying word 'virtually', because the *Credo* of the five-part Mass has the 'Ave Maria' antiphon as its true *cantus firmus*, but snatches of *Credo* I are worked into the polyphony also. Palestrina has five Marian Masses; in the four- and six-part settings, the same melodies for the Ordinary function as *cantus prius facti* without additional material, but the other three—all five-part, alternation Masses—are based on an identical group of Mantuan

---

[13] *Jacobi Arcadelt Opera omnia*, i, ed. Albert Seay (American Institute of Musicology, 1965), pp. 56–81.

[14] Mass *a 4* in *Cristóbal de Morales, Opera omnia*, i, ed. Higinio Anglés (*Monumentos de la Música española*, xi; Rome, 1952), pp. 1–34 (music section); Peter Wagner, *Geschichte der Messe* (Leipzig, 1913), pp. 457–533. Mass *a 5* in Morales, *Opera omnia*, iii (*Monumentos de la Música española*, xv; Rome, 1954), pp. 66–113 (music section).

[15] *Trésor musical*, xxv (*Musique religieuse*), ed. R.-J. van Maldeghem (Brussels, 1889), pp. 1–31.

[16] *Thomae Ludovici Victoria Abulensis Opera omnia*, ii, ed. Felipe Pedrell (Leipzig, 1903), pp. 93–118; Tomás Luis de Victoria, *Opera omnia*, i, ed. Higinio Anglés (*Monumentos de la Música española*, xxv; Rome, 1965), pp. 58–98 (music section).

chants, the Mantuan melody for the *Gloria* being closely related to *Gloria* IX.[17]

In Josquin's time, Brumel uses the eventually standard selection IX–IX–I–XVII–XVII in his Marian Mass[18] with one exception: he draws upon *Sanctus* IX instead of *Sanctus* XVII. The chants that he uses, therefore, are the ones that were to be adopted in 1614 by the Medicean Gradual. The fact that *Sanctus* IX and XVII begin similarly may be responsible for a certain interchangeability in their use. Josquin himself departs from Brumel's procedure by basing his last two movements on *Sanctus* and *Agnus* IV. The question naturally arises whether such differences in selection reflect local custom. Although it is reasonable to believe that they do, I cannot offer any evidence to this effect. When we gave brief consideration to Marian cycles in plainsong, we found *Sanctus* and *Agnus* IV in both the fourteenth-century Italian source now at Vercelli and a fourteenth-century French source now at Paris. Glareanus tells us that Brumel was 'approaching his last years'[19] when that composer and Josquin wrote their 'Missae de Beata Virgine', but he does not indicate where either one was living at the time or by what countries they might therefore have been influenced. Indeed, we were told at the symposium that Josquin's work may antedate the papacy of Julius II, which began in 1503.[20] Perhaps the discovery of additional evidence will some day show clearly that a connection between locality and choice of chant does exist.

Of the melodies that were eventually gathered into Mass IV, it is not just the *Sanctus* and *Agnus* that appear in Marian Masses, but also—though apparently less often—the *Kyrie*. The Machaut Mass[21] is, after all, designated as a 'Messe de Nostre Dame' in one source, the Vogüé MS., and the *cantus firmus* of its first movement is *Kyrie* IV. (Its *Sanctus* and *Agnus* are based on *Sanctus* and *Agnus* XVII.) The 'Missa de Nuestra Señora',[22] written

[17] Mass *a* 4: *Pierluigi da Palestrina's Werke*, xi, ed. Franz Xaver Haberl (Leipzig, 1881), pp. 1–20; *Le Opere complete di Giovanni Pierluigi da Palestrina*, vi, ed. R. Casimiri (Rome, 1939), pp. 1–25. Mass *a* 6: *Werke*, xii (1889), pp. 135–64; *Opere complete*, vi, pp. 175–215. Masses *a* 5: *Opere complete*, xviii, pp. 83–201. In 'The Recently Discovered Mantova Masses of Palestrina', *Acta musicologica*, xxii (1950), p. 46, Knud Jeppesen's important early report, he stated, not altogether accurately, that the 'three Missae B.M.V. . . . are built upon plainsongs quite unknown from other sources'.

[18] *Les Maîtres musiciens de la Renaissance française*, viii, ed. Henry Expert (Paris, 1898), pp. 1–76; *Antonii Brumel Opera omnia*, iv, ed. Barton Hudson (American Institute of Musicology, 1970), pp. 1–34.

[19] Henricus Glareanus, *Dodekachordon* (Basel, 1547), p. 366.

[20] See these Proceedings, pp. 712–13.

[21] *Guillaume de Machaut, Musikalische Werke*, iv, ed. Heinrich Besseler (Wiesbaden, 1954), pp. 192–210; *Polyphonic Music of the Fourteenth Century*, iii, ed. Leo Schrade (Monaco, 1956), pp. 37–64; etc.

[22] *La Música en la Corte de los Reyes Catolicos*, i, ed. Higinio Anglés (*Monumentos de la Música española*, i; Madrid, 1941), pp. 35–61 (music section).

jointly by Anchieta and Escobar, likewise has a Kyrie based on *Kyrie* IV. Its second movement is constructed on the normal *Gloria* IX with Marian tropes. The *Credo* begins like *Credo* I but proceeds differently; Msgr. Anglés, in his edition, reported the melody as unidentified. The *Sanctus*, unexpectedly, draws upon *Sanctus* VIII. The *Agnus* is based upon *Agnus* IX.

Among the Marian Masses I know, the one that is closest to Josquin's in its choice of chants is by Isaac. This composer has left us four 'Missae de Beata Virgine'; the Mass just referred to[23] is the only one of them for four voices. Its chants are *Kyrie* and *Gloria* IX and *Sanctus* and *Agnus* IV. The work has no *Credo* of its own. It is an alternation Mass, Isaac's polyphony for the *Agnus* being based on the second acclamation only. One of Isaac's five-part Marian Masses[24] and his Marian Mass for six voices[25] again draw on *Kyrie* and *Gloria* IX. In each Mass, the *Sanctus* melody is a variant of *Sanctus* IX that may be found in the Passau Gradual. Isaac's *Agnus* is based on the same *Sanctus* melody. The other five-part Mass[26] ranges farther afield. Edward R. Lerner, editor of the forthcoming complete edition of Isaac, has had the great kindness to inform me that the first two movements are based on *Kyrie* and *Gloria* melodies that appear in Erhard Ratdolt's *Graduale Augustense* of 1491–6. These melodies are quite different from those of *Kyrie* and *Gloria* IX, and make this Mass one of the few that depart from the norm in the two earlier movements. The last two movements are based on *Sanctus* and *Agnus* IV.

Close to Brumel, if not to Josquin, is Pierre de la Rue, whose 'Missa de Beata Virgine'[27] draws upon *Kyrie* and *Gloria* IX, *Credo* IV, *Sanctus* IX, and *Agnus* XVII. In other words, La Rue departs from Brumel only in his use of *Credo* IV instead of *Credo* I. This is the *Credo cardinalis*, dating from the fifteenth century, which was adopted also by certain other composers for their Marian Masses. Girolamo Cavazzoni, for example, in his *alternatim* Mass for organ and plainchant,[28] uses the melodies of Mass IX for his movements 1–2 and 4–5; he bases his third on the *Credo cardinalis*. The same *Credo* melody serves Giuliano Buonaugurio da Tivoli, one of the obscure composers brought to light by Knud Jeppesen in his *Italia sacra musica*. This composer constructs the first and second movements of his Mass[29] on *Kyrie* and *Gloria* IX and his last two on *Sanctus* and *Agnus* XVII.

We have mentioned the appearance of unusual *Kyrie* and *Gloria* melodies

---

[23] *Heinrich Isaac Messen*, ed. Herbert Birtner and Martin Staehelin (*Musikalische Denkmäler*, vii; Mainz, 1968), pp. 3–15.

[24] Ibid., pp. 16–40.   [25] Ibid., pp. 60–79.   [26] Ibid., pp. 41–59.

[27] *Drie Missen van Pierre de la Rue*, ed. René Bernard Lenaerts and Jozef Robijns (*Monumenta musicae belgicae*, viii; Antwerp, 1960), pp. 1–22.

[28] *Girolamo Cavazzoni, Dal I e II libro di Intavolature per organo*, ed. Giacomo Benvenuti (*I Classici della musica italiana*, Quaderni 23–24; Milan, 1919), pp. 48–60; *Girolamo Cavazzoni, Orgelwerke*, ii, ed. Oscar Mischiati (Mainz, 1958), pp. 32–9.

[29] Knud Jeppesen, ed., *Italia sacra musica*, ii (Copenhagen, 1962), pp. 14–35.

in one of Isaac's five-part Masses. Among other Masses incorporating similar rarities is the polyphonic 'Missa de Beata Virgine' by Benedictus Ducis, published in an edition by Hans Albrecht.[30] Its *Kyrie* and *Gloria* are based on melodies which, according to Albrecht's introduction, appear in German, Austrian, Swiss, and Bohemian manuscripts of the fourteenth and the sixteenth centuries. (The *Kyrie* melody is undoubtedly Melnicki No. 166[31]; the *Gloria* is very likely Bosse No. 49.[32]) The third movement is based on *Credo* IV, and the fourth movement on *Sanctus* IV in the version shown in Thannabaur No. 195 J.[33] Albrecht states that the source of the *Agnus* is not traceable.

Heinrich Finck's Marian Mass[34] departs from the norm in a still different way. The beginning of *Kyrie* IX is used as a head-motif in one or more voices at the beginning of most of the sections of the Mass. There may be a free paraphrase of the *Christe* of Mass IX in the bass of Finck's *Christe*, but no other chant melodies seem to have been identified.

The most unusual Marian Mass that *may* belong within our tradition is by Compère.[35] Professor Finscher has printed the words 'de Beata Maria Virgine' in brackets under 'Galeazescha' in the first caption in Vol. ii of his Compère edition. The work is one of those cycles of *motetti missales* that are sometimes referred to as 'substitution' Masses. Both because they are rooted in the Ambrosian liturgy and because they do not use the standard texts for the Ordinary, one would not expect to find traces of the normal Marian melodies in them—that is, 'normal' according to Roman standards. However, the two tenors in the motet 'Ave, virgo', which is *loco Introitus* in the 'Missa Galeazescha', both begin with the notes that form the opening of *Kyrie* IX. This could certainly be coincidence; however, the first tenor of the last motet, 'Virginis Mariae laudes', which is *loco Deo gratias*, opens with what is remarkably like the continuation of the same *Kyrie* passage that in plainsong Mass IX serves for the *Deo gratias*.[36] Several other parallels might be referred to as existing between the *motetti missales* of this

---

[30] *Musik alter Meister*, xi, ed. H. Albrecht (Graz, 1959).

[31] Margareta Melnicki, *Das einstimmige Kyrie des lateinischen Mittelalters* (Regensburg, 1954), p. 113.

[32] Detlev Bosse, *Untersuchung einstimmiger mittelalterlicher Melodien zum 'Gloria in excelsis Deo'* (Regensburg, 1955), p. 99.

[33] Peter Thannabaur, *Das einstimmige Sanctus* (Munich, 1962), p. 62.

[34] August Wilhelm Ambros, *Geschichte der Musik*, v (3rd ed., Leipzig, 1911), pp. 247–79.

[35] *Loyset Compère, Opera omnia*, ii, ed. Ludwig Finscher (American Institute of Musicology, 1959), pp. 1–25.

[36] The similarity may be due to nothing more than the melodic relationships between *Kyrie* IX and the sequence melody 'Victimae paschali laudes', which Compère has used with the Marian version of the text. ('Virginis Mariae laudes' dates from at least the twelfth century; see Carl Allan Moberg, *Über die schwedischen Sequenzen* (Uppsala, 1927), p. 73, and melody no. 5a.)

cycle and standard Roman chant melodies of the Mass Ordinary, but I do not wish to make too much of a case with regard to what may be only a group of coincidences. However, what appear to be parallels *are* present; and, in view of our need for information about possible relations between any body of chant and Milanese polyphony in the Josquin generation, the resemblances in question should perhaps not go unreported.

One of the characteristics of 'Missae de Beata Virgine' before the Council of Trent was the inclusion of tropes, and this is true not only in the *Gloria*. Thus, Anchieta's *Kyrie* includes the trope *Rex virginum*. Brumel's *Benedictus* likewise is troped, as is the *Benedictus* of each of Isaac's four Marian Masses, but the most characteristic insertions, certainly, are the six so-called Marian tropes, beginning with *Spiritus et alme*, that are normally inserted at this period in *Gloria* IX. They are included in Josquin's Mass and, among the Masses mentioned earlier, continue to be present in those of Anchieta, Brumel, La Rue, Cavazzoni, Arcadelt, and others. Complications arise with regard to their use in the Masses of Kerle and Palestrina. Kerle's Mass was first printed at Venice in 1562, with the tropes included. But when the Mass was reprinted in 1582—that is, after the Council of Trent—the tropes were removed. Palestrina's 'Missa de Beata Virgine' for six voices still, in the edition of 1570, has its tropes in their normal position, notwithstanding the late date; but, in the edition of 1599, although the music of the tropes is retained, the texts are replaced by repetitions of the liturgical words. However, the four-part Marian Mass of Morales included the tropes not only when it was first printed at Venice in 1540, but in all seven reprintings, extending beyond the time of the Council.[37] On the other hand, the ten sources of Morales' five-part Marian Mass vary in including or excluding the tropes.[38]

In short, even though a polyphonic 'Missa de Beata Virgine' of the Renaissance cannot be briefly and simply defined in musical terms, it may be said that it is a polyphonic Mass based upon plainsong melodies, these being characteristically *Kyrie* IX, *Gloria* IX (the six Marian tropes being included before the Council of Trent), *Credo* I, and *Sanctus* and *Agnus* XVII or IX or IV, these three occurring in descending order of frequency. The composer may use *cantus-firmus* or paraphrase technique, or both, but what he produces will not be a characteristic *cantus-firmus* or paraphrase Mass, since normally no two movements will be based on the same *cantus prius factus*.

Josquin's Mass, in many respects, belongs within the tradition. Not only

---

[37] See Robert Stevenson's review in *Journal of the American Musicological Society*, vii (1954), p. 142, and Anglés in *Monumentos*, xv, p. 27, n. 4 (text section), correcting his own statement in *Monumentos*, xi, p. 61 (text section), that the tropes were excised in the Roman edition of 1544.

[38] See Anglés in *Monumentos*, xv, p. 36 (text section).

do the Marian tropes appear in the *Gloria*, but the selection of chant melodies—which at first glance may seem abnormal as far as the presence of *Sanctus* and *Agnus* IV is concerned—is actually within the tradition also. What is not within it—what transcends it—is the expression of the master's radiant individuality. In the *Credo*, for example, at the words 'Qui cum Patre et Filio', he has what amounts to one measure of triple metre in the superius against two measures of duple metre in the other voices—this complexity clearing up and the superius joining in the duple metre and thus helping to provide descriptive text treatment when the word *simul* is reached.[39] The work is full of felicitous touches applied to its grand structure. But that is the subject for another paper. Although Brumel's Marian Mass is also a great work, one can in the main agree with Glareanus when he wrote of the two men, with regard to their 'Missae de Beata Virgine': 'Josquin excelled by far in my opinion—and so acquitted himself in this contest that it seems to me. . . that finer music cannot be created'.[40] If the present rather sketchy paper has been concerned not so much with the beauties of that work as with its background, the reasons for Glareanus' praise will, I believe, be in full evidence when you hear a performance of Josquin's Mass this evening.

[39] [For Spanish theorists' views on this passage, see Robert Stevenson, these Proceedings, pp. 239–40.—Ed.]

[40] *Dodekachordon*, p. 366.

VI Performance Practice

The Performance of Sacred Music in Italy during Josquin's Time, c. 1475–1525

FRANK A. D'ACCONE

The present paper is an attempt to study the performance of sacred music in Italy during Josquin's time by investigating the precise make-up of various chapels of the period on the basis of archival documentation. I am aware, of course, that the approach is one-sided. Iconographic and other evidence notwithstanding, however, it seems to me that it is primarily through examination and comparison of original documents that we can obtain some of the basic, accurate information we need.

In many local histories of music and musicians emphasis is placed upon famous composers or *maestri di cappella*, rather than on answering essential questions such as the number of singers and the distribution of voices in a given year, whether all of the *cantori* were in fact singers of polyphony, the presence or absence of instrumentalists, the participation of extraordinary personnel, whether singers performed at all services and, indeed, the days and services at which polyphony was performed. Only when these questions have been answered for all of Italy's major chapels shall we be able to form a clear idea about the performance of sacred music in that country during Josquin's lifetime. The present paper, although by necessity in the nature of a preliminary report, allows nevertheless some definite conclusions as regards the principal churches of several of the northern and north-central Italian cities.

The chapels examined here include those of the capitals of the five great political powers on the peninsula during the late fifteenth and early six-teenth centuries, that is, Rome, Naples, Milan, Florence, and Venice. The chapels of smaller political entities such as the city-state of Siena and the courts of Mantua and Ferrara have also been taken into account, as have been those of the subject cities of Verona, Treviso, Padua, and Bologna—the latter two being the seats of venerable and dynamic universities.[1] To a greater or lesser degree each of these cities made notable contributions to

[1] When available, data about chapels in a few other cities are also included.

the arts and letters of the time. In addition, several of them played host to the leading Franco-Netherlandish composers of the day (Obrecht, Isaac, Agricola, Compère, Ghiselin, van Weerbecke, Martini, de la Rue, de Orto, and Josquin himself) as well as to a younger generation of native composers (Coppini, Festa, Layolle, Gaffurio, Ruffino d'Assisi, Spataro, and Fogliano).

Mention of the political status of these cities introduces a point that is central to my thesis, that is, that politics, wealth, and social customs were principal elements in determining the formation and composition of various Italian chapels. When political power and state revenues were concentrated in the hands of one ruler, for example, a large, private chapel could be funded from the court's income. For many a Renaissance prince—in addition to a genuine love of music—maintaining a well-staffed chapel (like retaining illustrious writers and artists) was a matter of social pride; it reflected the magnificence and grandeur of his person and his office. Certainly, this was true for several of the Roman pontiffs as well as for some of the rulers of the other Italian states, both large and small. Religious music at such centres was performed before a select audience in the prince's own chapel; occasionally it may have reached a wider public.

In the cities a different situation prevailed. In Florence, for example, strong democratic traditions stood in the way of ostentatious personal display, even for a family as wealthy and influential as the Medici. In matters musical, they confined themselves to creating chapels for the town's major churches. Even in Venice, where the ruling oligarchy shared in the doge's power as well as in the public functions, the appointment of musicians was in the hands of an elected group of officials, as was also the case in Florence. The focal point of musical activities in Florence was the Cathedral of Santa Maria del Fiore, and in Venice it was St. Mark's, two magnificent churches that were the pride of citizens of all classes. The Basilica of San Petronio in Bologna and the splendid cathedrals of Siena and Modena strikingly reflect the civic spirit that prompted their construction and adornment. In these places religious and municipal events were often hard to distinguish; they were celebrated by all classes of society and music performed there reached the status of a public function. Rome and Milan present exceptional cases, for in addition to large private chapels, these cities also counted chapels in their principal churches. The performance of sacred music in Italy at Josquin's time, then, was affected not only by artistic, but also by political, social, and economic factors.

*　*　*

The first question to which we seek an answer concerns the number of singers of polyphony in some of the major Italian churches during the period from about 1430 to 1480. In studying Table I the reader should bear in mind that an organist was employed in all of the churches mentioned here and in the subsequent tables.

TABLE I

Singers of Polyphony in Italian Churches from about 1430 to 1480

Milan,[a] Cathedral	1430	4 adults, unspecified number of boys
	1459	Josquin becomes seventh member; chapelmaster dies: 6 adults, unspecified number of boys
	1460–80	7 adults (average), unspecified number of boys
Florence,[b] Cathedral—		
Baptistry	1439–69	4–6 adults
Cathedral	1478–81	5–6 adults (generally 2 each for the lower parts), 4 boys
Cathedral	1481–4	4 adults (chapelmaster, 1 alto, 1 tenor, 1 bass), 4–8 boys
Rome,[c] St. Peter's	1457–8	3 singers
	1465	5 singers (3 sopranos, 1 tenor, 1 contratenor)
	1478	7 singers (4 sopranos, 1 tenor, 2 contratenors)
Modena,[d] Cathedral	1456–70	3 adults
	1472–7	4 adults, unspecified number of boys
Padua,[e] Cathedral	1443	3 adults
	1466, 1470	5 singers
	1469, 1472	6 singers
Treviso,[f] Cathedral	1463	3 adults
	1472–6	4 adults (average), unspecified number of boys
Bologna,[g] San Petronio	1479	5 adults

[a] Claudio Sartori, 'Josquin des Prés cantore del Duomo di Milano (1459–1472)', *Annales musicologiques*, iv (1956), pp. 55–83; pp. 67, 77–81 passim.

[b] Frank A. D'Accone, 'The Singers of San Giovanni in Florence during the 15th Century', *Journal of the American Musicological Society*, xiv (1961), pp. 307–58; pp. 313, 316, 328–30.

[c] Fr. X. Haberl, 'Die römische "schola cantorum" und die päpstlichen Kapellsänger bis zur Mitte des 16. Jahrhunderts', *Vierteljahrsschrift für Musikwissenschaft*, iii (1887), pp. 189–296; pp. 236–8.

[d] Gino Roncaglia, *La cappella musicale del Duomo di Modena* (Florence, 1957), pp. 12–13.

[e] Raffaele Casimiri, 'Musica e musicisti nella cattedrale di Padova nei sec. XIV, XV, XVI', *Note d'Archivio*, xviii (1941), pp. 101–214; pp. 149, 158–61.

[f] Giovanni D'Alessi, *La cappella musicale del Duomo di Treviso* (Vedelago, 1954), pp. 48–9.

[g] Gaetano Gaspari, 'La musica in San Petronio. A continuazione delle memorie risguardanti la storia dell'arte musicale in Bologna', *Atti e memorie della R. Deputazione di storia patria per le provincie di Romagna*, serie I, ix (1870), pp. 1–35; pp. 17–18; reference here is to the reprint, G. Gaspari, *Musica e musicisti a Bologna* (Bologna, 1970), pp. 129–30.

From the information assembled in Table I it is clear that through the mid-1470s most chapels rarely employed more than six or seven adult singers. In smaller chapels polyphony may have been performed by one singer to a part, in larger ones by one or two voices, two for the lower parts and a somewhat larger number of sopranos. The evidence of this practice from St. Peter's in the years 1465 and 1478 is supported by a letter, dated 21 March [1469], from the singer Jachetto di Marvilla to Lorenzo the Magnificent, in which the writer states that, following instructions from the Medici, he had procured a tenor, a contratenor (himself), and 'three very high treble singers' for the Baptistry's chapel.[2] Manifestly, this combination was considered normal for performing pieces *a 3*. Jachetto further states that for the time being one of the singers could sing bass in pieces *a 4* and that later a contratenor, 'who is a good bass as well', could be brought from France. Another document, dated 8 July 1481, from the Cathedral of Siena complaining about a tenor who failed to return from a leave of absence, states that had this been known previously, the three sopranos and two 'contras' in the chapel would not have been retained, because 'senza tenorista non si può cantare'.[3] That more sopranos were required may have been due, in part, to the weakness of men's voices in the falsetto range. More importantly, the predominance of the soprano part may be related

---

[2] D'Accone, 'The Singers of San Giovanni', p. 324.

[3] Siena, Archivio dell'Opera del Duomo, *Debitori & Creditori* (1476–90), Vol. 717, fol. 304. The full document reads as follows:

MCCCCLXXXI

Nicholò di Lore da Firenze, tenorista, die dare a dì VIII di luglio lire quarantaquattro e soldi [blank] e quali sonno per salario abbiamo pagato a Ugo, Petraccino & Ruberto francioso, cantori, e a sser Biagio di Sansalvadore e a sser Domenicho di Mattio, chantori tutti; e questi abiamo tenuti istimando che decto Nicholò tenorista da Firenze, che aveva chiesto licenza a lo spectabile e degnissimo nostro operaro misser Alberto Aringhieri per quatro giorni per andare a la festa a Firenze, e questo fu a dì XX di luglio [*sic*; should read 'giugno'] che andò, stimando tornasse di dì in dì come ci dava sentore [*sic*]; e per non devviare la capella abbiam tenuti e detti sovrani e contri che sapendo non fusse tornato, chè senza tenorista non si può cantare, avemo dato licenza a' detti cantori. Ora avendo piena informatione come lui si acconciò questo dì essendoci chosì detto e affermato assai conveniente e che avvendoci fatta tenere questa spesa senza alcuno nostro frutto è paruto e così è l'onesto che la paghi lui; e però per comandamento del sopradetto misser Alberto l'abiamo qui [one word illegible: dichiarato?] vero debitore perchè a qualche tempo ce ne possiamo valere contra di lui o sue cose acciò che la chiesa nostra non perde ma che sta consicurata come è detto. L. XLIIII

Other accounts in the same volume also give the names of the singers mentioned in this entry: 'ser Biagio di Tommè, chappellano...e chanttatore' (fols. 277ᵛ–8); 'ser Domenicho di Mattio, prete...la chantoria di canto figurato' (fols. 278ᵛ–9); 'Ruberto Leudey picharddo, chantorre' (ibid.); 'Ugo di Gidio francioso, chantore' (fols. 281ᵛ–2); 'Pietro di Ghino, chantore sovrano in duomo' (fols. 307ᵛ–8). Payments to all of these musicians save for the last-named, who is not listed until August, are dated from April of 1481; payments for April and May are recorded instead to 'ser Giovanni a Sami (?) francioso, cantore in duomo' (fols. 278ᵛ–9).

Later entries in the same volume show that the chapel continued its existence despite this temporary setback. Payments are listed for December 1481 and January 1482 to 'Jachomo da Francia, chantore', 'per scriptura di uno libro di cantoria', while salaries for the last six months of 1482 are recorded to 'ser Piero de la piaza' [de platea], 'tenorista in duomo' (fols. 382ᵛ–3); 'Bartolomeo Casotris [de Castris], chantore'; 'Quintino di Martino, chantore'; and 'Giovanni di Giovanni francioso, chantore' (all on fols. 387ᵛ–8). Martin Staehelin believes that 'ser Piero de la piaza' was Pierre de la Rue. See his 'Pierre de la Rue in Italien', *Archiv für Musikwissenschaft*, xxvii (1970), pp. 128–37.

to the treble-dominated style of the mid-fifteenth century that would require reinforcement of the soprano part.

In contradistinction to these small musical establishments, the Italian courts of the time, probably in emulation of the dukes of Burgundy and similar northern centres, began to assemble much larger groups of singers. During the 1470s, for example, the Sistine Chapel[4] employed between fourteen and twenty adult singers, and the number went as high as twenty-four in 1483.[5] Similar numbers are found in the chapel of King Alfonso I of Naples, who as early as 1451 was employing twenty-one singers and two organists.[6] Also in 1480 twenty-one singers served the court of Naples.[7] The Milanese court chapel under Duke Galeazzo Maria Sforza boasted twenty-two *cantori de cappella* and eighteen *cantori de camera* in 1474, though the combined number of singers was apparently reduced in the following year, first to thirty-three and then to twenty-six.[8] Even a small court like Ferrara in 1472 had fifteen adult singers as well as a corps of boys.[9] In 1476 twenty-three singers were associated with the Ferrarese court; similar numbers are found until the year 1482, when war with Venice depleted the ducal treasury.[10]

★ ★ ★

During the late 1480s and 1490s the number of singers in the churches of some wealthier cities began to approach that of the courts. This change was doubtless due not only to a desire to emulate the courts but also to the requirements made by the new musical repertories of works by members of Josquin's generation, many of whom, indeed, found employment in these chapels.

As can be seen from the figures in Table II, by 1484 the Santissima Annunziata in Florence was employing eighteen adult singers. The Florentine Cathedral, whose chapel counted ten adults in 1485, also reached the figure eighteen in 1493. The number of adult singers serving at St. Mark's, Venice, grew from ten in 1486 to as many as seventeen in 1487, and during the next five years an average of fifteen adult singers was maintained.

[4] The Sistine chapel, founded by Sixtus IV (1471–84), flourished side by side with the singers of St. Peter's, who later became the choir associated with the Cappella Giulia, founded by Julius II.

[5] Haberl, 'Die römische "schola cantorum"', pp. 230–32, 241–2.

[6] C. M. Riccio, 'Alcuni fatti di Alfonso I. d'Aragona', *Archivio storico per le provincie napoletane*, vi (1881), pp. 411–61; pp. 411–12.

[7] Edmond Vander Straeten, *La musique aux pays-bas*, iv (Brussels, 1878), pp. 28–30.

[8] The personnel lists of the Milanese court have been published several times, most recently in Sartori, 'Josquin des Prés', pp. 64–6.

[9] I am indebted to Professor Lewis Lockwood for this information, which will be published in a forthcoming study of music at the Ferrarese court.

[10] Ibid.

TABLE II

Singers of Polyphony in Italian Churches from about 1480 to 1500

Florence,[a] SS. Annunziata,	1484	18 adults
Cathedral	1485	10 adults
	1487–8	13 adults (average)
	1493	18 adults
	1498–1501	4 adults, 8 boys
Venice,[b] St. Mark's	1486	10 adults, 12 boys
	1487	12–17 adults, 10–15 boys
	1490	15–17 adults, 12 boys
	1492	14–15 adults, 12 boys
Milan,[c] Cathedral	1483	9 adults, unspecified number of boys
	1484	10 adults, unspecified number of boys
	1491	13 adults, unspecified number of boys
	1496	15 adults, unspecified number of boys
Siena,[d] Cathedral	1481	6 adults (3 sopranos, 2 contratenors, 1 tenor)
Padua,[e] Cathedral	1484, 1488	4 adults, unspecified number of boys
	1497–8	9 adults, unspecified number of boys
Treviso,[f] Cathedral	1488–91	8 adults, not more than 5 boys
Modena,[g] Cathedral	1494	6 adults, unspecified number of boys
Rome,[h] St. Peter's	1485	9 singers (including 3 sopranos, 2 contratenors, 2 tenors)
	1491	10 singers (including 4 sopranos, 3 contratenors, 1 tenor, 1 bass)
	1497	8 singers

[a] D'Accone, 'The Singers of San Giovanni', pp. 337–8, 340–1, 345–6, 349. Savonarola's influence probably led to the disbanding of the chapel in 1493; it was re-established, with considerably fewer singers, in 1498 (ibid., pp. 346–9). Since no boys are listed in previous years, men must have sung the soprano part before 1498.

[b] Venice, Archivio di Stato, Procuratia de supra, Basilica di San Marco, *Chiesa, 1486–1493*, Reg. 1, fols. 8, 13, 17ᵛ, 19, 31, 35ᵛ, 40, 49ᵛ, 54ᵛ, 59ᵛ, 62ᵛ, 66ᵛ, 71, 76, 81ᵛ, 91, 95ᵛ, 101ᵛ, 111ᵛ, 116ᵛ, 120, 123ᵛ, 128ᵛ, 133, 137ᵛ, 142, 145ᵛ, 148ᵛ, 153ᵛ, 157ᵛ, 162, 165ᵛ. The relevant materials will be published in my study of musicians at St. Mark's in the late Quattrocento.

[c] Claudio Sartori, 'Franchino Gaffurio a Milano', *Universitas Europeae*, i (1952–3), pp. 13–16, 17–20; pp. 13, 17. The number of boys in the 1480s and 1490s was probably ten. At any rate, that is the number mentioned in a document of December 1481; see Claudio Sartori, 'La cappella del Duomo dalle origini a Franchino Gaffurio', *Storia di Milano*, ix (Milan, 1961), p. 738, n. 3.

[d] See footnote 3 above.

[e] Casimiri, 'Musica e musicisti', pp. 162–3, 173.

[f] D'Alessi, *La cappella musicale*, pp. 55, 62.

[g] Roncaglia, *La cappella musicale*, p. 14.

[h] Haberl, 'Die römische "schola cantorum"', pp. 238–9.

They were assisted by twelve *zaghi* or *zagi* (*chierici*) *cantadori*, that is, a group of older boys and young men who were in training for the priesthood. In the St. Mark's accounts, these *zaghi cantadori* are listed separately from the *zaghi menori*, or younger clerks, who were apparently called upon to sing only the chant. The chapel of the Milanese Cathedral, consisting of nine adults in 1483, by 1496 was employing fifteen adults as well as a number of boys. However, in the same period the churches of Siena, Padua, Treviso, and Modena retained much smaller groups of adult singers assisted, it would seem, by equally small numbers of boys, and as late as 1491 the chapel at St. Peter's in Rome included only ten singers.

★   ★   ★

For the early decades of the sixteenth century data are either incomplete or lacking for some of the cities mentioned above. We know nothing about the court chapels in Milan and Naples, for example, although the wars convulsing the Italian peninsula at that time must have seriously affected the composition and maintenance of those institutions.[11] For Venice, too, lists of the personnel at St. Mark's seem not to have survived, although we may again assume that war with the League of Cambrai and other powers between 1509 and 1513 did not allow—at least for those years—an expansion of personnel beyond the fifteen adults and twelve boys recorded during the early 1490s. That there was a large group of singers serving at St. Mark's again during the early 1520s, however, is borne out by the fact that a few surviving documents mention the existence there of two chapels, a *capella maior* and a *capella parva*.[12]

As for the other chapels for which reliable figures are available, the trend established during the late 1480s and 1490s is again discernible, except in a few cases. The Sistine Chapel still led the way. Records for the first decade of the century indicate that the number of singers employed ranged from sixteen to twenty-one.[13] On the basis of expenditures it has been calculated

[11] The Milanese court chapel apparently disappeared with the fall of Ludovico il Moro in 1500. The chapel maintained by the Spanish governors of Milan later in the sixteenth century 'seems to have been inconsequential'. See Carl Anthon, 'Some Aspects of the Social Status of Italian Musicians during the Sixteenth Century—II', *Journal of Renaissance and Baroque Music* [*Musica Disciplina*], i (1946), pp. 222–34; p. 226. At least one Italian court chapel, however, was unaffected by political events of the early sixteenth century. Some recently published data from Ferrara show that 'by about 1500 [Ercole I d'Este] had a larger musical establishment than the Pope or any political rival in Italy'. There were in fact 'at least 27 regularly paid singers' in the Ferrarese court chapel in that year, and similarly impressive figures (thirty-one singers in 1504, twenty-one singers in 1506, about twenty singers in 1508 and 1509) are mentioned for the following decade. See Lewis Lockwood, 'Music at Ferrara in the Period of Ercole I d'Este', *Studi Musicali*, i (1972), pp. 101–31; p. 107, n. 18. As indicated below, it was not until 1521 that the Sistine Chapel apparently achieved a total complement of thirty-one singers, the largest number employed during the period under discussion.

[12] Venice, Archivio di Stato, Procuratia de supra, Basilica di San Marco, *Actorum, 1517–1525*, Reg. 123, fol. 46, fol. 52, wherein are cited two musicians: 'Marci Antonii Aloysii cantori capelle maioris eccl. S. Marci' (on 29 April 1522) and 'pre. Laurentii ab organo cantoris capella parva' (on 22 July 1522). In his *Storia della musica sacra nella già cappella ducale di San Marco in Venezia* (Venice, 1854–5), ii, pp. 26–7, Francesco Caffi speaks of the musicians cited in these documents but makes no mention of their association with the two chapels. The year of the documents is misprinted as 1322.

[13] Haberl, 'Die römische "schola cantorum"', pp. 247–9; Manfred Schuler, 'Die Kapelle Papst Pius' III.', *Acta Musicologica*, xlii (1970), pp. 225–30.

TABLE III

Singers of Polyphony in Italian Churches from about 1500 to 1540

Milan,[a] Cathedral	1504	12 adults, 7 boys
	1507	12 adults, probably no more than 6 boys
	1516	14 adults, 6 boys
	1521	12 adults, probably no more than 6 boys
Bologna,[b] San Petronio	1505–6	7 adults, unspecified number of boys
	1512	9 adults, unspecified number of boys
	1513, 1521	10 adults, unspecified number of boys
	1525	13 adults, unspecified number of boys
	1540	15 adults, unspecified number of boys
Modena,[c] Cathedral	1505–13	9 adults, unspecified number of boys
	1513–20	11 adults, unspecified number of boys
Padua,[d] Cathedral	1511–12	5 adults, unspecified number of boys
	1523, 1529	6 adults, unspecified number of boys
	1532–3	7 adults, unspecified number of boys
Treviso,[e] Cathedral	1509–13	5 adults, not more than 5 boys
	1527–8	13 singers (2 *maestri*, 3 altos, 2 tenors, 2 basses, 4 boy sopranos)
	1532	12 singers (6 adults, 2 each for the lower parts; 6 sopranos, most of whom were probably boys)
Verona,[f] Cathedral	1524	7 adults, unspecified number of boys
	1527	11 adults, unspecified number of boys
	1530	7 adults, unspecified number of boys
	1533	9 adults, unspecified number of boys
Rieti,[g] Cathedral	1517	4 adults, unspecified number of boys
	1529	8 adults, unspecified number of boys
	1539	7 adults, unspecified number of boys
Rome,[h] St. Peter's, later Cappella Giulia	1501	7 singers
	1506–7	8 adults, 2 boys
	1514	5 adults, 3 boys
	1515	6 singers
	1525	11 singers
	1534	7 singers
Siena,[i] Cathedral	1508	6 adults
	1513	10 adults
	1517	14 singers
	1520	17 singers
Mantua,[j] Cathedral	1500	4 adults, unspecified number of boys
	1505	5 adults, unspecified number of boys
	1509	8 adults (2 each of standard ranges)
	1511–19	court singers also participated, exact number unknown; estimated at 25 singers of whom 15 were probably adults
	1523–6	15 singers
	1528	18 singers
Florence,[k] Cathedral	1502	16 singers (adults: 2 sopranos, 2 altos, 4 tenors, 2 basses, 1 teacher; 5 boys)
	1507	12 singers (adults: 1 soprano, 3 altos, 3 tenors, 3 basses; 5 boys)
	1512	8 adults (1 soprano, 2 altos, 3 tenors, 2 basses), 4–6 boys
	1513–26	6 adults (average), 4–6 boys
Baptistry	1510	8 adults (1 soprano, 2 altos, 3 tenors, 2 basses), 5 boys

	1515	13 adults (at least, including 2 altos, 5 tenors, 2 basses), 4 boys
SS. Annunziata	1526	12 adults, 3 boys
Cathedral and	1540	24 singers (chapelmaster, 7 altos, 4 tenors, 5 basses
Baptistry		and 7 sopranos, 4 of whom were boys)

---

a Sartori, 'Franchino Gaffurio a Milano', pp. 17–18.

b Gaspari, 'La musica in San Petronio', pp. 31, 33–5; reprint, pp. 143, 145–7. See also G. Gaspari, 'Miscellanea Musicale, Tomo San Petronio', pp. 21–44 (MS. in the Civico Museo Bibliografico Musicale, Bologna).

c Roncaglia, La cappella musicale, p. 21.

d Casimiri, 'Musica e musicisti', pp. 185, 192, 195.

e D'Alessi, La cappella musicale, pp. 64, 69–70, 93.

f A. Spagnolo, 'Le scuole accolitali di grammatica e di musica in Verona', Atti e memorie dell'Accademia d'Agricoltura Scienze Lettere Arti e Commercio di Verona, lxxx (1904–5), pp. 97–330; p. 142 and n. 5.

g A. Sacchetti-Sassetti, 'La cappella musicale del Duomo di Rieti', Note d'Archivio, xvii (1940), pp. 121–70; pp. 126, 129; xviii (1941), pp. 49–88; pp. 63–4.

h Haberl, 'Die römische "schola cantorum"', pp. 240, 251; Ariane Ducrot, 'Histoire de la Cappella Giulia au XVIe siècle', Mélanges d'Archéologie et d'Histoire de l'École Française de Rome, lxxv (1963), pp. 179–240 and 467–559; pp. 189–90, 192, 195.

i These statistics are drawn from Siena, Archivio dell'Opera del Duomo, Debitori & Creditori, 1506–1512, Vol. 719, fols. 51, 217, 227, 236, 265; and Debitori & Creditori, 1511–1522, Vol. 720, fols. 18, 45–47, 111, 163, 176, 195, 210, 211, 263, 313, 325, 329, 340, 358, 367, 380, 386, 403, 411, 422, 427, 443, 448, 462, 484, 500, 515, 521, 523, 531, 534, 568, 574, 575, 585, 593. Among the names of interest that appear on the Sienese rolls in these years are 'Maestro Eustachio, maestro di chapella' (1507–8) and 'Danello di Simone Lupi fiamengho, chantore' (1520).

j Pierre M. Tagmann, Archivalische Studien zur Musikpflege am Dom von Mantua (1500–1627) (Bern, 1967), pp. 32, 35–6.

k Frank A. D'Accone, 'The Musical Chapels at the Florentine Cathedral and Baptistry During the First Half of the 16th Century', Journal of the American Musicological Society, xxiv (1971), pp. 1–50; pp. 4, 9–10, 14, 16, 21–2, 25–6.

that under the music-loving Leo X the personnel rose to about thirty in 1516 and to thirty-one in 1521.[14] Under Clement VII during the later 1520s, however, the chapel was comprised of a more normal complement of twenty-two to twenty-four singers.[15]

As is evident from the figures in Table III, seldom if ever did the number of singers in other Italian churches approach that of the Sistine Chapel. During the first two decades of the century, for example, the Milanese chapel was more or less stabilized at twelve adults and about six boys. Between 1512 and 1525 San Petronio's chapel in Bologna grew from nine to thirteen adults and reached fifteen adults only in 1540. From 1505 to 1513 the Modenese chapel employed nine adults; this number was but slightly augmented during the next decade. Five adults are mentioned at the

[14] Herman-Walther Frey, 'Regesten zur päpstlichen Kapelle unter Leo X. und zu seiner Privatkapelle', Die Musikforschung, viii (1955), pp. 178–99; pp. 198–9.

[15] Haberl, 'Die römische "schola cantorum"', pp. 259–63.

Cathedrals of Padua and Treviso in 1511, and Treviso alone shows a significant increase by the late 1520s. There were seven adults associated with the
Veronese Cathedral chapel in 1524, and although their number rose to
eleven in 1527, by 1533 only nine adults were employed. In 1517 a chapel
consisting of four adults and a small number of boys was established at the
Cathedral of Rieti. By 1529 the group had reached its maximum complement of seven adult singers, one singer-organist and a few boys.[16] St.
Peter's chapel in Rome had seven singers in 1501 and ten in 1506–7. In the
decade after its reorganization as the Cappella Giulia, this chapel showed
little change, counting eight singers in 1514 and only eleven in 1525. The
Sienese Cathedral, on the other hand, increased the number of singers in its
service from ten in 1513 to seventeen in 1520.

In Mantua and in Florence the situation was more complex. As late as
1509 the Mantuan Cathedral was employing only eight adult singers.
With the formation of the ducal chapel in 1510, court musicians were called
upon to assist at the Cathedral. The exact figures for the next decade are
not known, although it has been estimated that as many as fifteen adults and
ten boys may have participated in the services. By 1523, when the Cathedral
chapel had become more independent, fifteen singers were on the rolls, a
number that grew to eighteen in 1528.

When the Florentine Cathedral chapel was reorganized in 1502 it
comprised sixteen singers. By 1512 the group was reduced to eight adults
and four to six boys. In the following years financial problems forced a
further reduction of singers so that by 1526, the year before all of the
Florentine chapels were disbanded because of the plague, only six adults
and about six boys remained. The Baptistry's chapel, however, which was
funded from a different source, began to grow after 1510, and by 1515 it
already included at least thirteen adults and four boys. Although exact
figures for the next decade are lacking, the expenditures for the chapel
mentioned in a report of 1527 suggest that the number of adults serving
there in that year was even greater than in 1515. In 1526 the Santissima
Annunziata, which had traditionally vied with the two major churches in
maintaining a well-staffed chapel, was employing twelve adults and three
boys. In 1540, when the Cathedral and Baptistry chapels were re-established
and united, there were twenty-four singers, including the chapelmaster.

★   ★   ★

At present, information regarding the days and services when polyphony
was performed by most of the chapels considered in this study is neither
complete nor precise. For example, a document from the Cathedral of
Rieti, dated 19 December 1529, states that the singers were to perform

---

[16] At least two boy sopranos were serving with the group in 1537. See Sacchetti-Sassetti,
'La cappella musicale del Duomo di Rieti', xvii, p. 129.

'figural music on feast days, as they have in the past, and at the Elevation of the Host on ferial days', but the feast days and specific services are not enumerated.[17] We know that in 1530 the Mantuan Cathedral chapel was performing at Mass on Saturday mornings, but no information seems to have survived regarding its duties on major feast days.[18] The Papal bull establishing the Cappella Giulia in 1513 states that the singers were to perform 'every day at the Canonical Hours'.[19] We do not know which of the Canonical Hours Pope Julius II had in mind, although a few later documents suggest that on certain occasions Vespers and Matins were celebrated with polyphony in St. Peter's.[20] Other documents from 1514 show that each year the chapel performed at an anniversary Mass in honour of its founder, on 20 February, and at Christmas and Easter.[21] Once again, however, no mention is made of the use of polyphony at these services.

We are more fortunate with regard to information concerning the duties of the various Florentine chapels.[22] Documents from before, during, and shortly after Josquin's lifetime show that polyphony formed a regular part of the services at both the Cathedral and the Baptistry throughout most of the fifteenth and sixteenth centuries. At the Baptistry the chapel performed at Mass on Sundays and on many major feast days. At the Cathedral, on the other hand, the chapel normally sang the fifth psalm at Vespers on Sundays and on feast days. On several of the latter, among them Christmas, Easter, and Corpus Christi, the first psalm at Vespers was sung instead. Presumably this change allowed the singers, on those few occasions when Vesper services were also celebrated with polyphony at the Baptistry, to move across the piazza in time to perform at the services conducted there. A similar arrangement seems to have been made on about nine days during the year when polyphony was sung at Mass at the Cathedral, with the chapel performing first in one church, then in the other. On the few occasions, such as Holy Week services, when polyphony was performed simultaneously in both churches, it became customary to divide the singers into two groups. Although our information for the Santissima Annunziata is less complete, we do know that during the period *c.* 1480–93 its chapel sang at Mass on Saturday mornings. The Annunziata's singers were also obliged to rehearse the music they performed there, 'whether it be a Mass, a motet, or a Magnificat etc., and that is for every occasion on which they must sing in the Church, not only on feast days, but also on ferial days'.[23]

Did all singers associated with the various chapels participate in each service accompanied with polyphony? For the court chapels of Naples,

[17] Ibid., xviii, p. 63.   [18] Tagmann, *Archivalische Studien*, p. 70.
[19] Ducrot, 'Histoire de la Cappella Giulia', p. 535.   [20] Ibid., pp. 509–10.
[21] Ibid., Table 2 (between pp. 510 and 511).
[22] D'Accone, 'The Musical Chapels', pp. 4–7, 26–9.
[23] D'Accone, 'The Singers of San Giovanni', p. 333.

Milan, and Ferrara there is at present no evidence one way or the other. Haas's assertion, however, that in this period each part, as a rule, was taken by only one or two singers—even in those chapels that employed large numbers—must be modified in view of what we now know.[24] For example, the singers of the three Florentine chapels (staffed at times as lavishly as many of the court chapels) as well as those of the Milanese Cathedral, were certainly full-time employees; if they were tardy or absent from any of the required services they were fined, and their fines duly noted and redistributed to others.[25]

As for the distribution of voices: again, our information is not as complete as we would like, but it is sufficient to give us an idea of the composition of a few of these chapels in certain years. The larger chapels may be considered first. In Florence, in the year 1493, eighteen adult singers served at the Cathedral, among them three altos.[26] If we can assume roughly equal numbers of tenors and basses, then it appears that there was an overwhelming number of sopranos in the group. Information from some twenty years earlier indicates that it might have been common practice to have a greater complement of sopranos in a large choral ensemble. In January 1473 the Duke of Milan sent Gaspar van Weerbecke to Flanders to engage a group of singers, among whom were to be ten sopranos, two basses, and two tenors.[27] The ducal chapel already included two tenors at the time.[28] A list of the personnel in the chapel, dating from July 1474, names twenty-two singers, and thus it would appear that almost half of them were sopranos.[29]

More definite information about the distribution of voices in larger groups comes both from Josquin's time and from a slightly later date; it concerns a chapel that employed adults and boys as well as one consisting of adults only. In 1502 the Florentine Cathedral employed sixteen singers, among them seven sopranos (two adults, five boys), two altos, three tenors, and two basses. In 1540, when the chapels at the Florentine Cathedral and Baptistry were re-established and united, the personnel included, in addition to the chapelmaster, seven sopranos (four of whom were boys), seven altos, four tenors, and five basses. This disposition of voices is almost the same as that found in the Sistine Chapel in 1533, when twenty-four adults are listed, among them seven sopranos, seven altos, four tenors, and six basses.[30]

24 Robert Haas, *Aufführungspraxis der Musik* (Potsdam, 1931), p. 108.

25 D'Accone, 'The Singers of San Giovanni', p. 333; 'The Musical Chapels', pp. 8, 19–20; Sartori, 'Franchino Gaffurio a Milano', p. 14.

26 D'Accone, 'The Singers of San Giovanni', pp. 345–6.

27 Vander Straeten, *La musique aux pays-bas*, vi, p. 6. Vander Straeten errs in dating the document '1474 (n.s.)'; the new year in Milan began on 1 January.

28 Ibid.   29 See note 8 above.

30 E. Celani, 'I cantori della Cappella Pontificia nei secoli XVI–XVIII', *Rivista Musicale Italiana*, xiv (1907), pp. 83–104; p. 85.

Although the figures are not as exact, it is also possible to trace the distribution of voices in the Sistine Chapel during the latter part of 1535, when twenty-four singers were still employed.[31] The chapel then included seven sopranos, nine altos or tenors, six basses, and two other singers, the ranges of whose voices have not been identified.

The distribution of voices in smaller chapels, when known, also shows a preponderance of sopranos. Between the years 1513 and 1526 the Florentine Cathedral generally employed six adult singers, two each for the lower parts, and from four to six boy sopranos. This group recalls in numbers and composition that of the late 1470s. It also approximates, at least in the number of adults, several of the other cathedral chapels in the first few decades of the sixteenth century. Indeed, Treviso's chapel as late as 1532 had twelve singers, among them six sopranos (most of whom were probably boys) and six adults, two each for the lower parts. When Pope Paul III travelled to Loreto in 1539, the eleven-man chapel accompanying him comprised four sopranos, four altos or tenors, and three basses.[32]

The situation in Venice between the years 1486 and 1492 was quite exceptional because of the large number of *zaghi cantadori* (twelve) associated with St. Mark's chapel. We do not know whether all of them were sopranos, for on a few occasions there were as many as five priests listed in their ranks; some of these young men may have sung parts other than the treble.[33] There must have been, on the other hand, a few sopranos among the fifteen to seventeen full-salaried members of the chapel—we know this to have been true in 1531.[34] In St. Mark's chapel sopranos also appear to have been preponderant.

The use of proportionally more sopranos in both large and small groups during the period 1475–1525 can perhaps be reduced simply to a matter of decibels, which falsettists were evidently incapable of producing in an equal amount. And though in most chapels boys' voices were used to augment the adults, the problem apparently still existed. Boys' voices, however piercing they may seem on occasion, are not of a power equal to the mature male voices singing in the lower ranges. But their employment offered

[31] José M. Llorens, 'Cristóbal de Morales, cantor en la Capilla Pontificia de Paulo III (1535–1545)', *Anuario musical*, viii (1953), pp. 39–69; pp. 45–6.

[32] Ibid., pp. 52, 46.

[33] See the volume cited above in Table II, note b, fols. 142, 145ᵛ, 148ᵛ, 153ᵛ, 157ᵛ, 162, 165ᵛ, payments for the months of September–October 1491 through September–October 1492. It may be that these young men had become priests in the meantime and were retained in the lower paid choir of *zaghi* because all of the salaried positions in the adult chapel were filled. They could, however, have also been falsetto singers.

[34] Two sopranos (fra Matteo fiorentino, minorita, and Andrea Salomono) are named in a list of singers dating from 20 May 1531. See Francesco Caffi, 'Musica sacra a Venezia, Appunti per aggiunte alla storia', fol. 55ᵛ (MS. in the Biblioteca Nazionale Marciana, Venice).

advantages; not only could they be paid much lower salaries than the adults, but the more gifted among them could be trained for eventual careers as professional singers. Nevertheless, many chapels, such as the Sistine Chapel, preferred adult sopranos. Although this preference may have had something to do with the quality of sound of a beautiful falsetto voice, adults may also have been sought after because they were better performers. With their extensive training, they could render long and difficult passages with clarity and ease. Many of them were, in fact, virtuoso singers, like the castrati of a later day by whom they were eventually replaced. Perhaps the preference for adult sopranos could also be grounded on liturgical solemnity, easily disturbed by the presence of boys. Some idea of how much these high voices were esteemed is given in a letter of 27 August 1484 from Duke Ercole of Ferrara to the soprano Cornelio di Lorenzo, who was then serving in the Florentine Cathedral chapel. In it the Duke remarks that he cannot yet give Cornelio an answer regarding 'that soprano, whom you say you'd risk your soul to send here!'[35]

Judging from the information assembled here, it seems clear that the performance of sacred music in Italy during Josquin's time varied considerably from city to city and decade to decade. This is not surprising, for then as now musicians differed on the balance of sound and the kind of group needed to produce a desired effect. Then as now the law of supply and demand and financial capacity exercised a dominating influence. Changing taste and fashion also were responsible for the size of a chapel, as is evident at the Florentine Cathedral in the late 1480s. In addition, the acoustics of the churches in which the music was performed obviously had a great deal to do with the size of choirs and distribution of voices. A document from the Florentine Cathedral, dated 4 December 1501, speaks of having to enlarge 'the platform existing in the choir of the said church'— the space under the cupola—so that the chapel, re-established only a few days earlier, could be better accommodated.[36] Unquestionably, the sixteen singers who began performing at that time were capable of producing a full and well-balanced sound, large enough to fill the area where services were being conducted.

*   *   *

There remains the thorny question of accompanied or unaccompanied performance in Italian church services during Josquin's time, which I can only touch upon lightly. I have considered documentary evidence solely from Josquin's time, differentiating strictly between sacred and secular practice.[37] I have likewise distinguished for reasons explained above be-

---

35 D'Accone, 'The Singers of San Giovanni', p. 343.

36 D'Accone, 'The Musical Chapels', p. 2, n. 3.

37 A differentiation not observed, for example, by Giacomo Benvenuti in *Andrea e*

tween practices of the court chapels[38] and those of the churches. Finally, I have specified whether the accompanying instruments were strings, winds, or brass on the one hand, or the organ on the other.

Surprisingly, evidence of instruments other than the organ in churches of Josquin's time is hard to find. None of the hundreds of documents from the Florentine Cathedral and Baptistry furnishes information on the use of instrumentalists during the services, either on a regular basis or for extraordinary occasions. The early decades of the fifteenth century have left us accounts of payments to instrumentalists employed at the Cathedral for processions on major feast days.[39] After the establishment of the chapel in 1439, however, accounts of such payments cease, and documents from Josquin's time attest to the exclusive use of instrumentalists for fanfares at public proclamations issued in the Cathedral.[40] Nor are there any records of the Florentine Signoria's band having assisted the singers at the Cathedral or at the Baptistry.[41]

Giovanni Gabrieli e la musica strumentale in San Marco (*Istituzioni e monumenti dell'arte musicale Italiana*, i, 1; Milan, 1931), pp. XLVII–XLVIII.

[38] Several descriptions of court practice, generally on festive occasions, are available in musicological literature. The following extract, from a letter of Beatrice d'Este Sforza to her sister Isabella d'Este Gonzaga, offers an excellent example. The writer describes the marriage ceremony of Bianca Maria Sforza and Maximilian I celebrated on 30 November 1493 in the Cathedral of Milan: 'When we were all in our places, the Most Reverend Archbishop of Milan entered in full vestments, with the priests in ordinary, and began to celebrate mass with the greatest pomp and solemnity, to the sound of trumpets, flutes, and organ music, together with the voices of the chapel choir, who adapted their singing to Monsignore's time'. (Quoted from Julia Cartwright, *Beatrice d'Este* (London, New York, 1926), p. 214.)

[39] The following accounts are typical of such payments: Florence, Archivio dell'Opera di Santa Maria del Fiore, *Stanziamenti, 1417–1421*, II. 4. 8, fol. 47ᵛ: 1419.

E de' dare a dì 26 di giugno L. 6 s. 16 ebe Michele di Dino chon 3 conpagni tronbetti per la processione della vigilia di Santo Giovanni. E a dì detto L. 6 s. 12 ebe Parissi piffero chon 2 compagni per detta processione.

fol. 116: 1421

A dì 1 di luglio L. 5 s. 10 portò Donato tronbetto per sè e chonpagni per sonare inanzi a loro li operai di S. Giovanni la mattina de la processione. E a dì detto L. 6 s. 12 portò Parissi piffero per sè e chonpagni per sonare per la detta festa.

The use of instruments in processions during the Renaissance needs investigation. Bellini's famous painting illustrates the use of winds and brass at these open-air occasions. Less documented is the use of other instruments, such as a harp and a lute, recorded at the Cathedral of Padua 'pro processione Corporis Christi 18 junij 1489' (see Casimiri, 'Musica e musicisti', p. 164).

[40] For a typical example see Florence, Archivio dell'Opera di Santa Maria del Fiore, *Stanziamenti, 1497–1500*, II. 4. 21, fol. 19ᵛ: 13 aprile 1498

Spese di giubileo per loro a trombetti e pifferi per bandire el perdono, cioè L. 10 a trombetti e pifferi e L. 2 a banditore.

[41] Giuseppe Zippel, *I suonatori della signoria di Firenze* (Trent, 1892), pp. 8–9, 18–22. Documents from the late fourteenth century show that these musicians played in the church

Venetian documents for the years 1486–92 make no mention of instrumentalists, whereas chaplains, sacristans, adult singers, *zaghi cantadori*, and others employed at St. Mark's are listed. Later in the sixteenth century the duties of the Doge's band of instrumentalists included assistance at the services in St. Mark's.[42] I have found no record of such practice during Josquin's time. Nor do the accounts of the Cathedral of Siena contain references to instrumentalists other than organists for the period in question.[43]

Significantly, the organ is the only instrument participating in several of the other Italian churches until later in the sixteenth century. At San Petronio in Bologna, a trombonist is recorded for the first time in 1560.[44] In 1565, a trombonist appears on the rolls of the Cathedral of Padua.[45] A trombonist is mentioned in the records of the Modenese Cathedral, again for the first time, during the period 1562–83,[46] whereas the Mantuan Cathedral registers do not speak of one until 1588.[47] Much earlier, during December 1546, a trombonist is listed on two occasions in the records of the Cappella Giulia, but no other mention of instrumentalists appears there until 1564, when a cornettist is recorded in the month of May.[48]

The above information poses two interesting questions. First, if Italian churches were regularly employing instrumentalists in Josquin's time, as several of them did later in the sixteenth century, why are there no records of this practice? Secondly, if the duties of town or court musicians in Josquin's time normally included accompanying the church service—thus making it unnecessary to record their presence—why is it that after the middle of the sixteenth century the names of instrumentalists and their

---

of Orsanmichele on Sunday mornings and on the mornings of certain other feast days. During this period, however, Orsanmichele's own complement of singers and instrumentalists performed in the afternoon and evening. See Frank A. D'Accone, 'Le compagnie dei laudesi in Firenze durante l'Ars Nova', *L'Ars Nova Italiana del Trecento*, iii (Certaldo, 1970), pp. 253–80; pp. 273–5.

[42] Denis Arnold, 'Brass Instruments in Italian Church Music of the Sixteenth and Early Seventeenth Centuries', *The Brass Quarterly*, i (1957), pp. 81–92; p. 85; idem, art. 'Venedig und venezianische Handschriften', *MGG*, xiii, col. 1378.

[43] Before the fall of the republic in 1559 the duties of the musicians employed by the Sienese Signoria included playing in processions, at guild festivals in the Piazza del Campo, during carnival times, and during the Mass, which was celebrated in the chapel to the side of the Palazzo della Repubblica. See A. Vessella, *La banda* (Milan, 1935), p. 95, n. 60, for information about the Statutes of this group, originally published in Luigia Cellesi, *Storia della più antica banda musicale senese* (Siena, 1906), p. 34.

[44] Gaetano Gaspari, 'Memorie risguardanti la storia dell'arte musicale in Bologna al XVI secolo', *Atti e memorie della R. Deputazione di storia patria per le provincie della Romagna*, serie II, i (1875), p. 24; reprint, p. 160, n. 1.

[45] Casimiri, 'Musica e musicisti', p. 132.

[46] Roncaglia, *La cappella musicale*, p. 26.

[47] Tagmann, *Archivalische Studien*, pp. 72, 84.

[48] Ducrot, 'Histoire de la Cappella Giulia', p. 506.

specific duties begin to appear in church records?[49] Can it be that practices in the church chapels began to change about that time? Definite answers must await the results of future research.

We do know, however, that organists were employed by all churches mentioned in this report. Indeed, at St. Mark's two were used simultaneously from as early as the 1490s.[50] As happens disconcertingly often, little explicit information has survived concerning the organist's role in these chapels. In a few cases, however, there is circumstantial evidence which seems to suggest that his duties included accompanying the singers. A document from the Florentine Cathedral, dated 5 February 1479, states that the chapel was 'to sing polyphonic music at all solemn Vespers on Sundays and feast days when the organist has to play'.[51] In addition, the chapel was to sing the *Te Deum* 'on solemn feasts when the organs are played'.[52] Both during the chanting of Vesper hymns and the singing of the *Te Deum* traditional practice alternated the performance of successive verses between choir and organ.[53] Also, the organ functioned as setting the pitch for the choir through the playing of toccatas in the various modes. Finally, the organ may have played the long-held notes of the traditional *cantus firmus* of certain major works of the period. But we have no conclusive proof that the organ accompanied the singers. The new style that spread throughout Italy (and the northern countries) during Josquin's time, with its equality of voices, the overlapping of contrapuntal parts, and the resulting homogeneity of sound, can be, and has been, performed effectively without the aid of instruments.

At the Santissima Annunziata during most of Josquin's lifetime two organists were often employed, the one to accompany the boy singers of *laudi*, the other to play in the Chapel of the Annunciation, where the

---

[49] Arnold, 'Brass Instruments in Italian Church Music', pp. 84–8. In a recent lecture at the University of California, Los Angeles, Professor Helmut Hucke maintained that various instruments were used to accompany chapels throughout the sixteenth century, even though payments to instrumentalists are generally lacking in chapel registers. Hucke explains this apparent anomaly as merely a matter of traditional administrative procedure. According to his thesis, instrumentalists at court chapels were readily available because they were at the courts in any case. Thus for performances in churches of cities where the court (or in place of the court, the Signoria) employed instrumentalists, these musicians' services could be lent for special occasions. This is an attractive thesis, but while it may be applicable to a few court chapels, it is doubtful, given our present state of knowledge, that it can be applied to most of the churches mentioned here.

[50] Caffi, *Storia della musica sacra*, i, p. 54.

[51] Albert Seay, 'The 15th-Century Cappella at Santa Maria del Fiore in Florence', *Journal of the American Musicological Society*, xi (1958), pp. 45–55; p. 50.

[52] Ibid.

[53] Such contemporary publications as Girolamo Cavazzoni's *Intabulatura dorgano*, which contains alternatim settings of Masses and hymns, document this practice; see Oscar Mischiati, ed., *Girolamo Cavazzoni, Orgelwerke*, 2 vols. (Mainz, 1958).

singers of polyphony generally performed.[54] A document, dated 30 March 1525, records a ceremony at the Cathedral of Arezzo and reports that afterwards 'the singers performed the *Te Deum laudamus* with organ and figural music'.[55] An undated early sixteenth-century document from the Cathedral of Verona states that the boy singers, and presumably the adults as well, were to perform the Mass 'with music and the organ' on certain feast days.[56] At the Cathedral of Mantua a document from 1522 reports that on one occasion a solemn Mass was sung 'with polyphonic music... [and] with the organ', while another document from 1530 states that the organist should play 'every Saturday when the singers perform the Mass'.[57] A lengthy document from the Florentine Baptistry, dated 17 March 1540, shows that the organist performed whenever the chapel sang, as well as on a number of other feast days.[58]

The arguments in favour of *a-cappella* performance in the Sistine Chapel during Josquin's time must have some validity because an organist appears never to have been employed there. On the other hand, the case for completely unaccompanied performance in the Italian church services, if indeed such an ideal existed at the time, is not a strong one.[59] But, then, neither is the case in favour of accompaniment by instruments other than the organ.

[54] D'Accone, 'The Musical Chapels', pp. 11–12.

[55] F. Coradini, 'La cappella musicale del Duomo di Arezzo', *Note d'Archivio*, xiv (1937), pp. 49–56; p. 52.

[56] Spagnolo, 'Le scuole accolitali', p. 149.

[57] Tagmann, *Archivalische Studien*, pp. 88, 70.

[58] D'Accone, 'The Musical Chapels', pp. 45–7.

[59] Professor Hucke, in the lecture cited earlier, remarked that because of its venerable and privileged position the organ was the only instrument to be used without question in services, and that it might, therefore, very well have become an integral part of 'a-cappella' performance. I tend to agree with him.

Musical Structure and Performance Practice in Masses and Motets of Josquin and Obrecht

RENÉ BERNARD LENAERTS

Research on performance practice of church polyphony at the time of Josquin has generally been based on written sources (theorists and chroniclers), lists of personnel of courts and chapels, and iconographic sources.

The information given by theorists is meagre; in their view, performance is a secondary problem. Their main concern is to state their personal doctrine on music. Moreover, some of them mention—as did Adrianus Petit Coclico in his *Compendium musices*—that experienced masters laid more stress on practical training in music than on the writing of treatises. 'In Belgian towns, where rewards are given to singers and where every effort is made and all pains taken to win the prizes and to attain the level of good singing, nobody writes or dictates a treatise on music. Take my master Josquin des Prez. He never lectured to us nor wrote a "Musica", but he succeeded in a short time in educating us as accomplished musicians, because he did not waste his pupils' time with long and frivolous instructions but taught the rules in a few words, by singing together, by exercise and practice'.[1]

Descriptions of historical events by chroniclers are not as rare, but they tend to deal with generalities, although they often mention specific instruments and state when they are used with the choir. Sometimes a simple conversation-book is more explicit, for example the *Collocutions bien*

---

[1] Adrianus Petit Coclico, *Compendium musices* (Nuremberg, 1552); facs. ed. by Manfred F. Bukofzer (Kassel, 1954), fol. Fij\ :'In urbibus Belgicis, ubi cantoribus praemia dantur, ac ob praemia adipiscenda nullus non modus & labor adhibetur, quo ad scopum bene canendi perveniant, nulla scribitur aut dictatur Musica. Item Praeceptor meus Iosquinus de Pratis nullam unquam praelegit aut scripsit Musicam, brevi tamen tempore absolutos Musicos fecit, quia suos discipulos non in longis & frivolis praeceptionibus detinebat, sed simul canendo praecepta per exercitium & practicam paucis verbis docebat',

familiaires composées par Jean Berthout, Maistre d'Ecole à Bruxelles of about 1540, where the performance of a Mass and a motet of Lupus Hellinck by the imperial chapel in the church of Our Lady of Sablon in Brussels is described in detail.[2]

The lists of personnel in church choirs and courtly chapels provide us with accurate data on the number of singers and their voice parts and the instrumentalists. Viewed over a certain period of time, they may even indicate changes in performance practice.

As far as iconographical documents are concerned, we have to proceed cautiously: whereas some are realistic and descriptive in detail, others are drafted with decorative or even allegorical intentions. Even when we find musical groups representing singers and players with all sorts of instruments, we cannot necessarily conclude that they indeed performed together.

In addition to these sources of information, the role of musical structure in determining performance bears investigation, particularly for the masters of the Josquin generation, in whose Masses and motets structure plays an outstanding part. Such an investigation should not be undertaken for the sole purpose of providing a phenomenological analysis that will lead to an authentic reconstruction of old music. In accordance with the scope of this conference it should also provide the listener of today with a proper understanding of this music, keeping in mind the modern sound media, but also taking into account older techniques of singing, the playing of accurate copies of old instruments, and the balance of sound—an acoustic value that was handled empirically in former times but can now be based on the subtle measuring of sound in laboratories.

To test the relationship between musical structure and performance practice, I propose to examine certain clearly defined procedures that can be neatly isolated. They influence entire compositions and hence are to be evaluated as structural components rather then ephemeral devices. Among these procedures are certain forms of *cantus firmus* treatment (the structural, isorhythmic *cantus firmus* and the so-called segmented *cantus firmus*), a double *cantus firmus*, a structural ostinato, certain canonic techniques, and the contrast of polyphonic and chordal sections. Immediately questions arise about choral or soloistic performance, vocal and/or instrumental ensembles, and about phrasing and tempo.

Most of the procedures cited occur practically only in works by masters from the Low Countries and are largely unknown to Italian, French, and Spanish contemporaries. From this it follows that these masters were educated in a school or tradition that strongly emphasized these devices. It would be surprising if such fundamental principles of composition should

[2] The text of the conversation is given in René Lenaerts, *Het Nederlands Polifonies Lied in de zestiende Eeuw* (Mechelen-Amsterdam, 1933), pp. 154-7. The Dutch title is: *Ghemeyne T'samenkoutinge gheordineert van Jan Berthout.*

have had no echo whatever in performance. Certainly, being structural principles of the composition, they should be made clear to the listener.

Obviously, a *cantus firmus* in exceptionally large augmentation, such as the tenor in Antoine Brumel's 'Missa Et ecce terraemotus',[3] is unsuitable for vocal performance. Such is also the case in Obrecht's motet 'Laudemus nunc Dominum'. This technique belongs to the period before 1500; it disappears gradually in the generation of Gombert and Clemens non Papa.

When a *cantus firmus* taken from a secular composition is written in long note-values and bears the chanson text, it will normally be performed on an instrument, the presence of a text notwithstanding. In works with several *cantus firmi* it is impossible to generalize. A rare example of liturgically related *cantus firmi* is found in Obrecht's 'Missa Sub tuum praesidium',[4] where the principal *cantus firmus*, sung throughout by the discant, is progressively joined by four Marian chants: 'Audi nos, nam te filius'; 'Mediatrix nostra'; 'Celsus nuntiat Gabriel'; 'Regina coeli laetare'. Two other Marian chants are quoted briefly. The principal *cantus firmus*—the only one present in all sections—is isorhythmically organized and represents a 'structural *cantus firmus*'. In each movement it is divided into three segments of unvarying length, except for the final note. Van Crevel's alleged discovery of this symmetrical form[5] tempts him to search for 'secret mathematical meanings'. He overlooks the fact that the presence of an isorhythmic *cantus firmus* rules out any result other than a mathematically equal number of breves, or an exact multiple or quotient of it. The emphasis laid on the principal *cantus firmus*, with its longer values, can best be expressed by giving the discant part to an instrument.

Other procedures of *cantus firmus* treatment call for different manners of performance. Two of Obrecht's Masses, 'Malheur me bat' and 'Maria zart', work with a 'segmented' *cantus firmus*. In the four-voice 'Missa Malheur me bat'[6] the superius of Ockeghem's chanson is divided into nine fragments and placed in the superius of the Mass; the complete chanson melody is heard in the last *Agnus Dei*. Each segment of the chanson melody is sung three times, in different note-values: the first two times in augmentation or double augmentation, the last time in *integer valor*. If the composer's intentions are to be made clear, the augmented version of the *cantus firmus*

---

[3] In the Introduction to his edition of this Mass (*Antonii Brumel Opera omnia*, iii; American Institute of Musicology, 1970), pp. IX–X, Barton Hudson refers to the Munich Mus. MS. 1 where the names of the singers in Lassus's time are entered in every voice part except the discant. The *cantus firmus* parts Tenor I and Tenor II also bear the names of singers, although the use of sackbuts seems appropriate here. Moreover, Hudson remarks: 'It is safe to conclude that the thirty instrumentalists mentioned by Praetorius would be applicable to Lassus's performance of Brumel's Mass' (p. X).

[4] *Jacobus Obrecht, Opera omnia*, vi, ed. M. van Crevel (Amsterdam, 1959).

[5] Ibid., Introduction, pp. XVII–XX.

[6] *Jacobus Obrecht, Opera omnia*, i/4, ed. A. Smijers (Amsterdam, 1955).

should be performed instrumentally (some passages are unsingable) and the normal values vocally, either with or without instrumental doubling. In the third *Agnus* the bass oscillates freely between E and A with rhythmic variations and occasional added notes. It is a characteristic 'fanfare' motive for a trombone, reminiscent of Dufay's 'Gloria ad modum tubae'.

The masterpiece of the segmented *cantus firmus* technique is undoubtedly Obrecht's 'Missa Maria zart'.[7] The melody of the German Marian song is split into twelve fragments, successively used as *cantus firmus* in the tenor of the Mass, and with striking symmetry: 1 and 2 in *Kyrie* (used twice, as in the original melody), 3–6 in the *Gloria*, 6–9 in the *Credo*, 9–12 in the *Sanctus*. In contrast to segmented repetition of fragments in the first four sections of the Mass, the complete melody appears in the *Agnus*: the bass sings it straight through in *Agnus* I and the superius does the same in *Agnus* III; in *Agnus* II, without tenor, it appears as *vagans* in alto, soprano, and bass. Two sections without tenor in the *Gloria* (the duets *Domine Deus* and *Qui tollis*) also present the *cantus firmus* as a whole, but this time slightly paraphrased.

The striking feature of these two works, even at first glance, is the care with which Obrecht incorporates the borrowed material. The *cantus firmus*, in its segmented form, impregnates the whole Mass. The complete version is put to the fore in the *Agnus Dei*, as a review of the whole work. In the 'Missa Maria zart' this even happens twice, in the *Gloria* and *Agnus*, at a distance that allows some perspective. Vast architectonic structures like those of the 'Missa Malheur me bat' and 'Missa Maria zart' cannot be intended for the analytical eye of the expert only; they call for a differentiated instrumentation that will translate structure into audible terms.

The use of ostinato in Obrecht's oeuvre, to which Peter Wagner called attention, but which is equally important in the works of Josquin and Pierre de la Rue, also leaves its mark on performance. We refer here not to the numerous incidental sequences or ostinato passages, but to the 'structural ostinato', when it appears as a principle of composition for a whole Mass. Hexachord alternation and transposition by step (*pes ascendens* and *descendens*) are indispensable to avoid monotony, but the core of the procedure is rhythmic variation. In Obrecht's work we find the curious form of an 'expanding ostinato', usually ascending, in which each repetition carries the theme one note further.[8] Josquin also used this technique in his 'Ut Phoebi radiis'. In the works of Obrecht and Josquin occur sections in which the ostinato appears in two or three voices (Obrecht, 'Missa Adieu

[7] Ibid., vii, ed. M. van Crevel (Amsterdam, 1964).

[8] Osthoff(*Josquin Desprez*, ii (Tutzing, 1965), p. 79) calls it an 'additiver Ostinato-Kanon'. For other examples in Obrecht, see 'Missa Salve diva parens' (*Opera omnia*, v), *Sanctus*, bass, mm. 77–108 (ascending), and 'Missa Fortuna desperata' (ibid., iii), *Benedictus*, superius, mm. 28–42 (descending).

mes amours', *Kyrie* II[9]; for Josquin, see the 'Missa Hercules Dux Ferrariae', *Kyrie* II, superius and tenor I, mm. 38–42, superius and bass, mm. 42–6).

Complete ostinato Masses are almost exclusively found in the works of Netherlandish masters. Famous examples are Josquin's Masses 'Faisant regretz' and 'La sol fa re mi'. 'Faisant regretz'[10] uses the four-note formula F D E D from Walter Frye's chanson 'Tout a par moy'[11] that Alexander Agricola had also used as ostinato in his own chanson by that name.[12] In the third *Agnus* Josquin quotes the complete chanson theme in the superius. The Mass offers numerous instances of stepwise transposition of the ostinato: as *pes descendens* at the end of the *Gloria* (mm. 85 to end), as *pes ascendens* in the *Credo* (mm. 8–13, 39–44). It is sung canonically by tenor and bass for most of the *Benedictus*.

[*The Sanctus and Agnus were played, with the ostinato given to a trombone.*]

The 'Missa La sol fa re mi'[13] belongs to Josquin's most popular Masses; its artistic value was praised time and again. In spite of more than 200 repetitions of the theme, the work never grows monotonous. The ostinato also plays an important role in the 'Missa Hercules Dux Ferrariae',[14] for example, the motive of a third appearing in descending sequence heard twelve times in the bass of *Kyrie* II; the pattern at the end of the *Gloria* (bass, five levels); the ostinato in dialogue between bass and superius at the beginning of the *Sanctus*. These are only a few examples; this monumental work deserves a study that would far exceed the limits of this paper.

I should like to mention in this respect the unpublished 'Missa Cum jucunditate' (*a 4*) by Pierre de la Rue, one of the four most widely circulated Masses among the thirty-one complete Masses by this composer. It is built on the theme G E G A G G, the *initium* of the antiphon at Lauds of the Nativity of Mary (September 8). This motive is used eighty-seven times in the course of the Mass, with constant variations of great ingenuity.

Ostinato compositions by Netherlandish masters are also found in the motet. The ostinato is essential to the comprehension of the work; it always bears an important text, either borrowed from the motet or another source,

[9] Modern edition of the Kyrie in A. Smijers, ed., *Van Ockeghem tot Sweelinck* (Amsterdam, 1940), pp. 54–7.

[10] *Werken*, Missen, xiii.

[11] Modern edition in *Walter Frye, Collected Works*, ed. Sylvia W. Kenney (American Institute of Musicology, 1960), p. 1.

[12] Gustave Reese has pointed out (*Music in the Renaissance* (New York, 1954), p. 244, n. 326) that Agricola's chanson, printed by Smijers, was not Josquin's model; 'that Josquin based his Mass directly on Frye is shown by the fact that he uses no material peculiar to Agricola, but does begin the superius of his Agnus III with an extensive quotation of material peculiar to the opening of Frye's superius'. In fact, Josquin quotes Frye's whole superius; see Sylvia W. Kenney, *Walter Frye and the Contenance Angloise* (New Haven, 1964), p. 189.

[13] *Werken*, Missen, ii.   [14] Ibid., Missen, vii.

that carries a meaning either contrasting with or complementary to the central idea of the motet. Text and melody are often chosen with symbolic intent. In Josquin's five-part 'Salve Regina'[15] the *quinta vox* sings an ostinato on the head-motive of the antiphon A G A D with symmetrical pauses, twelve times in the *prima pars*, four in the *secunda pars*, and eight in the *tertia pars*. This procedure very likely refers to Revelation 12:1 where the 'Mulier amicta sole', the woman clad with the sun, bears on her head a crown of twelve stars. There can be little doubt that the composer wanted the reference to be made clear, and this can be achieved by giving this motto to an instrument.[16]

In discussing the possible relationship of certain canonic procedures to performance practice, we shall confine ourselves, as before, to the structural canon, i.e., a canon that pervades the whole composition and functions as a structural principle. The examples differ considerably, and every instance has to be considered separately. Josquin's 'Missa Ad fugam', Ockeghem's 'Missa Prolationum', Noel Bauldewijn's 'Missa En douleur et tristesse', Willaert's six-voice 'Missa Mente tota', with its continuous four-voice canon, Pierre de la Rue's completely canonic four-voice 'Missa O salutaris hostia', notated in only one voice—they all present different versions of one basic technique, and they call in turn for different performing solutions. But when an additional voice in canon enters in the *Agnus Dei*—the traditional section for recapitulation and climax—it will most likely have to be brought out by instrumental performance.

Finally, there are the numerous abstract subjects, solmization formulas and *soggetti cavati*. Often a mere glance at the score reveals what should be brought out by the use of instruments (cornetts and trombones). An unusual example of canonic technique is found in Josquin's motet 'Ut Phoebi radiis' from Petrucci's *Motetti Libro quarto* (1505).[17] It is obviously a scholastic work from an early period of the master. The four-voice motet has two parts and is built entirely on a canon in breves for tenor and bass on the tones of the hexachord. In the *prima pars* the six notes are sung in canon at the upper fourth, adding one note in each statement: *ut, ut re, ut re mi*, etc.; the *secunda pars* repeats the procedure in descending progression, with a canon at the lower fourth. At the end of each part, the alto quotes the hexachord in shorter note-values. The two upper voices, soprano and alto, in contrast, are written in melismatic style; however, the quotation of a hexachord syllable always coincides with the singing of its proper note. The motet text is written in hexameters, seven in each part, the last line showing religious intention. The text was clearly written after the drafting of the

---

[15] Ibid., Motetten, Bundel ix, no. 48.

[16] See also my article, 'Zur Ostinato-Technik in der Kirchenmusik der Niederländer', *Festschrift Bruno Stäblein zum 70. Geburtstag*, ed. Martin Ruhnke (Kassel, 1967), pp. 157–9.

[17] *Werken*, Motetten, Bundel iv, no. 22.

musical frame of the work; Osthoff supposes that Josquin himself was the author.[18] The six hexameters, in cumulative succession, quote the hexachord notes 'Ut Phoebi radiis', 'Ut reges', 'Ut remi', etc. The resulting text lacks coherent meaning.[19] A mere glance at the score shows the structural contrast between the upper and the lower voices. There can be little doubt that Josquin intended to distinguish the tenor and bass from the two upper voices and this can be emphasized by assigning them to instruments.

Apart from the strictly structural procedures outlined above, the normal alternation of tutti sections with soloistic sections and the contrast of polyphonic and chordal passages serve as a guide to performance. In the field of ornamentation, the theoretical works tend more toward description than concrete examples, whereas ornamentation in instrumental music is extensively illustrated in Silvestro Ganassi's manuals, *Fontegara* of 1535 (improvisation) and *Regola Rubertina* of 1542–43 (viols). We ought to be grateful to Coclico for the series of cadence formulas offered in his *Compendium musices*.[20] Speaking about 'ornamentation, embellishment, or pronunciation in singing', he compares no fewer than twelve formulas in two or more versions: simple-ornate (*simplex-elegans*), plain-decorated (*crudus-coloratus*), ordinary-seasoned with salt and mustard (*communis cantus-caro cum sale & sinapio condita*). Moreover, he prints two ornamented voices (superius and bass) of the French chansons 'Languir me fault' and 'C'est à grand tort'. As far as church polyphony is concerned, ornamentation was chiefly applied to soloistic duo and trio sections in Masses and motets.[21]

In considering these problems, we must remember that the composers were all highly trained musicians, with a refined sense of sonority and balance; often they were also the conductors of the most famous chapels of their time. They used a composition not as a frozen *res facta*, but as a living organism suitable for more than one type of performance, in accordance with the size of the building, the specific occasion, and the available ensemble.

Many of the aspects under consideration here can be illustrated in Obrecht's five-voice motet, 'Laudemus nunc Dominum' (*2.p.*, 'Cantemus Domino canticum').[22] The texts are taken from the office of the Dedication of a Church. The motet is written for a solemn occasion, in the course of

[18] *Josquin Desprez*, ii, p. 79.

[19] [The meaning of the text has now been unravelled by Virginia W. Callahan; see these Proceedings, pp. 560–3.—Ed.]

[20] *Compendium musices*, fol. Hiv-I.

[21] G. Persoons, 'Orgels en Organisten in O. L. Vrouwkerk te Antwerpen 1500–1650' (Ph.D. diss., University of Leuven, 1968), p. 152, gives evidence of the practice: 'den duo en trio singen op dorgele' in the Antwerp Cathedral ca. 1560. In 1585 the Louvain theologian Johannes Molanus castigated the pride and conceit of church singers practising the 'fractio vocis'; see *De vita et moribus canonicorum* (Cologne, 1670), ch. xx, p. 139.

[22] *Jacobus Obrecht, Opera omnia*, ii/2, ed. A. Smijers (Amsterdam, 1958), pp. 58–74.

which chordal sections, very close to psalmody, alternate with two-part
and four-part passages in imitative technique. The *cantus firmus* in the tenor
has a second text set in long note values: 'Non est hic aliud nisi domus Dei'
(*prima pars*) and 'Vidit Jacob scalam' (*secunda pars*). Both are antiphons for
the same feast. The tenor of the *prima pars* is presented a second time in
shorter note values and slightly paraphrased. The work is a prime example
of the manner in which musical structure suggests the manner of performance.[23]

[23] To illustrate this paper, two examples were performed: Josquin, 'Missa Faisant
regretz', *Sanctus* and *Osanna* (*Werken*, Missen, xiii, pp. 46–7 and 49–50), and Obrecht,
'Laudemus nunc Dominum', *prima pars* (*Opera omnia*, ii, ed A. Smijers, pp. 58–65), with the
cantus firmus played on a trombone.

Historical Reconstruction versus Structural Interpretation in the Performance of Josquin's Motets

LUDWIG FINSCHER

In 1926, Friedrich Blume, in the foreword to his edition of four motets by Josquin, wrote:

Nowadays we have neither the instruments nor the vocal resources (say, boys' voices or male voices up to the range of countertenor) nor indeed the whole contemporaneous practice of singing and playing at our disposal. Hence any editor has an obligation to approximate, as far as possible, the original style in his performing proposals without losing sight of modern instruments. The individual structure of each composition offers the key to performance: homogeneous voice combinations call for realization by homogeneous groups of sound; heterogeneous combinations should be so executed that each voice has its own tone colour according to its structural and expressive meaning. The following proposals are not meant to be binding, but to oblige the performer to do justice to the textural and structural qualities of the music in the choice of the means of performance.[1]

This was written more than forty years ago. Clear and definite as Blume's ideas were—and yet cautious in their phrasing—few were the performers, professionals, or amateurs from the 'Wandervogel' and 'Jugendbewegung', who tried to translate them into practice. Today, we can boast of a large number of professional and amateur performers who play the old instruments (or at least modern copies of such instruments) with musical skill and historical insight; we know a number of choruses with countertenors and even boys' voices; yet I am afraid that the situation concerning historical performance practice is scarcely better than it was forty years ago. Blume had to stress the importance of structural interpretation not only because this music was new to most musicians, but also because a truly historical reconstruction of its sound was well nigh impossible at the time. Today, the

---

[1] Friedrich Blume, ed., *Josquin des Prés, Vier Motetten zu 4 und 6 Stimmen für Singstimmen und Instrumente* (*Das Chorwerk*, 18; Wolfenbüttel, n.d. (preface dated 1926)), p. 2.

sound of historical instruments has become a trademark (if not a fetish) and is applied to Josquin's works and to all 'old' music regardless of the texture of the individual work. In this situation, for which musicologists are no less responsible than musicians, an attempt to reconcile historical reconstruction and structural interpretation might be useful for both scholars and performers. The purpose of the present paper is to further such a reconciliation by pointing out not only the possibilities, but also the limitations of historical reconstruction and structural interpretation—things that may be obvious but nevertheless need articulation. 'The following proposals are not meant to be binding'. But they are intended to oblige the performer to reflect upon what he is doing.

My argument is quite simple.[2] We know a number of instruments which were, or at least could have been, used in Josquin's time; we know about certain types of instrumental ensembles and even something about the possible and actual use of, and preference for, certain instruments in church and chamber; we know the number of singers in church and court chapels all over Europe in Josquin's time; and we know of travelling groups of instrumentalists, specializing in fashionable types of instrumental sound and probably performing a specific repertory of compositions.[3] In some cases, we are even able to reconstruct historical performance situations in which specific pieces were played, for instance Dufay's 'Ave Regina', sung at the composer's funeral service, or Pierre de la Rue's Requiem, performed at the meeting of Maximilian and Philip the Fair at Innsbruck on 26 September 1503.[4] Moreover, we know many unrelated details of performance practice under specific local conditions, and we learn many more details from the visual arts, provided we can prove or reasonably assume to what degree pictorial representations of performance situations are realistic. In short, we know a lot and we will learn more as time and scholarly research proceed.

On the other hand, we do not know how many singers participated in the first performance of Josquin's 'Memor esto verbi tui' under the composer's direction (if the piece was really sung for the first time before Louis XII), nor do we know how many of the choir singers of the Papal or

[2] For a more general discussion, cf. Ludwig Finscher, 'Historisch getreue Interpretation— Möglichkeiten und Probleme', *Alte Musik in unserer Zeit* (*Musikalische Zeitfragen*, xiii; Kassel-Basel, 1968), pp. 25–34.

[3] For instance, the 'quattro compagni che suonano di viole d'arco, questa è una musica et è bon concerto' mentioned in the correspondence of Archbishop Bernardo Clesio of Trent, July 1530. Cf. Benvenuto Disertori, 'Il manoscritto 1947-4 di Trento e la canzone "i'ay prins amours"', *Rivista Musicale Italiana*, xlviii (1946), p. 28.

[4] Not Pierre de la Rue's 'Missa Assumpta est Maria', as stated in my edition: *Pierre de la Rue, Missa Assumpta est Maria*, ed. Ludwig Finscher (*Musica Divina*, 18; Regensburg, 1966), pp. (ii) and (v); cf. *Heinrich Isaac, Messen, Band 2*, ed. Martin Staehelin (*Musikalische Denkmäler*, 8; Mainz, 1973), p. 162.

the Milanese or some other chapel were sopranos, how many were counter-tenors, tenors, or basses.[5] We might reasonably assume that Passion motets were performed without instruments—which touches upon the possible performance practice of Josquin's 'Qui velatus facie fuisti' and 'O Domine Jesu Christe adoro te', among others—but we do not know how many and which instruments took part in the performance of great *cantus-firmus* settings like 'Miserere mei, Deus' or 'Domine Dominus noster'. We do not know if, to what degree, and in what manner instrumental parts were embellished. We know much about the timbres of instruments, but we know very little about vocal timbres of Italian, French, Spanish, or German singers in Josquin's time, although there were plenty of jokes about national styles of singing.[6] Nor do we know how they pronounced and accentuated their texts.[7]

This situation may change gradually as we learn more details about historical performance practice and weave them into a fairly comprehensive picture, but it is doubtful that it will ever change in principle. One thing seems certain: for the vast majority of works from Josquin's time, more than one manner of performance can be historically correct. If this is true, we must not aim at the reconstruction of details and of specific historical performance situations, but at a kind of ideal type of performance that makes use, as far as necessary, of our historical knowledge to realize in sound the compositional texture of each single work. One part of our historical knowledge seems to be that tone colour, vocal or instrumental timbre, the number of performers for each voice, were not concerns of

[5] See, however, the paper by Frank A. D'Accone, above, pp. 601–18.

[6] [Hermann Finck, in his *Practica musica* (Wittenberg, 1556), fol. Ssi^v, writes as follows: 'Germani boant: Itali balant: Hispani eiulant: Galli cantant' ('The Germans roar; the Italians bleat; the Spanish wail; the French sing'). Finck speaks of this saying as one that is 'in everybody's mouth'—and with a little trouble one could trace its pedigree. Needless to say, he objected to its nationalistic onesidedness, while at the same time blaming the powers that be for the lack of support of the arts in Germany. Similarly, Pietro Aron, in his *Lucidario in Musica* (Venice, 1545), Book IV, Chapter 1, quotes another version of the same saying: 'a Franciosi il cantare, alli Inglesi il giubilare, alli Hispagnoli il piagnere, a Tedeschi l'urlare, Et all'Italiani il caprezzare' ('the French sing, the English jubilate, the Spanish weep, the Germans roar, the Italians bleat'). Aron, too, objects, but with confidence and pride, and this is the point at which he gives his famous list of 'Cantori a libro' and 'Cantori al liuto'. But Aron recognizes national styles of music and of vocal rendering deriving from the various nations and their languages, and he mentions the derivation of certain national terms and titles therefrom ('per ritrovarsi…varie lingue, e populi, conseguentemente da quelli derivano diverse musiche, e pronuntie, si come della nostra, di quella de Franciosi, o delli Hispagnuoli, o delli Inglesi, o de Tedeschi, e di altre nationi si vede avenire, la onde da alcuni loro varij titoli, et appellationi sono state appropriati'). On the various types of voices and national styles of singing, see also Nanie Bridgman, below, p. 640.—Ed.]

[7] [Arthur Mendel, in the Workshop on Motets, proposes that Josquin's setting of the 'Stabat Mater' shows the influence of French accentuation; see below, pp. 660–2.—Ed.]

composers such as Josquin and his contemporaries.[8] Even the comparatively small number of instrumental pieces could be performed equally well, and equally correctly, by quite different instruments and instrumental combinations, as long as their technical capabilities conformed with the demands of the composition. If this be true, modern instruments would serve our purposes as well as historical ones, provided they do not impair the balance, and hence the clarity, of the compositional texture. At any rate, we have old instruments, but modern players and singers. The use of historical instruments would then be reduced to a demonstration of historical possibilities of sound and performance which, however, are not crucial for the composition and its structural interpretation.

Even so, a vast number of interpretational problems remain. If modern performance practice is to be guided by the principle of structural interpretation, careful analysis of the music must precede its performance; this analysis must needs be historically oriented: knowledge of the past and awareness of the present (within which the analyzing mind functions) must be reconciled. Such an analysis might result in a wider scope of performance possibilities, more rational and yet more differentiated than what we have today; it might result also in a restriction of experiments in instrumentation for experiment's—or for the instrument's—sake. While there is obviously a large number of historically correct ways to perform Josquin's motets, in many cases—though not in all—there remains only one way that is truly relevant from the structural point of view. The four-part 'Ave Maria ... Virgo serena' with which Smijers so aptly opened his Josquin edition is to such an extent developed out of the song-like melodiousness of the old sequence melody and the pious and inspired declamation of the text, and is so consistently constructed as a light and translucent fabric of four voices of almost equal weight and comparable structural importance, that the one body that would render the best interpretation of the score is certainly a small ensemble of two or three singers to each part, without instruments. Whereas a version adding historical instruments—cornett, alto shawm, alto trombone, and tenor trombone, as in Konrad Ruhland's recording[9]—is undoubtedly correct from the point of view of what is historically feasible, an *a cappella* rendering would appear to be the best version from the

8 [The tradition of writing laments for low voices and the setting of girls' songs, such as Arcadelt's 'Nous voyons que les hommes font tous vertu d'aimer', for high voices suggests that the concern for tone colour was not alien to the Renaissance composer. Even though it was not a topos of the theorists, instrumental timbre, too, was part of his world. Fifes, drums, and trumpets for military music, string ensembles for intimate chamber music, cornetts and trombones for solemnities—these are but a few examples of a consciousness of instrumental timbres deliberately fostered. But the joy of the Renaissance musician in experimentation prevented a rigid fixation of tone colour in definite groups of instruments as it became conventional later.—Ed.]

9 Telefunken SAWT 9480-A.

structural point of view. The same reasoning applies to those motets (most of them on biblical texts) that concentrate on declamation and expression in a musical texture of equally declamatory and expressive voices—'Planxit autem David', 'Memor esto verbi tui', 'Domine, ne in furore tuo arguas me', or 'Absalon, fili mi'. By virtue of their musical texture and their meaning, these motets are *a cappella* compositions, even if historical proof could be found that they were performed with instruments *colla parte* in Josquin's own time.

The situation is different but scarcely more complicated in *cantus-firmus* and ostinato settings such as 'Miserere mei, Deus' or 'Domine Dominus noster'. In both compositions, the outer parts are declamatory and expressive to such a degree that no rendering other than by human voices seems to be indicated. The *cantus firmus*, embedded in a tight fabric of closely interwoven melodic lines, must be stressed by interpretative means, but the choice of means can be fairly flexible, so long as the chief object of the performance is accomplished, which is to clarify the structural and expressive relationship of *cantus firmus* and outer voices. The only thing that matters is that the *cantus firmus* be sung to its own words, since the ostinato has a manifest declamatory quality in 'Miserere mei, Deus' and the repeats are always discernible as musical and textual units, notwithstanding their occasional augmentation (in 'Domine Dominus noster'). Everything else is of lesser importance: the singers of the *cantus firmus* may stress their phrases by dynamics, or the number of singers may be increased against that of the outer voices, or the singers may be supported by one or several instruments.[10]

Of course, the problems of structural interpretation become more complicated as the music itself grows in complexity of technique, style, and expression. In 'Praeter rerum seriem' no simple solution seems possible. In the first part of the motet, the *cantus firmus* is sung line by line, first by the tenor, then by the highest voice, but not quite consistently; both voices insert—apparently unsystematically—declamatory and ornamental phrases on text repetitions. The remaining voices are obviously instrumental in the beginning, but later on insert declamatory and expressive vocal phrases and even short sections from the *cantus firmus*. The last measures of the first part are completely declamatory and expressive in all voices; the contrast between the slowly moving *cantus firmus* and the lively melodic and rhythmic patterns of the outer voices is now abandoned. The second part shows the same development, but with less obvious contrasts between instrumental and vocal lines, and more subtle transitions between various levels of text and melody treatment. The rather strange work seems to have been composed with two principal objectives in mind, one to set a very

---

[10] A quite different problem is the *cantus firmus* of Josquin's 'Stabat Mater', both because of its original secular text, 'Comme femme desconfortée', and its mensuration in *longa* and *maxima* motion. Cf. the discussion at the Workshop on Motets, below, pp. 659–60.

simple *cantus firmus* in as complicated and as artistic a fashion as possible; two, to reduce the contrast between a (vocal) *cantus firmus* and (instrumental) outer voices within each part of the motet by a gradual process of assimilation. An attempt at a structural interpretation, consistent in itself, should render these two objectives clearly perceptible: either by beginning with singers and instruments in all parts and lending special stress to the *cantus firmus* sections, and then letting the instruments gradually drop out, or by beginning with vocal *cantus firmus* sections set sharply against the instrumental outer voices, and then adding singers to the instrumental parts and vice versa, step by step. Obviously, this is an extreme proposal inspired by an extreme composition. There is little doubt that in Josquin's time 'Praeter rerum seriem' was never performed like that. But if we take the texture and the meaning of Josquin's music seriously—and which music of its time deserves more serious consideration?—and if practical performance aims at structural interpretation (born out of our own state of awareness and insight) rather than at historical reconstruction (which will always retain its experimental and cognitive value), then we must not hesitate to come up with extreme conclusions so long as Josquin's music itself seems to call for them.

On the Discography of Josquin and the Interpretation of his Music in Recordings*

NANIE BRIDGMAN

In 1952, reviewing two recordings of Josquin's music that had just appeared in America, Otto Gombosi declared, 'With Josquin, I think, we are still experimenting.'[1] Since then the number of recordings of this composer's music has increased considerably and, thanks to more and more authoritative interpretations, the experimental stage is now past. Even so, it is surprising how many of his works remain unrecorded; one would like to see some enterprising person undertake an edition of Josquin's *Opera omnia* in sound. Unfortunately, urged on by a needlessly competitive spirit, interpreters often choose the same works, some of which have become positive warhorses, while many masterpieces are yet to be heard.[2] To prove this, we have only to consider the proportion of Josquin's work that has already appeared.[3] Of his twenty Masses, eight have been issued on twenty-five records. Of these, eight are devoted to the 'Missa Pange lingua'. Out of ninety-eight motets, thirty-four exist on 103 records, with the 'Ave Maria ... Virgo serena' well ahead with fourteen versions, while twelve recordings offer a mere excerpt from this same motet, 'Ave vera virginitas'. Thirty-four of his sixty-three songs are more evenly distributed on 105 records, the favourite being 'Mille regretz', for which there are twelve interpretations, closely followed by the nine of 'Basiez moi' and 'El Grillo' and the six of 'Bergerette savoysienne' and the 'Déploration d'Ockeghem'. Lastly, out of ten instrumental pieces (or considered as such), seven have

* I am indebted to Professor Gustave Reese and Mr. Philip Miller for a few suggestions and revisions on early recordings.

[1] *The Musical Quarterly*, xxxviii (1952), p. 663.

[2] Henry Leland Clarke is of the same opinion: 'It is hoped that the appeal of competitive comparisons will not breed warhorses here as it has in so many other fields. Before further duplications a first fine recording is needed of many masterpieces, for example, Josquin's *Missa Faysant regretz*' (*The Musical Quarterly*, lv (1969), p. 586).

[3] This obviously can only be an approximation, some foreign recordings having perhaps escaped my attention.

been chosen and constitute twenty-four recordings, the royal fanfare 'Vive le roy' leading with nine versions against the charming 'La Bernardina', favoured by four groups.

If the discography of Josquin's music opens with a sacred work, it is because the first recordings of his works were made in churches. In 1936 the monks of the Montserrat Monastery chose the motet 'Ave Christe immolate' as what appears to be one of the first recordings of his music.[4] Then the famous 'Ave Maria . . . Virgo serena', sung by the Cappella Giulia of Rome conducted by Monsignore Boezi,[5] began its brilliant discographic career, and other choirmasters followed suit. Joseph Samson in Dijon did the 'Ave verum', the Abbé Alphonse Hoch at the head of the choir of Strasbourg Cathedral and Gaudard conducting the St. Leon IX Choir the 'Ave vera virginitas', and Berberich with the Munich Cathedral Choir the *Sanctus* of the 'Missa Pange lingua'.[6] In 1938, Guillaume De Van with the Paraphonistes de Saint Jean des Matines (founded by himself in collaboration with Abbé Ducand-Bourget) recorded for the *Anthologie Sonore* the 'Stabat Mater' and the *Kyrie* of the 'Missa Hercules Dux Ferrariae'.[7] In 1939, attention turned to Josquin's secular music, the first work chosen being the six-part version of 'Basiez moi', not, as might be expected, by a French group, but by The Madrigalists for their series *Vocal Music of the Renaissance*,[8] which also included works by Janequin, Lassus, and others. Two short songs, 'Se congie prens' and 'Vive le roy', were recorded by De Van in 1942, but we have to wait until 1947 for Josquin's secular music to take its real place in the discographic world with the recordings of thirteen of his songs by the vocal ensemble of Marcel Couraud for the series *La chanson française de la Renaissance*.[9] In the meantime, the outbreak of the war notwithstanding, Josquin's sacred music continued its career, and in 1940 the first complete Mass, 'L'homme armé super voces musicales', was recorded by De Van and the Paraphonistes, together with the mighty 'Miserere' (for the first time, it seems) in 1942,[10] a remarkable accomplishment for the unfortunate

[4] *The Musical Quarterly*, xxii (1936), Record-List, p. 487 (Gram. GY 213). Before 1936 the *Et incarnatus* of the 'Missa Pange lingua' was issued by Curt Sachs in his series *Zweitausend Jahre Musik auf der Schallplatte*, performed by the Berlin State Academy Choir conducted by Pius Kalt. This recording is now available on Decca DX 106 and Parlophon B 37025.

[5] *The Musical Quarterly*, xxiii (1937), Record-List, p. 121 (Edition de Musique sacrée 48).

[6] *Disques* (Noël, 1938), p. 19; *The Gramophone Shop Encyclopedia of Recorded Music*, comp. R. D. Darrell (New York, 1936), p. 242.

[7] *Disques* (Noël, 1938), p. 19.

[8] *The Musical Quarterly*, xxv (1939), Record-List, pp. 125–6. [On the question of authenticity of the six-part version of 'Basiez moi', see Helen Hewitt, *Ottaviano Petrucci, Canti B* (*Monuments of Renaissance Music*, iii; Chicago, 1967), pp. ix–x and 71–2.—Ed.]

[9] *The Musical Quarterly*, xxxiii (1947), p. 434, and *Disques*, Nouvelle série, n⁰ 1 (15 January 1948), p. VII.

[10] *Disques* (1 October–31 December 1942), and *The Musical Quarterly*, xxxiii (1947), Record-List, p. 289.

country that France had become at that time. I have listed the pioneers only; after 1947, the discography of Josquin so swelled in number that it is impossible to enumerate all the records in detail here.

A production spread over more than thirty-five years is now available to the musicologist and discographer. One cannot fail to be impressed by the distance covered, if only in the technical progress made; the quality of the sound has been revolutionized by the introduction of long-playing records about 1950. We are far removed from the time when Van den Borren, hearing a recorded interpretation of music that he had known only through a 'mental reading', spoke of it as an impossible dream come true.[11] In 1952, Gombosi could still feel 'a real shock'—that of the 'musician of the desk'—when faced with 'the final, unalterable incarnation of the pure spirit, burdened with all the inherent weaknesses of flesh', that is, with a recording of old music.[12] We have now gone on to a more objective and perhaps more constructive stage of criticism—'objective' only in a manner of speaking, for this criticism disappoints us through the extreme contradictions it reveals. If art is difficult, so is criticism—certainly in this field—judging by the opposite impressions that one and the same interpretation can create. What one person considers 'un senso di raccolta meditazione, di doloroso stupore, di commosso compianto',[13] another will qualify as a 'lamentable tendency to perform the music of the 16th century at tempos that are more or less uniformly calm and sedate',[14] or what Gombosi more wittily calls 'the tempo of Cecilian piety'.[15] One critic deplores 'the cathedral resonances that often envelop recorded performances of sacred music',[16] while another will delight in this 'ambiance d'église'.[17] It is almost disturbing to compare two judgements made on the recording of Josquin's 'Miserere' by the Saint Eustache singers conducted by Père Emile Martin. Whereas François Pouget praises the extraordinary perfection of the interpretation and approves the absence of rigidity of the tempo which, he says, conforms exactly to the very spirit of the score and text,[18] Jeremy Noble objects that 'this sublime work . . . is treated (with the best possible intentions, I am sure) barbarously', adding: 'The non-commital black-and-white of a "clean text" edition of early music seems to tempt conductors to the projection of their fantasies with almost as much power as the ink-blots of a Rohrschach test; certainly Père Martin indulges in licences, such as halving and doubling the tempo

[11] 'Lecture mentale'; Charles van den Borren, 'La pureté du style et l'interprétation de la musique du Moyen âge', *La Revue internationale de musique*, ii (1938), p. 279.

[12] *The Musical Quarterly*, xxxviii (1952), p. 659.

[13] Carlo Marinelli in *Nuova rivista musicale italiana* (1969), pp. 1025-6.

[14] Leeman L. Perkins in *The Musical Quarterly*, lvi (1970), p. 495.

[15] *The Musical Quarterly*, xxxvii (1952), p. 663.

[16] Cecil Isaac in *The Musical Quarterly*, xlvii (1961), p. 563.

[17] François Pouget in *Disques* (Noël, 1956), p. 801.

[18] Ibid.

every few bars, that have no justification whatsoever in Josquin's notation or in anything we know of the musical practice of the time'.[19] Sometimes, though rarely, there is perfect harmony between the critics; the majority, for instance, agree in criticizing the too rapid tempi of Safford Cape,[20] and also in praising some particularly outstanding recordings by Noah Greenberg ('Missa Pange lingua'), Philippe Caillard ('Missa Pange lingua'), or even that same Père Martin ('Déploration de Johannes Ockeghem').[21]

After this little stroll in the world of discographic criticism, we must agree with Otto Gombosi that 'musical performance is still the most uncertain, the most controversial field of historical research'.[22] Faced with so many contradictory opinions, I shall attempt to settle some of the differences dividing the critics, such as the speed to be adopted, the regularity or irregularity of the tempi, the use of instruments, the number of singers, the style of singing, and style in general by turning to the old sources. Though most of them are dated slightly after the death of Josquin, they nevertheless constitute the only contemporaneous documents enabling us to execute the music of the past with a degree of authenticity. The earliest of these authorities, Franchino Gaffurio, during the last thirty-eight years of his life (1484–1522) occupied the position of choirmaster in that same cathedral of Milan where the young 'Juschino de Frantia' made his first appearance in 1459 as 'biscantore'. In 1473 Josquin became 'cantore di cappella' to the Duke Galeazzo Maria; in 1479 he left Milan, having spent at least twenty years of his musical life there.[23] Nothing in the writings of Gaffurio indicates that he held his brilliant colleague in especial esteem; he mentions him only once among those he calls 'pleasing composers' (*jucundissimi compositores*). Yet three Masses and a motet by Josquin appear in one of the *Libroni* that he compiled for use in his church. The rules of decorum in singing set forth in the last chapter of Book III of his *Practica musicae* (1496) contain remarks that are still useful today to anyone who wishes to interpret Josquin's sacred music. Gaffurio warns the singers against producing notes 'with a mouth gaping wide . . . or with an absurdly powerful bellowing'; he counsels them to 'avoid notes having a wide and ringing vibrato, since these notes do not maintain a true pitch and because of their continuous wobble cannot form a balanced concord with other voices'. He advises the tenor, with its longer and stronger notes, to support, but not overpower, the high and weak

[19] Jeremy Noble, 'Sixteenth-Century Music on Records. I: Sacred Music', *Music and Letters*, 39 (1958), pp. 154–5.

[20] Otto Gombosi, in *The Musical Quarterly*, xxxix (1953), p. 134. Denis Stevens, in *The Musical Quarterly*, lii (1966), p. 134.

[21] *The Musical Quarterly*, xlvii (1961), pp. 562–5; *Disques*, Nouvelle série, no. 75–6 (December, 1955), p. 829, and no. 103 (November, 1958), p. 842.

[22] *The Musical Quarterly*, xxxviii (1952), p. 659.

[23] Claudio Sartori, 'Josquin des Prés cantore del Duomo di Milano', *Annales musicologiques*, iv (1956), pp. 55–83.

voice of the *cantus*, and the bass and the alto to be 'mutually equal and congruent with the other voices'. He chides singers for 'exaggerated and unbecoming movements of the head and hands', pointing out that 'head and hands do not form a pleasing sound, but a well modulated voice [does]'.[24]

In the *Toscanello* (published in 1523 but written about 1518) Pietro Aron, after having enumerated the different sorts of voices—'thin, full, high, harsh, soft, and flexible' (*sottile, pingue, acute, dure aspere, molle e flexibile*), describes the perfect voice: 'high, sweet, and clear; high enough to be satisfactory in the top range, sweet enough to caress the souls of the listeners; clear enough to fill the ears. If one of these is lacking, it cannot be considered a perfect voice.'[25] Twenty years later, Lampadius, in his *Compendium musices* (1539), pays tribute to Josquin several times, and the *Dodekachordon* (1547) of Glareanus constitutes a veritable hymn of praise to the author's favourite musician; yet neither of these throws any light on the manner of execution. Only with Adrianus Petit Coclico do we find some answers to our questions. Priding himself on dealing with what his colleagues usually left unsaid concerning musical practice, this musician, professing himself a pupil of Josquin's, attempted to draw up what Bukofzer with slight exaggeration calls 'the unwritten code of performance'.[26] He cites many original details concerning his master's methods, but they are clothed in the vagueness customary to the writings of that time. Josquin taught his pupils to 'pronounce well, sing elegantly, and apply the text to the proper notes'.[27] He asked young singers to imitate those who sang from the throat and not through the nose (*ex gutture, non ex naso*), as the Germans probably did up to then, and which may indicate an evolution in the technique towards our present method.[28] If we rely on Vicentino, we shall perhaps move too far away from Josquin's time and adopt a style different from his. However, as theoreticians always lag behind creators, it may still be useful to know that Vicentino speaks of 'compositions that are sung without instruments'.[29] However, in churches, or other vast places, where voices, even with an

[24] Clement A. Miller, *Franchinus Gaffurius, Practica Musicae* (American Institute of Musicology, 1968), Book III, Ch. 15, pp. 148–9.

[25] '...alta, suave et chiara, alta accio che in soblime sia sofficiente, suave accio che gli animi de gli audienti accarezzi, chiara accio che empia gli orechi. Se di queste alcun manchera, non sara detta perfetta voce'; *Toscanello in musica* (Venice, 1529), fol. Bii.

[26] '...belle pronunciare, ornate canere, & textum suo loco applicare'; Adrianus Petit Coclico, *Compendium musices* (Nuremberg, 1552); facs. ed. by Manfred F. Bukofzer (*Documenta musicologica*, ix; Kassel, 1954), Postscript.

[27] Ibid., fol. Fijᵛ.

[28] Ibid., fol. Fiij; cf. also Thurston Dart, *The Interpretation of Music* (London, 1954), pp. 49–50.

[29] '...compositioni che si canteranno senza stromenti'; *L'antica musica ridotta alla moderna prattica* (Rome, 1555); facs. ed. by Edward E. Lowinsky (*Documenta musicologica*, xvii; Kassel, 1959), fol. 94 (misnumbered 88).

increased number of singers, would be too weak, he suggests using instruments in support of the voices,[30] and this can be of help in the performance of Josquin's music.

Unfortunately, none of this is of great assistance nowadays. Is it too much to hope, as Paul Collaer wrote in 1938, that it would be 'just as possible to render an old composition in its original sonority as it is to show a Memlinc or a Giotto that has not been arranged to suit today's taste'?[31] The answer, probably, is 'yes', to judge by the way certain interpreters are criticized, even when they have consulted musicologists before recording. Unless he is also a sensitive musician (which, alas, is not always the case), the musicologist too often achieves only a 'reconstruction of the diplodocus', giving rise to 'solemn boredom'.[32] In any case, even on purely scientific grounds, musicology is far from being able to solve the problems encountered by the performer, for, as Handschin says, 'we must not be too proud of our science in this affair; we should rather be conscious that in this field we can never arrive at more than an approximation'.[33]

Finally, why not try to reconstruct 'the human fact' by simply turning to Josquin himself, what we know of him and of his time? In so doing, and following the example of others, we could point to the complex personality of this musician, reflected in many aspects of his style. But this does not simplify the interpretation of his music, since each piece gives rise to new problems. What interpreter does not feel powerless to convey that 'something divine and inimitable' pointed out by Johann Ott in 1539?[34] First and foremost Josquin was a singer. He spent his whole professional life among the chapel singers; Glareanus refers to him as 'master of singers' (*cantorum coryphaeus*), 'chief of singers' (*cantorum imperator*).[35] The composer is often formed by the instrument he plays. This is as true today as it was then, so that the sacred music of Josquin must primarily be considered as vocal music, since it was in his quality of 'biscantore' that he wrote it for the use of the singers of the chapel to which he was attached. This does not mean that the voices, at times, were not accompanied by instruments; they were, but only to reinforce the voices, as Vicentino advises, not to replace them. In this connection, I for one do not believe that the *cantus firmus* of a Mass

---

[30] Ibid., fol. 85.

[31] Paul Collaer, 'Renaissance de la musique ancienne', *Atti del terzo congresso internazionale di musica* (Florence, 1940), p. 157.

[32] J. Hamon, 'Sur votre pick up', *Combat*, 20–21 February 1971.

[33] Jacques Handschin, 'Réflexions dangereuses sur le renouveau de la musique ancienne', *Atti del terzo congresso internazionale di musica* (Florence, 1940), p. 47: 'Ne portons pas trop d'orgueil scientifique dans cette affaire; soyons conscients que dans ce domaine nous ne réaliserons toujours qu'une approche'.

[34] *Novum et insigne opus musicum* (Nuremberg, 1537), Dedication: '...habet enim vere divinum et inimitabile quiddam'.

[35] Glareanus, *Dodekachordon* (Basel, 1547), pp. 441 and 214.

should be thrown into relief by the vigorous sound of a solo trombone, as is sometimes done.

Josquin's life, and the circumstances of his work, furnish some answers to questions that performers ask. For example, when it comes to the number of singers required for the execution of his Masses and motets, why not conform to that found in the churches or court chapels where he worked? At the ducal chapel in Milan there were about twenty-two 'cantori de cappella' (the 'cantori de camera' numbered between thirteen and eighteen);[36] from 1486 to 1494 we find his name mentioned in Rome among the seventeen to twenty singers of the Papal Chapel;[37] in Ferrara in 1503 he heads the list of twenty-four musicians of the Estense court.[38] These figures correspond to those of most of the court chapels of that time: in Malines (12 singers and 10 boys)[39] as at the court of Emperor Charles V (15 singers and 12 boys),[40] at the court of the King of France (there were 23 musicians at the funeral of Louis XII in 1515),[41] as at that of Henry VIII of England, who, in 1520, was accompanied to the Field of the Cloth of Gold by ten boys and twenty Gentlemen.[42] We also know that at the occasion of Emperor Charles V's visit to Cambrai in 1540, Josquin's motet 'Praeter rerum seriem' was sung in the cathedral by the *vicaires chantres* 'qui estoient XXXIII en nombre estans en bas au dit coeur'.[43] But if we do look to the chapels for guidance, then we must also face the question of the use of boys' voices. In the few recordings in which children's voices are used, we are struck by the freshness of sound; we begin to fathom that 'suavitas' that was the hallmark of Josquin's music in the judgement of his contemporaries. Moreover, the best recordings have been made with sopranos who have a very pure tone quality, without vibrato, but today few are trained to sing in that way.

Analysis of Josquin's style would tend to support the view that he did not favour singing by large masses; the sound of the full chorus is used judi-

[36] Sartori, 'Josquin des Prés', pp. 64–6. On the number of singers at other Italian centres, see Frank A. D'Accone, these Proceedings, pp. 601–14.

[37] Fr. X. Haberl, *Die römische 'Schola Cantorum'* (*Bausteine für Musikgeschichte*, iii; Leipzig, 1888), pp. 42–58. In Rome Josquin was able to hear his music performed frequently; no fewer than fifty-three of his works were copied into the manuscripts of the Sistine Chapel; cf. J. M. Llorens, *Capellae Sixtinae codices* (Vatican City, 1960), pp. 511–12.

[38] Helmuth Osthoff, *Josquin Desprez*, i (Tutzing, 1962), pp. 212–14.

[39] G. Van Doorslaer, 'La maîtrise de Saint Rombaut à Malines jusqu'en 1580', *Musica sacra* (1936), pp. 176 and 182.

[40] Joseph Schmidt-Görg, *Nicolas Gombert* (Bonn, 1938), pp. 47–72.

[41] Paul Kast, 'Remarques sur la musique et les musiciens de la chapelle de François Ier au Camp du Drap d'Or', *Les fêtes de la Renaissance*, ii (Paris, 1960), pp. 137–8.

[42] Hugh Baillie, 'Les musiciens de la chapelle royale d'Henri VIII au Camp du Drap d'Or', ibid., p. 148.

[43] Nanie Bridgman, 'La participation musicale à l'entrée de Charles Quint à Cambrai', ibid., p. 241.

ciously, and is relieved by prolonged episodes for two voices, designed as though to allow good singers to show what they are capable of. This brings us to the question of what the qualifications of a good singer were in Josquin's time. It is difficult to arrive at agreement on this point, complaints often being made of the 'heavy vibrato' of Italian voices.[44] As early as the Middle Ages, unfavourable criticism was levelled by one country against another. In a fifteenth-century Spanish manuscript it is said that 'the different nations dislike each other's way of singing; the Greeks consider that the Latins bark like dogs, and the Latins that the Greeks moan like foxes. The Saracens say that the Christians do not sing but rave; conversely, the Christians claim that the Saracens swallow their voices and gargle the melody from the bottom of the throat. The French assert that the Italians always rave in a frequent breaking of the voice, so that they disdain to hear them'.[45] In the sixteenth century, too, it was quite common to criticize the singing practised in a neighbouring country. It would seem useless to seek the realization of an ideal that is perhaps far removed from that of Josquin's, who, we must remember, had spent most of his adult life in Italy.

No amount of research and no document will ever throw light on the vexing question of tempo, which in certain recordings may range from simple to duple or even triple for the same work, to say nothing of the variations of tempo within the course of a work. 'The right tempo', says Père Martin, 'is one that restores life and warmth to this dull succession of longs and breves',[46] and he puts this theory into practice in his recordings. In this, incidentally, he conforms to the recommendations of Vicentino to 'change the beat to demonstrate the effects of the sentiments of the words'.[47] But when Vicentino wrote this Josquin had been dead for thirty years, and the madrigal, to which Vicentino mainly addresses himself, had reigned over all other forms of music for some twenty years.[48] As regards the interpretation of Josquin's works, we can do no better than adopt the opinions of Jeremy Noble, who condemns those 'broad effects of dynamics

---

[44] Noble, 'Sixteenth-Century Music', pp. 157 and 388.

[45] Handschin, 'Réflexions dangereuses', p. 53: 'Diversae nationes...diversimode sibi displicent in cantando. Graeci dicunt Latinos ut canes latrare et Latini dicunt quod Graeci gemunt sicut vulpes. Saraceni dicunt Christiani non cantare sed delirare fatentur. E converso referunt Christiani quod Saraceni voces transglutiunt et cantus in faucibus gargaricant. Asserunt Gallici quod Italici semper in crebra vocum fractione delirant. Unde illos dedignantur audire.'

[46] Émile Martin, *Josquin des Prez, Messe Hercules dux Ferrariae. Notes sur l'interprétation* (Abbaye Sainte-Marie de La Pierre-qui-vire [Yonne], 1958), p. 24.

[47] *L'antica musica*, fol. 94ᵛ (misnumbered 88). See Curt Sachs, *Rhythm and Tempo* (New York, 1953), p. 275.

[48] Gaffurio, in Book II, Ch. 3 of his *Practica musicae* (Miller, p. 75), equates a semibreve with the rate of diastole and systole of the pulse; see also Zarlino, *Istitutioni harmoniche* (Venice, 1558), p. 207.

and tempo so dear to most choral conductors'.[49] Here more than elsewhere, the choice is a question of personal taste, and it would be difficult to find decisive arguments in favour of one or another theory. As Wanda Landowska rightly said: 'Knowing the right tempo is a matter of guess-work; history and tradition are merely railings: they prevent you from getting lost, without necessarily indicating the true road.'[50]

To conclude on a subjective note, I confess that for my own part, after hearing a considerable number of recordings, I am in favour of artistic restraint, as opposed to the seeking of purely external effects. What can instruments add, for instance, to Josquin's admirable 'Miserere'? Why not concentrate on reconstructing a perfect vocal polyphony? I concede that the marriage of voices and instruments has sometimes led to very beautiful realizations, such as the 'Missa Pange lingua' recorded by Noah Greenberg with his New York Pro Musica Motet Choir and Wind Ensemble (Decca DL 9410), but here the purpose was to reconstruct a solemn Mass as it was heard at exceptionally grand ceremonies such as the Field of the Cloth of Gold. There, we know, not only the organ but also the sackbuts and fifers of the King supported the singers.[51] Rather than this brilliant and ephemeral entertainment, may we not be allowed to prefer the more meditative atmosphere of the medieval chapel, where Josquin conceived his works and where he sang them?[52]

[49] Noble, 'Sixteenth-Century Music', pp. 385–6.

[50] Bernard Gavoty, *Vingt grands interprètes* (Lausanne, 1966), p. 119: 'Reconnaître le bon mouvement est affaire de divination. L'histoire, la tradition, ne sont que des garde-fous: ils protègent des égarements, sans indiquer nécessairement le chemin de la vérité'.

[51] Kast, 'Remarques sur la musique', p. 136.

[52] To illustrate this paper, the speaker played a tape made of short examples taken from different recordings with widely contrasting interpretations:

'Miserere' by Guillaume De Van (A.S. 107/8–Vol. XI), Émile Martin (BAM LD 022), and Philippe Caillard (ERA. Stu. 70421)

'Missa Pange lingua', *Kyrie*, by Noah Greenberg (Decca DL 9410) and Philippe Caillard (ERA. LDE. 2010)

'Missa L'homme armé sexti toni', *Kyrie*, by Jeremy Noble (Historical Anthology of Music. HM. 3SD.)

'El grillo' by Renato Fait with I madrigalisti milanesi (MCA. 28009).

VII Workshops on Performance and Interpretation*

* Remarks of the discussants in the three workshops have been paraphrased by the reporters; i.e., ascription does not imply verbatim quotation. The comments and bibliographical information in the footnotes are the Editor's.

The Performance and
Interpretation of Josquin's Motets

International Josquin Festival-Conference, Tuesday, 22 June 1971, at 3 p.m.
Directors: Ludwig Finscher, Winfried Kirsch. *Discussants:* Clytus Gottwald,
Arthur Mendel, Konrad Ruhland. *Reporter:* Edward E. Lowinsky. *Tapes
transcribed by:* Leonardo Waisman.
Participating Ensembles: Capella Antiqua München directed by Konrad
Ruhland; Schola Cantorum Stuttgart directed by Clytus Gottwald.

FINSCHER: I shall introduce briefly each of the works to be performed
and discussed; then the conductors will say a few words about their specific
versions of each piece. After we have heard the performances, we shall
discuss them. We begin with a hymn setting, 'Ave maris stella', which has
been published in the 'Supplement' to the Josquin *Werken*. It appears in
MS. Capp. Sist. 15 as one hymn of the cycle that seems to have been put
together around 1500 and includes one verse by Dufay. First comes the
three-voice setting of Dufay, anonymously (all Dufay settings in this
fascicle of MS. Capp. Sist. 15 are anonymous), then a four-voice verse,
'Monstra te esse Matrem', ascribed to 'Josquin des pres', finally two verses,
'Vitam praesta puram' and 'Sit laus Deo', both anonymous. The odd verses
are in plainchant. In the Josquin edition the last two verses are printed as if
they were by Josquin, although only the verse 'Monstra te esse Matrem'
carries his name. I have doubts about the authenticity of these two verses,
whose style is quite different from that of the verse ascribed to Josquin.
There is another hymn in MS. Capp. Sist. 15 that might tend to support
this doubt. It contains (1) a three-voice verse by Dufay—anonymous, as
always in this manuscript—(2) a verse headed 'de Orto' (Mabriano de Orto,
member of the Papal Chapel), (3) a four-voice verse, anonymous, and (4) the
last verse, again headed 'de Orto'. By writing 'de Orto' over the last verse,
the scribe indicates that the previous verse, even though following another
verse by de Orto, is not by that composer.

Let me now ask the conductors to say a few words about their interpretation of the pieces.

GOTTWALD: The first problem concerns the relation of tempi

between the first verse, 'Sumens illud ave', by Dufay in *tempus perfectum*, and the second, 'Monstra te esse Matrem', by Josquin in *tempus imperfectum diminutum*. I propose to take the first verse by Dufay at approximately ♩ = 82–84 the other three verses slightly slower, at approximately ♩ = 68.

FINSCHER: Is this a ratio in accordance with the theoretical writings of the time, or is it just experimental?

GOTTWALD: It seems that in the fifteenth century the tempo becomes slower with regard to the breve as a tempo unit,[1] since smaller note values have been introduced more and more into the voice parts.

FINSCHER: I wonder what you think about the following problem: The first verse is by Dufay. The other verses are, if not all by Josquin, at least by Josquin and contemporaries. It is obvious from the source and from the style of the pieces that the additional verses, composed in order to modernize the Dufay cycle, were written at approximately the same time, about or probably before 1500. So we have a difference of two generations between the first composer and the composer of the three other settings. Do you think that with regard to tempo relations, one should try to perform the first piece as if it were a separate piece in a tempo adequate for Dufay's time and the other three in a tempo adequate for Josquin's time? Or do you think it is more important to have the uniform tempo relations between all the pieces of this cycle?

GOTTWALD: The problem of tempo relations is for me as a performer principally an artistic matter. Tempo relations are a means to differentiate the verses from one another without separating them.

FINSCHER: There is one principal problem of *musica ficta*, which again brings the historical dimension into our discussion, and that is the following: the cadences in the Dufay verse have no accidentals in the source (common practice of the time, of course); they are printed in the Josquin edition without *musica ficta*. Considering that we deal with an embellished faux-bourdon style, the cadences, seen from Dufay's own period, probably require double leading tones, that is, leading tones in two voices. How do you perform them?

GOTTWALD: With double leading tones.

FINSCHER: Of course, this is correct from the standpoint of Dufay's time, but is it still valid for the time in which these compositions were

1 See Heinrich Besseler, *Bourdon und Fauxbourdon* (Leipzig, 1950), p. 129.

written down as a cycle, together with younger compositions in which the cadence with double leading tones certainly is no longer used?

GOTTWALD: Were we to perform this Dufay piece with one leading tone in the superius only, then we would adapt this piece to Josquin's period.

FINSCHER: What are we to do in this conflict between historical correctness with regard to the date of composition of the Dufay piece, and historical correctness with regard to the date of the writing of this manuscript?

CARL DAHLHAUS [from the floor]: If you perform it as a cycle, you adapt it as a piece of the Josquin period, and therefore you must perform it in the style of the Josquin period, without double-leading-tone cadences.

EDWARD LOWINSKY [from the floor]: We must take into consideration that there was not only a manuscript tradition, but an oral tradition as well. If the oral tradition in the Sistine Chapel was so strong that as late as 1500 they wanted to perform works by Dufay, they knew exactly how it was done. In every organization you have old, middle-aged, and young people. It is the older people who carry the tradition. I find no difficulty in assuming that the Sistine Chapel performed Dufay believing that they knew how Dufay was to be performed, and then did the remaining verses as they would have been performed around 1500.

FINSCHER: Of course, it is a very special case. This is, as far as I can see, the only instance in the late fifteenth or early sixteenth centuries that compositions were apparently sung seventy years after their probable date of origin—a surprising testimony of historical consciousness within the strong tradition of the Papal Chapel.

QUESTION FROM THE AUDIENCE: Would it be possible to hear it both ways?

FINSCHER: Mr. Ruhland, do you sing the opening verse with double leading tones?

RUHLAND: Yes.

FINSCHER: The Schola Cantorum will sing the Dufay verse first with double leading tones and then with leading tones in the superius only.

[The Schola Cantorum sang both versions, then Capella Antiqua sang the version with double leading tones.]

QUESTION FROM THE AUDIENCE: What evidence is there that this type of double-leading-tone cadence was not in use in Josquin's time?

FINSCHER: It went out of use because a new combination of voices developed in which the only possibility to have leading tones was either in the subsemitone clausula of the upper voice or, in the Phrygian mode, the leading tone downward in the tenor. There is no longer any occasion for double leading tones, as a rule.

COMMENT FROM THE AUDIENCE: May I point out that most of the passages in which double leading tones appear to be possible in the music of Josquin are actually in three voices and that they are in fact adaptations of the fauxbourdon technique. Hence it is conceivable that the old style—since we are referring to an archaism—can indeed be used. I see no reason to assume that the double-leading-tone cadence was dead by the time Josquin came on the scene.

JAAP VAN BENTHEM [from the floor]: This type of cadence also occurs in the four-part chanson 'Plus nulz regretz',[2] which is a very modern chanson, and also in the late five-part chansons, where you can treat it with a double leading tone.

GUSTAVE REESE [from the floor]: Well, it's certainly true that the cadence with two leading tones was practically dead in Josquin's time. I wouldn't think of disputing that. The fact is that it was still known to exist even after his time; it is actually written in compositions by composers as late as Giaches de Wert—on rare occasions, to be sure. This being the case, I think we may assume that its existence was known, and that Professor Lowinsky's argument is valid, that the singers, or at any rate the choirmaster, would have known about the existence of such cadences and their applicability to a work as old as one by Dufay.

FINSCHER: Both ensembles have performed this piece *a cappella*. What about that?

RUHLAND: We always perform these hymn settings of Dufay *a cappella*, since they are very closely linked with the fauxbourdon style.

---

[2] See Ex. 2 on pp. 675–9, measures 15 and 67.

MENDEL: And of course, historically, because they are so closely connected with the Sistine Chapel.

FINSCHER: Let us go on to the problem of text underlay. Mr. Ruhland pointed out that the text underlay of the Dufay verse in the Josquin edition follows the text underlay of the hymn melody rather than that of the source. In MS. Capp. Sist. 15 there are two instances where the text underlay is different:

The question is: should we adhere to the manuscript insofar as it gives precise indications of text underlay (which MS. Capp. Sist. 15 does in the hymn cycle, but not consistently), or should we give our own text underlay according to the hymn?

RUHLAND: I think of Dufay's hymn settings as projections of the hymn tune and would therefore follow the text underlay of the hymn.

FINSCHER: But the composition is not a *cantus-firmus* setting; it is an embellished setting of the hymn tune in a three-voice fauxbourdon style. This being the case, I should prefer a version coming from the polyphonic manuscripts. Whether MS. Capp. Sist. 15 is the best version in every respect for this specific piece is another question.

QUESTION FROM THE AUDIENCE: Must we not consider the whole cycle of Dufay's hymn compositions in its various manuscript readings, and then compare their text underlay with that of the original hymn?

FINSCHER: Agreed.

COMMENT FROM THE AUDIENCE: The polyphonic setting of a monophonic tune brings into play problems of harmony and of metric stresses that would influence Dufay in how he sets the text.

FINSCHER: You would prefer then to decide details of text underlay according to the musical texture of this polyphonic setting rather than according to the original hymn tune. Of course, there always remains the difficulty of different text underlay in different manuscripts.

LOWINSKY [from the floor]: There is of course a more general question. In the sixteenth century we can determine the approximate period when it becomes important to the printer or the copyist that there be a clear text underlay. But in fifteenth-century manuscripts we need to do a lot more work from this point of view to determine to what extent scribes were interested in fixing the relationship between words and music.

FINSCHER: Apparently, exact text underlay is a development of the sixteenth century. We really know very little about the practice of text underlay in the fifteenth century.

LOWINSKY [from the floor]: I should like to ask the conductors, who after all have to perform fifteenth-century music, what their principles of text underlay are.

GOTTWALD: My chief principle is not to place unaccented syllables on long melismas.

RUHLAND: Certainly no melismas must be sung on unimportant syllables; on the other hand, the general principle should be to follow the text underlay of the Gregorian hymn verse.

FINSCHER: Let us proceed to the second verse of this cycle, the four-voice verse 'Monstra te esse Matrem', attributed to Josquin. We shall hear two different versions, introduced by the conductors.

GOTTWALD: Tenor and superius sing the embellished hymn tune in canon; the bass begins by imitating the canon but then proceeds freely. The only voice of this four-part setting which stands out melodically and rhythmically is the contratenor. I have given the contratenor to a light solo voice and have it accompanied by the three other voices that are not sung soloistically. It is not the *cantus firmus* that is accentuated in this performance, but the contratenor, the only voice which has, so to speak, a melodic life of its own.

[Recorded example 1, Schola Cantorum Stuttgart.]

RUHLAND: In our version, the canon voices are sung by four singers each; the two other voices are played by instruments, so that the canon structure comes out very clearly. The bass voice is the *fundamentum harmoniae* (not the *fundamentum relationis*[3]); the contratenor is a supplementary voice, not the voice that dominates the interpretation. Its melodic and rhythmic richness is, I feel, a secondary effect of its probably being composed as the last voice of the four-voice texture. The *cantus firmus* voices are supported by one instrument. The historical question whether the Sistine Chapel adhered exclusively to *a cappella* performance is of secondary importance for me. My aim is to bring out the canonic structure of the work as clearly as possible. We shall sing the preceding hymn verse, 'Solve vincla reis', before the Josquin setting.

[Recorded example 2, Capella Antiqua München.]

FINSCHER: The crux of the matter is that both ensembles have given us structural interpretations. If we maintain the position that in the Sistine Chapel, as far as we know at the moment, instruments were not allowed, then the vocal interpretation would be the correct one from a historical point of view. On the other hand, the vocal interpretation of the Schola Cantorum puts one voice into the foreground of the composition and

[3] The term is used by Tinctoris in his *Terminorum musicae diffinitorium* to designate the tenor, the part that traditionally carries the *cantus firmus*.

treats the canon structure and the bass as the background of this voice. Do you have any comment on these versions?

MENDEL: Lest I be thought to be representing the Sistine Chapel here, I should like, having been a choral conductor myself, to differentiate sharply between historical authenticity and artistic decisions. I think this music can take many different interpretations, and I'm not at all sure that the historical one is always the best one. But of course I do feel, and I'm sure the conductors agree with me, that a knowledge and understanding of the historical probabilities is useful, whether or not one decides to follow them.

LOWINSKY [from the floor]: I should feel very sorry if either of these two versions were to disappear; it's wonderful to have them both.

FINSCHER: That is the crucial point; these versions bring out two different aspects of the composition. All great music can take different interpretations which bring out different aspects of the composition.

We shall now proceed to the question of the performance of these settings as one cycle.

[The Schola Cantorum and Capella Antiqua perform.]

FINSCHER: One question which does not concern us immediately is the question of stylistic difference between these pieces; one hears that they come from different regions and different times. This is not a performance problem. But *musica ficta* is. In the last section, the *cantus firmus* is in the bass. The hymn melody always has B♮, but the harmonic setting would seem to demand a B♭ because the B frequently comes together with F in one of the other voices. Which is more important, the purity of the Gregorian melody, or the purity of the four-voice setting?

LOWINSKY [from the floor]: This question illustrates one of the many myths about *musica ficta*. First of all, let us be clear about the fact that the so-called sacrosanct Gregorian chant was never sacrosanct to the people who sang it, nor even to the people who wrote it. In different manuscripts we have different accidentals, different tones, a host of variant readings; and certainly, to the composer of polyphony, the chant was anything but sacrosanct. From the time of the organum and motet on, when the composer took a chant and fragmented, indeed mutilated, it in any way he pleased, we observe complete freedom on the part of the composer with regard to the chant. The composer uses it as the musician uses any materials: freely, to his own purposes. Specifically, we have evidence of various kinds proving that accidentals were in fact introduced into the chant. For one thing, if we studied the chant-books of the fourteenth, fifteenth, and sixteenth centuries, we would find that accidentals change and multiply in the succeeding generations of chant-books. Gafurius, in speaking about the 'Salve Regina' as a monophonic melody, says it should not be sung A–G–A–D but A–G#–A–D. I quoted this passage ten years ago at the New York Congress.[4] Secondly, I have begun to collect polyphonic compositions with *cantus firmi* from the chant in which accidentals are marked; this happens more frequently than seems to be generally known. Thirdly, this morning Professor Brown, in his paper on 'Instrumental Transcriptions of Josquin's Motets', illustrated how four sixteenth-century intabulators—one from Tyrol, one from Spain, one from Italy, and one from Germany—raised the F in the *cantus firmus* of 'Praeter rerum seriem' in cadential situations, whereas Smijers abstained completely from touching the *cantus firmus*. The notion of the sanctity of the chant that would forbid the use of *musica ficta* in the Gregorian *cantus firmi* of polyphonic compositions has no historical foundation.

FINSCHER: I think the question is answered. Actually, performing this piece with B♮ against F for the duration of a breve sounds terrible.

If you sing the hymn cycle as the two ensembles have done, first placing one of the four voices into the foreground in one verse, and then singing the next verse with equally balanced voices, you do something that differs from what was probably done in Josquin's time. In the Sistine Chapel the cycle was probably sung from beginning to end in the same fashion, without the detailed regard for the compositional structure of each verse that we tend to give it today.

KIRSCH: The intention might have been the historically well-documented *alternatim* performance, in which the first polyphonic verse, 'Sumens illud ave', is to be performed with solo voices, the second, 'Monstra te esse Matrem' with *tutti*, the third again with solo, and the fourth again with *tutti*. The proportions are fairly clear: 'Sumens' contains 23 measures, 'Monstra' has roughly double the number, namely 56, 'Vitam' has 22 measures, and 'Sit laus' has 49. Especially the setting of the 'Vitam' seems intended for solo voices.

QUESTION FROM THE AUDIENCE: Isn't the problem here one of tempo? We really ought to know how the tactus relates to the number of measures. Perhaps the total duration of these pieces is largely identical. What effect would this have on your proposal?

KIRSCH: Counting measures and fixing the tempo are two different

[4] International Musicological Society, *Report of the Eighth Congress, New York, 1961*, ii (Kassel, 1962), p. 61.

s, I admit. But my idea was prompted by the structure; stylistically
are quite different pieces, suggesting to me *alternatim* performance.
The question, above all, is: were these different pieces really composed
especially for this cycle, or were they perhaps combined from various
sources?

FINSCHER: I think the cycle was actually composed for this manuscript,
that means for the Sistine Chapel, but apparently by different composers
and composers of different rank as well. As for the tempo relations between
the verses set in *tempus perfectum* and those in *tempus imperfectum diminutum*,
I think these ensembles have made no attempt at an exact ratio. As far as I
could hear, there was a quite natural relationship of tempi.

Let us now proceed with the two versions of 'Absalon fili mi', the first
sung by the Schola Cantorum and the second by the Capella Antiqua.

[Recorded example 3, Schola Cantorum Stuttgart.]

[Recorded example 4, Capella Antiqua München.]

The Schola Cantorum chose a very low pitch, the Capella Antiqua a
high one. The two versions go back to different sources. 'Absalon fili mi'
has come down to us in three sources: one manuscript, which is probably
the oldest and the most reliable source (London, British Museum, MS.
Royal 8 G vii),[5] and two German prints of relatively late date—a characteristic they have in common with the general German Josquin tradition
(Kriesstein, *Selectissimae necnon familiarissimae cantiones* of 1540, and Montanus & Neuber, *Tertia pars magni operis musici* of 1559). The manuscript
source has the piece notated in the low pitch of the first version, going down
to D♭. The last note of the bass even touches Contra B♭; the two German
sources transmit it notated a ninth higher, closing on c. A decision is
difficult; on the one hand, the low version seems closer to the intentions of
the composer; it is not by chance that the piece is notated with such an
extraordinary key signature (B♭ and E♭ in the superius and alto, E♭ and A♭ in
the tenor, and E♭, A♭, and D♭ in the bass) and at such an extraordinary pitch;
nevertheless I feel that the German version comes out clearer since it obviates
the technical difficulties caused in the first version by the very low pitch,
even when we have such an exceptionally good ensemble as the Schola
Cantorum. Of course, at Josquin's time pitch varied from chapel to chapel;[6]
the original notation, rather than fixing an absolute pitch, may have served
merely as an indication, 'please sing as low as possible'. Moreover, MS.
London Royal 8 G vii is connected with the manuscripts written for the

---

[5] On the date of this manuscript, see the comment by Herbert Kellman, p. 657 below.

[6] See Arthur Mendel, 'Pitch in the 16th and Early 17th Centuries', *Musical Quarterly*,
xxxiv (1948), pp. 28–45, 199–221, 336–57, 575–93, especially the second instalment (also
available in *Studies in the History of Musical Pitch* (Amsterdam, 1968), pp. 88–169).

Burgundian and Hapsburg chapels, which contain many pieces by Pierre de la Rue in low notated pitch.

MENDEL: Of course, an exceptionally low pitch *might* mean nothing more than an exceptionally high pitch standard prevailing in the place for which the piece was written. I say, 'might mean nothing more', because it seems appropriate that a piece about David bewailing the loss of his son Absalom should be sombre in character; but we have no notion of what D♭ really sounded like wherever this piece was intended to be performed. There is no possible obligation, it seems to me, to sing it with A = 440 in mind, at the pitch at which it is notated.

GOTTWALD: If I had to perform this piece in a concert, I should certainly choose a higher pitch, but only slightly higher. It is of the essence to sing this piece as low as possible, as long as it is technically and musically feasible, because the low pitch is intended to express the meaning of the text. At the end of the piece, the descent into hell ('et descendam in infernum') is symbolized not only by the musical figure of the descending triads, but as a musical-rhetorical figure in the same sense that the tone region is as low as possible.

MENDEL: Perhaps that is right, although I must say that the descent by circle of fifths is already a striking enough figure for descending, no matter just how far it descends in pitch. Apart from that, I would say that one wants to descend to the limits not of the singable, but of the 'hearable'. If one descends so low that there is very little tone in the bass, is one not defeating one's own purpose?

RUHLAND: I am very glad that the two versions survive. When I asked Dr. Kirsch why two versions so different in pitch should exist in the sources, he said that the high version might have been introduced because the ordinary chapels could not sing this piece in the low pitch.[7]

FINSCHER: It is not very likely that the German prints—and the two German sources are printed editions—were conceived with regard to special chapel conditions.

KIRSCH: You speak of 'German sources'; I believe there is actually only

---

[7] If that alone were the reason, it might have been sufficient to raise the pitch, say, a fourth higher. But Kriesstein raised it a ninth higher and the reason probably lay in his intention to reduce the unusual key signature, which must have been especially baffling to German musicians, to more normal usage: one flat in the three lower voices, two flats in the superius.

one German source, the edition of Kriesstein in 1540; the edition by Montanus of 1559 is merely a copy of it.

QUESTION FROM THE AUDIENCE: If we transpose this piece to a higher pitch, do we not lose the feeling that Josquin had in mind when he prescribed the lower pitch?

MENDEL: Certainly, and not only the lower pitch, but the extreme keys. But how did Josquin's audience know what key the singers were intending to sing in, if there was no pitch standard? There were of course local pitch standards; each church had its own organ, and people in that church were used to that organ. This is a very difficult question.

FINSCHER: But this piece was probably not intended for the church, or am I mistaken in that, Professor Lowinsky?

LOWINSKY: I do not think that the piece was written for the church; it is not set to a liturgical text. The text does not come from one single source, but from three different biblical sources, each of which—and here I differ from Van Crevel[8]—depicts an Old Testament figure bewailing the loss of a son. This is reason number one why it is a special piece. Number two, the modulations (from B♭ to G♭) make it a very special piece at that time. And number three, there is the low pitch. Whatever the precise pitch was, this is an unusually low register in the history of the musical notation of the Renaissance. Now while I admit that the higher version makes it sound more lucid, I would say this is a lucidity that Josquin did not intend. What he wanted with these unusual means was to convey a sense of deepest mourning. In a paper given in 1968[9] I interpreted the piece as pertaining to the year 1497 when Alexander VI, who loved his children very deeply, lost his first-born son through a terrible murder and, inconsolate, did not eat or drink for three days. I have set out reasons why I believe that Josquin, at the behest of his patron, Cardinal Ascanio Sforza, wrote this piece as a consolation for the Pope. It is important not to destroy the special character of the work.

FINSCHER: I agree that this is certainly not a piece for the church. But where did the singers get their pitch, if not from the organ?

[8] Marcus van Crevel, *Adrianus Petit Coclico* (The Hague, 1940), pp. 97–8, identified correctly the first parts of the text as coming from the books of Samuel and Job, but the words 'sed descendam in infernum plorans' he derived incorrectly from two different sources instead of from Genesis 37:35 where Jacob, upon learning of Joseph's death, exlaims: 'Descendam ad filium meum lugens in infernum'.

[9] See Edward E. Lowinsky, 'Josquin des Prez and Ascanio Sforza', *Congresso Internazionale sul Duomo di Milano, Atti*, ed. Maria Luisa Gatti Perer, ii (Milan, 1969), pp. 17–22.

COMMENT FROM THE AUDIENCE: This is not the only piece that Josquin wrote with low pitches; one of the 'De profundis' settings also has a very low range.[10]

COMMENT FROM THE AUDIENCE: Glareanus, in referring to the 'De profundis', comments that Josquin did not transpose the piece upward, as is often done in this mode.[11]

MENDEL: And Morley specifically warns against transposing pieces up that are clearly intended to have a special meaning.[12]

COMMENT FROM THE AUDIENCE: Perhaps one workable solution would be to put the piece up one tone or a tone and a half. This would still leave us with a very low bass, but it would place the top line into a range for either a countertenor or an alto.

FINSCHER: Professor Kellman, is this manuscript linked with the group of Burgundian-Hapsburg manuscripts that contain compositions of Pierre de la Rue written in very low ranges?

HERBERT KELLMAN [from the floor]: Yes, the manuscript is definitely part of the Hapsburg repertoire. It was copied by Alamire between 1515 and 1523 and probably in the last-mentioned year. This places the manuscript close to Josquin's circle in his last years.

FINSCHER: Do you think it possible that in view of this specific Burgundian tradition at the beginning of the sixteenth century, and in view of the special forces of the court chapel at Brussels and Malines, 'Absalon fili mi' was perhaps transposed down when written into this manuscript?

KELLMAN: I have no reason to believe that it would have been transposed down.[13] The London manuscript contains several pieces that are very

[10] *Werken*, afl. 35, no. 47; the bass extends to E.

[11] *Heinrich Glarean, Dodecachordon*, trans. Clement A. Miller, ii (American Institute of Musicology, 1965), p. 266 (p. 364 in the 1547 edition).

[12] Thomas Morley, *A Plain and Easy Introduction to Practical Music*, ed. R. Alec Harman (New York, n.d.), p. 275: 'but you must understand that those songs which are made for the high key be made more for life, the other[s] in the low key with more gravity and staidness, so that if you sing them in contrary keys they will lose their grace and will be wrested, as it were, out of their nature. . . .'

[13] If we were to assume that the low range was due to a copyist's decision, we would also have to ascribe the unusual key signature and modulations extending so far beyond the customary range to a scribe. Their novelty and daring, however, are such that Josquin alone must be credited with the notation as it appears in the British Museum manuscript.

high; for example, Mouton's setting of 'Dulces exuviae', Dido's lament, is certainly a sad text. Yet, the top part is written in the G clef.[14] So if they left that piece in place, there is no reason why they should transpose Josquin's down. Concerning the question of the low bass parts, Praetorius speaks of some basses with extraordinarily low ranges; I don't recall if he mentions specifically Flemish singers or not,[15] but you do find pieces like this outside of the Hapsburg court as well, the most famous example being Pierre Moulu's lament on the death of Anne of Brittany in the Medici Codex, which I believe goes down to Contra A.[16]

VIVIAN RAMALINGAM [from the floor]: 'Dulces exuviae' is a woman's lament, so it would not be appropriate to transpose it down to the range of men's voices. Moreover, is it not probable that the lower voices of Josquin's 'Absalon' were supported by the organ?

COMMENT FROM THE AUDIENCE: Instruments in a court chapel would help in fixing the pitch as well as an organ. In performing Pierre de la Rue's Requiem with its very low bass, they may have used a sackbut.

MENDEL: A funeral motet with trombones would not be surprising; the trombone, of course, is the one instrument whose pitch is not fixed; only the limits are fixed. I do not know what the limit of the lowest sackbut in use at this period was.[17]

FINSCHER: Can we proceed to Josquin's 'Stabat Mater'? We shall hear it first sung by the Schola Cantorum, then by the Capella Antiqua.
    [Recorded examples 5 and 6.]

FINSCHER: In the performance of 'Stabat Mater' we face two chief

[14] Set for four voices in treble, mezzo-soprano, alto, and tenor clefs. But the manuscript contains other settings of 'Dulces exuviae' for four parts with the ordinary clef combination—which shows how difficult it is to make generalizations.

[15] Michael Praetorius, *Syntagma musicum*, ii (Wolfenbüttel, 1619), p. 17, calls the low C 'die rechte Tieffe eines rechten Bassisten in Fürstlichen Capellen, wenn er dasselbe mit voller und gantzer Stimme natürlich haben kan'. He then recalls certain famous bass singers of the court chapel at Munich under Lasso's direction who were able to sing a fifth lower according to 'Chor Ton', a major sixth lower according to 'Cammer Thon' and he fixes the latter as Contra E flat of 13 feet. See also Mendel, 'Pitch in the 16th and Early 17th Centuries', p. 200. Mendel believes that Praetorius' chamber tone is 'about a minor third higher than our standard' (ibid. p. 201). This means that Praetorius' 'low C' was our E♭.

[16] 'Fiere attropos' (*The Medici Codex, Monuments of Renaissance Music*, iv, pp. 311–17).

[17] Praetorius, *Syntagma musicum*, ii, p. 20, gives Contra E (= our Contra G) as the lowest normal note; D and C below that are indicated as possible notes. Thus the lowest sackbut could easily have doubled the bass line of 'Absalon fili mi'.

questions: first, how to execute the *cantus firmus* part, secondly, how to adapt the text to the music.

The *cantus firmus* is taken from the chanson 'Comme femme desconfortée'—a symbolic counterpoint to the Virgin's distress in the 'Stabat Mater', combining the sacred and the secular. Is it possible that the French text was sung? The Schola Cantorum sang the *cantus firmus* to the 'Stabat Mater' text. Dr. Gottwald, how did you arrive at this decision?

GOTTWALD: To sing the French text of the chanson together with the Latin text of the 'Stabat Mater' would be an over-interpretation of something that was probably intended only as a symbolic connotation.

FINSCHER: But considering the long notes in the tenor part, only a small portion of the 'Stabat Mater' text can be sung.

GOTTWALD: The first verse.

FINSCHER: One has to admit that if the tenor sang the original chanson text, the words could not be heard by the public, since the considerable augmentation of the original note values obstructs perceiving the text and even the melody (not to speak of the difficulty of hearing the French text of one part against the Latin text of the four other parts). This of course is also an argument against Dr. Gottwald's vocal performance of the tenor. Mr. Ruhland, what are your ideas?

RUHLAND: The singing of the chanson text, 'Comme femme', is not a good solution, for the reasons stated. The singing of the Latin text of the 'Stabat Mater' has also been shown to be impractical. To the reasons given must be added that the text underlay of the Josquin edition is quite arbitrary.

FINSCHER: True; we have no criteria whatever on what point to place what syllable.

RUHLAND: An instrumental performance therefore seems to be indicated, but this too has its difficulties: the piece is extremely long, the tenor has a wide range, and there is no pause from beginning to end. It is impossible, for technical reasons, to have it performed by one trombone, or any one wind instrument alone; in our performance the part was divided into two ranges, and the two instruments alternate according to range.

FINSCHER: Why not take the organ?

RUHLAND: It sounds and it looks rather absurd if one instrument player, an organist, or perhaps even the chapelmaster, sits at his instrument and plays the *cantus firmus* with one finger.

FINSCHER: The chapelmaster could use one hand for giving the beat, the other for playing the *cantus firmus*. Or another musician could play the *cantus firmus* with one hand.

WILLEM ELDERS [from the floor]: There is another instrument which is very appropriate for performing this part, the crumhorn. The alto crumhorn has just the ambitus of the tenor part.[18]

EDMUND BOWLES [from the floor]: Victor Ravizza, in his monograph on the use of instruments, shows that crumhorns hardly ever appear in ensembles in Italian paintings.[19]

FINSCHER: We proceed now to the last question concerning the performance, and that is the problem of text declamation in this piece. Professor Mendel has prepared a statement.

MENDEL: The setting of the text in the 'Stabat Mater' is particularly strange, and even more so in the *secunda pars* than in the first. Let me read you the soprano part of the beginning of the second stanza in the rhythm of the music:

♩ ♩♩○ ○ ○ ○ ○
Cu–jus a–ni–mam ge–men–tem

▬ ♩ ○ ○ ○ ○ ○ ○ ○
Con–tri–sta–tam et do–len–tem...

And later, the contratenor:

♩ ○ ○ ○
...et do–le–bat

▬ ♩ ○ ○ ○–♩ ○ ○ ○
Et tre–me–bat dum vi–de–bat...

[18] According to Praetorius (*Syntagma musicum*, ii, p. 24), the alto crumhorn has the range of a ninth, from c to d', four notes short of the range needed. The soprano crumhorn, on the other hand, ranges from g to a', and it would be capable of playing all the notes of the *cantus firmus* except f, which is needed frequently.

[19] Victor Ravizza, *Das instrumentale Ensemble von 1400–1550 in Italien* (Publikationen der Schweizerischen Musikforschenden Gesellschaft, Serie II, vol. 21; Bern and Stuttgart, 1970); only five of the 536 paintings he studied show crumhorns (see the table, pp. 80–96).

and so on. The accents of the words and the durations of the notes seem opposed (almost in the sense that Stravinsky sometimes sets words, in *The Rake's Progress*, for example). I have long wondered why the accents of the words should be so frequently inverted, both as to duration and metric position, in a piece with prevailingly syllabic declamation. Perhaps the reading of the Latin text by a Frenchman will answer the question. [Plays tape.] You see that instead of 'Stábat Máter dolorósa' we have 'Stabát Matér dolorosá', etc. I have two other readings on this tape, one by a Fleming, and one by an Italian. The Flemish and Italian readings are not in any way surprising: they put the accents where all the rest of us would, except the French. My suggestion is that Josquin, at least at this period of his life, was affected much more by the French language than by other languages.[20] This is assuming that the rhythm of French speech was essentially similar some 450 years ago to what it is today, or at any rate, that there was less tonic accent in French than in other languages of this period.

We have devised a method for determining 'good' and 'bad' accentuation in passages set syllabically. This method and its results will be described more fully in the workshop on the Masses (see below, pp. 702–4 and Table II). Suffice it to say here that of the syllabic passages in 'Stabat Mater', 5.4% exhibited poor declamation, 89% neutral, and 5.4% good declamation, whereas in the *secunda pars*, 24% of the syllabic declamation was poor, 62% neutral, and 13% good. Were one to examine this question systematically, and eventually by computer, one would perhaps arrive at tables demonstrating that Josquin's declamation develops gradually toward the natural grammatical accents. This was the tendency of the time, particularly in Italy where he spent so much time. On this basis, 'Stabat Mater' would seem to be a very early piece.[21] Obviously, I do not suggest that one single

---

[20] Gustave Reese (letter of 8 August 1972) has informed me that Albert Smijers, in a conversation in 1957, expressed the opinion that Josquin actually 'set Latin with care, but according to standards influenced by the French language'. This is true also for French contemporaries of Josquin. See, for example, the analysis of Boyleau's motet 'In principio erat Verbum' in *The Medici Codex*, iii, pp. 125–6. In the commentary on Moulu's five-part motet 'Vulnerasti cor meum' I wrote: 'The declamation is unusually syllabic, but the accentuation follows the well-known French proclivity toward emphasizing the last syllable, which, in the preceding motet, can be studied in its native habitat, the vernacular' (ibid., p. 204). The preceding work is Moulu's five-part setting of 'Fiere attropos', the epitaph on the death of Queen Anne of Brittany in 1514. This would seem to answer the doubt raised by Mendel in the next sentence whether French speech was essentially similar 450 years ago. A reading of French Renaissance poems confirms the French habit of stressing the last syllable; see, for example, Brian Jeffery, *Chanson Verse of the Early Renaissance* (London, 1971). But a careful study of the contemporaneous chanson literature would probably show that even in the setting of French texts the conflict between musical rhythm and speech rhythm can be observed, with the latter prevailing increasingly as the sixteenth century progresses.

[21] Osthoff, in his *Josquin Desprez*, ii, pp. 31–6, considers 'Stabat Mater' an early work on

characteristic is enough to determine chronology. I do suggest that if one ranks the pieces in ascending or descending orders according to many criteria, eventually some pattern might emerge.

FINSCHER: Alas, there is no time left for a discussion of the last piece, 'Paratum cor meum'.

QUESTION FROM THE AUDIENCE: Can we hear the last piece from each of the ensembles before we go home?
    [Schola Cantorum and Capella Antiqua perform the *prima pars* of
        'Paratum cor meum' without commentary.]
    [Professor Finscher thanks the ensembles and the speakers.]

---

the basis of general style and technique. Of course, a more intimate and precise relationship between text and music is the central core of his view of Josquin's evolution as a composer (see also note 1 to the workshop on the Masses, p. 701).

The Performance and Interpretation of Josquin's Secular Music

International Josquin Festival-Conference, Thursday, 24 June 1971, at 3 p.m. *Director:* Howard Mayer Brown. *Discussants:* Nanie Bridgman, George Hunter. *Reporter:* Howard Mayer Brown. *Tapes transcribed by:* Ellen T. Harris.
Participating Ensembles: Capella Antiqua München, directed by Konrad Ruhland; New York Pro Musica, directed by Paul Maynard; Prague Madrigal Singers, directed by Miroslav Venhoda.

BROWN: The following four compositions will be performed and discussed: 'Adieu mes amours on m'atent/Adieu mes amours', 'Plus nulz regretz', 'Je ne me puis tenir d'aimer', and 'Fortuna d'un gran tempo'. Each ensemble has been asked to prepare performances of these pieces in one or more of the following ways: (1) for voices *a cappella*, (2) for voices mixed with instruments, (3) for solo voice and instruments, and (4) for instruments alone. The following questions were sent to the participants:

1. What *musica ficta* have you added to each piece? Explain your choices.
2. How have you modified the text underlay given in the *Werken* and why? (In 'Adieu mes amours', should the contratenor be provided with text?)
3. Should the musical performance reflect the poetic form of the text? For example, must all the stanzas of 'Plus nulz regretz' always be sung? Should the repetition scheme of 'Adieu mes amours' always reflect the fact that the superius sings a *rondeau cinquain*?
4. What are your criteria for determining the tempo of each piece?
5. What are your criteria for deciding on the combination of voices and instruments used to perform each piece? Can all chansons be performed in all of the following ways: by voices *a cappella*, by voices doubled with instruments, by instruments substituting for some of the voices, by instruments alone?

Can chansons ever be performed by more than one singer to a part? Can some parts be doubled by more than one instrument? How freely can one transpose the instrumental parts up or down an octave? Can instruments drop in and out of the texture, or must they always play from beginning to end? Should the later stanzas of 'Plus nulz regretz' and the repetitions in 'Adieu mes amours' be 're-orchestrated', or must one use the same instrumentation throughout?

6. To what extent ought a performance to clarify the structure of a piece? For example, does the fact that the two lowest voices in 'Adieu mes amours' are *cantus prius facti* influence your scoring? May both texts be sung simultaneously, or should the *cantus prius factus* always be played on instruments?

7. To what extent should the performers make an effort to project the meaning of the words?

8. What dynamics have you added and why?

9. Would you add embellishments (improvised or written out by the performers)? Why? Why not?

10. The case for and against transposition.

11. Should a performance be historically accurate, or should it be a clarification of the piece for modern audiences, regardless of how it was performed at the time it was written?

Our discussion will centre on two questions: (1) how does a musician prepare a piece of early music for performance, and (2) to what extent does a performer need and want historical evidence? Before we begin I should like to stress that questions dealing with performing practice rarely have correct answers. Thus we are not asking the question: is group A giving us a correct or an incorrect performance? Instead we should be discussing the extent to which every performer needs to bring his own interpretation to a piece of early music.

Mr. Venhoda, will you tell us which instruments and voices will be used in your performances of 'Adieu mes amours'?

VENHODA: In the first version, the tenor and bass are sung (the bass doubled on the viol), the superius is played on the organetto, and the contratenor on soprano and tenor recorders, alternating. In the second version, the superius is sung as well.

[The Prague Madrigal Singers perform.]

BROWN: Mr. Maynard, will you tell us which instruments and voices will be used in your performances of 'Adieu mes amours'?

MAYNARD: Our first version uses treble viol for the superius, vielle for the alto, baritone voice and regal for the tenor, and bass voice, great bass recorder, and lute for the bass. It is very close to the version prepared by the Capella Antiqua München.

[Recorded example 1, New York Pro Musica.]

Our second version is the same as the first, but without the two singers. That is, the chanson will be performed instrumentally.

[The New York Pro Musica performs.]

BROWN: Mr. Ruhland, will you tell us which instruments and voices will be used in your performance of 'Adieu mes amours'?

Ex. 1   'Adieu mes amours on m'atent/Adieu mes amours'

Florence, Bibl. Naz. Centr., MS. Magl. XIX, 59, fol. 164ᵛ (text after Florence, Bibl. Ricc., MS. 2794, fol. 65ᵛ).

Text for superius (after Hewitt, *Odhecaton*, no. 14)

Adieu mes amours on m'atent.
Ma bourse n'enffle ne n'étend.
Et brief, je suis en desarroy,
Jusquez à ce qu'il plaise au roy
Me faire avancer du content.

Quant je voy que nul ne m'entent
Ung seul blanc en main il sentent,
Qu'il fault dire sans faire effroy
    Adieu mes amours, etc.

Ainsi qu'il vient il se despent,
Et puis après on s'en repent.
N'est-ce pas, cela je le croy.
Remède n'y voy quant à moy
Fors publier ce mot patent,
    Adieu mes amours, etc.

RUHLAND: Our first version is instrumental, very similar to the one just played, with two discant violas, tenor viol, and bass viol.

[Recorded example 2, Capella Antiqua München.]

In our second version the same instruments are used, and the tenor and bass are also sung. Since the canon between tenor and bass is not very strict, we felt that those parts could be supported by instruments.

BROWN: I should like to open the discussion by pointing out that all three conductors have chosen to beg the question I had in mind in choosing this piece. The superius sings a rondeau text; the tenor and bass are based on a *cantus prius factus* and have another text beginning with the same words, probably a popular song.[1] I should have thought that the two lowest voices were structural, and that the chanson was essentially the setting of a rondeau. Mr. Venhoda was the only conductor who had the superius sung. Mr. Ruhland, would you mind performing 'Adieu mes amours' with the top voice sung and the lower ones played on instruments?

RUHLAND: The girl who would sing the superius is playing an instrument. Would Mr. Venhoda lend us his soprano?

[The Capella Antiqua München performs 'Adieu mes amours' with a soprano from the Prague Madrigal Singers, all of the lower voices played on instruments.]

BROWN: In my view, this is the most normal way of performing the composition; the versions chosen by the conductors were splendid, but, I believe, rather special. I was hoping that we might discuss the problems of adding text to the contratenor—the edition in the Josquin *Werken* places the rondeau text only under the superius—but since none of the groups sang the contratenor, there is hardly any point in discussing that question. The version of the superius in Example 1 includes a good many repetitions of phrases that I myself added to make the part easier to sing. The version in the Josquin edition, edited by Antonowycz and Elders, does not have any repetitions, and some of the phrases are left without any text.[2] May I ask the soprano of the Prague Madrigal Singers if she found the superius very unvocal, that is, instrumental in character.

VENHODA: Yes, she found it quite instrumental.

HUNTER: I should like to take issue with the statement you made that

---

[1] The monophonic chanson has been edited by Théodore Gérold in *Le Manuscrit de Bayeux* (Strasbourg, 1921), p. 100.

[2] Smijers edited this chanson in *Van Ockeghem tot Sweelinck*, v (Amsterdam, 1949), pp. 156-7, after the version in the *Odhecaton*. He added text to the two lower parts only.

the lowest parts, because they are canonic, function as *cantus firmi*, and would then, 'of course', be played on instruments.

BROWN: I didn't really mean 'of course'.

HUNTER: The bottom voices constitute a complete song, which many people would have recognized. Since the function of secular music is simply to entertain, why would musicians not have sung these two parts, enjoying the fact that a well-known song was turned into a canon?

BRIDGMAN: Josquin may well have wished the words to be thrown into relief by the canon. Both voices keep repeating his request to the king—'Vivray-je du vent, se l'argent du roy ne vient plus souvent?' It is thus very important to sing the canon. Perhaps musically the result is not so good, but historically it is important to hear these words.

BROWN: You would really prefer to hear both texts simultaneously?

BRIDGMAN: Yes, especially the lower voices in canon.

HUNTER: The contratenor is stylistically similar to the superius, but does that mean that it necessarily be sung with words? Could a singer not have added solmization syllables to the contratenor?

BROWN: Why not? But surely that would depend on the place and occasion of the performance. A singer might not wish to sing solmization syllables when performing for an audience of hundreds of people.

HUNTER: But perhaps we ought to regard the audience as ...

BROWN: Irrelevant?

RUHLAND: Mme. Bridgman, does the text underlay in the superius make good sense linguistically? Is it good French?

BRIDGMAN: Yes, and I find the top line very vocal.

BROWN: At last someone agrees with me. It is very difficult to decide what is vocal and what instrumental in the fifteenth century. You cannot say the superius is instrumental and can't be sung, because we have just heard a brilliant contradiction of that statement.

BRIDGMAN: Everything can be sung. Take contemporary music, where the voice is sometimes used as an instrument.

BROWN: That is precisely why I am reluctant to say very strongly that a certain line is instrumental or vocal—almost anything can be sung. And I agree with Mme. Bridgman that the superius of 'Adieu mes amours' is vocal in character.

HUNTER: I agree, too. It is no less vocal than the top lines of many chansons by Dufay and Binchois.

BROWN: Would any of the conductors disagree with that statement?

RUHLAND: I find the text underlay rather contrived, especially in measures 38–40 (see Example 1). Since a new musical phrase begins in measure 40, the new line of text should begin there, too. Yet Mr. Brown begins the new line of text in measure 38.

BROWN: I regard those two measures (38–39) as anacruses. They constitute a crucial point in the structure of the piece. The medial cadence in the rondeau scheme occurs in measure 40. The form of the *cantus firmus* is ABA. The end of the B section occurs in measure 40. If you perform the chanson following the conventional repetitions of the rondeau, a curious mixture of the two forms (rondeau and ABA) results. In any case, I regard measures 38–39 as anacruses.

HUNTER: Why not consider measures 38–39 as ending the preceding phrase? Why not repeat the word 'desarroy' there?

BROWN: Then you would have to begin the word 'jusquez' in the second half of measure 40.

HUNTER: Why not add it to the first half of measure 40?

BROWN: That would not be to my taste.

HUNTER: But it would facilitate making a cadence.

BROWN: One crucial point emerges here: whatever we decide, we have to make an interpretation. The manuscript sources do not help us with such decisions. More than one version is possible.

RUHLAND: Are there other examples of chansons with two different texts in the works of Josquin? The two texts of 'Adieu mes amours' appear in only one manuscript.

BROWN: There are other chansons by Josquin with multiple texts mostly with Latin *cantus firmi*.[3]

HUNTER: Since there are some problems about the way in which the text must be set to the superius, is it not possible that a copyist, possibly for completely unmusical reasons, simply added a second poem without even checking to see whether it would fit the music?

BROWN: All things are possible, of course. I was delighted to hear Brian Jeffery say that there is often difficulty in determining the medial cadence in rondeau settings by Josquin. I should have thought a case could be made for leaving out some of the repetitions necessary to a rondeau scheme when performing these longer settings from the late fifteenth century. Perhaps only the refrains of Josquin's rondeaux were performed.

RUHLAND: Perhaps the two texts appear in 'Adieu mes amours' because someone confused the text incipits. Most of the sources, after all, contain only text incipits.

BROWN: That opens the Pandora's box of questions about the lack of texts in the *Odhecaton*. Were all of the compositions intended only to be played on instruments, or were some of them sung? I don't know. People have argued this question, and they will continue to do so.

VENHODA: It is important to understand the social rôle of the text. A song like this one was not only heard by an audience but actually performed by them. The words are filled with irony. Perhaps the society of that time sang the *cantus firmus*. Only by comparing the two texts does one understand that the superius, too, has a joking text.[4]

QUESTION FROM THE AUDIENCE: Mr. Ruhland's performance included some phrases which were not sung completely through. The voices began, but instruments alone finished the phrase. Can this have been a general practice? Could the superius in measures 38–39 be instrumental, with the voice entering in measure 40?

JOSHUA RIFKIN [from the floor]: Reiffenstein already was skeptical

---

[3] For example, 'Nimphes, nappés' (no. 21), 'Nymphes des bois' (no. 22), 'Cueurs desolez' *a 5* (no. 28), 'Fortune d'estrange plummaige' (no. 46), 'Que vous madame' (no. 47)—all with Latin *cantus firmi*—and 'L'amye a tous/Je ne viz oncques la pareille' (no. 25), the only other chanson with a double French text.

[4] See the discussion of the problem of the two texts in 'Adieu mes amours' by Brian Jeffrey, who arrives at a similar view, above, pp. 408–9. For the opposite view, see Osthoff, *Josquin Desprez*, ii, p. 197.

about singing the upper parts.[5] There are very good reasons why the superius appears with text in only one manuscript (Florence, Biblioteca Riccardiana, MS. 2794). The disposition of the sources shows unmistakably that the piece is instrumental and that placing the text in the superius in Florence 2794, which in effect turns the piece into a so-called combinative chanson, was an attempt to bring the chanson into line with prevailing French performance practice, which, unlike that of Italy, stressed vocal performance.[6]

BRIAN JEFFERY [from the floor]: The *cantus prius factus* is not a simple ABA form but a *bergerette*.

BROWN: I agree. I have a question for Mr. Venhoda. Why do you change the octave registration of the contratenor? Sometimes you play a phrase in the two-foot register and sometimes in the four-foot, and the contratenor often is heard above the superius line.

VENHODA: In the first place, I like the sound, and in the second place I change octaves according to the sense of the words. When the words are joking I play the phrase in the two-foot register; when they are serious I use the lower octave.

HUNTER: But the performer must be careful in making octave transpositions. In this particular piece the contratenor can sound above the superius without making any bad intervals, but sometimes when you invert lines unsatisfactory harmonies and unpleasant parallel motion result. When people got together to play this music for their own entertainment they probably put up with all sorts of unsatisfactory arrangements of this kind. But if one speaks of artistically valid performances, those of which Josquin himself might have approved, then perhaps one ought not to invert lines.

[5] Helmuth Reiffenstein, 'Die weltlichen Werke des Josquin des Prez' (Inaugural-Dissertation, Johann Wolfgang Goethe-Universität, Frankfurt am Main, 1952), p. 85.

[6] One reason why Italian chanson manuscripts frequently omit the text is the scribes' well known ignorance of French. When one contemporaneous source gives a text, it should be studied with the greatest of care. Whether a piece is instrumental or not cannot be left to a majority vote of sources, particularly when the sources come from a country in which the language of the song was not spoken. (See Helen Hewitt's thoughtful analysis of the problem in the chapter 'Significance of the Literary Texts' of her edition of the *Odhecaton* (Cambridge, Mass., 1942), pp. 31–42; cf. further the Introduction by Edward E. Lowinsky to Helen Hewitt's edition of *Ottaviano Petrucci, Canti B* (*Monuments of Renaissance Music*, ii; Chicago, 1967), pp. V–X. The ease with which many chansons from the more forward-looking repertory of *Canti B* can be sung to the texts that Professor Hewitt furnished from other sources is proof audible that the composers meant these works to be sung.)

BROWN: I have a question for each conductor. What would be an ideal performing edition of 'Adieu mes amours'?

MAYNARD: The only thing lacking in the version in the *Werken* is a complete text underlay of the superius, that is, one that also indicates how phrases are to be repeated. If one had been provided, the top line could have been sung, had we so wished. But, of course, it could also have been performed on an instrument.

RUHLAND: The ideal edition for me would be as close to the original as possible, that is, with old clefs and in the original notation. I would prefer to see the text only in the lowest voices, with the problematic places marked in brackets. And if text is placed beneath the superius, it, too, should be in brackets.

BROWN: The problematic places are in the bass at measures 18–20, 37–40, and 57–60. Mr. Ruhland left them instrumental—even though I had supplied text by repeating a phrase—because no text was placed beneath those phrases in the Josquin edition.

VENHODA: I think that Mr. Brown has given us an ideal edition.

BROWN: Let us now hear 'Plus nulz regretz'. Mr. Ruhland, which singers and instruments are you using?

RUHLAND: First we shall perform it *a cappella*, with two singers to each part.
   [Recorded example 3, Capella Antiqua München.]
Second, the canonic tenor and bass will be sung, two singers to each part, and the other parts will be played by a discant viola and a tenor viol.

MAYNARD: The Pro Musica will first perform 'Plus nulz regretz' as an instrumental piece with bass flute and lute playing the superius, organ the alto, vielle the tenor, and bass viol the bass. That is, we contrast the string sound of the two lower voices with flute sounds for the upper voices. We add the lute to the superius to bring it out a bit, to give it a slight edge over the alto.
   [Recorded example 4, New York Pro Musica.]
We shall also perform it *a cappella*, one singer to a part.

VENHODA: The Prague Madrigal Singers will perform it once only, with the superius (doubled by organetto) and tenor sung and the alto and bass played on vielle and bass viol.
   [The Prague Madrigal Singers perform.]

BROWN: I should like to comment on the use of *musica ficta*. I regret having added a flat to the B in the alto of measure 37.[7] I was interested to

Florence, Bibl. del Cons.,
MS. Basevi 2442, p. 4
(superius, alto, tenor);
Werken, Wereldlijke Werken,
Bundel iv, no. 35 (bass)

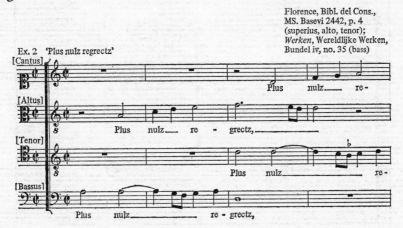

Ex. 2 'Plus nulz regrectz'

[7] The flat in the alto of measure 37 is undoubtedly correct—see the outline of the melodic tritone following B♮—but it needs consequence both backwards and forwards to make musical sense. Measures 18 to 29, dominated by B♮, move between Phrygian on E and A minor (see the cadence in mm. 28–9). Measures 30 to 43 are governed by B♭, introduced in the bass at measure 30 as a cadence on D minor approaches. The B♮ in the preceding sections

1) Orig.: escriptz

1) Orig.: escripz

regularly comes together with E in other voices; the B♭ of the present section appears just as regularly together with D and is followed by F. In measure 45 the B♭ reappears together with an E in another part, heralding a cadence on A minor (mm. 47–8). With the same logic, B♭ reappears as the harmony shifts back to D minor (see the cadence in mm. 52–3). B♮ follows as an approach to G major is made, ending deceptively on E minor (see mm. 60–61). The concluding section oscillates between A minor and D minor which interact so closely and avoid the subdominant of D minor so skilfully that a pure Dorian—questioned in the beginning of the chanson—is restored at the end.

In other words, the flats are the natural consequence of the change from A minor to D minor, and the rules of *musica ficta* were well designed to concord with such harmonic changes. While the world does not come to an end if they are violated, a sensitive and consistent implementation of the rules will uncover a new world of harmonic colour and order that heightens the artistic interest of the music of the period. All accidentals in parenthesis are suggestions of the Editor; the others are those of Professor Brown.

note that Mr. Ruhland's group sang B♭ in the superius in measure 5 but not in the alto at measure 37; that the Pro Musica did exactly the opposite, leaving the B natural in measure 5 and flat in measure 37; and that the Prague Madrigal Singers used a B♭ in both measures. And the world still has not come to an end!

BRIDGMAN: Mr. Ruhland, do you not prefer solo voices? Do you not think that they give better results than several voices to a part?

RUHLAND: I am not certain that the use of multiple voices for secular music is historically defensible. But I knew that the Pro Musica would use soloists, and I thought some variety would be a good thing for the workshop.

BROWN: 'Plus nulz regretz' was composed for a specific occasion.[8] Let me ask the conductors if they knew exactly how it was performed at that time, would they still feel free to arrange it as they wished? In other words, I am asking if Mr. Ruhland's last statement, which I would paraphrase, 'I do not know how this piece was actually performed, but I know what works well', is a valid viewpoint for a performer.

RUHLAND: If I definitely knew how the piece was performed, I would do it that way. We have performed Josquin's 'Cantio jocosa', written for King Louis XII, in this way.

MAYNARD: If the ten members of the Pro Musica could cope with the original manner of performance, we would do so. But if you told me that 'Plus nulz regretz' was performed by a group of forty musicians, in the first place I would not believe you, and in the second place we would choose another piece.

BROWN: My question is: to what extent does historical evidence change your ideas about performance practice?

MAYNARD: We always try to find out as much as possible about the conditions of the original performance and what the composer intended. We try to come as close as we can, and if we cannot come very close, we abandon the idea of performing that piece. Your question is really a theoretical one, since the Pro Musica, after all, does include in its repertoire music composed for larger forces than we have.

[8] See Osthoff, *Josquin Desprez*, i, p. 67, and Herbert Kellman, above, pp. 182–3. The complete text of the poem, as given in Brussels, Bibliothèque royale, MS. 228, is printed in Martin Picker, *The Chanson Albums of Marguerite of Austria* (Berkeley and Los Angeles, 1965), pp. 280–84.

BROWN: I have a question from the audience for you, Mr. Maynard. Why did you conduct the singers and not the instrumentalists? And why do the singers use vibrato but not the instruments?

MAYNARD: Let me answer in reverse order. Shelley Gruskin does use vibrato on the flutes and recorders, whereas Mary Springfels plays the viol without vibrato, and Lucy Cross, the lutenist, uses vibrato only occasionally on a long note. I myself feel that the instruments are compatible with the voices, and that there is no more objection to their combination in this music than there is when one hears a Schubert Lied sung with vibrato and accompanied on a piano without.

We are such a small ensemble that a conductor is not always necessary. If we had performed this piece in concert a few times, I would not have conducted the singers. As it is, I felt that I could help them do what we had planned in rehearsal.

BROWN: I have another question from the audience. Why do the ensembles not include ornamentation as a part of their interpretation?

MAYNARD. The instrumentalists of the Pro Musica are usually accused of adding too many ornaments, although, in this case, it is true, they simply played the notes as written. We thought of this chanson as having four equally important voices. We wished to keep the performance smoothly and evenly flowing, as in a motet. Any one of the four players could, of course, have improvised ornamentations.

RUHLAND: I am a purist in these matters. I do not wish to improve on Josquin. If *fusae* were appropriate, they would have been written down.

VENHODA: In a concert, the performance would have been quite different, an interpretation incorporating everything we had tried in rehearsals. In preparing this piece for a workshop, I had uppermost in mind the desire for contrast with the previous chanson. In 'Adieu mes amours' the tenor and bass were canonic and the words needed to be brought out. In 'Plus nulz regretz' it is better to express the serious meaning of the words by using one singer to a part.

EDWARD LOWINSKY [from the floor]: The problem of ornamentation merits attention. What musicologists have done with it so far is rather one-sided. There is a great body of evidence, much of it published and commented upon, that proves without a doubt that singers and instrumentalists used ornamentation. There is another body of evidence, not nearly so well known, much of it unpublished, and not commented upon very extensively, that proves that composers detested having their works performed with ornamentation. Zarlino[9] writes that ornamentation ought to be left out of choral performances because the composer has very carefully woven a contrapuntal fabric, and improvisation will disturb the texture. That statement shows that Zarlino might have tolerated ornamentation in solo but not in choral performance. He obviously reflects Willaert's opinion. Moreover, when a composer is so wonderfully inventive in his fioriture—in this respect Josquin resembles another favourite of mine, Chopin—and when you examine the mechanical figurations recommended by the writers on ornamentation, then you understand why Josquin, according to one well-attested anecdote, said to a singer who decorated a work by him, 'You ass! Tu asine! Why do you ornament my music? Had I wanted embellishments, I'd have written them myself. If you wish to improve upon well-made compositions, compose a piece yourself and leave mine alone!'[10]

HUNTER: The musicians who originally performed this music were not thinking of a modern concert audience for whom they were trying to give a definitive performance; they expected to have some fun with the music. One of the two examples of ornamentation in Mme. Thibault's paper was very restrained and beautiful. In spite of the anecdote about Josquin, I cannot feel that ornamentation should be totally excluded. I myself would rather not ornament these chansons of Josquin, but we must not lose sight of the social function of secular music. In a sense it was a toy for musicians to play with, and if singers wished to show off their imagination and their technique or if they wished to engage in contests, then they undoubtedly did so.

BROWN: What the evidence really shows is that musicians disagreed very much about this question in the sixteenth century. I see no reason why twentieth-century musicians can't also disagree.

MAYNARD: The New York Pro Musica has always used ornaments very freely. Shelley Gruskin, who has been with the group for a long time, is a genius at improvising ornaments. I would certainly never tell him to stop playing them. And I have yet to hear him play a piece exactly the same way twice.

[9] Zarlino, *Istitutioni harmoniche* (Venice, 1558), p. 204; Guy A. Marco and Claude V. Palisca, transls., *The Art of Counterpoint. Gioseffo Zarlino, Part Three of* Le Istitutioni harmoniche, *1558* (New Haven and London, 1968), p. 110.

[10] Osthoff, i, p. 222, n. 1. The anecdote comes from Johannes Manlius, *Locorum communium collectanea* (Basel, 1562), p. 542.

BROWN: If a performer wishes to emphasize the structure of a piece like 'Plus nulz regretz', he will probably wish to keep the four equally important voices as clear and balanced as possible. That is the point Mr. Maynard made. And yet some of the performances today stressed some of the parts at the expense of others. I should like to ask each conductor why he brought out some voices and suppressed others.

RUHLAND: The canon[11] must be brought out clearly; the other two voices are secondary in importance. But another interpretation is possible, which is why we also performed it *a cappella*.

VENHODA: It is not advisable to perform everything *a cappella*. It is hard for the singers, and hard for a modern audience, which requires more variety of sound.

BROWN: Let us turn now to 'Je ne me puis tenir d'aimer'. What instrumentation will you use? (see Ex. 3)

MAYNARD: Our first version is purely instrumental: regal on the top line, bass flute on contratenor, vielle on tenor (which seems to be the heart of the piece), lute on *quinta pars*, and bass viol on bass. Our choice of instruments is necessarily limited to those we have. We sometimes would like to use a cornetto, for example, but we don't have a cornetto player. And we sometimes would prefer four string players, but we don't have them. Within our limitations, however, we attempt to choose an instrumentation appropriate to the composition. This chanson is very motet-like, highly imitative. The imitation is made very clear by using five very contrasting sounds.

The second version we have prepared uses the same instruments and adds five voices.

[Recorded example 5, New York Pro Musica.]

VENHODA: We perform 'Je ne me puis tenir' *a cappella*, using one singer to a part.

[The Prague Madrigal Singers perform.]

RUHLAND: We shall perform the chanson in three versions, first with instruments alone (recorder and discant viola, discant viola, tenor viol,

---

[11] Strictly speaking, tenor and bass do not form a canon; time intervals, rhythm and pitches change. But they are certainly a pair of voices closely following each other. It looks as if Josquin had projected all four voices simultaneously, bearing in mind that he wished to tie tenor and bass together in a canon, but had to make concessions to the necessities imposed by the four-part harmony and counterpoint.

bass viol, with a trombone playing the tenor, which is a *cantus firmus*). Second, we shall use the same instruments, plus five solo singers. And third, we shall perform it chorally since we feel that this chanson is the one most like a motet.

[The Capella Antiqua München performs the first two versions.]

BROWN: Before you sing the third version, may I ask you to substitute C♮ for C♯ in the last six measures?

[Recorded example 6, Capella Antiqua München.]

BROWN: I prefer the C♯.

A member of the audience has commented, 'All their tempi are too fast'. I should like to ask each conductor about the tempo of 'Je ne me puis tenir d'aimer'. How did you arrive at the speed you chose?

VENHODA: The tempo is determined by the context. All of the tempi chosen today were good ones. In fact we all decided on approximately the same tempo.

MAYNARD: But there were some differences in tempo, though all were good. Tempo is a very subjective thing. Some people say Toscanini conducted Beethoven too quickly and others say Furtwängler conducted him too slowly. Tempo is not an absolute; it depends on the size of the group, the kind of phrasing, the diction, the style of singing, the instrumentation, whether the performer decides to keep a steady tempo or use rubato, and on many other factors.

BROWN: Were you influenced by theories of invariable tactus?

MAYNARD: No. I see the music before the rest of the ensemble does, and I have some idea about tempo before the first rehearsal. But very often my idea is modified as we rehearse, and we play the music a bit faster or a bit slower than I had originally thought suitable.

I usually decide on a tempo by considering the text. The second and third chansons today have thoughtful, sad words, and the music enhances them. Therefore I chose a somewhat slower tempo than usual. Beyond this simple observation, though, I cannot formulate any rules.

RUHLAND: In the first place, tempo is relative to the place where one performs. Here on a concert stage the acoustics are very dry and hence we play faster. In a Gothic cathedral we would probably choose slower tempi. The speed is also relative to the harmonic rhythm. Here the harmonies often change on the minim, and that influenced our choice of tempo.

BROWN: Mr. Ruhland seems to prefer the sound of unmixed consorts. In his performance of 'Je ne me puis tenir d'aimer' the superius was sounded at pitch and also doubled an octave higher. Mr. Maynard seems to prefer the sound of broken consorts, although he has explained to us that his choice of instruments is necessarily limited to the personnel of the group. Mr. Ruhland, do you use unmixed consorts for historical reasons, or merely because you prefer the sound and have the instruments available?

RUHLAND: The voices of this chanson are all equally important and the texture is imitative. These factors led me to a homogeneous instrumentation. One seldom has an ideal instrumentarium; one must accept what one has. Moreover, coming from Germany, we could not bring all the instruments we would have liked. For example, I should have preferred omitting the trombone and using two viols on the lowest voices in 'Je ne me puis tenir d'aimer'. In short, the style of this chanson seemed to me to warrant a whole and not a broken consort.

BROWN: Here is a question from the audience for Mr. Ruhland: 'Why does your ensemble use two Baroque violins rather then treble and alto viols?'

RUHLAND. We play on some instruments which may not be very familiar in this country but are more often used in Germany. For example, we use a tenor violin, and a discant viola (not viola da gamba). This is the seventeenth-century German equivalent of the eighteenth-century French pardessus de viole, an instrument with five strings tuned like a viola da gamba without its lowest string.

BROWN: I should like to ask Mr. Venhoda a question about his instrumentation in the chansons performed earlier today. Sometimes he lets an instrument play only for a few measures and then drop out, the line being continued by another instrument or by a voice. The result is a constantly changing instrumental timbre. Why do you do this, and what criteria do you use?

VENHODA: I first decide on the parts which must be sung. Then I ensure enough diversity to keep the attention of a modern audience for two hours. After that I feel quite free; I sit at my organetto and fill in parts that attract me. Then I try to emphasize the things the composer seems to want expressed; I follow the meaning of the text to support and strengthen certain expressive portions.

BROWN: Let us move on to 'Fortuna d'un gran tempo'. I gave each conductor three versions of the piece, the two in the Josquin *Werken*[12] and a version made by Jaap van Benthem and published in *Het Orgel*.[13] The first of the two versions in the *Werken* is completely without *musica ficta*, the second is the version proposed by Edward Lowinsky. I should like to ask each of the conductors which version he prefers, and which one(s) he will perform for us.

VENHODA: I understood that we were to perform all three. We shall perform all of them with the same instrumentation, using instruments only: tenor flute, organetto, and bass viol. I myself prefer Professor Lowinsky's version.

[Recorded example 7, Prague Madrigal Singers (version without *musica ficta*).]

MAYNARD: The Pro Musica would like to play Professor Lowinsky's version and also a version we prepared ourselves (see Ex. 4). We shall use soprano recorder, alto recorder, and organetto.

[The New York Pro Musica performs.]

RUHLAND: An interesting thing has just happened. We would have liked to perform the same version as the one you have just heard which was prepared by the Pro Musica. We agree with them down to the last accidental. But I thought that we could only choose one of the three versions that you sent to us. Therefore we have prepared a performance of Professor Lowinsky's edition, using discant viola, tenor viol, and bass viol.

[The Capella Antiqua München performs.]

JAAP VAN BENTHEM [from the floor]: I was quite surprised that my version of 'Fortuna d'un gran tempo' was sent to the ensembles. It is similar to that proposed by Mr. Maynard and Mr. Ruhland, but it was made for the organ and not for an ensemble of instruments, and this makes a difference in the way it sounds.

BROWN: I think that this is a case when we should let the music speak for itself. Rather than discuss the *ficta*, let me ask you all a question that several members of the audience have requested. What kinds of tuning do you use, mean-tone, equal, or just? Do you feel that the kind of temperament you use is an important element of the performance?

RUHLAND: We own two seventeenth-century trombones with a pitch slightly higher than A = 440. Therefore we adapt everything to them.

---

[12] Supplement, nos. 13a and 13b.

[13] Jaap van Benthem, 'Fortuna dun gran tempo', *Het Orgel*, lx (1964), pp. 170–74.

Werken, Supplement, no. 13a
(with *musica ficta* by Paul Maynard)

Ex. 4 'Fortuna dun gran tempo'

Fortuna　　　　Fortuna dun gran tempo

Fortuna　　　　Fortuna

Fortuna

Fortuna

BROWN: But what temperament do you use?

RUHLAND: Since we move our instruments around and sometimes rehearse in different places, it is much easier to tune them all to equal temperament, and especially the keyboard instruments, the positive organ and the virginals. Moreover, these instruments are also used by other groups and so we are not able to retune them.

MAYNARD: Although the players may correct me, I think that it is true to say that we do not play in any one temperament, although we come closest to equal. Our harpsichordist, Frederick Renz, sometimes tunes the harpsichord in mean-tone temperament for some compositions. But any instrumentalist will tell you that you have to make adjustments for accidentals, and so I think that we cannot claim to play in any one pure temperament. Moreover, since we do such a variety of music, both medieval and Renaissance, we must tune the instruments in a way that is best for our entire repertoire.

HUNTER: Couldn't you use a different kind of temperament when you perform *a cappella*, that is, when you are not tied down by the temperaments of lutes and keyboards?

MAYNARD: Yes. By and large an *a cappella* performance will tend toward Pythagorean tuning with higher leading tones.

HUNTER: Have you tried just thirds, in order to get pure triads?

MAYNARD: Only insofar as some of the performances with keyboards use mean-tone temperament in which some thirds are pure.

VENHODA: We normally use instruments from the National Museum in Prague, but we were able to bring only the organetto. The tuning differs a bit on the organetto because of differences in air pressure. However, we try to use equal temperament.

HUNTER: I am disappointed that none of the groups sings pure major triads. It might change the timbre of some of the compositions very much, especially in *a cappella* performances.

BROWN: The discussants suggested that we all rise and sing 'Adieu mes amours', but I have overruled them. We have at least been able to hear a great many points of view expressed today, although we have settled absolutely nothing. Thank you very much.

The Performance and
Interpretation of Josquin's Masses

International Josquin Festival-Conference, Friday, 25 June 1971 at 3 p.m. *Director:* Arthur Mendel. *Discussants:* Ludwig Finscher, Clytus Gottwald, Paul Maynard, Miroslav Venhoda, John Reeves White. *Translator for Dr. Venhoda:* Traute Marshall. *Reporter:* D. Kern Holoman, who also transcribed the tapes.
Participating Ensembles: New York Pro Musica directed by Paul Maynard; Prague Madrigal Singers directed by Miroslav Venhoda; Schola Cantorum Stuttgart directed by Clytus Gottwald.

MENDEL: Let me open the session by outlining the projected activities of the workshop. The first part of the afternoon will be devoted to discussion, and the second part to musical illustration and experiment. The first subject to be discussed will be how performers decide matters of performance or interpretation—what relative weight they give to historical considerations, to aesthetic considerations, and so on. Next will come the question of text distribution, then tempi and relations among them, and finally *musica ficta*.

I should like to ask each conductor how he chooses voices, instruments, tempi, dynamics, etc. What influences you: history, aesthetics, or personal taste? Mr. Venhoda?

VENHODA: Music is ambiguous as regards, for example, tempo. The same piece can be imagined at various tempi. It is the text that determines one's choice among these tempi. Until I realized this, my group and I always had difficulty in finding the true tempo. I consider this a very important question, because I am convinced that once you begin in one tempo, it cannot be changed. I think of this constant tempo as analogous, in a way, to the grid of lines that Albrecht Dürer draws as a framework for a drawing or painting—not that these lines are to be emphasized, but one must be constantly aware of them.

The text must be taken with utmost seriousness, with the attitude of a man of Josquin's time. When the words 'Tu pauperum refugium' are sung, they must be full of faith and hope. People of this time knew that they might die any day, perhaps of a mere toothache. To say 'Tu pauperum refugium' is like bearing a cross on one's back. Not only tempo but dynamics as well are affected by the meaning of the text. One must decide whether to sing

'Tu pauperum refugium' slowly, lyrically, romantically, or on the other hand quite strictly, out of conviction: 'Thou art mine, thou art my Zion.'

These things also affect the choice of voices and instruments. In the *Credo* I let only a single voice sing at the beginning, so that the expression of faith, 'Credo in unum Deum', may be as strong as possible.

In my interpretations, the linear and structural elements—the various canons, the interrelations—are not disturbed, since my tempo remains uniform and my dynamics are not subject to sharp and sudden changes. The music depends on these structural elements, as a body depends upon its skeleton, even though they remain in the background. What I find new in Josquin, as compared with Obrecht or Dufay, is his inventiveness. At every word, or at every sentence, he expresses something new—new for his time; and this always has to do more with the heart than with the intellect. Thus if I find something of this sort, I always emphasize it somewhat: solemnity perhaps with trombones; if the voices imitate a bell-like sound, I choose a psaltery or a *Cymbel* for support.

Performing musicians will perhaps have noticed that in *a cappella* singing, when it is really in tune, one often hears the overtones. That happens in this music so frequently that one must take it as a cue for instrumentation. People of Josquin's time probably had a particular sense of the balance between voices and instruments. They had a dream of beauty of sound that was brought to its culmination in the Romantic orchestra. I remember the first time I became aware of this. I heard this music in a church, and was sure that there must be a psaltery and recorders participating, but there were none.

MAYNARD: Instruments in polyphonic music of the Renaissance serve three purposes:

First, they add to and concentrate the sonority. A purely vocal performance with eight or ten voices to a part will produce a greater sonority than one with only two or three. But instruments add a kind of core to the sound that voices alone cannot have. Of course Pro Musica has been particularly dependent on instruments; since we perform with only one voice to a part, and some of our repertoire consists of choral music, we use instrumental doubling to add to the sonority.

Second, instruments contribute to clarity in at least two ways. Particularly in passages moving in quicker notes than the prevailing texture, instruments—especially wind instruments, which play all these notes separately anyway—point up the melodic line in a way that I do not think can be achieved with voices alone. This is especially true in passages that lie near the bottom of a vocal range. No singer can make details as distinct at the bottom of his range as in the middle or at the top. Another kind of clarity is produced by differentiation of timbre. It is true that the timbre of a countertenor is very different from that of a bass baritone or of a soprano. But if, say, one doubles the superius with recorder, the alto with vielle, the tenor with sackbut, the bass with bass viol, the difference in the resulting timbres helps make the polyphony clearer.

A third function of instruments is harder to define: it is the function they have in the orchestral music of later composers. In some way, recorders in a given case seem to frame the field or the quality of a piece; in another piece, the grainier sounds, of, say, crumhorns seem to be just right. That is, specific instrumental colours help to project the aesthetic or emotional effect of a piece.

GOTTWALD: The Schola Cantorum is not primarily an ensemble for old music, but specializes rather in avant-garde vocal music. Many avant-garde composers have written works for this group, Dieter Schnebel, Maurizio Kagel, and Pierre Boulez among them. About twice a year the group performs programs of old music, and in these programs the experience it has had with contemporary music is applied and tested. I am interested not only in sources and editions but also in compositional structure: the density of a setting, timbre, timbral melody, the composition of dynamics. For the motet 'Illibata Dei Virgo', which the group performed on Thursday evening, I chose a serial structure of dynamics, based upon the fourteen-letter (2×7) acrostic of the text. The dynamics and tempo of our performance of the 'Stabat Mater' have a structure related to the melodic structure of the *cantus firmus*. The interpretation of the chanson 'Baisez-moi' follows Monteverdi's 'Bacisoavi', as if Josquin's chanson were an anticipation of Monteverdi. The performance of the *Kyrie* of the 'Missa de Beata Virgine' shows the influence of Stravinsky, using absence of expression as a means of expression. I seek Utopian traces in old music and ways of carrying out their implications in performance. In this way, I believe old and contemporary music will not be divorced, but rather inter-related.

MENDEL: I should like, on the basis of previous conversation with Dr. Gottwald, to amplify slightly what Dr. Gottwald has stated so concisely. From one historical viewpoint, the question may be asked: What did the music sound like in Josquin's time, and how can we make it sound as much like that as possible? From another viewpoint, one may ask: What has happened since Josquin's time, what light does this shed on Josquin's music, and why should we deprive ourselves of this light? To my question: 'How can anyone grasp the serial structure of the dynamics which you attempted to apply in performance to the motet "Illibata Dei Virgo"?' Dr. Gottwald posed the counter-question: 'Does music consist only of what can be grasped in a single performance?'

Let me ask each of you the following question: 'If musicologists could say just how certain movements of a Mass were performed by Josquin's own choir, what effect would this have on your own performance?'

GOTTWALD: The question is irrelevant, since musicologists cannot give this information. We have so little knowledge of the answer to almost any question about Josquin's performance practice that the performer need not pay any attention to this question.

VENHODA: Even if I knew exactly how Josquin performed his music, I would probably not feel wholly bound to do it the same way. In my earlier records, the tempi are always rather slow. Gradually, I have adopted increasingly fast tempi. Audiences wish to hear twenty or thirty minutes of music. Besides, there are certainly different tempo relations between the *Credo* and the other sections of the Mass. The *Credo* must be sung a little faster, since it is very long, and there is no action before the altar. One must know these things. The *Gloria* is certainly faster than the *Kyrie*, but only by four or five metronomic degrees.

GOTTWALD: Even if I could know just how Josquin performed a piece, I would still reserve the right to perform it quite differently. As opposed to Venhoda, who considers the work in its liturgical framework, I consider the Mass a musical composition in itself, like a symphony. Since in a concert performance there is no action before the altar in any of the movements, there is no reason to treat the *Credo* differently from any of the other movements.

MAYNARD: One must always keep in mind that any concert performance of a Mass is to a certain extent artificial, because those five movements were composed in the context of the total liturgy, the Ordinary interspersed with the Proper. This telescoped concert version of the Ordinary is not the way it was originally intended to be heard.

FINSCHER: The Masses of Josquin's time were performed, as far as we know, during the liturgy; liturgical action and liturgical song were interspersed between the sections. But on the other hand, they were composed as a cycle, and the whole early history of the Mass is the story of how this cycle gradually became more and more a musical unit, with *cantus firmus*, identical incipits of movements, continuing through the parody Mass, and so on. So the telescoped performance of a Mass in concert today brings out exactly one point of the Utopian quality of this music: the Mass in the sixteenth century is much more than liturgical music; it is autonomous.

MENDEL: I recall a performance by the Pro Musica of the Ordinary of the Mass with the Proper interspersed; it was an interesting experiment. But without interpolation, one gets the concentrated picture of the whole composition, the sixteenth-century equivalent of a symphony or a sonata.

[Mr. Mendel read some questions from the floor.]

GOTTWALD [responding to a questioner]: I omitted the intonations to the *Gloria* and *Credo* because I consider that they are not a part of the musical work. They are irrelevant, compositionally speaking.

WHITE: In that case, what do you consider the relation between text and music?

GOTTWALD: To me, the text is simply a way of articulating the music; it is equivalent to the ways in which instruments articulate.

FINSCHER: I think Gottwald conceives of a Mass primarily as absolute musical structure. The problem is the 'spiritual meaning' of the music. Gottwald believes that this spiritual meaning cannot be expressed by imitative liturgical ceremony. It can only be developed from inside the music, from the music itself.

MAYNARD: Pro Musica certainly has always included intonations in its performances, and probably will continue to, but the main reason we include them is so that nobody could ever get the impression we didn't know better. The intonations have absolutely nothing to do with the polyphony. In a Mass where every movement opens with the same line of music, we nevertheless begin the *Kyrie* with no intonation, but the *Gloria* and *Credo* with them.

MENDEL: But I can think of cases where it seems to me the setting of the words 'Et in terra pax' complements the musical idea that was in the intonation.

[Mr. Mendel asked Kern Holoman to read a prepared report on text distribution in Josquin's music. The following is an abstract of those remarks:]

HOLOMAN: Our studies of Josquin's text distribution included the collection of data from the original sources and the evaluation of those data in an attempt to assess Josquin's declamation.

A particularly vexing and sometimes crucial question concerns the meaning of ligatures, their relation to problems of text distribution, and their concordance in the sources. There was considerable speculation that ligatures are scribal peculiarities and probably mean nothing at all. In the *Gloria* and *Credo* movements examined, there were as a rule no noticeable trends in sources for *specific* ligatures, but certain situations indicated that ligatures may in fact have suggested that the same syllable be sung to both notes. For example, there are many instances where there is one more note than syllable, and the ligature suggests where the melisma occurs. Moreover, except in an occasional tenor for which the sources contain little indication of text distribution, and which are therefore often considered instrumental, few instances were found where more than one syllable falls under a ligature. Smijers' text underlay often fails to take such ligatures into account. One example occurs in the *Gloria* of the 'Missa Pange lingua', measures 57–8, in the bass. Here the ligature in the source suggests a solution exactly opposite to the editor's.

Text underlay in the sources for the *Gloria* and *Credo* of the 'Missa Pange lingua' and the 'Missa Fortuna desperata' was investigated in detail. For the *Gloria* of 'Pange lingua' (as far as the *Qui tollis*) the sources show practically identical text distribution. But for the beginning of the *Gloria* of 'Missa Fortuna desperata', the text underlay differs considerably among the sources.[1] Table I shows the variant readings.

At the suggestion of Professor Mendel, the text passages containing internal parallelisms were examined in all the Masses to see if the placement of those phrases was obvious from the musical context. These passages were: 'Laudamus te, adoramus te, benedicimus te, glorificamus te'; 'Quoniam tu solus sanctus, tu solus Dominus, tu solus Altissimus'; and 'Deum de Deo, lumen de lumine, Deum verum de Deo vero'. Generally, these texts showed no higher correlation of obvious placement than the remainder of the movement to which they belonged. Thus, the placing of those texts was obvious only in the movements that were highly syllabic throughout. In melismatic movements—for example, the beginning of the *Gloria* in 'Missa Gaudeamus', or the *Credo* in 'Missa L'homme armé super voces musicales'—placement of the parallel structures was only slightly clearer than placement of other texts.

It was observed incidentally that text placement for the *Gloria* of 'Missa Pange lingua' and for the *Gloria* and *Credo* of 'Missa D'ung aultre amer' and 'Missa Mater Patris' is prevailingly syllabic, particularly for note-values greater than a semiminim. In these and a few other movements in Josquin's Masses, the placing of virtually every phrase is certain, as is the placement of a high percentage of syllables in those phrases.

[1] The difference in text distribution in the two settings of the *Gloria* may well be due to the fact that the 'Missa Pange lingua' is a late work, whereas the 'Missa Fortuna desperata' is considerably earlier. Josquin sets the text with greater care in his late works. Careful text setting on the part of the composer facilitates the work of copyist and typesetter and leads to greater agreement, since the composer has left fewer choices.

Another problem we investigated was one of evaluation: how good is Josquin's declamation in the Masses, and what are the criteria? There are three respects in which a musical setting of this period may emphasize primary-accented syllables: it may set them to longer notes than the adjacent unaccented syllables, or to notes in stronger metric positions, or to higher notes (or, in the lowest voice, sometimes to lower notes). Our impression was that in the late psalm-settings attributed to Josquin, as well as in the motets of Willaert and in music of the second half of the sixteenth century, of these three, it is the durational relationship that most commonly accords with the syllabic accentuation.

Ernest May of Amherst College devised in 1966 a scheme for analysis of this durational factor, which was briefly described in the workshop on the motets. He selected all passages in a given work where the number of syllables is equal to the number of notes. ('Passage' here was defined as a succession of notes bounded on each side by a rest, a fermata, a double bar, or the beginning of a work. Short ligatures were counted as single notes.) He then examined the setting of each primary-accented syllable in a syllabic passage in relation to the following unaccented syllable, and sorted these settings into three types. In *Type 1*, the note to which the accented syllable is set is *shorter* than the following (that is, relatively poor declamation); in *Type 2*, it is of the same length as the following; and in *Type 3*, it is *longer* than the following note (that is, relatively good declamation). Similar criteria were used for the unaccented syllables preceding the primary accent. This technique was applied to the *Credo* of the 'Missa L'homme armé super voces musicales' and to several motets, with the results printed in Table II. (So as to eliminate the mistakes and tedium of this operation, we are now developing a computerized program which will consider metric and melodic position as well as durational relationship.)

A reasonable editorial policy for text underlay, as we saw during the Symposium, is a complex matter, and disagreement on this matter is widespread. But we concluded from these investigations that ligatures can be meaningful in establishing solutions to some problems of text distribution,[2] and we feel that placement of phrases and words (as opposed to individual syllables), particularly in manuscripts of the early sixteenth century, is not generally haphazard.

---

[2] The same result was reached—and many illustrations were cited in its support—in the chapter on 'The Problem of Text Underlay' of the Introduction and Commentary to the edition of *The Medici Codex*, ed. Edward E. Lowinsky (*Monuments of Renaissance Music*, iii; Chicago, 1968), pp. 106–7; see also Index, under 'Text underlay, role of ligatures'. In the course of the study of the Medici Codex and over one hundred and thirty concordant sources it also became clear that the number and placement of ligatures is one of many characteristics distinguishing good from inferior sources. The frequently heard remark that ligatures have no meaning because they vary from source to source must be modified in the above sense.

TABLE II

Declamation in Latin-texted Works of Josquin

	Type 1	Type 2	Type 3
'O admirabile commercium'			
(Motetten, nos. 5–9)	1.5%	54%	44%
'Stabat Mater' (Motetten, no. 36)			
prima pars	5.4%	89%	5.4%
secunda pars	24 %	62%	13 %
total	13 %	79%	8.4%
'De profundis' *a 4* (Motetten, no. 47)			
prima pars	1.5%	64%	35%
secunda pars	0 %	63%	37%
total	1 %	63%	36%
'De profundis' *a 5* (Motetten, no. 90)	7.5%	66%	26%
'De profundis' *a 4* (Motetten, no. 91)			
prima pars	3.5%	74%	23%
secunda pars	4.5%	73%	23%
total	3.8%	73%	23%
'Missa L'homme armé super voces musicales', *Credo*			
Patrem	3 %	77%	20%
Et in Spiritum	11 %	45%	44%

MENDEL: We have two excellent guides to the ideal nature of text distribution in the sixteenth century: Zarlino's famous set of rules,[3] and one by Stoquerus, a pupil of Salinas, in a treatise discovered by Paul O. Kristeller at Columbia and described at length by Edward Lowinsky.[4] These complement each other and agree to a considerable extent. Their rules are very close to the practice of what we call the best declamation in the second half of the sixteenth century. My own feeling, however, is that these treatises describe a style that Josquin adhered to only in later works.[5] I would take declamation as one of the criteria of chronology, so that, for example, the 'Pater noster', in which almost all the declamation is the same as it would be in Willaert or Palestrina, seems, from this point of view, a late work.[6] But Josquin certainly did not set many of his Masses with such care.

[3] Gioseffo Zarlino, *Le istitutioni harmoniche* (Venice, 1558), pp. 340–1; translation in Oliver Strunk, *Source Readings in Music History* (New York, 1950), pp. 259–61.

[4] Edward E. Lowinsky, 'A Treatise on Text Underlay by a German Disciple of Francisco de Salinas', *Festschrift Heinrich Besseler* (Leipzig, 1961), pp. 231–51.

[5] This is true for Zarlino, not for Stoquerus. The latter's rules can profitably be applied to the works of Josquin's early and middle periods (see the chapter on text underlay, *The Medici Codex*, iii, particularly pp. 95–6 and 103–6).

[6] This is of course also the opinion of Helmuth Osthoff, already formulated in his paper 'Zur Echtheitsfrage und Chronologie bei Josquins Werken', *Kongress-Bericht, Internationale Gesellschaft für Musikwissenschaft, Utrecht, 1952* (Amsterdam, 1953), pp. 303–9. It was also the conviction of the Editor, who, in 1935, in his first essay, wrote: 'Josquin ist der

An important question is whether the words of the Mass were thought of as seriously as the words of each motet. The words of the Mass are rather more formulaic and perhaps hardly noticed, as when we sing familiar hymns, or 'The Star-Spangled Banner'. We mouth the words that we're familiar with and hardly think about them at all.

WHITE: How about Josquin's seemingly specific settings of 'Et homo factus est' and 'Dona nobis pacem'?

MENDEL: I don't mean that Josquin never paid attention to the words but that it is striking how often he did not, as compared with composers of twenty years later: Arcadelt, Morales, and, still later, Palestrina. In Palestrina, one has to hunt for inversions of declamation. In Josquin's late Masses, there are some on every page.

WHITE: Whose edition, though?

MENDEL: No, on every page of a source.

WHITE: But are the sources written with such care?

MENDEL: That's just the point: in the later part of the century, they are. I suspect that the singers were not more careful than the copyists: why shouldn't the copyists have copied with care respecting the words, if the singers sang with care respecting the words?[7]

I now want to ask each conductor: Do you sing the words approximately as you find them in the Smijers edition? Or do you redistribute them according to what seems to you better declamation?

GOTTWALD: I sing them from Smijers, with corrections: if an unaccented syllable falls on a long melisma, I tend to break this melisma up, so that the unaccented syllable will not take the whole melisma. In addition, I do not depend on ligatures, since they vary from manuscript to manuscript.

---

eigentliche Entdecker des Worts als unerschöpflicher Quelle musikalischer Inspiration. In der Vokalmusik seiner Vorgänger, in seinen eigenen Frühwerken gehen Wort und Musik lose nebeneinander her. In den Werken der Wende bilden sie eine innig verschmolzene Einheit' (Eduard Lowinsky, 'Zur Frage der Deklamationsrhythmik in der a-cappella-Musik des 16. Jahrhunderts', *Acta musicologica*, vii (1935), p. 62).

[7] Again, generalizations are difficult to arrive at in this area. 'Good' sources show great care in the text underlay; inferior sources are negligent in this as well as in other respects (see the chapter on text underlay in *The Medici Codex* and the individual commentaries under the entry 'text underlay' in the Index). But no scribe can provide a good text underlay if the composer did not concentrate on this aspect of his work.

MENDEL: But we know of cases in Gregorian chant where unaccented syllables, particularly final unaccented syllables, occur on long melismas. One reads frequently that the ligatures in polyphonic music vary considerably from manuscript to manuscript. In the little work that we did, however, we found much more agreement among the ligatures than we expected to, though far from universal agreement.

HERBERT KELLMAN [from the floor]: I have found that ligatures disagreed considerably in several manuscripts written by the same scribe, within perhaps a year or two of each other. One almost has the impression that a scribe is likely to write a ligature one day and break it up the next.

MENDEL: I suppose that it was the custom for each singer to put the words where he pleased at each performance, and this meant that declamation differed from one performance to another.

VENHODA: In a chanson, one cannot change anything at all, and the same is true in the 'Missa Pange lingua'; text underlay is all very precisely determined. The larger the form, the more features it has. If, for example, one sings the *Agnus* III of the 'Missa L'homme armé', it is always better to do it without words. I once did it exactly according to Smijers. Then I encountered an edition by van Crevel, which has far fewer words. It was much more beautiful to sing, since the syllables that occur serve only for the purpose of alignment. But musicologists should not ask performers; they should propose a version, and we will tell them whether it can be sung.

[Mr. Mendel read a note from AUSTIN CLARKSON]: Declamation varies with style level: lofty, middle, or low. Or as Tinctoris gives them: *magnus*, the Mass; *mediocris*, the motet; and *parvus*, the chanson. What we today confidently label good declamation is not relevant to Josquin's lofty style, but only to middle or low style.

MENDEL: Exactly! In the Masses, Josquin pays little attention to what we would call good declamation, as compared with what he does in the motets, and as compared with what everybody does later in the century with any Latin text. In the vernacular, in chansons and lieder, the declamation has been good for a long time.

MAYNARD: We have not hesitated at times to change the text underlay in the Smijers edition. As a matter of fact, there was a case in our performance of the 'Missa L'ami Baudichon' that was very similar to cases I think Mr. Venhoda had in mind. In the *Pleni sunt caeli*, which is one of the many duos in that Mass, the points of imitation come very close together. With the words 'gloria tua' it becomes even more active, and Smijers gives us in about a line of music ten repetitions of 'gloria tua'. It looks good on paper, and you would think it might help in phrasing. But it didn't work; it was very cumbersome. So, we did a couple of long melismas on the syllable 'o' in 'gloria', and it worked beautifully.

In an imitative piece, with each new point of imitation, the new text is given. But in a non-imitative piece, there will sometimes be disagreement with the editor about where the new phrase of text occurs. For example, if we have been in a quiet, legato, subdued section of music, and then come into a much more animated section, but with the animation coming at different times in different voices, I don't hesitate to change the underlay. When the new level comes, obviously the new text must come. Smijers may give it a measure or two earlier or later. One can freely make that kind of change.

[During a short break, the three ensembles came on stage.]

MENDEL: The second *Agnus Dei* of the 'Missa L'homme armé super voces musicales' is found at the end of the first staff of Plate 44, fig. a, reprinted from Petrucci's *Misse Josquin* (1502). This is a mensuration canon very familiar to American students, since it is found in the *Historical Anthology of Music*.[8] The movement has a triple signature: ₵3, C under it, and ₵ next to the words 'Agnus Dei'. It is to be sung by three voices, each one at a different tempo, indicated by the mensuration. Here is the melody sung by just one part:

[Recorded example 1, Prague Madrigal Singers]

The melody, or at least as much of it as they can get in, is sung by each of the other voices at a somewhat slower tempo: by the voice in ₵ at 2/3 of that tempo, and by the voice in C at 1/3 of that tempo:

[Recorded example 2, Prague Madrigal Singers]

Three mensuration signatures indicate three tempi, and when they occur simultaneously there is only one way they will fit: the way you have heard it sung. The semibreve or whole-note in ₵ is only half as long as the semibreve in C. When the 3 appears after the ₵, it stands for 3/2 and means one and one half times as fast as ₵; to put it differently: the ₵ means C divided by two and the ₵3 means C divided by 3.

Carl Philipp Emanuel Bach calls playing 2 against 3 'often disagreeable and always difficult',[9] and there have been various solutions proposed for getting rid of this difficulty. Glareanus, in the present case, proposes changing

8 Archibald T. Davison and Willi Apel, *Historical Anthology of Music*, i (Cambridge, Mass., 1964), no. 89.

9 Carl Philipp Emanuel Bach, *Versuch über die wahre Art das Clavier zu schlagen* (Berlin, 1753), Das dritte Hauptstück, § 27.

the voice in triple time so that an attack will always come in the middle of the measure.[10] Then you can think of the piece in 6 rather than in 3. This is obviously a way of doing the 3 against 2. Even Glareanus hopes that the singers will eventually catch on, for the last few measures of his example are not treated that way, though the first few are. Here is the superius of the Glareanus version, followed by the three parts together:

[The Prague Madrigal Singers perform.]

There is a more drastic way of simplifying 3 against 2, and that is to get rid of it. This technique was known in the sixteenth century and has been espoused in this century. You can replace 3◊ ◊|◊ with ₵◊◊◊ just as today you can play ♫ instead of ♪♪♪, if it's too difficult for you. There were poor musicians in the sixteenth century too. This is the solution offered in Berlin MS. 1175,[11] and here it is, first the superius alone and then the full version:

[Recorded examples 3 and 4, Prague Madrigal Singers]

Now the question is: what happens when these signatures do not come simultaneously, but one after another, as, for example, in the *Kyrie* of this same Mass, 'L'homme armé super voces musicales'. Plate 44, fig. b shows the *cantus firmus* on which this Mass is based and which recurs in most of the movements. This is the familiar 'L'homme armé' melody, slightly changed by Josquin for this Mass. It is in major prolation, with a mensuration signature of ⊙. The middle section has a ₵, and the last part returns to ⊙. In the first part there are three semibreves to a breve and three minims to a semibreve; in the second part there are two semibreves to a breve and three minims to a semibreve; the third part is the same as the first. Major prolation also means in Josquin's time that the minim is to be taken as if it were a semibreve, that is, it is to be read in augmentation.

Since the dot of major prolation indicates augmentation, the relation of the tenor to the other voices in *Kyrie* I, *Et in terra*, *Patrem*, *Sanctus*, and *Agnus* I is normal: the ♩ of ⊙ equals the ◊ of O. And since the stroke through the C or O theoretically means diminution in the ratio 2:1, the ♩ of ⊙ should equal the ▯ of ₵ or ₵; both augmentation of the *cantus firmus* and diminution of the other voices produces a ratio of 4:1, as in the *Christe* and *Agnus* III (see Table III).

But this strictly logical situation does not prevail in *Kyrie* II, *Qui tollis*, or *Et incarnatus*, where despite the presence of both the prolation dot and the stroke the ratio is only 2:1. This would seem to mean that the stroke in

---

[10] *Heinrich Glarean, Dodecachordon*, trans. Clement A. Miller (American Institute of Musicology, 1965), ii, p. 273 (see the 'resolutio' of the canon). Smijers published a transcription of Glareanus' version in the *Werken*, Missen, i, p. 33, that makes the point clear.

[11] Transcribed by Smijers, *Werken*, Missen, i, p. 33.

TABLE III

Mensural Proportions in the 'Missa L'homme armé super voces musicales'
(Original Signs and Note Values)*

	Cantus firmus	Other voices	Canons
Kyrie I	⊙	♪ = O ◆	
Christe	¢	♪ = ¢ ▱	
Kyrie II	⊙	♪ = Ⓞ ◆	
Et in terra	⊙, ¢, ⊙	♪ = O ◆	
Qui tollis	⊙, ¢, ⊙	♪ = ¢ ◆	
Patrem	⊙, ¢, ⊙	♪ = O ◆	
Et incarnatus	⊙, ¢, ⊙	♪ = ¢ ◆	
Confiteor ('Gaudet cum gaudentibus')	⊙, ¢, ⊙	♪ = ¢ ♪	
Sanctus	⊙, ¢	♪ = O ◆	
Pleni		C ▱	
Osanna ('Ut jacet')	⊙, ¢, ⊙	♪ = C3 ♪.	
Benedictus			Bassus I C♪ = Bassus II ¢ ◆
Qui venit.			Altus I C♪ = Altus II ¢ ◆
In nomine			Superius I C♪ = Superius II ¢ ◆
Agnus I	⊙, ¢	♪ = O ◆	
Agnus II			Superius ¢3 ▱ = Altus C ◆ = Bassus ¢ ▱
Agnus III	⊙, ¢, ⊙	♪ = ¢ ▱	

Five of the sub-sections listed above are in ¢ in all voices except the one having the *cantus firmus*:

    a. In two of them (*Christe* and *Agnus* III), the ♪ of the *cantus firmus* equals a note four times as long as ♪ in the other voices.

    b. In two (*Qui tollis* and *Et incarnatus*), the ♪ of the *cantus firmus* equals a note twice as long as ♪ in the other voices (as it does in the sub-sections marked O and Ⓞ).

    c. The *Confiteor* is exceptional. In it, the 'canonic' instruction ('[The tenor] rejoices with [the other] rejoicers') is an enigmatic way of saying that the ♪ of the *cantus firmus* equals the ♪ of the other voices.

    * The signatures here tabulated are those of Petrucci's 1502 edition. Some sources have 3 (rather than ¢3) for the superius in *Agnus* II, but the meaning cannot be different. Cappella Giulia XII.2 seems to lack the stroke through the tempus sign in the superius and bass but not in the alto in *Kyrie* II, and in all voices in the *Et incarnatus*. Otherwise all manuscript sources agree, so far as can be ascertained from microfilm, except perhaps Berlin, Deutsche Staatsbibliothek, Mus. MS. theor. 1175, Cappella Sistina 197, and Toledo 9, which we have not seen.

these movements is meaningless—that, for example, the signature of the *Qui tollis* and *Et incarnatus* might just as well be C. This latter signature is very infrequent in Josquin; most pieces in imperfect tempus have a signature of ¢. It may well be that the original meaning of ¢ had been nearly forgotten by this time, and that for all intents and purposes it had simply replaced C, without any difference in meaning in most cases. In this Mass, at any rate, C occurs (except for the *Pleni*) only simultaneously with ¢, and here the proportions are those called for by theory. So it would seem that in the *Christe* and the *Agnus* III, the stroke really means diminution in the ratio 2:1, while elsewhere it does not.

Accordingly, the Prague Madrigal Singers will now sing the *Agnus Dei* III (₵) at approximately the same tempo as the ₵ voice in *Agnus* II, about ◆ = 88. Then the Pro Musica will sing *Kyrie* I (O) at about ◆ = 44, *Christe* (₵) at about ◆ = 88, and *Kyrie* II (Φ) not twice as fast as *Kyrie* I but at a tempo between those of the two previous movements, about ◆ = 66. (The tempi actually sung were:

Agnus II	₵◆ =	100
Agnus III	₵◆ =	80
Kyrie I	O◆ =	50
Christe	₵◆ =	94
Kyrie II	Φ◆ =	69

After the first singing of the *Agnus*, the Prague group sang a few measures of the *Agnus* III again, at a tempo of Mr. Venhoda's own choosing, which turned out to be about ₵◆ = 76. The Pro Musica repeated the whole *Kyrie*, too, for which Mr. Maynard chose:

Kyrie I	O◆ =	60
Christe	₵◆ =	66
Kyrie II	Φ◆ =	60)

[Recorded example 5, Prague Madrigal Singers
Recorded example 6, New York Pro Musica]

In short, the problem is, should the half-note, or minim, of the *cantus firmus* always be at the same tempo? If so, this will make some movements very fast in comparison with others. Or are we not to take this seriously: is the breve of the *Christe*, a note ostensibly twice as long as the semibreve of *Kyrie* I, only a little longer, or what? We have tended to believe that the stroke through the C, when it does not occur simultaneously with other voices, means 'somewhat faster than without the stroke'. And the same with the circle. But it is a strange solution in a piece which is so obviously playing with mensurations, a piece that has been called a tribute to Ockeghem, and which certainly seems to have been written somewhat in imitation of Ockeghem's 'Missa Prolationum'.

We now pass to the inevitable subject: *musica ficta*. I want to approach this question from the same point of view: what do the sources tell us, and how much attention should we pay to them?

We have three pieces as examples. First the *Sanctus* of the 'Missa Ave maris stella'. The movement offers problems.

The trouble with the 'rules' of *musica ficta* is that you cannot apply them all, because one of them may conflict with another. And the question is: 'In what order of priority should we apply them?' or, better yet, 'were they applied?'

Table IV reviews the situation regarding accidentals in the sources of the

Sanctus of the 'Missa Ave maris stella'. Any E♭ in Smijers' score that does not appear in one of the parallel columns of the original sources constitutes an editorial addition.

TABLE IV

Accidental E♭s in the Sources of the *Sanctus* of the 'Missa Ave maris stella'

	Smijers edition (after Petrucci 1505)	Petrucci 1505	Basel F.IX.25	Brussels 9126	Jena 3	Milan E 46	Milan 2267	Rome Capp. Sist. 41	Stuttgart 44	Vienna 1783	Vienna 4809
Sanctus											
Bass, m. 15	edit.	–	♭	–	♭	–	–	–	–	♭	♭
Bass, m. 16	edit.	–	–	–	♭	–	–	–	–	–	–
Sup., m. 16	edit.	–	–	–	–	–	–	–	–	–	–
Pleni											
Alto, m. 76	spec.	♭	♭	♭	♭	♭	–	♭	♭	♭	–
Bass, m. 76	edit.	–	–	–	–	–	–	–	–	–	–
Bass, m. 77	edit.	–	–	–	–	–	–	–	–	–	–
Osanna											
Alto, m. 106	spec.	♭	♭	♭	♭	♭	–	♭	♭	♭	♭
Bass, m. 106	spec.	♭	♭	♭	♭	♭	♭	♭	♭	♭	♭
Alto, m. 107	edit.	–	–	–	–	–	–	–	–	–	–
Benedictus											
Sup., m. 1	edit.	–	–	–	–	–	–	–	–	–	–
Sup., m. 2	edit.	–	–	–	–	–	–	–	–	–	–
Alto, m. 10	edit.	–	♭	–	–	–	–	–	–	–	–
Alto, m. 11	spec.	♭	♭	–	–	♭	♭	–	♭	–	♭

Abbreviations: edit. = editorial
spec. = specified in the original source

The particular problem in this movement is that there are a number of tritones and diminished fifths that do not sound particularly good. The tritones and diminished fifths all occur between E and B♭. There are two ways to avoid them. One is to make the Es flat, the other to make the Bs natural. If the Bs are made natural, there is a strange succession of B♭s and B♮s in rather close order. Here is the piece sung both ways:
[The New York Pro Musica performs.]

Now we have the *Et in Spiritum* of the 'Missa Malheur me bat', preceded by the chanson attributed to Ockeghem on which the Mass is based. The chanson has no problems of *musica ficta*. The *Et in Spiritum* seems to be a very innocent little piece, free of *musica ficta* problems until just near the end, when suddenly some B♭s come in, and then a B♮, making a very noticeable cross-relation (Ex. 1). It's a little hard to find a solution for this. My solution has no historical background, as far as I know. Professor

Ex. 1 mm. 209-216

Lowinsky, however, arrived at the same solution, so I suppose it does have one.[12] This seems to me, strangely enough, to get rid of the problem, but I don't expect universal agreement on this. Here, then, are the chanson and the Mass section with the proposed solution.

[12] The passage occurs in a lengthy sequence—often the place of unavoidable tritones and diminished fifths justified by the logic of the sequential pattern. Even at the beginning (m. 211), the progression of B♭ major-E minor, with its double false relation, shocks. Josquin could have avoided it by providing an F♯ in the alto and leaving the B♮ in the bass untouched. But, as always, he takes the long view. The B♮ in the beginning that might have been avoided is the preparation for the B♭ at the end of the passage (m. 214), indicated in both alto and bass parts, and indeed unavoidable. Now, the B♭ major chord is followed by a C major chord. The Phrygian ending on E demands the leap of a major sixth in the alto from D to B♮ in measures 214-15. Just as unconventional—but also inescapable—is the step of the diminished third from B♭ to G♯ in the bass, the only progression musically viable, and entirely defensible in its subsemitone function toward A, common in plagal endings and foreshadowed in the final cadence of *Kyrie* II. (Smijers avoided the G♯ in the Phrygian endings of the Mass in accordance with the second phase of his *musica ficta* policy; see the discussion in the Symposium, this volume, p. 738). If the passage has a historical background, it resides in Josquin's fecundity of harmonic invention. It is only one in a multitude of harmonic finds that one encounters in his music. The boldness of its design has many parallels in Josquin's harmonic language.

[Recorded examples 7 and 8, Prague Madrigal Singers]
(Because of a misunderstanding, the *Et in Spiritum*, instead of being sung once with the bass singing Bb–G♮ and then with the bass singing Bb–G♯, was sung in the latter version both times. For this reason, only one performance appears on the recording.)

We pass now to the 'Missa de Beata Virgine'. I will ask Richard Sherr to read a summary of the situation in the sources.

SHERR: The eighteen sources for the *Credo* of the 'Missa de Beata Virgine' consulted for this study may be divided chronologically into three groups:

> *Group I* (before 1521)
>
> Rome, Biblioteca Vaticana, Cappella Sistina, MS. 23
> Rome, Biblioteca Vaticana, Cappella Sistina, MS. 45
> Jena, Universitätsbibliothek, Codex Mus. 7
> Munich, Bayerische Staatsbibliothek, Mus. MS. 510
> Rome, Biblioteca Vaticana, Cappella Sistina, MS. 160
> Wolfenbüttel, Herzog-August-Bibliothek, MS. A
> *Missarum Josquin Liber tertius*. Petrucci, 1514
> *Liber quindecim Missarum*. Antico, 1516
>
> *Group II* (c. 1521)
>
> Vienna, Oesterreichische Nationalbibliothek, Cod. 4809
> Jena, Universitätsbibliothek, Codex Mus. 36
>
> *Group III* (after 1530)
>
> Munich, Bayerische Staatsbibliothek, Mus. MS. C
> Modena, Biblioteca Estense, MS. Lat. 452 = MS. α N 1.2
> Bologna, Archivio di San Petronio, MS. A31
> Cambrai, Bibliothèque Municipale, MS. 18
> Stuttgart, Württembergische Landesbibliothek, MS. 44
> Milan, Biblioteca Ambrosiana, MS. Mus. E46
> Rome, Cappella Giulia, MS. XII.2.C.48 (section containing this Mass)
> *Liber quindecim Missarum*. Petreius, 1539

The chronology indicated cannot be said to be definitive, but certain things are known about some of the sources.

For example, the coat of arms appearing toward the end of MS. Capp. Sist. 23, often referred to as that of Pope Julius II (1503–13), is in fact that of his family (della Rovere), surmounted not by the tiara and crossed keys of a pope but by a cardinal's hat. It may refer to the Cardinal Giuliano della

Rovere before he became Pope (i.e., 1471–1503), or to any of several other cardinals of this family, some of them created by Julius II himself.

MS. Capp. Sist. 45 has been dated between 1523 and 1527; it contains a French inscription referring to the sack of Rome (6 May 1527), and shows, near the beginning, the coat of arms of a Medici pope; Clement VII, a Medici, reigned from 1523 to 1534. Since the repertory and scribal evidence point to the period of the Medici Leo X, I think the manuscript more probably dates from his reign (1513–21); the inscription, of course, could have been added at any time.

For others I have relied on experts: Herbert Kellman (the Alamire MSS. Iena 7, 1516; Capp. Sist. 160, 1518–19; Vienna 4809, 1521–c.1525);[13] Martin Bente (Munich 510, before 1519);[14] Karl Erich Roediger (Jena 36, 1500–20);[15] Joshua Rifkin (the section of Capp. Giul. XII. 2 that contains this Mass, 1530s).[16]

Much of the San Petronio manuscript (including this *Credo*) is in the hand of Spataro, whose years as *maestro di cappella* of San Petronio were 1512–40.[17] The Stuttgart, Cambrai, and Milan manuscripts all seem quite late.

The geographical origin of the sources is as follows:

Italian	*Northern*	*Unknown*
Capp. Sist. 23	Jena 7	Milan
Capp. Sist. 45	Capp. Sist. 160	
Capp. Giul.	Vienna	
Modena	Jena 36	
San Petronio	Wolfenbüttel	
Petrucci	Stuttgart	
Antico	Munich C	
	Munich 510	
	Cambrai	
	Petreius	

[13] See above, pp. 212–13.

[14] Martin Bente, *Neue Wege der Quellenkritik und die Biographie Ludwig Senfls* (Wiesbaden, 1968), p. 207.

[15] Karl Erich Roediger, *Die geistlichen Musikhandschriften der Universitäts-Bibliothek Jena*, Textband (Jena, 1935), pp. 12–13.

[16] The presence of a Mass by Animuccia, whose first publications appear in the late 1540s, is presumably the reason why Smijers, in his description of the manuscript (*Werken*, Missen, xviii, p. VIII), dated it as of the middle of the sixteenth century. But Animuccia's Mass that appears on fol. 208ᵛ is written in a hand different from the bulk of the manuscript, which can be dated 'about 1520' (*The Medici Codex*, iii, pp. 60–61); in my opinion, it is safe to include this manuscript in Group II.

[17] Professor Mendel later read a communication from Frank Tirro, graduate student at the University of Chicago, who is writing a dissertation on Spataro's choirbooks, to the effect that MS. A 31 of the Archivio di San Petronio probably belongs in the second rather than the third group.

Many of the Northern manuscript sources are lavish in the number of B♭s they notate either as accidentals or by signature, whereas the Italian manuscripts (with one notable exception) have hardly any flats[18] (see Table V).

TABLE V

Accidentals before B and E in the Sources of the *Credo* (mm. 1–102) of the 'Missa de Beata Virgine'

measure	voice	Wolfenbüttel A	Stuttgart 44	Vienna 4809	Jena 7	Jena 36	Capp. Sist. 160	Cambrai 18	San Petronio A 31
10	B	♭	♭	♭*	♭*	♭*	—	♭*	♭
19	B	♭	♭	♭*	♭*	♭*	—	♭*	♭
21	S	♭*	—	—	♭*	♭*	—	—	—
23	B	♭*	♭	♭*	♭*	♭*	—	♭*	♭
23	C		♭						♭
25	S	♭*	—	—	♭*	♭*	—	—	—
25	B	♭*	♮	♯	♭*	♭*	—	♭*	—
26	B	♭*	—	♭*	♭*	♭*	—	♭*	—
27	S	♭*	—	—	♭*	♭*	—	—	—
28	S	♭*	—	—	♭*	♭*	—	—	—
32	B	—	—	♭*	♭*	♭*	♭*	♭*	—
36	B	♭	♭*§	♭*	♭*	♭*	♭*	♭*	♭
36	C	♭*							♭
36	S	—	—	♭*	♭*	—	—	—	
37	S	♭*	—	—	♭*	♭*	—	—	—
38	B	♭*	♭*§	♭*,E♭	♭*,E♭	♭*	♭*,E♭	♭*	—
39	C	♭*							—
40	B	—	♮	♭*	♭*	♭*	♭*	♭*	
42	B	♭	♭	♯	♭*	♭*	♭*	♭*	♭
43	B	♭	♮	♭*	♭*	♭*	♭*	♭*	♭
43	A	♭*	♭	—	♭*	♭*	—	—	♭
44	A	♭*	(♭)	—	♭*	♭*	—	—	(♭)
44	S	♭	—	—	♭*	♭*	—	—	♭
45	B	♭	—	♭*	♭*	♭*	♭*	♭*	—
45	A	♭*	♭*?	—	♭*	♭*	—	—	—
48	B	—	—	♭*	♭*	♭*	—	♭*	—
49	C		♭*						—
51	B	—	♮	♭*	♭*	♭*	♭*	♭*	—
52	C		♭*						—
58	B	♭	—	♭*	♭*	♭*	♭*	♭*	—
58	S	♭*	—	—	—	♭*	—	—	—
59	S	♭*	—	—	—	♭*	—	—	—
60	S	♭*	—	—	—	♭*	—	—	—
62	B	—	—	♭*	♭*	♭*	♭*	♭*	—
63	S	♯	—	—	—	♭*	♯	—	—

[18] In the edition of the Medici Codex, a systematic attempt has been made to list variants in the setting of accidentals in the diverse sources; also lists of varying key signatures in the sources transmitting Josquin's works have been published there (see Vol. iii, pp. 131–33).

measure	voice	Wolfenbüttel A	Stuttgart 44	Vienna 4809	Jena 7	Jena 36	Capp. Sist. 160	Cambrai 18	San Petronio A 31
69	B	—	—	♭*	♭*	♭*	♭*	♭*	—
72	B	♭	♭	♭*	♭*	♭*	♭*	♭*	—
72	C		♭						—
73	B	♭	—	♭*	♭*	♭*	♭*	♭*	—
74	A	—	—	♭	♭	♭*	♭	♭*	—
75	A	—	—	(♭)	(♭)	♭*	(♭)	♭*	—
87	B	—	—	♭*	♭*	♭*	—	♭*	—
88	B	♭*	—	♭*	♭*	♭*	—	♭*	—
91	B	♭*	—	♭*	♭*	♭*	—	♭*	—
93	B	♭*	♭	♭*	♭*	♭*	—	♭*	—
93	S	♭*	♭	♭	♭	♭*	♭	♭	—
95	S	♭*	—	—	—	♭*	—	—	—
95	C		♭						—
96	S	♭*	—	—	—	♭*	—	—	—
97	B	♭*	—	♭*	♭*	♭*	—	♭*	—
100	B	♭*	—	♯	♭*	♭*	—	♭*	—
101	S	♭*	—	—	—	♭*	—	—	—

Sources without flats:
Capp. Sist. 23
Capp. Sist. 45
Capp. Giul. XII.2
Petrucci
Antico
Modena
Munich C
Munich 510
Petreius
Milan

1. Unless otherwise specified, all accidentals refer to the note B.

2. If a flat appears at the beginning of a staff, it is taken to apply to all Bs in that line; if it appears anywhere else, it is taken to apply only to the note it precedes and to successive repetitions of that same note indicated thus: (♭).

3. In Jena 36 (throughout the *Credo*) and in Jena 7 (up to m. 50) there are key signatures of one flat in the superius and alto. These manuscripts, because of their key signatures, have more B♭s than are shown in this table.

4. The dash means: no accidentals. The blank space means that the canonic voice (C) is not written out in the source, which therefore provides no explicit evidence for or against the accidental. The canonic voice is written out in San Petronio and in Stuttgart.

★ Under the rule stated in Note 2 above the note is governed by a flat at the beginning of the staff and there is no explicit flat immediately preceding it.

§ The ♭ in m. 36 comes at the beginning of the staff and seems to function for the moment as a signature-flat, since the B in m. 40 has an explicit ♮ while the one in m. 38 has no accidental. (Cf. the situation in the other manuscripts.) Both the ♭ and the ♮ may be later interpolations, but in general there is no way of knowing whether such interpolations were made a half-hour or a half-century after the original copying. Accordingly, this table reflects the situation in the manuscripts as they now appear.

Table by Richard Sherr.

A glance at the music of this *Credo* shows the problem. The piece contains a canon at the lower fifth. In most of the sources the melody of the canon is written in one voice-part only; the second voice is to read it a fifth lower and two measures later. If it is to follow exactly, it will have to sing a number of B♭s. Some of these unnotated flats occur against notated Bs for the bass, who, because of this and also because of many other cases of *mi contra fa*, would be required to sing a large number of B♭s to avoid the forbidden intervals. The scribes or editors of some Northern sources apparently thought that their singers were incapable of arriving at a solution by themselves, and tried to give some indication of the correct manner to proceed. But they don't agree. The method chosen by Alamire, the scribe of Jena 7, Vienna 4809, and Capp. Sist. 160, was to flat all or most of the Bs in the bass and to indicate this by a signature in the bass part. Unfortunately, Alamire is not consistent in these three manuscripts as to exactly how many Bs should be flatted.[19] (In Jena 7 the signature holds for the entire *Credo*; in Vienna 4809 it disappears at m. 125, and in Capp. Sist. 160 it appears sporadically on certain staves only.) He makes little attempt to bring the other voices into line. In Jena 7, someone has tried to reconcile the voices by placing flat signatures in the superius and alto parts (the signature, for some reason, disappears at m. 50, only to resume at the *Et in Spiritum*). Jena 36 has consistent flat signatures in the superius, alto, and bass for the entire *Credo*.

But putting signatures into the superius, alto, and bass does not completely solve the problem. If the canon is to be preserved, it is impossible to place a flat signature in the tenor, the leader of the canon. This in turn means that there are going to be some cross-relations between B♮s in this voice and B♭s in the others. The only Northern source which attacks this problem is Wolfenbüttel A; it employs a combination of signatures and accidentals. When all these flats are tabulated, it can be seen that this source has been carefully edited with a mind to reconciling all the parts.

The Italian sources notate none of the many flats we find in the Northern ones. The only exception is the Spataro manuscript. Now, Spataro was a theorist who argued for more explicitness of accidentals (see K. Jeppesen, 'Eine musiktheoretische Korrespondenz des frühen Cinquecento', *Acta Musicologica*, xiii (1941), p. 28).[20] A glance at the notated flats in his edition of the *Credo* shows that every one is there to correct *mi contra fa* in a fourth,

[19] It cannot be assumed that Alamire personally wrote every note in the manuscripts that originated from his busy workshop (on this problem see Martin Picker, *The Chanson Albums of Marguerite of Austria* (Berkeley and Los Angeles, 1965), p. 34). The fact that both Herbert Kellman and Martin Picker saw themselves forced to change their opinions as to Alamire's authorship of a number of manuscripts is indication of the difficulties encountered in making incontestable attributions to one scribe (ibid., p. 103, notes 6 and 16).

[20] It would seem that Spataro, writing the choirbooks for the use of his singers, was moved by obvious practical purposes.

fifth, or octave. Spataro also wrote out the canonic follower and supplied it with flats only where such flats avoid the above intervals, which means that this voice sings many fewer flats than it would if it were sung from the leader part. There is, unfortunately, a slight complication in that someone later inserted a flat signature into this part (it is clearly squeezed in), and still later this signature was erased. So Spataro, or someone after him, may have had different ideas about this voice later on.[21]

It should also be noted that none of the sources regularly indicates the use of the subsemitone which, we have good reason to believe, was usually employed in suspension formations.

The large number of sources (some of them quite early) which contain no flats, and the large number of sources (some of them quite early) in which flats are notated inconsistently, suggest the following hypothesis:

The original source for this *Credo* had few notated flats, but required some to be sung according to certain rules. In Italy, it was not thought necessary to spell out these flats. There, the only one who did so was a choirmaster and a theorist; if we were to take him as typical, it would then seem that the piece was sung in Italy only with the flats necessary to correct *mi contra fa* in fourths, fifths, and octaves. In the North, however, it was decided that the piece should be edited and the flats put in. In so doing the editors added many B♭s not required by any rule we know of, but simply *causa pulchritudinis*.[22] This, then, represents a performance tradition which was probably quite different from the Italian one.

MENDEL: We will now hear four different versions of the first section of the *Credo* of the 'Missa de Beata Virgine', with increasing numbers of accidentals. First, according to the Italian sources, without addition, except for the following: the canonic follower, which is a fifth below the canonic leader, sings B♭ whenever the leader has sung F. He was presumably singing

[21] It is quite possible that Spataro, who was in correspondence with the Florentine theorist Pietro Aron over many years, added the signature of one flat to the canonic follower upon publication of the latter's *Trattato della natura et cognitione di tutti gli tuoni* (Venice, 1525). Here Aron remarks that one can find the key signature of one flat in the tenor or contrabassus parts of certain compositions, a procedure not proper and correct 'except if done with judgement and ingenuity as did the eminent Josquin in the *Patrem* of the 'Missa de Beata Virgine''' (see Willem Elders' reprint, Utrecht, 1966). See also Oliver Strunk, *Source Readings in Music History*, note d to p. 211, where he remarks: 'As published in Heft 42 of *Das Chorwerk*, the Credo of Josquin's *Missa de Beata Virgine* has no signatures whatever. But it is clear from Aron's comment and from the composition itself that the Tenor secundus, following the Tenor in canon at the fifth below, should have the signature one flat.')

[22] This remark should not be construed to mean that the sixteenth-century musician could add any accidentals he pleased by calling them *causa pulchritudinis*, which, on the contrary, operates under rules as precise as those of *causa necessitatis* (see *Monuments of Renaissance Music*, i, pp. X ff).

from the same music (the solution was not written out) and when he saw a semitone, he presumably sang one. And where a diminished or augmented octave would result, we have corrected that by the addition of a flat. But diminished fifths and augmented fourths remain uncorrected in this version:

[The Schola Cantorum Stuttgart performs.]

The next version has the same accidentals, plus sharps for the leading tone in suspension cadences, except where an augmented or diminished octave would occur. This solution assumes that these cadences were so performed, and that this was understood.

[The Schola Cantorum Stuttgart performs.]

The next version is the one found in the manuscript written by Spataro, a theorist who, in some ways, was very theoretical; he described certain things that were certainly not the practice of the time. He is at times more interested in what should have been than in what was. In this case, he was rather sparing with added accidentals, but he did add them to avoid simultaneous augmented fourths and diminished fifths. This version adds those to most of the other accidentals you've already heard. But Spataro, as Mr. Sherr said, wrote out the realization of the canon, and he did not place a flat before every B, in spite of the fact that it represented an F in the canonic leader; at times, then, there is a B♮ in the tenor in this version that was not present in the versions previously heard.

[The Schola Cantorum Stuttgart performs.]

Finally, there is the version of the Wolfenbüttel manuscript, which more or less represents all the German manuscripts, in the sense that it contains more flats than any of the other sources. The explanation is one of two: either the Italians knew enough to put all these flats in without having them written, *or* the Germans put in a lot more flats than the Italians.[23] Here is the Wolfenbüttel version:

[The Schola Cantorum Stuttgart performs.]

QUESTION FROM THE AUDIENCE: All the stress has been on how the modern editor solves *musica ficta* problems. How did the sixteenth-century singer make up his mind?

MENDEL: This is precisely what we are trying to imitate. As scholarly editors we ask ourselves: what would a sixteenth-century singer have done according to the rules? No doubt sixteenth-century singers at times stumbled into such violations of the rules as the augmented octave that was just sung here in the Spataro version—in this case because in the copies of that version furnished to Dr. Gottwald we carelessly omitted one of Spataro's flats.

---

[23] The overwhelming evidence provided by Italian writers on *musica ficta* would point to the first alternative.

No doubt not only all these versions but twenty-five or a hundred-and-twenty-five more could have been heard in the sixteenth century.

(Mr. Mendel closed the workshop with thanks to Mr. Venhoda and the Prague Madrigal Singers, to Dr. Gottwald and the Schola Cantorum, and to Mr. Maynard and the New York Pro Musica.

Lewis Lockwood, speaking for Claude Palisca, who was unable to be present, thanked both Josquin des Prez and Edward Lowinsky for the unique experience of the week. Mr. Lowinsky responded by expressing his gratitude to the audience for its singular devotion and unflagging attention throughout the five-day event.)

Symposium:
Editing the Music of
Josquin des Prez

Problems in Editing the Music of Josquin des Prez: A Critique of the First Edition and Proposals for the Second Edition

International Josquin Festival-Conference, Wednesday, 23 June 1971 at 3 p.m.
Moderator: Gustave Reese. *Panellists:* Myroslaw Antonowycz, Ludwig Finscher, René B. Lenaerts, Lewis Lockwood, Edward E. Lowinsky, Arthur Mendel.
Transcribed from tape by: Ellen T. Harris. *Reporter:* Edward E. Lowinsky.*

REESE: In his welcoming speech, the Director mentioned that the *Gesamtausgabe* of the works of Josquin des Prez is now completed. It may be too much so, because we are afraid that some of the pieces are not genuine. On the other hand, perhaps some pieces should be added. The time has arrived to consider a second edition. Not that it should follow immediately on the heels of the first; there has to be a cooling-off period. We have to find out what changes need to be made. The first edition, as everyone in this hall knows, is the production of the Vereniging voor Nederlandse Muziekgeschiedenis, and we are tremendously indebted to the Dutch Society. Without their initiative there would be no edition of the works of Josquin des Prez. Now the Dutch Society itself seems to recognize that if we are to have a second edition, it should be an international undertaking, and I hope we are preparing for such international co-operation right now. The object of today's session is to discuss what editorial procedures might possibly be improved upon. The first contribution will be made by Arthur Mendel.

MENDEL: In the numerous public or semi-public discussions of editorial problems in which many of us have engaged, we have often argued back and forth the merits of reduced time values, bar-lines, *Mensurstriche*,

---

* Remarks of the discussants have been paraphrased by the reporter except for the contributions of Professors Mendel, Antonowycz, and Lenaerts, which were submitted in writing. Notes are those of the speakers. Editor's notes appear in brackets.

modern clefs, indications of *musica ficta*, etc. What I think we have not often enough or deeply enough considered is the *purposes* of modern editions. In directing attention to this question, I shall doubtless mention many truisms. But the prospect of a second complete edition of the works of Josquin des Prez is so important that we ought to take nothing for granted and carefully consider the premises on which such an edition should be based. The Dutch Society for Music History plans a second edition. It is already engaged in a second edition of the works of Obrecht. Whatever one thinks of the volumes of that edition (and opinions certainly vary widely), we should all salute the openminded attitude of the Dutch Society in sponsoring bold experiments in editorial techniques. A Society that has shown itself so hospitable to new ideas cannot fail to welcome such a re-examination of the foundations of the editing of music of this period.

In his role as mediator between the composer of 1500 and modern musicians and musicologists, the editor's lines of communication are obstructed at both ends. He has received the message he seeks to transmit not from the sender but at second or third or nth hand, and has no way of knowing just how closely it resembles what the sender wrote. He does not quite know who the recipients are to be. What he does know is that he cannot perfectly fulfill his obligations either to the composer or to the eventual users of his edition. This is because some of the users expect from an edition what the composer never thought of providing them with: a fully explicit notation of his music. Musical notation has become steadily more explicit over the centuries, so that for example the musicians of an ensemble who sit down to play a work by Stravinsky do not need any understanding of the piece as a whole: the composer has indicated explicitly just which notes are to be played, just when, and just how. That is approximately what the modern musician has come to expect (though not always in such completeness) from the printed music from which he performs, whether it is by Stravinsky, or Brahms, or Schütz—or Josquin. It did not occur to the composer of Josquin's time to make any of these things fully explicit. Not only did he give no indication of how loud or soft, how legato or how staccato, with what crescendi or diminuendi (if any) his music was to be performed, or what voices or instruments, or how many of each, were to perform it; if he had definite ideas about tempo, we cannot be sure what they were; we are not certain even about the tempo relations between different sections of the same movement. And finally—what the modern musician finds perhaps most puzzling of all—he did not even specify explicitly all of the notes to be sung or played; so that while there is no doubt about some of them, there is considerable doubt about others, and it has been suggested with great persuasiveness that he often did not have specific choices in mind.

That, I suggest, is the core of the editor's dilemma: how can he satisfy the modern user's demand for an edition in which everything is made clear, when so many things are not clear even to him, some of which were perhaps not clear (in the sense of definite choices having been made among alternatives) to the composer himself, let alone to performers of the period?

Consider briefly the three parts of the editor's task:

I. Representing as faithfully as possible what the composer's original manuscript was probably like, modified or completed in accordance with what the consensus of recent scholarship believes to be the conventions governing it (these modifications being of course clearly identified as such).

II. Determining to what extent he will adapt his edition to the habits of modern users, and to what extent it will be fruitful as well as realistic to expect modern users to be ready to expand their repertory of habits.

III. Deciding to what users his edition is to be addressed, and to what extent he can reconcile their sometimes opposed needs.

I

No autograph exists of Josquin's music, and since we do not even have a copy or edition that we know he approved, the editor's first task must be to approximate as closely as possible what Josquin wrote. For this purpose he has available anywhere from a very few to a great many sources, both printed editions and manuscripts. For the 'Missa de Beata Virgine', which circulated more widely in manuscript in the sixteenth century than any other Josquin Mass, there are no less than thirty-one sources—five printed editions and twenty-six manuscripts. Except as regards a few isolated pieces and excerpts quoted in didactic or theoretical works, these sources have one characteristic in common: they are all *performing* versions of the work. To judge their value, the modern editor would have to copy them out in score. Thanks to Dr. Smijers and Dr. Antonowycz, the editors of a new edition need only compare the early sources with the printed scores of the existing edition.

Must the editor read every note, every accidental, every text syllable, and every ligature of every one of these sources? Some of them seem remote in both date and place of origin from any close connection with Josquin. An edition printed in Nuremberg twenty years after Josquin's death, or a Spanish manuscript copied even later, may seem unlikely, *prima facie*, to be closely related to the original source of the work. But how do we know how far the Spanish copyist or the representative of the German publisher travelled—where and from what earlier source he copied the version he presents? In most cases we can only infer the answers by reading if not every note at least a great many notes, which may establish the probability that the source in question was copied from another source we already know, and can therefore be ignored. On the other hand, this process may show that the version derives from a source that we do *not* know—in which case it represents this earlier unknown source, and may acquire much greater authority than we should at first have attributed to it. By combining what the editor knows or believes probable on the basis of external evidence of many kinds—documents, handwritings, watermarks, the repertory represented in the manuscript, the kinds of linguistic mistakes or idiosyncracies of the copyist, the similarity of the source in any of these respects to other sources about which more evidence is available—with what he learns from comparing the readings of the music and text, he establishes a ranking of the sources according to what he believes to be their relative authority. By 'authority' we mean, of course, the degree of presumptive similarity to the lost Josquin autograph.

Establishing the filiation of musical sources when we do not know the identity of most of the copyists, and therefore do not know how much musicianship to attribute to them—what emendations they have made on their own initiative—is not an exact science.[1] The editor must explain *why* he takes one source to be more authoritative than another. The comparison of readings in many sources is an extremely laborious and lengthy business, and if Smijers had attempted it at all systematically we should not even now be in possession of the complete edition. A few sentences written ten years ago by our old friend Father Weakland, now Abbot Primate of the Benedictine Order, reviewing Volume i of Part IV of the Roman Gradual in the critical edition of the monks of Solesmes,[2] are relevant here:

...the grouping [of sources] was done by two sets of experiments....For the first experiment 263 manuscripts...were related to each other on the basis of 150 variants....In the second experiment only 33 manuscripts, the most representative from the first experiment, were compared to each other on the basis of 310 variants....
...The fear that too many compromises had to be made because of the large

---

[1] In this connection, perhaps I may be permitted a comment on Professor Hoffmann-Erbrecht's paper of this morning. In the field of filiation of manuscripts as in other branches of editorial technique, early Bach scholars (Rust, Spitta, and Bischoff) and the editors of the *Neue Bach-Ausgabe* (Georg von Dadelsen, Alfred Dürr, and Werner Neumann) have been pioneers. There are approximately as many sources for the 'Well-Tempered Clavier' as for the 'Missa de Beata Virgine'. In Bach research, too, it is often easy to rule out the derivation of manuscript B from manuscript A on the ground that manuscript A contains a mistake which is not reproduced in manuscript B. But sometimes it is *too* easy. There are copyists who are musicians enough to correct a mistake when they see it. Among Bach's copyists, they are rare; I don't know how rare they were in the fifteenth and sixteenth centuries, but perhaps Professor Kellman or Professor Rifkin can tell us whether they would count Alamire among them.

[2] In *Notes*, ser. 2, vol. xix (December 1961), pp. 62–4.

number of manuscripts and variants and that the approximate nature of the conclusions may easily be turned into absolutes remains....One wonders if such a mass of data could not have been set up on IBM computers with fuller and less compromising results. We have before us, it seems, a perfect example of a case in which modern techniques could have been used to advantage.

Now that we do have the complete Josquin edition, we can afford to wait a while for the next one. We can use the readings Smijers offers us as working hypotheses, and if the second edition is to be an improvement on the first it must give a detailed account of every source, or convincing reasons for disregarding certain sources. This doubtless means that no one or two men can undertake the editing of all of Josquin's works but that, as in other collected-works editions, not more than a few works can be assigned to a single editor. Since many of the sources involved contain several or many works by Josquin, study of the problems in one work can often be greatly aided by study of other works occurring in the same sources. This means that the assignments of works to individual editors must take these over-lappings into account; it does not necessarily mean that one editor should be responsible for all the works occurring in a particular group of sources. What I think should in any case be avoided is the piecemeal issuance of different works contained in the same sources, about which the later volumes would almost surely have to correct the earlier ones. Nor would these corrections be confined to the critical reports (which, as can be seen, would have to be many times as long as those in the Smijers edition): the re-evaluation of sources would in many cases mean changes in the music itself, as it became clear that a reading that had been considered authoritative was in fact less so than an alternative reading.

Teamwork could also contribute greatly to the *accuracy* of the new edition, a quality which seems to become more difficult of attainment every year.

II

The habits of modern musicians to which the edition might be adapted are principally three:

A. The habit of expecting one clear reading, rather than having to choose among readings.

When different readings are more or less equally plausible, and found in what seem more or less equally authoritative sources, is it enough to present one reading, others being relegated to the critical apparatus or to footnotes? (Do performers consult the critical apparatus or read the footnotes?) On the other hand, the editor cannot escape responsibility for making obvious corrections in the sources, even if the sources should be unanimous in presenting an erroneous reading.

For example, in the *Osanna* of the 'Missa Mater Patris' (m. 97), the Smijers edition reproduces a reading from Petrucci that is obviously mistaken: it violates rules of sixteenth-century counterpoint, and since the melody is motivic, the correct reading is obvious.[3]

B. The habit of reading only time signatures of which the lower figure represents quarters or smaller values, or at the very most, halves. Must note values be reduced? To the point where notes that were originally separate quarters become beamed together in groups of eighths and sixteenths? (The later volumes of the Josquin edition reduce the mensuration signs C, ₵, O, and Ⴔ in the proportion 2:1, while signs containing the figure 3 are reduced in the proportion 4:1—and this without any indication of the difference. Totally inadequate and it seems to me purposeless, is the inclusion of incipits at the beginnings of the large Mass sections if they are not included also at the beginnings of sub-sections.) If musicians can read $\frac{3}{2}$ and $\frac{3}{4}$, why not $\frac{3}{1}$, or even 3 breves (as in O2)?

Concerning both points A and B above, how shall the editor present everything he knows that is relevant and differentiate it from what he does not know and only guesses? How much of what he guesses (e.g., tempi and tempo relations, sharps and flats, text distribution) needs to be included at all in a critical edition?

C. The habit of reading only violin and bass clefs. Wolfgang Osthoff[4] makes an eloquent plea for preservation of the original clefs. But while I share his preference, I am about ready to consider that battle lost for the present. Notation in modern clefs does not, at any rate, affect the way the music is performed (as the introduction of eighth-note and sixteenth-note beams, for example, is likely to), provided the original clefs are indicated.[5] It is certainly true that the old multiplicity of C and F clefs suits this music much better than the modern limitation to two forms of G clef and one form of bass clef, and I do not see how people become musicians without thorough familiarity with them. As the music of earlier centuries gains wider and wider currency, I venture to believe that more and more features of its original notation will become current too, including old clefs.

---

[3] The parallel octaves in measures 20–21 of the *Credo* of this Mass referred to by Helmuth Osthoff (*Josquin Desprez*, i, pp. 153–4) are present only as a result of misprints in Osthoff's book; those in measure 97, on the other hand, occur in both Petrucci and Modena, Archivio Capitolare, MS. IV, and there is no such obvious clue to a correct reading as in measure 97 of the *Osanna*.

[4] 'Per la notazione originale nelle pubblicazioni di musiche antiche e specialmente nella nuova edizione Monteverdi', *Acta musicologica*, xxxiv (1962), pp. 101–27.

[5] The sources do not always agree as to clefs, and the clef of one voice is often changed within a work or a section or sub-section in order to avoid ledger-lines. But this is an argument against preserving 'original clefs' rather than for it.

But those of us who think so are still, I gather, in a small minority, so the time is apparently not yet.

III

Who will the users of the new edition be? One way of classifying them would be:

A. Musicologists and students of musicology, and
B. Performing musicians, who may be divided into
   1. Professionals, and
   2. Amateurs (choruses, collegia musica, madrigal groups, etc.)

Another way is:

A. Score readers, and
B. Readers of individual vocal or instrumental lines.

Different solutions of editorial problems favour different classes of users. For example, bar-lines, with ties where needed, best show the macro-rhythm and are of the greatest assistance to score readers, who should be among the more sophisticated users, best able to discount this feature of notation to the extent necessary. *Mensurstriche* or other less conspicuous indications of macro-rhythm are most favourable to the attentiveness of each individual performer to the rhythm of his own line.[6]

The choice of solutions to this and other problems ought to be affected by the answer to the question: who will the users of the edition be?

Ideally, performing musicians would make their own 'practical editions', though in practice only the most conscientious of them will do so, and others will use 'practical editions' made by editors of varying qualities. But—and I speak from seventeen years' experience as conductor of an amateur chorus, most of those years prior to my work in musicology—what all makers of

---

[6] We have learned from Professor Lowinsky ('Early Scores in Manuscript', *Journal of the American Musicological Society*, xiii (1960), pp. 126–73) that bar-lines and ties exist in virtually all scores dating from the sixteenth century, and I am ready to believe that composers may have used them in composing, though so far as I know no such scores survive from Josquin's time. But scores did not serve as *performing materials*, except for keyboard players and conductors, and the choirbooks and separate partbooks that were sung and played from do not have bar-lines and ties. I believe this is an important distinction. Each individual participant in the performance of a polyphonic piece ought to have mainly the rhythm of his own part in mind—the 'micro-rhythm', regular only in the large, and often irregular in the small. The macro-rhythm—the metre common to all parts—will *emerge* from the sum of the micro-rhythms. I therefore favour *Mensurstriche* or similar expedients for performing editions, and personally believe they can be made quite practical for scholarly editions as well, though I do see the advantages of bar-lines to the score reader. These ideas are more fully expressed in the Introduction to my practical edition of *A German Requiem (Musicalische Exequien)* by Heinrich Schütz (New York, 1957).

'practical editions' need as a basis is what I think the new Josquin edition should furnish them: everything we know from the sources, and nothing (or as little as possible) more. On that basis, performers, editors, and transcribers can make whatever versions they want. I should be the last to underestimate the value of the Busoni Bach editions, the Schnabel editions of Beethoven Sonatas, indeed the transcriptions by Liszt, Webern, and Schönberg. Years ago, performers were satisfied with Czerny, Bülow, Joachim, or Tovey editions. Today, the word *Urtext* is what helps to sell copies. The word is often used carelessly or irresponsibly, but I hope and believe that the growing maturity of performers to which its popularity bears witness will continue to increase. We should do everything we can to aid and encourage it. What we need is a truly *Urtext* edition of Josquin.

REESE: Thank you, Professor Mendel. We shall postpone any discussion of Professor Mendel's contribution until later, and ask Dr. Antonowycz to continue.

ANTONOWYCZ: So much has been said about the techniques of editing older music and with so little practical result that I am afraid I will have some difficulty in displaying the necessary enthusiasm. Still, there is a point in speaking about this matter, and I am grateful to the organizers of this impressive conference that this symposium is taking place.

Many things could be said about a new edition of the works of Josquin, about the grouping and order of various works, questions of authenticity, editorial accidentals, and so on. I will confine myself to one specific aspect of editorial technique and speak about the necessity of reproducing *modus*, *tempus*, and *prolatio* in new editions of older music. I shall not say anything revolutionary, but concern myself with old and well-known questions of methodology. Some of the viewpoints formulated here have already been disseminated in a limited circle in Holland. It gives me pleasure to discuss them before this international audience.

1. The necessity of reproducing all mensuration signs

In new editions of music of the fifteenth and sixteenth centuries, two main tendencies can be discerned:

(a) In most editions, the *modus*, *tempus*, and *prolatio* are indicated with the help of bar-lines drawn either through or between the staves.

(b) In some editions, they are more or less ignored. Either only the tactus is indicated (as, for example, in van Crevel's Obrecht edition) or more than one breve of the original tempus may fall within one measure of the new edition, as for instance in Brumel's 'Missa L'homme armé' as edited by Carapetyan:[7]

[7] *Kyrie*, m. 1 (alto); *Antonii Brumel Opera omnia*, i (Rome, 1951), p. 1.

Ex. 1

I disagree with both of these methods of transcription, interesting though they may be, because I am convinced that the *modus*, *tempus*, and *prolatio* must be reproduced in modern editions: they constitute the rhythmic and metric matrix within which the composers of the fifteenth and sixteenth centuries thought and worked. For that reason they must be visible in modern editions, even if at times they seem to have no manifest influence on the performance of the old music. (However, it is not so simple to decide where they have an influence and where not.)

2. Representation of *modus*, *tempus*, and *prolatio*

How should the rhythmic and metric categories be represented in modern editions? The clearest and the most effective means is by the use of bar-lines, be they drawn through or placed between the staves. Any fear that the bar-lines would lead to an incorrect accentuation seems to me farfetched: the bar-lines in newer music, too, have only a relative meaning for the accentuation. Not all compositions where the bar-lines indicate a 3/4 scheme have to be performed like a waltz, and not all compositions in 2/4 or 4/4 like a march. Fear not the bar-lines!

Replacing the commonly used bar-lines by personal inventions like commas or dots or wedges does not lead to a solution of the problem, but to mere replacement of one sign by another, causing confusion and fatigue. The advantages of the traditional method are its visual clarity and almost universal use.

3. Representation of tactus

Leaving *modus*, *tempus*, and *prolatio* out of consideration and confining oneself to tactus alone, as is done by van Crevel, means too large a simplification of the metrical problems of older music, and in some situations offers no solution. We know that the tactus shifted in time from longer to shorter notes—from long to breve, from breve to semibreve, and from semibreve to minim. This was a gradual development. The changes in meaning and understanding of the tactus can already be deduced from the occurrence of terms like *tactus maior*, *tactus minor*, *tactus tardior*, and *tactus celerior*. In such a continuous evolution, tactus cannot always be tied with certainty to a specific note.

A concrete example where tactus theory is helpless occurs in the 'Missa La sol fa re mi'. According to most sources, the *Pleni sunt coeli* is written in *tempus perfectum* (*integer valor notarum* O), in other sources in *tempus perfectum diminutum*:[8]

Ex. 2

Where then is one to put the tactus signs?

I have raised my voice against the tendency to apply experimental methods of transcription in expensive editions of collected works for general use. These experiments in themselves are valuable, but they should be limited to specialized scientific publications. As teachers and as practicing musicologists and musicians, we are best served by the traditional and the most widely accepted system.

REESE: Thank you, Dr. Antonowycz. And now may we hear from Professor Lenaerts?

LENAERTS: Pursuing Dr. Antonowycz's line of thought, I should like to make some further remarks on mensuration signs. The manuscript A.R. 879 of the Proskesche Musikbibliothek in Regensburg bears numerous contemporary annotations in the form of numbers over pauses, ligatures, and blackened (imperfected) notes. They occur, among others, in Josquin's 'Veni Sancte Spiritus' (6 v.) and in the *Agnus Dei* of his 'Missa L'homme armé super voces musicales'. (The manuscript is incomplete; the *quinta vox* is missing.) The copyist has dated his transcription at the end of the above-mentioned *Agnus Dei*: 'Finis 1569, 13 Julii'.

The numbers represent the beats within the *tempora*; they occur mostly in sections in *tempus perfectum*. Important is the fact that the figures stand for the semibreves in the pauses: 15, 4, 5, etc., whereas the grouping of the rests strictly respects the mensuration signs O, O2, C, ₵. At the beginning of the composition, added numbers are found in each voice. This seems to indicate that the performers needed help in observing the right mensuration (see Pl. 44, figs. c–d).

The annotations of the Regensburg manuscript may be compared with those of the *Concentus 4 Missarum Obrecht*, published by Gregorius Mewes (Basel, n.d.), the unique copy of which is found in the Universitätsbibliothek Basel. The tenor partbook contains marginalia, extensively studied by M. van Crevel in his edition of the 'Missa Maria zart'.[9] These marginal notes

---

[8] See *Josquin des Prez, Opera omnia*, i/2, p. xiii.

[9] *Jacobus Obrecht, Opera omnia*, Missae, vii (Amsterdam, 1964). He gives the annotated pages in seven facsimiles (pp. xix–xxii).

explain the mensuration signs and add up the number of tactus in certain Mass sections. (Incidentally, van Crevel mentions that they contain a number of mistakes.) While we cannot follow van Crevel in his deductions concerning the secret mathematical structure of Obrecht's Mass, he is right in stating that these marginal notes confirm the practical use of the tactus; it is the unit of counting.

The Regensburg case differs in two points: (1) the manuscript presents numbers that are clear and accurate and appear to have been entered systematically and by an expert hand, perhaps by the copyist himself. (2) They have a purely practical aim in aiding the performer to interpret the mensuration signs. There is no hint whatsoever at a possible secret cosmological or cabalistic structure.

From this example—to my knowledge a rather rare one—I should like to draw a practical conclusion with regard to a future second edition of Josquin's works. I completely agree with Dr. Antonowycz's statement about the need for reprinting all the original mensuration signs (*modus, tempus, prolatio*), including those of the sub-sections. The numbers in the Regensburg manuscript clearly prove that *modus, tempus,* and *prolatio* were indeed the rhythmic and metric matrix within which the composers thought and worked. But they show even more clearly that the performance depended as well on the interpretation of these mensuration signs: the singers simply counted the beats dividing the *tempora* and added them up.

In further agreement with Dr. Antonowycz, I consider it a mistake to indicate merely the tactus units by means of dots, commas, or bar-lines. This procedure gives a false impression of the ancient mensuration system and opens the way to all sorts of difficulties. In my opinion, both scholarly and practical editions can best serve their purpose by using the traditional system of complete bar-lines, not *Mensurstriche*.

REESE: Thank you, Professor Lenaerts. And now may we hear from Professor Lockwood.

LOCKWOOD: I should like to focus upon the question of the choice of a primary source. To keep this discussion within reasonable boundaries, I wish to draw my examples only from the Josquin Masses. This morning two papers dealing with manuscripts were delivered, one by Professor Hoffmann-Erbrecht and one by Professor Kellman. I have found it necessary to modify my contribution in the light of these two papers.

The edition of Josquin's Masses occupied Albert Smijers for thirty years. The first Mass published by him, the 'Missa L'homme armé super voces musicales', came out in the year 1926, the last, 'Missa Allez regretz', in 1956. Over this long period Smijers changed his views on the choice of a specific primary source. (I refer to the stipulated primary source that Smijers used, but there is the further question as to whether the source stipulated as the primary source is indeed the one on which the edition was based.) When Smijers began his work, large-scale studies of individual sources were not yet available. Smijers was confronted with the necessity of studying the source material, while at the same time making an edition of the Masses intended to respond both to practical and scientific needs. His achievement is the more heroic for having been concluded at all, not to speak of the high level of scholarship at which, in general, the work was executed.

Josquin's Masses were published during his own lifetime by Petrucci, in the famous three volumes of 1502, 1505, and 1514. Smijers followed Petrucci's order in publishing the Masses, but not necessarily his texts. For example, as source for the first Mass in the first book, 'L'homme armé super voces musicales', Smijers chose MS. Cappella Sistina 154, written about thirty years after Josquin's death.[10] The basis for the 'Missa L'homme armé sexti toni', number five in the first book, is an untitled print of circa 1558 preserved in Wiesbaden, a source whose authority is difficult to ascertain. In fact, all Masses of Petrucci's first book as published by Smijers are taken from unusual and in some cases manifestly unauthoritative sources, for reasons it is difficult to be sure about. In the third Mass, 'Gaudeamus', the stated source is MS. Jena 32, but some of the variant readings given are those of Jena 32, as if the edition rested on a source other than the Jena manuscript. This even includes such matters as stipulated accidentals. Starting in 1935, Smijers changed his procedure. Continuing with the original Petrucci canon, he now published the Masses, it would appear, from the Petrucci prints.

Smijers' knowledge of the relationships between the sources, contemporary and posthumous, must have been slight, even as our own is still today. I shall attempt here to present four types of relationships:

I. Works known only from printed sources. The unique example is the 'Missa Di dadi', in Petrucci's third book. This is in many ways a peculiar work. The chief question posed by its tradition is: why is this work available only in one printed source? In the absence of any information on how Petrucci obtained the works that he printed, it is difficult to answer this question or to assess the authority of the Petrucci print.

II. Works of which the sources are about evenly distributed between early prints and manuscripts (e.g. 'Missa Gaudeamus').

III. Works transmitted chiefly by manuscripts. The most outstanding example is the 'Missa de Beata Virgine', discussed by Professor Mendel in the Mass Workshop.[11] In view of the large number of manuscripts, the

[10] [Cf. the remarks on the same subject in Edward Lowinsky's welcoming address, above, p. 15.]

[11] See above, pp. 712–18.

choice of the best source is more difficult. The earliest group of sources includes three manuscripts belonging to the Cappella Sistina: (1) MS. Capp. Sist. 160, which Herbert Kellman assigns to the workshop of Alamire;[12] (2) MS. Capp. Sist. 45, usually ascribed to the papacy of Clement VII (1523–34), but possibly dating from a period within Josquin's lifetime,[13] in which case it would assume a higher priority rating than it now receives; (3) MS. Capp. Sist. 23, traditionally related to the papacy of Julius II (1503–13); Richard Sherr has suggested that this manuscript might be earlier than the papacy of Julius II.[14] Should this be true, Capp. Sist. 23 would reveal that the 'Missa de Beata Virgine' was a work of Josquin's middle period, and not a very late work, as now suspected.

IV. Works transmitted in contemporary and late manuscripts, but printed only after Josquin's death. The only printed sources of the 'Missa Pange lingua' are late German publications. The earliest manuscripts for the Mass are associated with the Papal Chapel and the papacy of Leo X: (1) MS. Capp. Sist. 16; (2) MSS. Pal. lat. 1980–81[15] and 1982;[16] (3) MS. Santa Maria Maggiore J.J.III.4, now housed in the Vatican. Richard Sherr suggests that its repertoire may be older than those of the manuscripts of the Leo X period. It contains Busnois' 'Missa L'homme armé' and Masses by Obrecht, Josquin, Brumel, Weerbecke, Févin, and Moulu. The manuscript bears the French royal arms on one folio, together with an as yet unidentified heraldic emblem. The 'Missa Pange lingua' has always been thought to be a very late work by Josquin. There is no good historical reason to associate Josquin directly with the Cappella Sistina or with Rome generally during the papacy of Leo X. The question arises: does the nucleus of the early manuscripts which may be the earliest group of sources for this Mass suggest that it could have originated through some connection between Josquin and the Papal Chapel? I can raise the question. I don't know of anyone even here who can answer it. This is the question to which any editor will sooner or later have to address himself if he wishes to make decisions on what he considers to be a primary source. This suggests the close interrelationship of textual, biographical, historical, and stylistic problems.

Primary sources can be used in two ways: (1) As the literal basis for the

[12] See above, p. 209. I am indebted to Professor Kellman for background information.

[13] For the reasons, see Richard Sherr's presentation in the Mass Workshop, above, p. 713.

[14] Ibid., p. 712.

[15] [Edward E. Lowinsky, *The Medici Codex of 1518*, iii, p. 64, attributes the ownership of this manuscript to Cardinal Giulio de' Medici, later Pope Clement VII, on the joint evidence of the coat of arms, the biographical data, and the extraordinary closeness of musical readings with the Medici Codex. Its probable date would fall after the writing of the Medici Codex in 1518 and before the Cardinal became Pope in 1523. (On the relationship between the Cardinal and his nephew Lorenzo II de' Medici, see ibid.)]

[16] I am indebted for these references to Professor Joshua Rifkin.

edition, with variants of other sources relegated to the critical notes. Such an edition has the advantage of furnishing an original text in its entirety. (2) As the basis for composite or conflated readings, in which case preference may be given to one particular source, while other sources furnish versions of parts and passages that the editor prefers to his primary source. Such an edition constructs a text that exists in no single source of the period. Few recent scholarly editions of early music follow the first method; most follow the second. Two eminent exceptions are Heinrich Besseler's edition of Dufay's works and Nino Pirrotta's edition of the music of fourteenth-century Italy.

In 1960, in the preface to his edition of volume ii of Dufay's *Opera omnia*, Besseler wrote: '...only one source is used as a basis for both music and text. If a conflation of several manuscripts is used for the transcription, it is impossible to recognize the principal source, and, to avoid confusion on this point, a single main source is used. . . .'[17] Professor Pirrotta, in the preface to his first volume, said: 'The transcription of each composition is based on only one source. . . . The choice of the source, in the case of compositions found in more than one source or in more than one version of the same source, has been determined by an examination of each composition in its various versions and not by an order of preference in the sources.'[18]

The interrelations of sources and the interrelations of the pieces they contain do not necessarily coincide. A source that constitutes the primary source for one piece does not necessarily fulfill the same function for another piece. At times this is also true for the sub-sections of a piece, or even for different voice parts. Now, how widely can an editor cast his net in trying to make these decisions? This morning Professor Hoffmann-Erbrecht spoke very cogently on the subject of filiation of manuscripts.[19] I am going to take the liberty, with his kind indulgence, to raise a question. Among the sources cited for his example 2, 'Domine ne in furore tuo', he listed two manuscripts, each of which exists only in the form of a single partbook: London, British Museum Add. MS. 19583 (alto) and Modena, Biblioteca Estense, MS. α.F.2.29 (tenor). I saw the latter manuscript in 1962 and remarked on its mutilated condition. Two years later Professor Martin Picker pointed out to me that the two partbooks belong to one and the same set, originally of four partbooks, two of which (soprano and bass) are now lost.[20] Professor Hoffmann-Erbrecht, unaware of the relationship,

---

[17] Heinrich Besseler, ed., *Guglielmi Dufay Opera omnia*, ii (American Institute of Musicology, 1960), p. xvi. A similar statement may be found ibid., vi (1964), p. xxiii.

[18] Nino Pirrotta, ed., *The Music of Fourteenth-Century Italy*, i (American Institute of Musicology, 1954), p. iii.

[19] See above, pp. 285–93.

[20] [This is a discovery that a number of scholars seem to have made independently of each

placed MS. London (L) on one side and MS. Modena (M) on the other side of the stemma, which must mean that the two parts follow different lines of textual transmission. It would seem, however, that some other hypothesis about the relationship of the two sources will have to be developed.

Filiation of manuscripts, an essential part of musicological study, as was pointed out this morning, is only one dimension of what must go into the choice of a primary source. The other dimension is the study of manuscripts from the point of view of their origin, function, destination, contents, and scribal characteristics, that is, study along the lines that Professor Kellman discussed. What we need is a fusion of the approaches of Professors Hoffmann-Erbrecht and Kellman.

REESE: Thank you, Professor Lockwood. Since Professor Lockwood has mentioned Professor Pirrotta and he is here, he may wish to make some comments.

PIRROTTA: I have long formed the conviction that not all works contained in one source have the same origin. Therefore they do not all have the same degree of authority. One manuscript may have the most authoritative version of one composition, and a poor version of another. I believe that an edition based on a conflation of many sources is ideally an approach to the possibility of an *Urtext*. Practically, it does not correspond to any historical reality, because it is a version that never existed in time, or, at least, we have no evidence that it ever existed in time. This, then, is a falsification of history insofar as it combines a number of historically different versions of the same composition.

I may perhaps be forgiven for introducing a note of scepticism. I feel we insist too much on the idea that an edition be 'scientific'. Of course, every

---

other. It was published for the first time, as far as I am aware, in *The Medici Codex*, iii, p. 117, and credited to Dr. Bonnie J. Blackburn, Assistant Editor of the *Monuments of Renaissance Music*. An anonymous reviewer in the *Times Literary Supplement* of 17 July 1969 wrote: 'It is certainly not true that a student of the editor's discovered the relationship between the handwriting of a tenor part-book in Modena (α.F.2.29) and that of British Museum Add. MS. 19583, for this fact was noted by a British scholar some ten years ago in the catalogue in question shelved in the reading room'. Does the reviewer think it impossible that scholars can make discoveries independently of each other? Does he regard a hand-written note in a catalogue of a library as a scholarly publication? Or does he believe that Dr. Blackburn saw the catalogue in question? Neither the editor nor Dr. Blackburn worked in the British Museum before the publication of *The Medici Codex*. Recently, Joshua Rifkin discovered that the beginning of the alto part-book, containing chansons, is to be found in the Bibliothèque Nationale, Paris, MS. nouv. acq. fr. 4599; see Lawrence F. Bernstein, '*La Courone et fleur des chansons a troys*: A Mirror of the French Chanson in Italy in the Years between Ottaviano Petrucci and Antonio Gardano', *Journal of the American Musicological Society*, xxvi (1973), pp. 1–68; p. 20.]

edition has to be scientific in the sense that it should be done in the best possible way. But I strongly feel that the aim should not be to show how scientific we are, but how good and how worthwhile the music is. Our attention should be focussed on how best to bring out the quality, the essence of the music.

REESE: Professor Lowinsky, will you take over?

LOWINSKY: Ladies and gentlemen, the moment of truth has come. I must confess that I have not done my homework as well as I had hoped to. I am going to read the statement that I sent to my colleagues on the Symposium; then I shall improvise on it. This will be the easier for me since, through the unexpected intervention of the Goddess Fortuna whom Professor Reese invoked so effectually at the very beginning of our meeting, I have had the generous offer of assistance in illustrating certain points from the New York Pro Musica and the Prague Madrigal Singers.

No aspect of editorial policy affects the actual sound of the music more crucially than the policy governing *musica ficta*—the editor's adding of accidentals to the score. It is of particular importance in an edition of the works of Josquin des Prez, because his works, as transmitted in prints and manuscripts, are marked by a most liberal use of accidentals, varying significantly, however, from one source to another. It is in the realm of *musica ficta* that Josquin's innovative spirit shows evidence of remarkable pioneering. My chief criticism of the first edition of Josquin's works is that it has not one, but at least three different *musica ficta* policies. Surprisingly, they go from good to bad to worse.

'Smijers I', if I may so call it, is Smijers' *musica ficta* policy for most of the 1920s. It was a policy of liberal application of *musica ficta* rules. I have long wondered what the roots were of Smijers' original ideas, and what caused him to switch later to a new policy that I might call 'Smijers II', beginning approximately in the 1930s, when he followed a policy of a distinctly more restricted use of editorial accidentals. Never having talked with Professor Smijers about the subject, I cannot be certain that I am right, but I think that the following points are worth considering:

Smijers started his scholarly career with a dissertation on Carolus Luython (c. 1556–1620), a student of Philippe de Monte. Unlike his master who, as Praetorius confirms, did not believe in writing out accidentals implied by *musica ficta*, Luython followed the opposite course, strongly supported by Praetorius: he wrote out most of the accidentals usually reserved to the singers' discretion, and thus demonstrated to the young Dutch scholar *ad oculos* how accidentals ought to be used in sixteenth-century music. Smijers may also have been influenced by the edition of Obrecht's works by Johannes Wolf, completed in the year in which Smijers began his edition of

Josquin's works. Johannes Wolf used a very liberal policy of editorial accidentals. Like Ambros, of whom we heard this morning from Professor Harrán, he had read the theorists very thoroughly.

Why, then, did Smijers change in the 1930s to what I consider a less fortunate and less successful policy of restriction in the setting of accidentals? I have the notion that the review of Smijers' edition by Otto Ursprung may have had something to do with it. Actually, the article that Otto Ursprung wrote was more than just a review of the edition. It was a review of the music of Josquin des Prez as it revealed itself in the early volumes of Smijers' edition. Here Otto Ursprung wrote that Smijers was much too liberal in his policy. 'In general', said Ursprung, 'Josquin keeps to the modes as they are used in learned music, much more strictly than one could suspect from Smijers' edition, which has so many editorial accidentals.'[21] What is the basis for saying that Josquin kept much more strictly to the modes? Ursprung does not say; nor do many of those who followed him, as was pointed out very ably by my colleague, Howard Mayer Brown, in a paper that eases my task considerably.[22] In the last generation, many editors saw a great virtue in using 'the utmost reserve in the setting of accidentals'. But a scholarly approach to the problem would require the raising and answering of the following question: Do we have documents that show that musicians were expected to add these accidentals? We indeed have these documents, many of them available in modern editions. Others are available in old editions, in early printed books, and in manuscripts. I have collected these materials over many years, and I hope that the time will come when I can put them all together. The mass of theoretical utterance on the singer's need to add *musica ficta* is not only great, it forms a continuous tradition, and the testimonies are, perhaps with one single exception, unanimous. The one exception is Henricus Glareanus, who was not a practising musician but a humanist, and who, having created the system of twelve modes, had a vested interest in preserving Lydian with a B♮ and Mixolydian with F♮, because were Lydian to have B♭ and Mixolydian F♯, where then would be the difference between Lydian, Mixolydian, and Ionian that was indispensable to his theoretical system? Maurice Cauchie, in embracing the idea of the purity of the modes,[23] seems to have followed Glareanus' view—I say 'seems', for he mentions Glareanus as little as he does any other theorist of

---

[21] 'Im allgemeinen hält Josquin die in der gelehrten Musik ("Ars") üblichen Tonarten doch viel strenger ein, als die in der Gesamtausgabe beigesetzten vielen Akzidentien erscheinen lassen'; Otto Ursprung, 'Josquin des Prés, Eine Charakterzeichnung auf Grund der bisher erschienenen Gesamtausgabe der Werke Josquin's', *Bulletin de la Société "Union musicologique"*, vi (1926), pp. 11–50; p. 43.

[22] See above, pp. 475–522.

[23] Maurice Cauchie, 'La pureté des modes dans la musique vocal franco-belge du début du XVIᵉ siècle', *Theodor Kroyer Festschrift* (Regensburg, 1933), pp. 54–61.

the time. Passionately, he opposed in particular the notion of the *sub-semitonium modi*, basing himself on nothing more than a few examples in which sixteenth-century composers demanded a whole-tone cadence by introducing the seventh note in a lower voice simultaneously with the soprano. But one cannot deduce general rules from exceptions. The rules governing the correct performance of polyphonic music that include the use of the subsemitone at cadence points were formulated, time and again, by the musicians, composers, and theorists of the fifteenth and sixteenth centuries, and they have of course a venerable tradition going back to the Middle Ages. The strictures of Otto Ursprung, more so than the ideas of Maurice Cauchie, may have had an influence upon Smijers in shaping what I call the second policy of *musica ficta* observable in the edition of Josquin's works.

The third policy I would call the policy of Antonowycz and Elders, who continued the work of Smijers, and to whom we owe it that the edition of Josquin's works now lies before us completed. At first Antonowycz and Elders seemed to follow 'Smijers II' in a general way. But eventually, in a series of works in the Supplement, they did away with *musica ficta* altogether, completely abandoning the principles of Smijers' policies I and II. I am delighted to have both of these gentlemen here so that they can explain to us the reasons for this great switch.

Now in each of these policies there is considerable latitude in application, to the point where the same harmonic progression in the same mode is treated differently in different pieces for no discernible reason. I shall only give one example here concerning what I should call a grammatical aspect of *musica ficta*. There are errors in the application of *musica ficta* that should not really be open to debate because we deal with the syntax of the harmonic language of the time, the construction of cadences. At the end of the *Credo* of the 'Missa La sol fa re mi',[24] we find a sequence of chords forming a Dorian cadence:

Ex. 3

24 *Opera omnia*, i/2, p. 61.

It should be sung as:

Three measures later the same sequence of chords comes in what we might call Aeolian, that is, in a cadence on A:

While refraining from raising the seventh in the Dorian cadence, Smijers adds a sharp to G here. But more impressive is the fact that in another part of the same Mass (*Gloria*, m. 77), the same cadence is given the subsemitone. No error is more frequent in modern editions than the misconstruction of the Dorian (and the transposed Dorian) cadence. The rules are clear; they are unanimous. Dozens of theorists support them.

Josquin is one of the most imaginative harmonic inventors of all times and unquestionably the outstanding harmonic inventor of his own time. There is no conceivable doubt that, like his fellow composers, he counted on the singers' use of *musica ficta*. When he does not want *musica ficta*, he writes in a manner rendering its use impossible. For instance, the 'Missa La sol fa re mi' contains a number of Phrygian cadences on a full chord, and they demand the major third, G♯, at the end. But Josquin, always striving for harmonic and expressive variety, having used the major third both at the end of the first and of the second *Kyrie*, writes a progression at the end of the third *Kyrie* that insures a minor ending by going from D to G in the alto.

We often hear it said that *musica ficta* should be applied only to final, not to intermediary cadences. There is not one shred of evidence in the numerous treatments of *musica ficta* for such a proposition. Nor is it supported by the evidence of tablatures, as has been shown in the two papers of Geneviève Thibault and Howard Brown. We also hear it said that the demand for variety imposes an obligation on the modern editor to observe *musica ficta* rules at times and ignore them at others. But a careful study of Josquin shows that he did it all himself. If he has a number of cadences with sub-semitones, he so orders and gradates them that they are different in nature and effect. On the other hand, if he wishes to have a whole-tone cadence, and often he does, he leads the voices so that a whole-tone progression is unavoidable.

Josquin is his own best editor. In our attempt to discover his true intent, we must start from the same premises as he himself did, that is, from the *musica ficta* rules of his time. If we follow them we shall find how Josquin created a harmonic world of new and surprising colour and variety.

And now I wish to present a witness stronger than words, one too little invoked in musicological debates: the sound of the music itself. I asked Paul Maynard to help me in this problem. He proposed to perform 'Quando natus est', the *secunda pars* of 'O admirabile commercium', which he did with his group last Monday night from the edition of the Medici Codex. The divergency in the interpretation given in the Josquin edition[25] and in that of the Medici Codex[26] in his judgement was substantial enough to illustrate the effect of two different *musica ficta* policies. The New York Pro Musica will sing the piece first in Smijers' edition and then in that of the Medici Codex.

[The New York Pro Musica performs 'Quando natus est'.]
Thank you very much, Mr. Maynard and singers!

I wonder whether, with the chairman's and Professor Mendel's permission, and while we have the singers here, we could undertake a little experiment on an issue that Professor Mendel has raised with regard to reduced and unreduced note values. If, as Professor Mendel believes, the reduction of unbeamed quarter-notes into beamed eighths makes a difference in the singing, then could we not agree that that difference must be heard?

MENDEL: It makes a difference in the *reading* of the music. It is perfectly possible to erase that difference in rehearsal.

LOWINSKY: You and I agree that we must concentrate in editorial matters on those things that make a difference in sound. Do you claim

25 *Werken*, Motetten, Bundel i, no. 6.
26 Edward E. Lowinsky, *The Medici Codex of 1518*, iv, pp. 33–7.

that when we perform a piece from an unreduced score, it will sound differently, and that you can recognize whether a piece is sung from a reduced or an unreduced version?

MENDEL: I would say that singers with this much experience in the music of the period can certainly sing unreduced notation as if it were reduced and reduced notation as if it were unreduced.

LOWINSKY: Very well, my experiment is made then. For if that is the case, then we have established the fundamental difference between the problem of *musica ficta* and that of using notation with reduced note values. The latter will not come out in sound in the performance of experienced singers. But if we perform a Dorian cadence without accidentals, we will hear it under all circumstances, be the performers experienced or not. We can agree at least that the difference between reduced and unreduced values is not a critical one since it will not register in sound when we deal with an experienced group.

MENDEL: Of course, of course. May I just say this? A piece that has no accidentals in the written version can be sung with accidentals if the singers know the rules. That's what was done, obviously, in the period, but to different extents at different places. A piece that is written in reduced notation with the eighths beamed in twos can be sung as if they were not so beamed, of course. One can, in performance, make up for what I would call the deficiencies of the score if one is an experienced musician. People easily play music with cross rhythms that is barred regularly. But inexperienced people may have trouble doing this the first time; they have to learn to fight the bar-line.

LOWINSKY: Thank you, Professor Mendel.

I should now like to go on to my proposals. If we are to have a second edition of the works of Josquin des Prez, then we ought to formulate a coherent policy on *musica ficta*. We ought to formulate it, state it, and follow it. At the same time we must remain aware that Josquin's attitude in this, as in other respects, is often experimental. At times he poses problems that cannot be solved without taking some decided liberties within the set of rules governing *musica ficta*. In such cases there is only one solution: detailed study of the whole harmonic context of the work in question and of related works. I shall give you one example from a Mass that I consider the acid test for any editor in regard to *musica ficta*. It is the 'Missa Una musque de Buscaya', a most difficult work. In this Mass the astonishing progression of the chords E♭ major–A minor seems to me unavoidable.[27] There is a

27 *Werken*, Missen, x. On the words 'suscipe deprecationem nostram', 'receive our

most interesting relationship between this relatively early Mass and the relatively late 'Déploration d'Ockeghem'.[28] The same progression of E♭ major and A minor chords occurs in the latter work, but only in one manuscript, the Medici Codex. In Smijers' edition, based on Susato's print of 1545,[29] the sequence appears in this form:

Ex. 6

But the Medici Codex[30] eschews the diminished fifth chord in measure 124, and instead ends the sequence with this progression:

Ex. 7

prayer' (*Gloria*, mm. 66–72), Josquin writes a homophonic passage which Smijers left untouched, allowing a diminished fifth chord in semibreves to emerge on the first beat of measure 69. An E♭ in the bass is required (a) by the rule *una nota supra la*, (b) by the melodic progression of the bass, which after two more notes ends on B♭, (c) by the simultaneous B♭ in the alto calling for a perfect fifth in the bass. True, we now land in a double false relation. The question is which of the two solutions is artistically more convincing—a question that calls for a study of the harmonic personality of the Mass as a whole. Shocking as this sequence of chords appears on first hearing within the fifteenth-century idiom, Josquin used it deliberately throughout the Mass for reasons of harmonic colour and expression; he places it in new musical contexts and makes its appearance both technically and musically compelling.

28 The latter work may now be dated after 6 February 1497, the date of Ockeghem's death; see 'Johannes Ockeghem overleed op 6 februari 1497', *Johannes Ockeghem en zijn tijd* (Dendermonde, 1970), pp. 279–80. I agree with Osthoff's dating of the 'Missa Una musque de Buscaya' as before Josquin's entry into the Papal Chapel in 1486; see Osthoff, *Josquin Desprez*, i, p. 142; see also the discussion in Edward E. Lowinsky, above, p. 67.

29 *Werken*, Wereldlijke Werken, Bundel ii, no. 22.

30 Lowinsky, *The Medici Codex*, iv, no. 46.

We have here the same chord progression as in the 'Missa Una musque de Buscaya': E♭ major, A minor,[31] and we have documentary proof from a source written in Josquin's lifetime that indeed such a double false relation was not only within the realm of Josquin's harmonic imagination but also of his artistic skill. It is one thing to invent an extraordinary harmonic combination, it is quite another to make it musically convincing and effective.

It would appear then that in formulating a coherent policy, a differentiation ought to be made between the ordinary rules of *musica ficta* governing, for example, cadential behaviour in the various modes, and the extraordinary uses of the rules that Josquin loves to indulge in, never without a purpose, even though that purpose may not be immediately obvious.

Secondly, the accidentals in the various sources should be carefully noted in the critical apparatus; better still, differing accidentals ought to be noted in the text itself. This is a practice that, I believe, Helen Hewitt initiated in her edition of the *Odhecaton*, using footnotes. This gives the broadest possibility of choices from the original sources to the performer. I agree with Professor Mendel that we are hiding too much in the critical notes, and we do it in such an indigestible form that it takes a very tough performer to want to study it. But that can be improved, and in the *Medici Codex* I've tried to show how it can be done.

My third point concerns the key signatures: they should faithfully follow the source on which the edition is based. Variants in key signatures should be carefully noted, possibly in the text, certainly in the critical apparatus. In the edition of the *Medici Codex* I have discussed examples in which, for reasons I do not understand, Professor Smijers, who was a model of conscientiousness, simply went against the sources.

Finally, while it is undoubtedly true that Josquin's works were performed in his own time in varying versions of *musica ficta*, the editors ought to keep in mind that performers can give only one performance at a time. For that reason, an editor ought to strive to find the best possible solution. This will require, in addition to knowledge of the rules, thorough familiarity with the work and style of the composer, and with the works of the whole period, with the instrumental transcriptions of the composer's works—the latter to be used with caution, more as signposts than as models—and with a sense of musical logic as well as imagination. For, in shaping a *musica ficta* policy, the editor takes on the responsibility for being the interpreter of the master's harmonic, melodic, and poetic design. Although it has been

---

[31] Except for one thing: in the Mass the E♭ major chord appears in root position, A minor in first inversion as a sixth chord; in the 'Déploration' the reverse is the case: E♭ major appears as a sixth chord, A minor in root position.

fashionable to dismiss this responsibility, it is in fact one of the most challenging tasks of an editor of fifteenth- and sixteenth-century music, and, I am confident, will be increasingly regarded as such.

Now the Prague Madrigal Singers will sing for us one passage from the 'Misericordias Domini',[32] which they interpreted last night 'with so much soul', to quote a student who spoke to me. The passage in question, which they will sing first with Smijers' accidentals, then with the accidentals proposed by me (in parentheses), is the following:

Ex. 8

[The Prague Madrigal Singers perform the first version.]

Now, we will have the same passage again in my interpretation. You will now hear the net of modulations that results from a coherent policy of *musica ficta*, in which the same motive, appearing in imitation through a number of successive fifths, will take on the logical accidentals leading to a modulation of which Josquin is one of the first masters.[33]

[The Prague Madrigal Singers perform the second version.]

Thank you very much, Mr. Venhoda and Prague Madrigal Singers!

[33] Technically speaking, this is a modest modulation. The appearance of a flat before B in the alto of measure 57 blocks interpretation of B in the bass of measure 55 as B♮. Musically speaking, the addition of the flat to the bass enhances the great and coherent line of the whole passage; without it the flat printed in measure 57 would be incomprehensible. Symbolically speaking, the Lord's mercy—the subject of this passage—denotes a divine mutation benefitting the human race, the change from justice to mercy.

If the question is raised why Josquin fails to make his purpose clear by signing a flat to the B in the bass in measure 55, the answer lies in one aspect of *musica ficta* that is almost generally overlooked today, although it is often enough stressed by the theorists of the time. Pietro Aron remarked, not without some asperity, on Josquin's use of canon mottoes that demonstrate 'how abstruse and shrouded in deep obscurity he wanted his idea to be'; see Edward E. Lowinsky, 'The Goddess Fortuna in Music, with a Special Study of Josquin's *Fortuna dun gran tempo*', *The Musical Quarterly*, xxix (1943), pp. 45–77; p. 63. But he defended the composer's right 'to use an easy or a difficult, an ordinary or an unusual, a *diatonic* or a *chromatic* way ([*modo*] *naturali et accidentali*), as he pleases' (ibid.). And Zarlino, in treating the transposition of modes by *musica ficta*, says of these transpositions: 'At times the musicians transpose the mode a tone, or another interval, higher and lower, not out of necessity, but as a humorous riddle and caprice and, perhaps, because they want to puzzle and intrigue, as it were, the singers'; see my Introduction to the first volume of *Monuments of Renaissance Music*, H. Colin Slim's edition of *Musica nova* (Chicago, 1964), p. xi b. Do not these remarks by such illustrious writers, and especially the direct allusion of Aron to Josquin, tell us that a *musica ficta* policy, to do justice to the composer's mind, must entail something more than applying accidentals to cadences? But Josquin does not leave us in the dark without lighting a candle. The unusual procedure of imitation in the circle of fifths, the signing of a flat in measure 57, the transpositional logic, the resulting musical coherence of the whole passage, and the symbolic expression of *misericordia Domini* as an act of divine mutation, they all point the way to the *modus accidentalis* that the composer wishes to see used here.

REESE: And now Professor Finscher, will you take over, please?

FINSCHER: Since it is half past five now, I don't wish to make a formal statement. But I should like to take up a few points of the *musica ficta* discussion, which is the one problem on which the people assembled here are apt to come to different conclusions. And, of course, I disagree with many solutions given here by the participants.

First of all, there is the question of Smijers' *musica ficta* policy in the examples cited from the 'Missa La sol fa re mi'. As far as I can see, Smijers added accidentals to every cadence that occurs at the end of a sentence; cadences occurring in the middle of a sentence of the text are left without accidentals. I completely agree with Professor Lowinsky on this point. This is one kind of editorial policy which is, to put it bluntly, unpardonable, first of all because it is not explained, and secondly because it is an interpretation that is at complete variance with the theoretical writings of the time and results, as Professor Lowinsky has stated, in hiding Josquin's own differentiation of cadences.

On the other hand, I see the danger that we might arrive at this same position by opposite means if we use *musica ficta* extensively, that is, beyond the very few cadential situations for which we know with certainty that *musica ficta* must be applied. For instance, in 'Quando natus est', the passage on 'descendisti': why do you insert F♯ in the first point of imitation but not C♯ in the second one? The whole section loses consistency.

Ex. 9

LOWINSKY: The answer to this question is simple. The F♯ that I use follows the rules. The C♯ that Professor Finscher proposes would follow no known rule of *musica ficta*.[34] In the preceding passage we have a minor third moving toward a unison.

FINSCHER: But not in measure 57.

LOWINSKY: Granted, but we do in measures 58, 59, 60, and here the question of the context comes into play. These things take a great deal of deliberation, but let me say that this sort of difference of opinion does not worry me. It is not fundamental. I wouldn't mind having this done in this or the other way, whereas I would mind if the same passage were to appear in a four-part context in slow, suspension cadences, and the leading-note were omitted. This, I think, belongs to the large realm of permissible variants; there are certainly no 'grammatical' rules involved here. And one reason for this is the fast motion; this too is an important point.

FINSCHER: Perhaps a more fundamental point is raised by a piece like 'Absalon fili mi'. It is, without doubt, an exceptional work, an experimental work. I think it is very interesting that all accidentals are noted, apart from a very few accidentals which need to be added in cadences according to the rules of *musica ficta*.[35] If an experimental composition like this was notated with such great care, it probably means that the normal use of *musica ficta* was confined to certain cadential formulas; hence it was necessary to note everything else that went beyond this region of comparatively simple and clear formulas. If that is the case, it means that we must restrict ourselves to this very limited region of cadential *musica ficta* and not try to go beyond it. I think that this is a central point.

LOWINSKY: May I ask Professor Finscher what he would do with a piece like 'Fortuna dun gran tempo', which is written for three voices, with no key signature in the first, one flat in the second, and two flats in the third, and has no accidentals throughout? It is evident to all of us that the clash of these voices with three different key signatures produces dissonances that not only are impossible for the time, but are intolerable for our own ears.

[34] Moreover, in measures 62 and 64 the semitone is obtained by the tenor's signed E♭ against the C of the soprano.

[35] [More needs to be added to the great modulation that crowns the ending of 'Absalon fili mi' than a few cadential accidentals. I mention the G♭ in the tenor of measure 68 and the flats before A and D in measures 69 to 71 in superius and tenor. For Howard Brown's testimony that the lute transcription of the work by Sebastian Ochsenkun has the same accidentals as those I added, see his paper, above, p. 520.]

FINSCHER: There are two versions of 'Fortuna dun gran tempo' in the modern edition,[36] and clearly from my position I must say that the first version, the version with as few accidentals as possible...

LOWINSKY: None. The Supplement gives one version with my accidentals, and one with no accidentals.

ANTONOWYCZ: The subject touched on by Professor Lowinsky is unquestionably very important, and further research should be undertaken. But I feel that it will be difficult, if not impossible, to arrive at a consistent method of adding editorial accidentals. Indeed, one and the same person, in performing a work, might change the accidentals he had previously added. Concerning the rules of *musica ficta*, we know from Glareanus that Josquin was no great friend of rules, especially concerning modes. The freedom in Josquin's compositions is so great that unification is simply impossible, and perhaps not necessary, or even useful. I draw your attention to this only as a practical observation. Otherwise I am in full agreement with the proposals made by Professor Lowinsky.

LOWINSKY: May I just ask Professor Finscher now that he has the music before him whether I'm correct in saying that in the Supplement the first edition of 'Fortuna dun gran tempo' appears without any editorial accidentals?

FINSCHER: Yes, it does. And I think it can be executed in this fashion, though certainly with some clashes. The question is whether these clashes are substantial ones. We must, I think, go through the composition measure for measure.

LOWINSKY: May I play 'Fortuna' without accidentals and then with?
[Lowinsky plays the version without accidentals.]
This is the 'polytonal' version, if you wish, and it remains to be asked whether it makes musical sense and indeed was possible at the time. Now comes what I call the logical result of the extraordinary key signature, the imitation in successive fifths, and the rules of *musica ficta*.
[Lowinsky plays the version with accidentals.]

FINSCHER: Nice piece.

ANTONOWYCZ: Nice piece!

FINSCHER: The second version is possible; it sounds quite nice.

[36] *Werken*, Supplement, nos. 13a and 13b.

LOWINSKY: How about the first?

FINSCHER: The first version is not so bad. I think the musical joke and the musical experiment—which this piece quite certainly is—comes out in a different way, but, I think, with equal clarity and inner consistency even in the first version. Your symbolic interpretation of the piece could even be applied to the first version.

LOWINSKY: I would like to keep this at the moment just on the grounds of musical sound and logic.[37] I simply do not believe that a cadence involving C in the bass, B♭ and E♮ on an accented beat in a three-part structure in a piece that is obviously so tonally designed is possible, particularly not when it resolves into B♭ major. I'd like to see evidence that these sounds are possible according to the theory and practice of the time.

MENDEL: If we're going to issue challenges, I'd like to say that until Professor Lowinsky produces what I have been begging him to produce for twenty-five years, namely, his collection of the theoretical sources and the examples, he cannot expect us to take on faith his digest of what those say.

LOWINSKY: Professor Mendel, it is not that I have done nothing in these twenty-five years. First of all, we now have three huge volumes of music in my series, *Monuments of Renaissance Music: Musica nova*, edited by H. Colin Slim, *Canti B*, edited by Helen Hewitt, and the *Medici Codex*, edited by myself. The *musica ficta* policy laid out and practically applied is formulated by myself. In these three volumes, sixteenth-century instru-

---

[37] The symbolic interpretation that I gave to Josquin's 'Fortuna' hinges on the double meaning of *mutatio*. This is the term under which Horace, Boethius, Dante, Boccaccio, and many other writers comprehend and represent the function of Fortuna in human affairs; it is 'also the musical term of the time indicating a tonal change or transposition'; see Edward E. Lowinsky, 'The Goddess Fortuna in Music', p. 67. Hence there is a close—and, I believe, unbreakable—tie between the musical, that is 'chromatic', and the symbolic interpretation. This is also the view of Dietrich Kämper, in his '"Fortunae rota volvitur". Das Symbol des Schicksalsrades in der spätmittelalterlichen Musik', in *Der Begriff der Repraesentatio im Mittelalter*, ed. Albert Zimmermann (*Miscellanea Mediaevalia, Veröffentlichungen des Thomas-Instituts der Universität zu Köln*, 8; Berlin, 1971), pp. 357–71; p. 368. This study—based on much of the same primary and secondary literature but also adding more recent publications—is largely a recapitulation of the ideas developed in my two Fortuna studies.

I believe that Kämper goes too far when he claims that in his 'Fortuna dun gran tempo' Josquin 'postulates the equal temperament of twelve degrees' (p. 369). This work can still be managed in the old meantone tuning. Only with Willaert's 'Quidnam ebrietas' of *c.* 1519 do we arrive at the point at which equal temperament becomes inescapable; see my 'Adrian Willaert's Chromatic "Duo" Re-examined' cited below in n. 40.

mental, secular, and sacred music is presented in what I believe to be a coherent policy of *musica ficta*. Moreover, the introductions to these three volumes contain lengthy discussions on *musica ficta*. Secondly, in the course of my writings I have given a considerable number of theoretical and practical examples. Were one to deny not only the possibility, which Professor Finscher does not do, but the likelihood, say, of my interpretation of 'Fortuna dun gran tempo', then how would one judge the amazing and much bolder modulations in that remarkable work, 'Absalon fili mi', by the same composer, which in fact goes beyond the Db that I introduce in 'Fortuna dun gran tempo' to Gb—and the Gb is signed? The key signatures are amazing, starting with Eb, then Ab, then Db.[38] Furthermore, how do you deal with a work such as Matthaeus Greiter's 'Fortuna' that starts on F and ends on Fb, modulating through the circle of fifths and also signing all accidentals? I have published an extensive study on Greiter's work. I haven't just left you alone with the *Secret Chromatic Art*.[39] I may also recall the new evidence presented in my essays on 'Adrian Willaert's Chromatic "Duo" Re-examined'[40] and 'Echoes of Adrian Willaert's Chromatic "Duo" in Sixteenth- and Seventeenth-Century Compositions'.[41] What happens too often is that the critics of one piece do not look at the rest of the evidence.

WILLEM ELDERS [from the audience]: In his book *Secret Chromatic Art in the Netherlands Motet*, Professor Lowinsky has shown that several works have a symbolic meaning and I believe that in these works the accidentals proposed by him must be accepted. We have only a few works in which Josquin has gone further than his contemporaries, works such as 'Absalon fili mi' and 'Fortuna dun gran tempo'. We published 'Fortuna dun gran tempo' twice in the *Works* of Josquin because Dr. Antonowycz and I could not agree. Hence we gave the piece first precisely as Petrucci printed it, without any additions, and then with Lowinsky's solution, which was only possible because the piece had a symbolic meaning. When we

[38] One cannot make much of the fact that 'Fortuna' has no accidentals, whereas 'Absalon' does, since we deal not with Josquin autographs, but with sources of heterogeneous origin and period. Moreover, the inconsistency in the writing of accidentals, rich in some sources, sparse in others, is part and parcel of a tradition going back over centuries and reflecting more the idiosyncrasies of various scribes, printers, and places of origin than demonstrable differences in sound. Finally, the absence of any modulatory accidentals in Petrucci's print is symbolic of Fortuna's invisibility and cryptic designs of which Dante, Boccaccio (and others) spoke so eloquently ('The Goddess Fortuna', p. 68).

[39] Since then another essay has appeared, 'Secret Chromatic Art Re-examined' (*Perspectives in Musicology*, ed. Barry S. Brook et al. (New York, 1972), pp. 91–135) in which a new series of theoretical sources on *musica ficta* of German and Spanish origin has been published.

[40] *Tijdschrift voor Muziekwetenschap*, xviii (1956), pp. 1–36.

[41] *Studies in Music History: Essays for Oliver Strunk*, pp. 183–238.

go beyond this and add accidentals in motets and Masses where there is no symbolic meaning, we will not all agree that this was intended by the composer.

LOWINSKY: Thank you, Dr. Elders, for the lovely revelation that the two editors of the Supplement each published the version of 'Fortuna dun gran tempo' that he approved of. To your last point I would say that *musica ficta* can be discussed fruitfully only when we have individual examples before us; any other discussion remains too vague.

ANTONOWYCZ: I find Josquin's 'Fortuna dun gran tempo' in your interpretation very nice, and I agree with Dr. Elders.

FINSCHER: I agree with Dr. Elders that there is a small corpus of experimental compositions, and Professor Lowinsky has examined these experimental compositions very carefully. But the question is whether we can draw conclusions as regards accidentals from this small group of obviously experimental works. What you said about 'Absalon' was just what I had meant to say. The fact that the accidentals in 'Absalon' are notated up to G♭ should make us very careful in suggesting solutions of *musica ficta* by adding our own accidentals.

LOWINSKY: I have shown in the editions of the *Monuments of Renaissance Music* that under no circumstances must we draw general rules from pieces that are special cases. I very much agree with Dr. Elders that throughout the sixteenth century significant modulation and chromaticism in vocal music are not used without symbolic or expressive justification. The question narrows itself now to this: is the 'Fortuna dun gran tempo' such a special case?[42]

FINSCHER: Yes, I think it is clearly an experimental piece belonging together with Greiter's 'Fortuna' and, in a certain sense, with the so-called 'duo' by Willaert.

LOWINSKY: If this is true, then it is allowable to look at a piece like Greiter's 'Fortuna', composed about 1550, in a country that had absolutely no known tradition of bold chromatic modulation or direct chromaticism, in the light of the early 'Fortuna' piece. Greiter modulates logically through

[42] Reference should be made here to the astonishing affirmative testimony furnished by Jean Molinet (1435–1507), illustrious poet and musician, who praises the miraculous things done by Fortuna 'par sa fainte musique'; see Helen Hewitt, *Ottaviano Petrucci, Canti B* (*Monuments of Renaissance Music*, ii; Chicago, 1967), p. 57.

the circle of fifths from F major to F♭ major, even using B double flat in the last cadence.

FINSCHER: But the fact that there is a tradition of a small group of experimental pieces concerned symbolically with 'Fortuna' and stretching over a period of some fifty years does not mean that the kind of technical experiment used to express the 'Fortuna' symbolism in 1550 is identical with that used in a piece of 1500.

LOWINSKY: It is not identical: Josquin's 'Fortuna' goes only to D♭; Greiter's moves beyond that to G♭, C♭, F♭, and B double flat; it is written not for three, but for four parts; and it shows a significantly expanded harmonic and modulatory concept.

FINSCHER: Yes, but it comes down to the same principle of written or implied modulation, does it not?

LOWINSKY: Absolutely, but I can explain where Matthaeus Greiter got it from. How do *you* explain a phenomenon such as Greiter's piece?

FINSCHER: I confess I don't have the facts.

MENDEL: Where did Josquin get it from?

LOWINSKY: There is a very interesting theoretical development. John Hothby, writing around 1480, demanded hexachords on all notes up to D♭ and F♯. The question is: do we believe that such a theoretical demonstration would be possible unless there were practical examples of it that the theorists had to theorize for?

MENDEL: This discussion may seem ended shortly; it will not be. On Friday we will hear a piece in which there is a surprising use of accidentals which occurred to me on quite unhistorical and merely musical grounds, and occurred independently to Professor Lowinsky on both musical *and* historical grounds, which illustrates the word 'Amen'.[43]

REESE: Maybe 'Amen' is a cue. It is time for me to thank the speakers.

43 On this see the Workshop on the Masses, pp. 710–11 above.

Index